# Green Building:
## Project Planning & Cost Estimating
### Third Edition

## RSMeans

**WILEY**

John Wiley & Sons, Inc.

No part of this publication may be reproduced, stored in a retrieval system, or transmitted in any form or by any means, electronic, mechanical, photocopying, recording, scanning, or otherwise, except as permitted under Section 107 or 108 of the 1976 United States Copyright Act, without either the prior written permission of the Publisher, or authorization through payment of the appropriate per-copy fee to the Copyright Clearance Center, Inc., 222 Rosewood Drive, Danvers, MA 01923, 978-750-8400, fax 978-646-8600, or on the web at www.copyright.com. Requests to the Publisher for permission should be addressed to the Permissions Department, John Wiley & Sons, Inc., 111 River Street, Hoboken, NJ 07030, 201-748-6011, fax 201-748-6008, or online at http://www.wiley.com/go/permissions.

Limit of Liability/Disclaimer of Warranty: While the publisher and author have used their best efforts in preparing this book, they make no representations or warranties with respect to the accuracy or completeness of the contents of this book and specifically disclaim any implied warranties of merchantability or fitness for a particular purpose. No warranty may be created or extended by sales representatives or written sales materials. The advice and strategies contained herein may not be suitable for your situation. You should consult with a professional where appropriate. Neither the publisher nor author shall be liable for any loss of profit or any other commercial damages, including but not limited to special, incidental, consequential, or other damages.

Product Manager/Editor: Andrea Sillah. Production Manager: Michael Kokernak. Editor/Production Coordinator: Jill Goodman. Composition: Jonathan Forgit. Proofreader: Mary Lou Geary. Book Design: Jonathan Forgit.

For general information on our other products and services, or technical support, please contact our Customer Care Department within the United States at 800-762-2974, outside the United States at 317-572-3993 or fax 317-572-4002.

Wiley also publishes its books in a variety of electronic formats. Some content that appears in print may not be available in electronic books.

For more information about Wiley products, visit our Web site at http://www.wiley.com.

Library of Congress Cataloging-in-Publication Data:
ISBN 978-0-87629-261-7

Printed in the United States of America

10    9    8    7    6    5    4    3    2    1

# Table of Contents

# Acknowledgments

The preparation of this book involved a team of experts, support from industry organizations, and input from a number of individuals. The primary and contributing authors and reviewers are listed in the "About the Contributors" section following these acknowledgments. Others who provided guidance and assistance during various stages of the book's development are listed below.

We would like to particularly thank *Building Design & Construction* and David Castelli of *Design Cost Data* for allowing permission to reprint case studies originally published in the magazines. We also want to express our gratitude to the National Association of Home Builders Research Center for granting us permission to use information from their organization.

We are grateful to the following organizations for allowing us to reprint logos representing their green building standards and guidelines: the American Lung Association, Building Green Inc., the Climate Neutral Network, the Collaborative for High Performance Schools, the Forest Stewardship Council, the Global Ecolabelling Network, the Green Building Initiative, Greenguard, Green Seal, the International Living Building Institute, the National Association of Home Builders, Natural Resources Canada, the Natural Step, Rate It Green, TerraChoice Environmental Marketing Inc., the U.S. Environmental Protection Agency, and the U.S. Green Building Council.

Finally, we would like to acknowledge the many organizations and businesses that granted us permission to reprint photographs of their green projects, including: Abundant Renewable Energy in Newberg, Oregon, and Marty Aikens, Business Agent at IBEW, Boston, Massachusetts, for their wind turbine photos; Ann Grimes of the City of Dallas Office of Economic Development for brownfield rejuvenation photos; Pat Bellestri of Soledad Canyon Earth Builders for photographs of the company's rammed earth homes; Sarnafil for reflective roof photos; Whitman-Hanson Regional High School and Selectman Jim Armstrong for allowing us to photograph the school; the International Dark-Sky Association for photographs representing responsible nighttime lighting; and the landscape architect of Chicago City Hall's living roof, the Conservation Design Forum, for providing images of that project. Special thanks to the Federal Energy Management Program (FEMP) for their efficiency recommendations tables, and James Ziobro, PE, of Griffith & Vary Engineers for his rainwater recovery system drawing.

# About the Contributors

**Arthur Adler,** PE, CEM, author of Chapter 12, "Commissioning the Green Building," is principal of Applied Energy Engineering & Commissioning located in Manchester, Massachusetts. He has more than 20 years of experience in operating, analyzing, and optimizing HVAC systems for commercial, high tech, industrial, and institutional clients. His company performs energy analysis, commissioning, and retro-commissioning of building mechanical, electrical, and control systems. Mr. Adler has extensive knowledge of sustainable building design and construction practices and is an accredited professional with the U.S. Green Building Council's Leadership in Energy and Environmental Design (LEED) green building rating system.

**Jodi Smits Anderson,** AIA, LEED AP, author of the Foreword, is the Director of Sustainability Programs for the Dormitory Authority, State of New York. She is an architect, board member of the NY Upstate Chapter of the USGBC, LEED accredited professional, AIA member, and a member of the Architectural Advisory Council for SUNY Delhi. She is a graduate of RPI School of Architecture and has practiced architecture with many firms in the New York State Capital Region as a designer and as a construction administrator. She has given presentations on green building and sustainable choices throughout New York state, trained contractors about greening their work, worked with a talented and knowledgeable committee on "Greening the Executive Mansion," and had the pleasure of speaking at Greenbuild 2009 as a panelist on "Becoming a Green Government Guru." She is currently working with interagency councils on several executive orders for New York state, including green procurement and reduction of greenhouse gas emissions.

**James Armstrong,** CPE, CEM, LEED AP, author of Chapter 4, "Efficient Use of Energy & Other Resources," and co-author of Chapter 7, "Health, Comfort & Productivity," is senior energy engineer at Siemens Industry Inc., Building Technologies Division, where he develops and manages building optimization, commissioning and energy efficiency services for Siemens customers around New England. He has been responsible for commissioning projects as a program manager/account executive for energy and engineering consultants for NSTAR Electric & Gas and as senior project/application engineer for Shooshanian Engineering and Trigen Boston Energy Corporation. Mr. Armstrong's earlier experience includes managing utilities and facilities for MassDevelopment at the Devens Commerce Center (formerly Fort Devens) and for institutions such as Colby Sawyer College and the Boston Museum of Science. He also served on the Green Schools Certification Task Force, which developed MASS CHPS, now part of the school construction legislation in Massachusetts. Mr. Armstrong is a graduate of the Calhoon MEBA Engineering School and a retired marine engineer and U.S. Navy Veteran engineering officer.

**The American Wind Energy Association** (AWEA) provided the text for Chapter 6, "Wind Power." AWEA is a national trade association that represents wind power plant developers, wind turbine manufacturers, utilities, consultants, insurers, financiers, researchers, and others involved in the wind industry. In addition, AWEA represents hundreds of wind energy advocates from around the world. The association provides up-to-date information on wind energy projects operating worldwide; new projects in various stages of development; companies working in the wind energy field; technology development; and policy developments related to wind and other renewable energy development.

**G. Bradley Guy,** Associate AIA, LEED AP, is the author of Chapter 3, "Building Deconstruction." He is an assistant professor in the Master of Science in Sustainable Design Program, School of Architecture and Planning, at The Catholic University of America in Washington D.C., where he teaches the course, "Building Deconstruction and Design: Recover, Rediscover, Redesign." He is also on the faculty of the Yestermorrow Design/Build School, Warren, VT, where he teaches the course "Design for Deconstruction and Reconstruction." Mr. Guy is a member of the USGBC LEED Materials & Resources Technical Advisory Group (TAG), and has consulted on numerous LEED green building projects, including in post-Hurricane Katrina New Orleans. He is also a consultant d/b/a Material Reuse. His areas of expertise include, building deconstruction, reuse and recycling of materials, and design for adaptability and deconstruction in the built environment. He developed the "Green Demolition Certification" to qualify environmentally responsible building removals, and has written books and guides to deconstruction, materials reuse, and design for deconstruction. Mr. Guy holds an MS in Architectural Studies from the University of Florida.

**Sieglinde K. Fuller**, PhD, author of Chapter 13, "Economic Analysis & Green Buildings," is an economist with the Office of Applied Economics of the National Institute of Standards and Technology, a non-regulatory federal agency within the U.S. Commerce Department's Technology Administration. Her areas of expertise include benefit-cost analysis, economic impact studies, and the pricing of publicly supplied goods and services. As project leader of the NIST/DOE collaborative effort to promote the use of economic analysis for energy and water conservation and renewable energy projects, Dr. Fuller has been involved in developing techniques, workshops, instructional materials, and computer software for calculating the life-cycle costs and benefits of such projects in accordance with federal legislation.

**Mark Kalin**, FAIA, FCSI, LEED AP, is the author of Chapter 11, "Specifying Green Products & Materials." He is a registered architect, author of the original *GreenSpec*, and is currently national chair of CSI's Sustainable Facilities Practice Group. Kalin Associates is one of the nation's leading independent specifications consultants, and has prepared specifications for over 150 projects seeking USGBC LEED certification, and *Master Specifications* for the new sustainable Masdar City.

**Alexis Karolides**, AIA, author of Chapter 1, "Green Building Approaches," and Chapter 2, "Introduction to Green Building Materials & Systems," is a registered architect and principal with the Rocky Mountain Institute (RMI) in Snowmass, Colorado. Her projects at RMI have included a prototype energy-efficient supermarket for Stop & Shop, a green renovation of a historic building at Hickam Air Force Base, campus-wide energy planning and building retrofit strategies for Berea College, a Hines residential development, the greening of the California State Capitol, and a monastery in Tibet. She is a frequent speaker at national and international conferences and has presented educational seminars and design workshops for communities, businesses, and institutions, including Shell; Perrier; Sherwin Williams; the cities of Milwaukee, Pittsburgh, and Cincinnati; and the Departments of Environmental Protection and Urban Planning in Tianjin, China.

**M. Magda Lelek**, PE, CEM, co-author of Chapter 15, "Evaluation, Analysis & Data Tools," is a registered mechanical engineer and a principal with Andelman and Lelek Engineering Inc. in Massachusetts. She specializes in building energy modeling, energy efficiency studies, commissioning services for energy efficiency and LEED projects, and sustainable building development as related to mechanical systems. Ms. Lelek has more than 11 years of professional experience on commercial, institutional, and industrial projects. She has been a member of the Green Schools Task Force, where she was involved in the development of green guidelines for the Massachusetts CHPS High Performance Green School initiative. Currently, Ms. Lelek serves on the Massachusetts Sustainable Design Roundtable in the Metrics Working Group. She is a LEED-accredited professional and certified energy manager. She holds a master's degree in mechanical engineering with a specialty in HVAC and environmental sciences.

**Barbara C. Lippiatt,** author of Chapter 14, "Evaluating Products Over Their Life Cycle," is an economist with the Office of Applied Economics of the National Institute of Standards and Technology. Her primary interest is in developing economic decision methods and tools primarily for efficiently designing and managing buildings. She has applied these decision tools to a wide variety of building problems. In 2003, Barbara was honored for her BEES work with the U.S. Department of Commerce's silver medal.

**Joseph Macaluso,** CCC, is the author of Chapter 9, "Rating Systems, Standards & Guidelines," Chapter 10 "Budgeting & Financing" and co-author of Chapter 15, "Evaluation, Analysis & Data Tools," and is one of the book's primary editors. He is a certified cost consultant, chairs the Government and Public Works Special Interest Group of the Association for the Advancement of Cost Engineering, and received their 2008 Technical Excellence Award. He also the chairman of the New York Interagency Engineering Council, and organized their *Greening the Apple* green building technical conference. Mr. Macaluso is the construction cost estimator for Empire State Development Corporation in New York, a state agency that provides funding and technical assistance for a wide range of projects throughout the state. Over the past 24 years, he has prepared construction cost estimates and schedules, negotiated change orders, and reviewed budgets and contractor qualifications for major public works projects. In addition he has taught cost estimating courses at Long Island University and the City University of New York.

**Phillip R. Waier,** PE, LEED AP, is the author of Chapter 16, "The Greening of Commercial Real Estate." He is a principal engineer at RSMeans, and senior editor of the annually updated publication, *Building Construction Cost Data*. Mr. Waier manages the activities of Means' editors, cost researchers, and consultants who collect data from public and private agencies and firms throughout the United States. He has spent 30 years in the construction industry, serving as president and chief engineer for a mechanical contracting firm, project manager for numerous industrial construction projects, and structural engineer for major foreign and domestic projects. Mr. Waier is a registered professional engineer and a member of Associated Builders and Contractors (ABC) and Associated General Contractors (AGC).

**Andy Walker**, PhD, PE, is the author of Chapter 5, "Solar Energy Systems" and Chapter 8, "The Green Design Process & Associated Costs," and co-author of Chapter 7, "Health, Comfort & Productivity." He is senior engineer at the National Renewable Energy Lab. Dr. Walker supports the U.S. DOE Federal Energy Management Program Technical Assistance Task, conducting engineering and economic analysis of energy efficiency and renewable energy projects in federal buildings. He has also taught several energy-related classes in the Mechanical and Architectural Engineering Departments at the University of Colorado at Boulder, the Colorado School of Mines, and Metropolitan State College of Denver. He serves on the Executive Committee of the American Society of Mechanical Engineers Solar Energy Division and has been an Associate Editor for the *Journal of Solar Energy Engineering*. Prior to joining NREL, Dr. Walker worked as the Renewable Energy Coordinator for the Colorado Office of Energy Conservation and as a research associate at the Solar Energy Applications Laboratory at Colorado State University. As a Peace Corps Volunteer in Nepal, he taught math and science and completed several projects, including a passive solar school dormitory and a village-scale biogas generator. He has conducted solar thermal and photovoltaics training for developing countries for the U.S. Agency for International Development. Dr. Walker is the author of more than 28 book chapters, journal articles, and conference papers and has been recognized with 11 awards from professional associations and government agencies. He is inventor of a stochastic algorithm to evaluate integrated renewable energy technologies. Dr. Walker's credentials include a BS, MS, and PhD in Mechanical Engineering, and he is a registered Professional Engineer in the State of Colorado. He has solar heating and PV on his passive solar house, drives a hybrid electric car, and buys 100% of his home's electric power from wind energy.

# Foreword

Green building has moved from its start as a concept for "tree-huggers," through being a marketing ploy for products and technologies and special services, past that irritating realm of "it's a cool thing to do if you can afford it," and finally into its rightful place as a way of building better, smarter, more useful buildings. Ray Anderson of Interface Flooring Company would call this a "so right, so smart" approach to design and construction. For the writers of this book, and many other people who are helping to demystify green building, it is truly common sense—building well for the money, looking at long-term goals for the building users, the environment, and the budget, as well as looking at the shorter term realities of project costs, material availability, and project schedule.

Our class song in college was "The Future's so Bright, I Gotta Wear Shades." Unfortunately, our current world is a bit different than the one we envisioned 20+ years ago. It's a little tougher and more cautious about money, and from this vantage point our future world is very much in debate.

Will we have fossil fuel to burn in 50+ years, and, if so, what will be the cost of this fuel?

Will the temperature of NYC in 2075 be like Atlanta, Georgia, is now?

Will our suburbs be abandoned, as envisioned by James Kunstler in his book *World Made by Hand*?

What building materials will be developed?

Will prime ocean real estate be worthless, or even gone?

Will we be mining landfills for the metals we will need?

What new codes will we be adopting?

I'm sure dozens of other questions have occurred to you in just reading those few I have presented.

This book does not hold all the answers to these questions, but it does present useful knowledge from a wide range of savvy professionals, along with tools and references about how to design and build buildings *today* that will also deal with that uncertain future. We must all design and build to reduce waste in operations, protect the health of the building's users, and program for resilience in the use of the buildings. These buildings will perform better for their owners and users, while outlasting their traditional counterparts. To make the point even more clear: the value of green buildings exceeds that of non-green buildings, rental rates have proven to be higher, and even insurance companies are beginning to offer special premiums for proven green construction.

We are finally moving past the egocentric view that we can build whatever we like and then engineer the systems that will condition the spaces to make them comfortable for others to live and work in. We realize that we can save money and energy as well as improve our health, if we use the relatively free things that nature gives us by incorporating location-based diversity into how we design and build and renovate buildings.

We also see that construction work is the one endeavor that will nearly always improve the local economy, and we can intensify this benefit by sourcing local materials when possible, and using local talent that understands the regional landscape, flora, fauna, and workforce issues. Renovation of existing buildings is even more powerful, because it improves our existing building stock, helps to reduce greenhouse gas emissions, reduces energy costs, and usually improves local appeal and tax base.

We now know that balancing triple bottom line (people, planet, and profit) will give us the best project for the dollars we spend. Clients are demanding it. Laws are requiring it. Incentives and grants are supporting it. Even the planet is calling for it.

Green Building is a complex puzzle. It's hard work to design and build and cost out even a simple project well, and many people are only at the start of the long learning curve that will culminate in true green building. Green building tends to be more complex, because it makes use of the benefits of the natural world and combines that with a deeper understanding of program and space needs—all the while introducing highly integrated technological systems and controls. Architects need to not only figure out what the owner wants, but work more directly with the team structural engineers, MEP engineers, landscape architects, and contractors. All of these items multiply the intricacies. Then, add in the fact that typically unpredictable people will live in, use, and maintain these buildings, and you've got a boatload of challenges inherent in every project.

There is a *perceived* budget hit with green building. It is easy to allow the famed "additional cost" to derail planning for a green building. Green construction does not need to cost more, and it can actually cost less up front if the team is willing to work together to make the many tough trade-off decisions that are part of the complexity of project planning—it's not easy, but it's possible. And remember, a green building is not one that is completely designed as normal and then "greened up" with materials and PV panels on the roof. Finally, green building will certainly save the owner money in operations and maintenance over the life of the building, so long as the building users are also trained regarding the proper use of the building and its systems.

It's a busy and ever-changing world out there. Products and technologies have changed and increased in number. Green building seems to have opened up the creative juices of product manufacturers, engineers, architects, scientists, students, and others who are finding ways to reduce waste, remove toxins from manufacturing processes, and to more efficiently condition the buildings we inhabit. The tools and resources, third party verification systems, and rating systems are also numerous and sometimes confusing. Life cycle analysis, energy modeling, charrette leadership, green consultants, commissioning authorities, etc. are all fairly new pieces of the building process that is green.

This book is an excellent resource to help you deal with the complexities we all face in building greener. It touches on this broad world of products, tools, rating systems, and technologies, as well as some of the less quantifiable value aspects of green buildings. Health and productivity, integrative design, general concepts inherent in green building, and, finally, the beauty that is often created in building green are all explored in these pages. *Green Building: Project Planning & Cost Estimating* is a lot like the green buildings it will help us to build. It is a practical guide that also inspires us, making it not only a useful resource book, but an enjoyable read as well. Green building is "common sense," but until common sense is indeed as common as we would wish, this is one of the best tools out there to help you to integrate green building into all of the work that you do.

Read on, and build ever greener.

*Jodi Smits Anderson*
*AIA, LEED AP*
*Director, Sustainability Programs, Dormitory Authority,*
*State of New York*

# Introduction

Green, or sustainable, building has experienced rapid growth and matured in the four years since the second edition of this book was published. Central to this movement are the now clearly established economic benefits of building green. Large and small businesses; educational, health care, and other institutions; government facilities at all levels; and home builders/homeowners are profiting from resource efficiencies and improved comfort and productivity. The commonly held belief that green building necessitated higher initial costs has proven a false assumption, as design and building professionals, together with product manufacturers, have found ways to achieve savings in up-front costs.

This third edition is revised and updated with particular emphasis on the most applicable green building guidelines and standards, which have greatly evolved over the past several years.

Two new chapters have also been added: on wind energy and green building's added value to commercial real estate. Other chapters have been updated, including several cost and technology-focused topics such as economic incentives, funding sources, and software programs and other methods used to evaluate the cost/benefit of green methods. The book also includes efficiency tables for HVAC equipment and requirements for rating systems, including checklists for LEED.

The case studies in Part 4 of this book are completely new—a diverse collection of building types and green strategies. The majority of the projects have been completed over the past three years and have achieved USGBC LEED ratings. The case studies include overviews of project goals, special challenges, materials, and systems, along with cost breakdowns.

This book is intended as a resource for anyone who seeks to incorporate green features into structures that they are conceiving, designing, specifying, estimating, constructing, remodeling, or maintaining. Its mission is to provide, in one volume, an understanding of green building approaches, materials, project management, and estimating requirements. Many excellent additional green building resources are listed at the back of this book.

The construction industry consumes a major share of resources. Its products are the places in which we live and work, and its materials and methods can either enhance or detract from both our environment and our budgets. Choosing green is now recognized for its merits as improving both the quality of our lives and our fiscal health.

# Part 1 Green Building Concepts

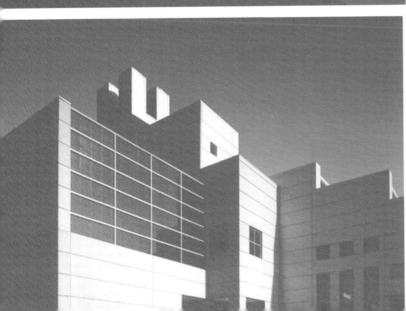

# Chapter

# 1 Green Building Approaches

*Alexis Karolides, AIA*

Acommon assumption in recent years is that the built environment will necessarily degrade the natural environment. But for most of Earth's history, structures built for shelter have typically enhanced bio-diversity and benefited the surrounding community. Beaver dams, for instance, create pools where wetlands form, supporting a vast array of diverse life not possible in the original stream. Why should an office building be any different?

Green building is a way of enhancing the environment. Done right, it benefits human well-being, community, environmental health, and life cycle cost. This means tailoring a building and its placement on the site to the local climate, site conditions, culture, and community in order to reduce resource consumption, augment resource supply, and enhance the quality and diversity of life. More of a building philosophy than a building style, there is no characteristic "look" of a green building. While natural and resource-efficient features can be highlighted in a building, they can also be invisible within any architectural design aesthetic.

Green building is part of the larger concept of "sustainable development," characterized by Sara Parkin of the British environmental initiative, Forum for the Future, as "a process that enables all people to realize their potential and improve their quality of life in ways that protect and enhance the Earth's life support systems." As the World Commission on Environment and Development (the Brundtland Commission) phrased it, "Humanity has the ability to make development sustainable—to ensure that it meets the needs of the present without compromising the ability of future generations to meet their own needs."

Ideally, green building is not just an assemblage of "environmental" components, nor a piecemeal modification of an already-designed, standard building. In some cases, these incremental approaches add to the building's cost, while producing marginal resource savings. It is much more effective to take a holistic approach to programming, planning, designing, and constructing (or renovating) buildings and sites. This involves analyzing such interconnected issues as site and climate considerations, building orientation and form, lighting and thermal comfort, systems and materials, and optimizing all these aspects in an integrated design.

To capture the multiple benefits of synergistic design elements, the "whole system" design process must begin early in the building's conception and must involve interdisciplinary teamwork. In the conventional, linear development process, key people are often left out

**Figure 1.1**
The Phipps Conservatory and Botanical Gardens Welcome Center in Pittsburgh, PA, was built targeting a LEED Silver rating. Photo courtesy IKM Incorporated – Architects *(Photographer: Alexander Denmarsh Photography.)*

of decision-making or brought in too late to make a full contribution. Thorough collaboration, on the other hand, can reduce and sometimes eliminate both capital and operating costs, while at the same time meeting environmental and social goals. In addition, the process can anticipate and avoid technical difficulties that would have resulted in added expense to the project. Collaboration can also produce a "big picture" vision that goes beyond the original problem, permitting one solution to be leveraged to create many more solutions—often at no additional cost.

It is precisely the integrated approach described above and the multiple benefits thereby achieved that allow many green buildings to cost no more than standard buildings, even though some of their components may cost more. Green design elements may each serve several functions and allow other building components to be downsized. For example, better windows and insulation can allow for smaller heating systems; photovoltaic panels can double as shade for parking or can replace a building's spandrel glazing.

The U.S. Green Building Council's (USGBC's) LEED® (Leadership in Energy and Environmental Design) rating system for commercial, institutional, and high-rise residential buildings is an instrument used to evaluate environmental performance from a "whole building" perspective over a building's life cycle, providing a definitive standard for what constitutes a green building. It should be used not just to "rate" a building, but as a tool to facilitate greening the building early in the design process. The USGBC has asserted that a LEED-certified or Silver-rated building should not cost more than a conventional building. (Gold- or Platinum-rated buildings may cost more, but they also may involve cutting-edge technologies or significant energy-generation capacity not found in standard buildings.)

Recent studies have corroborated that LEED buildings, in general, fall within the typical cost ranges of their conventional counterparts.[1] One study that did show up to a nominal 2% first cost premium for LEED buildings, demonstrated a tenfold return on this initial investment in operational savings over the life of the building.[2]

Many cities also have local green building guidelines or rating systems that are similarly useful and are sometimes associated with incentives (such as rebates, reduced fees or taxes, and/or an expedited permit process). Some cities *require* that LEED or their local green building guidelines be followed (typically for government buildings). *(See Chapter 9 for more on the LEED rating system, and Chapter 10 for financial incentives.)*

Players in the real estate market are realizing that green development is good business. Developers, builders, and buyers are discovering that green enhances not only health and quality of life, but also the bottom line.

## Potential Benefits of Green Building

- Reduced capital cost
- Reduced operating costs
- Marketing benefits (free press and product differentiation)
- Valuation premiums and enhanced absorption rates
- In some cities, streamlined approvals by building and zoning departments
- Reduced liability risk
- Health and productivity gains
- Attracting and retaining employees
- Staying ahead of regulations
- New business opportunities
- Satisfaction from doing the right thing

## Resource Efficiency

Buildings make up 40% of total U.S. energy consumption (including two-thirds of the country's electricity) and 16% of total U.S. water consumption. They are responsible for 40% of all material flows and produce 15%– 40% of the waste in landfills, depending on the region.[3] Clearly, large-scale improvements in resource productivity in buildings would have a profound effect on national resource consumption. According to *Natural Capitalism*, a book by Paul Hawken, Amory Lovins, and Hunter Lovins, *radical* improvements in resource efficiency are readily possible—today's off-the-shelf technologies can make existing buildings three to four times more resource-efficient, and new buildings up to ten times more efficient.[4]

Reducing energy use in buildings saves resources and money while reducing pollution and $CO_2$ in the atmosphere. It also leverages even greater savings at power plants. For instance, if electricity is coming from a 35%-efficient coal-fired power plant and experiencing 6% transmission line losses, saving a unit of electricity in a building saves three units of fuel at the power plant.[5] Process losses exaggerate the problem. Take a typical industrial pumping system, for instance. Insert 100 units of fuel at the power plant to produce 30 units of electricity; 9% of this is lost in transmission to the end user, 10% of the remainder is lost in the industrial motors, 2% in the drivetrain, 25% in the pumps, 33% in the throttle, and 20% in pipes. Of the original 100 units of fuel, the final energy output is a mere 9.5 units of energy.[6]

As Amory Lovins has said, "It's cheaper to save fuel than to burn it." But full financial benefits will *only* be realized by using an integrated, resource-efficient approach. (High-performance windows *will* increase first costs unless the reduction in heating and/or cooling load is factored into the sizing of the mechanical system.) Just as important as what goes into a green building is what can be left out. Green building design eliminates waste and redundancy wherever possible.

One of the key ways of reducing resource consumption and cost is to evaluate first whether a new building really needs to be built. Renovating an existing building can save money, time, and resources, and can often enable a company (or a family, if it is a residential building) to be located in a part of town with existing infrastructure and public transportation, enhancing convenience and reducing sprawl. Next, if a new building is required, it should be sized only as large as it really needs to be. Smaller buildings require fewer building materials, less land, and less operational energy.

The American cultural assumption is that we should buy (or lease) as much square footage as we can afford. In the residential sector for instance, the average new house size has steadily increased from 983 square feet in 1950 to 2,349 square feet in 2004, while the average number of people per household has shrunk from 3.38 in 1950 to 2.60 in 2004.[7] Yet smaller houses and commercial buildings allow the budget to be spent on quality, rather than what may be underused quantity.

## Energy

The easiest and least expensive way to solve the "energy problem" is not to augment energy supply, but to reduce the amount of energy needed. In buildings, great opportunity lies in simple design solutions that intelligently respond to location and climate. For instance, for most North American sites, simply facing the long side of a building within 15 degrees of true south (and using proper shading to block summer, but not winter sun) can save up to 40% of the energy consumption of the same building turned 90 degrees. *(See Chapter 5 for more on solar heat gain.)*

Attention to making the building envelope (exterior walls, roof, and windows) as efficient as possible for

Each year in the U.S. about $13 billion worth of energy—in the form of heated or cooled air—or $150 per household escapes through holes and cracks in residential buildings.
— *American Council for an Energy-Efficient Economy*

the climate can also dramatically reduce loads, especially in "skin-dominated" buildings (residences and other small buildings). For this type of building, optimal sealing, insulation, and radiant barriers, combined with heat-recovery ventilation, can reduce heat losses to less than half that of a building that simply meets code.[8]

Heat travels in and out of buildings in three ways:  radiation, convection, and conduction, all of which must be addressed to reduce unwanted heat transfer effectively.

**Radiation** is the transfer of heat from a warmer body to a cooler one (regardless of position). The way to stop radiation heat transfer is by using reflective surfaces. A reflective roof, for instance, can reduce solar heat gain through the roof by up to 40%. Radiant barriers in attics or crawl spaces can also be used to reflect heat away from or back into occupied spaces of a building. Using light pavement surfaces (or better yet, reducing pavement as much as possible) will lower ambient air temperature around a building, thus reducing the building's cooling load. High-performance window glazing often includes a thin film or films to reflect infrared light (heat) either out of a building (in a hot climate) or back into a building (in a cold climate). Passive solar design in cold climates usually involves allowing the sun's radiation to enter a building and be absorbed into thermal mass for re-release later.

**Convection** is the transfer of heat in a fluid or gas, such as in air. Green buildings achieve natural ventilation by using convective forces, such as wind, and differences in humidity and temperature. Typically, we experience convection as unwanted heat loss. It is what we experience when we feel a cold draft next to a leaky window or when a door is opened and cold air rushes in. Methods of preventing convective heat transfer include providing an air barrier; sealing gaps around windows, doors, electrical outlets, and other openings in the building envelope; providing air-lock entrances; and using heat recovery ventilators, which transfer 50%–80% of the heat from exhaust air to intake air in cold climates, and vice versa in hot ones. They are an excellent way to ensure adequate ventilation in a tightly sealed house, while maintaining high energy efficiency.

**Conduction** is the transfer of heat across a solid substance. Every material has a specific conductivity (U-value) and resistance (the inverse of the U-value, called the R-value). Insulation is made of materials with particularly high resistance to conductive heat transfer (high R-values). In climates with significant indoor/outdoor temperature differentials, it is important to insulate the entire building envelope—roof, walls, and foundation. Although heated or air conditioned buildings in any climate benefit from insulation, the greater the indoor/outdoor temperature differential, the more insulation is needed.

## Windows

Much of a building's heat transfer occurs through its windows. Therefore, one of the most critical ways to reduce all three types of building heat loss (or gain) is by selecting the appropriate, high-performance window for the given conditions. Important window properties include solar heat gain coefficient (SHGC), heat loss coefficient (U-value), and visible transmittance. The appropriate combination of these properties will depend on the climate, solar orientation, and building application. Ultra-high-performance windows combine multiple glazing layers, low-emissivity coatings, argon or krypton gas fill, good edge seals, insulated frames, and airtight construction. Because metal is a particularly good conductor, metal window frames need a "thermal break" (an insulating material inserted to block the conductive heat transfer across the metal) to achieve high performance. High-performance windows have multiple benefits besides saving energy. These include:

- Enhancing radiant comfort near the windows (thereby allowing perimeter space to be used and sometimes enabling perimeter zone heating/cooling to be eliminated).
- Allowing the HVAC (heating, ventilation, and air conditioning) system to be downsized (thereby reducing first costs).
- Reducing fading from ultraviolet light.
- Reducing noise transfer from outside.
- Reducing condensation and related potential for mold and extending the life of the window.
- Improving daylighting—quantitatively and qualitatively.

## Heat Load

Besides entering through the building envelope, heat can also be generated inside the building by lights, equipment, and people. Especially in large, "load-dominated" buildings, many of which tend

**Figure 1.2**
Daylighting should be considered early in a building's design. In the case of Whitman-Hanson Regional High School in Whitman, MA, large, highly-insulated low-E coated windows paired with straight corridors bring outdoor light deep into the school's interior, thereby reducing energy costs as less artificial light is required to light the building.

today to be air-conditioned year-round, installing efficient lighting and appliances (which emit less heat) will significantly reduce the building's cooling load. Using daylight as much as possible will reduce cooling loads even more, because daylight contains the least amount of heat per lumen of light. (Incandescent lights are the worst—and thus the least "efficient"; they are basically small heaters that happen to produce a bit of light.)

## Integrated Design

Integrated design makes use of the site's natural resources, technological efficiency, and synergies between systems. Once the building envelope is efficiently designed to reduce heat flow, natural heating and cooling methods can be used to greatly downsize, or even eliminate, fossil-fuel-based mechanical heating and cooling systems. Techniques include daylighting, solar heating, natural ventilation and cooling, efficient and right-sized HVAC systems, and utilization of waste heat.

### *Daylighting*

Daylighting provides important occupant benefits, including better visual acuity, a connection to nature, and documented enhancements to productivity and well-being; it also reduces operational energy costs when electric lights are turned off or dimmed while daylight is ample. This emphasizes the importance of integrating all the mechanical systems—daylighting, lighting, and HVAC. It is also important to design systems to modulate with varying loads. *(See Chapter 7 for more on daylighting.)*

### *Passive & Active Solar Heating*

Many methods of solar heating are available. They include passive solar (direct, indirect, and isolated gain), solar water heating, and solar ventilation air preheating. **Direct solar gain** occurs when sunlight strikes a high-mass wall or floor within a room; **indirect gain** (or a Trombe wall approach) is achieved by installing glazing a few inches in front of a south-facing high-mass wall, and letting the collected heat radiate from the wall into the adjoining occupied space; and **isolated gain** involves an attached sunspace, such as a greenhouse. Active solar heating systems can be used for domestic hot water and for hydronic radiant heating (warm fluid, typically piped in a floor slab or below a finish floor, radiates heat directly to people in the room, which is generally more efficient than heating air). *(See Chapter 5 for more on solar heating.)*

## Other Efficient Cooling Methods

There are multiple techniques for natural ventilation and cooling. For example, in hot, dry climates, **thermal chimneys** and **evaporative cooling** are effective (and have been used for thousands of years in the

Middle East). A thermal chimney uses solar energy to heat air, which rises and is exhausted out the top of the chimney, causing a natural convection loop as cooler air is drawn into the building (sometimes through a cool underground duct) to replace the exhausted hot air. Evaporative cooling draws heat from the air to vaporize water, making the resultant air cooler and more humid. This works in dry climates, where it may be desirable to add humidity. **Earth sheltering** and **earth coupling** take advantage of the vast thermal mass of the ground, which remains a constant temperature at a certain depth below grade (the depth depending on the climate). Earth sheltering can also protect the building from inclement weather, such as strong wind.

In a climate with a large diurnal temperature swing, **thermal mass cooling** can be accomplished by allowing cool nighttime air to flow across a large indoor building mass, such as a slab. The cool thermal mass then absorbs heat during the day.

Though not a passive technology, **radiant cooling** is more efficient than conventional systems that circulate conditioned air. Typically, radiant cooling involves running cool water through floor slabs, or wall or ceiling panels. In a hot dry climate, the water can be cooled evaporatively and radiatively by spraying it over a building roof at night, then collecting and storing the cooled water for use the next day. In a humid climate, dehumidification is needed in addition to cooling, but lowering humidity and providing airflow can enable people to be comfortable at temperatures up to nine degrees warmer than they otherwise would be.[9]

## Renewable Energy

According to the National Renewable Energy Lab, "each day more solar energy falls to the earth than the total amount of energy the planet's 5.9 billion people would consume in 27 years." Solar energy is the only energy income the earth receives. (Wind, tidal, and biomass energy are all derived from solar energy.) Of course, the less energy we need after applying all the energy-efficiency measures, the less it will cost to supply the remaining energy demand with renewable sources.

After all practical steps have been taken to reduce energy loads, appropriate renewable energy sources should be evaluated. These include wind, biomass from waste materials, ethanol from crop residues, passive heating and cooling, photovoltaics, geothermal, tidal, and environmentally benign hydro (including micro-hydro) technologies. Clean, distributed energy production methods include fuel cells and microturbines. If a building is more than a quarter-mile from a power line, it may be less expensive to provide "off-grid" power than to connect to a grid.[10] This is a particularly valid consideration in developing countries. (In the U.S., building remote from the grid probably means pushing further into wildlands, which usually poses other sustainability issues.)

## Third-Party Commissioning

Building commissioning—independent assessment of systems to ensure that their installation and operation meets design specifications and is as efficient as possible—can save as much as 40% of a building's utility bills for heating, cooling, and ventilation, according to Lawrence Berkeley National Laboratory.[11] The commissioning agent ideally gets involved with the project at its outset. Throughout the life of the building, ongoing, regularly-scheduled maintenance and inspection as well as formal "re-commissioning" ensure proper, planned performance and efficiency of the building and its mechanical systems. *(See Chapter 12 for more on commissioning.)*

## Enhanced Security

An important benefit of widespread construction of energy-efficient buildings, building-efficiency retrofits, and renewable energy generation is the reduction of dependence on foreign fossil fuels, a trend that could greatly enhance U.S. security, while creating a more trade-balanced, resource-abundant world. Security is further enhanced by efficient buildings and distributed energy production lessening the need for large centralized power plants that could provide strategic targets for terrorist attack.

## *Demolition/ Construction Practices*

With any site development, it is important to protect the watershed, natural resources, and agricultural areas, and therefore to be especially vigilant about erosion control and pollution prevention. Rather than degrading the surrounding environment, development can actually enhance it.

Demolition and construction should be carefully planned to reduce or eliminate waste. Typically, demolition and construction debris account for 15%–20% (in some places, up to 40%) of municipal solid waste that goes to landfills, while estimates are that potentially 90% of this "waste" could be reusable or recyclable.[12]

Ideally, planning for waste reduction begins not when a building is about to be demolished, but with initial building design. Buildings can be designed for flexibility to accommodate changing uses over time, for ease of alteration, and for deconstructability should the building no longer be suited for any use. Planning for deconstruction involves using durable materials and designing building assemblies so that materials can be easily separated when removed. For example, rather than adhering rigid foam roof insulation to the roof surface, installing a sheathing layer in between allows the insulation to be reused. Window assemblies can also be designed for easy replacement, which is not unlikely during a building's life.

Reusing and recycling construction and demolition waste is the "environmentally friendly" thing to do, and could also result in cost savings while promoting local entrepreneurial activities. A waste reduction plan, clearly outlined in the project's specifications, would require the following:

- Specification of waste-reducing construction practices.
- Vigilance about reducing hazardous waste, beginning by substituting nontoxic materials for toxic ones, where possible.
- Reuse of construction waste (or demolition) material on the construction site (for instance, concrete can be ground up to use for road aggregate).
- Salvage of construction and demolition waste for resale or donation.
- Return of unused construction material to vendors for credit.
- Delivery of waste materials to recycling sites for remanufacture into new products.
- Tracking and reporting all of this activity.

It is critical to note that reusing, salvaging, and/or recycling materials requires additional up-front planning. The contractor must have staging/storage locations and must allot additional time for sorting materials, finding buyers or recycling centers, and delivering the materials to various locations. *(See Chapter 3 for more on deconstruction practices.)*

## Recycling

"Americans produce an estimated 154 million tons of garbage—roughly 1,200 pounds per person—every year. At least 50% of this trash could be, but currently isn't, recycled," according to Alice Outwater.[13] Recycling doesn't stop at the job site. The building should be designed to foster convenient recycling of goods throughout the life of the building. This usually entails easily accessible recycling bins or chutes, space for extra dumpsters or trash barrels at the loading dock, and a recycling-oriented maintenance plan.

## Environmental Sensitivity

### Learning from the Locals

Every region of the world has a traditional building culture or a "vernacular" architecture. Because people in the past could not rely on providing comfort through the use of large quantities of resources extracted and transported over long distances, they had to make do with local resources and climate-efficient designs. Thus structures in the hot, dry U.S. Southwest made use of high-thermal-mass adobe with water-cooled courtyards. New England homes used an efficient, compact "saltbox" design. In the South, "dogtrot" homes with high ceilings provided relief from the hot, humid climate.

But how did the first settlers decide how to build? It could be that they—and we—have a lot to learn from other types of "locals"—from the wisdom of the natural world. For example, according to their descendants, the original Mexican settlers of the San Luis Valley of Colorado, wondered how thick to make the walls of their adobe homes in the new climate. To answer the question, they measured the depth of the burrows of the local ground squirrels and built to those exact specifications.

Looking to nature for design solutions makes a lot of sense. Over the course of 3.8 billion years of evolution, poorly adapted or inefficient design solutions became extinct—those that are still with us can give us clues as to how our own buildings and site solutions can be better adapted. For instance, human-engineered drainage systems use concrete storm drains to remove water as fast as possible from where it falls, often channeling it to municipal sewage systems where it is mixed with sewage. As more and more of a city gets covered with impermeable surfaces, these combined stormwater/sewage systems cannot handle the load of big storms, which can overflow into streets and erode and pollute streams. By contrast, a solution modeled on natural drainage would have surface swales, check dams, depressions, temporal wetland areas, and ecologically appropriate plants to absorb water over a large area, closer to where it falls. Clustering development to allow for open areas where natural drainage can occur provides natural beauty and an effective stormwater solution, reduces the strain on the sewage treatment plant, provides habitat for other species, and costs less to build.

As is true with so many green building solutions, a roof covered in native grasses provides multiple benefits—it helps solve the stormwater runoff problem, increases roof insulation value, greatly extends roof life (due to blocked ultraviolet radiation), lowers ambient air temperature (by reducing radiation from the roof) thereby lowering the urban "heat island" effect, improves air quality (by producing $O_2$, absorbing $CO_2$, and filtering the air), increases wildlife habitat, adds beauty, and can provide pleasant, usable outdoor space, even in a crowded city. With growing awareness of all these benefits, an increasing number of cities around the world are providing incentives for green roofing, even mandating it for some buildings.[14]

## Site Selection & Development

How can development leave a place better than the way it was found? A key tenet of green development is to promote health and diversity for humans and the natural environment that supports us. One approach is to restore degraded land to enhance long-term proliferation of life. Responsible site development also involves attention to human culture and community, as well as to the needs of other species in a diverse ecosystem.

**Renovating** existing buildings should be considered before looking for new building sites. This reduces construction costs, while salvaging an existing resource. Sometimes it keeps a building from being demolished, which is critical because a building's biggest energy use is typically associated with its construction. This approach may even preserve cultural heritage by keeping a historic building in use and maintained.

If no suitable existing building can be found, "brownfield" or infill sites should be evaluated next. **Brownfield** sites are abandoned industrial areas that often require remediation prior to new construction. If hazardous wastes are present, the use of the site should be carefully considered, even though remediation will be performed *(See Figure 1.3 for an example of an award winning brownfield rejuvenation project.)* **Infill** simply means building on a vacant site within an established urban area, rather than on the outskirts.

All three of these options—building renovation, brownfield, and infill development—preserve farmland and ecologically valuable natural areas and limit "urban sprawl." These options also tend to have lower infrastructure costs, because transportation infrastructure and utilities such as sewage, electricity, and gas are usually already in place. Finally, these sites are usually located close to existing schools, businesses, entertainment, and retail, enhancing convenience and potentially reducing automobile use.

When choosing a new building site, important considerations include the availability of a sufficient, rechargeable water source and access to renewable energy sources (such as solar, wind, geothermal, or biomass). Developing land that is ecologically sensitive (including wetlands or rare habitats), prime farmland, culturally/archeologically significant, or vulnerable to wildfire or floods should be avoided.

Where should a building be sited? "Buildings must always be built on those parts of the land that are in the worst condition, not the best."[15] Open space should not be the "leftover" area. After preserving (and sometimes restoring) the most ecologically valuable land in its natural state, additional open spaces for outdoor activities should be as carefully planned as the spaces within buildings.

Green development includes regional planning that gives priority to people, not to automobile circulation. The design of a green development should accommodate people who are too old, too young, or financially or physically unable to drive. Such developments include

Before

Before

After

The new Jack Evans Police Headquarters facility made use of abandoned commercial property, formerly occupied by Sears Automotive. The first two photos show the unoccupied automotive service center and its basement prior to its demolition in 2000. The third photo shows the new police headquarters, up for LEED Gold certification. This project was a recipient of the EPA's Phoenix Award in 2003 for brownfield redevelopment. *(Photos courtesy of Ann Grimes of the Dallas Office of Economic Development.)*

**Figure 1.3**
Brownfield Rejuvenation

public transit (preferably pollution-free), parks, pedestrian and bike trails, an unsegregated mix of housing types (from low- to high-income, all in the same neighborhood), and a balance of housing, business, and retail in close proximity. Other goals of a green development are to limit sprawl (with urban growth boundaries, for instance) and to provide distributed electricity generation systems (those located close to the user, such as fuel cells, photovoltaic arrays, wind microturbines, biomass, and geothermal).

## Water/Landscape

A myriad of problems can result from impervious surfaces: urban heat islands (asphalt-laden cities that are several degrees hotter than surrounding areas), altered stream flows (lower lows and higher highs, increased flooding), and polluted waters (from unfiltered road- and parking-surface runoff). Fortunately, cities are starting to see the economic and social value of preserving and restoring natural capital. Shade trees can reduce ambient air temperature by 15 degrees. Natural drainage can be far less expensive up-front, and far less costly in avoided flooding, pollution, and stream damage in the long run. There are many options for reducing stormwater runoff from a site, including reinforced grass paving, porous asphalt, rainwater-collection cisterns, infiltration islands in parking lots, swales, dry wells, and planted stormwater retention areas.

One type of landscape often overlooked in development is edible plantings. Gardens, orchards, or crops can and should be incorporated into both residential and commercial projects. These plantings can serve all the functions of non-edible landscaping (e.g., cooling and stormwater absorption) and produce food as well. The Village Homes community in Davis, CA, for instance, has a revenue-producing almond orchard, as well as a wide variety of fruit trees interspersed along pedestrian paths.

Although turf grass serves to facilitate many functions, such as play and picnic areas, it need not be planted ubiquitously in areas that are not going to be used for those functions. The turf grass that is planted on lawns and corporate campuses is typically a non-native, monoculture crop that requires constant human input (mowing, watering, fertilizing, and dousing with pesticides and herbicides). These inputs are neither cheap nor environmentally sound. By contrast, native landscape is perfectly adapted to thrive in the local environment and therefore needs no irrigation or fertilizer, is ecologically diverse enough to resist pests, and provides free stormwater management. When landscape architect Jim Patchett replaced turf grass with native prairie on the Lyle, Illinois, campus of AT&T, multiple problems were solved, while maintenance costs dropped from $2,000 to $500 per acre.

## Sewage Treatment

The average U.S. effluent production is about 100 gallons per capita per day, which creates a tremendous sewage burden. Most cities run sewage through primary and secondary treatment plants that use both mechanical and chemical processes, which typically remove about 90%–95% of the solids in the wastewater. Tertiary treatment can remove 99% of solids, but is rarely done because costs are considered too high for the marginal benefit. This means that in most cities, up to 10% of everything that is flushed down the toilet escapes the treatment plant and ends up in the waterways.[16]

The first goal for more sustainable sewage systems is to reduce the amount of effluent that needs to be treated in the first place with water-efficient (or waterless) plumbing fixtures. Waterless urinals not only reduce water consumption, they are also more sanitary and odor-free than standard urinals, because bacteria prefer wet surfaces. Composting toilets detoxify human waste without water (and produce usable fertilizer), but they do require a lifestyle adjustment.

After sewage is minimized, the most ecologically sound methods of treating it should be evaluated. Biological sewage treatment systems detoxify the waste from standard toilets and can treat sewage to tertiary levels. They can take several forms, including constructed wetlands, greenhouse systems, and algal turf scrubber systems. Whether the wastewater is being purified by bacteria, plants, invertebrates, fish, and sunlight in a series of tanks in a greenhouse, or by an outdoor wetland ecosystem, the idea is to use natural processes. This significantly reduces chemical use, energy use, and potentially, operational costs. Unlike conventional systems, these alternative systems also provide an amenity—they are appealing, typically odor-free, and can provide plants for sale to nurseries and purified water for reuse in the landscape. Some biological sewage treatment systems have even become tourist attractions.

## Designing for People: Health & Productivity

## Building Design & Materials

The recent exposure that "Sick Building Syndrome" has been given in the news media has raised awareness around the issue of how buildings affect the people occupying them. This is significant, because the average American spends 90% of his or her

**Sick Building Syndrome**

**High-risk people:** Elderly, children, and people with allergies, asthma, compromised immune systems, or contact lenses.

**Symptoms:** Headache; fatigue; congestion; shortness of breath; coughing; sneezing; eye, nose, throat, and skin irritation; dizziness; and nausea.

**Multiplicative effects:** Combining chemicals, poor temperature and lighting, ergonomic stressors, and job stress.

time indoors. Sick Building Syndrome has been attributed to tighter buildings and poor air quality caused by off-gassing of volatile organic compounds (VOCs) from modern finish materials (such as paints, adhesives, carpets, and vinyl); poorly vented combustion appliances; equipment and chemicals (such as copiers and lab or cleaning compounds); tobacco smoke; soil gases (such as radon, pesticides, and industrial site contaminants); molds and microbial organisms; and intake of outdoor air contaminated with pollen, pollution, or building exhaust.

Air quality should be protected by ensuring adequate ventilation and locating air intakes away from dumpsters, exhaust vents, loading docks, and driveways. Carbon dioxide monitors can be installed to ensure adequate (but not excessive) ventilation, thereby optimizing both air quality and energy efficiency. Heat recovery ventilators can capture heat from the exhausted air (or pre-cool the incoming air, depending on the climate). Most important, however, is to ensure the best possible air quality in the first place, when the building is constructed. Properly vent radon, use nontoxic building materials, and design wall, roof, and foundation assemblies to avoid mold growth by keeping rain and condensation out of them in the first place and providing a way for it to dry out if it does get in. *(See Chapter 7 for more on indoor air quality.)*

## Maintenance

Protecting the indoor environment does not stop when building construction is completed. Air quality must be ensured through routinely scheduled maintenance and housekeeping. If roof or plumbing leaks are undetected or neglected, hazardous molds can develop. Also important is *how* a building is maintained and with what type of housekeeping products. A building can be carefully designed with nontoxic finishes, only to have the fumes from noxious cleaning products absorbed into soft finish materials.

Some systems are easier to maintain than others. For instance, it is more difficult for microbes to grow on metal air ducts than on those lined with fiberboard insulation, and the metal ducts are also easier to clean. Regularly changing air filters and maintaining carpets and other finishes is critical. Occupants and custodial staff should be educated so they understand how to protect a building's healthfulness and performance, as well as its appearance. Human exposure to harmful chemicals should be minimized, and procedures should be established to address potential accidents with hazardous chemicals.

## A More Natural Indoor Environment

Despite the difficulty of pinpointing the cause of health problems, there is currently little doubt that poor indoor environmental quality plays a role in many common maladies such as headaches, eyestrain, fatigue, and even more serious illnesses such as asthma and chemical sensitivity. If poor lighting, stale air, harsh acoustics, and lack of connection to nature can compromise people's health at work or at home, what effect does improving these conditions have? Several studies of green office, school, and hospital buildings have shown that factors such as high levels of daylighting, views to nature, individual control of workplace environment, and improved acoustics are strongly related to improved health and productivity, including faster healing in hospitals, higher test scores in schools, lower absenteeism in offices, and generally lower stress levels.[17]

> **Factors that Enhance Productivity and Health**
> - Quality lighting, including high levels of daylighting
> - Increased individual control of workplace, including lighting
> - Heating and cooling
> - Improved acoustics
> - Improved indoor air quality
> - Views to nature

Researchers in a field called "biophilia" are studying the correlation between building ecology (specifically more "natural" environments that feature views to nature, daylight, and fresh air) and good health. Their theory is that human evolution predisposed us to thrive in the natural environment, and thus connecting to it at work or at home positively impacts our performance and well-being. There may be other benefits as well. For instance, NASA research has shown that significant quantities of plants can purify many toxins from the air.[18]

# Quality Lighting
## *Daylighting*
Quality lighting starts with well designed daylighting, which is more than just providing windows. In order to avoid glare (the difference in luminance ratio between a window and its adjoining spaces), daylight must be introduced—or reflected—deep into the building, and direct-beam light (such as that from standard skylights) should be diffused or reflected onto a ceiling. These goals can be accomplished using light monitors, clerestories, light shelves, advanced skylight systems, atria, courtyards, and transom glass atop partitions. Light-colored finishes greatly enhance the ambient brightness of the room. *(See Chapter 7 for more on daylighting.)*

## Indoor Electric Lighting

With daylighting and electric lighting designed as an integrated system, the amount of electric lighting needed during most of the day can be reduced. For instance, if linear fluorescent fixtures are run parallel to window walls, those that are close to the window can be dimmed with automatic dimming controls when daylight is ample. Rather than dropping a set number of footcandles of light into an area, quality lighting is the careful art of directing light onto surfaces where it is specifically needed—primarily on walls and ceilings (not on floors).

Fixtures that provide mainly indirect, but also some direct light will create an even, glare-free ambiance, to which task lighting can be added to accommodate specific activities and individual preferences. Accent lighting can be added to create sparkle and to draw people into or through a space. Within a well-designed lighting system, efficient lighting fixtures, such as fluorescent tube lights, compact fluorescent lights (CFLs), and light emitting diodes (LEDs) will further reduce energy use.

## Outdoor Lighting

Glaring outdoor light should be avoided in new installations and replaced in existing ones. Bright, glaring light can be intrusive and dangerous (elderly people often take minutes to adapt back to lower light levels), and it imparts light pollution to night skies. This is a serious issue, not only for astronomers, but also for natural systems such as the nesting and migration of birds. Hooded fixtures are a good choice to protect nighttime darkness. For security lighting, it is preferable to provide uniform glare-free illumination on horizontal surfaces (rather than bright spots of light) and to highlight important vertical surfaces—such as destination doorways. White light provides the best peripheral vision. Yellow light, as provided by low- and high-pressure sodium lamps, accommodates no peripheral vision at all.

## Individual Environmental Control

Operable windows, furniture with adjustable ergonomic features, dimmable lighting, and available task lighting are all examples of provisions for individual environmental control. Adjustable thermostats or, even better, under-floor air distribution with an airflow diffuser for each occupant, can provide individuals with temperature control. Such provisions allow people to maximize their personal comfort and provide psychological benefit as well. Even people who rarely open their windows appreciate being able to do so.

**Figure 1.4**
Hooded outdoor lamps, such as this one, help protect nighttime darkness by directing light flow down, only where it is needed. *(Photo courtesy of the International Dark-Sky Association.)*

## Green Building Hurdles

If green building has so many advantages, why isn't everyone doing it? There are currently several impediments to the universal practice of green building. First, although it has grown tremendously in the past few years, it is still a relatively new field, with the knowledge base continuing to grow among design and construction professionals. Second, developers and builders tend to try to keep things as simple as possible because "experimentation" adds time to a project, and time means money. Moreover, tried and true methods avoid liability risk, because lawsuits are often based on deviation from standard practice.

Market expectation also plays a role in a "Catch-22" fashion. Developers build what is selling on the market, while people buy what is available on the market. Without a large sample of green buildings to choose from, there is little room for market demand to drive construction of green buildings. Developers and builders who take the risk to build green are typically well rewarded, but if no one in the area has tried it yet, there may be few who are bold enough to be the first.

Misguided incentives cause yet another problem. Usually design decisions are made by developers and their hired design teams, but most of the financial and other benefits of a green building accrue to end users—owners or tenants who typically have no input in the design. Other less quantifiable benefits accrue to the community and society at large. Although there is growing evidence that green buildings provide lower operational costs and better quality environments, the mainstream market hasn't recognized this yet. Only when this happens will mainstream developers have the full incentive to build green, knowing that they will enjoy premium rents, lower turnover, fewer liability risks, and a better reputation.

## Conclusion

Termites live in inhospitable climates of Africa, Australia, and the Amazon by building air circulation passages in the walls of their structures that can cool the inside by as much as 20°F. These termite mounds are as hard as concrete, but constructed out of locally collected soil, wood fiber, and the termites' own saliva.

We don't have to live in termite mounds to benefit from the ingenuity of their design. Nature's innovations—structures made and operated with local materials, current solar income, and no toxicity—should be the role models for our own built environment. We need to stop asking the question, "how can we do less harm?" and ask instead how we can *enhance* the human experience in the built environment, while enhancing the natural environment at the same time. Toxic building materials, energy-inefficient building systems and methods, and reliance on non-renewable energy sources are short-term, ultimately detrimental solutions. We need to start relying on solutions that are well adapted for life on earth in the long run.

Green building is a turn in the right direction. Sustainably designed new buildings can produce more energy than they consume; use local, nontoxic, low-energy materials; and enhance occupant experience, all while benefiting the surrounding community. And green buildings make good, long-term economic sense. When systems are properly integrated, overall first costs may be lower for green buildings than for standard buildings, while operational costs are almost always lower for green buildings.

Even more important, studies have shown that in green buildings, workers are more productive and take fewer sick days, students learn faster and are absent less often, and hospital patients heal more quickly and require less medication.[19] Green buildings are fundamentally better buildings; it's time for them to become the norm, not the exception.

1. Mattiessen, Lisa Fay, and Peter Morris. *Costing Green: A Comprehensive Cost Database and Budgeting Methodology.* 2004.

2. Kats, Greg, et al. "The Costs and Financial Benefits of Green Buildings. A Report to California's Sustainable Building Task Force." October 2003.

3. Roodman, D., and Lenssen, N. "A Building Revolution: How Ecology and Health Concerns Are Transforming Construction." Worldwatch Paper #124. Worldwatch Institute, Washington, DC, 1995.

4. Hawken, Lovins & Lovins. *Natural Capitalism: Creating the Next Industrial Revolution.* Little Brown & Company, 1999.

5. Barnett, Dianna Lopez, and William D. Browning. *A Primer on Sustainable Building.* Rocky Mountain Institute, 1995.

6. E SOURCE, Inc. *Drivepower Technology Atlas.* Chapter 1. 1993.

7. Hobbs, Frank, and Nicole Stoops. "Demographic Trends in the 20th C. Census 2000 Special Reports". U.S. Census Bureau; U.S. Census Bureau website: United States and States R1105, Average Household Size: 2004; and National Association of Home Buildings (Housing Facts, Figures and Trends for March 2006).

8.  Barnett, Dianna Lopez, and William D. Browning. *A Primer on Sustainable Building*. Rocky Mountain Institute, 1995.

9.  Ibid.

10. RMI literature.

11. Lawrence Berkeley National Laboratory literature.

12. Triangle J. Council of Governments. "WasteSpec: Model Specifications for Construction Waste." 1996-2002.

13. Barnett, Dianna Lopez, and William D. Browning. *A Primer on Sustainable Building*. Rocky Mountain Institute, 1995.

14. Some of the most aggressive green roof programs are in Portland, OR; Chicago, IL; Basel, Switzerland; Muenster and Stuttgart, Germany: from "Making Green Roofs Happen," November, 2005, www.toronto.ca/greenroofs/pdf/makingsection2_nov16.pdf

15. Alexander, Christopher, et al. *A Pattern Language*. Oxford University Press, 1977.

16. Alice Outwater. *Water: A Natural History*. Chapter 11. Basic Books, 1996.

17. Romm, Joseph J. and William D. Browning. "Greening the Building and the Bottom Line: Increasing Productivity through Energy Efficient Design." 1994; Heshong Mahone Group. "Daylighting in Schools: An Investigation into the Relationship Between Daylighting and Human Performance." 1999; Ovitt, Margaret A. "Stress Reduction of ICU Nurses and Views of Nature," 1996.

18. Wolverton, Bill, http://www.wolvertonenvironmental.com

19. Romm, Joseph J. and William D. Browning. "Greening the Building and the Bottom Line: Increasing Productivity through Energy Efficient Design," 1994; Heshong Mahone Group, "Daylighting in Schools: An Investigation into the Relationship Between Daylighting and Human Performance," 1999; Ovitt, Margaret A. "Stress Reduction of ICU Nurses and Views of Nature," 1996; Ulrich, R.S. 1984. "View Through a Window May Influence Recovery from Surgery." Science 224: 420-421.

# 2 Introduction to Green Building Materials & Systems

## Alexis Karolides, AIA

S ince cave dwellers first placed brush or animal skins in front of the cave opening, humans have used building materials for shelter. In fact, most animal species alter their immediate environments by building dwellings with collected or self-manufactured materials. Nothing could be more natural. So what is it about our current manufacture and use of materials that raises concern?

Animals' dwellings made from nontoxic, energy-efficient materials allow them to survive. The materials are recycled back into the environment after their useful life as a dwelling. Human use of materials, until recent history, followed these same principles. Things began to change with the advent of metals, but it was the industrial revolution that really accelerated the change. Suddenly we had an industrial production system dependent on the most intense energy source yet known, the stored energy of millions of years of photosynthesis buried beneath the earth's crust as fossil fuels. We learned to manufacture all imaginable materials from steel to plastic, and we could transport them across the world. The seemingly endless abundance of fossil fuels, and the vastness of the surrounding environment to absorb the toxic by-products of burning them, seemed to negate the evolutionary rules followed by all other animal species: local supply, low embodied energy, nontoxic, and recyclable.

But here the problems begin. First of all, using a stored resource is like dipping into a savings account, and the United States' savings account of fossil fuel reserves, once seemingly endless, is dwindling. Second, the earth's ability to assimilate the toxic and slow-to-degrade by-products and end-products of human manufacturing is no longer guaranteed— all of the earth's major life support systems are either stressed or in decline. Finally, many of our own products are made with chemicals that are making us sick. Exacerbating this problem, our buildings are increasingly airtight, and those of us in industrialized nations are spending on average 90% of our time indoors.[1]

The use of our "natural resource savings account" to construct and operate buildings is by no means trivial. The construction and operation of U.S. buildings uses 40% of the country's energy, 16% of its fresh water, and three billion tons of raw materials per year, which is 40% of total global use. Moreover, building industry "by-products" include air and water pollution, as well as the solid waste that comprises 15%–40% of U.S. landfills.[2]

Equally significant is the concern that many contemporary building materials contribute to indoor air quality problems. For weeks or months after installation, standard products such as paints and adhesives off-gas volatile organic compounds (VOCs) that are harmful to humans.

Indoor air quality problems do not stop with material composition; material assembly can also be a culprit. In hot, humid climates, for instance, vapor impermeable vinyl wall covering can encourage mold formation when humid air condenses on the back of the wall covering. Certain mold spores, when inhaled, can be toxic and even deadly to humans.

So what can be done, given the myriad of products to choose from and the complex construction decisions to be made? One place to start is from the perspective of improving the indoor environmental quality for building occupants. Reducing exposure to toxic substances, such as VOCs, lead, mercury, and harmful molds and microbes, can help protect occupant health. Methods to achieve this goal include specifying low-VOC substitutes for conventional products (including paints, adhesives, and millwork); detailing interior finishes to minimize porous surfaces that can accumulate mold (for example, if tile is used, seal the grout); carefully designing building assemblies to avoid water entry; and, in some cases, avoiding microbial growth by eliminating certain finishes altogether (such as impermeable wall coverings in hot, humid climates or basement finishes that don't permit drying).

Equally important as indoor environmental quality is consideration of the larger environment. One way to address this goal is to favor products that reduce waste or environmental degradation. For instance, if carpet is to be used, modular carpeting (carpet tile) is recommended, because only those tiles in the wear pattern need frequent replacement. Recyclable carpet further enhances waste reduction and raw materials savings. Another material that fosters environmental health is wood that is certified from sustainably managed forests.

Purchasing local products reduces transportation and its associated energy consumption and pollution, supports the local economy and culture, and maintains regional identity by promoting the use of indigenous/traditional materials.

A more technical way of evaluating a material is to consider its embodied energy, an approximate measure of the energy (per unit mass) typically needed to produce a building product—most statistics refer to the process energy requirement for raw-material acquisition and product manufacture, but not other energy factors associated with producing and installing the product (such as upstream energy used in constructing and operating the factory itself or transportation of the product and workers to the building site).

Estimated embodied energy of some common materials (in mega joule/kg) are:[3,4]

- Baled straw = 0.24
- Concrete = 1.9
- Kiln-dried hardwood = 2.0
- Clay brick = 2.5
- Glass = 12.7
- Virgin steel = 32
- Recycled steel = 10
- Plastics (general) = 90
- Virgin aluminum = 180
- Recycled aluminum = 9

The high embodied energy associated with producing products such as plastic and aluminum makes it all the more important to recycle these products—recycling saves most of the energy for certain plastics, and 95% of the energy for aluminum.

Embodied energy fits into a larger energy-use picture: it is important to consider the climate, site, building design, and life cycle as a whole system. For instance, a large mass of a low-embodied energy material (such as concrete) adds up to high total embodied energy—this may be justified in a passive-solar building in a climate with a high diurnal temperature swing (where the mass can offset operational energy use over the life of the building), but not in a hot, humid climate or an inappropriately designed building. Other important factors associated with a material are its durability, reuse/recycling potential, and the environmental impacts associated with its production, use, and end-of-life disposition.

A much more comprehensive process for evaluating building materials is life cycle assessment (LCA), which considers the complex interaction between a product and the environment throughout the product's cradle-to-grave life cycle, including the associated environmental impacts of resource extraction, manufacturing, transportation, on-site construction, operations, maintenance, demolition and disposal (or recycling/reuse). In addition to embodied energy, LCA examines environmental impacts such as water use, resource depletion, toxic emissions, global warming potential, waste generation, etc. LCA is necessarily complex (its protocols and methodologies are defined by an international standard, ISO 14040); but it is useful as a tool that can inform product development, planning, and policy making, helping the building industry move toward maximizing long-term environmental and human benefit. *(See Chapter 14 for more on the environmental life cycle.)*

In summary, "green" building materials are those that:

- Are **healthy for the interior environment**—do not produce indoor air quality problems due to the release of harmful VOCs (such as urea-formaldehyde, which is carcinogenic) or harmful fibers and do not cause health problems for the factory workers who manufacture the product.

- Are **healthy for the outdoor environment**—do not increase the potential for smog, cause environmental degradation, deplete scarce resources, produce hazardous by-products or excessive processing waste, and do not cause health problems for the people who extract the resources used in the product.

- Help **minimize building energy use**—by preventing heat gain or loss, reducing electricity consumption, and simplifying maintenance.

- Have **low-embodied energy**—do not result from energy-intensive material acquisition and manufacturing processes. (Materials with a high amount of recycled content may meet this criteria as long as they don't require energy-intensive remanufacture.)

- Are **durable, reusable, recyclable, and/or biodegradable**—will not quickly need to be replaced and become "waste" or, worst of all, hazardous waste.

- Are **locally obtained**—support the local economy and do not require excessive transportation from resource collection and product manufacture to installation.

Applicable building codes and standards limit the choice of materials and assemblies for dwellings and most types of commercial buildings. Before specifying an unconventional material, such as straw-bale or adobe brick, check with code officials having jurisdiction to determine if it will be approved, or if a variance may be granted.

# Green Material Alternatives by CSI Division

## Division 01 – General Requirements

The general requirements should include on-site sorting of materials to facilitate their reuse on the construction site, salvaging for resale or donation, or recycling into other products. While demolition and construction debris consumes on average 15%–20% (up to a staggering 40%) of U.S. landfill capacity, estimates are that potentially 90% of this "waste" could be reusable or recyclable.[5] Because reusing, salvaging, and/or recycling materials requires additional up-front planning, the contractor must have staging/storage locations and must allot additional time for sorting materials, finding buyers or recycling centers, and delivering the materials to various locations.

## Division 02 – Existing Conditions

Reuse existing materials where practical. For example, gypsum board scrap should be separated on the job site to allow pieces to be recycled. What cannot be recycled back into gypsum board product can be ground up to be used for a soil amendment (provided it is free of toxic paints or wall coverings).

## Division 03 – Concrete

Concrete is a strong, durable material with high heat storage capacity that can be used to moderate building temperature swings. Because traditional concrete is one of the most inert building materials, it is also a good product from an indoor air quality standpoint, even for chemically sensitive people. (This is not completely true for high-tech concretes that contain chemical agents for workability and air-entraining.)

Concrete does, however, have some environmental drawbacks. It can cause water pollution if wash-out water from equipment at concrete plants or on job sites finds its way to local waterways. The pH of washout water is so high, it is toxic to aquatic life. Another concern is the production of cement, the binding agent used in concrete, which accounts for about 10%–15% of concrete's mass, but 92% percent of its embodied energy. Cement manufacture is a major contributor to atmospheric greenhouse gases due to both its production and process emissions. According to a U.S. EPA report, in producing a total of 90 million metric tons of cement in 2001, the U.S. cement industry emitted 77 million metric tons of $CO_2$. About 46% of these emissions are attributed to combusting fuel, predominantly coal and coke, to fire cement kilns to temperatures up to 3,400 degrees Fahrenheit; the remaining 54% of the emissions result from the chemical process of making cement, which involves converting limestone to calcium oxide and $CO_2$.[6] Cement production accounts for 1.5% of all U.S. $CO_2$ emissions (according to the Portland Cement Association); *worldwide,* however, cement production causes over 8% of the total $CO_2$ emissions attributed to human activity.[7] To its credit, the cement industry has made great strides in recent decades to increase energy efficiency and reduce emissions. For instance, the chemical process in cement production that releases $CO_2$ can be used to capture other combustion emissions such as sulfur dioxide and nitrogen oxide.

Furthermore, ongoing developments in concrete production can reduce environmental impacts by substituting other materials for cement. Up to 60% of the cement content used in traditional concrete may be replaceable with "supplementary cementitious material" (SCM) salvaged from industrial waste (or derived from natural soil or rock), depending on the concrete application, the type and quality of the substitute, and the results of batch testing. Industrial by-product SCMs include fly ash, a waste product from coal-fired power plants, **blast furnace slag**, a waste product from steel production, **silica fume**, a waste product from the silicon metal industry, and **rice hull (or husk) ash,** which is generated when agricultural rice waste is burned to produce power.

Replacing a percentage of the cement in concrete with an SCM reduces energy consumption and $CO_2$ production, reduces solid waste, and can *improve* concrete strength, performance, and durability.[8] Because power plants are common in most cities, fly ash can usually be obtained locally. Global implications of using rice hull waste are tremendous. Rice is the world's main staple crop, generating 100 million tons of hulls annually, which is traditionally burned along with the straw in the fields, causing pollution and health problems. Burning the crop waste in small power plants could generate electricity, dispose of the waste, and provide a high-quality cement substitute.

To minimize the environmental problems with concrete, the following measures should be taken.

- Reduce concrete waste by recycling crushed concrete for fill material or road base, or grinding it up for aggregate. (Currently only 5% of concrete is recycled. By weight, it represents up to 67% of construction and demolition waste.)[9]
- Carefully estimate the amount of concrete required to avoid ordering excess amounts that become waste.
- Consider less material-intensive alternatives to poured-in-place concrete, such as insulation-form walls and autoclaved cellular concrete block. Precast concrete is factory-made to order, which, due to controlled production processes, also reduces concrete waste.
- Use insulated shallow foundations in northern climates; consider pier-and-beam foundations instead of slabs on grade.

- Protect aquatic ecosystems by washing forms and equipment where runoff will not contaminate waterways.
- Use the maximum amount of fly ash or other SCM appropriate to the construction application, location, and material quality.

## Division 04 – Masonry

Masonry includes brick, block, and stone. Because masonry components are common in many regions of the world, it is generally quite easy to use locally obtained masonry. However, as with many products, it is not a given that a locally obtained masonry product will also be locally manufactured. (A local stone may be selected, only to be shipped overseas for manufacture.) Thus, careful masonry specification is important to avoid energy- and pollution-intensive transportation and to support the local economy.

Masonry is resistant to deterioration from moisture and insects, and is well-suited for warm climates where less insulation is required. Adobe is an especially environmentally friendly masonry product, using a small fraction of the production energy of fired brick, making it a very low-embodied energy material. Unlike standard brick, adobe does not require oven-curing. It is made from clay, sand, and water, then cured in the sun and assembled with mud-based mortar. (Traditionally, straw was sometimes added to avoid cracking, but the correct 20% clay/80% sand ratio can prevent cracking.)[10]

## Division 05 – Metals

Metals have become such a common element in so many building applications, from nails to plumbing fixtures, that it would be hard to imagine building without them. Metals are strong, durable, and generally do not cause indoor air quality problems. (Airborne dust from lead paint is a notable exception.)

Sometimes metals are just one of several viable material choices, in which case it is instructive to compare options. Structural framing is one such example. The debate over which is the "greener" framing material—steel or wood—has no unanimous resolution. Although steel is highly recyclable and its raw materials are plentiful, wood is a renewable resource, is recyclable and biodegradable, and has much lower embodied energy than steel (even recycled steel has five times the embodied energy of kiln-dried wood). Wood is also a natural insulator, whereas steel is a conductor. (It is 400 times more conductive than wood.) The "thermal bridging" that occurs at exterior walls where steel studs span from the inside out can halve the overall R-value[11] of a wall with cavity insulation (as compared to the R-value of the same wall framed with wood). This presents a major energy-efficiency problem for steel-framed exterior walls. Providing a layer of continuous exterior insulation, while it does not completely solve the thermal bridging problem, can significantly increase the overall R-value of the steel-stud wall.[12]

On the other hand, steel framing is lighter than wood, more regular and dimensionally stable, and offers the advantage of resistance to insects. It does not require (as wood does) treating the soil with termiticides, and therefore is better for air quality. Steel is easily separated at the demolition site using a magnet, and steel scrap has a ready market. The overall recycled content of U.S. steel (on average for all steel products) is 46%, but this doesn't account for the steel scrap that is exported (11% of the total manufactured steel) rather than re-manufactured in the U.S.[13]

Both the wood and steel industries have caused serious environmental problems. Clear-cutting forests has caused habitat destruction and siltation of streams (and pesticide-laden, monoculture plantation forests are not much of an improvement). Strip-mining for the iron and limestone used in steel has caused severe erosion, ecosystem destruction, and leaching from tailings piles into water systems. Fortunately, both industries are making environmental and efficiency improvements.

In an application that allows the use of either wood or steel (especially if *untreated* wood can be used), wood *from a certified, well-managed forest* would be the most environmentally sound choice. Overall, its manufacturing process uses much less energy and creates less pollution and environmental degradation than mining and processing steel.[14]

The mining and manufacture of other metals presents environmental concerns similar to those associated with steel, and often much more severe. For instance, the embodied energy of copper is about twice that of steel, while virgin aluminum has as much as seven times the embodied energy of steel.[15]

Like steel, other metals used in building are highly recyclable. Although remanufacturing metals uses significant energy, it is much less than the energy and environmental impacts of starting with the virgin resource. Because metals are highly durable and could be recycled indefinitely, their environmental impact (extraction from the earth and the fact that they are nonrenewable resources) is significantly reduced.

Finally, metals offer clear advantages for certain applications. For example, if water collected from a roof surface is to be used for drinking, a steel roof will not leach petro-chemicals into the water, as an asphalt-based roof might. Although stone or clay tile roofing could also be used, their greater weight would require more structural support than the lighter steel.

# Division 06 – Wood, Plastics, and Composites
## Wood
**Certified wood** should be used for any wood application for which it is available. Certified wood comes from well-managed forests that seek to balance the sometimes competing economic, community and environmental concerns associated with lumber harvesting and production. Certified wood suppliers can be found by using the interactive website **http://www.certifiedwood.org** and clicking on Certification Resource Center.

## Structural Support Members
Years ago, the dwindling supply of old growth timber spurred the wood industry to manufacture structural products that can be made with smaller diameter, lower-strength, faster-growing tree species. Engineered wood products include glu-lam beams, I-joists, and oriented strandboard. These products enhance quality control while reducing pressure on natural forests. They can make use of up to 80% of each log, as compared to solid-sawn lumber, which only uses about 50%.[16]

Glu-lam beams are composed of wood boards glued together to create high-strength beams with depths ranging from 5" to 4" or more (depths and spans are limited only by shipping concerns). Similarly, prefabricated I-joists are more structurally efficient than solid joists, thus they require less wood. Engineered trusses are also an excellent option for creating predictable strength while reducing the amount and size/quality of materials required.

A potential downside of engineered wood is that it may contain toxic adhesives. Off-gassing of these toxins, such as formaldehyde, is particularly hazardous during curing in the factory (unless protective measures are taken), but still can be an issue after curing, especially for chemically sensitive people. These products may also release deadly gases in a fire. Fortunately, substitute products are now available.

## Sheathing
Composite sheathing and small-dimensional lumber products that are made with recycled wood fiber or that use sawmill waste or small-dimensional lumber help to conserve old growth forests. For applications that do not require high strength, sheathing products are currently available that are made of recycled wood fiber (up to 100%) and are themselves recyclable (up to 99%). These products use a relatively nontoxic bonding agent and are manufactured using less energy than oriented strand board (OSB) or plywood. To reduce air infiltration with any sheathing product, joints and edges must be sealed with air-barrier tape.

## Decking/Outdoor Wood Applications

Traditionally, naturally rot- and insect-resistant redwood and cedar were used for outdoor applications. Unfortunately, the popularity of these woods, combined with irresponsible logging practices, began to destroy the majestic old-growth forests in which they grew. Pressure treating wood with preservative made it possible to use species that were not naturally rot-resistant, but this produced other problems. Chromated copper arsenate (CCA) was the wood preservative most commonly used until 2003, when it was phased out due to its high toxicity to humans and other species, both during use and after disposal.

Fortunately, more sustainable alternatives exist today, including third-party certified redwood and cedar and wood treated with less toxic preservatives, such as alkaline copper quaternary (ACQ) and copper boron azole (CBA) for wood exposed to weather, or borate for wood not exposed to weather, but requiring pest-resistance. Wood treated with the copper-based ACQ and CBA should be avoided near aquatic ecosystems, however, since copper is highly toxic to many aquatic organisms.

Though initial costs are higher, recycled plastic lumber and composites that comprise recycled wood fiber and recycled plastic provide a decking alternative with some performance advantages, compared to real wood. These include reduced maintenance, increased longevity, and increased slip-resistance. They do raise a new set of environmental issues, such as the production and ultimate disposal of the materials used in their manufacture.

Other alternatives to preservative-treated or naturally rot-resistant wood include metal (especially for structural applications), landscape blocks or rocks for landscaping projects, and steel pilings filled with concrete (in lieu of creosote-treated underground pilings).

## Architectural Woodwork

Use of reclaimed timbers, where available, helps preserve old growth forests while making use of, rather than discarding, a valuable existing resource.

## Cabinetry

To improve indoor air quality, formaldehyde-free, low-VOC glues should be specified for both binders and laminate adhesives. Wheat-based fiberboard and other products from agricultural by-products are also excellent choices. If standard particleboard or fiberboard is used, it is important to ensure that the millwork is completely wrapped in laminate (including the edges) to reduce the off-gassing of VOCs (particularly urea-formaldehyde).

## Materials Made from Recycled Plastics

This type of recycling is more accurately termed **down-cycling** when, for instance, plastic soda containers are made into park benches rather than reused or remade into soda containers. Nevertheless, this approach is far preferable to the alternative—disposing of plastic in a landfill right away. Even though most down-cycled products cannot be recycled themselves, they keep the plastic out of the landfill much longer, buying time for engineers to develop better waste-elimination technologies. Examples of products available with 100% recycled content include:

- Wheel stops and speed bumps
- Park furnishings and trash receptacles
- Shelves and shower seats
- Drain pipes
- Toilet compartments
- Plastic signage
- Loading dock bumpers

# Division 07 – Thermal and Moisture Protection
## Insulation

Figure 2.1 shows the maximum R-values and features of common types of insulation.

The following are considerations when choosing an insulation material:

- Does the insulation retard airflow? (Spray foams and rigid insulations with sealed joints do; loose-fill, batt, and cellulose products do not.) Even if no perceptible gaps in the insulation are present, air under pressure will travel through products that are not airflow retarders. If gaps are present, the issue becomes even more critical. Even small gaps in fiberglass insulation have been found to decrease its effectiveness by up to almost 50%.[17]

- What type of insulation will provide the best R-value within a reasonable thickness for the particular application?

- Does the insulation pose potential health risks to installers or manufacturers, and if so, can proper precautions be used to prevent these risks?

- Does the insulation contain ozone-depleting chemicals?

- Does the insulation have the potential to release gaseous pollutants into the building interior?

- In a retrofit situation, what type of insulation is most practical? For instance, it may be possible to retrofit a conventionally framed structure by blowing insulation into the voids between studs (using holes drilled at the top and bottom of a wall and then resealing them). For a masonry building, however, unless there is a cavity between wall wythes, insulation must be added on either the inside or outside of the walls, which might impose space constraints or other considerations.

It should be noted that providing adequate insulation levels, even given the disadvantages of particular insulation products, is better than providing minimal insulation or none at all. The energy saved by the insulation will occur year after year, reducing the amount of heating and cooling required in the building and the burning of fossil fuels typically associated with that heating and cooling. That said, the best insulation for the job may depend on the circumstances. For instance, if space constraints are a critical issue, the high insulation value per inch of polyisocyanurate and high-density polyurethane foams (4" provides about R-30) may make them the best choices.

If chemical sensitivity is the most critical issue, the structure should be designed to accommodate adequate amounts of a product that does

| Type of Insulation | R-Value per Inch |
|---|---|
| Loose-fill: | |
| Cellulose | 3.1-3.7 |
| Fiberglass | 2.2-4.2 |
| Rock wool | 2.2-2.9 |
| | |
| Batts: | |
| Fiberglass | 2.9-3.8 |
| Cotton | 3.0-3.7 |
| | |
| Sprayed insulation: | |
| Polyurethane foam | 5.6-6.2 |
| Icynene foam | 3.6-4.3 |
| Wet-spray cellulose | 2.9-3.4 |
| Spray-in fiberglass | 3.7-3.8 |
| | |
| Foam board: | |
| Expanded Polystyrene | 3.9-4.2 |
| Extruded Polystyrene | 5 |
| Polyisocyanurate | 5.6-7.0 |
| Polyurethane | 5.6-7.0 |
| Phenolic (closed cell) | 8.2 |
| Phenolic (open cell) | 4.4 |
| | |
| *Source: DOE Insulation Fact Sheet www.eere.energy.gov/buildings* | |

**Figure 2.1**
Insulation Fact Sheet—Maximum R-Values

**Green Building: Project Planning & Cost Estimating**

not off-gas harmful pollutants, such as cementitious foam insulation. Alternative building materials that provide high insulation value without toxicity (such as straw bale construction) may also be a good choice for chemically sensitive people. *(See the "Alternative Materials" section later in this chapter.)*

Another general consideration is the reduction of insulation waste. Trimmings from insulation batts can be recycled into loose-fill insulation and cellulose excess can be reused during the installation process. Rigid foam roofing insulation can be salvaged during roofing retrofits if during the original installation a sheathing layer was installed between the insulation and the roof surface.

For roof insulation, loose-fill/blown or batt insulation can be added on top of the upper-story ceiling or, if the attic is to be used for storage, insulation can be installed between the rafters. In addition, a radiant barrier, which reflects radiant heat back (either into or out of a building, depending on the climate) can be attached to the underside of the rafters (or the underside of the insulation), with the shiny side facing down into the attic. It can also be attached on top of the ceiling joists (shiny side facing up into the attic). The radiant barrier must be adjacent to an air gap to work; otherwise heat will travel through the radiant barrier via conduction.

Foundation slabs should be insulated to the climatically appropriate degree by installing rigid insulation around the perimeter and underneath them before the concrete is poured. Pier and beam foundations can be insulated by filling the floor cavities over the crawl space with insulation. Thermal protection can also be achieved by installing a radiant barrier in the floor joist air space above an unheated basement or crawl space.

The R-value of a radiant barrier will vary greatly depending on its location (attic or basement) and whether it is the heating or cooling season. During the heating season, the radiant barrier will be effective in the floor joist air space above an unheated basement because the warm air above the basement will tend to stratify, eliminating convection and making radiation the prime mode of heat transfer. By contrast, in the attic space, during the heating season, convection will carry heat right past a radiant barrier. In the cooling season, however, a radiant barrier located in the attic will reflect the heat of a hot roof out of the cooler attic.

## Moisture Protection

Uncontrolled moisture transport is a very serious issue that can affect the health of the occupants and threaten the longevity of the building.

When moisture condenses or is trapped within a wall, roof or floor assembly, it can cause structural damage as well as mold and mildew, a major cause of indoor air quality problems.

Moisture can enter a building envelope in three ways—rain transport from outside, diffusion of water vapor through the envelope materials, and transport of water vapor in air that leaks through cracks in the envelope. Rain transport must be controlled with proper drainage planes in the wall assemblies. A properly located vapor diffusion retarder will help retard diffusion through a building envelope assembly. Much more significant than vapor diffusion, however, is the amount of moisture that can be carried through currents of air escaping through cracks and voids; thus the importance of sealing these cracks. As warmer air rises, it causes high pressure at the top of a building and low pressure at the bottom, resulting in what is called the **stack effect**. *(See Figure 2.2.)* At these points of greater pressure differential (namely the attic and basement), it is especially crucial to seal air leaks and use airflow retarders.

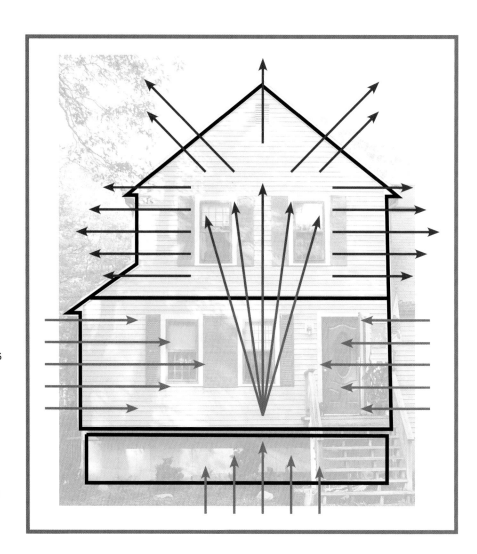

**Figure 2.2 Stack Effect**
As warmer air rises when surrounded by cooler temperatures outside, it causes high pressure at the top of the building and low pressure at the bottom. Cold air is drawn in through leaks and openings, such as doors and windows. At points of greater pressure differential, such as the attic and basement, it is especially crucial to seal air leaks and use airflow retarders.

Water build-up can be avoided by controlling air pressure, ventilation, and humidity, and through building envelope design (notably the placement of insulation, vapor diffusion retarders, and airflow retarders). To avoid condensation within the building envelope, a vapor diffusion retarder should be on the side of the envelope that is typically warmer and more humid.

Warm, moist air travels from inside to outside in cold climates (and in mixed climates, during the winter), but from outside to inside in warm climates (and in mixed climates, during the summer). Consequently, There is no one "correct" location for a vapor diffusion retarder for all climates and seasons. No matter how well detailed the building design or renovation is, moisture will still find its way into the envelope assembly. It is therefore critical that the assembly allow for drying to either the exterior or interior. The designer should evaluate the potential for condensation in each unique building envelope assembly over the annual outdoor temperature range and build forgiveness (drying potential) into the system.[18]

## Vapor Diffusion Retarders

Vapor diffusion retarders are materials with low permeability to water vapor (low "perm" rates). Materials that are considered to be "impermeable" include polyethylene, rubber membranes, glass, aluminum foil (commonly used as facing on insulation and sheathings), sheet metal, oil-based paints, and bitumen-impregnated kraft paper. Materials that are generally considered to be "semi-permeable" and can sometimes be used as vapor diffusion retarders depending on the specific design conditions include plywood, oriented strandboard (OSB), unfaced EPS and XPS, heavy asphalt-impregnated building paper, and most latex paints.[19]

## Airflow Retarders

Airflow retarders are continuous materials that are able to resist differences in air pressure caused by mechanical systems, the stack effect, and wind. Materials that are effective at retarding airflow include gypsum board, sheathing materials, rigid insulation, and sprayed foam insulation (assuming all joints, cracks, and penetrations have been properly sealed).

## Waterproofing & Dampproofing

If a structure is to be durable, nothing is more important than preventing water entry—from rain above ground and hydrostatic pressure below ground. The rainier the climate, the more rain control is needed. Gravity, wind pressure, momentum, surface tension, and capillary action can all cause rain to penetrate into a building surface. Each has been traditionally prevented by the following design techniques:

- Providing ample roof overhangs can help keep rain off the building surface to begin with.
- Avoiding straight-through openings in walls can prevent rain entry by momentum.
- Providing kerfs or drip edges can interrupt rain entry via surface tension.
- Providing flashings can direct gravity-flow rainwater back toward the building exterior.
- Providing a pressure-equalized or pressure moderated space in the air cavity behind the exterior wall face can prevent water entry via air pressure.[20]

Under the most severe rain exposures, providing a pressure equalized (vented) space behind the exterior cladding, combined with a "drainage plane" behind that, can prevent all these modes of water entry. For low-precipitation areas, an adequate approach (with a long track record) is to provide a face-sealed exterior wall of high mass masonry or concrete, which allows rain to be stored in the wall assembly mass for later drying. The least forgiving system is a face-sealed approach with no rain-storage mass, such as **external insulation finish systems** (EIFS). This system should be used only in the driest climates, unless a water management system (a drainage plane) is included.

Asphalt-impregnated felt (or tar paper) has been traditionally used as a drainage plane, but water-resistant sheathings, such as rigid insulation or foil-faced structural sheathing, can also serve the purpose. Window, door, and roof/wall intersections must be carefully detailed to ensure drainage plane continuity. Because the drainage plane is toward the outside of the wall assembly, impacts to indoor air quality from the tar paper or rigid board are typically only an issue for chemically sensitive people.

Hydrostatic pressure can drive water through basement walls unless they are properly detailed. Proper detailing involves sloping the ground away from the foundation and capping it with water-shedding clay, using free-draining granular backfill (such as sand) next to the foundation wall or installing a drainage board (such as rigid fiberglass), and providing perforated subgrade perimeter footing drains (to drain water so it does not build up around the foundation wall). The drains must be piped to daylight or a sump pump.

Foundations also require dampproofing to resist absorption of water through a foundation wall by capillary action. (Dampproofing is not designed to resist hydrostatic pressure and should not be confused with waterproofing.) Low-VOC dampproofing coatings that will not leach into the groundwater are the environmentally preferable option.

## Foundation Ventilation Systems

To keep moisture vapor, as well as radon, methane, and pesticide gases, out of foundations, the pressure next to them must be controlled. This is accomplished by creating negative pressure in the gravel drainage pad under the slab (or in the crawl space) with a ventilation system piped to daylight through the roof. Soil gases are removed by passive stack action or by exhaust fans.

Since no waterproofing system will avoid all moisture entry, and since concrete starts out wet to begin with, concrete slabs must be allowed to dry. With a polyethylene vapor diffusion retarder under the slab to keep ground moisture out, slabs can only dry into the building. Installing vapor-retardant flooring (such as carpet or vinyl) over a slab in a manner that does not permit drying, especially if the concrete has not had sufficient curing time to dry out, can lead to buckled flooring, as well as mold, mildew, and associated indoor air quality problems—which can be quite serious. Installing vapor-retardant finishes (or insulations) on interior basement walls that have dampproofing on their exterior surfaces can create similar problematic scenarios.

It is possible to allow slabs to dry to the outside by installing vapor permeable (or semi-permeable) rigid insulation under them, in lieu of a polyethylene vapor diffusion retarder. The insulation causes the slab to be warmer than the ground and, as long as there is no major vapor diffusion retarder, moisture will flow from warm to cold, even if the ground is saturated. Drying to the outside also works for foundation walls when dampproofing is replaced by rigid fiberglass or mineral wool insulation (which are vapor-permeable, but also provide drainage and a capillary break), but designers should be wary that this approach could provide an avenue for termites, if they are an issue in the region.

Unless the floor assembly over a crawl space is constructed like any other exterior envelope assembly (with insulating sheathing and vapor diffusion retarders), crawl spaces should not be vented with exterior air, but should be treated like basements (enclosed, heated during the winter, and cooled during the summer). Otherwise, venting crawlspaces with warm, humid summer air will cause condensation (and potential mold), because the crawl space surfaces will be cooler than the outside air. As mentioned above, crawl spaces should be kept under negative pressure, with soil gases exhausted to the outside. *(See Chapter 7 for more on mold issues.)*

## Roofing

Durability is critical in a roofing system, because failure can cause serious building damage and because frequent re-roofing is highly resource-intensive. For single-ply membrane roofs or built-up asphalt roofs, it is preferable to separate the rigid insulation from the roofing membrane so that when the roof needs to be replaced, the insulation can be reused. Use of a polystyrene insulation that will not be damaged by wetting/drying is also preferable. If water is to be harvested off the roof, a roofing material should be used that does not leach heavy metals or petro-chemicals into the rainwater.

If renewable energy is a priority, the marginal costs of upgrading to PV-integrated roofing panels or PV shingles (when installing a new roof or replacing an old one) should be considered, because this will be less expensive than providing a roof plus stand-alone PV panels. Finally, environmental impacts of the roofing choice should be considered. These include pollutants released from some types of roofing, such as hot-melt asphalt built-up roofing.

## Reflective Coatings

Even in mild climates, the sun beating down on a roof all day can cause it to reach extreme temperatures and drive considerable heat into a building via conduction. Ways of reducing heat gain through a roof include:

- Adding insulation underneath it
- Installing a radiant barrier
- Installing a reflective roof (or painting an existing roof with a reflective coating)

A reflective roof prevents the building from getting hot, reduces heat island effects, and prolongs the life of the roof. Multiple studies of buildings in hot climates (including California, Texas, and Florida) have documented 10%–50% energy savings when roofs were retrofitted with reflective coatings.[21] Reflective coatings can be applied to any roof surface and can reflect about 82% of total sunlight. Non-petroleum, water-based reflective coatings are the best environmental choice. However, modeling indicates that in colder climates, such as Colorado, increased winter heating energy is more than the savings in summer cooling energy. *(See Chapter 4 for more on reflective roofing.)*

## Rainwater Catchment Systems

Capturing rainwater for irrigation greatly reduces the use of treated water, and the collected rainwater—oxygenated, non-mineralized, and non-chlorinated—is much better for plants. Rainwater can also be used for household applications, including drinking water. In fact, people in many regions of the world, including some parts of the United States, have traditionally relied on harvested rainwater for their water supply. Typically a building's roof and gutters double as its rainwater collection device.

For potable water collection, it is critical to ensure that the roofing will not leach lead, copper, asbestos, or other hazards. Today's steel roofing is claimed to be the safest option as long as the coating does not contain heavy metals. (Old metal roofs with toxic coatings and lead fastening systems should never be used to collect drinking water.) Cisterns for rainwater storage can be made out of metal, concrete, or plastic. Note that in some cases, rainwater may contain pollutants that make it unsuitable for drinking or for aquatic life.

Water treatment requirements depend on whether the water will be for potable (or non-potable) domestic use, or just for irrigation. The first step in water treatment is to remove large debris with gutter screens and a "roof washer" (a system that diverts the first flush of water from a rain event so that it doesn't end up in the catchment system). Sediment can be allowed to settle within the tank or can be removed with cartridge filters. If disinfection is needed, chemical options include chlorine and iodine.

**Figure 2.3**
The Pensacola Civic Center in Florida features a Sarnafil EnergySmart Roof.® *(Photo courtesy of Sarnafil.)*

While chlorine's dependability, availability, and low price have made it the most common disinfectant, its manufacture and use pose environmental, taste, and health concerns. Although it can be filtered out at the tap with activated charcoal, there are still larger environmental issues with the widespread use of chlorine. Ultraviolet light, a good, nonchemical option, can be used to kill most microbial organisms once the water has been filtered of particulates, but it is energy intensive. A more expensive chemical-free disinfection system is ozonation (ozone is a form of oxygen produced by passing air through a strong electric field), which kills microorganisms and oxidizes organic matter into $CO_2$ and water.[22] *(See Chapter 4 for more on rainwater catchment systems.)*

## Living "Green" Roof

Living green roofs provide UV-protection for the roof membrane—extending the life of the roof up to 100% and potentially longer, while providing environmental cooling (reduced heat island effect), habitat, added insulation, storm water management, natural beauty (excellent for habitable roofs or roofs visible from above), not to mention cleaner air. Providing a green roof is an easier undertaking for new construction than for retrofits, because of structural requirements.

## Blue Roof

Blue roofs, like green roofs, are built to manage and re-use storm water, but do so through the use of mechanisms rather than vegetation. Blue roofs have controls on the roof's downspouts that channel and regulate the flow of rainwater, thus mitigating the effects of runoff. The water can be stored temporarily in tanks on the roof and later used for purposes such as irrigation or as cooling water makeup.

## Cladding

Most cladding materials, when properly maintained, can provide protection from the elements that can last the life of a building. Wood, steel, aluminum, fiber-cement, and vinyl all have their strengths and weaknesses. Vinyl siding is relatively maintenance-free, but like other vinyl products, is made with polyvinyl chloride (PVC), which has been linked to cancer, birth defects, and groundwater contamination. Wood and wood composite products, when harvested from certified forests, are excellent choices, but require periodic painting (though some manufacturers will now guarantee paint for up to 25 years). Fiber-cement siding is durable and insect resistant (although, like wood, it requires periodic painting), but it has a higher embodied energy content than wood. Aluminum and steel typically do not require painting, but both have higher embodied-energy content than wood. Both of these materials are highly conductive to heat and cold and have issues associated with their mining and production.

# Division 08 – Openings
## *Windows*

The goal when selecting windows is to specify a product that will provide the climatically appropriate insulating value, while also letting in a high percentage of visible light for daylighting, and providing the appropriate solar heat gain coefficient (SHGC). Due to advances in glazing, there are many options and manufacturers to choose from, and it is possible to "tune" the glazing carefully for the particular orientation and desired conditions.

Following are several key terms that apply to windows:

**Daylight Transmittance:** The percentage of visible light a glazing transmits.

**Solar Heat Gain Coefficient (SHGC):** The percentage of solar energy either directly transmitted or absorbed and re-radiated into the building. SHGC ranges from 0.0 to 1.0; the lower the number, the lower the solar heat gain. *(Note: SHGC has replaced the older term SC, or Shading Coefficient; SHGC = 0.87 × SC.)*

**U-Value:** Measures the heat loss or gain due to the differences between indoor and outdoor air temperatures (BTU/hr/SF). U = 1/R; the lower the U-value, the better the insulating performance.

**R-Value:** Measures the insulation effectiveness of the window (R = 1/U); the higher the R-value, the better the insulating performance.

**Low-Emissivity (low-E) Coatings:** Applied coatings that allow short-wave energy (visible light) to be transmitted through glass, but reflect long-wave infrared radiation (heat); the lower the emissivity, the lower the resultant U-value.

In the most extreme climates (very cold), the best windows provide low-emissivity, high visible transmittance, insulating gas fill (argon or krypton), good edge seals, insulated frames (with thermal breaks if frames are metal), and airtight construction. Some window manufacturers use low-E coatings applied not to the glass as with regular low-E windows, but to a suspended plastic film in between double panes of glass. Triple-pane windows are also an option, although weight and window depth may be a serious consideration.

Newer materials on the market include innovative gels or semiconductor coatings that can be applied to glazing layers to turn a window from clear to white or tinted when it is exposed to a certain heat (thermochromic) or sunlight (photochromic) threshold or to an electric voltage (electrochromic). These could be used in skylights to provide full daylighting on cloudy days, while avoiding glare and overheating on hot sunny days. (In their light-blocking white form, they still transmit 10% of incident solar energy—potentially enough for glare-free daylighting.) Another innovative product that could become revolutionary for window technology is a silica gel, which allows over 70% visible light transmission but blocks heat transfer. (Its R-value is three to four times that of common insulation products, such as rigid foam and fiberglass.)[23]

Ordinary glass has a visible transmittance similar to its solar heat gain coefficient. Selective glass has a semiconductor coating to absorb the ultraviolet in infrared portions of the solar spectrum, but allow the visible portion to pass through, resulting in a visible transmittance of 0.70. They have a solar heat gain coefficient of only 0.37. Selective glass would be specified where the designer wants to maintain a clear appearance, but reduce solar heat gain.

Frames are available in wood (clad or unclad), metal (which need to be thermally broken to prevent conduction through the frame), fiberglass, and vinyl. Although vinyl is a low-maintenance option, it is made from PVC, making it less environmentally healthy than other types of window frames.

As with many products, it is worthwhile to ask window manufacturers whether their products contain recycled materials. Even if the manufacturer does not use recycled content, knowing that customers are requesting it helps move the marketplace in this direction.

### Doors
Glass (or partially glazed) doors should be designed with all the same considerations as windows. In addition, door frames should be carefully detailed, with door sweeps and weatherproofing, to prevent air infiltration. Non-glazed doors should also be insulated, preferably with non-ozone depleting EPS. In cold climates, airlock entryways can save considerable energy. *(See Chapter 4 for more on doors for loading dock applications.)*

## Division 09 – Finishes
### Interior Wall Systems
Particularly green interior wall systems, if available, are those made from pressed agricultural "waste," such as straw. Some products use 100% agricultural waste product, avoid toxic binders, are fire-resistant (with a fire rating from one to two hours), and do not require structural studs.

As mentioned earlier in this chapter, in the Division 02 discussion, if gypsum board is to be used, recycled content product should be specified if locally available, and gypsum board scrap should be separated on the job site to allow pieces to be recycled.

## Acoustical Panels

When selecting acoustical panels, considerations should include durability and flexibility, low or no toxicity in the panel fabric, and recycled content in both panel and fabric.

Acoustical ceiling tiles often have recycled content and are recyclable. At least one ceiling tile company has a recycling program that will take old tiles, even from other manufacturers. Specifying ceiling tile with recycled content is critical to foster this reuse of resources.

## Paints, Coatings & Adhesives

Paints, coatings, and adhesives for finishes, such as flooring and wall coverings, commonly off-gas VOCs, including formaldehyde, or other toxic chemicals that affect installers as well as building occupants. Therefore, it is critical to specify low- or zero-VOC products, which are readily available today. Off-gassed VOCs can be re-absorbed into soft surfaces, such as fabrics. Because most VOCs are emitted during the application and curing process, this problem can be greatly reduced by providing good ventilation and ensuring a minimum of exposed absorptive surfaces during installation.

## Wall Coverings

Low- or zero-VOC paint is preferable to wall covering applied with toxic adhesive. The best wall coverings from environmental and air-quality standpoints are nontoxic textiles adhered with low-or zero-VOC adhesives. Vinyl wall coverings pose environmental concerns in their production & disposal and health concerns associated with off-gassing. When vinyl decomposes (a process that is accelerated when it gets hot), it off-gasses toxic fumes. Furthermore, as previously mentioned, vinyl should not be installed on the walls of air-conditioned spaces in hot, humid climates, due to the potential for moisture to condense and mold to form behind the vinyl.

## Floor Finish

Solvent-based floor finishes can cause indoor air quality problems, especially during and immediately following installation. Alternatives, such as water-based urethane finishes for wood floors, are increasingly available.

## Carpet

Each year in the United States landfills acquire millions of tons of carpet that may take 20,000 years to decompose. To stop this needless waste, it is important to select carpet that has high-recycled content and is itself recyclable. Carpet that can be recycled back into carpet is preferable to carpet that will be "down-cycled" into other plastic products. By specifying carpet tile instead of broadloom, 100% of the carpet does not have to be removed when only 20% of it (the part in the traffic pattern) shows wear. Finally, low toxicity is another important consideration in carpet selection.

Carpet underlayment should also have recycled content, be nontoxic (formaldehyde-free), and provide both insulation value (commonly R-12) and sound barrier properties.

## Resilient Flooring

Like other vinyl products, vinyl flooring is not the most environmentally sound choice. Several other types of resilient flooring can be used, including cork, natural linoleum, recycled-content rubber, or chlorine-free polymer resin tile.

## Ceramic Tile

Tile is a low-toxic, durable finish material for floors, walls and other applications. Several manufacturers offer products with up to 70% recycled content, mainly post-consumer glass, but sometimes also including post-industrial content such as soil/rock waste from the sand and gravel industry. In addition to making use of a post consumer product, adding recycled glass to ceramic tile can provide the tile with interesting textures and colors.

## Wood Flooring

As with all wood applications, certified wood should be specified, and locally or regionally grown and processed products are preferable to those that require significant transportation. Endangered species of tropical woods should absolutely be avoided. Bamboo is becoming a popular flooring option. Not actually a wood, but rather a grass, bamboo is exceptionally strong (it can be used for structural applications) and rapidly renewable (shoots are mature and ready to harvest in three to seven years). Unfortunately, the type of bamboo used in the building industry is not native to the United States and is currently imported from Asia.

# Division 10 – Specialties
## Toilet Compartments

100% recycled-plastic toilet partitions are available from multiple manufacturers and should be specified. Steel is also commonly available.

## Access Flooring

Access flooring allows for both wiring and air distribution to be provided in the same plenum, eliminating the need for overhead ductwork and cable trays, which can reduce the overall floor-to-floor height of a building design. Access flooring enables very convenient data system upgrades and office moves (since wiring and air are available under any floor tile). These systems also allow for energy efficiency benefits from under-floor air distribution. *(See the "Displacement Ventilation" section later in this chapter.)*

## Fireplaces & Stoves

Although wood is a renewable resource, burning it can cause considerable air pollution and can compromise indoor air quality, especially if fireplaces and stoves are not properly vented. Furthermore, fireplaces can actually impart an overall heating penalty by drawing heat from the fire and the building up the chimney. A typical masonry fireplace has a heating efficiency of –10% to +10%. Radiant wood-burning stoves burn cleaner and achieve higher efficiency—typically 50%–70%. Fireplace efficiency can be improved by installing a fireplace insert—basically a wood burning stove that fits into the fireplace.[24]

Pellet stoves (which burn compressed sawdust or agricultural waste) have higher combustion efficiency and lower particulate emissions than standard wood burning stoves, but overall efficiency (which factors in both combustion efficiency and heat delivery to the occupied space) is similar or only slightly better than EPA-certified wood stoves, about 65%–80%.[25]

Masonry stoves can achieve overall efficiency of 70%–90%, due to the fact that flue gases travel along circuitous routes through high-mass masonry chambers, which absorb the heat and radiate it into the occupied space.[26]

## Sun Control Devices

Sun control devices, such as awnings, exterior light shelves, louvers, and fins, can shade interior spaces from glare, while also reducing unwanted heat gain. Interior light shelves can enhance daylighting by bouncing light deeper into a building, thereby creating a more even distribution of light in the spaces immediately adjoining and more distant from the window. *(See Chapter 7 for more on daylighting.)*

## Walk-off Mats

Much of the dust and dirt in a typical building comes from people's shoes. The simple provision of a walk-off mat in the building entryway can improve indoor air quality by greatly reducing dust and dirt. A well-designed system consists of at least three different surface types, working from removal of coarser material (through a grate that is designed to allow for passive draining of water) to a final mat that brushes dust from shoe bottoms.

# Division 11 – Equipment
## Efficient Equipment

Today's appliances use dramatically less electricity and water than standard older models, yet offer improved performance. The ENERGY

STAR® label appears on the most energy-efficient in-class residential appliances (including washing machines, refrigerators, air conditioners, dishwashers, stoves, home electronics, and other appliances), commercial appliances (such as kitchen and office equipment), and lighting. The ENERGY STAR® website (**www.energystar.gov**) features a search function for selecting ENERGY STAR-qualified appliances.

An ENERGY STAR-qualified refrigerator uses at least 20% less energy than required by current federal standards (but due to industry-wide improvements in the first part of the century, a 2006 ENERGY STAR refrigerator uses 40% less energy than a conventional 2001 model).

A revolutionary technology that has been incorporated into high-efficiency refrigerators is vacuum insulation (thermos bottles operate on the same principle), which can, in theory, achieve a center-of-panel insulating value of R-75.[27] The insulation is made without ozone-depleting foams, and its high insulating efficiency means that refrigerator walls can be thinner, allowing for more usable space.

When replacing a washing machine, choose a horizontal-axis model (now available from most major manufacturers). Compared to top-loading models, horizontal axis washing machines use 60% less energy and 40% less water and detergent. They spin faster to remove more moisture from a load of laundry, which saves time and energy drying the clothes if using a dryer. They also clean more effectively and reduce wear on the clothes because they spin rather than agitate, and wash more effectively. Clotheslines dry for free without polluting, but if a line is not available, the next best option is an efficient dryer with a moisture sensor to prevent excessive drying, while saving energy.

Select the most energy-efficient office equipment available, including copiers, fax machines, and printers. For major office equipment, consider leasing rather than purchasing to encourage manufacturers to provide durable, upgradeable, recyclable machines, and to ensure that the most efficient models are provided as leases expire.

Note that ENERGY STAR machines (such as copiers and cathode ray tube [CRT] computer monitors) must be set in ENERGY STAR mode in order to conserve energy when not in use. Flat screen LCD monitors and laptops outperform CRT monitors optically, and also use less energy, reduce harmful electro-magnetic fields, and save desk space. *(See Chapter 9 for more on ENERGY STAR® and other standards for appliances and equipment.)*

## Division 12 – Furnishings

Furniture selection should be considered part of the whole building design. Green furnishings are those that provide adjustable ergonomic comfort and are made without toxic, off-gassing fabric dyes and adhesives or unsustainably harvested woods. Selecting light-colored finishes reduces the lighting level required, and specifying unupholstered materials in cooling climates and upholstered furniture in heating climates reduces energy use (because people feel more comfortable with less required air conditioning or heating).

Durability, reusability, and design for recycling are other important features. Finally, renovating or remanufacturing furniture can reduce its embodied energy.

# Division 13 – Special Construction
## *Solar Energy Systems*

Except for the manufacture of solar energy equipment, collecting and using solar energy results in none of the greenhouse or acid gas emissions associated with the combustion of fossil fuels. Moreover, sunlight is a widespread resource—according to National Renewable Energy Laboratory, the amount of it that reaches the earth each day is more than the planet's 5.9 billion people would consume in 27 years. Solar systems collect current solar income—as opposed to solar income stored millions of years ago in the form of fossil fuels. Only cost and public perception limit the increased use of solar energy systems.

Solar energy can be passively collected through building designs that allow entry of sunlight and storage/re-radiation of resultant heat; or it can be actively collected by systems that contain moving parts, such as fans, pumps, or motors. Active systems include those that collect and distribute (or store) solar-heated air or water for building heating and domestic water heating, and those that generate power.

Power generation systems include solar (photovoltaic) cells— semiconductor devices that convert photons from the sun into electricity, and solar power plants that concentrate solar energy to super-heat a fluid that is used (or stored for later use) to run a steam turbine or a Stirling engine. Solar power plants tend to be large-scale utility-run operations, but photovoltaic systems vary from utility-scale to building-scale to the scale of a single device such as a calculator or an off-grid light fixture.

## *Solar Water Heating*

After reducing water-heating loads with efficient plumbing fixtures, solar thermal technology can be used to heat water for domestic, commercial, and industrial purposes. Even if a backup system is required, using the available sun to heat water will save money over the long run (with payback periods in the 6–12 year range),[28] while reducing environmental impact. There are several different types of reliable, freeze-protected systems on the market. For backup water heating, select an ENERGY STAR® water heater model. *(See Chapter 5 for more on solar energy.)*

## Photovoltaic (PV) Systems[29]

A photovoltaic system can produce clean, renewable energy, without greenhouse gasses, for 20–30 years or more. Claims by critics that it takes more energy to make a PV cell than the cell produces in its lifetime are false—empirical studies have shown that PVs recoup their production energy in two to four years;[30] *financial* paybacks for PV systems range dramatically, depending on electric utility prices, up-front cost of the system, availability of rebates, daily solar radiation, the installation angle of the solar array, etc., but in a location with an average of five sun-hours per day and $.10/kWh electricity costs, the payback for a PV system, without rebates (assuming a 0% discount rate), can be as long as 43 years.[31] Currently more than 20 states have incentives to make PV cost-effective from the perspective of the building owner.

The original and most common semi-conducting material used in PV cells is single crystal silicon. These cells have proven their durability and longevity in space applications and are also generally the most efficient

**Figure 2.4**
This 51kW photovoltaic system supplies approximately 6% of the electricity needs for Whitman-Hanson Regional High School, a 234,500 SF award-winning pilot project for the Massachusetts Green Schools Initiative.

type of PV cells, converting as much as 17% of incoming solar energy into electricity. The main disadvantage of single crystal silicon cells is their production costs; growing large crystals of silicon and then cutting them into thin (0.1–0.3 mm) wafers is slow and expensive.

Alternative PV cells (15%–17%) include poly-crystalline silicon cells, "thin film" PV cells, and concentrating collectors. Although poly-crystalline silicon cells are less expensive to manufacture than single crystal silicon (because they do not require the growth of large crystals), they are also slightly less efficient. Thin films (0.001–0.002 mm thick) of "amorphous" or uncrystallized silicon are inexpensive compared to crystal silicon and may be easily deposited on materials such as glass and metal, making them the mass-produced PV material of choice for the electronics industry and for a variety of other applications. The advantage of amorphous silicon cells for building applications is that they can be deposited on roof tiles or spandrel glass panels. Achieving the double function of building envelope and electricity production in one product can enhance overall building cost-efficiency. They are also flexible and can conform to a curved surface. The disadvantage of amorphous silicon cells is that they are less efficient (9.5%). Thin film PV cells made from other materials have been developed in an attempt to overcome the inefficiency of amorphous silicon thin films, while retaining low production costs. Gallium arsenide (GaAs), copper indium diselenide ($CuInSe_2$), and cadmium telluride (CdTe) have all been used as thin film PV cells, with varying efficiencies and production costs.

In yet another effort to improve the efficiency and reduce the cost of photovoltaics, scientists have developed collectors that concentrate light from a large area onto a small PV cell. Special silicon cells were designed to withstand the increased light levels. Efficiencies as high as 30% have been achieved, and concentrating lenses and reflectors are much less expensive to produce than PV cells. The disadvantage is that only direct sunlight, not light scattered by clouds or reflected off surfaces, can be concentrated; thus concentrating collectors only achieve optimal efficiency in areas that receive a great deal of direct sunlight, such as deserts. *(See Chapter 5 for more on photovoltaics.)*

## *Wind Turbines*

Small wind turbines are commercially available for individual building applications. They can either provide off-grid power or they can augment the power supply of a grid-connected building. Building-scale turbines can have heights as low as 45 feet and can operate in wind speeds as low as 5 miles per hour. The payback period for such a turbine can be about 12 years.[32] In many locations, combining wind turbines with a photovoltaic system can ensure a more stable power supply than would be provided by either technology alone.

## Micro-Hydro

With access to an acceptable watercourse, micro-hydro can be an effective and inexpensive way to provide reliable constant power. In the United States, micro-hydro technologies have a promising potential. A 2004 study of U.S. waterways found that the total annual mean power potential for micro-hydro systems, currently undeveloped, is as high as 85,000 MW.[33] This means that if the U.S. took advantage of all its watercourses that have a flow that is acceptable for micro-hydro power generation, as much as ten percent of U.S. power could be supplied by this renewable, reliable, ecologically friendly, distributed technology.

Micro-hydro systems work best in waterways that provide year-round laminar (not turbulent) flow at a rate of at least 2 or 2.5 meters per second (five knots). On an ideal river, a micro-hydro system can have a payback period as short as three to four years.[34]

**Figure 2.5**
This residential-scale wind generator, Abundant Renewable Energy's model ARE110, is grid-tied on a 127-foot tilt-up tower in Newburg, Oregon. *(Photo courtesy of Abundant Renewable Energy, Newberg, OR. Website: www.AbundantRE.com)*

# Division 14 – Conveying Systems

## Elevators

As with all motorized equipment, selecting the most efficient model possible will reduce energy use for the life of the elevator. Durability is essential—broken elevators are frustrating, and manufacturing new ones is highly resource- and energy-consumptive. As with office equipment, consider leasing rather than purchasing elevators. This gives manufacturers a major incentive to make their product durable and easily maintainable.

# Divisions 22 & 23 – Plumbing & HVAC

## Plumbing Fixtures

*When the well is dry, we know the worth of water.*
— Benjamin Franklin, 1790

Humans cannot live without water, but the western world's practice of using exorbitant amounts of drinking-quality water to transport sewage is not a sustainable practice. This is becoming increasingly evident as the population grows, and water becomes increasingly scarce in the dry regions of the United States. Plumbing fixtures that use low or no water are available from a number of manufacturers. These include:

- Composting toilets, waterless urinals, and low-flow toilets (models range from 0.8–1.6 gallons per flush, including standard gravity-flush, pressure-assist models, and dual flush toilets, which can deliver either a 1.6 gallon or a 0.8 gallon flush, as needed).
- Low-flow showerheads (various models using less than 2.5 gallons per minute).
- Low-flow faucets (using less than 2.5 gallons per minute) and metered faucets (to ensure that faucets in public bathrooms will not be left on).
- Shutoff valves for kitchen faucets and showerheads that enable the temperature setting to be "saved" while the water is temporarily shut off.

## Gray Water Systems

Treating gray water like black water is not the most efficient strategy. Once-through gray water from sinks and washing machines can often be reused directly for toilet flushing or for subsurface irrigation (depending on regional codes). Gray water can also be used on (non-edible) plantings after treatment with a commercial filter or site-built sand filter.

For showers or other hot-water fixtures, gray water waste heat recovery systems can capture the heat from the hot water as it goes down the drain and transfer it to incoming water. These systems are especially effective in high-use shower areas, such as in locker rooms.

## Cogeneration

This technology produces both heat and electricity and makes use of them in a large building or campus system. Because the heat associated with standard electricity production is often wasted (simply exhausted into the atmosphere), cogeneration is a much more efficient process. In fact, cogeneration raises fuel utilization efficiency to more than 90% (compared to typically 35% efficiency for plants generating electricity alone) and reduces fossil fuel use by over half.

## Displacement Ventilation

Instead of mixing high-velocity air from overhead ducts to "dilute" the stale air in a room, a displacement ventilation system supplies fresh, cool air from a pressurized floor plenum (similar to the access floors used for computer rooms) or from low, wall-mounted diffusers. The fresh air displaces the warmer, stale air, which is removed via a ceiling plenum.

Compared to a conventional system, a displacement system moves a larger volume of higher-temperature air at a lower velocity and lower pressure drop, thereby reducing required fan power. Low-velocity air is quieter and less drafty. Also, displacing rather than diluting the air results in better pollutant removal. Pollutants and heat from copy machines and other equipment, lights, and people tend to be drawn straight up in a "plume" rather than being mixed laterally in the conditioned air. Furthermore, the warmer supply air means the chillers are more efficient. Finally, the under-floor plenum can also be used for wiring, providing superior convenience.

Materials required for under-floor air distribution typically include an access floor system (usually covered with carpet tiles or resilient floor tiles) so that sections of floor can easily be removed to access the floor plenum. In applications where spills may be an issue, such as grocery stores, labs, hospitals, etc., displacement ventilation can be supplied low in the room, through millwork, rather than through the floor.

## Natural Ventilation

In conventional building operation a considerable amount of energy is used in circulating air for ventilation. Using natural forces to move air can result in effective ventilation without the energy input. Examples include providing cross ventilation to make use of wind, building chimneys to induce stack ventilation, and using water-evaporation systems in hot dry climates to induce cooling and air movement. (Humid air is more buoyant than dry air.)

# Division 26 – Electrical

## *Lighting*

First and foremost, lighting should be designed effectively and efficiently, avoiding glare and providing light where it is needed (primarily on wall and ceiling surfaces) rather than simply assigning a set number of footcandles of light to a space. Specifying highly reflective (light-colored) interior surfaces is important to evenly distribute light and enhance occupant well being. Ambient overhead lighting should be minimal. For most applications, a direct/indirect lighting fixture will provide the most appealing and efficient ambient light source. It should be dimmable to integrate with daylighting and to afford user-flexibility. *(See Chapter 4 for more on lighting efficiencies and Chapter 7 for daylighting.)*

Task lighting provides for flexibility, and accent lighting enhances visual interest. Automatic lighting controls can greatly reduce lighting energy consumption. They include occupancy sensors that turn lights off when a room is not in use (especially appropriate for infrequently used rooms) and photosensitive dimmers that dim lights when daylight is ample. Finally, lights should be easily maintainable.

Today's **fluorescent lighting** is efficient, has excellent color rendition and is appropriate for most applications. Current fluorescent technology includes T-8 and T-5 lamps with dimmable electronic ballasts. Compared to the older T-10 and T-12 lamps, the newer lamps contain less mercury and significantly improve energy efficiency. Compact fluorescent lights (CFLs) should be used instead of inefficient incandescent lamps. CFLs come in pleasant color spectrums, use 75% less energy than incandescent lights, and last ten times as long. Electronic ballasts (rather than magnetic ballasts) should be used in all linear luminaires.

**LED (light emitting diode) lighting** has many unique benefits that have already made it competitive in many niche applications, despite its high cost relative to conventional sources. LEDs typically produce about 30–35 lumens per watt (though researchers have achieved 50 lumens per watt), making them much more efficient than incandescent lights (which produce 12–15 lumens per watt), but not typically as efficient as compact fluorescents (which produce at least 50 lumens per watt). LEDs last 10 times as long as compact fluorescents (133 times as long as incandescents), are extremely durable and emit light in one direction, providing a disadvantage for ambient lighting but an advantage for task lighting (LEDs can light the task with a smaller total lumen output than incandescents or fluorescents, which illuminate in 360 degrees). Currently common in exit signs, traffic signals, pathway lighting, flashlights and other niche applications, LED technology is being developed for broader use.[35]

**Disposal** of fluorescent, mercury vapor, metal halide, neon, and high-pressure sodium lamps is a critical issue, as they all contain mercury, direct exposure to which is toxic. Magnetic ballasts for fluorescent lights made before the late 1970s also contain highly toxic PCBs (polychlorinated biphenyls). All lamps containing mercury should be recycled with a qualified lamp recycling company and protected from breakage during transport. If lamps do break, they should be collected (with proper protection) and stored in a sealed container. Expired PCB ballasts should be stored in sealed containers and disposed of with extreme caution and scrupulous labeling, using a PCB disposal company that is registered with the Environmental Protection Agency.[36]

**Exterior Lighting:** The luminous Milky Way that spans majestically across the night sky is never seen by 75% of Americans, due to nighttime light pollution.[37] Recent research has also shown harmful physiological effects that result from interrupting sleep by viewing light.[38] Minimizing **light pollution** and **light trespass** will help protect dark skies for humans and nocturnal animals alike. Strategies include eliminating unshielded floodlighting and providing "cut-off" luminaires.

Full cut-off (FCO) luminaires considerably reduce wasteful upward lighting by directing all light down toward the intended area of illumination. (None is allowed above the horizontal plane.) Replacing defective, nonfunctioning, or non-cut-off luminaires with FCO luminaires allows for substantial lowering in the wattage of the new fixture, thereby realizing a cost and energy savings. Cut-off luminaires also enhance safety for both pedestrians and drivers by eliminating glaring light.

Uniform outdoor light distribution is important for comfort, safety, and energy efficiency. Light levels need not be high. In fact, studies have shown that about three footcandles is all that is needed for security purposes.[39] Much brighter light (often 100 footcandles or more), which has become prevalent at all-night gas stations and other stores, is actually dangerous, because drivers (especially the elderly) can take two to five minutes to readjust their vision.

Exterior lighting controlled by motion detectors can enhance safety while reducing energy use. Some schools have reduced both energy use and vandalism by keeping the campus dark after hours. Police are informed that light seen on campus should be treated with suspicion. The security director at one San Antonio school, where vandalism dropped 75% with the dark campus approach, suggested that vandalism loses its appeal when people cannot see what they are doing.[40]

High-pressure sodium lamps (the characteristic yellow parking lot lights) should be avoided in most applications, as they reduce peripheral vision. White light sources, such as metal halide and fluorescent, improve visibility with less light.

## Plug Loads

Plug loads are the electric loads drawn by all the equipment that is plugged into outlets. Computers, printers, and faxes do not draw energy at one constant rate. Energy use spikes when equipment is turned on and then falls to a much lower operating level. Rating labels on the equipment are for start-up loads (maximum energy draw) and should be used to size the wires and devices in the electrical system.

Adding up the nameplate ratings of various pieces of equipment in an office and dividing by the area will typically result in the determination of a "connected" load of 3–4 watts per square foot. This connected load is not, however, the same as the average operating, or "as-used" load, which is likely to be less than 1 watt per square foot. (A study of U.S. office buildings found it to be 0.78 watts per square foot on

**Figure 2.6**
Responsible outdoor lighting at the University of Arizona Medical School in Tucson. *(Photo courtesy of the International Dark-Sky Association.)*

average.) This as-used load, rather than the connected load, should be used to calculate the sizing of mechanical systems, which must compensate for the actual heat generated by the equipment, not the amount of heat that would be generated if the equipment remained in start-up mode. The resultant downsizing of the mechanical system can have a significant impact on the first cost of the facility.[41]

## Division 31 – Earthwork
### Erosion & Sedimentation Control
Controlling erosion is essential to protecting air and water quality and avoiding loss of topsoil. An erosion plan should ensure that topsoil is stockpiled, that soil is not carried away by storm water runoff or wind, and that particulate matter from construction activities does not cause sedimentation of receiving waterways. Unless local standards are stricter, the management practices outlined in the Environmental Protection Agency's *Storm Water Management for Construction Activities* should be followed.[42]

### Pest Control
Using the least toxic integrated pest management approach to protect from insects, rodents, and other pests will benefit building occupant health as well as the environment. Tightly detailing building penetrations and joints to avoid cracks and moisture leakage is the first step. Termites have traditionally been kept at bay by highly toxic chemicals. Chlordane, the most common insecticide until recently, was taken off the market due to health and environmental problems. Substitute chemicals, though less toxic than chlordane, are not problem-free. One nontoxic solution is to install a sand barrier that termites cannot easily penetrate around the foundation.

Boric acid is relatively nontoxic and used to retard many types of household pests. Added to cellulose insulation, it serves the triple function of retarding fire, inhibiting mold, and deterring insects and rodents.

## Division 32 – Exterior Improvements
### Site Work/Landscaping
The conventional development practice of replacing native landscape with impervious surfaces (conventional buildings and paving) has caused a myriad of problems, including polluted water runoff, combined storm/sanitary sewer overflows, fluctuating stream levels, flooding, erosion of stream beds, and wildlife impacts. These problems can be ameliorated by avoiding paving where possible in favor of vegetation (also by vegetating building roofs) and, unless turf grass is necessary for recreational or other purposes, using native/well-adapted vegetation.

Vegetation (especially non-turf plants with long roots) allows water to soak in naturally to the ground, rather than quickly running off. If paving is necessary, porous pavement is preferable. Porous paving products include reinforced grass paving and gravel (for low-traffic areas), block interspersed with gravel, and porous concrete and asphalt (which are similar to their standard products, but missing the fine aggregate).

## Ponds/Reservoirs

Retention and detention ponds serve the single purpose of managing storm water, while constructed wetlands can manage storm water while providing multiple human and environmental benefits. When designed according to natural models, wetlands become a diverse ecosystem of plants and animals that filter polluted run off and provide habitat (that may be threatened elsewhere by development). Unlike engineered ponds with steep concrete sides and barbed-wire fences, constructed wetlands are shallow, vegetated site amenities. Like natural ponds, they do not need fences.

## Efficient Irrigation Systems

Drip irrigation systems are more efficient than sprinklers because less water evaporates before reaching the plant. The best irrigation timers include buried moisture sensors that ensure that just the right amount of water is delivered to the plant's root zone. Systems programmed to water deeply every several days, rather than shallowly every day or two, use less water and promote healthier plant growth.

## Alternative Materials

A chapter on green building materials would not be complete without discussion of nonconventional building materials. Several natural, low-tech building techniques—including straw bale, adobe, rammed earth, and cob—have a long history of use around the world, but are just beginning to regain popularity in the U.S. Although these building techniques are labor-intensive and unfamiliar to the conventional contractor, they provide many environmental and health advantages. Typically they are associated with very low-embodied energy, no harmful off-gassing of pollutants, locally sourced materials, and good energy performance in appropriate climatic regions.

## Straw Bale

Straw is a very low-embodied-energy by-product of the farming industry. While it would be a bad idea to remove all the straw from the field, as some of it needs to be tilled into the soil to provide aeration and organic matter, current agricultural practices produce excess straw, much of which is typically burned as "waste," creating air pollution.

Use of straw for straw bale construction not only makes use of this "waste" product, it also provides good insulation, fire-resistance (because the tight packing in bale walls eliminates the necessary oxygen for burning), and even protection from most termites. (Only one species will eat straw.) The primary concern with straw bale construction is protection from moisture, but this has been successfully addressed with big overhangs, high foundations with a capillary break next to the straw, and proper interior and exterior plaster detailing, including flashing around openings.

## Adobe

Earthen, sun-cured brick is another relatively labor-intensive, but low-embodied-energy material with a long history of use in hot, dry climates. Adobe lacks the insulating properties of straw, but provides instead a large thermal heat sink that soaks up excess heat during the hot day and re-releases it during the cool night, thereby moderating the building's internal temperature. *(Adobe is discussed earlier in this chapter, under "Masonry.")*

## Other Earthen Materials

**Rammed earth** (earth formed into thick, durable monolithic walls) and **cob** (earth and straw molded by hand into sculptural walls) are two building methods that work in hot, dry climates along the same principles as adobe. Any of these materials can be (and are) used in other climates, but require supplemental insulation or additional heating or cooling. *(See Figure 2.7 for examples of rammed earth construction.)*

## Alternative Factory-Made Materials

A myriad of alternative factory-made materials (such as autoclaved cellular concrete, structural stressed skin panels made with agricultural waste, and fiber-concrete block) are also available. They combine the ease and familiarity of conventional, modular construction techniques (a big plus for buildings that are to be built by conventional contractors) with benefits that often include better energy efficiency, lower toxicity, use of waste products, and lower embodied energy than their conventional counterparts.

## Conclusion

Choosing green building materials is not a cut-and-dried process. There is a myriad of considerations—sometimes conflicting with each other—including indoor environmental quality, energy use, embodied energy, location of product source, durability, end-of-life considerations, resource renewability, and environmental impact. No project will be composed of a perfectly green set of materials and strategies; rather, designers and owners must determine the most important goals and

These rammed earth homes in New Mexico feature walls 18" thick built by tamping a mixture of soil, 3% portland cement, and 6%–10% moisture content. Photo 1 shows a 10' wall section formed up with 4' forms on the bottom and middle, and 2' forms on top. Photos 2 and 3 show the walls after the forms have been removed. Photo 4 shows a finished home. *(Photos courtesy of Pat Bellestri, Soledad Canyon Earth Builders, http://www.adobe-home.com)*

**Figure 2.7**
Rammed earth homes

characteristics for a particular project and design a holistic building system to achieve those goals, incorporating as many green features as possible.

Green building design is an integrated, holistic process with a goal greater than the sum of its individual material components. More important than each technical detail is the process of creating a "living building" with wonderful, healthy spaces that provide human contact to the natural environment, derive energy from renewable sources, enhance the surrounding environment (avoiding waste and toxicity), and support local economies and cultures.

1.  U.S. Environmental Protection Agency, Office of Air and Radiation. "Report to Congress on Indoor Air Quality." Volume II: Assessment and Control of Indoor Air Pollution, pp. I, 4-14. EPA 400-1-89-001C, 1989.

2.  Roodman, D.M and N. Lenssen. "A Building Revolution: How Ecology and Health Concerns are Transforming Construction." *Worldwatch Paper 124*. Worldwatch Institute, Washington, DC, March 1995, p.5.

3.  CSIRO website: www.cmit.csiro.au/brochures/tech/embodied

4.  Lawson, B. "Building Materials Energy and the Environment: Towards Ecologically Sustainable Development." RAIA, Canberra, 1989.

5.  Triangle J. Council of Governments. *WasteSpec: Model Specifications for Construction Waste, Reduction, Reuse, and Recycling*, 1989.

6.  Portland Cement Association. "Manufacturing Fact Sheet, 2006." www.cement.org/concretethinking/manu_facts.asp AND *Environmental Building News*, Vol 2, No. 2, March-April, 1993. Hanle, Lisa J., et al. $CO_2$ Emissions Profile of the U.S. Cement Industry, U.S. Environmental Protection Agency.

7.  Ibid.

8.  King, Bruce, PE. "A Brief Introduction to Pozzolans." Ecological Building Network website, www.ecobuildnetwork.org, excerpted in part from *Alternative Construction – Contemporary Natural Building Methods*, edited by Lynne Elizabeth and Cassandra Adams, John Wiley & Sons, 2000.

9.  American Institute of Architects. *Environmental Resource Guide*. John Wiley & Sons, 2006.

10. http://www.epsea.org/adobe.html

11. R-value is a measure of thermal resistivity, the opposite of conductivity. The higher a material's R-value, the better it will insulate against heat transfer. The overall R-value of a building envelope assembly (an exterior wall, for instance) is determined by adding up the individual R-values of the components of the assembly. If, however, a conductive material spans from one side of the assembly to the other, heat will travel along this "path of least resistance," just as it will rush through an open window in an otherwise sealed wall.

12. *Environmental Building News* (July-August, 1994). Vol 3, No. 4.

13. Ibid.

14. Ibid.

15. http://www.physics.otago.ac.nz/eman/403downloads/AS4_EmbodiedEnergyCoeffs.pdf

16. Truss Joist MacMillan product literature (1998).

17. Energy Design Update. "How Thermal Shorts and Insulation Flaws Can Degrade an 'R-19' Stud Wall to a Measly 'R-11'" and Johns-Manville Research and Development Center "Effects of Insulation Gaps," November 1979. Information cited at http://www.westerngreen.com/miscellany.htm

18. Building Science Corporation and Energy Efficient Building Association (1998) Builder's Guide.

19. Ibid.

20. Ibid.

21. Mahone, Doug. "Inclusion of Cool Roofs in Title 24: California Building Energy Efficiency Standards," Revisions for July 2003 Adoption, 2001.

22. Texas Water Development Board and Center for Maximum Potential Building Systems. *Texas Guide to Rainwater Harvesting*, 1997.

23. http://www.photonics.com/Content/Aug97/techMatsu.html

24. *Design Handbook for Residential Woodburning Equipment.* Auburn, Alabama, June 1981.

25. *Environmental Building News*, Vol. 1, No. 2, September/October, 1992.

26. Lyle, David (1984). *The Book of Masonry Stove: Rediscovering an Old Way of Warming.* Brick House Publishing Co., Inc., 1984.

27. Canadian Housing Information Centre, Canada Mortgage and Housing Corporation. "Support for IEA Annex 39: High Performance Thermal Insulation Systems." Current Housing Research, Volume 11, No. 2, Winter 2004-2005.

28. Center for Resource Conservation. "Renewable Energy Basics." http://www.conservationcenter.org/e_basics.htm

29. Energy Educators of Ontario. *Energy Fact Sheet, 1993.* http://www.iclei.org/efacts/photovol.htm

30. "What Is the Energy Payback for PV?" U.S. Department of Energy Energy Efficiency and Renewable Energy (EERE) fact sheet, December, 2004; and Knapp, Karl E. and Theresa L. Jester. "PV Payback." Home Power #80, December 200/January 2001.

31. "Economic Payback of Solar Energy Systems," http://www.solarbuzz.com/Consumer/Payback.htm

32. Martin, Justin. "Your Own Windmill." *Fortune Small Business*, May 1, 2006.

33. Caroll, Gregory, et al. *Evaluation of Potential Hydropower Sites throughout the United States.* Prepared for 2004 ESRI User Conference, San Diego, CA.

34. The 3-4 year payback estimate assumes a micro-hydro capacity cost of $2,500/kW installed (estimate from Verdant Power), and 10,654 kWh/yr (2001 U.S. average household consumption according to U.S. Department of Energy, Energy Information Administration, www.eia.doe.gov) and an average $.07-.10/kWh utility electrical rate.

35. U.S. Department of Energy, Energy Efficiency and Renewable Energy website, "FAQs on Market-Available LEDs"; also Eartheasy website, www.eartheasy.com, "LED Lights."

36. *Environmental Building News*, Vol. 6, No. 9, October 1997.

37. *Environmental Building News*, Vol. 7, No. 8, September 1998.

38. Light viewed during the night interrupts melatonin production, according to Nancy Clanton, PE, IESNA, President of Clanton Engineering, Board Member of the International Dark Skies Association.

39. *Environmental Building News*, Vol. 7, No. 8, September 1998.

40. Ibid.

41. E Source, Inc. "Cooling Demands from Office Equipment and Other Plug Loads: Less than One Watt per Square Foot." Report #TU-96-9, 1996.

42. EPA Document No. EPA-832-R-92-005, Chapter 3.

# Chapter 3 Building Deconstruction

**G. Bradley Guy, Associate AIA, LEED AP**

Building deconstruction is an alternative to traditional demolition for the renovation of buildings or the removal of buildings at end-of-life. Relocation of a structure, its renovation or adaptive reuse, are environmentally preferable to building demolition and deconstruction as a means to preserve materials resources in all of these processes.

In the pre-industrial era, materials conservation was driven by the energy and labor intensity to harvest, prepare, and transport them. Reuse of materials provided an economic advantage. In the mid-to-late 20th century, the emergence of machine-made and mass-produced materials, chemically complicated materials, and the relatively low cost of oil allowed this basic idea of "waste not, want not" to fall from usage in the creation of built environment. This trend has begun to reverse as:

- The price of key materials such as metals increases.
- Disposal costs increase and landfill capacity decreases.
- The price of transportation increases.
- Some building materials become scarce or degraded in quality (e.g. old-growth lumber).
- Demand for green buildings increases.
- Legislation requiring construction and demolition materials recycling increases.
- Technologies to make productive use of "waste" increases.
- There is recognition of the contribution that building materials production and waste make to greenhouse gas emissions.

A recent study by the U.S. Environmental Protection Agency indicated that approximately 170 million tons of building waste is generated annually from construction, renovation and demolition activities, as of

2003. Approximately 50% of the total is generated by demolition and 41% is generated from renovation activities, with only 9% generated from new construction activities (U.S. EPA, 2007). Approximately 30% of the materials resulting from buildings (excluding road and bridges) are recycled, with less than 1% being reused.

Furthermore, state and local legislation requiring C&D waste diversion has increased dramatically over the past 5 years. In 2006, the State of Massachusetts enacted the first landfill ban on selected construction materials of asphalt, brick, concrete, clean wood and metals. As the construction industry and markets become more mature at handling this stream of diversion, more states and municipalities will likely increase restrictions on the disposal of CRD debris materials.

Another factor supporting deconstruction is the increasing number of used building materials stores. There are over 1,600 building material reuse stores in the U.S.[1] and Canada. Of this number, approximately 700 are Habitat for Humanity (HfH) ReStores, according to HfH International. The average ReStore is over 10,000 square feet and, in aggregate, they produce about $40 million in net revenues per year for their affiliates.[2] For more information, refer to Habitat for Humanity (**www.habitat.org/env/restores.aspx**).

## What Exactly Is Deconstruction?

Building deconstruction is the disassembly of buildings to recover the maximum amount of reusable and recyclable materials in a safe, environmentally responsible, cost-effective manner. Generally, buildings are deconstructed in the reverse order of how they were constructed— last on, first off (LOFO). All salvageable items are removed and reused on the site for a new project, sold, or donated. Non-salvageable items are recycled to the extent possible, and the remaining debris is taken to the landfill. Deconstruction can be applied to total building removal, and also to remodeling. Partial deconstruction can also be compatible with a renovation process where it necessitates careful removal of elements while maintaining the integrity of the portions of the building that are to remain.

### Deconstruction versus Demolition

Standard demolition practices may include elements of deconstruction, such as "cherry-picking" or "skimming,"—or removing high-value items before demolition. Demolition practice may also include recycling otherwise unusable items, such as concrete for use as aggregate for new foundations or walkways.

The principal distinction between deconstruction and demolition is deconstruction's goal of diverting as much material as possible from landfills. Deconstruction may involve both reuse and recycling, depending on the technical requirements of a safe process and the highest and best use of the constituent components and building materials. Demolition tends to have a much lower threshold for recovering reusable materials and is typically focused on speed and the mechanical reduction of the mass of a building in order to make the disposal of materials as efficient as possible. As a result, standard demolition practices are more compatible with recycling than reuse.

## Reusing Salvaged Materials on the Same Site

In some cases, the materials that are removed from the old building can be cleaned, refurbished, and/or reconfigured as components for either a new building or for added/remodeled space on the same site.

Incorporating these salvaged materials into the new project is the most environmentally and economically effective approach to deconstruction and reuse. In this scenario, logistical transport and storage burdens can be reduced, while at the same time greater control over the alignment of the design and materials selection can be achieved. Just as with the new materials brought to the site, the reclaimed materials will need to be stockpiled and protected from weather and damage from construction activities. Other benefits include avoidance of seeking external markets, retrieving a 1:1 value in substitution for new materials, and LEED credits for Construction Waste Management, Materials Reuse, and Regional Resources. Some of the challenges will be the iteration between the palette of available reclaimed materials and the design and functional aspirations of the project, and any additional efforts such as re-certifications of materials, cleaning, refurbishing, and modifications to the materials. The old materials would, of course, have to fit in with the new building design and specific applications, in consideration of limitations such as ungraded lumber and lack of warranties. Extra time might also need to be scheduled to clean and modify materials at the site before they are reinstalled.

## Who Performs Deconstruction?

The recovery of materials for reuse has been taken up to a large extent by specialty companies that either focus on high-end commodities in particular (such as antique door hardware and old-growth, high-quality lumber components) or lower-value components (such as windows, doors, fixtures, cabinetry and casework, roof joists, bricks, and common wood stair treads and strip flooring). Deconstruction as a specialty is typically carried out by smaller entities, either for or by non-profit organizations.

The vast majority of deconstruction/salvage services are combined with building materials reuse sales operations and have less than twenty employees. While there are national directories such as the Whole Building Design Guide (**www.wbdg.org**), the most effective way to find deconstruction/salvage services proximate to a potential project is to start with the yellow pages of the city or region where the project is taking place. Headings to search under include: Building materials, Demolition, Salvage, Surplus, Recycling, Used, Waste, and Wrecking. If there are local or regional green building organizations such as chapters of the U.S. Green Building Council (**www.usgbc.org**), these can also be good resources. While there are national directories such as the Whole Building Design Guide **http://www.wbdg.org/**, the most effective way to find deconstruction/salvage services proximate to a potential project is to start with the yellow pages of the city or region where the project is taking place.

## *The Deconstruction Process*

## Feasibility & Planning Requirements

Several factors must be considered when investigating the feasibility of building reuse for a particular project, and then planning for it. Among the most important are the condition of the building and materials, the types and quantities of potential reusable and recyclable materials, and the closest markets for the resulting "harvest". The markets for reclaimed materials can be broken down first into two main categories: the raw commodity materials of timbers, dimensional lumber, stone, brick for reuse and metals for recycling; and the more refined products of windows, doors, cabinetry, interior finishes, mechanical, electrical and plumbing components, etc. Unlike new construction, which consumes disparate materials of choice to make a completed building, deconstruction, or "un-building," does the reverse, producing a stock of materials that are pre-determined by the structure to be removed, with all the historical, environmental, and physical characteristics that come with them.

Two early feasibility and planning requirements:
1. Site assessment

2. Identifying the local market for salvaged materials

**Site assessment** involves analyzing the building and site, including salvageable materials, space for equipment and storage/processing of removed materials, presence of hazardous materials, and site and safety constraints for deconstruction. Assessment includes evaluating potentially reusable materials based on type, quality level and condition, quantity, and the installation methods that were used (which will affect their value and the labor to uninstall them). Figure 3.1 provides some guidelines for site assessment.

Because the materials are "as-is", it is important to ascertain from the potential internal project reuse or external markets, the conditions, quantities, and logistical requirements for the materials that might be produced. Minimum lengths for salvaged dimensional lumber,

## Figure 3.1
### Materials Assessment Form

Assessing a building to be deconstructed starts with collecting some basic information, such as the age of the building and its overall dimensions. For each salvageable material, note its condition, installation methods or finishes that will affect disassembly or its value, and evidence of any hazardous materials, such as asbestos or lead.

retaining all the hardware for doors, full versus partial sheets of plywood, palletizing full lots of brick or stone might be some of the considerations of maximizing value in the markets for these reused materials.

Buildings and the components in the buildings must also be assessed for potential hazards such as asbestos, lead-based paint, PCBs, mercury in lamps and thermostats, refrigerants, etc. A common problem in older

| Building Materials | Material | Type | Number | Dimensions | Total | Condition/ Finish Treatment | Hazardous Materials | Reuse % | Recycle % | Disposal % |
|---|---|---|---|---|---|---|---|---|---|---|
| Roof<br> Frame<br> Sheathing<br> Shingles or other roof covering | | | | | | | | | | |
| Gutters & Downspouts | | | | | | | | | | |
| Exterior Walls<br> Framing<br> Hardware (e.g., connectors)<br> Sheathing<br> Siding | | | | | | | | | | |
| Interior Wall Framing<br> Load-bearing<br> Partition walls | | | | | | | | | | |
| Foundation | | | | | | | | | | |
| Plaster/Gypsum Wallboard | | | | | | | | | | |
| Flooring<br> Finish | | | | | | | | | | |
| Stair treads | | | | | | | | | | |
| Cabinetry, Shelving | | | | | | | | | | |
| Millwork | | | | | | | | | | |
| Light Fixtures | | | | | | | | | | |
| Plumbing Fixtures | | | | | | | | | | |
| Appliances (Note age, condition) | | | | | | | | | | |
| HVAC Components (including radiators) (Note age) | | | | | | | | | | |
| Doors & Windows | | | | | | | | | | |
| Door & Cabinet Hardware | | | | | | | | | | |

buildings and from post-disaster situations is the presence of mold. Older wood structures can also suffer from damage due to rot and various wood-boring organisms. An Environmental Site Assessment may be conducted by a professional inspector, following established standards.

**Identifying the local market for reclaimed materials** involves weighing costs versus benefits for those that can be recovered from the site and sold or donated to local organizations or individuals. The current price for new materials will affect the value of salvaged ones, as will the season (as it affects construction activity) and the strength of the local construction market as a whole.

Other factors that affect salvaged materials' value include their condition, grade (e.g., code-approved framing lumber versus lumber with outdated grading stamps or none at all), and whether the items are restricted to a specific use (for example, a window) versus a number of potential uses (e.g., lumber).

Materials can be sold to salvage retailers or brokers and advertised in various ways, including in newspapers and on the Internet. Generating advance interest is important so that they can be sold promptly for efficiency. If sold directly from the site, transportation costs are avoided. A plan should also be in place for materials that are not sold, but can be donated to nonprofit organizations. The third option, after resale and donation, is recycling, and the last, disposal at a landfill.

## The Phases of Deconstruction Work

There are generally three phases of disassembling building components, each requiring more effort than the last:

1. Pre-demolition salvage ("cherry-picking" or "skimming")

2. Non-structural deconstruction ("soft-stripping")

3. Structural deconstruction ("whole-building")

As materials are taken from the building, they must be moved to a storage or pickup location and possibly processed (cleaned, de-nailed, etc.), then bundled for removal. Before disassembly begins, space should be allotted for processing, and a plan developed for storage or timely removal so that materials do not have to be moved more times than necessary. Under severe time constraints materials might be removed off-site for processing. Protection from theft and weather may be needed. A plan also needs to be developed for prompt removal of non-reusable debris that is targeted for the landfill or recycling.

The locations for processing or loading out materials are based upon site access, access from the building location where materials are being removed at any given time, coordination with other work, and space.

Processing is best completed at a point as close to where the materials were located at the building so that they can be made "handling friendly" to maximize the safety and efficiency of loading, transporting, unloading, and inventory. Processing and loading out locations do not have to be static, and should be adjusted as the work locations and materials-types change.

## Safety

As with all construction projects, safety is a key concern in planning and executing deconstruction. The order in which tasks are performed on-site must be carefully planned to ensure that workers are not at risk from structural collapse. One of the benefits of deconstruction is that it produces less airborne dust than demolition, including dust from lead-based painted materials. Because deconstruction typically involves more hand labor than destructive forms of demolition, personnel safety training and personal protective equipment (PPE) protocols and use are critical. Attention should be paid to possible increased risk of fire hazard because of stored materials.

Like demolition, deconstruction must be performed according to OSHA and EPA rules and requirements for both handling and disposal of materials. Whole-building deconstruction is, in fact, building removal, and follows the same basic regulatory procedures that apply to demolition. When engaging a deconstruction service for residential renovation work, an owner should determine that the supervisors have been certified under the guidelines of the EPA Lead, Renovation, Repair and Painting Rule that went into effect in April, 2010. The EPA has proposed to create a similar rule for the commercial sector.

## Economic Benefits

Aside from the LEED credits and environmental benefits (saving natural resources and energy, minimizing site disturbance and dust, and reducing landfill waste), deconstruction has clear economic benefits. Deconstruction to divert materials from landfill reduces disposal costs. Reuse of salvaged materials in lieu of new materials can reduce materials costs not only by substituting for traditional materials, but also by sometimes providing materials of unique quality that would be prohibitively expensive to reproduce. The donation of building materials to nonprofit organizations like HfH ReStores provides tax benefits for building owners and makes lower-cost materials available for affordable housing and do-it-yourselfers.

Owners who work with nonprofit organizations to conduct salvage and deconstruction can offset the higher costs that these efforts may require (versus traditional demolition and disposal) with the retention of the materials for their own use, sale of the materials, or tax deductions from donations of the materials.

# Creating Jobs/Project Funding

Deconstruction is also a source of green jobs and entry-level employment because it requires manual labor that cannot be outsourced to other countries, and not all activities of a deconstruction

**Breaking Down Disposal Costs**

Materials can be categorized based on "variable disposal fees," which are becoming the norm in a growing number of communities. These fees are based on individual materials and their condition (e.g., separated from other debris) and are also determined by the materials that local recovery facilities and landfills are able to process. Those that can be handled most efficiently, in terms of disposal and recycling, will have lower charges (or sometimes no charges), as compared to disposal of commingled debris.

**Some examples follow:**

- Clean concrete—unpainted and not mixed with other organic materials or contaminants.
- Clean wood—unpainted, untreated, with or without nails, and not mixed with other materials or contaminants.
- Clean asphalt—asphalt materials not mixed with organic or other materials.
- Clean asphalt shingles—not mixed with other materials and not containing asbestos.
- Organic land-clearing debris—"green" waste not mixed with other C&D debris or household waste.
- Metals—Non-ferrous metal, such as copper and aluminum, commands a higher price, though ferrous metals, such as steel and iron, also have a positive value.

Generally speaking, there will always be charges for disposing of commingled construction and demolition debris. The threshold at which disposal becomes a better economic option than deconstruction with source separation of materials will be determined by:

- The value of the recovered materials
- The cost of disposal
- Transportation costs
- Whether the value (either a revenue or an avoided cost) produced by deconstruction can offset the added labor and transportation costs for reclaiming for reuse, or separation for lower-cost recycling.

The most sensitive cost factor in this equation is the amount of added labor needed to achieve sufficient value in recovered materials.

process require a high level of skill. Research by this author has found that approximately the same amount of labor-hours are typically spent in processing materials (~25%) as in the actual removal of the materials from the building (~25%). The remaining ~50% of time is spent in set-up activities, clean-up, less careful materials removal for disposal, loading materials, etc.[3] The majority of work in deconstruction is well-suited for entry level construction worker training.

Estimates of the job creation and local economic development benefits from deconstruction as opposed to demolition and disposal vary. One metric is the income multiplier effect, which is the measure of how many additional dollars of income are created in a local economy by $1.00 of expenditure in a job-sector. This accounts for the fact that deconstruction workers may not be paid the same wage as other industries. According to the U.S. EPA's (**http://www.epa.gov/waste/ conserve/rrr/rmd/rei-rw/pdf/n_report.pdf**) study of the economic impacts of reuse and recycling industries, reuse and recycling generate similar income effects to manufacturing and construction, which are approximately 2 times higher than for the service and retail trade industries.

*Cost Considerations*

According to a growing collection of case studies, deconstruction and/or aggressive construction and demolition materials recycling are producing cost-savings in projects throughout the U.S., particularly in the West Coast and Northeast where disposal costs are high. Anywhere that disposal fees start to exceed $75.00 per ton is the first and possibly most important indicator that deconstruction and/ or aggressive recycling will provide a clear economic advantage over traditional demolition and disposal without recycling. A study of deconstructions by the author of six wood-frame homes built between 1900–1950 at the University of Florida Powell Center for Construction and Environment found deconstruction costs on average to be 37% lower than demolition, after accounting for the value of the salvaged materials.

## Materials

The materials economics are relatively simple. There is the revenue (for sale—or tax benefit of donation to a nonprofit) from reused or recycled materials. There is then the "value" of avoiding the cost of disposal. For every ton of material diverted from a landfill, there is one less ton of disposal costs. To the extent deconstructed materials can be incorporated into a new building or space on the same site, the savings are two-fold—reduced disposal costs and new material costs.

A potential emerging market over the next decade will be the carbon value of reclaimed building materials, especially wood. By extending the lives of building materials and substituting them for otherwise new production of materials, reused and recycled materials provide for an avoidance of greenhouse gas (GHG) production. In any carbon offset market program, either voluntary or legislated, reclaimed materials will be able to have an additional value based on the market rate per ton of GHG equivalent.

The most salvageable materials tend to be finish and structural wood, windows and doors, cabinets and casework, masonry, metals (structural steel, doors, grates, grilles, railings, gutters and downspouts, etc.), lighting and plumbing fixtures, and even ceiling tiles and carpet. Among the more difficult items to profitably salvage include any that incorporate hazardous materials and inefficient fixtures (such as toilets, lighting, and mechanical) and appliances. Ductwork from an old building may be contaminated with mold and/or other harmful substances, so would have to be thoroughly cleaned so that there is no possibility of indoor air quality problems.

## Labor

Labor costs are higher for deconstruction than for demolition because of the manual work required to uninstall materials and then process them, plus the time required to plan and organize and market/sell the salvaged materials. Figures 3.2 and 3.3 are tables from a deconstruction case study by the National Association of Home Builders Research Center published in 1997. The tables show a labor summary and time required per salvaged building component as a percentage of overall labor hours.[4]

**Figure 3.2**
Time Required per Building Component
*Reprinted with permission, NAHB Research Center, Upper Marlboro, MD (www.nahbrc.org)*

|  | Building Component | Percent of Total Labor Hours |
|---|---|---|
| **Structural** | Masonry (incl. chimney)<br>Wood framing, sheathing | 41.00<br>28.00 |
| **Weather-proofing** | Asphalt shingles<br>Windows | 4.80<br>1.60 |
| **Finish** | Plaster<br>Oak strip flooring<br>Doors, door frames, baseboards, trim<br>Plumbing fixtures, appliances, cabinets<br>Bathroom tiles | 10.90<br>5.90<br>2.60<br>2.30<br>0.40 |
| **Other** | Piping, wiring<br>Gutters, fascias, rakes | 1.34 |

| Component | Tasks (hours) | | | | Component Total | Labor-hours/unit |
|---|---|---|---|---|---|---|
| | Disassembly | Processing | Prod. Support | Non-prod. | | |
| **Interior** | | | | | | |
| Interior doors, frames, trim | 5.75 | 5.25 | --- | --- | 11.0 | 0.55/each |
| Baseboards | 4.75 | 5.0 | | | 9.75 | 0.19/lf |
| Kitchen cabinets | 2.75 | 0.5 | --- | --- | 3.25 | 0.27/each |
| Plumbing fixtures | 7.75 | 1.75 | | | 9.5 | 0.59/each |
| Radiators | 1.5 | 0.5 | | | 2.0 | 0.13/each |
| Appliances | 0.25 | 2.75 | | | 3.0 | 0.60/each |
| Bathroom floor tile | 2.50 | 0.50 | --- | --- | 3.0 | 0.038/sf |
| Oak strip flooring | 19.25 | 27.0 | 0.25 | --- | 46.50 | 0.038/sf |
| Plaster - upper level | 34.25 | 10.0 | 5.50 | --- | 49.75 | 0.012/sf(plaster area) |
| Plaster - lower level | 23.75 | 10.75 | 2.0 | --- | 36.50 | 0.009/sf(plaster area) |
| Piping and wiring | 6.75 | 3.25 | 0.50 | --- | 10.50 | 0.0072/lbs |
| Interior partition walls | 6.25 | 24.75 | 3.0 | --- | 34.0 | 0.18/lf |
| Windows and window trim | 10.0 | 2.50 | 0.50 | --- | 13.0 | 0.54 each |
| Ceiling joists | 1.0 | 4.75 | 0.5 | --- | 6.25 | 0.0075/lf |
| Interior load-bearing walls | 2.75 | 15.5 | 1.75 | --- | 20.0 | 0.027/lf |
| Second level sub-floor | 16.0 | 6.0 | 1.25 | --- | 23.25 | 0.023/sf |
| Second level joists | 7.25 | 16.25 | 1.5 | --- | 25.0 | 0.027/lf |
| First level sub-floor | 7.75 | 8.0 | --- | --- | 15.75 | 0.016/sf |
| First level joists | 7.0 | 10.0 | --- | --- | 17.0 | 0.020/lf |
| Stairs | 2.5 | 0.75 | 0.75 | --- | 4.0 | 0.3/riser |
| **Exterior** | | | | | | |
| Gutters, fascias, rakes | 2.25 | 1.0 | --- | --- | 3.25 | 0.014/lf |
| Chimney | 33.25 | 40.5 | 4.75 | --- | 78.5 | 0.16/cu.ft. |
| Gable ends | 8.0 | 3.0 | 0.75 | --- | 11.75 | 0.053/sf |
| Masonry walls - upper section | 14.75 | 104.5 | 20.5 | --- | 139.75 | 0.25/sf(brick area) |
| Masonry walls - lower section | 15.75 | 84 | 5.25 | --- | 105.0 | 0.078/sf(brick area) |
| **Roof** | | | | | | |
| Roofing material | 17.75 | 18.25 | 1.75 | --- | 37.75 | 2.68/100 sf |
| Roof sheathing boards | 21.25 | 14.5 | 1.5 | --- | 37.25 | 0.028/sf |
| Roof framing | 7.25 | 9.75 | 7 | --- | 24.0 | 0.021/lf |
| Shed roof framing at entry | 1.25 | 2.25 | --- | --- | 3.5 | 0.036/lf |
| Building Subtotal | 291.25 | 433.5 | 59 | --- | 783.75 | |
| Talk shop | --- | --- | 29 | 29.5 | 58.5 | |
| Supervision | --- | --- | 9.5 | --- | 9.5 | |
| Meetings, paper work, daily roll-out and roll-in of tools, etc. | --- | --- | 38 | 43.5 | 81.5 | NA |
| Research monitoring | --- | --- | --- | 89.5 | 89.5 | |
| Lunch, breaks, idle | --- | --- | --- | 118.75 | 118.75 | |
| Business Subtotal | --- | --- | 76.5 | 280.25 | 357.75 | |
| Grand Total | 291.25 | 433.5 | 135.5 | 280.25 | 1141.5 | |

**Figure 3.3**
Labor Summary of Tasks Performed
*Reprinted with permission, NAHB Research Center, Upper Marlboro, MD (www.nahbrc.org)*

## Effect on the Project Schedule

Because it takes longer to salvage and process materials for deconstruction, versus demolition, additional time needs to be scheduled for it. This can be challenging in a tight time-frame project. It's important to identify the likely savings up-front in order to make the case for deconstruction. Building owners need to understand the economic and environmental benefits in order to buy into the schedule impact.

New methods and equipment, such as de-nailing guns, are being brought into deconstruction to save time. With Bobcats, forklifts, and conveyor belts, quantities of salvaged materials can be handled more efficiently. Planning ahead and finding buyers or nonprofit recipients for materials also saves time.

## Permitting

New permit requirements for construction and demolition waste management and diversion goals are being created in real-time. While many C&D waste diversion permits do not distinguish between reuse and recycling, in fact there are emerging permits requirements that specifically target deconstruction and reuse. Two notable ones are from the City of Seattle and the City of Boulder. Multiple cities in California now have construction and demolition debris deposit (CDDD) programs. The first one was San Jose. To reclaim the deposit, the owner or contractor must document the diversion of 50% of the expected waste to certified reuse and recycling companies in the region. (The certification is made by the city to validate that these businesses are legitimate and will process the materials that might be claimed as having been delivered.) If the full 50% diversion is not achieved, the owner or contractor will still receive a portion of their deposit back, relative to the percentage they did, in fact, divert.

## Conclusion

Building deconstruction is best considered as one aspect within a continuum of sustainable and green building practices. While it is highly preferred to building demolition and disposal, it may not be rated above other strategies such as reusing at least some portion of a building in place.

A ranked environmental preference might be:
1. Preservation

2. Rehabilitation and renovation

3. Building relocation

4. Disassembly and reassembly

5. Deconstruction and reuse, remanufacture, and recycle

6. Building demolition and disposal

Ultimately, economics, building use, available time, and environmental and social considerations all play a part in these decisions. It is clear, however, that deconstruction and the resulting availability of salvaged materials offer a significant opportunity in sustainable design and construction. For the informed owner, there are several potential benefits:

- Reduced overall costs for removing a building
- Additional LEED points for construction waste management and materials reuse
- The value of marketing a green project
- If using salvaged materials, lower price and potentially better quality (e.g., for old-growth lumber)
- Added aesthetic qualities of rustic or unique materials

For contractors, deconstruction offers:

- Potential permitting advantages
- Good publicity

The community gets the benefit of cleaner building removal methods (with less hazardous dust in the environment) and reduced demand on landfills. And society is rewarded with the preservation of natural resources.

1. Hamer Center for Community Design, 2006.

2. Personal communication, Mary Zimmerman, HfH

3. Guy, B., "Six-House Building Deconstruction Case Study: Reuse and Recycling of Building Materials," Powell Center for Construction and Environment, University of Florida, prepared for Alachua County, FL Solid Wastes Management Innovative Recycling Project Program, 2000, at www.lifecyclebuilding.org under "Resources."

4. National Association of Home Builders Research Council. "Deconstruction–Building Disassembly and Material Salvage: The Riverdale Case Study." 1997. http://www.smartgrowth.org/pdf/deconstruction.pdf

# Recommended resources for more information:

Asphalt Shingle Recycling
http://www.shinglerecycling.org/

*Business Magazine.* "Green Builders Get Big Help from Deconstruction." September-October, 2004. Vol. 26, No. 5, p. 20.
http://www.jgpress.com/inbusiness/archives/_free/000648.html

City of Boulder Deconstruction Plan and Construction Waste Recycling
http://www.bouldercolorado.gov/files/PDS/green_points/attachment_c__decon_plan_const_waste_recycling_edits1_09.pdf

City of San Jose Construction & Demolition Diversion Deposit Program
http://www.sjrecycles.org/construction-demolition/cddd.asp

City of Seattle Demolition and Deconstruction Permitting
http://www.seattle.gov/dpd/Permits/Process_Overview/Demolition/default.asp

Concrete Recycling
http://www.concreterecycling.org/

Deconstruction Studies and Reports
http://www.wiserearth.org/user/BradleyGuy/section/gallery

Design for Reuse Primer
http://www.publicarchitecture.org/design/Design_for_Reuse_Primer.htm

Drywall Recycling
http://www.drywallrecycling.org/

Lifecycle Building Challenge
www.lifecyclebuilding.org

The Deconstruction Institute
www.deconstructioninstitute.com

USEPA, Estimating 2003 Building-Related Construction and Demolition Materials Amounts
http://www.epa.gov/osw/conserve/rrr/imr/cdm/pubs/cd-meas.pdf

Whole Building Design Guide
http://www.wbdg.org/

# Efficient Use of Energy & Other Resources

## James Armstrong, CPE, CEM, LEED AP

A green design team develops a vision of a facility that considers the entire facility and how it interacts with its surroundings, occupants, and internal operations. This chapter will explore the ways in which the building systems design can drastically impact the consumable resources (energy, water) required to meet the desired design conditions, including occupant comfort. We will first review the factors to consider, and then outline some strategies for reducing energy and water use. It should also be noted that energy equipment and building technologies are continually improving, and designers must make an extra effort to evaluate new alternatives rather than merely repeating the last successful design solution.

## *Understanding Occupants' Needs & Expectations*

Early in a project, during the "programming" phase, the occupants and/ or owners need to convey to the design team (including the architect and project manager, as well as the LEED® or green consultant) what the required uses of the building will be—and when those uses will occur. The main objective is to understand occupancy, use, usage patterns, and/or potential synergies between spaces. This is when customers need to clearly define—to the best of their ability—what they need from the new facility. This is also when the customer and the design team identify the goals of the project regarding "greenness." For example, is energy efficiency the priority, or is sustainability more important? Or are there other green issues, such as water conservation, that are major goals for the project? Once the team understands what the customer's expectations are, they can begin to design spaces—and all the building systems that will come together to achieve those goals. The next section explores these systems and how they can help achieve green building goals. It is critical when the needs have been identified that the design team document those needs and perform a final review of what they understood the needs to be with the owner/occupants as a way of completing the circle.

## The Building Envelope & Systems Interactions

The building envelope must be considered as surrounding a dynamic and constantly changing environment, rather than as a static box for which architects and engineers design systems to perform based on extreme conditions. Many states have been adopting "energy codes" or referencing ASHRAE 90.1 (American Society of Heating, Refrigerating, and Air-Conditioning Engineers) energy design standards for required system and envelope efficiencies. These include references to building simulations that truly model the interaction between building components and systems. ASHRAE has recently completed a green design standard in January of 2010, ASHRAE 189.1, which is a green design standard or stretch standard modeled after many of the voluntary standards such as USBC models.

Every building in use has many processes and interactions taking place within it every minute of every day. The concept of green design requires the designer to meet these varying conditions in an energy-efficient manner, using systems, or assemblies, and components that appropriately interact. These interactions can be as simple as daylight entering a space, or as complex as manufacturing processes running within the facility, and they affect the dynamics of the building's consumption of resources. We can no longer afford to design buildings to run like a car with the gas pedal to the floor while we control the speed with the brake, as we have been doing for too long. We now need to run the car like a hybrid, taking advantage of coasting, using braking to recharge the battery, and minimizing the waste by taking advantage of regenerative energy. The building's systems capability and/or reactions with other systems must be taken into account in order to achieve the desired design conditions.

The interaction processes can be divided into four categories:
1. Ventilation
2. Envelope
3. Occupancy
4. Process

## Ventilation

Ventilation, or movement of air in and out of a building, is accomplished in one of two ways: **mechanical infiltration** and **ventilation**. Infiltration occurs even without a mechanical ventilation system installed. Infiltration is the entering and/or escaping of air from one space to another, usually due to pressure or temperature differential. Infiltration occurs in routes established during construction, and over time through cracks that form as the building settles.

**The temperature differential**—between different spaces within the building, or between the indoor and outdoor temperature—can cause the air to migrate through open doors, windows, and other means of egress or settlement cracks. The temperature differential causes a buoyant pressure difference and natural convection currents. Warm air tends to leak out the top of a building, while cold air comes in through lower openings. Infiltration is also caused by the pressure difference between the windward and leeward sides of a building.

The moisture content or relative humidity between spaces can cause **vapor migration**. This is one of the keys to green building design—the calculated dew point for an exterior wall. Architects have come to realize that they need to pay attention to details that affect dew point in their wall sections. Ideally, any moisture that may condense in or on the wall will occur after the frost point. This keeps the walls from causing frost pockets in extreme climates. Designers also want the walls to "breathe" in order to remove the moisture.

Infiltration may be adequate to ventilate the space if there is no requirement for, or any existing, mechanical ventilation. Depending on the building type, mechanical ventilation may or may not be required. For example, infiltration augmented by operable windows is usually sufficient for residences or small commercial facilities.

Mechanical ventilation brings into the "box" outside air, which must be conditioned (filtered, heated, cooled, humidified, or dehumidified) prior to entering the space—to meet the design criteria for the space. Depending on the era of the facility's construction, ventilation varies widely. The ASHRAE guidelines, such as ASHRAE 62.1, specify ventilation requirements for the building depending on usage, type, and/or the projected occupancy for the space.

Proper ventilation is one of the cornerstones of green building design. The key to achieving energy efficiency while maintaining a proper amount of fresh air (10–20 CFM of OA, or outside air, per person) is recovering the thermal energy from the exhausted air and using it to pre-heat or pre-cool the entering air. This energy recovery reduces the required energy needed to condition the air. Energy recovery type desiccant wheels can exchange moisture between the fresh air and exhaust air, allowing "enthalpy" recovery as well. (*See "Heat Recovery Systems" later in this chapter.*)

Ventilation requirements are usually driven by human occupancy, and a control system that measures and responds to varying occupancy has the potential for tremendous savings. For example, most courtrooms are ventilated according to their design (maximum) occupancy, which might only occur once every five years. Installing controls to detect occupancy and modulate the ventilation rate can reduce significantly the amount of outside air that needs to be conditioned. Laboratories are another matter. The ventilation rate is typically determined by the processes being performed in the labs. Some labs may require 10–20 air changes an hour as designed. This is a lot of air to be conditioned prior to entering the labs. This number is also dependent upon the process and or chemicals that are within the process. Labs 21, which is an EPA standard for energy benchmarking of laboratory facilities, is a good starting point.

Often the movement of air has three purposes: to act as a flowing medium to heat and cool the space; to act as a medium for space pressurization, such as in laboratories or hospitals; and to provide fresh air (oxygen) to the occupants. A green design approach (advocated by Vivian Loftness of Carnegie Mellon University) is to separate the fresh air function from the space-conditioning function, which enables the designer to optimize each independently and reduce the overall fan power.

## The Building Envelope

The building envelope is a major determining factor in a building's energy consumption. The envelope controls the impact of outside conditions on the interior spaces, while the HVAC systems strive to maintain the specified design conditions. An example is sunlight entering the space through the windows, doors, and/or skylights. Sunlight adds solar heat to the space. Depending on the climate, the design set point for temperature can be exceeded due to the thermal solar gains. The building systems will then strive to achieve set point by attempting to condition, or cool, the space.

### Solar Heat Gain & Natural Light

In North America, a space with a south-facing façade with large window walls will require more cooling than a north-facing space with similar window walls. Heat must be added to the north-facing space and removed from the south-facing space. This is a normal dynamic for many office buildings in northern climates, even in the middle of the winter. Adding to this equation is the heat gain from building occupants, lighting, and computers or other equipment, which may require that the building be cooled year-round, and, in many southern climates, may never need heat at all. Solar gain through windows accounts for 32% of needed cooling energy in U.S. buildings. Another 41% is caused by heat from electric lighting, 17% from equipment, 7.5% from people, and the rest from heat conduction through roofs and walls.

The perimeters of these same buildings may at times have too much light, and yet the buildings' lighting systems are still on. With green design, it is possible to shut off or dim the electrical lighting to maintain even lighting levels, and to incorporate skylight shafts, clerestory windows, glass interior walls, and other daylighting techniques, to bring natural light deeper into the building. A green design would also transfer heat from the overheated to the under-heated sections and use outside air economizer systems to cool whenever the outdoor ambient temperature meets the design conditions without the use of mechanical cooling.

Green design also relies on trees to provide seasonal shade, thereby reducing the need for mechanical cooling. A deciduous, or leaf-bearing, tree planted on the south-facing wall will provide shade during the summer months, and natural cooling. These trees will lose their leaves in the fall and allow the space to receive natural lighting and solar heat in the winter months. Trees also reduce the water consumption of the lawn underneath by two-thirds. Trees are effective for shading west walls when the sun is low in the sky. This is true green design—using natural elements to reduce the consumable energy required to condition a space.

Insulation and vapor-retardants are other components of the building envelope that can have a tremendous impact on the consumable energy required for a space. (*See "Wall & Roof Insulation" later in this chapter for more on insulation.*)

## *The Roof*

Roof design has made major strides where sustainability is concerned. Because the roof is the most weather-impacted part of a building envelope, designers must consider long-term solutions to the conditions caused by weather exposure. Selection of roof materials for a green building involves health, environmental, and energy considerations. The available materials have pros and cons. Coal tar and gravel, for example, can be produced from recycled materials, whereas EPDM roofing is made from virgin materials. (LEED provides a listing of roofing materials with their environmental impacts that can be helpful in making selections.) Some green roofing approaches include using light-colored roofing materials to reduce the thermal gains by reflecting solar heat, using recycled or recyclable material (such as shingles manufactured from slate dust), and using material that has a longer life (such as metal or polymer roofing systems). A protected-membrane roofing system allows reuse of the rigid insulation during future re-roofing, substantially reducing material use.

Some roofs have become a resource as well as a shield. Rain can be collected by a roofing system connected to a cistern (collection tank) so that the water can be used for other purposes. (*See "Rainwater Collection Systems" later in this chapter.*) Living roofs become their own ecosystem, with plantings and grass contained within the membrane. This strategy provides insulation, alleviates runoff, and helps to meet the impervious surface requirements on some facilities so that more building can be accomplished with less land.

The key to understanding the impact of the envelope is to be aware of the interactions and changes that occur within and through it. Changing the envelope to become a more dynamic component of the building is a critical part of green design.

**Figure 4.1**
The glass dome ceiling near the main entrance of the Phipps Conservatory and Botanical Gardens Welcome Center in Pittsburgh, PA, allows sunlight to enter the space. *(Photo courtesy IKM Incorporated – Architects, photographer: Alexander Denmarsh Photography.)*

## Occupancy & Controls

The human body gives off heat at various rates, depending on activity level and inherent characteristics. Human beings also require oxygen, the primary reason for ventilation of a space. The higher the occupancy of a space, the more ventilation will be required, with less heat required in colder climates or seasons, and a higher cooling load in warmer climates or seasons. This is the human impact on the space design conditions.

Occupancy is also a variable that can be monitored in a facility's energy use. The type of usage of a facility can drastically change the energy requirements of a space. Typically, the cubic feet of space per person is the main criterion for ventilation. In most residential situations, this factor has minimal impact, since the cubic feet per person tends to be much higher than in commercial spaces. An exception is a multi-occupant dormitory or bunkroom, which requires more air exchange than an apartment.

Auditoriums, conference spaces, and gymnasiums are extreme examples. A conference room may have an occupancy capacity of 100 people. This same space may be normally occupied for only five hours per day, and is only at capacity on six occasions per year. The space has HVAC and lighting systems that were designed to maintain the entire space at peak, or design, conditions. This brings in too much fresh air and more lighting than is needed most of the time. This space could benefit from "smart controls," such as sensors, for a combined net impact of as much as one-third of the total required energy. The occupants are just as comfortable, yet the consumable energy required is reduced.

Technology is currently available that monitors the $CO_2$ levels of the space, or you can detect this using a return air sensor, which are both good indicators of a space's occupancy. This sensor, when integrated into a building management system, can modulate the fresh air requirements based on desired conditions. Occupancy sensors can also be used to turn off lights in unoccupied spaces. Time clock systems shut down the air handlers and other mechanical systems (as well as lights) when a space is scheduled to be unoccupied. These interactions make the building more dynamic and more efficient. Some simpler versions of this same process include the integration of occupancy sensors, that are currently installed to meet energy codes, into the building automation system. When the room is occupied the fresh air is enabled, when the room becomes unoccupied the fresh air is minimized.

## *Process*

Many facilities in North America use vast amounts of energy or water to complete a process, whether it is making photocopies or manufacturing automobiles. The processes should be reviewed to reduce the waste by-products or reuse these products in some fashion. Many facilities require year-round air conditioning due to the heat gain from their internal processes. Existing facilities and planned new construction need to be reviewed as a whole. The interactions of each process should be considered, including water usage, heat requirements, emissions, and cooling and ventilation requirements. All of these should be measured and catalogued. (*Chapter 15 provides information on available energy modeling programs.*)

Sub-metering of equipment and processes is a component of green building design and operation. It allows for the operator to better understand the various components of a facility and can be used to make further improvements and/or to establish operating requirements that minimize the consumption of energy and natural resources.

I recently worked on a facility for the injection molding process, where they used the same cooling tower water as the condenser water for their chillers and for the oil cooling for the hydraulic oils in the presses. We separated the processes and used one tower for the oil cooling and another for the chilled water system. This separation allowed the condenser water to be dropped, which drastically improved the chiller's efficiency and increased its capacity.

In another facility, an offset printing plant, large volumes of air are blown across the press to dry the ink and remove the ink vapors. The next step in the process is to "burn off" the ink and blow the hot air into the atmosphere. In the same facility, there is another process that requires large volumes of hot water. We simply recovered the heat from the burn off process and used it as the heating source for the hot water.

Both of these strategies to improve efficiency were devised by taking the time to understand the thermal properties of each process and then matching two processes together!

## *Energy Efficiency Strategies*

## Roofs
The following sections explore energy considerations related to roofing materials. Insulation for roofs and exterior walls is addressed in "Wall and Roof Insulation" later in this section.

### *Reflectivity*
Research by energy service companies, product manufacturers, and organizations such as the Lawrence Berkeley National Laboratory (LBNL) are demonstrating the potential of reflective roofing to conserve energy, mitigate urban heat islands, and improve air quality. Development in areas such as the U.S. Sunbelt has resulted in increased temperature and smog, as green areas and shade trees

have been replaced with dark paving and roofs. Black roofs (such as EPDM, asphalt, and modified bitumen) have been shown to have a 6% reflectivity and temperatures 75°–100° hotter than the ambient temperature, while white, reflective roof membranes can reflect 80% of the heat, with roof temperatures only 15°–25° warmer than the ambient temperature.

Cooler reflecting roofs not only release less heat into the environment, but have a major effect on the building's interior temperature, thereby reducing cooling costs by as much as 30%. The net yearly impact depends on the building's particular location. (Lower reflectivity may be preferred in extreme northern conditions, as heat gain may be required for other reasons, such as snow melting.) In addition to saving energy by reducing solar heat gain, cooler roofing materials can increase the longevity of the roof system itself.

A variety of coatings and materials can provide light colors and reflectivity. Like all products, selection of these systems should include evaluation of demonstrated life cycle and maintenance costs and a good warranty, supported by a reliable manufacturer. The ENERGY STAR® program has established specifications for roofing products, including a solar reflectance of at least 65% for low-slope and steep-slope use,

**Figure 4.2**
The National Fire Protection Association Headquarters in Quincy, MA, features a Sarnafil EnergySmart Roof®.
*(Photo courtesy of Sarnafil.)*

and 81% for low-slope only, when the product is initially installed. (For more information go to **www.energystar.gov** and click on Roof Products.) It should be noted that durability and maintenance influence reflectance, as the percentage can be reduced by surface weathering and dirt accumulation.

Appearance may be a factor in the selection of reflective roofing, particularly in residential applications where sloped roofs are more visible than the low-slope roofs that are common on commercial buildings. Houses may also have attics to help reduce the effect of heat gain on air-cooling requirements.

I recently worked on a facility that implemented a cool roof strategy using a white PVC roof. The facility also used a water recovery system, where the water from all of the roof drains was collected in a 20,000 gallon inground tank before being diverted to the retention basin. We were quite surprised when we found out that the white roof did not evaporate the water very fast, which allowed us to collect more water in the hot summer months than any of us expected. Most of the water collected came from the condensate drains from the rooftop air handlers!

## Living Roof System

Living roofs, or "green roofs," involve a waterproof membrane applied on a roof deck, covered with earth that will grow grass or other vegetation to collect the rain and minimize the impact of the site's impervious surfaces. Living roofs also provide thermal insulation and generate oxygen, causing a net reduction in a facility's $CO_2$ generation.

**Figure 4.3**
Living roof at Chicago City Hall. *(Photo courtesy of the project's landscape architect, the Conservation Design Forum.)*

Green roof considerations include:

- Structural requirements (The sod and plantings can weigh as little as 2 lbs/SF in some systems to as much as 150 lbs/SF in others.)
- Careful waterproofing (Leaks can be extremely difficult to pinpoint once the growing materials are in place.)
- Maximum roof pitch of 17%
- Climate (Best suited to wetter areas; can be a fire hazard in hot, dry climates.)
- Maintenance requirements
- Required certification by the contractor installing the membrane

Green roofs can be as simple as 6" grass growing in sod (or grasses indigenous to the area, which require little water and no fertilizer), or as large and elaborate as a whole garden with seating areas. In addition to tremendous energy savings, green roofs provide aesthetic benefits, and, properly cared for, can last much longer than conventional roof decks, since the sod and plant materials protect the waterproof membrane from ultraviolet light. Carefully consider the structural review of the facility when choosing a green roof to make sure it can accommodate the weight of the plants and/or infrastructure associated with the plantings. National and state green building organizations can be good sources of additional information.

## Exterior Walls
### *"Active Walls"*

In addition to using recycled framing, sheathing, and insulation materials, walls can be green by virtue of their energy efficiencies—both passive (for example, sunspaces that collect and store heat) and active. Active walls act as a generator or collector of energy. An example is a double glass wall designed to collect solar energy, but reflect thermal energy when the interior envelope temperatures have been reached. This combination reduces a facility's net heating and cooling loads.

Another example of an active wall is one comprised of solar collectors. An office tower that might normally have a glass façade could instead be faced with active photovoltaic panels that generate electricity to be used in the building. This approach reduces the overall construction requirements because the engineered active panels replace the glass or brick typically used. (*See Chapter 5 for more on photovoltaic systems.*)

## Wall & Roof Insulation

Adding insulation to an existing building is the simplest of all measures and one that homeowners have been practicing for years. The building's insulation value is increased to a point where its thermal energy is contained, and the impact of outside environmental conditions on interior conditions is reduced. This approach has a limited opportunity in commercial facilities due to the volume of fresh air they require. Selecting appropriate insulation for a new, sustainable building is key to strategies to reduce energy use.

The many insulation systems available today offer a variety of R-values and other features. However, it is important to consider the entire building envelope, not just insulation, and to design to eliminate moisture (from the wall pocket), while minimizing the thermal conductivity between the indoor and outdoor air. This is true for any design, not just green design. As mentioned earlier in this chapter, the dew point of walls must be considered. Water will condense in the coldest part of a wall. Since humid air can travel through the insulation but heat cannot, the vapor barrier is placed on the warm side of the insulation (outside in a cooling climate, inside in a heating climate).

This is a sustainable design issue for other reasons besides energy efficiency, as a poorly designed wall will fail in 10–20 years, and the mold growth promoted by the moisture will be a source of indoor air quality problems. Constructing replacement walls can result in significant cost, disruption, and waste of natural resources. The design should consider and minimize the environmental impact over time, and allow for the building dynamics.

The thermal resistance of insulation, as measured in R-value, is the resistance to heat flow (in °F per hr/BTU/SF, degrees of temperature difference divided by wall area and heat loss rate in BTU/hr). Common forms of insulation used in the building envelope are loose-fill, batt, rigid board stock, and foamed-in-place. Material selection criteria should include cost and R-value, but also effects on indoor air quality and health, energy, and other environmental impacts during manufacturing.

Cellulose, fiberglass, and cotton can all have high-recycled content, depending on the supplier. (Cotton batt insulation has the additional advantage of being easy to handle.) When selecting foam insulation, it is important to specify that no harmful gases (chlorofluorocarbons, or CFCs) be used to expand the foam. Any insulation selected should meet all applicable fire rating, pest-resistance, and insulation value product standards set forth by ASTM and others. ASHRAE 90.1 specifies required insulation criteria for building envelope components, dependent on heating degree days and other factors. (*See Chapter 2 for more on the health and environmental impact of insulation choices.*)

Insulation's limitations should also be taken into account. Buildings need to breathe somewhat in order to provide fresh air for the occupants and remove moisture. Insulation, as part of the wall and roof systems, should be considered in the context of all the other building systems, not just the HVAC system.

## Fenestration

### Low-Emissivity (or Low-E) Glass

Emissivity is defined as the ability of a product to emit or receive radiant rays, thus decreasing the U-value. (U-factors represent the heat loss per unit area per degree of temperature difference, BTU/SF/°F. They are reported by the National Fenestration Rating Council, NFRC.) Most non-metallic solids can emit or receive radiant rays and, therefore, have a high degree of emissivity. Fenestrations that reflect radiant rays have a low emissivity. Use of low-E glass windows allows the daylight to enter the building, but reduces the amount of thermal energy from the sun that enters the building envelope. The result is a reduction in the facility's net cooling requirements.[1]

### Heat Mirror Technology

This type of fenestration uses a low-emissivity coated film product suspended inside or between the panes of an insulating glass unit. This is a lower-cost alternative to low-E glass double-pane units.[2]

### Window Films

Films can be applied to the surface of an existing window to change the optical properties. Unlike the wavy, bubbly polyester films of the past, today's acrylic films are hardly noticeable. These films are designed to reduce the amount of solar heat transmission through window glass by increasing the solar reflection (not necessarily visible reflection) and decreasing solar absorption of the glass.[3]

### Opaque Insulated Fenestration

This composite fenestration combines controlled, usable, natural daylight with highly energy-efficient properties. This product has R-values (insulation values) from R-4 through R-12. (Typical windows have an R-value of 1.) The translucent wall panels allow for natural lighting without the thermal energy loss normally associated with windows. The panels are lightweight and shatterproof, and have impressive structural integrity.[4]

## Doors

In addition to seeking sustainable door materials made from recycled material or certified lumber, it is important to look for energy efficiency in the form of exterior door R-value and appropriate door seals. Jamb materials merit attention, as they can also reduce conductive heat loss on exterior doors.

## Vestibules

A vestibule is an area between two sets of doors, serving as an air lock at a building's entrance. Vestibules minimize the infiltration of exterior conditions into the space within the building envelope.

## Air Doors

Air doors, sometimes called air walls, are typically used for garage- or loading dock-type doors to reduce infiltration and ex-filtration. An air door creates an invisible barrier of high-velocity air that separates different environments. Air enters the unit through the intake and is then compressed by scrolled fan housings and forced through a nozzle, which is directed at the open doorway. The system utilizes centrifugal fans mounted on direct-driven, dual-shafted motors. The result is a uniform air screen across the opening with enough force to stop winds up to 25 mph.[6]

At Mount Wachussett Ski area base lodge in Massachusetts, the building is heated with over 400 kW of electric resistance heat. A utility-sponsored energy study demonstrated that the building would be more comfortable and reduce its electric heating load by 40% with the installation of vestibules. After installation, not only was the energy reduced, but the ticket agents no longer had to wear gloves because the existing systems could now keep up with the heat loss at the main door.[5]

## Plastic Curtains

Plastic curtains reduce infiltration and ex-filtration. They are an economical solution for protecting employees and goods from adverse environmental conditions. Plastic curtain or strip doors are inexpensive, easy to install, and save energy.

## Fast Closing Doors

Many walk-in or drive-in refrigerated spaces are converting to "fast-closing" doors that sense the need to open for a delivery or worker, then close quickly. For refrigerated spaces, vapor migration is almost as big an energy loss as the temperature migration. Therefore a tight seal in the space is key to saving energy. A plastic curtain will help with temperature, but not moisture.

# HVAC Systems
## Right-Sizing Systems

As mentioned earlier in the chapter, buildings are typically designed based on extreme conditions. The heating system is sized based on a "design day" (the average coldest day in that location) and the maximum occupancy. The cooling system is sized based on a "design day" (the average hottest day) and design occupancy. Buildings may operate at these design conditions for only 1% of the year. When specifying equipment sizes, engineers might allow design conditions to be exceeded 1%, 2.5%, or 5% of the time. (For critical applications, such as artifact storage or hospitals, exceeding the design conditions might be allowed for only a very small fraction of the time, say 0.1%.) While the capacity of an HVAC system might be designed to be exceeded only 1% of the time, in reality there would be no consequences if it were exceeded 2.5% or even 5% of the time.

An example of right-sizing is the Whitman Hanson Regional High School in Whitman, Massachusetts. This 235,000 SF facility operates year-round, though it is not fully occupied in the summer months. The design team analyzed the actual load during the school year versus the design load requirements' using the ASHRAE guidelines for load calculation. The peak load came in at just over 400 tons of cooling. When the actual school year was plugged into the model, the peak load during the "fully occupied" portion of the year was around 200 tons. The design team specified a hybrid chilled water plant using a 200-ton packaged evaporative-cooled chiller and an efficient 200-ton air-cooled chiller. This enabled the team to meet the load "peak calculations," while focusing on "efficiency" when the building needs cooling the most, during certain months of the school year.

Right-sizing rather than over-sizing is essential for green design of mechanical systems. It is important for the designer to ascertain what the requirements are, and then specify an efficient mechanical system to meet, but not exceed, those sizing requirements. To be fair, owners must agree in the contract that the designer will be free from liability if the environmental conditions exceed the design conditions for some fraction of the year. Clearly, there are huge savings in first cost and operating cost if engineers would stop over-sizing equipment in order to avoid liability should indoor conditions stray slightly from desired conditions (too warm, too humid) for a limited number of hours per year.

The key to right-sizing is to truly understand the load or "need" of the building. A school project I worked on had a model that showed we needed 419 tons of cooling. Because a school is typically not fully occupied in the hot days of August, we talked the designer into only sizing the system at 400 tons. Then, we went one step further and prepared a bin analysis of the weather in the geographic location as compared to the unloading curve of the systems and the occupancy of the facility. We discovered that during the school year (end of August through the middle of June) our load was actually 200 tons. We installed a 200 ton evaporative-cooled chiller and a 200 ton air-cooled chiller side by side. We also found out that we hardly ever run the air-cooled unit (typically, only when the other unit is being serviced).

## Heating Systems

To "right-size" boilers and furnaces to meet the building's actual load and operating requirements, two basic conditions need to be understood:

1. Standard efficiency units are more efficient when fully loaded.

2. Condensing units are more efficient when part-loaded.

Remember, the efficiency is simple math—BTUs in to net BTUs out. The theoretical due point for combustion gas is 246°F (about 119°C). This means that the stack temperature has to be around 280°F (about 138°C) or above, or the combustion gas will condense in the breaching. This causes the combustion gas to become the boiler waste (goes up the chimney). Condensing boilers are designed to condense the combustion gas and allow a much lower exhaust gas temperature, thereby putting the BTUs where you want them—into the water that will be used to heat the building.

Because engineers and facility managers depend on the reliability of heating systems, they traditionally have installed multiple units—often two or three boilers. One was supposed to be sufficient to heat the building, and the second was a backup. This evolved into a three-boiler system with two units sized for the peak load and the third as a backup for either base unit. With new energy code requirements (ASHRAE 90.1 2007), the over-sizing of systems is no longer permitted. Designers must now size systems for the actual conditions, without backup factors. (The other method is to use staged systems to meet the peak load, especially with cooling systems.)

When selecting components for a facility, it is important to understand the types and efficiencies of available equipment. The most common way to obtain equipment efficiency is the ASHRAE efficiency rating, a measure of how effectively a gas or oil heating system converts fuel into useful heat. This measure is defined by the BTUs of fuel going into a unit as compared to the effective number of BTUs of heat output by a unit. The difference is the energy that goes up the stack. There are two common types of efficiency ratings:

- **Combustion Efficiency** (CE): The system's efficiency while it is running. Combustion efficiency is analogous to the miles per gallon a car gets when it is cruising at a steady speed on the highway. This measurement is typically used to categorize boilers and hot water heaters.

- **Annual Fuel Utilization Efficiency (AFUE):** This seasonal efficiency rating is a more accurate estimation of fuel use. It is a measure of the system efficiency and accounts for start-up, cool-down, and other operating losses that occur under normal operating conditions. AFUE is similar to a car's mileage over all kinds of driving conditions, from stop-and-go traffic to highway driving. This measurement is typically applied to furnaces and direct-fired forced hot air systems.[7]

Following are brief system descriptions and operating efficiencies, which can vary by manufacturer.

## *Boilers: Hot Water*

- Standard efficiency: 80% Combustion Efficiency (CE).
- High-efficiency oil/gas units: 84%–87% CE. These boilers operate with lower stack temperatures.
- Condensing propane and natural gas boilers: 88%–96% CE.
- Condensing boilers operate with stack temperatures below 246°F. At this temperature, the water in the exhaust gas condenses in the stack. The lower stack temperatures effectively cause less stack losses and a net increase in combustion efficiency.

One unique characteristic of some cast iron boilers is the possiblity of thermal shock. That happens when the boilers are sized inadequately, and the differential temperature running to and from the boiler plant exceeds 40 degrees. This will cause thermal stresses beyond what the boiler is designed to perform, and the shock can cause cracking of the cast iron. Therefore, some systems are over-sized to avoid the thermal stress on the boiler plant.

Many burners are sized to ensure that the turn down of the flame does not go below 40% of the boiler rating. This is due to the potential for condensation in the boiler from low stack temperatures. If you find white streaks on a gas-fired boiler breeching or yellow/brown streaks on an oil-fired boiler breeching, thermal stress is occurring and prematurely decaying the boiler system. The gases or combustion are eating away at the boiler. Gas-fired boilers create carbonic acid and oil-fired boilers create sulfuric acid in the breeching. This is also a key point that designers must consider.

Ironically, boilers are the most efficient when they have a large differential temperature (within limits). One of the easiest ways to allow for flexibility without breaking the bank is to have a hybrid boiler plant. What I mean by this is sizing your load and run a bin analysis to match the weather and the load; then, size the boilers to take advantage of outdoor air reset and install condensing boilers side by side with cast iron boilers sized to match the load. I worked on a school that had two cast iron boilers side by side. One cracked, due to thermal stress.

We engineered and installed a propane-fired condensing boiler next to the cast iron boiler. Not only was it one-third the size, it increased the system range of operation and we reduced fuel consumption by 32% in the facility!

## *Boilers: Steam*
- Standard efficiency: 80% CE
- High-efficiency oil/gas units: 82%–84% CE

## *Makeup Air & Air Side Systems*
These are the building's fresh air systems that require some pretreating or preheating. High AFUE is a measure of the system efficiency
- Standard-efficiency systems can range from 80%–85% AFUE.
- High-efficiency systems can range from 85%–95% AFUE.[8]

*(Also consider solar preheat of ventilation air using the perforated collector described in Chapter 5.)*

## *Efficiency Controls*
Efficiency controls for boilers and furnaces include:
- **Pressure Reset Systems:** Used on steam systems to allow for wide fluctuations in pressure. As a result, the burners can be shut off longer and stay on longer, with fewer cycles. Avoiding short cycles increases the net system efficiency.
- **Dead Band Widening:** Used on steam systems to allow for a wide system dead band, or time delay, from the set point. Again, the burners can be shut off longer and stay on longer, with fewer cycles. Avoiding short boiler cycling increases the net system efficiency.
- **Reset Controls:** Used in hot water systems to inversely control the hot water loop set point as compared to the outdoor temperature. For example, the system may be set for 180°F when the outdoor temperature is 0°F and, inversely, the loop temperature could be 120°F when the outdoor air temp is 45°F. The lower water temperature setting allows more efficient heating when outdoor temperatures are less severe.

Other methods to improve boiler efficiency include the following:
- Decentralize systems (to reduce distribution losses).
- Modernize boiler controls. (Install feed-forward control-type systems.) Feed-forward controls react more quickly by monitoring the entire system. Rather than reacting to swings in operating pressures or temperatures, these systems maintain the loads based on actual usage.
- Install an economizer heat exchanger in the flue to preheat the boiler feed water.

- Install an oxygen trim system to optimize the fuel/air ratio that monitors stack conditions and continuous stack gas analysis for combustion control.
- Reduce excess air-to-boiler combustion.
- Consider opportunities for cogeneration (combined heat and power), including the use of fuel cells and microturbines as the heat source.

## Radiant Heat

Under-floor systems use much lower water temperatures (typically 110°F–120°F/43°C–49°C). These systems are tied to condensing boilers or other low-temperature systems, such as ground-source heat pumps. This approach takes advantage of lower water temperatures, which are otherwise only effective with oversized radiation systems. Radiant heating systems maintain one of the most constant building temperatures, as they retain heat for long periods of time. The floor becomes a large thermal mass, or thermal storage system. This results in comfortable and more consistent space temperatures. The only downside to radiant systems is that you cannot reset the temperatures when a space is unoccupied, and they tend to be more expensive than traditional heating systems.

## Low Temperature Design

Many fan coil units are designed around a hot water temperature of 180°F. If the design team increases the surface areas of the heating coils, a lower hot water temperature can be used. The lower temperature, combined with the condensing boilers, almost doubles the system efficiency. Remember, condensing boilers are most efficient when part loaded (lower temperatures).

## Heat Recovery Systems

Heat wheels, or enthalpy wheels, remove moisture from the ambient air, while also cooling the ventilated air by passing all incoming air over a desiccant-coated wheel. The wheel rotates, and this same desiccant migrates from the incoming air to the exhaust air, where the moisture is exhausted outdoors. This process removes up to 85% of the heat and moisture from the exhaust air and transfers that heat to the intake air in winter. These systems also remove heat from intake air in summer and transfer it to the exhaust air. In both conditions, the result is a reduction in the net load of the fresh air systems on the facility's energy requirement for conditioning.

Heat recovery systems contribute in two different ways to a sustainable, healthy building. They reduce humidity to a level that is not conducive to dust mite and mold growth, and their ability to recover heat and moisture greatly reduces the energy required to heat or cool the ventilation air. Heat recovery systems also enable a reduction in the heating and cooling capacity of the system.[9]

## Air-to-Air Heat Exchangers

An energy recovery ventilator (ERV) is a type of mechanical equipment that features a heat exchanger, combined with a ventilation system for providing controlled ventilation into a building. Typically this is an air-to-air, plate-type heat exchanger.[10]

## Heat Sink Systems

This is also an ERV, but uses the principal of exhausting over a thermal heat sink, and then switching the incoming air to travel over the heat sink that was heated by the exhaust air.[11]

## Alternative Heating Systems

Infrared heaters include electric, propane, or natural gas units that heat the materials and equipment, not the air within the space. These units typically have lower combustion efficiency, but a higher heat transfer or emissivity, yielding higher efficiency.

## Solar Thermal Systems

Solar collectors gather energy when the sun is shining and use thermal storage or an auxiliary system to supplement the heat when the sun is not shining. Solar water heating is often cost-effective. For space heating, passive solar architecture is preferred over solar mechanical solutions.[12] (*See Chapter 5 for full coverage of solar electrical and heating and hot water systems.*)

# Cooling Systems

## Cooling & Refrigeration

Refrigeration is the process of lowering and maintaining the temperature in a given space for the purpose of chilling foods, preserving certain substances, or providing an atmosphere conducive to bodily comfort. Storing perishable foods, furs, pharmaceuticals, or other items under refrigeration is commonly known as **cold storage**. Such refrigeration prevents both bacterial growth and adverse chemical reactions that occur in the normal atmosphere.

In mechanical refrigeration, constant cooling is achieved by the circulation of a refrigerant in a closed system, in which it evaporates to a gas and then condenses back again to a liquid in a continuous cycle. If no leakage occurs, the refrigerant lasts indefinitely throughout the entire life of the system. All that is required to maintain cooling is a constant supply of power, and a method of dissipating waste heat. The two main types of mechanical refrigeration systems used are the **compression system**, used in domestic units for large cold-storage applications and for most air conditioning; and the **absorption system**, now employed largely for heat-operated air-conditioning units, but formerly also used for heat-operated domestic units.[13]

Three things must be considered when choosing a "green" cooling system:

1. **Refrigerant Type:** Depending on the type of cooling system, the refrigerant can be carcinogenic, flammable, ozone-depleting, or totally neutral and drinkable (water). For green systems, only the non-CFC type refrigerants are acceptable—whether for air conditioning or refrigeration of food products or process equipment. To establish the type of refrigerant and alternatives, check the following website: **http://www.epa.gov/ozone/index.html**

2. **Energy Usage:** One of the fundamentals of green building design is the use of energy-efficient equipment. A later section in this chapter will review typical energy usage for various types of energy use for delivered cooling. The actual usage should be supplied by the manufacturer and certified by the ARI (American Refrigeration Institute). Refer to the following website for an explanation of the calculations of efficiency ARI Standard 550/590-2003: **http://www.ari.org/standardscert/standards/550590-2003.html**

3. **Waste Heat Removal:** All types of cooling remove heat from one space and convey it to another. The type of waste heat removal has a direct relationship to the energy efficiency. Following are the basic types of waste heat removal systems: air-cooled, evaporative-cooled, water-cooled, and air-cooled coil.

## Air-Cooled Systems

The most common type of waste heat removal is air-cooled, which requires a fan to move air across a coil to remove heat. This method has the lowest temperature differential between the refrigerant and the atmosphere. Air is also a fair to poor heat transfer medium. This is not the preferred method for optimum energy efficiency. There are some oversized condensers that have a higher EER than smaller condenser systems; these are an allowable exception.

## Evaporative Cooling

This method uses technology similar to air-cooled, except that water is added to the airstream and is allowed to evaporate in the cooling process. The result is a larger temperature differential. Introducing water into the airstream also creates a better heat transfer medium. The water is typically collected into a sump, and pumps are used to spray the water over the coils. Some of the water is evaporated, and some is recirculated. The sump typically has a makeup water system for the water that has been evaporated. For green building design, gray water recovery can be used, as opposed to fresh water, for the makeup supply.

## Water-Cooling

These systems are heat exchanger-based. The refrigerant passes through a heat exchanger on one side, and water is passed through the heat exchanger on the other. The water is then sent outside to a waste heat removal system.

## Air-Cooled Coil

This method is most commonly used on smaller systems that require year-round operation (e.g., computer cooling systems). The cooling medium may have glycol added to allow the system to be operated throughout the seasons and to reduce the potential for freezing. If using this system in a green building, the designers should strive to recover this heat. In some facilities, this waste heat is used to preheat domestic water or the return lines from a hydronic heating system. In green design, the air-cooled coil should only be used for heating domestic water after the heat has been recovered for other uses. Excess heat must still be rejected from the water; therefore, it should only be used for this purpose as a last resort.

## Cooling Towers

Cooling towers take advantage of the evaporative properties of water. Water is sprayed over large surface areas, and large volumes of air are forced over the surfaces. The air and water mixture causes evaporation and latent heat removal. Depending on the cooling tower design and the ambient wet bulb temperature (outdoor temperature), the water temperature may actually become cooler than the ambient dry bulb temperature. In some manufacturing facilities, this process is used as the process thermal heat removal system. The following website provides more information regarding the evaporative cooling principle: **http://www.piec.com/page3.htm**

For green building design, recovered gray water (as opposed to fresh, potable water) can be used in the makeup supply. One of the keys to effective cooling tower design is increasing the surface area and using propeller-type fans. These fans use one half the energy of "squirrel cage fans," but require larger towers.

## Mechanical Cooling Systems

**Air-Cooled Direct Expansion Systems (DX):** In DX systems, the refrigerant expands through the TXV (thermal expansion valve), and then removes heat from the airstream by way of the DX coil. For DX systems to operate, the refrigerant must be compressed from a low-temperature, low-pressure gas to a high-temperature, high-pressure gas in the compressor, where the heat is then removed by air or liquid cooling. Gas coil-to-air heat exchange is not as efficient as gas coil-to-liquid heat exchange, as the thermal conductivity is typically lower than water. Therefore, in general terms, air-cooled refrigeration systems are not as efficient as water-cooled systems. However, some manufacturers have increased the efficiency of air-cooled equipment by increasing heat surface area and using larger fans.

Evaporative-cooled condenser systems will typically drop the energy usage of any compressor system by 10%–20%, depending on weather conditions. Evaporative cooling involves the spraying of water over the condenser of a refrigeration system and allowing the water to evaporate. This evaporation increases the system's ability to remove heat.[14]

**Free Cooling Systems:** Plate and frame heat exchangers, or "free cooling systems," are used when there are wide swings in outdoor conditions, and there is a building need for cooling most of the year. This system uses the evaporative cooling of the cooling tower system and a plate and frame heat exchanger to remove heat from the chilled water system directly to the condenser water system without the need for mechanical cooling.

Free cooling systems have also been described as "airside free cooling." They bring the cool outdoor air into the space and mix it with the treated air to achieve the desired conditions without mechanical cooling.

**Compression-Type Refrigeration Technologies:**
- Electric scroll compressors: electric-powered rotary compressors for small 1–5-ton systems that use less electricity than conventional reciprocating refrigeration compressors, typically .9–1.4 kWh/ton hr.[15]
- Electric screw compressors: electric-powered rotary compressors for larger 10–100-ton systems. These also use less electricity than traditional reciprocating refrigeration compressors, typically .7–.95 kWh/ton hr.[16]

**Natural Gas-Fired Air-Conditioning Systems:** Natural gas-fired air-conditioning systems are an option for green building designers, due to their net energy savings. With any electric system there are inherent losses associated with the distribution of electricity. The average power plant has a heat rate or efficiency of 20%–35% of energy output in kWh to energy input BTUs. There are also energy losses due to the transmission of electricity over wires over many miles. If a facility operates with gas-fired equipment, the heat rate for internal combustion equipment is typically 35%, with no transmission losses. Natural gas-fired units can have the following:

- Reciprocating compressors (used for 10–100-ton systems typically use 12–14 MBTU of natural gas per ton-hour of cooling).[17] These are equally efficient, yet have none of the electrical transmission losses associated with conventional electric power.
- Screw compressors (used for 10–100-ton systems typically use 12–14 MBTU of natural gas per ton-hour of cooling).[18]

## Chilled Water Systems

In chilled water systems, the refrigerant expands through the TXV (thermal expansion valve), then removes heat from the chilled water medium, which is circulated through a facility and into the air stream by way of a chilled water coil. As with air-cooled DX systems, chilled water system refrigerant needs to be compressed from a low- to a high-temperature, high-pressure gas in the compressor, with the heat removed in the condenser. Again, the condenser can be air- or liquid-cooled. The system loses some efficiency due to the multiple heat exchanges; however, the heat exchange, typically liquid-to-liquid, is very efficient, as the thermal conductivity tends to be higher in water.

In general terms, water-cooled systems are more efficient than air-cooled systems. They are rated by their IPLV (integrated part load value). Refer to the following website for details: **http://www.trane. com/commercial/library/vol281/table2.asp**

## IPLV Ratings
### Air-Cooled Chillers:

- Chillers with Screw Compressors (25–100 tons), typical IPLV .6–.9 kWh/ton hr
- Air-Cooled Scroll Chillers (1–25 tons), typical IPLV .95–1.2 kWh/ton hr
- Evaporative-Cooled Chillers (25–100 tons), typical IPLV .65–.85 kWh/ton hr

### Water-Cooled Chillers:

- Screw Chillers (25–100 tons), typical IPLV .6–.8 kWh/ton hr
- Centrifugal Chillers (100–3,000 tons), typical IPLV .45–.7 kWh/ton hr
- Centrifugal Chillers with VFDs (100–3,000 tons), typical IPLV .35–.6 kWh/ton hr

## Absorption Chillers

One of the oldest artificial cooling systems available, absorption cooling is a chemical reaction type of cooling system that uses heat to separate water from lithium bromide. Once the solutions have been separated, heat is rejected through a condenser heat exchanger, which condenses the steam and cools the lithium bromide. The two chemicals are then allowed to mix in the absorber where the lithium bromide absorbs the water, and an isothermal reaction causes cooling. This isothermal reaction is similar to an ice pack where the liquid (water) is mixed with a solid (lithium bromide), causing cooling. For green building design, absorption is a perfect heat sink or way to use waste heat. Some commercially available absorbers can use waste heat (under vacuum) as low as 140° (lower than the waste heat temperature in many facilities). For more information, consult: **http://www.hydronics.com/yazaki.htm** or **www.broadusa.com**

## BCS Building Control System: Energy-Saving Strategies

1. **Discharge Reset** of hot water or air handling units based on the load requirements in the spaces.

2. **Static Pressure Reset:** adjusts the system static pressure set point based on the area with the greatest load.

3. **Enthalpy-Based Economizer Controls:** utilizes air with the lowest heat content for cooling, by controlling a space based on total heat, not just temperature. (*See Chapter 7 for more detail.*)

4. **$CO_2$ Control (often called demand controlled ventilation):** Modulates the fresh air into a space above the minimum required, depending on the $CO_2$ level in the space. This becomes a truly dynamic control and maintains the building $CO_2$ level within recommended parameters. This approach is very effective in spaces that have large fluctuations in occupancy.

5. **Energy Monitoring and Trending:** The BCS system can monitor energy usage to identify large energy users or spikes. This allows a facility manager and commissioning agent to identify anomalies in a building's energy usage, saving thousands of dollars in energy costs by identifying short cycling or changes in schedules that are normally missed by the operators.

6. **VFD (Variable Frequency Drives) Modulation:** Fans and pumps can be "slowed down" by the VFD with properly located sensors. This ensures that only the volume required is delivered and not recirculated, thereby reducing wasted energy in the form of unnecessary recycling of air. VFDs are usually controlled by a combination of the above-mentioned strategies to deliver only the required volumes.

7. **Occupancy Control:** Occupancy sensors or supervisory access cards enable the fresh air louvers to open when people are in a space, a method similar to $CO_2$ control, but without the calculations. The outdoor air louvers are shut when there is no occupancy and opened when someone enters the space. This type of control is cost-effective when using smaller air handlers.

# Lighting

Lighting accounts for 20%–25% of electricity use in the United States: 5%–10% of it in households, and 20%–30% in commercial facilities. In most of these buildings, at least 50% of this energy is wasted because of inefficient fixtures or equipment, poor maintenance, or inappropriate use.

One of the best ways to understand your lighting requirements is by using the IES guidelines (Illuminating Engineers Society). As part of lighting design they are encouraging engineers to run a photometric analysis of the design before it is built. In many cases the light level may be higher or lower than what was expected. This allows modifications to the design to meet the ideal light level. Many design changes are as simple as changing the selection of lamps and ballasts. Figure 4.4 is a sample photometrics analysis.

Following are several approaches to saving energy expended on lighting:

- **Daylighting:** Designing buildings for optimum use of natural light. Daylighting can save 40%–60% of energy costs compared to conventional design practices. It involves strategies to avoid glare and excess heat gain, while reflecting light into the building. *(See Chapter 7 for more on daylighting.)*

- **Using lower wattage lamps** in existing or new fixtures, providing the illumination is adequate for the task, purpose, and users. Replacing lamps with new ones of a more appropriate (lower) wattage, smaller tungsten halogen lamps, or CFLs (compact fluorescent lamps) is one method. New fixtures with lower wattage lamps can be a better solution, since they are likely to be more efficient and reliable over time.

- **Controlling the amount of light and the time lights are on** through devices such as dimmers, occupancy sensors, photocells, or timers (clock or crank timers), or encouraging users to turn lights off when they are not needed. Occupancy timers are well-suited to spaces used infrequently and are effective as a security measure. Dimmers can be used with both incandescent and fluorescent lamps. They prolong the life of incandescent lamps, but reduce their lumen output, making them less efficient. Fluorescent lamps must have dimming ballasts and lamp holders that accommodate dimmers, but are no less efficient with dimming.

- **Proper maintenance:** Keeping fixtures dusted and cleaned, and replacing yellowed lenses. Maintaining wall and ceiling finishes also increases light efficiency, since dirt decreases light reflection on the walls.

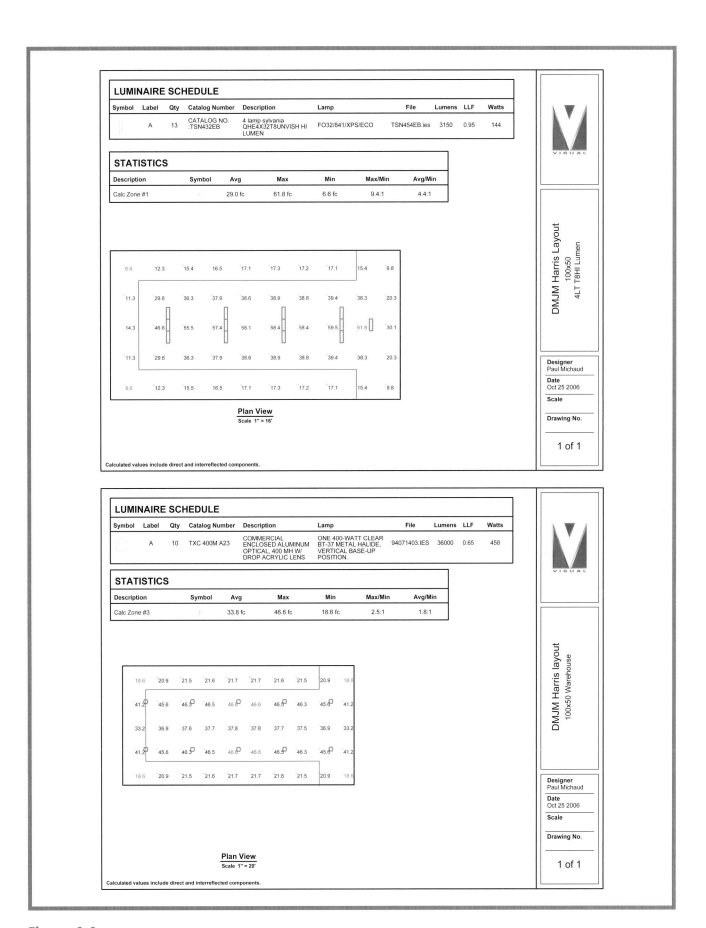

**LUMINAIRE SCHEDULE**

| Symbol | Label | Qty | Catalog Number | Description | Lamp | File | Lumens | LLF | Watts |
|---|---|---|---|---|---|---|---|---|---|
| | A | 13 | CATALOG NO. :TSN432EB | 4 lamp sylvania QHE4X32T8UNVISH HI LUMEN | FO32/841/XPS/ECO | TSN454EB.ies | 3150 | 0.95 | 144 |

**STATISTICS**

| Description | Symbol | Avg | Max | Min | Max/Min | Avg/Min |
|---|---|---|---|---|---|---|
| Calc Zone #1 | + | 29.0 fc | 61.8 fc | 6.6 fc | 9.4:1 | 4.4:1 |

**Plan View**
Scale 1" = 16'

DMJM Harris Layout
100x50
4LT T8HI Lumen

**Designer**
Paul Michaud

**Date**
Oct 25 2006

**Scale**

**Drawing No.**

1 of 1

Calculated values include direct and interreflected components.

**LUMINAIRE SCHEDULE**

| Symbol | Label | Qty | Catalog Number | Description | Lamp | File | Lumens | LLF | Watts |
|---|---|---|---|---|---|---|---|---|---|
| | A | 10 | TXC 400M A23 | COMMERCIAL ENCLOSED ALUMINUM OPTICAL, 400 MH W/ DROP ACRYLIC LENS | ONE 400-WATT CLEAR BT-37 METAL HALIDE, VERTICAL BASE-UP POSITION. | 94071403.IES | 36000 | 0.65 | 458 |

**STATISTICS**

| Description | Symbol | Avg | Max | Min | Max/Min | Avg/Min |
|---|---|---|---|---|---|---|
| Calc Zone #3 | + | 33.8 fc | 46.6 fc | 18.6 fc | 2.5:1 | 1.8:1 |

**Plan View**
Scale 1" = 20'

DMJM Harris layout
100x50 Warehouse

**Designer**
Paul Michaud

**Date**
Oct 25 2006

**Scale**

**Drawing No.**

1 of 1

Calculated values include direct and interreflected components.

**Figure 4.4**
Sample Luminaire Schedule. *(Courtesy of Paul Michaud)*

Both the IES (Illuminating Engineering Society) and ASHRAE advocate for proper lighting power density calculations to provide adequate light for the type of space and not "over lighting." Lighting design just 10 years ago averaged 2 watts per square foot; current technology and design can provide the proper light evenly displaced at less than 1 watt per square foot. There are three key design components:

1. **The space itself,** including the reflectivity of the walls, ceiling, and furniture within it. The reflectivity of these items may require a designer to increase and or decrease the lighting levels.

2. **The fixture's photometrics** (how well will it distribute the light to where it is needed, evenly and without glare). Photometrics are often overlooked, and buildings end up with hot spots and cold spots or uneven light distribution. Look around your space—is the light evenly distributed, or do you have areas that are brighter than others (other than task lighting that is intended to focus on a certain area)?

3. **Lamp technology:** Fluorescent fixtures are the most prevalent type of lamp. For the same light output, you can use 2 T-12 4' lamps with an electronic ballast that will use 85 watts, or 2 T-8 4' lamps with electronic ballasts that will use 65 watts—or the new technology called "high performance T-8 4' lamps" that use 47 watts. Close to half the power, yet these new lamps put out the same (approximate) 3100 lumens per lamp as the other two types.

## Types of Lamps[19]

The most common and newly emerging types of lighting include: incandescent, fluorescent, high-intensity discharge, low-pressure sodium, and light-emitting diode (LED).

**Incandescent:** These lamps, used primarily in homes, have the lowest purchase price, but the highest operating cost. Incandescent lamps have shorter lives and are less efficient than the other types of lighting, but can be made more efficient by choosing the most appropriate lamp for the situation. Common types of incandescent bulbs include:

- Standard, or Type A bulbs, which are the least efficient. "Long-life" bulbs do have a longer service life, but are less efficient than the regular Type A bulbs.
- Reflector, or Type R bulbs are used for floodlighting and spotlighting, often in stores and theaters. They spread light over a wider area than Type A bulbs.
- Tungsten halogen bulbs, most often used in commercial settings, are more efficient than either standard or reflector bulbs, but also more costly.

- Parabolic aluminized reflectors (Type PAR) bulbs are used outdoors for floodlights.
- Ellipsoidal reflectors (Type ER) are used for projecting light downward from recessed fixtures, where they are twice as efficient as Type PAR bulbs.

**Fluorescent:** These lamps are used in commercial indoor lighting and to some extent, in homes, where they offer efficiency and produce less glare than incandescent bulbs. Fluorescent lamps are three to four times more efficient than incandescent bulbs and last ten times longer. They are best used in situations where they will be left on for at least a few hours at a time.

Fluorescent tube lamps are common, and are often seen in 4', 40-watt or 8', 75-watt sizes. Compact fluorescent lamps (CFLs) provide efficiency and convenience, since they fit into standard incandescent bulb fixtures and save as much as 75% of the energy incandescent bulbs would use. CFLs last 10–15 times as long as incandescent bulbs. They can cost about 5–10 times as much, but their long life and energy savings over time make them well worth the extra investment.

Fluorescent light efficiency can be improved by replacing the fixtures themselves with more efficient models, by replacing their lamps with lamps of a lower wattage (where appropriate), or by replacing their ballasts. Electronic ballasts have made a big difference in the conservation of electricity. However, designers must consider the effect of electronic noise that is produced when using large quantities of electronic ballasts or other electronic equipment. Harmonic mitigation (measures to control electronic noise) has become a requirement when the installed kW of electronic components exceeds 10% of the total harmonic load. (Preventing excess noise is also a goal of green building, to enhance the comfort and productivity of building users.)

Low- or no-mercury fluorescent lamps should always be used in green construction to minimize the waste impact on the environment. Manufacturers' data should provide this information. (One of the best research organizations is the Illuminating Society of America: **http:// www.iesna.org**) The tubes should be recycled and not disposed of in landfills. Existing fixtures are also potentially hazardous since the older tubes contained larger quantities of mercury, and older ballasts may contain PCBs (polychlorinated biphenyls).

**High-Intensity Discharge (HID):** These lamps, used for outdoor lighting in stadiums and other large spaces, provide the highest **efficacy** (ratio of light output from a lamp to the energy it consumes, measured in lumens per watt, LPW) of all the lighting types. HID lamps are 75%–90% more efficient than incandescent lamps. HID lighting includes mercury vapor, metal halide, and high-pressure sodium.

- Mercury vapor, the oldest of the HID lighting types, casts a cool (blue-white) light. Often used for street lighting, HID light fixtures have been replaced in many indoor applications, such as gymnasiums, by metal halide systems, which are more efficient and have better color rendition.

- Metal halide lamps offer not only the superior color rendition advantage, but deliver a higher output of light with more lumens per watt than mercury vapor lights. Applications include indoor arenas and gymnasiums, as well as outdoor spaces where color rendition is a factor.

- High-pressure sodium lights, highly efficient at 90–150 lumens per watt, produce a warm white light, variable color rendition, and have long lives with good reliability.

**Low-Pressure Sodium:** This is the most efficient type of lighting, with the added advantage of long service life. The applications are, however, limited to highways and security, where color rendition is not a factor, since the light produced is mostly yellow or gray.

**Induction Lighting:** This is one of the best lifetime investments in lighting technology. This technology lends itself to ten plus years' bulb life and efficiencies approaching LED at a lower cost than LED lighting.

**LEDs (Light-Emitting Diodes):** These lamps have a long life of ten plus years and low energy usage. There are some LEDs now available that will allow for multiple lamps to be grouped together serving as one light source, increasing the light output.

## Electrical Power Generation

### Fuel Cells

These units provide electrical power for many of the manned space craft and unmanned space probes and have finally become commercially available. They are, however, very expensive. Fuel cells use hydrogen, and since hydrogen is not a common fuel, many fuel cells are equipped with "reformers" to produce hydrogen from natural gas, propane, or other fuels. Reformer systems have been demonstrated (Frieberg, Germany, and Humboldt, California) to produce the hydrogen by solar electrolysis of water. While still largely dependent on fossil fuels, fuel cells utilize a noncombustion chemical process that produces no emissions (except a small amount of carbon dioxide and water vapor). The chemical efficiency is not limited to the Carnot efficiency, which limits the efficiency of heat engines (spark ignition, diesel, rankine, or brayton cycle engines). Fuel cells are available in sizes from 0.5 kW to 200 kW. They are characterized by their electrochemistry: proton exchange membrane, alkaline fuel cell, phosphoric acid, molten carbonate, or solid oxide. (*See Figure 4.5.*) Fuel cells may eventually replace heat engines as the prime movers of our society. The nonprofit information center for all fuel cell manufacturers can be accessed at: http://www.fuelcells.org

## Renewable Energy & Distributed Generation Technologies

Renewable energy is truly the best source of power for all of our project needs. Nonrenewable energy forms, such as fossil fuels, are not sustainable over the long term. Each type of renewable energy outlined below has advantages and challenges, including initial installation expense. However, appropriate application of these technologies can be economically advantageous over the long run, as major corporations and homeowners alike are discovering in their facilities and homes.

### Distributed Generation & Cogeneration

Distributed generation is a technology that is used to create the power required for a facility at the point of use. Cogeneration is a form of distributed generation. In cogeneration systems, the system produces power at the point of use and also uses the waste heat generated by the process for other purposes within a facility. In green design, we strive to minimize waste and effectively use as much of a process as possible. Examples of cogeneration are described in the chiller portion of this chapter. The combined heat and power challenge website offers other examples at: http://www.aceee.org/chp

### Photovoltaic Systems (PV)

Photovoltaic systems produce DC power, which can easily be converted to AC through an inverter. (*See Chapter 5 for complete coverage of photovoltaic systems.*) You may also want to consider PPA (Power

## Fuel Cell Types and Applications

| Fuel Cell Type | Applications | Operating Temp. | Comments |
|---|---|---|---|
| Alkaline | Space | 80–100°C | Needs pure fuel/oxidant |
| Phosphoric Acid | Stationary | 200–220°C | Long life, useful heat |
| Proton Exchange Membrane | Stationary Transportation | 80–100°C | Short start time, easily manufactured Small size/scalability Limited co-generation |
| Molten Carbonate | Stationary | 600–650°C | High efficiency, good co-generation |
| Solid Oxide | Stationary | 650–1000°C | High efficiency, good co-generation |

Figure 4.5

Purchase Agreement) which is a financial arrangement in which a third party invests in your facility by installing solar panels , on space they lease, and selling you the power.

## Wind Power

Wind turbines are being constructed throughout the world at an impressive rate, as utility and other private and public companies and organizations invest in a long-term, reliable energy source that is not subject to dramatic price increases or shortages caused by civil unrest, political changes, or the economy. Although small wind energy systems can be constructed to reduce a customer's electricity bill, wind turbines are more often built by utility companies, private corporations, or government entities. *(See Chapter 6 for more on wind power)*

Stand-alone wind systems can offer power in areas that are far from the nearest utility grid. Wind systems can also be connected to utility grids provided they meet certain criteria. Factors such as wind resource maps,

**Figure 4.6**
This 100 kW wind turbine at Local 103 IBEW in Boston, MA, provides 20% of the electricity needs to the facility's state of the art training center. *(Photo taken by Martin Aikens, Business Agent, IBEW Local 103.)*

local terrain, size of the property, and local zoning codes determine the suitability of a wind system for a particular location. These systems generate AC power, which is then converted to DC, and back to AC to regulate the voltage. The technologies continue to change and vertical axis turbines, horizontal axis turbines, and many other new innovations continue to arise. Do your homework, keeping in mind that for commercial facilities, it is most prudent to know your wind patterns and durations before you make any decisions.

Wind energy systems involve a significant initial investment, but are competitive with conventional energy sources over time. The life cycle cost analysis will include factors such as the type of system, wind resource at the site, electricity costs, and how the wind system will be used. The increasing volume production of wind system equipment is expected to continue driving overall costs down.

Not without its controversies (including aesthetics and danger to birds), wind power offers tremendous potential for renewable energy, provided it is managed correctly. This includes measures such as proper site assessments before constructing wind turbines and avoiding high-risk areas such as breeding grounds, flyways, and habitats for endangered species. With wind power suppliers increasingly working together with environmental organizations like the Audubon Society, there is great potential to take advantage of this endlessly renewable energy source. For more information about wind power, visit the American Wind Energy website at **http://www.awea.org** and the Audubon Society at **http://www.audubonmagazine.org/features0609/energy.html**

## Water Power (Hydroelectric)

Hydroelectric power is obtained from the potential energy of water. It may use dammed or kinetic water, which drives a water turbine and a generator. These systems supply both public utilities and private commercial companies.

Hydroelectric systems generate AC or DC power. They require a minimum of 3' of steady head (height between the water source and its outflow) to be buildable. Like wind turbine systems, permitting is often the biggest issue with hydroelectric power.[20]

## Water Conservation

There are several practical approaches to conserving water, including reducing the quantity used—by such measures as low-flow plumbing fixtures, and by landscaping approaches including xeriscaping and drip- and finely tuned-irrigation systems with rain sensors. Other methods include reuse of gray water for irrigation or HVAC systems; and collecting rainwater for similar uses, depending on the filtration methods. A green building project should incorporate as many of these methods as possible.

# Potable Water Reduction

Conservation is the first line of defense in any green building project. Therefore, any use of water must involve conservation equipment. Such devices are required by code in many areas of the country.[21]
They include the following:

1. Water-saving, low-flow showerheads and toilets

2. Water-saving or automatic shut-off sinks

3. Waterless urinals (using a chemical seal and highly polished surface to eliminate the need for flushing water)

**Figure 4.7**
Rainwater Recovery System Overview. *(By James Ziobro, PE, Griffith & Vary Engineers, Wareham, MA.)*

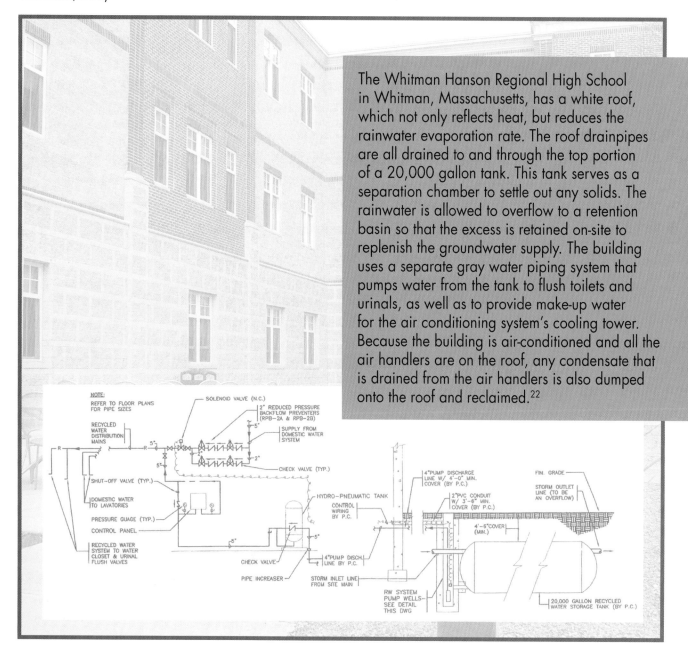

The Whitman Hanson Regional High School in Whitman, Massachusetts, has a white roof, which not only reflects heat, but reduces the rainwater evaporation rate. The roof drainpipes are all drained to and through the top portion of a 20,000 gallon tank. This tank serves as a separation chamber to settle out any solids. The rainwater is allowed to overflow to a retention basin so that the excess is retained on-site to replenish the groundwater supply. The building uses a separate gray water piping system that pumps water from the tank to flush toilets and urinals, as well as to provide make-up water for the air conditioning system's cooling tower. Because the building is air-conditioned and all the air handlers are on the roof, any condensate that is drained from the air handlers is also dumped onto the roof and reclaimed.[22]

4. Recirculating dishwashers for commercial applications

5. Steam trap programs (Since water is the basic component of steam, all steam trap programs inherently conserve water.) In commercial facilities that require steam for process, the steam condenses to become water. The percentage of water that is reused is a key component in water conservation[23]

## Non-Potable Substitution Systems

These systems collect and use by-product water to replace potable water for various purposes. Sources of substitution, reclaimed water include:

- Storm water systems: rainwater collected in tanks for non-potable water usage (can be used as potable water in some cases, if properly filtered, in areas where air or other pollution does not create toxicity)
- Process water: can be recycled and collected for non-potable systems

Some of the uses for non-potable reclaimed water include:

- Cooling systems heat sink
- Irrigation systems
- Toilet flushing
- Process cooling

## Storm Water Collection & Infiltration

This is the single most significant way we can preserve water for the future. For years, we have been letting water run off into rivers and streams and back to the ocean. Meanwhile, we are pumping it out of the ground faster than it can recharge. All green building designs must minimize the amount of runoff from impervious surfaces on a property. Rainwater falling on these surfaces should be collected and channeled to a recharge area, so it can go back into the ground, or should replace municipal water used for irrigation, cleaning, process cooling, or even drinking, if properly purified.[24]

### *Rainwater Collection Systems*

Rainwater has been collected and used in the Caribbean islands and other communities and homes for centuries. It has traditionally been collected at downspouts from a residential roof and directed to storage tanks or cisterns. Many green buildings are using this age-old technology to reduce their water consumption.

Rainwater catchment or collection systems offer several advantages, in addition to saving water and money. The water has no minerals and is therefore "soft" and better for washing and watering plants. It also provides building owners with an independent supply. The technology used for these systems is fairly simple and low-maintenance. Collecting rainwater also helps reduce the burden on municipal drainage systems and water treatment plants.

**Suitability:** Collection tanks have traditionally been used in locations such as islands with salt-contaminated ground, remote areas far from water sources, and tropical regions where annual rainfall is plentiful, but there is also a dry season. Recently, many have discovered that even in areas without those criteria, rainwater can be a money-saving source of high-quality water.

Some considerations include:

- Monthly rainfall (Use data from national weather agencies for at least the previous ten years.)
- Total catchment area—the area of the roof that is available for collecting rain
- Loss factor—the water that does not go into the tank
- How much water is needed to accommodate building uses (If the facility is air conditioned, you must also accommodate the condensate from the AHUs drains as well.)

**Tank Size, Type of System & Cost:** Rainwater collection tanks can range in size from 50–30,000 gallons. The need for water and amount of rainfall, as well as periods of drought, will help determine the appropriate tank size. In areas of evenly distributed rainfall, the tank might be sized to hold a month's worth. In regions with both rainy and dry seasons, a bigger tank might be desirable to store water for times of drought. The intended purpose of the collected water is another key factor. A simple 50-gallon drum placed under the downspout might be adequate for watering plants, depending on the climate. (One-fourth inch of rainfall from an average home's roof would fill the barrel.) Larger needs will require a bigger tank. The planned use of the water will also determine the need for filtration systems and other features.

The cost of rainwater receptacles varies widely, depending on materials and size. A small 75-gallon rain barrel made from recycled plastic can be purchased for about $150. A large, high-end, underground tank could cost roughly a dollar per gallon of capacity ($5,000 for a 5,000-gallon tank). Galvanized tanks are less expensive than polyethylene, but tend to rust and will need to be replaced at some point. Fiberglass tanks range in size from several hundred to 30,000 gallons. These cost roughly $2,000 for a 4,000-gallon tank.
*(See Chapter 7 for more on the comfort and health benefits and precautions of using collected rainwater.)*

## Conclusion

Green design is not a bunch of gadgets one can acquire in order to reduce energy and water use. Green design is an interactive, holistic approach that sets environmental standards for the building's operations and life cycle, while meeting the requirements of building users and owners. Passive systems are encouraged as they truly work without the impact of human or machine.

Increasing efficiency does not require drastic, high-tech, or expensive measures. What is needed is a conscious effort to incorporate healthy, resource-saving features into a facility design, but also to make sure the facility has the flexibility to change as its use changes. Green is very much a common sense approach to building design— but we all realize that common sense is not that common!

1. http://www.askbuild.com/cgi-bin/column?097
2. http://www.southwall.com/products/heatmirror.html
3. http://solutions.3m.com/wps/portal/3M/en_US/WF/3MWindowFilms/
4. http://www.kalwall.com/about.htm
5. http://www.wachussett.com
6. http://www.tmi-pvc.com/air/index.html
7. http://elpaso.apogee.net/res/rehcomb.asp
8. Ibid.
9. http://www.gri.org/pub/solutions/desiccant/tutorial/dw_dw_vs_enthalpy.html
10. http://www.greenbuilder.com/sourcebook/EnergyRecoveryVent.html
11. http://www.regenteco.com
12. http://www1.eere.energy.gov/solar/
13. http://www.ari.org/consumer/works/
14. http://www.achrnews.com/CDA/ArticleInformation/features/BNP__Features__Item/0%2C1338%2C18149%2C00.html
15. http://www.nypha.com/prodhp.htm http://www.engr.siu.edu/staff2/abrate/scroll.htm
16. http://www.york.com/products/esg/products/YorkEngineeredProducts.asp? cnt_Model_ID=122&Display=24&View=ON&ShowSubsID=122&Model=122
17. http://www.tecogen.com/chiller.htm
18. Ibid.

19. U.S. Department of Energy, Office of Energy Efficiency and Renewable Energy, Consumer Energy Information: EREC Fact Sheet, "Energy-Efficient Lighting," available at http://www.eren.doc.gov/erec/factsheets/eelight.html

20. http://www.fwee.org/TG/nwaterpwr.html

21. http://wwwga.usgs.gov/edu

22. http://www.epa.gov/ow

23. http://www.geocities.com/RainForest/7575/#bath

24. http://www.whrsd.org

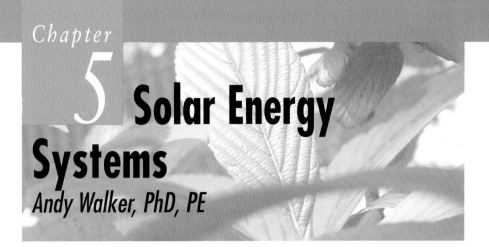

# Chapter

# 5 Solar Energy Systems

*Andy Walker, PhD, PE*

Developments in solar energy are accelerating so rapidly it's hard even for experts to keep up. The last edition of this book could not have anticipated the explosive growth or the price declines wrought out of technology improvements in just the last year. Technologies coming out of the lab only a couple of years ago are already having an effect on the designer's choices and on the marketplace. We could not have anticipated, for example, that thin-film non-silicon photovoltaic modules would be manufactured for less than $1 per watt and would unseat older technologies to lead U.S. photovoltaics manufacturing; that electro-chromic glass, which can be controlled from clear to opaque, would be commercially competitive; and that transpired collectors for solar ventilation air preheating would be available in a range of colors from a mainstream building component manufacturer. Another remarkable change is that, in 2008, 43% of new electric generating capacity additions were provided by renewables, compared with only 2% of new capacity additions in 2004.[1] These and many other exciting developments are described in this new edition. With technology changing so quickly, future editions will look back at our efforts as quaint.

We can expect future advancements in solar buildings to be rapid and profound. We may not be able to predict the future, but we can perceive some of the characteristics of what must be over the horizon. It must be carbon neutral in this climate changing world. Now we realize that we can't put all our eggs in one basket, and whatever energy picture we evolve to is going to incorporate a lot more diversity of supply than it does now. It's going to have to be efficient. It's going to have to involve local jobs. It's going to have to have a low impact on the environment, on the facilities, and on the infrastructure of the facilities where it's installed. It's going to have to be affordable, and it's going to have to be secure.

Let's discuss the solar energy technologies within the context of these characteristics. Energy is an issue at the intersection of security, economics, and the environment, where there are certainly risks and vulnerabilities, but also opportunities. The ability of solar energy to solve problems in one of these sectors may alleviate problems in some of the other sectors.

Life on Earth has always depended on energy from the sun. Our food energy comes from photosynthesis caused by the sun in plants. The fossil fuels that we currently rely on are solar energy, captured and saved by plants over the span of 50 to 450 million years. We have been using that stored fuel at a rapid rate for more than 100 years, and, in the process, moving carbon from the lithosphere to the atmosphere. Even before fossil fuels run out—which they inevitably will—we may be forced to consider alternatives because of the environmental consequences of burning them. One alternative, solar energy, has long been used in buildings; Socrates made reference to it thousands of years ago.[2] A recent reawakening interest in the health and comfort benefits of natural systems has caused its revival for use in building design

Principal ways of using solar energy in buildings include the following:
- Daylighting
- Passive solar heating
- Solar water heating
- Photovoltaics (electricity)
- Solar ventilation air preheating

Also important to the designer is avoiding solar glare and overheating—two common problems in buildings, described more in Chapter 7.

New technologies, such as photovoltaics that convert solar energy cleanly and silently into electricity and super-insulated windows that admit visible light while screening out ultraviolet and infrared rays, provide today's designer with powerful new tools in the utilization of solar energy. It is now technically feasible to provide all of a building's energy needs with solar energy. Solar is even the least costly option in areas where delivery of fossil fuels or provision of electric power is expensive. Many solar energy applications are cost-effective already, and, as the price of conventional utilities continues to rise, more and more solar energy features will find their way into green buildings.

The sun is a nuclear reactor 93,000,000 miles from Earth, streaming radiant energy out into space. The intensity on a sunny day is around 317 BTU/SF/hour (1,000 watts per m$^2$), a value respected by anyone who has been sunburned or momentarily blinded by the brightness.

Enough solar energy reaches the Earth to power the world economy 13,000 times over.[3] In fact, 20 days worth of solar radiation is equal to the capacity of all our stored fossil fuel from gas, coal, and oil resources.[4] There is no question that solar energy is of adequate quantity to meet our energy needs. The emphasis is rather on how it can be integrated into building design, given the distributed and intermittent nature of the solar resource.

## Background: Energy, Economics, Environment, Health & Security

## The True Cost of Conventional Energy Sources

The first law of thermodynamics tells us that energy is neither created nor destroyed, but may be converted from one form to another. For buildings, the important forms of energy are electric power and chemical energy stored in fuels, such as natural gas. The second law of thermodynamics tells us that whenever energy is converted from one form to another, some fraction is irretrievably lost as heat. To generate electricity for building consumption, about twice as much energy is wasted as reject heat at the power plant, and losses also occur in transmitting and distributing the electricity over power lines. Partially as a consequence of these thermodynamic inefficiencies, electric energy costs an average of $27.89 per million BTU in 2009, almost three times more than the $10.50 per million BTU for heat from natural gas.[5]

Energy provides comfort in buildings and powers our automated economy, but at a price. Expenditures for energy in the United States reached $1,157 billion in 2008—$174 billion of this for commercial buildings, and $242 billion for residential buildings. The remainder went toward transportation and industrial processes. Energy expenditures in homes averaged $2,084 per home per year, a significant percentage of household income. In commercial buildings, energy expenditures averaged $2.28 per square foot per year. Significant increases in the cost of energy for both homes and businesses in recent years has dramatically sparked interest in renewable energy. In 2009, the cost of natural gas delivered to commercial buildings averaged 19% higher than in 2005.[6]

Estimates of the long-term availability of fossil fuels vary widely, and are frequently revised as new reserves are discovered, technologies to extract fuels improve, and the needs for different fuels change. Current estimates of proved reserves include 192 trillion cubic feet of natural gas in the U.S. and 6,343 trillion cubic feet worldwide. Even at the current rate of consumption of 21.9 trillion cubic feet per year in the U.S. and about 100 trillion cubic feet worldwide, the end of this fuel is in sight. Production of natural gas in the U.S. peaked around 1995 and has been in decline since, requiring more imports.[7] In order to secure our children's energy future, renewable energy technologies must be developed and deployed before these reserves are exhausted.

Energy cost savings is the number one motivation to consider solar energy. I've pinned my whole career on trying to find places where renewables are justified solely by the utility energy cost savings. That involves traditional life cycle cost analysis, by which cash flows are calculated in a very specific way (for example, regulation 10 CFR 436 and the BLCC computer program for federal agencies). Almost all buildings have some cost-effective solar opportunities, even if it is limited to heating ventilation air or photovoltaics on irrigation valves. Some buildings can get a significant portion of their needs from cost-effective projects and, in a few places where energy is expensive, such as Hawaii, could even get 100% of their energy from cost-effective, on-site solar projects.

There are some other reasons to consider renewable energy that might have a value equal to, or in excess of, energy cost savings. One reason is to avoid the cost of infrastructure. I installed my first PV system, an off-grid water pumping station, back in 1981. At that time all of our projects were off grid, so what we were really saving was the cost of running a power line out to a remote location.

Another reason is to reduce the volatility of fuel prices. Many people talk about energy escalation rates and hearings at the utility commissions to establish rates and increases in rates; but not too many people pay attention to the little charge on the utility bill called the "fuel adjustment charge," which changes every month. Basically, the utility is passing on to the consumer the cost of the fuel used in their power plants. That price can be very volatile, as we saw recently with the price of natural gas. In a recent solar project analysis, industrial customers asked us to consider rate increases of up to 15 percent a year for natural gas. It wasn't just out of some kind of morbid curiosity; they were actually thinking that the cost of natural gas might increase at that high rate. If they know what the cost of energy will be, they can add it into the price of their products, but a factory cannot adjust production to fluctuating energy costs.

Not included in this economic accounting are the environmental impacts of energy use. In 2009, atmospheric emissions associated with energy use in U.S. buildings included 2,337 million metric tons of $CO_2$ (carbon dioxide) of the country's 5,978 tons. Buildings in the U.S. account for 39% of U.S. carbon emissions, and 7.7% of all global carbon emissions.[8] Emissions have a demonstrated negative effect on health and threaten the stability of the ecosystem that nourishes us. Fuel cells (which use electrochemical reactions rather than combustion) have been suggested to avoid $SO_x$ and $NO_x$ emissions, but emission of the global warming gas $CO_2$ is unavoidable with the use of any hydrocarbon fuel. It's been said the Stone Age didn't end because we ran out of stones; it ended because we found something better.

Unlike the combustion of fossil fuels, the use of solar energy emits no pollution. Environmental impacts of exploring for, extracting, refining, and delivering fossil fuels are also avoided, since solar energy is available in all locations.

Local trades are employed to install, operate, and maintain solar energy systems. That helps with balance of trade issues, especially now that we import so much energy into our communities. Domestic production of natural gas peaked around 1994. Domestic production of oil peaked way back in 1978. Since then we have had to import more energy from other countries, and that adds to our balance of trade deficit.

## A Renewable, Safe Alternative

The use of solar energy avoids many security and reliability problems. Our interconnected power system is brittle, with small problems cascading to affect millions of customers. Since solar energy can be produced and stored in a distributed fashion (e.g., at each building), it is not vulnerable to such an accident or to sabotage. Instead of panicking in the dark when the power goes out, occupants of daylit rooms can see, and perhaps even keep on working. Pipes are less likely to freeze in a home with passive solar heating. Solar energy provides a decentralized, robust energy source capable of withstanding local power interruptions, if so designed. This can have a very high value for remote communities powered by, say, a diesel generator. Sunlight is delivered to those remote locations every day for free, so it mitigates the chance of supply interruptions. It provides a redundant energy supply. A photovoltaics system may be configured to act as an uninterruptible power supply, although it may add about a third to the cost. I've had personal experience with the reliability of solar energy: when the natural gas boiler in my home went out, I still had hot water at the tap because my solar water heating system continued to deliver it. That kind of redundant electric power supply or hot water supply can have a value associated with it.

On a larger scale, global conflicts over energy supplies are certain if we acknowledge that energy supplies are crucial for a nation's interest and will be secured by military force. As an equitable resource available to all, the increased use of solar energy lessens global conflicts over energy resources.

## Energy Use in Different Types of Buildings

Because commercial and residential buildings use energy differently, they require different solar energy strategies. (*See Figure 5.1.*) In an office building, lighting is paramount. Occupancy is during the day, and daylighting is a principal strategy. For a motel, water heating may be the largest use of energy, and daylighting may be less important, since rooms are occupied primarily at night. While it might be appropriate

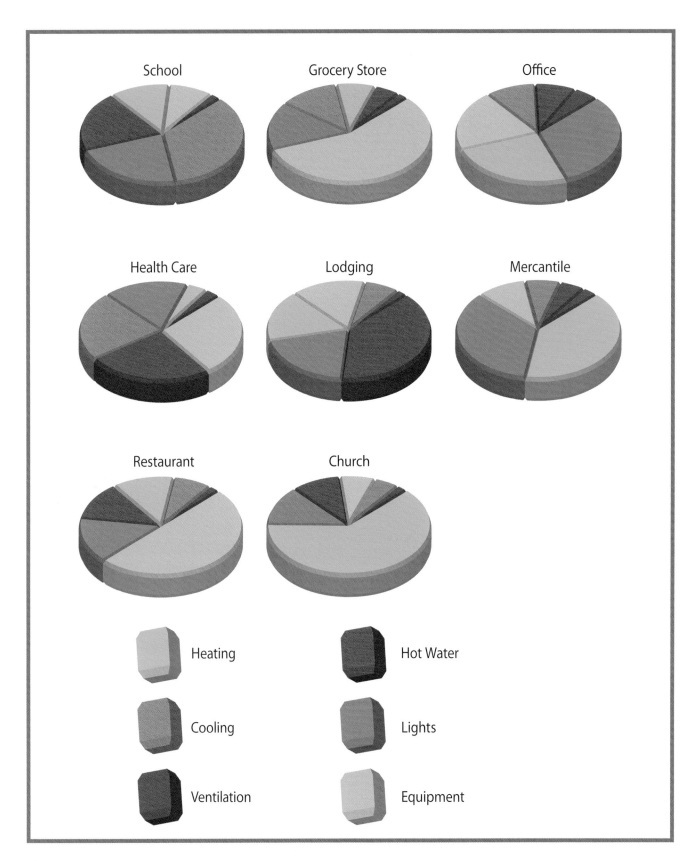

**Figure 5.1**
**Energy Use Breakdown for Different Types of Buildings**
The average energy use is 120 K/BTU/SF per year. *(Data from DOE OBT Building Energy Databook.)*

Green Building: **Project Planning & Cost Estimating**

to consider daylighting and solar water heating for all buildings, the differences of these end-uses have implications for the building design. The solar energy strategies used to address these differing requirements will influence both the building envelope and mechanical systems in different ways, as discussed in this chapter.

## The Solar Resource

Solar power systems can be designed to operate anywhere on Earth, and they are even used extensively in outer space. In polar regions, the systems would provide power only in summer. A solar energy system design includes a solar collector area large enough to capture sunlight to meet the load, and storage capacity to span long winter nights and cloudy periods. The solar collectors should be oriented to optimize collection for the location and the climate. The path of the sun across the sky has implications for building layout, solar collector orientation, and shading geometries. The amount of sunlight on a surface throughout the day is factored into the design of solar energy systems.

### The Effect of Latitude

At lower latitudes, such as near the Equator, the sun rises almost directly to the east, passes nearly overhead, and sets to the west. This path does not change much throughout the year, so the seasons are less pronounced at lower latitudes. As we move north to higher latitudes, the path of the sun across the sky causes more seasonal variation. In summer, the sun rises slightly north of due east, passes a zenith that is just south of directly overhead, and sets to the north of due west. In winter, the sun rises south of due east, cuts a low arc across the sky, and sets south of due west.

In the Northern Hemisphere and in summer, building surfaces that receive the most sun are the roof and the east- and west-facing walls (east in the morning, west in the afternoon). In winter, the sun cuts a lower arc across the sky, and the south-facing wall receives the most sun. The north wall of a building receives sun only in the morning and evening in summer, and then only at a very oblique angle. Extending the long axis of a building in the east-west direction has two advantages: it limits overheating of west-facing exposures during summer afternoons, and it maximizes south-facing exposure for solar heating on winter days. (Low sun angles in the morning and evening are a source of glare when daylighting with east and west-facing windows.) For the Southern Hemisphere, the geometry would be reversed. Figure 5.2 shows solar energy incident on a horizontal area per day in units of 300 BTU/ft²/day (kWh/m²/day). It is seen that solar radiation in much of the continental U.S. varies, from 900 BTU/ft²/day (3 kWh/m²/day) in winter to 2,200 BTU/ft²/day (7 kWh/m²/day) in summer with an annual average of 1,500 BTU/ft²/day (5 kWh/m²/day).

## Solar Collectors in Photovoltaic & Thermal Systems

There are two types of collectors used to gather sunlight. Focusing collectors use only direct beam radiation (parallel rays) due to the reflective optics. Flat plate collectors use both the direct and scattered diffuse components of solar radiation. Most collectors are of the non-focusing type, although focusing collectors are sometimes used in large-scale applications.

### *Tracking Systems*

For solar collectors in photovoltaic or solar thermal systems, it is possible to construct a tracker that rotates with both the azimuth (degrees west of south) of the sun and the altitude (degrees of the sun off the horizon) throughout the day, thus keeping the collector facing directly toward the sun at all times. Tracking systems are usually pole-mounted on the ground, rather than on a building. Tracking is more common with photovoltaic systems than with thermal systems because electrical connections are more flexible than plumbing

**Figure 5.2**

Maps of daily average solar energy on the horizontal for the months of March, June, September, and December. *(Courtesy of NASA LARC SSE 2.)*

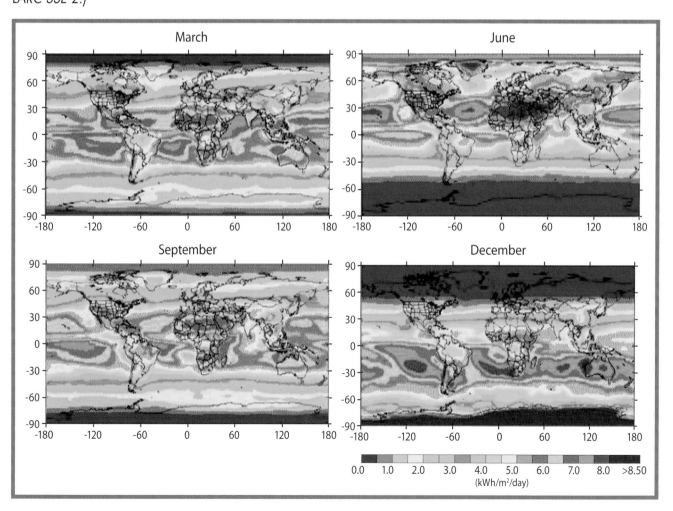

connections. Tracking the sun from east to west increases energy collection by as much as 40% in summer, but does not significantly improve performance in winter due to the path of the sun in the sky. This benefit of increased collection would be weighed against the cost of an additional solar collector area in deciding whether tracking is appropriate for a particular application. (*See the section on photovoltaics later in this chapter for a discussion on the cost of tracking hardware.*)

### Fixed Systems

Fixed (non-tracking) systems are often favored for simplicity and lower cost. A fixed PV array may be mounted on the ground, on the roof, or built into the building. It is important to determine the best fixed angle at which to mount the collector. In general, a south-facing surface tilted up from the horizontal at an angle equal to the local latitude maximizes annual energy collection.

## *Passive Solar Heating*

Every building with windows is solar-heated, whether to the benefit or detriment of occupant comfort and utility bills. In cold climates, the goal may be to capture and store as much solar heat as possible, while in warm climates the objective is to keep heat out. In general, a building must perform both functions, using solar heat in winter and rejecting it in summer. Passive solar features can be woven into any architectural theme, from New England Cape Cod style to Santa Fe Pueblo style. Figure 5.3 shows a passive solar home in the Victorian style.

**Figure 5.3**
Passive solar design can be of any style, such as this Victorian passive solar home in Denver, CO. *(Photo by Melissa Dunning, courtesy of NREL.)*

In a typical commercial building, 16% of annual energy use is for space heating, while in a typical residential building, the percentage is much higher at 33%. The heating load can be significantly reduced by deliberate orientation of the building on the site and by careful design of the size and orientation of each window. Buildings designed in this way, using standard construction methods, are known as **sun-tempered**. Strategies to meet a higher percentage of the heating load through architectural design solutions are known as **passive solar heating**. The word "passive" means that the architectural elements, such as windows, insulation, and mass, operate as a system without the need for power input to mechanical equipment. Passive solar designs are categorized as **direct gain, sunspaces,** or **Trombe walls** (named after a French inventor). All three types have the same major components: windows to admit the solar radiation; mass to store the heat and avoid nights-too-cold and days-too-hot by smoothing out the temperature fluctuations; and a superior level of insulation in walls, roof, and foundation.

An understanding of solar radiation and of the position of the sun in the sky is essential to effective building design. In the northern hemisphere, winter sun is at its maximum on the south side of a structure, so this is the façade most affected by passive solar heating design. All passive solar heating features have a southerly orientation. The building floor plan would be laid out to provide sufficient southern solar exposure, with the long axis of the building running from east to west. The extent of this elongation must be optimized for the climate, since it also increases surface area and associated heat loss. Some east-facing windows are also recommended in areas with cool mornings. One strategy to maintain a compact plan while also admitting solar gain into the northern rooms of a building is to use high, south-facing clerestory windows. The fact that the clerestory windows are high up also ensures high-quality daylight, along with passive solar heat gain. It is important to take into consideration any surrounding objects that might shade the solar features, such as hills, other buildings, and trees.

## Window Efficiencies

Advances in window technology have revolutionized passive solar heating design. Excessive heat loss from large window areas used to limit the application of passive solar heating to moderate climates. The well-insulated glass assemblies available today allow large windows even in very cold climates and high elevations, albeit at higher cost.

The designer may now select glass with a wide range of optical and thermal properties. The heat loss from a glazing assembly is described by the loss coefficient, or U-value in units of (BTU/SF/hour/F or W/m$^2$/C). The lower the U-value of a window, the less heat loss.

Manufacturers construct windows with multiple layers of glass separated by gaps of air or other low-conductivity gas to reduce convective heat loss, and apply a low-emissivity (low-E) coating to reduce radiative heat loss. The U-value of a window ranges from 1.23 for single-pane with metal frame to as low as 0.24 for triple-pane with low-E coating and gas fill. Standard double-pane glass has a U-value between 0.73 and 0.49, depending on the type of frame.[9] A low U-value is of benefit in both warm and cold climates.

Other properties to consider include the **solar heat gain coefficient** (SHGC), and the **visible transmittance**. The SHGC is the fraction of solar heat that is transmitted directly through the glass, plus the fraction absorbed in the glazing and eventually convected to the room air. SHGC varies from 0.84 for single-pane clear glass to as low as zero for insulated opaque spandrel glass. Standard double-pane clear glass has an SHGC of 0.7. A high SHGC is of benefit on the south side to admit solar heat in winter, but on east and west sides, or in warm climates, a low SHGC is best. The visible transmittance of glass is an important consideration for daylighting goals. New developments in glass technology include photochromic (changes with light level), thermochromic (changes with temperature) and electrochromic (changes with application of an electric voltage). These new glass products will offer a versatile palette to the designer when commercially available.

Vertical south-facing windows are recommended over sloped or horizontal glazing for passive solar buildings in the northern hemisphere. Sloped glazing provides more heat in the cool spring, but this benefit is obviated by excessive heat gain in the warm autumn and also the additional maintenance caused by dirt accumulation and leaks. Overhangs admit the low winter sun while blocking the high summer

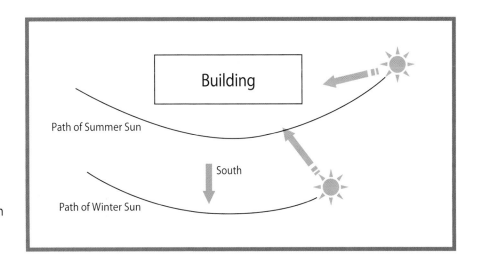

**Figure 5.4**
A building with the long axis stretched out in the east-west direction minimizes solar heat gain in summer and maximizes solar heat gain in winter.

sun, but since the ambient temperature lags behind the sun's position in the sky (cool on the spring equinox, warm on the autumnal equinox), there is no single fixed window overhang geometry that is perfect for all seasons. Therefore movable external awnings, plant trellises (which are usually fuller in autumn than in spring), or internal measures, such as drapes and blinds, are often used to improve comfort.

## Thermal Storage Mass

Thermal storage mass is often provided by the structural elements of a building. It is important that the mass be situated such that the sun strikes it directly. Mass may consist of concrete slab floor, brick, concrete, masonry walls, or other features such as stone fireplaces. A way to add some mass to a sun-tempered space is to use a double-thickness of drywall. There are some exotic thermal storage materials including liquids and phase-change materials, such as eutectic salts or paraffin compounds, that store heat at a uniform temperature. These materials are not commonly used, however, due to their cost and the need to reliably contain them over the life of the building.

Optimum levels of insulation in a passive solar building are frequently double those used in standard construction, not only to reduce back-up fuel use, but also to help limit the size of the required passive solar heating features to reasonable proportions. The need to add insulation has implications for selection of wall section type and choice of cathedral versus attic ceiling, since an attic can accommodate more insulation. Insulation on slab edges and foundation walls is especially important, because these massive elements are often used to store solar heat. In all cases, the insulation should be applied to the outside of the mass in order to force the mass to stabilize the interior temperature. The mass should not be insulated from the occupied space, so that it easily heats the room air. Furring out from the mass wall or carpeting the floor slab is not recommended. Finished concrete or tile floors are preferred. Durable insulated finish systems are available for exterior application to concrete or block walls. Although advanced glazing assemblies are already well-insulated, drapes and movable insulation are sometimes used to provide additional insulation at times when solar gain is not a factor, such as at night.

It is not reasonable to expect passive solar energy to heat mass that is not directly in the sun, or to distribute widely throughout a building. The reason is that natural (passive) convection is caused by the temperature difference between the hot area and the cold area, and we want that temperature difference to be minimized for comfort reasons. Distribution to other parts of a building requires a mechanical solution involving pumps or fans.

# Direct Gain

Direct gain spaces admit the solar radiation directly into the occupied space. This strategy is most effective in residences or within atriums and hallways of commercial buildings. Direct gain is generally not recommended for workspaces, or where people view computer screens or televisions, due to excessive glare and local heat gain. In a residence, occupants can move to a chair that is not directly in the sun, but in workspaces, people usually have to remain in place to accomplish a task.

The required window area varies from 10%–20% of floor area for a temperate climate, to 20%–30% for a cold climate.[10] The percentage of the heating load that can be met with solar energy in a direct gain application is limited by the need to maintain comfortable conditions. The space cannot be allowed to get too hot, which limits the amount of solar heat that can be stored for nighttime heating; nor can it get too cold, which means it will require the use of a back-up heater at times.

# Sunspaces

A sunspace avoids the limitations of a direct gain space by allowing the temperature to vary beyond comfort conditions. In sunspaces, the mass can overheat and store more energy when sun is available. Sunspaces can also reuse fuel by allowing the spaces to subcool at night or during storms. As a consequence, the sunspace may not be comfortable at all times, and its uses should be programmed accordingly. Appropriate uses for a sunspace include casual dining area, crafts workspace, or an area for indoor plants.

Skylights or sloped glazing in sunspaces are common in practice, but are not recommended, since the high sun is not gladly received in summer, and since the sun hits the horizontal skylight only at an oblique angle in winter. (Skylights are available that address this issue by incorporating shades and louvers to control direct heat gain in summer.) It is also common to see sunspaces that project out from the house wall, another approach that is not recommended. It is better to have the house partially surround the sunspace (except on the south side) to reduce heat loss from both the sunspace and the house. Thus, the sunspace differs from a direct gain space more in terms of temperature control and the use of the space than it does in terms of architecture.

The recommended amount of glazing in a sunspace varies from 30%–90% of floor area in temperate climates to 65%–150% of sunspace floor area for cold climates.[11] In most applications, the wall between the sunspace and the building acts as a massive thermal storage wall. In very cold climates or if the sunspace windows are poorly insulated (high U-value), it may be necessary to insulate this wall. Operable windows and doors between the sunspace and the building are opened and closed to provide manual control. Vents and fans are also used to extract heat from the sunspace under automatic control based on the temperature of the sunspace.

## Trombe Wall

A Trombe wall is a sunspace without the space. It consists of a thermal storage wall directly behind vertical glazing. This passive solar heating strategy provides privacy and avoids glare and afternoon overheating. Over the course of the day, the wall heats up, and releases its heat to the space behind the wall over a 24-hour period. The outside surface becomes very hot during the day, but due to the thermal inertia of the mass, the interior surface remains at a rather constant temperature. Since the wall is not insulated, care must be taken to ensure that the heating cycle by the sun matches the cycle of heat loss to the interior and exterior. Well-insulated glazing can reduce this heat loss, but multiple panes, low-E coatings, and ultraviolet filters also reduce the amount of solar heat that gets through the glass, so the trade-offs must be evaluated to optimize cost.

**Figure 5.5**
Thermal storage Trombe wall at the National Renewable Energy Laboratory, Colorado. *(Courtesy of NREL.)*

**Green Building: Project Planning & Cost Estimating**

Trombe wall area varies from 25%–55% of floor area in temperate climates, and from 50%–85% of floor area in cold climates.[12] The wall is covered with a thin foil of blackened nickel called a **selective surface**, which has a high absorbtivity in the short wavelengths solar spectrum, but a low emissivity in the long wavelength infrared spectrum, thus reducing radiant heat loss off the wall. The heat must conduct into the wall from the selective surface, so proper adhesion to avoid blistering or peeling of the surface from the wall is critical to performance. Rather than hollow block, the wall should be solid to allow the heat to conduct through uniformly. Since the space between the mass wall and the window can exceed 180°F, all materials, including paint and seals, must be able to tolerate high temperatures. Similar to direct gain spaces and sunspaces, an overhang over the glazed trombe wall reduces unwanted summertime heat gain.

## Design Tools

Analysis techniques useful for passive solar design include rules-of-thumb, correlation tables, and computer simulations. Rules-of-thumb relate the size of windows and amount of mass (as well as details such as overhang dimensions and mass thickness) to the square footage of the space to be heated. Rules-of-thumb can be found in books on passive solar heating.[13] Correlation tables are the results of detailed calculations that relate passive solar design parameters to conditions such as average temperature, local latitude, and other factors that affect system performance. In recent years, computer simulations have overtaken these methods. Two popular simulations that analyze passive solar heating are Energy-10 and DOE-2. Another program called EnergyPlus is being introduced to succeed DOE-2. Both simulate solar gains, thermal losses, and resulting temperature of the indoor space for each of 8,760 hours of a typical year, using representative weather data for the site.

- Energy-10 is very easy to use for direct gain and sunspaces, but currently does not have the feature of modeling Trombe walls.
- DOE-2 can model any passive solar heating strategy in a large number of zones. Newer versions of DOE-2 include a geometric representation of the building and account for self-shading of building areas.
- Energy-Plus combines the best features of previous programs.

Both programs account for the interactions between solar heat gain, internal heat gain from lights, people, and equipment, mechanical system performance, and other simultaneous effects. (*See Chapter 15 for more on Energy-10 and DOE-2.*)

## Cooling Load Avoidance

Since heat sources internal to the building, such as lighting and computers, are often constant throughout the year, the peak cooling load and the size of the air conditioning system required to meet this peak are often determined by solar heat gain on the building envelope. On a national average, space cooling represents 10% of annual energy use in residential buildings, and 12% in commercial buildings. In commercial buildings, 33% of the cooling load is due to solar heat gain through the windows (of the remainder, 42% is due to heat from lights, 18% to heat from equipment, and 7% to heat from the people inside).[14]

Since the sun cuts a high arc across the sky in summer, a building with small east and west dimension is recommended for cooling load avoidance, as it is for solar heating in winter, when the sun cuts a much lower arc to the south. In the summer, the sun is at a maximum on the roof and on the west façade, which is why these faces deserve the most attention regarding strategies to reduce solar heat gain. While solar heat gain on well-insulated opaque surfaces is negligible, the size and orientation of windows is key. Solar heat gain on west-facing windows is at a maximum on summer afternoons, so the size of these windows should be no more than what is required to take advantage of an important view or to meet daylighting goals. Windows on the south side are beneficial for winter heat gain, and an overhang over them blocks the sun when it is higher in the sky in summer. An overhang can be designed to provide shade in summer and sun in winter, but only

**Figure 5.6**
As demonstrated on this office building, overhangs are effective at reducing cooling loads on the south side, but are not needed on the north side and ineffective on the east and west. *(Photo by Warren Gretz, courtesy of NREL.)*

on the south side. On the north side, an overhang is never needed, and on the east and west sides is not effective due to low sun angles in the morning and at night.

Solar heat gain can also be controlled by careful selection of window glazing properties. Glazing with a low solar heat gain coefficient (SHGC) attenuates solar heat gain. The low SHGC is achieved by absorbing the energy in the tint of the glass or reflecting it with a surface coating. Reflection is the most direct way to reject solar heat, since some of the light absorbed in the tinted glass will be re-radiated or convected into the room air. If a clear appearance is desired, or if a high visible transmittance is required to meet daylighting goals, a selective glazing is recommended. Selective glazing screens out the infrared and ultraviolet portions of the solar spectrum, but allows much visible light to pass. A double-pane assembly of selective glazing typically has an SHGC of 0.35. Occupant comfort may be improved by the use of shades and blinds to block the sun. However, once solar heat makes it through the window glass, it must be removed by the building mechanical system, with associated energy cost and environmental impacts. In other words, blinds and drapes only stop the heat flow after the heat is already in the house.

Several measures can be taken outside of the building to mitigate solar heat gain if it is unwanted. Deciduous trees provide shade in summer, but in winter they lose their leaves, allowing about 60% more sun to pass through for solar heating. Vegetation can also be provided on a trellis to block the sun from a window or porch. **Green roofs** are roofs with a thin layer of planted soil to dissipate solar heat, absorb water runoff, and give the roof space a pleasing garden-like appearance. (*See Chapter 4 for more on living or green roofs*.) Reflective white or aluminized coatings are also used to reflect solar heat. Water-spray systems have been demonstrated to cool the roof, but the drawback is significant water consumption.

## Design Tools

Design tools for cooling load avoidance are the same as those already discussed for passive solar heating. (*Figure 5.7)* shows an application of the DOE-2 computer program to evaluate external shades as a cooling load avoidance measure at a new GSA federal courthouse in Gulfport, Mississippi.

## Photovoltaics

Photovoltaics (PV), as the name implies, are devices that convert sunlight directly into electricity. PVs generate power without noise, without pollution, and without consuming any fuel. These are compelling advantages for several applications, especially where utility power is not available (such as remote ranger stations) or inconvenient (such as watches and calculators). One disadvantage of photovoltaics is that they require a large surface area to generate any significant amount of power. This is because the sunlight comes to us distributed over a wide area, and because today's PVs can only convert about 10% of the solar power to electricity. Efforts to make systems more efficient (to convert more sunlight to electricity) and to utilize unused roof space mitigate this problem. A second disadvantage is that PV is rather expensive due to the high-technology manufacturing processes. Still, in many applications they cost less initially than alternatives, and even when they cost more initially, they often recoup this investment in fuel and operations savings over time.

Rather than describing PV systems in terms of square feet of array area, it is more common to describe them in terms of "watts," the amount of power the system would generate under standard rating conditions, which are typical of a sunny, cool day. Costs for complete PV systems in 2009 varied from $6.80 to $9.90 per watt for grid-connected systems with an average of $7.50/watt. Operation and Maintenance of PV systems is reported at $40/kW, including inverter replacement[15]. Off-grid systems with batteries average about $13.00/watt. The PV industry has been growing tremendously as demand for the technology has been fueled by government incentives in the U.S., Japan, and Europe and by the need for remote power in developing countries. U.S. production of PV rose from 7 MW in 1980, to 14 MW in 1990, to 75 in 2000 and to 412 in 2008. U.S. installations in 2008 were reported at 1,106, indicating the amount imported over U.S. production. Worldwide,

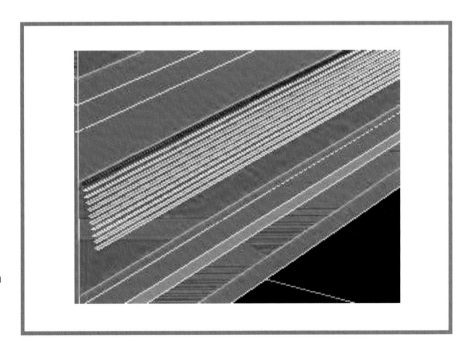

**Figure 5.7**
The DOE-2 computer program (with PowerDOE interface) was used to model the performance of these louvers.

production of PV grew from 46 MW in 1990 to 288 MW in 2000 to 6,941 MW in 2008.[16] PV is most cost-effective when used in remote locations where utility power is not available (also called off-grid). However, more and more utility customers are adding grid-connected PV to buildings in order to realize the utility cost savings, improved reliability and power quality, and the environmental benefits associated with displacing utility power (which would most likely come from a gas- or coal-fired power plant).

## Photovoltaic Cells & Modules

The electric power that PV produces is DC (direct current), similar to that coming from a battery. The voltage of each cell depends on the material's band gap, or the energy required to raise an electron from the valence band (where it is bound to the atom) to the conduction band (where it is free to conduct electricity). For silicon, each cell generates a voltage of about 0.6V. The voltage decreases gradually (logarithmically) with increasing temperature. The current generated by each cell depends on its surface area and intensity of incident sunlight. Cells are wired in series to achieve the required voltage, and series strings are wired in parallel to provide the required current and power. As increasing current is drawn from the cell, the voltage drops off, leading to a combination of current and voltage which maximizes the power output of the cell. This combination, called the **maximum power point** (MPP), changes slightly with temperature and intensity of sunlight. Most PV systems have power conditioning electronics, called a **maximum power point tracker** (MPPT) to constantly adjust the voltage in order to maximize power output. Simpler systems operate at a fixed voltage close to the optimal voltage.

Each PV cell is a wafer as thin and as fragile as a potato chip. In order to protect the cells from weather and physical damage, they are encapsulated in a "glue" called ethyl vinyl acetate and sandwiched between a sheet of tempered glass on top and a layer of glass or other protective material underneath. A frame often surrounds the glass laminate to provide additional protection and mounting points. Such an assembly is called a **PV module**. The current and voltage of the module will reflect the size and series-parallel arrangement of the cells inside. The **rated power** of a PV module is the output of the module under standard rating conditions which are: 317 BTU/ft$^2$/hour (1 kW/m$^2$) sunlight, 77°F (25°C ) ambient temperature; and 3.28 ft/s (1 m/s) wind speed). Other standard tests conducted on PV modules include the "hi pot" test (where a high voltage is applied to the internal circuits, and the assembly dipped in electrolyte solution to detect imperfect insulation). Another test involves 1" simulated iceballs fired at 55 mph at different parts of the module to evaluate hail-resistance.

Similarly, modules are wired in series to increase the voltage, and then series strings of modules are wired in series to provide the required current and overall power output from a **PV array**.

For small DC systems, 12V, 24V, and 48V configurations are common to match the voltage of lead-acid batteries often used in these systems. Higher voltage results in less current and less loss in the wiring. For large systems, voltage as high as 600V is used to minimize line losses. There is a trade-off, however, between line loss and reliability, since if any module in a series fails (by shading or damage), that whole series string is affected. Note that **Power = Current × Voltage**, and power will be limited by the lowest voltage in parallel and the lowest current in series.

The cost of PV modules depends on size and type. Types of PV include: crystalline silicon; multi-crystalline silicon; amorphous silicon; Cadmium Telluride (CdTe); and Copper Indium Galium Selenium (CIGS). Crystalline silicon is the oldest type of PV and has achieved the highest efficiency range of 14%–19%. The highest efficiency modules may have prices on the order of $2/watt. Multi-crystalline is 13%–17% efficient modules may cost $1.50 to $2 per watt. The thin film technologies are 6%–11% efficient. CdTe is not the most efficient and not the cheapest, but represents a very competitive ratio of cost to performance and the largest U.S. manufacturer, First Solar, employs this technology and manufactures modules for less than $1/watt in 2008 and 2009 (although they sell for $1.50/watt). Exciting developments promise even higher efficiency and lower cost in the future.

**Figure 5.8**
In this photovoltaic system at Joshua Tree National Park, batteries are included to store electrical energy and a generator provides power when the solar is insuffient.

There are two types of solar panels Monocrystalline/Polycrystalline, and thin film panels. Monocrystalline uses silicon grown from a single crystal, where as Polycrystalline use multifaceted silicon crystals. Since the crystals are fragile they must be mounted on a rigid surface and protected by glass or plastic. Thin film panels, a newer technology, uses a thin film of silicon that can be applied directly onto different types of materials, which may be flexible. Monocrystalline/Polycrystalline panels are more efficient (approximately 16 watts/SF for Nonocrystalline, and 12 watts/SF for Polycrystalline) than thin film panels (approximately 8 watts/square foot) but cost more to produce than thin film panels.

## PV System Components

PV modules may be the most expensive component in a PV system and efficient modules are more expensive on a $/watt basis. But higher efficiency modules require less area (ft$^2$) for a required amount of power so, when one considers the foundation, rack, conductor, conduit and installation labor, the more expensive module may result in a lower whole-system cost. A PV system may consist of some or all of the following components, depending on the type of system and the applications:

- PV array to convert sunlight to electricity
- Array support structure and enclosure to protect other equipment
- Maximum power point tracker to match load to optimal array voltage
- Batteries to store charge for when it is needed
- Charge controller to protect battery from over-charging
- Low-voltage disconnect to protect battery from over-discharging
- Inverter to convert direct current (DC) to alternating current (AC)
- Automatic generator starter/stopper to start a generator when battery is too low, and a battery charger to re-charge the batteries with generator power

For miscellaneous balance-of-system components, such as wires, conduit, connections, switches, breakers, and AC and DC disconnects, add 4% to 8% to the total system price.

### *Array Support Structures*

Ground-mounted structures can be mounted on the tops of poles or on various types of truss racks with foundations. The mounting structure is 5%–7% of the system cost, $0.30/watt to $0.55/watt, depending on system size and configuration. The cost of a tracking mount varies from $0.50 for large systems to as high as $1.50 to $3.00/watt for small systems. Often, a designer determines the trade-off between the cost of more PV area and the cost and maintenance requirements of a tracker in order to decide between fixed-tilt and tracking mount.

## Batteries

There is an acute need to store electrical energy for many purposes besides PV systems, and researchers are investigating alternatives. Battery manufacturers continue to implement innovations to improve performance. Battery technology is raging headlong into the 1700s, with designers specifying the same old lead-acid technology because of its low cost.

Batteries do have some dangers. They contain several toxic materials, and care must be taken to ensure that they are recycled properly. In some cases, batteries are shipped dry, with the electrolyte added on-site. During installation, care must be taken to ensure that battery electrolyte (battery acid) is not ingested by an installer or an unaware bystander. Storing battery electrolyte only in well-labeled, child-proof containers can reduce this risk. Finally, batteries are capable of rapidly releasing their stored energy if they are shorted; care must be taken to avoid electrocution and fires caused by sparks.

The amount of battery capacity required depends on the magnitude of the load and the required reliability. A typical battery capacity is sufficient to meet the load for 3–5 days without sun, but in applications that require high reliability, 10 days of battery storage may be recommended. In 2005, battery prices for PV systems averaged $163 per kWh of battery storage.

## Charge Controller

The function of the battery **charge controller** is very important for system performance and battery longevity. The charge controller modulates the charge current into the battery to protect against overcharging and an associated loss of electrolyte. The low-voltage disconnect protects the battery from becoming excessively discharged by disconnecting the load. It seems unfortunate to disconnect the load, but doing so avoids damage to the battery, and not doing so would simply delay the inevitable, since the load would not be served by a ruined battery. The set point of the low-voltage disconnect involves a cost trade-off. For example, allowing the battery to get down to a 20% state of charge (80% discharged) would result in a short battery life. Limiting it to an 80% state of charge (20% discharged) would make the battery last considerably longer, but would also require 4 times as many batteries to provide the same storage capacity. The cost of a charge controller may be estimated at $5.80 per amp of current regulated.

## Inverter

Utility power in U.S. buildings is 120V or 240V AC (alternating current) of 60 Hz frequency (50 Hz in many countries overseas). Since many appliances are designed to operate with alternating current, PV systems are often furnished with power conditioning equipment called an **inverter** to convert the DC power from the PV array or the battery to AC power for the appliances. Inverters use power transistors to achieve the conversion electronically. Advances in inverter technology have resulted in systems that deliver a pure sine wave form and exceptional power quality. In fact, except for the PV array, the components of a PV system are the same as those of an uninterruptible power supply (UPS) system used to provide critical users of power with the highest power quality. Inverters are available with all controls and safety features built in. The cost per watt for residential-sized inverters may be estimated at $0.80/watt and for commercial-sized inverters it is $0.59/watt.

## Generator

For small stand-alone systems it is often cost-effective to meet the load using only solar power. Many residential systems and some commercial ones include batteries and generator even if they are grid-connected so that they can run during a power outage. Such systems are called multi-mode systems and add about 30% to the cost of a grid-connected-only system. However, during extended cloudy weather this approach requires a very large battery bank and solar array. To optimize cost, the PV system can incorporate a generator to run infrequently during periods when there is no sun. This **hybrid PV/generator system** takes advantage of the low operating cost of the PV array and the on-demand capability of a generator. In this configuration, the PV array and battery bank would ordinarily serve the load. If the battery becomes discharged, the generator automatically starts to serve the load, but also to power a battery charger to recharge the batteries. When the batteries are fully charged, the generator automatically turns off again. This system of cyclically charging batteries is cost-effective even without PV, as it keeps a large generator from running to serve a small load. A hybrid system would be designed to minimize life cycle cost, with the PV array typically providing 70%–90% of the annual energy, and the generator providing the remainder. PV is also often combined with wind power, under the hypothesis that if the sun is not shining, the wind may be blowing.

## Grid-Connected Systems

Grid-connected systems don't require batteries because the utility provides power when solar is not available. These systems consist of an array, DC disconnect, inverter, AC disconnect, and isolation transformer. Several utility and industry standards must be satisfied, and an agreement with the utility must be negotiated, before a customer's system can interact with the utility system. The Institute of Electrical and Electronic Engineers, Inc. (IEEE) maintains standard 1547 which describes recommended practice for utility interface of PV systems and which allows manufacturers to write "Utility-Interactive" on the listing label if an inverter meets the requirements of frequency and voltage limits, power quality, and non-islanding inverter testing. Underwriters Laboratory maintains "UL Standard 1741, Standard for Static Inverters and Charge Controllers for Use in PV Power Systems" which incorporates the testing required by IEEE 1547 and includes design (type) testing and production testing. Photovoltaics are most cost-effective in remote applications where utility power is not available and alternatives such as diesel generators are more expensive. Historically, remote applications have been the bulk of the market. However, in 2004, for the first time, grid-interactive electricity generation became the dominant end-use of PV, with a market share of 71% (129,265 peak kilowatts), up from 39% in 2003. Grid-connected applications have averaged a compound growth rate of 64% per year during the 1999–2004 period.

## Building-Integrated Photovoltaics (BIPV)

An exciting trend is building-integrated photovoltaics, or BIPV, where the photovoltaic material replaces a conventional part of the building construction. About 90% of grid-connected systems in 2004 were rooftop or building-integrated (BIPV). One-for-one replacements for shingles, standing seam metal roofing, spandrel glass, and overhead skylight glass are already on the market. The annual energy delivery of these components will be reduced if walls and roofs are not at the optimal orientation, but it has been demonstrated that PV installed within 45 degrees of the optimal tilt and orientation suffers only a slight reduction in annual performance. Tilt less than optimal will increase

**Figure 5.9**
The house on the right-hand side incorporates 2.2 kW of building integrated photovoltaics in the standing seam metal roof but is barely distinguishable from the other houses in the photo. *(Courtesy of the National Association of Homebuilders, Bowie, MD.)*

summer gains, but decrease the annual total, and panels facing east will increase morning gains, but decrease the daily total.

## *Design Tools*

Design tools for PV systems are simple hand calculations and hourly simulations of PV system performance. Hand calculations are facilitated by the fact that PV systems are rated at a solar radiation level of 317 BTU/hr/ft$^2$ (1 kW/m$^2$), so a PV array can be expected to deliver its rated output for a number of hours (called **sunhours**) per day equal to the number of kWh/m$^2$/day presented in the solar resource data.

## Solar Water Heating

Solar water heating systems are relatively simple extensions to buildings' plumbing systems, which impart heat from the sun to preheat service hot water. Water heating accounts for a substantial portion of a building's energy use, ranging from approximately 9% of total energy use in office buildings to 40% in lodging facilities. Averaged across all buildings, hot water represents 15% of energy use in residential buildings, and 8% in commercial buildings.[17]

Solar water heating systems are usually designed to provide about two thirds of a building's hot water needs, and more where fuel is very expensive or unavailable. Solar water heating applications include domestic water heating, pool and spa heating, industrial processes such as laundries and cafeterias, and air conditioning reheat in hot, humid climates. Solar water heating is most effective when it serves a steady water heating load that is constant throughout the week and year (or at a maximum during the summer). For example, a prison that is occupied seven days a week would accrue 40% more cost savings than a school open only five days a week.

In 2006, a total of 18 million ft$^2$ of collector area was shipped by suppliers (mostly from New Jersey, California, and Israel) to the U.S. market, up from 14 million ft$^2$ in 2004. Growth in solar water heating is spurred by federal tax credits, incentives in some states, and the rising cost of natural gas. Low-temperature swimming pool heating was by far the largest application, with over 14 million ft$^2$. Flat-plate collectors to supply service hot water accounted for about 2.5 million ft$^2$ and high temperature collectors also accounted for 388,000 ft$^2$ of collector area shipped.

Advanced technology and production economies of scale have led to significant cost reductions. The value of shipped low-temperature collectors was $1.89/ft$^2$ in 2008. The average cost of thermosyphon systems with the storage integral to the collector was $ 24.27; the price of flat plate collectors was $17.40/ft$^2$; the price of evacuated tube solar collectors was $25.69/ft$^2$; and the price of parabolic trough solar collectors was $11.96. These values are based on factory revenue divided by output, so retail prices would be roughly double, and the installed system price with all the other components is on the order of $75 to $225/ft² depending on project size and location.[18]

Solar water heating can be used effectively in almost any geographic location, but is especially prevalent and effective at low latitudes, where the constant solar resource matches a constant water load. In 2008, 5.1 million ft² of solar thermal collectors were shipped to Florida, 3.7 million ft² to California, 939,000 ft² to Arizona, and 780,000 ft² to Hawaii.[19] Appropriate near-south-facing roof area or nearby unshaded grounds would be required for installation of a collector. System types are available to accommodate freezing outdoor conditions, and systems have been installed as far north as the Arctic and as far south as Antarctica. The "drain-back" schematic protects against both freezing and over-heating.

There are different types of solar water heating systems; the choice depends on the temperature required and the climate. All types have the same simple operating principle. Solar radiation is absorbed by a wide-area solar collector, or solar panel, which heats the water directly or heats a nonfreezing fluid which, in turn, heats the water by a heat exchanger. The heated water is stored in a tank for later use. A backup gas or electric water heater is used to provide hot water when the sun is insufficient, and to optimize the economical size of the solar system.

Solar water heating systems save the fuel otherwise required to heat the water, and avoid the associated cost and pollution. A frequently overlooked advantage of solar water heating is that the large storage volume increases the capacity to deliver hot water. As one residential system owner described it, "With 120 gallons of solar-heated water and the 40- gallon backup heater, I can take a shower, my wife can take a bath, we can have the dishwasher and the clothes washer going, and we never, never run out of hot water."

## Types of Collectors for Solar Water Heating

Solar thermal collectors can be categorized by the temperature at which they efficiently deliver heat. Low-temperature collectors are unglazed and uninsulated. They operate at up to 18°F (10°C) above ambient temperature, and are most often used to heat swimming pools. At this low temperature, a cover glass would reflect or absorb solar heat more than it would reduce heat loss. Often, the pool water is colder than the air, and insulating the collector would be counterproductive. Low-temperature collectors are extruded from polypropylene or other polymers with UV stabilizers. Flow passages for the pool water are molded directly into the absorber plate, and pool water is circulated through the collectors with the pool filter circulation pump. The simple collectors available for swimming pool systems cost around $4 to manufacture and retail for $9 per square foot.

**Mid-temperature systems** place the absorber plate in an enclosure insulated with fiberglass or polyicocyanurate, and with a low-iron cover glass to reduce heat loss at higher temperatures. They produce water 18°–129°F (about 10°–50°C) above the outside temperature, and are most often used for heating domestic hot water (DHW). Reflection and absorption reduce the solar transparency of the glass and reduce the efficiency at low temperature differences, but the glass is required to retain heat at higher temperatures. A copper absorber plate with copper tubes welded to the fins is used. To reduce radiant losses from the collector, the absorber plate is often treated with a black nickel selective surface, which has a high absorptivity in the shortwave solar spectrum, but a low-emissivity in the long-wave thermal spectrum. Such flat plate systems cost as high as $250/SF installed for a single residential system to around $90/SF for a large commercial system.

**High-temperature collectors** surround the absorber tube with an evacuated borosilicate glass tube to minimize heat loss, and often utilize mirrors curved in a parabolic shape to concentrate sunlight on the tube. Evacuating the air out of the tube eliminates conduction and convection as heat loss mechanisms, and using a selective surface minimizes radiation heat loss. High-temperature systems are required for absorption cooling or electricity generation, but are used for mid-temperature applications such as commercial or institutional water heating as well. Due to the tracking mechanism required to keep the focusing mirrors facing the sun, high-temperature systems are usually

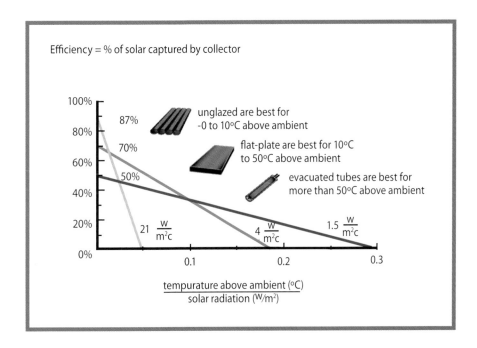

**Figure 5.10**
At low temperatures, an unglazed uninsulted collector offers the best performance, but as temperature increases, glazed insulated flat plate or evacuated tube collectors are more efficient.

very large and mounted on the ground adjacent to a facility. These collectors are usually used in very large systems and a typical installed system cost is on the order of $75/SF.

Selecting the best type of collector will depend on the application. Figure 5.10 shows the efficiency of different types of collectors as a function of the temperature difference between the inside of the collector and the outdoor temperature, and the intensity of the solar radiation. Notice that at low temperatures, the inexpensive, unglazed collectors offer the highest efficiency, but efficiency drops off very quickly as temperature increases. Glazed collectors are required to efficiently achieve higher temperatures, and very high-temperature applications require an evacuated tube in order to deliver any useful heat.

Although solar water heating systems all use the same basic principle, they do so with a wide variety of specific technologies that distinguish different collectors and systems. The distinctions are important because certain types of collectors and systems best serve certain applications in various locations.

The following nomenclature describes types of solar water heating systems:

- **Passive:** relies on buoyancy (natural convection) rather than electric power to circulate the water.
- **Active:** requires electric power to activate pumps and/or controls.
- **Direct:** heats potable water directly in the collector.
- **Indirect:** heats propylene glycol or other heat transfer fluid in the collector and transfers heat to potable water via a heat exchanger.

## Design Tools

Solar water heating systems should be designed to minimize life cycle cost. It is never cost-effective to design a system to provide 100% of the load with solar because of the excessive investment in collector area and storage volume. The economic optimum is usually on the order of 70% of the load met with solar. One strategy is to design a system that meets 100% of the load on the sunniest day of the year. This approach will ensure that the investment in solar hardware is always working to deliver energy savings, with no over-capacity. Other design considerations include maintenance, freeze protection, overheating protection, and aesthetics of the collector mount and orientation.

In the Northern Hemisphere, solar hot water collectors should be oriented to face toward the equator within 30° of true (not magnetic) south. Collectors tilted up from the horizontal at an angle of latitude plus 15° maximize winter solar gains and result in a solar delivery that is uniform throughout the year. This would be the appropriate tilt angle for a solar water-heating load that is also constant throughout the year. A collector tilted up from the horizontal at an angle of latitude minus 15° maximizes summer solar gains, and would be appropriate for a summer-only applications, such as swimming pool heating or beach showers. It is usually acceptable to mount the collectors flush on a pitched roof as close to the optimal orientation as possible in order to reduce installed cost and improve aesthetics.

Design tools include simple hand calculations, correlation methods, and hourly computer simulations. Hand calculations are facilitated by the assumption that solar water heating systems have a typical efficiency of 40%. (*See Figure 5.11.*) Accurately accounting for the changing effects of solar radiation, ambient temperature, and even wind speed requires an hourly simulation. Correlations of simulation results, such as an F-Chart, were popular before computers were ubiquitous. FRESA[20] and RETScreen®[21] are two computer programs used for preliminary analysis. The hourly simulation program TRNSYS[22] is widely used for precise engineering data and economic analysis and to optimize parameters of solar water heating system design. The new version 1.8 of Energy-10 also models solar water heating.

## Codes & Standards

The Solar Rating and Certification Corporation (SRCC) is an independent, nonprofit trade organization that implements solar equipment certification programs and rating standards. SRCC ratings are used to estimate and compare the performance of different collectors and systems submitted to SRCC by manufacturers for testing. SRCC developed a solar water heating system rating and certification program, short-titled OG 300, to improve performance and reliability of solar products.[23]

---

Solar water heating, four-person residence in Denver, Colorado:

Mass of hot water used each day, M

$$M = 4 \text{person} * 40 \text{gal/person/day} * 3.785 \text{ kg/gal} = \textbf{606 kg/day}$$

Energy load to heat water each day, L

$$L = MC(T_{hot} - T_{cold}) = 606 \text{ kg/day} * 0.001167 \text{kWh/kgC} * (50C-18C) = \textbf{22.6 kWh/day}$$

Divide load by peak solar resource and efficiency to size collector, AC
For Denver, Imax = 6.1 and I ave = 5.5 kWh/m2/day

$$Ac = L/(\eta_{solar} I_{max}) = 22.6 \text{ kWh/day}/(0.4*6.1 \text{ kWh/m2/day}) = \textbf{9.3 m2}$$

Multiply collector size by average solar resource and efficiency to estimate energy savings, and divide by boiler efficiency to estimate annual fuel savings, Es

$$Es = A_c I_{ave} \eta_{solar} 365/\eta_{boiler} = 9.3 \text{ m2} * 5.5 \text{ kWh/m2.day} * 0.4 * 365 \text{days/year}/0.97 = \textbf{7,665 kWh/year}$$

**Figure 5.11**
Example of hand calculation to evaluate solar water heating.

Other standards include the following from the American Society of Heating, Refrigerating, and Air Conditioning Engineers:

- ASHRAE 90003: Active Solar Heating Design Manual
- ASHRAE 90336: Guidance for Preparing Active Solar Heating Systems Operation and Maintenance Manuals
- ASHRAE 90342: Active Solar Heating Systems Installation Manual
- ASHRAE 93: Methods of Testing to Determine the Thermal Performance of Solar Collectors

From the American Water Works Association (AWWA):

- AWWA C651 Disinfecting Water Mains

From Factory Mutual Engineering and Research Corporation (FM):

- FM P7825 Approval Guide

From the National Fire Protection Association (NFPA):

- NFPA 70 National Electrical Code
- MIL-HDBK 1003/13A Solar Heating of Buildings and Domestic Hot Water
- SOLAR RATING AND CERTIFICATION CORPORATION (SRCC) SRCC OG-300-91 Operating Guidelines and Minimum Standards For Certifying Solar Water Heating Systems

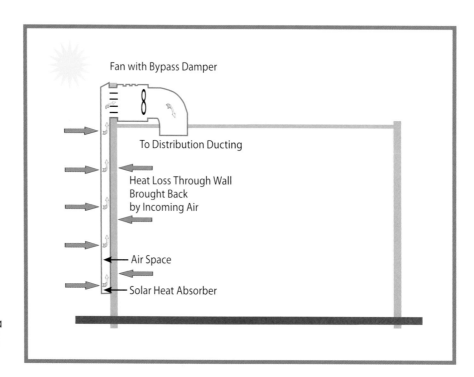

**Figure 5.12**
Solar ventilation air preheating is a solar technology that is simple and cost effective.

- ASCE/ SEI-7 – American Society of Civil Engineers – "Minimum Design Loads for Buildings and Other Structures".
- NRCA – National Roofing Contractors Association

# Solar Ventilation Air Heating

Solar ventilation air preheating is a cost-effective application of solar energy thanks to an innovative transpired collector that is both inexpensive and high-performance. Heating of ventilation air accounts for about 15% of the total heating load in an average commercial building, much more in buildings that require a lot of ventilation, as factories and laboratories. Preheating the air with solar energy before it is drawn into the space can save much of this energy. Solar ventilation air preheating technology is simple, low-cost, extremely reliable (no moving parts except the fan), very low in maintenance requirements, and high in efficiency (up to 80%). There are no problems with freezing or fluid leaks, but there is also no practical way to store the heated ventilation air for nighttime use. Well over two million square feet of transpired collectors have been installed since 1990.

## Transpired Collector Principle

The key to low cost and high performance is an elegant solar technology known as the **transpired collector**. A painted metal plate is perforated with small holes about 1 mm (0.04 in) in diameter and 3 mm (0.12 inch) apart. At this small scale, within 1 mm of the surface of the plate, flow within the laminar boundary layer is dominated by viscosity of the air, and heat transfer is dominated by conduction. This is in contrast to the air flow even a few more mm away from the plate where the flow is dominated by the momentum of the wind, and the heat transfer is dominated by convection. These two differences between the boundary layer of air within 1 mm of the plate and the air farther away are key to the operating principle of the transpired collector. Sunlight strikes the black surface of the plate and is absorbed. Solar heat conducts from the surface to the thermal boundary layer of air 1 mm thick next to the plate. This boundary layer of air is drawn into a nearby hole before the heat can escape by convection, virtually eliminating heat loss off the surface of the plate. Since the plate operates at less than 20°C warmer than ambient air, heat loss by radiation is not overly consequential. There is no cover glass to reflect or absorb radiation.

To operate effectively, the fan-induced flow through the wall must be sufficient to continuously draw in the boundary layer. Consequently, efforts to increase the temperature of delivered air by reducing the flow rate will adversely affect performance. Don't get greedy. They don't call it ventilation *preheating* for nothing. On cold winter days, supplemental heating by gas or electricity will be required to ensure comfortable conditions.

The transpired collector is mounted about six inches away from the south wall of a building, forming a plenum between the wall and the collector. The collector is fastened to the wall, and the edges are sealed using standard metal building flashing techniques. A fan is installed in the wall to draw air from the plenum into the supply ductwork. The solar preheated air can be delivered to the air handler for the heater or directly into the space to be ventilated. The bypass damper could be thermostatically controlled, and fan operation will depend on the ventilation needs of the space.

The transpired collector makes an efficient sunlight-to-air heat exchanger that tempers the incoming fresh air. It is not possible to recirculate the room air back to the collector for reheating because the fact that it pulls air into the face of the wall is necessary to the operating principle. The amount of temperature increase that the air experiences coming through the collector depends on the air flow rate and on the incident solar radiation. The recommended air flow rate is about 4 CFM per square foot of collector area. At flow rates less than 2 CFM/SF, the boundary layer can blow away before it is sucked through a hole, and at flow rates higher than 8 CFM/SF, the required additional fan power begins to erode the cost savings.

## Typical Applications for Solar Ventilation Air Preheating

The transpired collector technology is appropriate for preheating ventilation air in industrial and maintenance buildings, school and institutional buildings, apartment buildings, commercial buildings, and penthouse fans. Examples include factories, aircraft hangers, chemical storage buildings, and other facilities that require ventilation air. Industrial process uses for heated air, such as crop drying, can also be addressed with this technology.

Due to its metal construction, the transpired collector matches well with other metal construction, which is most common in industrial applications. The design of a new building is the best time to consider solar ventilation preheating, but it can be used in retrofit applications as well. It can even improve the appearance of a dilapidated façade. There must be sufficient south-facing vertical wall to mount the collector, and the wall must be largely unshaded by surrounding buildings, trees, hills, or other objects.

Design considerations for solar ventilation air preheating include some flexibility with wall orientation and color. A south-facing wall is best, but not absolutely necessary: +/- 20° of south gives 96%–100% of heat delivery, while +/- 45° of south gives 80%–100% of the heat delivery of a south-facing wall. Black is best for absorbing solar radiation, but a

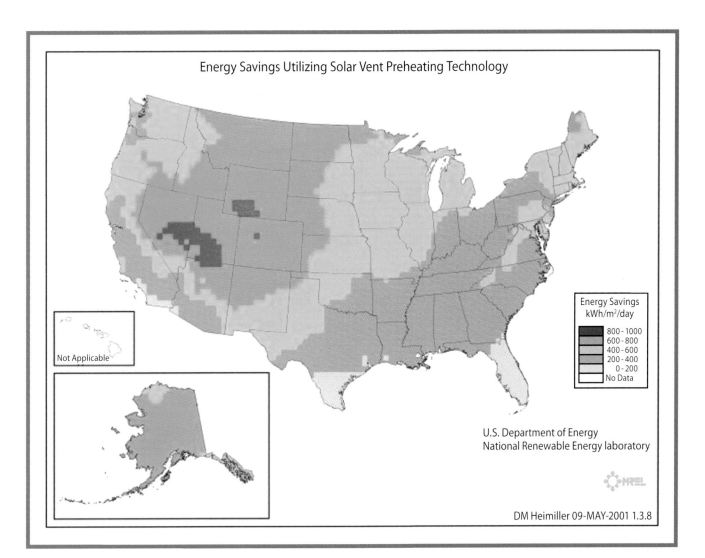

Energy Savings Utilizing Solar Vent Preheating Technology

| Energy Savings kWh/m²/day |
| 800 - 1000 |
| 600 - 800 |
| 400 - 600 |
| 200 - 400 |
| 0 - 200 |
| No Data |

Not Applicable

U.S. Department of Energy
National Renewable Energy laboratory

NREL

DM Heimiller 09-MAY-2001 1.3.8

**Figure 5.13**
Map shows annual energy savings
of solar ventilation air preheating
systems, including effects of
solar radiation and ambient air
temperature. *(GIS map by Donna
Heimiller, NREL.)*

| Installation Costs in Retrofit Applications | |
|---|---|
| Absorber, supports, flashing, fasteners | $14.70/SF |
| Freight | $1.00/SF–$2.00/SF |
| Design | $1.00/SF–$2.00/SF |
| Installation | $8.00/SF–$11.00/SF |
| Other costs and connection to mechanical equipment | $5.00/SF–$10.00/SF |
| Total | $30.00/SF–$40.00/SF |

**Figure 5.14**

wide choice of dark to medium colors may be used with efficiency loss of less than 10%, and about 20 colors are available standard from the supplier, with custom colors possible.

## Design Tools

The solar resource information presented earlier in this chapter cannot be used directly to analyze specific solar ventilation preheating systems, since performance depends not only on the solar resource, but also on the simultaneous need to heat the ventilation air. (Buildings in southern climates have great solar resource, but cannot use much of the heat.) The map in Figure 5.13 has been developed to assist in the design of solar ventilation air preheating systems. This map indicates energy savings including the effects of solar radiation and ambient air temperature. It assumes that the building is occupied seven days a week. If it is occupied only on weekdays, multiply the savings by 5/7. FRESA and RETScreen® both have modules to analyze solar ventilation air preheating systems, and SWIFT is available for more detailed simulation of transpired collector performance.

## Cost of Solar Ventilation Air Preheating

For a small system less than 2,000 SF, a solar ventilation air preheating collector typically costs $15/SF, and the total system cost may cost $40/ft². For systems larger than 10,000 SF may be estimated at $30/SF. This cost is for the collector, flashing fasteners, design, installation, and ductwork for the solar collector only and does not include the cost of the fan. The fan would be part of the existing or conventional ventilation system. For fan costs, see *RSMeans Mechanical Cost Data*.

## Conclusion

The effects of solar energy on a building are unavoidable. If we ignore the sun in building design, we are often left with complaints about glare and uncomfortable conditions, as well as excessively high utility bills. On the other hand, if we harvest and control the useful daylight and solar heat, we can improve occupant comfort and health, enhance lighting quality, and reduce or even eliminate utility costs. The solar energy technologies described in this chapter provide a useful checklist for considering solar in building design: passive solar heating, cooling load avoidance, solar water heating, photovoltaics, and solar air ventilation preheating. Of course, these systems need to work together as part of a holistic building design, including mechanical and lighting systems working in concert with the sun.

We can learn a lot about architectural measures, such as passive solar heating, cooling load avoidance, and daylighting, from quality historic buildings that were constructed before utilities were available. Solar water heating and photovoltaics, on the other hand, are evolving modern technologies. Photovoltaics, for example, were initially developed to power spacecraft, but are finding more and more cost-effective applications on Earth. Many buildings, especially off-grid homes, now rely on solar energy for 100% of their space heating, water heating, and electricity needs.

In remote areas not served by a utility or with high costs to deliver fuel, solar energy can be the lowest-cost way of serving energy requirements. As the cost of solar technologies continues to decline, and as their performance continues to improve, there will come a day when clean, silent solar power is actually cheaper than the economic and environmental consequences of fossil fuel use. Many in the green building design industry believe that day is today.

1. U.S. Department of Energy, Energy Efficiency and Renewable Energy "EERE Renewable Energy Databook", October 2009, http://www1.eere.energy.gov/maps_data/pdfs/eere_databook.pdf

2. Butti, Ken and John Perlin. *A Golden Thread, 2500 Years of Solar Architecture and Technology*. Palo Alto, Cheshire Books.

3. Assuming 1,353 W/m² solar radiation, 1.27 E7 m earth diameter, and 382 Quad annual global energy use.

4. Brower, M. *Cool Energy: Renewable Solutions to Environmental Problems*. Cambridge: MIT Press, 1992.

5. Energy Information Administration. *Annual Energy Outlook 2008* Available at: www.eia.doe.gov/oiaf/aeo

6. Ibid.

7. Natural Gas Navigator. Available at: http://tonto.eia.doe.gov/dnav/ng/ng_sum_top.asp

8. Office of Energy Efficiency and Renewable Energy, U.S. Department of Energy. *2009 Building Energy Databook*. Available at http://buildingsdatabook.eren.doe.gov

9. Ibid.

10. Steven Winter Associates. *The Passive Solar Design and Construction Handbook*. John Wiley and Sons.

11. Ibid.

12. Ibid.

13. Ibid.

14. "Greenhouse Gas Report." Available at: http://www.eia.doe.gov

15. "Tracking the Sun II", Lawence Berkeley National Laboratory, October 2009.

16. "Solar Thermal Collector Manufacturing Activities 2008" http://www.eia.doe.gov/cneaf/solar.renewables/page/solarreport/solar.html

17. "Greenhouse Gas Report." Available at: http://www.eia.doe.gov

18. Steven Winter Associates. *The Passive Solar Design and Construction Handbook*. John Wiley and Sons.

19. Ibid.

20. FRESA software, available at http://www.analysis.nrel.gov/fresa

21. RETScreen® software, available at http://www.retscreen.net

22. TRNSYS software, available at http://sel.me.wisc.edu/trnsys

23. Solar Rating and Certification Corporation (SRCC). *SRCC OG-300-91 Operating Guidelines and Minimum Standards for Certifying Solar Water Heating Systems*.

# 6 Wind Power

## The American Wind Energy Association

Peple have been harnessing the energy of the wind in this country for more than a hundred years. In the late 1800s and early 1900s, millions of windmills were installed on farms to pump water from deep underground. Large-scale commercial wind energy development began in California in the early 1980s, and produced large arrays of turbines, generating power on windy ridges or passes, and more recently, on the prairie. Small wind electric systems—a single turbine, much smaller than the utility-scale models, were very common in the 1930s, producing clean, affordable electricity for a rural home, farm, or business. These small turbines with aerodynamic blades were much more efficient than the old fashioned windmill. The systems can still be found, but began disappearing when the Rural Electric Administration (REA) brought utility power to farms.

Why is wind energy gaining so much momentum? Spiraling utility bills, the need for uninterrupted service, the high cost of accessing the utility's electric grid from a remote location, and concerns over environmental impacts. Reducing dependence on potentially volatile prices for electrical power is another key motivator for many home-scale windsmiths.

Depending on the local wind resource and utility rates, a small wind energy system can reduce a customer's electricity bill by 50%–90%. It can be installed as a stand-alone system, eliminating the high cost of extending utility power lines to a remote location, or it can be connected to the power grid, enabling the customer to sell excess power to the utility or buy additional power as needed. Over its 20- to 40-year life, a small residential wind turbine can offset approximately 1.2 tons of air pollutants and 200 tons of carbon dioxide and other "greenhouse" gases. And it can do so at one-third to one-half the installed cost of the most competitive solar electric technology.

Stand-alone or hybrid off-grid wind systems can be appropriate for homes, farms, or even entire villages that are far from the nearest utility lines. (The cost of running a power line to a remote site to connect with the utility grid can be prohibitive, ranging from $20,000 to more than $30,000 per quarter mile, depending on the terrain.)

Many areas of the country qualify as having sufficient wind resources for small wind systems. Wind resource maps give only a rough estimate of whether a particular location is windy enough to make small wind energy economical. Local terrain and other factors also influence the wind power available at a specific site.

The maps in Figure 6.1 and 6.2 provide an idea of the wind resources available in different parts of the United States and Canada. Annual average wind power is classified from lowest (Class 1, shown in figure 6.1 in white) to highest (Class 7). Large-scale turbines require a minimum of a Class 3 wind regime (and prefer a Class 5). However, small wind systems can be successfully installed in Class 2 or better

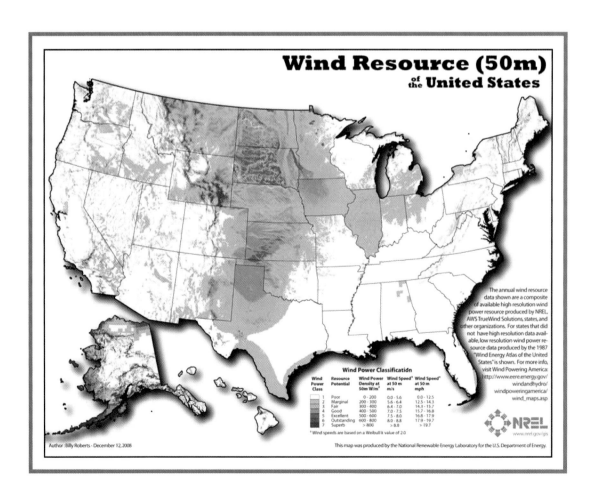

**Figure 6.1**

wind regimes. Class 2 corresponds to average annual wind speeds of 9–11 miles per hour, or 4–5 meters per second.

Indicators of good topography include:

- Gaps, passes, gorges, and long valleys extending down from mountain ranges
- High elevation plains and plateaus
- Plains and valleys with persistent downslope winds associated with strong pressure gradients
- Exposed ridges and mountain summits
- Coastlines and immediate inland strips with minimum wind barriers and vegetation
- Upwind and crosswind corners of islands
- Wind-deformed vegetation: flagging of trees and shrubs
- Surface materials deposited by the wind to form playas, sand dunes, and other types of "eolian" landforms

Power generated by small wind systems is used to reduce the demand for utility-supplied electricity or is sold to the utility, often at retail prices. Thus the value of this widely available energy resource depends

**Figure 6.2**

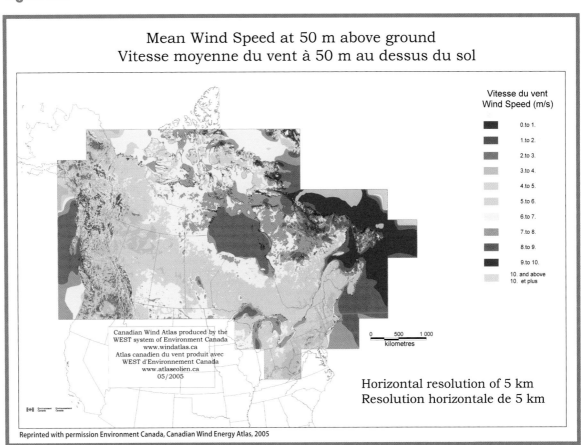

Mean Wind Speed at 50 m above ground
Vitesse moyenne du vent à 50 m au dessus du sol

Reprinted with permission Environment Canada, Canadian Wind Energy Atlas, 2005

on the retail cost of electricity in a particular location. In general, the value of power generated by small wind energy systems ranges from 6 to 18 cents per kilowatt-hour.

## Applications & Concerns: An Overview

Small wind energy systems are sometimes referred to as "residential" applications, and indeed they are. But they also can and do provide power to farms, schools, and other rural businesses. A small wind turbine along with solar photovoltaic panels can provide supplementary power for a grid-connected, all-electric home (which includes a heat pump and an electric car). However, small systems may also be installed to power a specific application, such as pumping water distant from the utility grid. The size of the system required to meet a given customer's needs depends on how much energy the customer uses and the annual average wind speed.

For example, a home or farm using 1,400 kWh per month in a location with Class 4 winds could cover virtually all its electricity needs with a 10 kW turbine. A larger ranch or facility using 10,000 kWh per month would require a 50-60 kW system to meet its electricity needs, depending on the wind resource available. Some commercial customers may even consider negotiating a power purchase agreement with their local utility to purchase back excess electricity generated.

Concerns that may arise regarding use of wind turbines include noise, aesthetics, potential harm to birds, and interference with television and radio signals. The noise level of most modern residential turbines is around 52–55 decibels. They are audible outdoors, but no noisier than the average refrigerator.

Because small turbines are mounted on tall towers, they are visible from a distance. To minimize any objection from neighbors, the wind industry recommends customer property sizes of ½ acre or more for turbines up to 2 kW, and 1 acre or more for larger wind turbines.

While birds can collide with any structure, reports of small wind turbines killing birds are very rare. A sliding glass door is more dangerous to birds than a small wind turbine.

Small wind turbines have not been found to interfere with TV or radio reception. The rotors are made of fiberglass or wood; both materials are transparent to electromagnetic waves, such as radio or TV.

Wind can supply electricity during a utility power outage if the system includes storage batteries and a way to disconnect from the utility grid (for those that are connected).

Small wind turbines are equipped with overspeed protection and are designed to furl out of the wind during extreme gusts.

## Other Considerations

### Connecting to the Utility Grid

Whether or not to connect a wind system to the local utility grid depends on a number of factors. In general, grid-connected small wind systems can be practical if the following conditions exist:

- Average annual wind speed is at least 10 miles per hour (4.5 meters per second).
- The market rates for power are fairly high (10-15 cents/kWh).
- Utility requirements for connecting to the grid are not prohibitive.
- There are tax credits or rebates for the purchase of wind turbines or good incentives for the sale of excess electricity.

*(Utility grid connection is discussed in more detail later in the chapter.)*

### Net Metering

The idea of net metering is to allow the electric meters of customers with generating facilities to turn backwards when their generators are producing more energy than the customers demand. Net metering allows customers to use their generation to offset their consumption over an entire billing period, not just at the time the electricity is produced. This way the customers can receive retail value for more of the electricity they generate.

Net metering programs vary by state and by utility company. Net excess generation (NEG) may be carried on a monthly basis, or it may be credited for up to a year. Annual NEG credits allow wind turbine owners to use energy produced in the winter, when weather tends to be windier, to displace large summer loads such as air-conditioning or pumping water for irrigation. *(Net metering is covered in more detail later in this chapter.)*

## Basic Criteria for Using a Wind System

In considering whether to incorporate a small wind energy system into new construction or retrofit projects, the following factors should be reviewed:

- **A good wind resource.** Wind resource maps *(See Figure 6.1)* indicate whether a property is in a Class 2 zone or better, but terrain and other factors also affect windiness at a particular site. In general, the more exposed, the better.
- **Size of the property.** At least one-half acre is typically enough for the smallest small wind systems (up to 2 kW), but the general rule-of-thumb is one acre or more.
- **Average monthly electricity bill.** A monthly bill of $100 or more means small wind is more likely to be economical.

- **Local zoning codes or covenants.** If local codes specifically allow wind turbines, the permitting process can be expedited.
- **State or local incentive programs.** Incentive programs for small wind systems can help improve the economics.

## Small Wind System Components

Wind is created by the unequal heating of the Earth's surface by the sun. Wind turbines convert the kinetic energy in the wind into mechanical power that runs a generator to produce clean, nonpolluting electricity. Today's small-scale turbines are versatile and modular. Their rotors consist of two or three blades that are aerodynamically designed to capture the maximum energy from the wind. The wind turns the blades, which spin a shaft connected to a generator that makes electricity. A mainframe supports the rotor, generator, and tail that aligns the rotor into the wind.

Turbines are mounted on towers—typically 80–120 feet high, which place the blades high enough to be exposed to the wind. There are many tower options, but in general the taller the tower, the more power the wind system can produce. The tower also raises the turbine above air turbulence created by objects (buildings, trees, etc.) closer to ground level. As a rule of thumb, the bottom of the rotor blades should be at least 30 feet above any obstacle within 300 feet of the tower. Towers may be self-supporting, but more commonly use guy wires. Some small tower models can be tilted down to facilitate maintenance work. Towers constructed as a lattice are strong and inexpensive, but attract birds by providing perches.

In addition to the tower and turbine, small wind energy systems require:
- A **foundation,** usually made of reinforced concrete
- A **wire run,** to conduct electricity from the generator to the electronics
- A **disconnect** (or safety switch,) which allows the electrical output to be isolated from the electronics
- A **power processing** (or conditioning) unit, which makes the turbine power compatible with the utility power
- A **system energy meter,** which records energy production

If the system is designed to stand alone or operate during a power outage, it will need deep-cycle batteries (like the ones used for golf carts) to store power, and a charge controller to keep the batteries from overcharging. A grid-connected system not designed to operate during a power outage does not need batteries.

## Evaluating the Local Wind Resource

Wind resources can vary significantly over an area of just a few miles due to local terrain influences on the wind flow. As a first step in evaluating whether there is enough wind on the site to make a small wind turbine system economically worthwhile, wind resource maps *(See Figure 6.1)* can be used to estimate the potential wind power density in the region. The highest average wind speeds in the U.S. are generally found along seacoasts, on ridgelines, and across the Great Plains; however, many areas have wind resources strong enough to power a small wind turbine. The wind resource estimates on this map generally apply to terrain features that are well exposed to the wind, such as hilltops, ridge crests, and high plains.

New, high-resolution wind resource maps are being produced using state-of-the art computer modeling tools to give a better estimate of wind regimes at different heights above ground level. The models help predict daily and seasonal patterns which can be compared to on-site energy usage patterns. Other ways to indirectly quantify the wind resource include obtaining long-term wind speed information from a nearby airport and observing the project site's vegetation. (Trees, especially conifers or evergreens, can be permanently deformed by strong winds. For more information on the use of "flagging," see *A Siting Handbook for Small Wind Energy Conversion Systems,* available through the National Technical Information Service, at **www.ntis.gov**)

Direct monitoring by a wind resource measurement system at a site provides the clearest picture of the available resource. Wind monitoring equipment can be purchased for $1200–$4,000, depending on tower height. This expense may not be justified for one small wind turbine project. The anemometers, or wind sensors, must be set high enough to avoid turbulence created by trees, buildings, and other obstructions. The most useful readings are taken at turbine hub-height, the elevation at the top of the tower where the blades will connect.

Finally, if there is already another small wind turbine system installed in the area, it may be possible to obtain information on the annual output from the owner.

## Estimating the Cost of Wind Systems

Although wind energy systems involve a significant initial investment, they can be competitive with conventional energy sources when accounting for a lifetime of reduced or altogether avoided utility costs. The length of the payback period depends on the system selected, the wind resource at the site, electricity costs, and how the wind system will be used.

A guideline for estimating the cost of a small wind system is $2–$4 per installed watt, with larger turbines costing less. For example, a 10 kW system costs $30,000–$40,000 installed, and a 50 kW system costs

$100,000–$150,000 installed. A comparable photovoltaic (PV) solar system would cost over $90,000 including wiring and installation. Wind turbines become more cost-effective as the rotor size increases in diameter. Although small wind systems cost less in initial outlay, they are proportionally more expensive than larger machines, unlike PV systems that have basically the same cost per watt independent of array size. At the 50 watt size level, a small wind turbine may cost up to $8/watt, compared to approximately $6/watt for a PV module.

Installed costs for small wind turbines are expected to decrease to $1.50/kW by 2010. Volume production is expected to drive overall costs down 15%–30%, and new technology breakthroughs are further reducing manufacturing and installation costs.

It is important to evaluate the trade-off between the incremental cost of a taller tower and increased wind turbine performance. Wind speed increases with height above ground, and increasing speed increases wind power exponentially. Thus, relatively small investments in increased tower height can yield very high rates of return in power production. For instance, installing a 10 kW generator on a 100-foot tower rather than a 60-foot tower involves a 10% increase in overall system cost, but can result in 29% more power.

## Determining Payback

A typical home consumes 800–2000 kWh of electricity per month, and a 4–10 kW systems can meet this demand. For customers paying 12 cents/kWh or more for electricity in an area with average wind speeds of 10 mph or more, payback periods will generally fall in the range of 8-16 years. After this payback period, the energy from the wind system will be virtually free (except for upkeep costs) for the remainder of the system's 20–50 year life.

Key factors in calculating payback are the cost and value of the electricity produced, and whether rebates, buy-down funds, or other financial incentives, such as net metering, tax exemptions, and tax credits, are available. For example, combining a California-type 50% buy-down program, net metering, and an average annual wind speed of 15 mph (6.7 m/s) would result in a simple payback of approximately 6 years.

Turbine manufacturers can help estimate the energy production and the expected payback period based on the particular wind turbine power curve, the average annual wind speed at the site, the height of the planned tower, and the wind frequency distribution—that is, the number of hours the wind blows at each speed during an average year. The calculation will be adjusted for the site's elevation, which affects air density and thus turbine power output.

# Obstacles & Incentives

There are 21 million U.S. homes and 4.6 million commercial buildings located on properties of one or more acre, 60% of them in areas with Class 2 winds or better. Why, then, are there not more small wind energy systems already in place? Part of the reason is that low production volume and historic lack of public funding have led to relatively high costs for this technology. Efforts by the U.S. Department of Energy and state agencies to promote small wind have only recently begun to help.

Other barriers include zoning regulations with height restrictions of 35 feet and concerns about potential noise from turbines. The process of obtaining approval for interconnection with the utility grid can be expensive and time-consuming.

Fortunately, a number of promising developments are bringing down these barriers. The U.S. Department of Energy has made small wind a major emphasis of its current outreach efforts. DOE's Advanced Small Wind Turbine Program, combined with industry research and development, is improving small wind technology, while lowering the manufacturing costs.

As the market begins to expand, higher volume production is also expected to lower costs, perhaps by as much as 30%. New low-cost "micro" 1.5 kW systems are able to generate 100-300 kWh per month for a total installed cost of under $4,000.

A host of programs and policies are already in place to nurture the rural residential wind market. More are in development. At the federal level, the Public Utility Regulatory Policies Act of 1978 (PURPA) requires utilities to connect with and purchase power from small wind energy systems. However, there are currently no federal tax credits for small wind systems. (These expired in 1985.)

## Economic Incentive Programs

State incentive programs include rebates, buy-down programs, and grants; loan funds and industry recruitment programs; sales tax and property tax exemptions; personal and corporate tax incentives; and net metering policies. These states (CA, IA, IL, IN, MA, MI, MT, and NJ), have rebates, grants, or buy-down programs which offer the strongest financial incentive for the small wind turbine market. Fifteen states (AK, AZ, CA, CT, ID, IA, MD, MN, MO, NE, NY, OR, TN, VA and WI) offer loan funds, and six (AZ, CA, CT, MT, NC, and WA) offer industry recruitment incentives. Ten states (AZ, IA, MA, MN, ND, NJ, OH, RI, VT, and WA) have sales tax incentives. Eighteen states (CT, IL, IN, IA, KS, MD, MN, MT, NV, NH, ND, OH, OR, RI, SD, TX, VT, and WI) have property tax incentives. Fourteen states (AZ, HI, ID, MA, MN, MT, NC, ND, OH, OR, RI, TX, UT, and WV) have personal or corporate tax credits, deductions, exemptions, and accelerated depreciation policies for installation of wind energy systems.

## Zoning Ordinances

Other state polices include zoning ordinances allowing tall towers, wind access laws, and line extension requirements. FL, MN, MT, OR, and WI have wind access or easement rights laws to secure property owners' wind resources, which include restrictions against neighborhood covenants that prohibit the use of renewable energy systems. Texas has a unique line extension policy which requires utilities to provide information on on-site renewable energy technology options to customers required to pay for the construction of utility power lines to a remote location.

## Net Metering Policies

At least thirty-three states (AZ, AK, CA, CO, CT, DE, GA, ID, IL, IN, IA, ME, MD, MA, MN, MT, NV, NH, NJ, NM, NY, ND, OH, OK, OR, PA, RI, TX, VT, VA, WA, WI and WY) have net metering policies that allow customers to offset power consumption up to 100% at the full retail value over the billing period. Net metering rules are determined on a state-by-state basis and sometimes by individual utility. Some state laws apply only to private investor-owned utilities that are regulated by public utility commissions, and as a result many rural electric cooperatives are not required to offer the option to their customers. This is unfortunate, since small wind turbines have historically been used and have a larger market in rural settings.

Without net metering, small wind system owners are considered to be qualifying facilities under the Public Utility Regulatory Policies Act of 1978 (PURPA), and are paid only the utility's avoided fuel cost (often under 2 cents/kWh) for their "instantaneous" excess generation. Combined with requirements to purchase a second meter, this arrangement gives little financial incentive to consumers to install wind systems.

## Building Permit Issues

Many jurisdictions restrict the height of structures permitted in residentially zoned areas, although variances are often obtainable. A conditional use permit may be required, which could specify a number of requirements the installation must meet. Most restrictions occur in populated areas where height, safety, or aesthetics are issues. In addition to zoning issues, neighbors might object to a wind turbine that blocks their view, or potential noise.

Most zoning and aesthetic concerns can be addressed by supplying objective data, such as the ambient noise level of 52–55 decibels, with sound dropping sharply with distance. In many cases, the perception of visual and noise impacts prior to wind turbine installation is worse than the actual impact.

## Tower Height

County ordinances that restrict tower height may adversely affect optimum economics for small wind turbines. Unless the zoning jurisdiction has established small wind turbine as a "permitted" or "conditional" use, it may be necessary to obtain a variance or special use permit to erect an adequate tower.

The 35-foot height limit in many zoning ordinances dates back to the early 1900s as the height to which the typical firefighting engine could pump water, and is clearly not pertinent for modern residential wind turbines. Small wind advocates may want to encourage local governments to allow wind turbine towers up to at least 80 feet as a permitted use.

The Federal Aviation Administration (FAA) has regulations on the height of structures, particularly those near the approach path to runways at local airports. Objects that are higher than 200 feet (61 meters) above ground level must be reported, and beacon lights may be required. A proposed wind system within ten miles of an airport, no matter how tall the tower, requires contacting the local FAA office to determine if it is necessary to file for permission to erect a tower. A general rule of thumb for proper and efficient operation of a wind turbine is that the bottom of the turbine's blades should be at least 10 feet (3 meters) above the top of anything within 300 feet (about 100 meters).

## Noise

The most characteristic sounds of a wind turbine are the "swish . . . swish . . . swish" of its turning blades and the whirring of the generator. Improved designs have made wind turbines much quieter over the last decade. Within several hundred feet of a machine, these sounds may be distinguishable from the background noise of local traffic or the wind blowing through the trees, but they usually are not disruptive or objectionable. The impact on any particular neighbor will depend on how close they live, whether they are upwind or downwind, and the level of other noise sources, such as traffic. Some permitting agencies have set up noise complaint resolution processes.

## Visibility

The visibility of a particular wind system will depend on many factors, including tower height, proximity to neighbors and roadways, local terrain, and tree coverage. Some neighbors may object to a wind turbine being in their field of view, and this could be an issue when applying for a zoning permit. In most areas, modern wind turbines are an uncommon sight, so it is natural to expect some reservations about their introduction. Objections are more likely to occur in populated and tourist areas. Opposition is least likely to surface in rural settings and after some small turbines have been installed in the area.

## Connecting Wind Systems to Utility Grids

Federal regulations under PURPA require utilities to connect with and purchase power from small wind energy systems. Local utilities should be contacted before connecting to their distribution lines to address any power quality and safety concerns.

A grid-connected wind turbine can reduce the home or business' consumption of utility-supplied electricity. When the wind system produces more electricity than is used, the excess is sent or sold to the utility. If the turbine cannot deliver the full amount of energy needed, the utility makes up the difference. A grid-connected system requires no batteries for storage; only a power conditioning unit (an inverter) or an induction generator is needed to make the turbine output electrically compatible with the utility grid. The output is connected to the household breaker panel on a dedicated breaker, just like a large appliance. In effect, the utility acts as a big battery bank, and the utility sees the wind turbine as a negative load.

Electrical code requirements emphasize proper wiring and installation and the use of components that have been certified for fire and electrical safety, such as Underwriters Laboratories (UL). Most local electrical code requirements are based on the *National Electrical Code* (NEC), published by the National Fire Protection Association.

The utility's principal concern will be that the wind turbine automatically stops delivering any electricity to power lines during an outage. Otherwise line workers and the public, thinking that the line is "dead," might not take normal precautions and might be injured. Another concern among utilities is that the power from the wind system synchronize properly with the utility's grid, and that it matches the utility's own power in terms of voltage, frequency, and power quality.

Most utilities and other electricity providers require a formal agreement before interconnecting a wind turbine to the utility grid. In states with retail competition for electricity service, such as California and Pennsylvania (where the utility operates the local wires, but the customer has a choice of electricity provider), it may be necessary to sign separate agreements with each company. These agreements are usually written by the utility or electricity supplier, and the terms and conditions of those with investor-owned utilities must be reviewed and approved by state regulatory authorities.

Several state governments are developing new standardized interconnection requirements for small renewable energy generating facilities. At least five states (CA, DE, NY, OH and TX) have conducted proceedings on interconnection of distributed generating facilities. In most cases the new requirements are based on standards and testing procedures developed by consensus through independent third-party authorities, such as the Institute of Electrical and Electronic Engineers (IEEE) and UL. Sixteen states (CA, DE, GA, MD, MT, NJ, NM, NV, NY, OH, OR, RI, VT, VA, WA, and WY) have adopted interconnection standards based on UL/IEEE. As existing safety standards developed specifically for photovoltaics, UL 1741 and IEEE 929 have been successfully used to certify inverters for small wind turbines. The IEEE has published standard IEEE P1547 for inter-tied "distributed generation" technologies, including small wind turbines.

A number of states have also required utilities to develop simplified, streamlined agreements for interconnecting small-scale renewable generating facilities, including wind turbines. These shorter agreements are designed to be relatively consumer-friendly and avoid complicated legal or technical jargon.

Some utilities require small wind turbine owners to maintain liability insurance of $1 million or more, claiming this is necessary to protect the utility from liability for facilities it does not own and control. Such insurance requirements quickly make small wind turbine systems uneconomical.

In eight states (CA, GA, MD, NV, OH, OK, OR, and WA), laws or regulatory authorities prohibit utilities from imposing any insurance requirements on small wind systems that qualify for "net metering." In five other states (ID, NM, NY, VA, and VT), regulatory authorities have allowed utilities to impose insurance requirements, but have reduced the required coverage amounts to levels consistent with the conventional residential or commercial insurance policies (such as $100,000–$300,000).

Owners of small wind systems may be asked to indemnify their utility for any potential liability arising from the operation of the wind turbine. Indemnity provisions should be fair to both parties. Customer charges can take a variety of forms, including interconnection fees, metering fees, and standby fees, among others. PURPA prohibits utilities from assessing discriminatory charges to customers who have their own generation facilities.

Grid-connected small wind turbines can provide many benefits to utilities, as well as turbine owners. In rural areas with long power lines, they can improve power quality (by boosting voltage) and reduce line losses. They can also provide extra generating capacity and reduce power plant emissions.

## Conclusion

Although important challenges exist for the domestic small wind market, small wind turbines have significant potential to contribute to the nation's electricity supply, and to reduce the environmental impacts of generating electricity. Approximately 21 million U.S. homes are built on one-acre and larger lots, and 24% of the U.S. population lives in rural areas. Recent reductions in costs and increased public, political, and institutional support for small wind energy systems are helping this potential to be realized. (For updated information on wind power, contact The American Wind Energy Association (AWGA), 1501 M Street, NW, Suite 1000, Washington, DC 20005, phone: (202) 383-2500, website: **www.awea.org**)

James Armstrong, CPE, CEM
Andy Walker, PhD, PE

Green buildings include, as a part of their mission, the provision of conditions that are healthy, comfortable, and enhance productivity. Average energy use in commercial buildings in 2005 was $1.77/SF/year. That same year, the cost of an average employee (at $42,100/year, occupying a 64 SF cubicle) would have been $626/SF/year. Clearly, even a small improvement in employee comfort and productivity would be of tremendous economic benefit and actually dwarf the energy cost savings resulting from green building methods. The bottom line is that both these factors are very significant in successful sustainable building design.

Green building includes not only using energy-efficient, recycled, and recyclable materials and products, but also creating a healthy, comfortable indoor environment. The rewards have been demonstrated: higher property values on more desirable space, higher productivity among building users, enhanced ability to attract and retain employees, and valuable public relations for the owner and/or tenants.

There are many comfort/health/productivity factors in the green indoor environment, including:

- Indoor air quality: healthy, properly humidified, odorless air—and operable windows to admit outside air
- Thermal comfort, with individual control over one's space, including effects of air temperature, radiant heat gain from the sun or surroundings, air movement, and humidity
- Views of the outdoors and ample natural light with task lighting, including effects of color rendition, and positioning of fixtures to avoid glare and reflections
- Clean water

- Comfortable noise levels and speech privacy
- Comfortable, climate-appropriate furnishings

## Indoor Air Quality

Indoor air quality (IAQ) has been much discussed over the past several years. Today's buildings are more tightly constructed than ever. This means that less airborne dirt and dust can infiltrate buildings from outside, but it also means that airborne particles generated in the space or brought into a building on clothing or by other means, or from construction or other materials installed in the building, cannot get out and are recirculated over and over again. These particles can cause unnecessary physical discomfort and illness. Particulates can be a variety of substances, including dust, pollen, and mold spores. Some harmful bacteria and viruses can also exist in the airstream.

The American Society of Heating, Refrigerating, and Air-Conditioning Engineers (ASHRAE) Standard 62 "Ventilation for Acceptable Indoor Air Quality" specifies ventilation rate limits on formaldehyde, lead, and carbon monoxide and also provides procedures for achieving acceptable indoor air quality. While pure air is an ideal, the objective is to maintain concentrations of pollutants below threshold values. Ventilation rates are prescribed to achieve this.

## Mold

Mold is the most common medium for growth and development of airborne bacteria. Molds are small organisms found almost everywhere there are organic (carbon-based) materials, indoors and out, including on drywall, wood framing and flooring, concrete, insulation backing, carpets, furniture, HVAC equipment and vents, plants, foods, and dry leaves. Mold can be nearly any color, including white, orange, green, and black. Very tiny and lightweight, mold spores travel easily through the air. Most building surfaces provide adequate nutrients to support the growth of mold. When mold spores land on material that is damp, they can begin to multiply.

While molds are beneficial to the environment and are needed to break down organic material, if they are present in large numbers they may cause adverse health effects, including asthma and allergic symptoms such as watery eyes, a runny nose, sneezing, nasal congestion, itching, coughing, wheezing, difficulty breathing, headache, and fatigue. The same amount of mold may cause health effects in one person, but not in another, because some people are more sensitive to molds than others. This group includes infants and children, elderly persons, immune-compromised patients (e.g., people with HIV infection, cancer, lung or liver disease, or who are undergoing chemotherapy), and individuals with existing respiratory conditions, such as allergies and asthma.

Airborne mold spores in large numbers can also cause skin irritation and allergic reactions and infections. Exposure to high spore levels can actually stimulate the development of a mold allergy.

Mold needs a food source (material to grow on) and a source of moisture. These can come from things like flooding, leaky roofs, humidifiers/air handlers, damp basements or crawl spaces, constant plumbing leaks (common under sinks and behind dishwashers and clothes washers), and clothes dryers that are vented indoors.

Mold is the natural process by which organic materials are broken down or decay. Since many construction components (including structural elements) are derived from organic materials such as wood or pulp, they can be damaged by unchecked mold growth.

Stachybotrys is a greenish-black, slimy type of mold found only on cellulose products (such as wood or paper) that have remained wet for several days or longer. Stachybotrys does not grow on concrete, linoleum, or tile. Stachybotrys is reported to have caused serious respiratory, skin, and gastrointestinal conditions.[1] According to the U.S. Centers for Disease Control and Prevention (CDC), all molds should be treated the same with respect to potential health risks and removal.

## Preventing Mold through Construction Practices

Prevention of mold requires prevention of moisture intrusion from the outdoors, as well as attention to potential moisture leaks inside the building. Moisture can also accumulate as warm humid air condenses on a cold surface (either the inside wall layer of a cooled building, or the outer layer of a heated building). Humidity can build up to high levels in a space due to tighter buildings with reduced air infiltration, the result of added insulation and better-fitting windows and doors. Another contributor is oversized cooling systems, which run less frequently, providing less opportunity to remove humidity from the building interior. Improper building maintenance or operating procedures, and compromised air filtration, can also lead to mold. Mold often grows in wall cavities, under impervious floors, or in cavities in cathedral ceilings where it is difficult to detect and treat.

Manufactured homes have had their share of moisture-inducing problems, including duct leakage and tears in the "belly board," the material that protects the structure from ground moisture. These homes also use nonporous finish treatments, such as vinyl and plastic, which encourage condensation.

Construction techniques to address moisture intrusion from outside include vapor diffusion retarders, airflow retarders, waterproofing and dampproofing, flashings (with special attention to HVAC equipment on rooftops), vented spaces with drainage planes, proper slopes in grading and use of granular backfill or drainage board next to the foundation, perimeter drains as needed, and low-VOC dampproofing coatings.

**Mold-Resistant Materials**: The construction industry has recently responded to mold problems and their effect on indoor air quality by producing a number of mold-resistant materials. Some, like paperless drywall, avoid use of materials that allow mold to grow. Others use chemical processes, such as Microban®, in carpet, paint, caulk, and grout to kill microbes. Mold-resistant paint contains a mildewstat, or mildewcide, while mold-resistant insulation products contain fungicides. There are several other mold-resistant products available, from house wrap to ceiling tiles.

Careful design and selection of materials can avoid conditions that are conducive to mold growth. For example, potentially problematic plumbing connections and floor drains should be accessible for easy cleaning and frequent detection of leaks. (*See Chapter 2 for more on green approaches to prevention of moisture intrusion.*)

## Monitoring Humidity

Special-use buildings, such as schools, laboratories, libraries, and museums, may require humidity monitoring systems and control methods. Schools, especially in the southeastern part of the United States, experience mold problems related to shutting off the cooling/ventilation systems in summer or in the afternoon when the school day ends. Both humidity and contaminants tend to build up during those "off" periods. The additional problem with schools is that children are more susceptible to IAQ problems, including mold. Some studies recommend desiccant systems to remove moisture and to reduce $CO_2$.

## Cleanup of Mold

It is important to make sure that the source of moisture is stopped before mold is cleaned up. If this is not done, it will grow again. The appropriate cleanup measures will depend on the surface where mold is growing. A professional should be consulted if large areas (more than 30 SF) are contaminated with mold. The first step is to clean surfaces with soap and water. When most of the staining and all of the mold have been removed, a water and bleach mixture (10:1 ratio) can be used to kill the mold spores. Bleach must not be mixed with any other chemicals or cleaners. The space should be well-ventilated, not only because of the bleach's toxicity, but to help dry the wet surfaces.

During the cleanup of molds, many spores may be released into the air. Mold counts in air are typically 10–1,000 times higher than their background levels prior to the cleaning and removal. To prevent health effects, several protective measures can be practiced. Anyone with a chronic illness, such as asthma or emphysema, should not perform the cleanup. A HEPA (high efficiency particulate air) filter respirator will reduce the mold spores that can be inhaled. Protective clothing should be worn, along with rubber gloves that are easily cleaned or discarded.

Bystanders should not be present when the cleanup takes place. Work should be done over short time spans and breaks taken in a fresh-air location. Windows should be open and air handlers turned off, except for exhaust fans. Fans can also be used in windows to blow air out of the affected room to the outside during and after the cleanup. (Make sure the air is being blown outside the building, not into another room.) Contaminated materials should be double-bagged before they are removed from the area.

Dehumidifiers and other equipment, such as negative air machines, HEPA-filtered air scrubbers, and HEPA-filtered vacuums, are typically used on large remediation jobs. Furniture and furnishings in the mold-contaminated area must be cleaned and then stored in a dry, mold-free area. Containment areas should also be set up to prevent cross-contamination. Post-remediation testing is a crucial part of a mold remediation job—to ensure the mold levels are acceptable.

## HVAC Condensate Drainage Systems

When air is cooled, it may dip below its dew point—the point at which any moisture in the air condenses. This moisture must be removed effectively; otherwise it will collect in the airstream and become a breeding ground for mold and or algae. Because the moisture is typically removed before the air reaches the fan, the air handler is in a negative pressure. Therefore, the key to moisture removal is installing a P-trap at the drain. This allows the air handler to maintain a vacuum while removing the moisture. This is one of the most common problems in HVAC systems and has been known to be the source of many airborne diseases, including Legionella.

## Gases

Other threats to indoor air quality include noxious gases, such as radon, carbon monoxide, propane, methane (natural gas), and formaldehyde—from natural sources, appliances, and man-made construction materials. Hospitals, labs, parking garages, gas stations, sewage treatment plants, airports, and factories may additionally have to control exposure to hydrogen, ammonia, and fluorocarbons (Freon). Identifying such gases, their sources, and amounts enables professionals to determine an appropriate treatment. (*See also "Gas Detectors & Alarms" later in this chapter.*) Monitoring $CO_2$ can have an additional "green" benefit as some of the new energy management systems automatically adjust the temperature based on occupancy—as determined by $CO_2$ level.

## Off-Gassing of Construction Materials

Many forms of construction materials and products introduce contaminants into a facility, both initially and for many years after construction is completed. This is due to the off-gassing of contaminants over time until the product becomes stabilized, sometimes years later. Selecting natural carpeting, fabrics, flooring, and finish materials (including natural wall covering or, preferably, low- or no-VOC paints and wood floor finishes), and framing, sheathing, and cabinetry materials without harmful chemicals, is the green approach.

Materials constructed with potentially harmful chemicals, such as particleboard with formaldehyde resin, can sometimes be wrapped or sealed to reduce exposure (for example, millwork completely wrapped in laminate or coated with a nontoxic coating). Gypsum board and acoustic panels and ceiling tiles should also be investigated for toxic components before specifying. Natural floor materials, such as cork, bamboo, or linoleum are a better choice than vinyl, which contains potentially toxic chemicals. (*See Chapter 11 for more on these materials.*)

Insulation is another potential source of indoor pollutants, from fibers and chemicals in materials such as cellulose, fiberglass, and mineral wool (which uses phenol formaldehyde binders), polyurethane spray foam, and polystyrene. Safer choices include Perlite, Icynene, and Air Krete, as well as scrap cotton. Formaldehyde-free fiberglass insulation is available from the major insulation manufacturers.

**Formaldehyde**: Formaldehyde is a chemical used widely to manufacture building materials and products, such as glue in fiberboard. Formaldehyde is also a by-product of combustion and certain other natural processes. Thus, it may be present in substantial concentrations both indoors and out. Sources of formaldehyde include building materials; smoking; household products; and the use of un-vented, fuel-burning appliances, such as fork lifts, gas stoves, or kerosene space heaters. Formaldehyde, by itself or in combination with other chemicals, is used for a number of purposes in manufactured products. For example, it is used to add permanent-press qualities to clothing and draperies, as a component of glues and adhesives, and as a preservative in some paints and coating products.

In smaller facilities and homes, the most significant sources of formaldehyde are likely to be pressed wood products made using adhesives that contain urea-formaldehyde (UF) resins. Pressed wood products made for indoor use include: particleboard (used as subflooring and shelving and in cabinetry and furniture); hardwood plywood paneling (used for decorative wall covering and in cabinets and furniture); and medium-density fiberboard (used for drawer fronts, cabinets, and furniture tops). Medium-density fiberboard contains a higher resin-to-wood ratio than any other UF pressed wood product and is generally recognized as emitting the highest levels of formaldehyde.

Other pressed wood products, such as softwood plywood and flake or oriented strand board, are produced for exterior construction use and contain the dark, or red/black-colored phenol-formaldehyde (PF) resin. Although formaldehyde is present in both types of resins, pressed woods that contain PF resin generally emit formaldehyde at considerably lower rates than those containing UF resin.

Since 1985, the Department of Housing and Urban Development (HUD) has permitted the use of plywood and particleboard only if they conform to specified formaldehyde emission limits in the construction of prefabricated panels. In the past, some construction using prefabricated panels had elevated levels of formaldehyde because of the large amount of high-emitting pressed wood products used in their construction.

The rate at which products such as pressed wood or textiles release formaldehyde can change. Formaldehyde emissions generally decrease as products age. When products are new, high indoor temperatures or humidity can cause increased release of formaldehyde.

During the 1970s, many properties had urea-formaldehyde foam insulation (UFFI) installed in the wall cavities as an energy conservation measure. However, many of these properties were found to have relatively high indoor concentrations of formaldehyde soon after the UFFI installation.

Use of this product has been declining. Studies show that formaldehyde emissions from UFFI decrease with time; therefore, homes in which UFFI was installed many years ago are unlikely to have high levels of formaldehyde now.

Formaldehyde, a colorless, pungent-smelling gas, can cause eye, nose, and throat irritation; wheezing and coughing; fatigue; skin rash; and severe allergic reactions. High concentrations may trigger attacks in people with asthma. There is evidence that some people can develop a sensitivity to formaldehyde, which has also been shown to cause cancer in animals and may cause cancer in humans.[2]

The average concentration of formaldehyde in older properties without UFFI is generally below 0.1 PPM (parts per million). In properties with significant amounts of new pressed wood products, levels can be greater than 0.3 PPM. Coatings may reduce formaldehyde emissions for some period of time. To be effective, the coating must cover all surfaces and edges and remain intact.

Since release of formaldehyde may be affected by the humidity level (as well as heat), dehumidifiers and air conditioning can help reduce emissions. (Drain and clean dehumidifier collection trays frequently so that they do not become a breeding ground for microorganisms.) Increasing the rate of ventilation will also help reduce formaldehyde levels. *(See Chapters 2 and 11 for more on construction materials that minimize exposure to contaminants.)*

# Tools for Improving Air Quality
## *Monitoring Systems*
Monitoring systems serve two important services:

1. To document that allowable limits are not exceeded.

2. To control demand-control-ventilation (variable outdoor air).

## *Gas Detectors & Alarms*
Detectors and alarms are available to identify carbon monoxide, radon, propane, methane, and formaldehyde. These devices generally plug into 110-volt wall sockets, are UL-listed, and offer battery backups. Industrial air monitors are used in hospitals and labs, parking garages and gas stations, chemical and pharmaceutical industries, food and beverage industries, process plants, sewage treatment plans, and airports. These systems test for gases such as hydrogen, ammonia, carbon monoxide, and fluorocarbons (Freon).

## *Air Purification Systems*
Operable windows are becoming more popular in a variety of facility types, as part of the movement toward a more comfortable, natural environment in workplaces and in homes. Being able to open a window to admit "fresh" outside air when the outdoor air temperature is comfortable and having some control over one's immediate space conditions is a valuable feature, and can greatly enhance the quality of the indoor air. (Tuberculosis hospitals built early in the 20th century were located in the countryside at high altitudes for fresh, healing air.)

More and more building managers are also using high-efficiency air filtration systems, increasing the amount of fresh air brought into a building, as well as the exhaust volumes. Of course, all of the air introduced into the facility must be conditioned (heated, cooled, filtered)—processes that require large quantities of energy. Fortunately, the new generation of HVAC motors and controls allows more economical air cleaner operation, while also lowering overall operating costs, reducing noise, and providing greater levels of comfort.

A variety of systems are available for homes, offices, and other types of facilities using HEPA filters and other methods, such as ionization, to remove particulates and odors from the air. The ionization method restores the negative ions in the air to a healthy level. (Clean-air environments, such as national forests, mountains, and waterfalls, have a negative ion level of roughly 2,000 per cubic centimeter, whereas typical urban indoor environments may have only 200 negative ions, due to the buildings' airtightness and the effect of man-made materials, such as concrete and asphalt.) It should be noted, however, that some ozone-generating ion air purifiers may increase indoor ozone levels above federal health limits. Ozone at high levels has been shown to trigger asthma.

## Cleaning the Air in Large Facilities

Larger facilities use technologies such as "hot process dynamics" (particles rising with hot air). Indoor air enters the base of the air purifier, which releases and recirculates clean air. Each system covers an area up to 1,600 square feet, and offers features such as adjustable louvers that enable users to customize the air flow patterns. Some other approaches include:

- **Activated charcoal filtration:** An air-side filtration system that can be activated to pull certain chemicals and components from the airstream.

- **Electrostatic precipitators:** Filtration systems that ionize the air. The ionized particles are attracted to an electric anode, which can be cleaned to remove the particulates.

- **Desiccant systems:** Moisture-removal systems that remove waterborne contaminants. A method used to maintain operating room air quality, while providing 100% outside air.

- **Ultraviolet lighting:** A system that kills mold and bacteria in the airstream. Ultraviolet systems require a switch to shut them off when the door is opened to prevent the UV rays from causing harm to people. The UV lighting is directed on the coils, which increases the effective surface area of the lamps. UV light can kill many forms of bacteria.

- **Providing more outside air:** The easiest method, made more efficient by the use of heat recovery to mitigate the requirement for air-side treatment (heating or cooling) of the fresh air.

## Air Purification in Homes & Smaller Facilities

Residential and small commercial facilities can be treated with portable air cleaners. Factors to consider when selecting these devices include:

- **Capacity for removing particulates:** Typical systems remove particulates between 0.01–0.3 microns, the size that tends to cause asthma and allergic reactions.

- **Method used to purify air**: Negative ion, ozone air cleaners, HEPA filters.
- **Size**: Stationary filters clean the air only in their nearby surroundings. Even air cleaners with motors or fans require multiple units to purify the air in a whole house or similar space, since walls, floors, ceilings, and doors act as barriers. Another approach is an in-duct air purifier. In considering size, portability may be a factor, depending on the intended use of the system.
- **Type of system**: Filters can harbor mold and bacteria, and glass plates can be fragile, whereas stainless steel and ceramic plates are more durable. "Needlepoint" ionization is capable of producing a high density of negative ions, which increases its effectiveness in removing allergens. HEPA filters are disposable and can cost up to $170/year. Washable filters produce savings and avoid waste.
- **Cost**: To evaluate cost, one must consider not only the cost of filter replacements and other maintenance, but also the system's coverage in square feet, and its annual consumption of electricity. HEPA filters, ozone, and negative ion air cleaners may be priced in the same range, but the latter two tend to cover a larger area. The cost of replacement parts and maintenance are other considerations.
- **Noise**: Motors that draw air through a filter can produce significant noise. Negative ion and ozone generators use quieter fans. Some ionizers rely on natural air flow; they have no fans or motors and are very quiet. In small spaces, the purifier may be effective set on the lowest speed, which is also the quietest and uses less energy.
- **Warranty** (typically two years) and guarantee.

## Whole-House Air Filters

For existing homes and spaces that have central air, pleated, electrostatic filters can be installed. For more stringent air cleaning, electronic precipitator cleaners can be used, collecting particulates on electrically charged plates.[3] At least one major manufacturer now offers whole-house air cleaning technology that is claimed to remove up to 99.98% of airborne allergens, a significantly higher efficacy rate than HEPA room air filters, and vastly more effective than standard 1" filters.

## Home Carbon Monoxide Detection & Alarms

The U.S. Consumer Product Safety Commission recommends a minimum of one carbon monoxide (CO) alarm in every home. This requirement is currently legislated in several states and municipalities. The UL standard for CO alarms requires that they activate within a period of 4 hours at 70 PPM.

Many HVAC contractors test for CO using hand-held instruments when maintaining or repairing systems. Some detection devices require training, available from manufacturers or industry institutes. These practices enable the contractor to identify and then repair any faulty equipment.

The capabilities and sensitivities of CO alarms vary significantly. Excessive false alarms have been a problem with many systems. Others have to be replaced frequently since their electrochemical sensors have a limited lifespan. Metal Oxide Semiconductor (MOS)-based detectors are capable of cross-sensitivity, which can lead to false alarms. The other drawback of MOS-based detectors is that they may be less sensitive over time, and are unable to read levels below 100 PPM. More sensitive equipment may be needed for buildings used by infants, seniors, and pregnant women, as well as people with compromised respiratory systems. Appropriate CO detection/alarm systems for this population should be capable of reading below 60 PPM. Manufacturers of digital carbon monoxide systems offer low-level alert and other features, including improved response time and accuracy, and a wider range of monitoring.[4]

## Indoor Plants to Improve Air Quality

Indoor plants support green building in two ways—they bring nature inside, which improves the outlook of many building users, and they help clean the indoor air. Research has shown that indoor plants increase oxygen and humidity, and absorb off-gassed chemicals such as carbon monoxide, benzene, and formaldehyde. In *Your Naturally Healthy Home*, author Alan Berman suggests that at least one plant should be provided for each ten square yards of floor space with ceiling heights between eight and nine feet.[5] The following types of plants are recommended for their particular effectiveness in improving air quality (based on a NASA research study and other articles and publications):

- Areca, Reed, and dwarf date palms
- Boston and Australian sword ferns
- Janet Craig dracaena
- Bamboo palm
- English ivy
- Peace lily
- Rubber plant
- Weeping fig
- Chrysanthemum
- Gerbera daisies
- Philodendron

- Spider plant
- Golden pothos

Proper watering and maintenance of plants (including removing dead leaves) are essential to ensure that the pots do not become sources of air quality problems because of mold.

## Thermal Comfort

Perhaps the most urgent need that humans have of buildings is protection from the elements. The space inside a building provides conditions that allow us to survive freezing cold or blistering hot outdoor conditions. Clearly temperature is important, but several other factors also contribute to thermal comfort. Air temperature, humidity, and velocity all play a part, as do other sources of heat, such as solar radiation through a window or thermal radiation from a hot tin roof. Heat radiation from hot ceilings or other objects in the room can also cause discomfort, if they are more than 18°–45°F (10°–25°C) warmer than the other surfaces in the room. Drafts in excess of 0.25 m/s velocity (turbulent drafts greater than 0.1 m/s) can also cause discomfort.

Another factor in thermal comfort is human metabolism, which generates heat. The amount of heat people generate depends on their level of activity, and varies from about 430 BTU/hr (125 W) for a resting adult, to as high as 1,700 BTU/hr (500 W) for strenuous activity. Comfort is a condition of the mind that depends on the physiological processes the body must perform (as controlled by the hypothalamus in the brain) to maintain a constant 98.6°F (37°C) body temperature. At low temperatures, blood vessels in the skin constrict, causing the skin to serve as a layer of insulation. The body can induce muscle activity, including noticeable shivering, to increase the rate of heat production. At high temperatures, blood vessels in the skin dilate and dissipate heat from the core of the body. Sweat glands in the skin, pump water to cool the skin by evaporation.

Indoor thermal comfort is achieved by providing a temperature that avoids the body's need to perform these physiological responses. ASHRAE Standard 55, "Thermal Environmental Conditions for Human Occupancy," specifies summer and winter comfort zones to account for differences in clothing. Most people are comfortable at an air temperature between 70°–79°F (21°–26°C).

Humidity influences human comfort because it affects the rate at which sweat can evaporate from the skin. Comfort criteria of ASHRAE 55 are satisfied at low humidity, but humidity has other effects too. Overly dry air can dry out mucous membranes, leading to more frequent colds, respiratory illness, and associated absenteeism. On the other hand, overly humid air causes sweat to accumulate on the skin and clothing. Relative humidity of 30%–60% usually ensures comfort. Higher humidity is acceptable at low temperatures, and lower humidity is more comfortable at high temperatures. Most environments in North America are dry in the winter and humid in the summer. These conditions require humidification in the winter and dehumidification in the summer.

The HVAC system required to achieve comfortable conditions will depend on the local climate. In many areas and building types, for example, air conditioning is not required. In warm climates, heating might be needed only infrequently, and amply provided by a low-cost electric heater. A complete HVAC system would provide control of both temperature and humidity; air distribution systems would be designed to provide everyone with adequate ventilation air and positioned so as to avoid drafts. A new approach is to separately filter or otherwise purify outdoor ("fresh") and indoor air, in combination with energy recovery ventilators or heat exchangers, with an overall decrease in the amount of air that needs to be heated or cooled.

## Tools for Thermal Comfort

Building envelope considerations, such as reflective roofing, low-E windows, and window tinting, are some of the tools that enable designers to optimize thermal comfort while also improving energy efficiency. Some strategies can be modified to suit the season, such as tinted window shades that can be up in winter and down in summer. Enthalpy-controlled HVAC systems (EMS) are dynamic and focus on humidity as well as temperature, as factors in human comfort. Siting the building according to seasonal heat gain and use is another key to thermal comfort, as is landscaping (e.g., shade trees). Individual control over one's space is also a key comfort item. Operable windows provide part of the solution.

## Quality of Light

The quality of lighting in a space is a key element in the *comfort, health, and productivity* category of green building. Effective lighting can enhance the mood, energy, and effectiveness of people using the space. Light also affects people's circadian rhythms, an important factor in maintaining healthy sleep cycles. This section will focus on these aspects of lighting. Discussion of energy efficiencies in lighting design can be found in Chapter 4.

### Lamps

Compact fluorescent light bulbs (CFLs) provide both quality light and energy savings. They have a much longer bulb life (ten times longer). Other new lighting technologies in development include various types of LEDs (light-emitting diodes), which produce less heat, have a longer life than incandescents, and save energy over both incandescent bulbs and CFLs. LEDs are not widely available yet and still need improvements to increase their brightness, but they should soon be a standard option with additional features such as the ability to change light color.

## Daylighting

Daylighting has numerous benefits. Daylight allows us to dim or switch off artificial light, resulting in energy and cost savings. Our eyes, having evolved in sunlight, respond better to daylight than artificial light, which also may flicker and hum. Daylight also admits less heat into a space than artificial light per unit of light. Incandescent lamps are essentially electric heaters that happen to give off a little light, and fluorescent lights also introduce heat into a space, exacerbating cooling loads. Finally, it can be disturbing for people to work in windowless cubicles with no awareness of the weather and no connection to the outdoors. Occupants of daylit spaces are certainly happier, and evidence shows that they are more productive.

Daylighting is more than just having windows. It is admitting natural light into the space, but it also includes controlling and distributing light for uniform lighting levels, avoiding glare and reflections, and controlling artificial light to achieve energy and cost savings.

Daylight is very bright compared to the light we need in a built environment. As a result, small apertures in building walls and roofs are sufficient to meet daylighting goals. Daylighting works best in a

**Figure 7.1**
Sealed for many years, this beautiful skylight in a historic Washington D.C. federal building has been restored to operation.

Green Building: Project Planning & Cost Estimating

task-ambient lighting strategy, where daylight is used to maintain a low ambient light level everywhere, and task lights (such as desk lamps) are used to provide a higher light level only when and where needed.

Daylighting was a practical requirement in historic buildings built before the advent of electric lights, and much can be learned from the study of old office buildings and factories. In many cases, historic features, such as numerous high windows, clerestory windows, transom windows, skylights, and narrow floor plates to provide all rooms with perimeter windows, have been compromised by subsequent changes to the building. Restoring the daylighting system to its original intent could be both cost-effective and improve the quality of the space.

## Cautions

It is important to discuss potential pitfalls related to daylighting so that they may be avoided. The pupil of the human eye constricts in response to bright light. If brightness is not uniform throughout the room, this constriction makes it hard to see in the darker areas, requiring people to install and use even more artificial light. A daylighting strategy should not admit more light than is needed for recommended lighting levels, so that additional artificial light is not needed in areas not daylit. Similarly, even in daylit areas, the difference in lighting level between the brightest spot and the darkest spot in a room must be minimized. This requires not only special measures to distribute light to the dark spots, but also to attenuate light in areas that are readily daylit.

Computer screens, increasingly common in all environments, are best viewed in low ambient light levels. Surrounding sources of light are reflected to the eye from the surface of a computer screen, causing an annoying veil over the image on the screen. Computer workstations can be oriented to avoid reflections of windows and lighting fixtures. Fixtures with sharp cut-off angles may be specified so that reflections of light sources do not appear on computer screens. Another issue is backlighting, for example, when a person stands in front of a window and appears only as a silhouette. This can be avoided with proper design.

The temperature a person feels is a combination of the surrounding air temperature and radiant heat gain. Radiant heat gain from sunlight is intense, and direct exposure to sunlight indoors almost always causes thermal discomfort. Direct sun may be acceptable in circulation spaces (such as an atrium or hallway) or in residential buildings where occupants can move out of the sun, but should be avoided on all workstations.

## Building Layout for Daylighting

To achieve daylighting goals, the designer must be involved early in the programming phase of a project, when the relationships between spaces are being laid out. In general, daylight cannot be expected to penetrate more than 15–20 feet into a room from a perimeter window. Overhead skylights can provide light in areas farther from walls, but only on the top floor or in single-story buildings. Several devices have been invented to project daylight deep into the core of a building, including window reflectors, light pipes, and fiber optics. A building design that puts occupants in the proximity of perimeter windows results in high-quality daylighting and high occupant satisfaction (by providing a visual connection to the outdoors). This requires a more articulated plan, which may increase wall heating and cooling loads, but can also fit well with natural ventilation and passive solar heating objectives.

Historic buildings have provided a good lesson in effective daylighting, with designs such as the double-loaded corridor (two rows of rooms separated by a corridor, so that every room has an exterior wall). Premium daylight is available to all rooms through the outside wall, and the lower light level required in the hall is "borrowed" through transom windows between the hall and the room. Often these windows are high (above the doors) and translucent to provide privacy. While a double-loaded corridor with room windows facing north and south would be best, it can be configured around a courtyard, an E shape, or an infinite variety of other shapes.

## Glazing Properties

A wide variety of window glass options are available, and careful selection of glass is an important element in any daylighting strategy. Developments in glazing technology have revolutionized architecture by addressing the limitations caused by excessive heat loss, and also by controlling the amount and nature of light passing through the window. Light striking a window is reflected off the surface, absorbed by the tint in the glass, or transmitted to the other side. These properties are described by the transmittance and reflectivity of the glass. The visible transmittance (VT) is the fraction of visible light that makes it through the glass, while the total transmittance includes the infrared and ultraviolet parts of the solar spectrum. Some of the heat absorbed in the tint of the glass is convected to the room air. The parameter used to describe the sum of transmitted solar radiation plus this absorbed heat

| Properties of Three Different Types of Window Glazing | | | |
|---|---|---|---|
| | Visible Transmittance | Solar Heat Gain Coefficient | U-value (heat loss) |
| Double-pane clear | 0.82 | 0.78 | 0.46 |
| Low-E | 0.78 | 0.58 | 0.25 |
| Selective | 0.72 | 0.37 | .27 |

Figure 7.2

that eventually makes it into the room air, is called the Solar Heat Gain Coefficient (SHGC).

For passive solar heating applications, it may be desirable to transmit as much sunlight as possible. It is common to add a UV coating to protect occupants and items inside from ultraviolet radiation. Such coatings effectively remove 99% of ultraviolet radiation.

A reflective coating such as silver or gold rejects solar heat but adds a mirror-like appearance. A tint such as blue, green, or bronze also reduces the SHGC, but affects the view out the window.

If a clear appearance is desired or required for daylighting, but solar heat is not wanted, selective glazings are available that screen out the ultraviolet and infrared, but maximize visible transmittance. Selective glazings would be specified in cases where the control of solar heat gain is important, but a clear appearance is also desired. Selective glass can have a SHGC as low as 40%, but a visible transmittance in excess of 70%. A SHGC less than 40% usually requires attenuation of the visible spectrum by tint or reflective coating. The interior and exterior appearance (reflectivity and color tint), the daylighting and passive solar heating goals, and the orientation of the window are considerations when specifying glazing properties.

Heat loss through glazing is described by the heat loss coefficient (U-value), which is multiplied by the indoor-outdoor temperature difference to calculate the heat loss rate. Multiple layers of glazing result in a lower heat loss coefficient, with air or a lower conductivity gas, like argon, used in the spaces between the layers. Low emissivity (low-E) coatings are applied to the interior surfaces to reduce the radiant heat transfer from one pane to another through the air gap. In some products, the low-E coating is applied to a thin film that serves as a third pane suspended between two glass panes. The glazing assemblies are sealed, often with a desiccant in the frame, to avoid unsightly water condensation between the panes.

Clear glass represented 44% of the market in 2003, tinted 20%, and reflective 6%. Thirty percent had low-E coatings. Selective glass costs $2/SF more than standard two-pane assemblies and low-E coating adds $1/SF to the cost. Despite this slightly higher cost, many architects are using selective low-E as their standard choice in glazing.

## Daylighting Apertures: Windows, Skylights, & Light Pipes

Windows are most effective when they introduce daylight very high into a space. Variations on windows include clerestory and roof-monitors, which are vertical windows installed in articulations in the roofline.

The effectiveness of windows as daylighting apertures also depends on their orientation.

- North-facing windows are good sources of daylight. The sun hits north windows only in the early morning or late evening, and then only at a very oblique angle. The diffuse, indirect sunlight coming from the north prevents the glare and heat gain of other orientations, and no overhangs, shades, or special glazing treatments are required.

- South-facing windows require shades to control direct solar gain in the winter, when the sun is low in the sky. South-facing windows receive maximum sun at midday in winter, and are essential components of a passive solar heating strategy. In summer, overhangs over south-facing windows are effective at blocking direct solar gain. Specific overhang geometry is calculated using the sun angle equations. (*See Chapter 5.*)

- East-facing windows receive maximum sun and very low sun angles on summer mornings. West-facing windows receive maximum sun on summer afternoons. In general, low sun angles are a source of glare and unwanted heat gain, and east- and west-facing windows would be minimized depending on the views and other program requirements. However, in some climates, such as the high desert, some heat gain in the morning mitigates the night chill, and may be acceptable. Views can often be framed in small windows to avoid the problems that large windows or floor-to-ceiling glass would create on east or west faces. Where east or west windows are required, the most elegant way to reject the solar heat is with a highly reflective glass. Occupants would also use internal shades and drapes to achieve comfort.

**Figure 7.3**
Interior and exterior views of light shelves at a building at the National Renewable Energy Laboratory, Colorado. *(Photo by Warren Gretz, courtesy of NREL.)*

**Light shelves**, such as those shown in Figure 7.3, are used to bounce light off the ceiling, project light deeper into the space, distribute it from above, and diffuse it to produce a uniform light level below. Like overhangs, light shelves are designed using the sun path geometry described in Chapter 5. The upper surface of the light shelf would have a high reflectivity, and may be specular (like a mirror). The ceiling in the space would also have a high reflectivity, but would be diffuse (as in flat, white paint).

The sun is at its maximum on a roof during midday in summer. As a result, skylights were previously discouraged as sources of unwanted heat gain. However, new developments in glazing and shading designs, shown in Figure 7.4, have made it possible to use skylights to provide daylight above core zones in single-story buildings, or on the top floor of multi-story buildings.

Getting daylight into the core of large buildings has proved challenging. **Light pipes** are lined with highly reflective film to reflect light down the length of the pipe from a roof aperture to a room fixture. Light pipes are becoming popular in residential construction, and have found application in industrial facilities as well. Due to the relatively small size of each pipe, they seem to be best suited for small spaces like bathrooms or hallways. The cost of light pipes, also called solar tube skylights, is $450 for the plastic top dome, flashing kit, and bottom diffuser plus $20 per foot of light pipe length for a 10" diameter pipe.

**Figure 7.4**
Advanced solar luminaires use reflectors to increase light level and mitigate the glare and heat gain of horizontal skylights. *(Photo courtesy of Soluminaire.)*

**Fiber optics** have also been demonstrated as a means to introduce light deep into the core of buildings, and may become feasible as glass fiber used for telecommunications becomes more affordable.

## Daylighting Controls

Controls are required to realize the energy and cost savings of daylight by dimming or switching off the artificial lighting. Available daylighting controls are of two types: multi-level switching or continuous dimming.

**Multi-level switching** turns off some or all of the lights in response to daylight. Equipment consists of a light level sensor and relays. Standard lamps and ballasts are utilized. For example, a three-lamp fluorescent fixture with a one-lamp ballast and another two-lamp ballast would have four lighting levels: all off, one on, two on, or three on. The switching of circuits on and off is noticeable to occupants, and a potential cause for complaints. Lighting circuits must be laid out such that they correspond to the natural light levels in a room. Rows of lights would be laid out parallel to the windows such that lights near the windows could be off, while those far away from the windows are on. The difficulty and expense of reconfiguring lighting circuits limits the use of multiple-level switching in retrofit projects. A multi-level control module would cost around $485 and could control several zones. Each zone would require a photocell sensor at a cost of $115 and power relay at a cost of $180.

**Continuous dimming controls** address the shortcomings of multi-level switching, albeit at a higher cost. Equipment consists of a light level sensor, which supplies a low-voltage control signal to each electronic, dimmable ballast. The electronic controls within the ballast modulate light output in response to the signal from the sensor. Since the control wiring is independent of the power wiring, there is no need to reconfigure the power circuits in a retrofit project, although installation of the low-voltage control wiring is required. A dimming control module would cost around $150 per zone controlled. Typical size of a lighting zone is about 2,500 SF. Each zone would require a photocell sensor at a cost of $115. The dimming ballasts cost around $110 apiece. The cost of dimmable ballasts is significantly higher than non-dimmable electronic ballasts; however, some of the newer self-addressing dimmable ballasts are showing promise in driving down the market price.

Placement and orientation of the light sensor is of paramount importance in daylighting system design. Usually, the light sensor is located in the ceiling overhead (measuring light reflected off the work surface below, between the windows and the light fixtures to prevent artificial light from causing control feedback). Daylighting sensors

Skylights provide daylight in the cafeteria at Whitman Hanson Regional High School in Whitman, MA. "We have known for years that research has shown that natural light in classrooms improves teaching and learning. It also improves the attitudes of staff and students." – Dr. John F. McEwan, Superintendent of Schools, Whitman-Hanson

**Figure 7.5**

**Figure 7.6**
NREL researcher Paul Torcellini checks the accuracy of the daylighting sensor that controls artificial light at the Thermal Test Facility in Golden, Colorado. Notice that the electric light in the background is turned off in this daylit photo. *(Photo by Warren Gretz, courtesy of NREL.)*

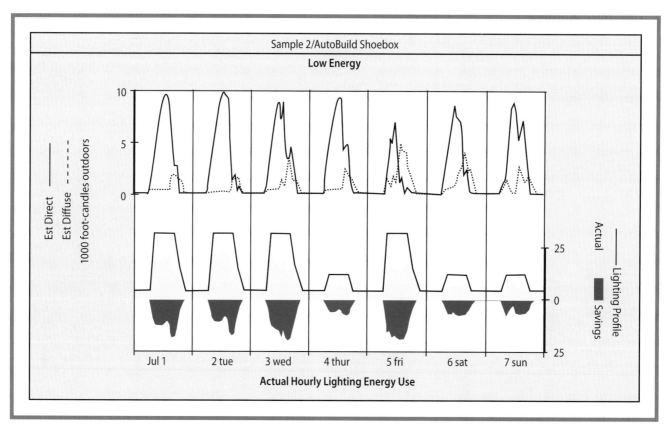

**Figure 7.7**
Savings due to daylighting in a small commercial building for the first week in July as calculated by the hourly simulation program Energy-10. *(Energy-10 graphic by Andy Walker.)*

can also be built into the switch plate, mounted on a vertical wall, providing an easy and inexpensive retrofit. The desired light level is selected by programming or dip switches on the sensor. Lower light level settings will result in higher energy and cost savings, since daylight will allow artificial light to be off for more hours of the year. (If necessary, task lights can augment daylight to provide the required light level on the work surface.)

## Daylighting Design Tools

Daylighting design is complicated by the fact that sunlight varies in both magnitude and position throughout the day and year. Handbooks

**Figure 7.8**
This photorealistic Radiance® simulation, at noon and at night, was done to evaluate daylighting and efficient electric lighting retrofit options for an historic office building in Washington D.C. Notice how the model correctly represents glare on the computer screen and reflection in the window glass. *(Model by Lawrence Berkeley National Laboratory, photo courtesy of NREL.)*

provide useful correlation of indoor to outdoor light levels for several common window and room geometries. Sophisticated computer programs, such as those listed below, have been developed to analyze daylighting and the effects on building systems.

- **DOE-2** takes window and room geometry, wall reflectivity, and sensor placement into account to calculate electric light savings and effects on heating and cooling load in an hourly simulation. *(See chapters 5 and 15 for more on DOE-2.)*

- **Energy-10** can automatically divide a small building into daylighting zones (north, south, east, west, and core) to calculate daylighting savings and effects on whole building energy use. *(See Chapter 15 for more on Energy-10.)*

- **Radiance®** is a ray-tracing program that displays light level contours and produces lifelike renderings. Radiance was developed by the U.S. Department of Energy and Lawrence Berkeley National Laboratory and is available from: **http://radsite.lbl.gov/radiance/ HOME.html**

Because photons of light are so much smaller than the physical dimensions of a building or even of a small model of a building, physical models are very useful in predicting light levels in a building. The model can be placed on a rotating and tilting platform to replicate the sun's angles at different times of day and year.

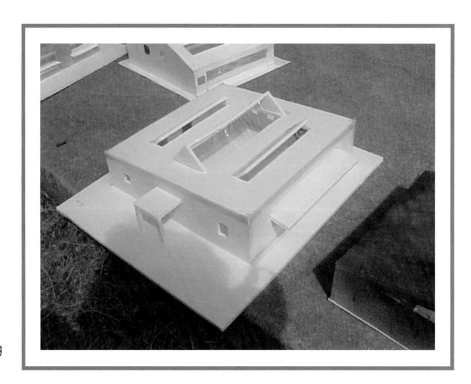

**Figure 7.9**
Models, such as these produced by students in the author's class at University of Colorado at Boulder, are useful for analyzing daylighting designs.

# Water Quality

Chapter 4 has addressed **water conservation** strategies such as low-flow plumbing fixtures, landscape considerations, and rainwater catchment systems. This section focuses on the health and comfort (taste, "feel") aspects of water. Even coming directly from a private well, water can be contaminated with chemicals and particulates that can be unhealthy, foul-tasting, or malodorous. The minerals in water can affect not only the taste of water, but can make it too "hard" to use effectively for bathing or washing, and can be harmful to HVAC equipment and piping. A healthy indoor environment should include clean water, appropriate to all purposes.

## Purification Systems

There are a variety of purification systems available to address water problems throughout the home or facility—for drinking, bathing/washing, and other purposes. Reverse osmosis filter systems are one option. Ultraviolet lamps may be incorporated to reduce contaminants by 90%, and biological hazards, such as anthrax, E. coli, Giardia, viruses, and salmonella, by up to 99.9%. These systems are capable of reducing compounds including chlorine, PCBs, VOCs, arsenic, copper, iron, cyanide, and lead, as well as filtering out particles and sediments. Shower head systems designed to remove chlorine are now available.

Major faucet manufacturers now offer "filtering faucets," a convenient advantage over bulky home filtration systems. Some of these devices have two separate channels, one with filtered water, the other unfiltered. Pressing a button selects the desired channel. The cost of these units depends on the features and available types of filters, some of which filter out chlorine, microorganisms such as Giardia, and lead.

### Carbon Absorption

This system is most often used for residential water treatment, as it is effective in removing the odor and unpleasant taste sometimes found in municipal water supplies. Carbon filters are not certified for removing VOCs, lead, coliform, or asbestos. Carbon systems use either granular activated carbon (which removes several chemicals, gases, and microorganisms) or solid block carbon (compressed carbon with binding medium). Potential problems with carbon systems include:

- **Bacteria growth** from accumulated impurities
- **Chemical recontamination** of water from filters saturated with impurities
- **Channeling,** or pathways that allow water to pass without proper filtering

Carbon block systems avoid the above problems by providing complete filtration of organic impurities (no channeling). These filters are available with a fine filtering mechanism to remove coliform and other bacteria, and pathogenic cysts such as Giardia, as well as lighter-weight

VOCs. Carbon block filter density does not permit bacteria growth. Carbon block filters, available in types to fit under the sink, on the faucet, or on the counter, need to be replaced more frequently than granular carbon filters.[6]

Typical water purification systems include a storage tank, special faucet, and filters, as well as the filtering mechanisms. Mechanisms include microfiltration, molecular (which captures broad spectrum adsorption), electrochemical separations, and ultraviolet light disinfection. Solar-powered systems are even available, used mostly for remote areas or emergency, power-outage situations. Larger systems can produce up to 1,000 gallons per day.

Maintaining water purification systems involves changing cartridges regularly (every 6–12 months for residential applications). The frequency depends on the area and water content.

## Healthy Use of Gray Water & Rainwater

Gray water is wastewater recycled from showers, baths, and laundry. *(See Chapter 4 for more on equipment and other considerations.)* Gray water can be used, especially in warm months of the year when it is most needed, to provide moisture for plants. Using gray water as part of a healthy, green approach can reduce water utility expenses significantly, while decreasing demand on local water supplies. Some precautions are necessary, however, since gray water is not disinfected and could contain contaminants.

Gray water systems must be clearly labeled and must not have any cross-connects to potable water systems. Gray water should never be consumed as drinking water, nor should it be sprayed on anything that might be eaten. Gray water should not be used in a manner that would allow it to run off of the property, or to puddle. Recycled water should only come from bathing, the bathroom sink, or clothes washing. Water used to flush toilets, clean soiled diapers, or used by someone with an infectious disease should never be reused. The same is true for water that has contacted meat or poultry. Laundry wastewater that contains chlorine bleach or phosphates should not be used to water plants. (Biodegradable soaps are recommended.) Ornamental plants and fruit and nut trees can be watered with gray water, but not the following plants:

- Vegetables and herbs
- Seedlings
- Potted plants
- Acid-loving plants, such as rhododendrons, azaleas, other evergreens, and begonias

Plants watered with gray water should be watered with clean water every other time to prevent any harmful build-up.

Landscape irrigation has been estimated to account for 40% of residential water consumption. While xeriscaping (use of native plants) is key to reducing landscape water demand, accumulated rainwater, in rain barrels or cisterns, is another resource- and money-saving approach that can help maintain the landscape. Chapter 4 includes a section on the equipment, and cost and design considerations for rainwater collection systems. Here we will address health and comfort issues.

## Benefits

Water collected from rooftop runoff is free. It contains no chlorine, calcium, or lime and generally has far fewer salts and sediments than city or most well water. Rainwater is not "hard," so it feels better and cleans more effectively, with less soap or detergent. Collected rainwater can be used for organic vegetable gardening and potted plants (indoors and out), and is especially healthy for tropical plants such as orchids, as compared to chlorinated city water. Rainwater is also good for washing vehicles and windows. Stored rainwater can be especially valuable in an emergency and in locations frequently hit by storms or drought.

## Precautions

In many areas of the country, and especially cities, collected rainwater should not be used as drinking water because of air pollution, which is slightly acidic and contains VOCs, lead, and petrochemicals. In an emergency, an appropriate filtration system could be used to make rainwater safer to drink. If rainwater in a particular location is deemed safe for drinking, it is still necessary to consider the roofing material to make sure no harmful contaminants are leaching from it. Many systems include a roof washer to dispose of the first water collected during a rain shower, as this will contain the most impurities, such as bird droppings, soot, and dirt. The rainwater must also be stored out of ultraviolet light to prevent growth of algae, and filtered to remove all debris.

It is important to provide barriers to mosquito infestation in the barrel or cistern by use of screens or plastic lids. Even with these barriers, there is a chance of mosquito eggs dropping into the receptacle from the gutters. Nontoxic water treatments can control this problem in an environmentally friendly way. Leaves and other forms of debris can also find their way into the rainwater collection barrel or cistern. Using a mesh or other gutter guard is helpful.

Other contaminants occurring in collected rainwater in some parts of the country can be identified through water testing. In some states, such as Hawaii, home test kits are available.

## Plumbing Fixtures

One health issue that may be associated with plumbing fixtures is the emission of lead, especially from porcelain bathtubs. Lead, which is typically associated more often with piping than fixtures, can be particularly harmful to infants and children. Lead testing kits are available. Re-glazing is an option to contain potential lead emission.[7]

# Noise Management

Noise inside a building can come from a variety of sources—outside road and air traffic; and inside—elevators, plumbing, and mechanical equipment, and copiers, phones, radios/computers, and conversations. A healthy, comfortable, and productive indoor environment should be as free as possible not only from the stress and distraction of loud, distracting noise. It should also provide appropriate speech privacy. There are several approaches to this goal which should be incorporated into the design of new construction or remodeled space.

## The Building Site

Preventing noise pollution starts with selecting an appropriate site for a facility. For example, you would not want to build a school or library next to an airport, major highway, factory, or railway. Part of the site selection process is investigation into plans that may be under way to build other types of potentially noisy facilities in the same area.

## Laying out Interior Spaces

If the building is adjacent to a noisy highway, interior spaces should be assigned based on their respective need for quiet. Spaces with noisy functions (such as mechanical and electrical equipment rooms, cafeterias, gyms, restrooms, and stairwells) and other areas where there is more tolerance to noise, should be closest to the side of the building where there is the most highway noise.

## Windows, Walls & Roofs

Proper selection of windows, wall insulation, and wall framing and materials is essential to reducing noise from outside. Some sound-insulating materials, such as acoustic ceiling tile and straw-bale construction, can offer the advantages of recycling or using natural materials as an added green benefit. Walls constructed with insulated concrete forms can reduce noise from outside the building. Green, or "living roofs," can absorb sound, in addition to their other benefits.

Hard versus absorbent surfaces also have a major impact on noise level inside a space, as do interior wall framing and insulating techniques. Acoustic or sound-absorption panels are effective in mitigating the noise in gathering spaces. A preferred design approach is to reduce the number of parallel surfaces, using more curved and angled walls to diminish the acoustic bounce and the noise.

## Noise from HVAC Systems

Proper design of air duct systems can further reduce noise transmission. For example, one of the main sources of noise from HVAC duct registers results from balancing dampers just inside, or behind the grille. If the dampers are substantially closed in order to balance the system, noise levels can rise by as much as 5–20 decibels above their ratings. If dampers are installed farther upstream in the supply duct, noise is reduced. Small diffusers and large air intakes also tend to create more noise. Insulating elbows can help reduce noise, although other issues may also need to be investigated, such as vibrating turning vanes or bars, rattling dampers, or imbalances in fans and other rotating equipment. Placement of furnace closets is crucial in building design, as some noise is unavoidable in the adjacent areas.

The key to ductwork noise control is velocity control, which is achieved by designing the ductwork to reduce velocity throughout the distribution system, while maintaining constant velocity and balanced air distribution. Most mechanical engineering firms understand this, as do many contractors. Again, it is a key factor that must not be overlooked.

A commissioning plan should include checking for problems when the system is installed. The building management staff can respond to problems such as vibration and eliminate them, but it is important to prevent them wherever possible in the initial installation.

Selection of the type of mechanical system can also affect noise. For example, scroll compressors are significantly noisier than centrifugal compressors in cooling systems.[8]

## Noise from Light Ballasts

Lighting designers must consider the electronic noise produced by numerous electronic fluorescent light ballasts, especially when combined with other electronic equipment. Harmonic mitigation is required when the installed kW of electronic components exceeds 10% of the total load. (Refer to **http://www.powerquality.net/problem.htm** for more detail.)

## Audio Masking (or Sound Conditioning) Systems

In existing facilities, audio masking systems offer one solution to noise attenuation. These devices provide electronically generated background sound at a certain level and frequency. They can reduce the distraction of intrusive noise, such as speech or equipment noise. These systems also increase speech privacy—which can not only boost productivity, but also security, by protecting against eavesdropping. Some systems provide protection from laser beams and other high-tech sound detection devices. ASTM defines three levels of speech privacy:

1. **Confidential privacy:** heard, but not understood

2. **Normal privacy:** sometimes heard and understood, but for the most part not intrusive

3. **Poor privacy:** all speech in the area can be heard and understood

Privacy is sometimes measured in terms of the Privacy Index (PI), based on the Articulation Index (AI). Audio masking systems can incorporate music and paging, and offer varying levels and types of masking. For example, *white noise* is thought to have more of a "hiss" sound, as compared to *pink noise*. Sound masking systems are typically wall- or shelf-mounted, but can also be installed above ceiling tiles in plenums with sound-masking speakers located at intervals (such as every 12–15 feet) in a large space.[9]

## Furniture & Furnishings

Furniture and furnishings appropriate for a green building should be comfortable, healthy, and environmentally friendly. The selection of products that meet these criteria is no longer confined to futons, yoga mats, candles, and incense burners. This ever-expanding market offers a wide array of interesting, comfortable furniture and fabrics for those with discerning tastes, environmental awareness, and chemical sensitivities.

Several furniture companies provide a range of products that support both the environment and healthy indoor air quality. The best of these produce furniture that contains no toxic chemicals such as formaldehyde and polyurethane, use FSC certified wood, and fabrics produced with safe vegetable dyes and tanning processes. The finishes used on environmentally friendly wood furniture are typically water-based or traditional oils and waxes, and are nontoxic.

Green furniture choices also include used furniture from flea markets and auctions and "new" pieces made from recycled materials. Some furniture is made from old wood from recycled barns, 80–100 years old, and from shipping pallets, which would otherwise be discarded in landfills. (It has been estimated that the amount of wood thrown away in pallets is equal to the quantity of framing lumber used annually in 300,000 average-size U.S. homes.) Another green choice in wood furniture is second-growth, rather than old-growth, wood, often oak or maple.

Other materials are being recycled into furniture as well. Some creative examples include Adirondack chairs made from skis and snowboards, and tables, chairs, and shelving made from bicycle parts.

The type of furniture and upholstery also affects thermal comfort. In general, un-upholstered wood or metal furniture is preferred in warm climates, and thick upholstery is favored in cold climates.

## Qualities to Look for in Furniture[10]

- Longevity/durability (well-made furniture, preferably from local materials that can be repaired)
- Safely biodegradable materials
- Certified woods
- Rapidly renewable materials such as agriboard
- Recycled materials, including plastics
- Organic fabrics
- Washable components
- Solid wood, rather than veneer, that can be refinished, if necessary
- Obtained locally to reduce transportation pollution

## What to Avoid[11]

- Tropical hardwoods
- Particle board containing urea or formaldehyde glue
- PVC, nylon, and other petroleum-based plastics
- Finishes with a high level of VOCs or other toxic chemicals, such as polyurethane
- Laminated and veneer finishes, which will eventually show wear and have to be replaced
- Plastic and foam
- Upholstered furniture that cannot be washed and therefore has a shortened life
- Bromines, formaldehyde, or halogens used for fireproofing
- Stain-resistant substances that contain formaldehyde, fluorocarbons, or PFOs (polymer, perfluorooctane sulfonate)

## Office Furniture & Furnishings
### Reused or Recycled

The EPA estimates that approximately three million tons of used office furniture are being discarded annually by U.S. businesses, much of it because of fabric wear, out-of-date appearance, or poor construction that rendered it irreparable. Fortunately, there are some good alternatives. Many organizations are saving 30%–50% over new furniture costs by purchasing refurbished or remanufactured furniture for a new look or purpose, or having their own used furniture reconditioned. Others are purchasing new furniture made from recycled content, including metal, PVC, pressboard, and fabrics. The cost of new furniture made of recycled content is similar to new, nonrecycled furniture.

The basic options for recycling or reuse are:

- **Reused:** as is, without improvements or repairs
- **Refurbished or remanufactured:** disassembled, with the parts cleaned and repaired or replaced, then reassembled
- **New, recycled content**

Green office furnishings include such items as reupholstered chairs, refinished tables, and office partitions made with cores of recycled cellulose, recycled aluminum frames, and upholstery from recycled soda bottles. Other office items, such as appointment books, briefcases, bulletin boards, and mouse pads, are available in recycled rubber and other materials. Energy-saving devices, such as solar PC chargers, are additional ecological choices for the office. Specifications for refurbished office furniture could include indoor air quality issues, such as not allowing materials that off-gas toxic fumes or that require use of toxic cleaning solvents. The specifications might also require availability of replacement parts and accessories.

## New Furniture & Furnishings

Office furniture was traditionally manufactured using processes that emitted volatile organic compounds (VOCs) from finishes, glues, and stains. The major suppliers have all developed lines of furniture that use sustainable wood and nontoxic, or at least less wasteful finishes, such as powder-based coatings.

The Greenguard Environmental Institute (GEI) has established performance-based standards for office furniture and furnishings, as well as building materials, electronic equipment, and cleaning, maintenance, and personal care products. Greenguard's focus is on products that have low chemical and particle emissions for use indoors. The standard involves certification relating to testing methods, allowable emissions levels, and other criteria. (*See Chapter 9 for more on GEI.*)

Green furniture vendors can be found through various sources including the U.S. General Services Administration, which publishes a vendor list. TerraChoice, the Canadian eco-rating organization, has an office furniture guide (**www.environmentalchoice.com**). GreenBiz offers "Recycled Office Furniture: Good for the Environment, Good for Business" (**www.greenbiz.com**).

## Flooring & Wall Finishes

Ecological flooring options include reclaimed American antique hardwood, bamboo, linoleum, and ceramic tiles made with recycled glass. There are natural wall covering materials available, and while most adhesives contain harmful chemicals, healthy living websites and publications feature "recipes" for natural, nontoxic adhesives.[12]

Paints should be low- or no-VOC. Milk paint, also known as casein, has been found in many historic buildings, and was popular in the first half of the 20th century and until today in the paper industry and for painting theater scenery. Milk paint is gaining popularity again now as a natural coating. The original milk paint used the protein found in milk as a binder, with oil or other additives to increase durability.[13]

## Carpeting, Rugs & Mattresses

### Carpet

There are several green factors to consider when selecting carpet, including use of recycled materials, reduction of waste, and others. Chapters 2 and 11 explore these considerations. Here, we'll focus on comfort and health.

Epidemiologists have discovered a connection between asthma and exposure to wall-to-wall carpeting. Carpet made of wool is a safer, natural choice, along with area rugs made from wool, or braided hemp or cotton scraps, which can be removed for cleaning and airing.

Since 1992, the Carpet and Rug Institute (CRI) has administered the "Green Label" IAQ testing and labeling program for carpet, adhesives, and cushion materials. The purpose is to be able to identify low-emitting products that meet established standards for good indoor air quality.

### Mattresses

Healthy mattresses are made with wool, pure latex, and organic cotton without chemical sizing or fabric softeners, and without metal, virgin paper cardboard cording, or mechanically tufted batting. Cotton mattress materials are often recommended for people with back and joint problems or chemical sensitivities. Some crib-size waterproof mattress covers made from polyvinyl chloride covered with cotton and/or polyester layers, or polyolefin, have been shown to emit toxic fumes. Wool offers several advantages as a mattress material:

- Absorbs and releases moisture
- Is naturally resistant to fire, mold, and dust mites
- Is resilient

Organic wool is recommended to avoid pesticides commonly used as a pesticide-control dip for sheep. Organic cotton is a better choice than standard cotton because no pesticides are used in its production. Fire-retardance, required by federal law for mattresses, can be achieved with boric acid, which is nontoxic and releases no vapors.

Standard mattresses can be enclosed in a barrier cloth made of tightly woven cotton to prevent dust mites.

Pillows are available in organic cotton and wool. Sheets, towels, shower curtains, and table linens are also available in organic cotton.

## Green Cleaning & Maintenance

A healthy indoor environment also requires use of nontoxic cleaning and personal care products. The availability of these items is widespread and growing. The Greenguard Institute is one organization that offers standards for these products. (*See Chapter 9 for more on Greenguard.*) Some traditional substances used for cleaning have been proven unhealthy: for example, ammonia is corrosive, poisonous, and irritating to eyes, lungs, and nose and produces lethal gases when combined with bleach. In addition, ammonia is explosive when exposed to flames.

Natural substances such as vinegar, can be used for cleaning, and others such as essential oils, tannic acid powder, and boric acid can be effective in neutralizing allergens in dust mites and pet dander, and repelling insects and rodents.

There are *key words* used on product labels to define the risk to people and the environment. Being familiar with this terminology is important to selecting healthy products. Four key terms are:

1. **Poison/Danger:** highly toxic—a few drops could be fatal.

2. **Warning:** toxic—a teaspoonful could be fatal.

3. **Caution:** somewhat less toxic—two tablespoons to a cup could be fatal.

4. **Strong Sensitizer:** could cause allergic reactions.

According to The Environmental Research Foundation, the *most dangerous substances* that should be avoided are:[14]

- Pesticides
- Toxic gases, including chlorine and ammonia
- Heavy metals, such as lead and mercury
- VOCs, such as formaldehyde

## Conclusion

The holistic theme that permeates green building projects is evident in the indoor environment, where many different components must interact to create healthy and comfortable air, water, lighting, and furnishings, as well as quiet surroundings where people can concentrate and feel comfortable learning or working. The interior space is where building owners and users are likely to spend the most time experiencing the long-term benefits of thoughtful, ecological design—and to enjoy an awareness that they are saving natural resources while taking care of their health.

1. "Morbidity and Mortality Weekly Report," 10 March 1999. http://www.cdc.gov/mmwr/preview/mmwrhtml/mm4909a3.htm

2. The Environmental Protection Agency's Integrated Risk Information System profile, http://www.epa.gov/iris/subst/0419.htm

3. *The Green Guide,* The Green Guide Institute.

4. http://www.snipsmag.com

5. Berman, Alan. *Your Naturally Healthy Home.* Rodale Press, 2001.

6. Schaeffer, John, ed. *Real Goods Solar Living Source Book: The Complete Guide to Renewable Energy Technologies & Sustainable Living, 9th Edition.* Real Goods, 1996.

7. http://www.leadcheck.com

8. http://www.snipsmag.com/CDA/ArticleInformation/features/BNP_Features_Item/0,3374

9. http://www.armstrong.com/commceilingsna/

10. http://www.care2.com and http://www.valuecreatedreview.com/news60.htm

11. Ibid.

12. Ibid. also Berge, Bjorn. *The Ecology of Building Materials.* Architectual Press, 2001.

13. Swanke Hayden Connell Architects. *Historic Preservation: Project Planning & Estimating.* RSMeans, 2000.

14. *Toxic Turnaround.* The Environmental Research Foundation.

# Part

# 2 Designing, Specifying & Commissioning the Green Building

# Chapter

## 8 The Green Design Process & Associated Costs

*Andy Walker, PhD, PE*

An integrated design process is important in green design, and cooperation among disciplines is critical to meet sustainability goals. New methods and software tools have been introduced to facilitate teamwork and cooperation. Adding green measures as an afterthought necessarily costs more. Conversely, integration of green features early in the process can minimize cost. In an integrated design process, the full team has input into the building's conceptual or schematic design, and decisions are made based on their impact on the whole building. On many conventional projects, the architect hands an already evolved building design to the mechanical engineer, who sizes a mechanical system to meet the peak load. By that time, decisions regarding building orientation, massing, and fenestration—all of which affect energy use—have already been made. This late in the process, there is limited or no opportunity to optimize the building as a system. The mechanical engineer can only optimize the HVAC subsystem, which is usually the task. Similarly, in order to have proper daylighting, the lighting designer would have to be consulted even as early as the building is being laid out on the site.

Everyone involved in a building project may wish to coordinate closely at the outset, but the way competitive design fees are conventionally structured and procured, there is no financial incentive to participate in meetings and correspondence, evaluate alternatives, and reach a true consensus. A 2004 report by NIST estimated the costs of inadequate interoperability to U.S. industry at $2.6 billion in the design phase, $4.1 billion in construction, and $9.1 billion in operating and maintenance.[1]

## Technology & Information Sharing

```
<xsd:element name="Material">
<xsd:complexType>
<xsd:element ref="Name"
    minOccurs="0" />
<xsd:element ref="Description"
    minOccurs="0" />
<xsd:element ref="R-value"
    minOccurs="0" />
<xsd:element ref="Thickness"
    minOccurs="0" />
<xsd:element ref="Conductivity"
    minOccurs="0" />
<xsd:element ref="Density"
    minOccurs="0" />
<xsd:element ref="SpecificHeat"
    minOccurs="0" />
<xsd:element ref="Permeance"
    minOccurs="0" />
<xsd:element ref="Porosity"
    minOccurs="0" />
<xsd:element ref="RecycledContent"
    minOccurs="0" />
<xsd:element ref="Cost"
    minOccurs="0" />
</xsd:complexType>
</xsd:element>
```

**Figure 8.1**

The value of the team's time spent coordinating early in the design process is likely to be returned several times over in lower construction and operating costs. Several trends promise better design integration. Powerful new communication technologies enable design team members in different locations to share information, analyze data, and generate results efficiently. Many design and construction professionals are also making maximum use of collaborative websites to share drawings and coordinate schedules. Finally, efforts are under way by industry and national laboratories to integrate computer-aided design drawings, energy analysis computer programs, cost estimating procedures, and all processes where information is shared. *(See Chapter 15 for more on computer programs for energy analysis.)*

The term "building energy model" describes this integration of design information. The difference between a model and a drawing is that anyone can take the model and look at it from the perspective of their discipline. For example, a length of beam might be tagged with its modulus of elasticity for the structural engineer, its thermal conductivity for the energy engineer, its recycled content for the sustainability consultant, and so forth. If the length of the beam is changed during design, this change is instantly made available to all disciplines. A standard proposed to link the information is the use of extensible markup language (XML), which uses "tags" and has proven itself useful in all aspects of internet business. For more information, contact the International Institute for Interoperability at the National Institute of Building Sciences (**http://www.iai-na.org**).

Figure 8.1 shows lines are from Green Building XML schema (key to the information's format found at **http://www.gbxml.org/schema/ 0-34/GreenBuildingXML.xsd**). Notice how any information of interest could be identified by "tags" and associated with any material, and thus available to all design disciplines.

## Team Building & Goal Setting

There is no single design process that is "green" and another that is "not green." Rather, there is continuous improvement in processes that results in better and better buildings. Key to the process is abandoning the habit of replicating what worked last time, and instead continuously evaluating new products and methods to seek improvement. Team members must have a common interpretation of what constitutes improvement. Defining measurements and setting goals are important aspects of team building.

Sustainability goals require a clear definition and criteria that can be used to determine whether or not the design team has succeeded in meeting the goal. Sustainability ratings provide a convenient means to do this. For example, the building program might set the goal of a Silver

LEED® rating. Several sustainability rating criteria exist including: LEED (Leadership in Energy and Environmental Design), Green Globes, ENERGY STAR®, ISO 14000, ISO 14001 Environmental Management Standard – International Standard Organization, and others. These are described in Chapter 9, "Rating Systems, Standards, & Guidelines."

## Cost of a LEED® Rating

As this book goes to press, the U.S. Green Building Council charges a fee of at least $900 for registration, $2,000 for design review, and $500 for construction review. The fee for larger buildings is as high as $0.45/SF. In a study for the General Services Administration, Steven Winter Associates Inc. estimated "soft costs" to obtain a LEED rating for new courthouses and office building major renovations. (Soft costs refer to professional services for all aspects of design and documentation, other than hardware and installation labor.) For new courthouses, for example, the cost to take a project through the LEED-certified level is $0.41 to $0.46/SF; for Silver, it's $0.41 to $0.55/SF; and for gold, $0.61 to $0.81/SF if the LEED expert is a consultant hired from outside the design team. If the design team prepares the LEED rating, the cost is $0.43 to $0.45/SF for Certified, $0.44 to $0.54/SF for Silver; and $0.56 to $0.73/SF for Gold. For major renovations of office buildings, the values are $0.41/SF for Certified, $0.44 to $0.49/SF for Silver, and $0.69 to $0.70/SF for Gold for outside consultants. If the design team does it themselves, the cost is $0.35/SF for Certified, $0.36 to $0.44/SF for Silver, and $0.58 to $0.59/SF for Gold.

## The Design Team

Every project involves an **owner** or a developer with legal power to improve the property. The **architect** ascertains the owner's requirements, creates the building design, and administers the construction contract, and thus is the key determinant of the sustainability of the resulting building. The **landscape architect** affects sustainability of the grounds themselves, including water and chemical requirements (insecticide, fertilizer, and so forth), but may also impact energy use by siting and planting to provide shade and/or wind breaks.

The **structural engineer** integrates a variety of design requirements, including window openings, the storage of heat in mass, and the need to withstand physical forces. The **civil engineer** decides issues of site sustainability, in the sense that issues such as reduction of surface water runoff are addressed by this member of the team. The **mechanical engineer** calculates energy use and thus informs all the other team members of the life cycle energy use implications of design decisions. In addition to designing an efficient system, the **electrical engineer** may have an opportunity to integrate use of innovative sources of power, such as co-generation or solar energy. The **plumbing engineer** can save resources initially, with fixture and pipe layouts and material selection, but also over the building life cycle by specifying low-flow fixtures and minimizing pumping power.

If consulted early in the process, the **interior designer** has an opportunity to specify recycled and recyclable furniture, furnishings, and fixtures, as well as appropriate colors and reflectivity, which allow a lower lighting level, and furniture upholstery options that are durable and comfortable over a wider range of temperatures.

The **lighting designer** makes decisions critical to both the occupants' well-being and life cycle energy use. Recommendations of an **HVAC consultant** might include right-sizing the system or using innovative methods, such as displacement ventilation or solar or geothermal heat, that can save energy and improve indoor environmental quality. An **environmental building consultant** would make recommendations regarding the impact of building materials as they are produced, and the waste they generate in the construction process and over their product life cycle. A **waste management consultant** might have ideas on how to minimize construction waste and also how to enhance the facility's recycling capacity over its life.

The **contractor** and the trades should be consulted early, not only to ensure the constructability of the design, but also because the trades are often the best source of ideas for innovative improvements. The **commissioning agent** should be involved from the pre-design phase, beginning with the end in mind. *(See Chapter 12 for more on commissioning.)*

It is tempting to map out a process with each professional pigeonholed into his or her discreet discipline, but this approach would be disastrous to the sustainability of the result. With a team approach, the structural engineer would be responsible for ensuring that the structural members did not interfere with the distribution of daylight, and the landscape architect's job would include consideration of the effects of plantings on summer solar heat gain inside west rooms. Integration of these otherwise disparate activities requires more than communication. It requires that sustainability goals established in early program documents be shared across the team, and that the tasks required to integrate with the work of others be included in the contract documents.

## Teamwork in the Design Process

Teamwork is collaboration and cooperation, and the priority of a shared goal. Team members work together better if they are all involved in setting the project goals early in the design process. Deliberate and planned efforts to communicate at each step help to ensure success in green design.

Pre-design planning includes **project identification**, a **feasibility study**, and **programming**. The healthier environment and lower operating cost of a green building are key features in a marketing plan, and would enhance the feasibility of a project by commanding higher rates and higher occupancy. Some nonprofit organizations have discovered that donors are much more enthusiastic about supporting a project with superlative goals than a business-as-usual building. Environmental compliance, once seen as a barrier, now presents opportunities for green-minded designers, whether the project is a redevelopment of a brownfield or using solar energy to avoid running a new power line over pristine land.

Subsequent activities include the procurement of architectural and engineering services including preliminary or **schematic design, design development**, and **construction document preparation**. The **Statement of Work** describing these services must include the additional work required to arrive at an exemplary design, such as:

- More specific research of the client's needs and the most effective way to meet them
- Detailed energy modeling
- Life cycle analysis
- Evaluation of alternative systems and materials
- Development of documentation related to sustainability rating criteria

The design process also involves complying with the National Historic Preservation Act and the National Environmental Policy Act. These processes, which involve people with diverse interests, must remain collaborative rather than confrontational to avoid impeding project implementation. Green design strategies may assuage the community's concern with pollution, noise, or inappropriate development. Measures that may be required to mitigate such impacts can be real assets to a green project. A good example is preservation of wetlands adjacent to a project.

| Design Fees | Conventional Building | Green Building |
|---|---|---|
| Architectural | 3.1% to 11% | 3.1% to 16% |
| Structural | 1.0% to 2.5% | 1.0% to 3.5% |
| Mechanical | 0.4% to 1.3% | 0.6% to 2.6% |
| Electrical | 0.2% to 0.5% | 0.2% to 0.5% |
| Landscape Architect | 0.1% to 0.3% | 0.1% to 1.3% |
| Construction Manager | 2.5% to 10% | 3.5% to 15% |
| LEED® Process | 0% | 0.25% to 0.5% |

**Figure 8.2**

Schematic design, design development, construction documents, bidding and negotiation with contractors, and construction contract administration are considered the architect's basic services.[2] A suite of comprehensive services would also include project analysis, feasibility studies, programming, land-use studies, analysis of financing options, attending or facilitating meetings to set goals and monitor progress, management of construction, energy analysis, surveys of the sustainability attributes of various materials, or other special consulting services.

## The Building Program

The building program is a document conveying the conditions and requirements of a project. Along with specifying the number of square feet of different types of space (office, assembly, laboratory, etc.) and the need to meet code requirements, the program should state clear and quantitative sustainability performance goals. For example, the building program may specify a desired LEED level (Silver, Gold, Platinum), or it may specify a maximum dollar amount per square foot per year operating cost. Other goals frequently described in the program relate to achievement of a project that is beautiful, safe, reliable, or comfortable, or that provides superior air and light quality.

Some organizations, such as federal agencies, have developed their own architectural guidelines regarding sustainability that would be referred to in the building program. The building program would also document the energy-related needs of users—a critical first step in designing systems to meet those needs efficiently, and an indicator of the suitability of various renewable energy sources.

Goal-setting should be considered a team activity. Team members must proceed with a keen awareness of, and commitment to, project goals. This is much more likely to happen if they have a sense of control by sharing in setting goals and also in determining how success will be measured. If a goal is stated very generally, as "to minimize life cycle cost through sustainable design principles," it would be difficult to judge whether it was met in the end. This is why a more quantitative goal could be more useful.

Energy performance goals can be set with different objectives. Annual energy use per gross square foot (BTU/SF/year) is a common metric among federal projects because that is the way progress toward statutory goals is tracked.[3] Shortcomings of BTU/SF/year as a measurement standard are that BTUs supplied by different fuels have different costs, and there is no differentiation between time-of-use or demand rates.

Another option is to specify an energy use goal as a certain percentage less than that required by code. For example, a goal might be to use

25% less energy than allowed by 10CFR434/435 for federal projects, ASHRAE 90.1 for commercial buildings, or the California Title 24 energy efficiency standards. A useful metric is annual operating costs ($/year), which accounts for costs of different fuels and time-of-use and demand savings, and integrates well as a figure of merit with all other annual costs, such as operation, maintenance, water, and disposal.

It is important to use the same yardstick to measure performance as was used to set the goal in the first place. Disputes often arise when goals set using a computer model are compared to actual utility bills. There are many variables, including schedules, occupancy, and plug loads, that affect energy use after a building is occupied. These are outside of the designer's control. Although the performance of the building will ultimately be evaluated by measuring the actual resource use (such as utility bills) of the completed building, the performance of the design team should be evaluated by simulating the final design with the same computer program and uncontrolled parameters (weather file, utility rates, occupancy, schedules, plug loads) that were used to set the goal.

How are the energy goals set before anyone knows what the building looks like? One approach is to model a default building in the shape of a shoebox with the same floor area and number of floors, the same occupancy schedules, and the same kinds of space (office, circulation, kitchen, meeting rooms, storage, etc.) as called for in the building program. First, a **reference case** is defined to serve as a benchmark with which the performance of the evolving design will be compared. For the reference case shoebox model, the properties of walls, roofs, windows, and mechanical systems are the minimum required by applicable codes. The annual energy performance of the reference case shoebox model is evaluated using climate data and utility rates for the site. Then a suite of energy-efficiency measures is modeled using the shoebox to determine which strategies are most effective. For example, if evaporative cooling is effective on the shoebox model, it is likely to be effective for the actual design. Measures are evaluated in combination with each other to account for interactions.

The shoebox model with the most cost-effective package of measures implemented provides an estimate of what should be achievable in the design, but the goal is usually set above this level. For example, a reference case might be 100 KBTU/SF/year, the shoebox with all ideal cost-effective measures implemented might be 30 KBTU/SF/year, and the actual goal for the project might be set at 40 KBTU/SF/year, a reasonable goal for the design team. The Energy-10 computer program has been developed especially to implement this pre-design analysis and to aid in setting energy-use goals.[4] *(See Chapter 15 for more on Energy-10 and other design programs.)*

## Design Team Selection Criteria

Selection of capable, enthusiastic individuals to be on the design team is perhaps the most important step in green design. The right team will always strive for success; inclusion of disinterested people is a formula for failure. A good proposal:

- States commitment to superior performance.
- Includes a team that demonstrates capability to respond to sustainability and energy targets set in program documents.
- Includes a team that responds to sustainability rating and energy analysis results with an effective combination of communication and decision-making authority.
- Includes an energy/sustainability expert on the design team.
- Demonstrates familiarity with new materials and energy technology and familiarity with analysis tools (such as Energy-10 or DOE-2).
- Demonstrates proficiency with sustainability rating criteria (for example, includes a LEED®-accredited professional).
- Demonstrates understanding of code requirements.
- Cites completed (and measured) successful projects. Advanced degrees and qualifications are good, but there is no substitute for an established track record of projects recognized as successful advancements in green design.

## Design Team Statement of Work

To continuously improve sustainability, the design team must research new technology and rank many alternatives, as well as employ sophisticated methods of evaluating performance. These additional tasks must be included in the scope of work to ensure that they get done, and that the designer has enough hours budgeted for the additional analysis and design team meetings.

The **performance goals** from the building program should be written by the architect and owner or consultant into the statement of work for all

| Example - LEED Consulting Costs for a 100,000 SF Building | | | |
|---|---|---|---|
| Task | Fee | Cost/SF | % of Fee |
| Charrette/Preliminary Assesment | $ 5,000 | $ 0.05 | 16% |
| Evaluation of Credits | $ 7,000 | $ 0.07 | 22% |
| Documentation and Submissions | $ 17,000 | $ 0.17 | 53% |
| Specification Review | $ 2,000 | $ 0.02 | 6% |
| Misc | $ 1,000 | $ 0.01 | 3% |
| TOTAL | $ 32,000 | $ 0.32 | 100% |

**Figure 8.3**

subsequent architectural and engineering services. This establishes the contractual obligation to create a sustainable project and also creates a mutual understanding between parties of what that means in terms of specific tasks. The statement of work should involve the mechanical engineer and lighting designer as early as possible in the design process.

Green design can take 40%–100% more effort on the part of the mechanical engineer or energy analyst over the work required to simply size the mechanical system. The mechanical engineer would use the shoebox model analysis to investigate various mechanical system strategies early in the design, and then maintain an ongoing energy analysis of the evolving design in order to continuously inform designers of the energy use and cost implications of design decisions.

**Energy modeling** with hourly computer simulation programs is essential for green design, but energy modeling is a specialized field, and the programs are very detailed. Someday, computer-aided design software will link directly to an energy analysis program. In the meantime, the task of doing **takeoffs** (reading dimensions off plans and entering them into the energy program) falls on the mechanical engineer. The energy analysis requires several iterations to analyze multiple design alternatives, including:

- Building envelope and orientation
- Size and type of HVAC plant
- Type of distribution system
- Control set points
- Daylighting apertures and control
- Efficient lighting
- Renewable energy supplies

Time must be budgeted to conduct regular meetings of the project designers to communicate energy use and cost implications and recommend alternatives. The task of investigating utility rates and programs should be included and should integrate with the hourly computer simulation. The statement of work for the energy analyst should include assistance with compiling the building commissioning handbook.

Whole-building analysis is needed to account for interactions between systems. Exploiting these interactions is a key strategy in green building design. For example, energy-efficient lighting reduces the heat gain from lights, resulting in a smaller chiller and significantly less energy required for cooling. On the other hand, competing measures suffer from the fact that the same kWh cannot be counted twice. For example, a daylight sensor, which turns off the electric lights in a room whenever ample daylight is coming in the window, will not save anything if an occupancy sensor has already turned the light off because nobody is in the room. Most interactions are well represented by hourly simulation computer programs such as DOE-2, Energy-10, and Blast. These programs are based on first principles (laws of physics), rather than correlation, enabling them to evaluate an infinite variety of design configurations. The hourly simulation consists of an equation balancing energy in and out of each and every building component, and these equations are solved simultaneously for each of the 8,760 hours of a typical year. Solving the system of equations at each hour accounts for interaction between envelope, heating, cooling, and lighting systems, as well as solar heat gain, heat gain from occupants in the space, and any other energy flows specified by the user.

During pre-design, the energy analyst develops the code-compliant reference case, identifies and evaluates energy efficiency and renewable energy strategies, and sets performance goals based on a case with all

**Figure 8.4**
The performance goal for a new courthouse in Miami was set by GSA at 550 mega joule/gross square meter/yr (48k BTU/SF/yr), or 21% less than an ASHRAE 90.1 prototype building, whichever is less. (Rendering by ARQ/HOK, courtesy of General Services Administration.)

effective strategies implemented. During preliminary design, the task is to evaluate schemes and the sensitivity of results to variable inputs, such as utility rates, and then select strategies for further development. Schematic design will determine rough sizes of components (such as array, batteries, and inverter for a photovoltaic system). During design development, the analyst assists with determining precise sizes and complete descriptions of the designs, and will have the most input before the design is 35% complete. By the time it is 90% complete, the role of the analyst has been reduced to confirming that performance goals have been met.

## Costs of Energy Modeling

The cost of energy modeling varies depending on the size and complexity of the building and its mechanical distribution systems and central plant. A reasonable expectation of cost can be estimated by multiplying the square footage of the building by $0.15/SF for large or simple buildings to $0.30/SF for small or complicated buildings, but typically not less than $5,000 per project.

While far from business-as-usual, several projects have piloted the concept of basing the professional fees on the level of performance as designed. Performance-based fees reward the effort of minimizing the project's life cycle cost and reward the designer for not over-sizing equipment. The elements of a performance-based fee include:

- A clear goal, along with a specification, of how performance relative to that goal is to be measured

> [The process]…should build on performance-based fees—providing a better understanding of the most effective allocation of fees to different phases of the design process.
> — Greg Kats,[6] California Sustainable Building Task Force Report

- A schedule showing how the fee relates to success in meeting the goal
- A method of evaluating the design
- A protocol for resolving disputes without expensive litigation

To mitigate the risk of this new approach, some projects have retained a minimum fee, and based a special incentive fee on the documented performance of the design.[5] Several efforts to develop performance-based fee contracts have been scuttled by contracting officers or legal advisors unfamiliar with the technology required to evaluate performance. It is essential to involve legal counsel in the very earliest stages of contract development.

# Schematic/ Preliminary Design

In this phase, the team prepares schematic design studies showing the scale and relationship of the project components. Submittals include drawings, specifications, and a cost estimate. This package provides the owner with a description of the design for review and approval and addresses both the project requirements and cost. Clearly, any suitable sustainability measure must be included in the schematic design, because subsequent phases only develop these concepts and rarely add new ones.

The schematic design submittal should include the size of major energy system components and how strategies interact. In addition to floor plans, elevations, and type and size of mechanical system components, the following information should be included:

- **Building Plan:** Building dimensions and layout accommodating green building design strategies. For example, a double-loaded corridor often suits daylighting and natural ventilation. The design team would consider any strategies that affect the shape of the building (open or private offices, perimeter circulation spaces, orientation, earth protection, articulated or compact plan, atrium, and sunspaces, to name a few).

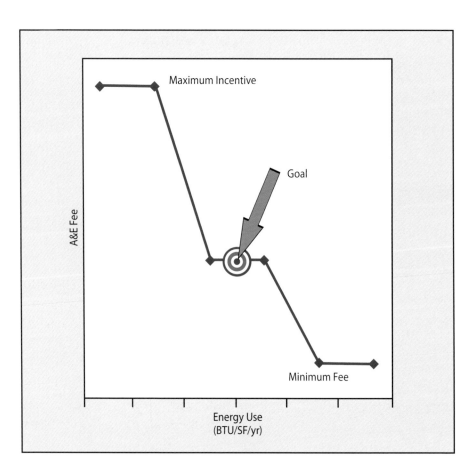

**Figure 8.5**
A performance-based fee might include a minimum fee plus an incentive up to a budgeted maximum.

- **Daylighting:** Size, number, and position of apertures (windows or roof monitors); relative dimensions of shading overhangs and light shelves; type of control (switching or dimming); number and locations of light sensors; and requirements for room surface finishes and window glazing.
- **Passive Solar Heating:** Window areas and glazing properties, amount of thermal storage material and relative position of glazing and mass, optimal levels of envelope insulation, size and relative position of shading, and overheat protection.
- **Natural Ventilation:** Size and relative position of apertures (operable windows or vents), controls, and interface requirements for HVAC system.
- **Solar Energy Systems:** System type, solar collector area and orientation, amount of storage (water tank for solar hot water or batteries for photovoltaics), size of heat exchangers and pumps, controls, and power conditioning equipment.

For each energy savings measure, and for the optimal combination of measures, the schematic design should include estimates of energy use and operating cost, along with probable construction costs. This information informs decisions of features that should be included in the schematic design based on life cycle cost effectiveness. Concepts included in the schematic design proceed to design development.

The energy analysis would include an hourly simulation to evaluate different schematic designs and the interaction between measures. Measures can be considered independently (single measure included). Elimination parametrics can also be used (single measure excluded) to evaluate the impact of a measure on the building as a whole system. The analyst can then rank strategies based on their performance and life cycle cost.[7] The objective is to select systems for design development. As the design develops, it will be too late to add new strategies or technologies. Thus, it is important that complete information for decision-making, such as a design charrette or advice of consultants, be sought prior to completion of the schematic design.

## Design Charrette

A design charrette is an intense effort to complete a design in a short period of time. Charrette participants first listen in order to understand the goals, needs, and limitations of a project, and then envision creative, but realistic solutions. Charrettes often consist of plenary sessions and specific break-out sessions. The break-out sessions might treat topics such as lighting, mechanical systems, material use, water and wastewater, site and landscape, or other specific areas of interest to charrette participants. During plenary sessions, participants deliberately expose and exploit interactions between topics discussed in the break-out sessions, and bring discussion back to a whole-building perspective.

It is important to record ideas as they are mentioned, and to express these ideas effectively in a charrette report. An independent recorder helps to ensure that the record includes not only the views of the most vocal, or of the facilitator, but every concept, no matter how timidly presented. The work of volunteer scribes rarely measures up to that of a professional recorder. The report will carry the ideas generated at the charrette forward into the design process.

Since each aspect of the design affects all other aspects, and thus whole-building performance, it is best to involve a wide range of stakeholders in a charrette. Often, charrette topics do not end at the building walls. In addition to the owner and representatives of all disciplines and firms on the design team, a charrette may include electric, gas, and water utilities; surrounding community associations; water quality and air quality management districts; industrial partners and technology experts; financial institutions; and environmental organizations.

## *Charrette Costs:*

Experience with 14 charrettes conducted by the U.S. DOE Federal Energy Management program indicates that total charrette costs are typically between $25,000 and $40,000, as described by the following:

- LEED® facilitator: $5,000
- Report editor: $5,000

**Figure 8.6**
Design Charrette

- Professional recorder: $3,000
- Expert facilitiator for each break-out group: $3,000 (often 3–5 break-out groups depending on topics)
- Copying charrette materials and reports: $500

## Team Decision-Making

Disagreements between team members are inevitable, and are perhaps most acute in the schematic design phase. A structured approach to decision-making anticipates disagreement and enhances communication by stimulating team dialogue before competing options are identified, or before any team member falls in love with any design option.

Any decision-making process must evaluate priorities and goals. Sometimes, the team revises its initial goals in the schematic design

**Figure 8.7**
Sample criteria and weights for project design

| Criteria | Default Weight | Sub-Criteria | Default Sub-Weight |
|---|---|---|---|
| **Life-cycle cost** | 1/6 | Construction cost | 0.68 |
| | | Annual operation cost | 19.4 |
| | | Annual maintenance cost | 19.4 |
| **Resource use** | 1/6 | Annual electricity, $kWh/m^2$ | 3 |
| | | Annual fuels, $kWh/m^2$ (of heat equivalent) | 1 |
| | | Annual water, $kg/m^2$ | 0.15 |
| | | Construction materials, $kg/m^2$ | 0.03 |
| | | Land, $m^2/m^2$ | 300 |
| **Environmental** | 1/6 | $CO_2$ emissions from construction, $kg/m^2$ | 1 |
| | | $SO_2$ emissions from construction, $kg/m^2$ | 90 |
| | | $NO_x$ emissions from construction, $kg/m^2$ | 45 |
| | | Annual $CO_2$ emissions from operation, $kg/m^2$ | 30 |
| | | Annual $SO_2$ emissions from operation, $kg/m^2$ | 3000 |
| | | Annual $NO_x$ emissions from operation, $kg/m^2$ | 1500 |
| **Architectural quality** | 1/6 | Identity | 0.25 |
| | | Scale/proportion | 0.25 |
| | | Integrity/coherence | 0.25 |
| | | Integration in urban context | 0.25 |
| **Indoor quality** | 1/6 | Air quality | 0.35 |
| | | Lighting quality | 0.25 |
| | | Thermal quality | 0.20 |
| | | Acoustic quality | 0.20 |
| **Functionality** | 1/6 | Functionality | 0.45 |
| | | Flexibility | 0.15 |
| | | Maintainability | 0.25 |
| | | Public relations value | 0.15 |

phase. The dialogue about priorities should be kept alive throughout the design process. An effective decision-making process unites the team's focus and direction and fosters an awareness of effects on the building system as a whole, rather than just the subsystem (such as lighting or mechanical) that most concerns an individual team member. To evaluate the implications of a design option on whole-building performance, the team can establish a weighting system in order to evaluate dissimilar criteria, including cost, environmental impacts, noise, functionality, and resource use. One approach would be to convert all criteria to present-value dollars. Many costs, such as construction costs, are already in present-value dollars. Methods to convert life cycle operating costs to present value are well established. Several efforts in Europe and the U.S. have attempted to assign dollar values to emissions such as $CO_2$ and $SO_2$ based on the impacts to public health, but assigning dollar values to intangible attributes, such as architectural quality, has little precedent. Still, a design team may agree on an approach to do so, perhaps based on projected rental rates.

Documenting the decision-making process is important in order to maintain the awareness of how the design got to where it is and also to inform the owner or new team members, thus avoiding a need to revisit decisions that have been made. The dual needs of weighting criteria and documentation can be satisfied by setting up a bookkeeping system for priorities, numerical values of various weighting criteria, and a convenient format for reporting the rationale of design decisions.

The LEED® rating criteria offers a method to quantify green building design measures, and may be useful as a system of weighting criteria for a team.

## Design Development

During design development, drawings and documents are developed to describe the entire project in detail. Drawings and specifications describe the architectural, structural, mechanical, electrical, materials, and site plan of the project. During design development, the team arrives at sustainability strategies and systems based on the brainstorming and selection that took place in the schematic design phase of the project. The energy analyst performs a more detailed analysis, including cost and performance trade-offs between alternative systems. The architect, mechanical engineer, and electrical engineer work together to place renewable energy sources (solar water heating, solar ventilation preheating, photovoltaics) in such a way that they do not look like afterthought add-ons. Mechanical system options (thermal storage, economizer, night cooling, HVAC controls, evaporative cooling, ground-exchange) are specified at the component level. The lighting system design development integrates daylighting, equipment, fixtures, and controls. Communication during design development is key, since a change in any system, such as lighting power, could affect all other systems, such as the cooling load on the mechanical system.

It is wise to conduct design reviews that are both internal and external to the project team. The focus of design review efforts should be on the early schematic design submittals. By the time the design is 35% complete, it is usually too late to make major changes. An objective party who has not been involved in the design might be recruited to review it. These reviewers might include consultants, advocates from state and local governments or national laboratories, and experts on sustainability topics such as energy, materials, and indoor environmental conditions. Reviewers point out strengths as well as weaknesses, and try to be constructive with solutions to perceived problem areas.

It is important that reviewers do not put the designer on the defensive or embarrass him or her in front of the owner (their client). To do so would rupture the team approach and make sharing of information problematic in subsequent reviews. A reviewer without all the answers might take a Socratic, or questioning, approach. Design reviews can be accomplished by marking up plans and specifications and by supplying product literature and other information to facilitate implementation of the recommendations. A meeting can be called where reviewers convey more complicated concepts from reviewers to the design team.

## Value Engineering

During value engineering, the design is scrutinized to see how the same or better result can be achieved at a lower cost. Value engineering sometimes focuses on the functional mission of a building. It is important that sustainability goals key to the design intent not be compromised. Value engineering should be based on life cycle cost rather than first cost. Energy analysis should be incorporated into the value engineering process to inform the value engineer of the consequences of deleting important energy features and to ensure that energy targets and goals are maintained through the value engineering process. The energy analyst would have to perform analysis and computer simulation as necessary to determine the effects of proposed cost cuts and to defend justified measures.

Value engineering is not always the enemy of the sustainability advocate. Sometimes it represents a final opportunity to include a sustainability measure that saves on first cost or has compelling benefits.

## Construction Documents

During this phase of the project, the design team prepares working drawings and specifications from design development work approved by the owner and confirmed as meeting the sustainability goals set in the building program. In addition, the design team may prepare necessary bidding information, determine the form of contract with the contractor, and specify any special conditions of the contract. The construction documents contain all the information necessary for bid solicitation, and thus all the information that bidders need to provide an accurate costing of labor and materials. At this time, the team ensures that architectural, mechanical, and lighting details and specifications meet energy goals. They then perform a final energy analysis to confirm that the energy goals have been met, and also to provide necessary documentation required for LEED certification or other purposes.

The task of collecting documentation to evaluate LEED or other environmental performance criteria must be planned and budgeted. There is a considerable amount of work involved in preparing green specifications. Certainly the detail that describes the green attributes of the specified material or method must be added, and often information must be included to find suppliers and assist the installing subcontractors in adopting a new material or technique. Careful specifications are key to keeping the cost down while promoting sustainable construction methods among suppliers and subcontractors.

The result of this final design effort is a package of drawings and specifications for use in the construction contract documents. Forms certifying that the construction documents comply with all applicable codes and standards (including those related to energy and environmental requirements) are signed, and the plans are stamped by the architect and professional engineer. Contract documents are often organized according to the structure presented in Figure 8.8.

## Bid Solicitation & Contract Award

During the bidding phase of a project, bidders submit offers to perform the work described in the construction documents at a specified price. Bids describe the costs proposed for all construction described by the construction documents, as well as other direct construction costs. (Bids do not include design team fees, the cost of the land, rights of way or easements, or other costs defined as being the responsibility of the owner or otherwise outside of the scope of the construction contract.)

The design team supports the owner in bid solicitation and negotiation. This way, the team has an opportunity to maintain sustainability goals if cost cutting is required. Again, the energy analyst might have to perform studies to analyze trade-offs or substitutions. Also, since the contractor is providing all labor and materials to complete the construction, bidders may want to substitute materials they are familiar with or have easy access to, for those specified for their sustainability benefits. In such cases, it is important that a sustainability expert and advocate remain involved in order to advise the owner toward a compromise that optimizes the benefits of material selection.

| Bidding Requirements | Invitation |
| | Instructions |
| | Information |
| | Bid Form |
| | Bid Bond |
| Contract Forms | Agreement |
| | Performance Bond |
| | Payment Bond |
| | Certificates |
| Contract Conditions | General |
| | Supplementary |
| Specifications (in divisions) | General Requirements |
| | Site Construction |
| | Concrete |
| | Masonry |
| | Metals |
| | Wood, Plastics, & Composites |
| | Thermal & Moisture Protection |
| | Openings |
| | Finishes |
| | Specialties |
| | Equipment |
| | Special Construction |
| | Conveying Equipment |
| | Plumbing/HVAC |
| | Electrical |
| | Earthwork |
| | Exterior Imporvements |
| | Utilities |
| | Sustainabilty |
| Drawings | Site |
| | Architectural |
| | Electrical |
| | Mechanical |

**Figure 8.8**
Elements of a Construction Contract

## Construction

Administration of the construction contract is often included in the architect's and design team's basic services. The green design team specifically monitors sustainability and energy-related aspects during construction. The commissioning agent, although involved from the beginning, would be most active at this stage in order to correct problems early in construction. Many energy efficiency measures, such as insulation and vapor barriers, require special attention to detail during installation. The oversight of the commissioning agent helps to ensure that the benefits of these measures are realized. It is often too late to correct problems if they are discovered after installation. For example, it is much more expensive to correct sagging or missing insulation after the drywall and interior finish are installed. Again, the design team maintains adherence to sustainability goals as change orders are issued and if cost-cutting is required. Additional analysis may be required to evaluate cost and performance trade-offs.

Sometimes it is possible to include the construction contractor in the design process, but more often the contractor is not selected until the design is complete. In either case, it is important to get input from the construction trades early in the design process. Advice from the construction contractor, or a construction expert hired as a consultant, serves several useful purposes in the design process. The contractor can advise team members on the constructability of a design concept (e.g., how difficult or expensive it would be to implement). Trades are also an excellent source of ideas on how a design objective can be realized with fewer materials or at a lower cost, if they are made aware of the strategies being pursued.

## Commissioning

Commissioning, addressed in more detail in Chapter 12, is the procedure used to confirm that building systems are installed according to the design intent. Commissioning should not be considered optional, as it provides the owner and design team with needed information and often uncovers problems that are easy to correct, but would have dire consequences if not detected. Unlike testing and balancing, which is part of the construction contract, commissioning is performed by a third-party **commissioning authority** on behalf of the owner. The commissioning authority should be involved very early in the design process. Early involvement will help the commissioning authority develop a record of the design intent with respect to energy efficiency and sustainability. The commissioning authority's recommendations to the design team will result in system designs that are not only easy to evaluate in field installations, but more reliable. The team should develop and implement a commissioning protocol with reference to *ASHRAE Commissioning Guidelines*.

### Commissioning Costs

Basic commissioning such as that required as a prerequisite in a LEED® rating might cost between $0.40 and $1.00/SF and an additional 20% for enhanced commissioning.[8] Enhanced commissioning, often required to fully realize the benefit of sustainability systems such as that associated with a one-point LEED credit, adds $0.08 to $0.20/SF. Additional services required in the HVAC contract to support enhanced commissioning ranges from $0.15 to $0.20/SF.

## Operations & Maintenance

Operations and maintenance (O&M) staff from the owner's other buildings are usually available to advise the design team. If O&M staff members understand and support the sustainability goals of a project, they are more likely to make an extra effort to see that the systems perform. On the other hand, if the staff does not like a system, it will quickly be disabled and forgotten. Involving O&M staff in the design process gives them an understanding of the rationale behind system selection, the design intent of sustainability measures, and the importance of new or unusual systems to the performance of the building as a whole.

It is important to train both occupants and maintenance staff on the energy-related features of a building and also on sustainability features, such as recycling and gray water systems. Since staff change jobs frequently, the training should be videotaped, and good documentation (such as videos and manuals) should be well-organized and protected as a resource for new maintenance staff.

## Measurement & Verification

Measurement and verification (M&V) provides continuous post-occupancy evaluation of how systems are performing. This is a requirement for performance contracting, but provides critical information for all projects. Sustainability features often provide more than one way to meet a service. For example, if the solar water heater fails, the electrical system provides hot water; if the recycling bins are full, a person can use the trash can. Managers are often unaware when these redundant sustainability features fail, because they get no complaints from the occupants. Measurement and verification provides diagnostic information so that systems continuously realize their intended benefits. The International Performance Measurement and Verification Protocol (**www.ipmvp.org**) describes options for structuring and implementing such a program.

### The Costs of M&V

Metering is often the central aspect to any M&V program. Costs of an electric meter with advanced capabilities might range from $1,700 for a single-phase meter to $2,500 for a three-phase meter, but the additional costs associated with polling computer and balance of system brings total installed cost of a metering program to $3,000 to $5,000 per meter. Costs to collect data and generate useful reports range from $10 to $30 per month per meter. Similar costs can be expected for other types of utility meters such as gas or water.

## Establishing a Green Team in an Existing Facility

Designing new buildings or major remodeling projects provides an excellent opportunity to create a facility that will benefit from green construction and operations practices. However, existing buildings—even without major renovations—can also become significantly greener, with a plan and an internal team to champion this effort. The American Society of Hospital Engineering published a monograph, "Green and Healthy Buildings for the Health Care Industry," which recommends a short- and long-term plan for implementing green practices into facilities operations. The short-term steps include:

- Establishing a "green team."
- Requiring project designers to specify cost-competitive green products for new projects, and requiring procurement managers to put in place procedures that include green attributes in procurement decisions for all supplies (paper products, cleaning materials, etc.).
- Providing seminars on healthy building practices and efficient resource management. Occupant awareness and behavior is credited with $500 million of the $1.2 billion energy savings achieved by the federal government from 1985 to 1995.
- Occupant cooperation helps ensure that efforts to optimize resource use are successful, and in fact, occupants hostile to changes can ensure that those measures fail.
- Expanding the Environmental Health & Safety Department's responsibility to include monitoring air quality.
- Measuring resource consumption (energy and water), emissions, and waste generated, and establishing goals to improve efficiencies.
- Consider alternative financing, such as Energy Savings Performance Contracting (where the cost of a measure is paid back over time from energy cost savings) to fund projects that the facility does not have money for.
- Establishing recycling practices.
- Using LEED® as an evaluation tool and modifying if appropriate.

The medium- and long-range recommended goals include:
- Establishing life cycle measurements for environmental, human health, and natural resource performance.
- Designing for 50-year plus building life expectancy.

- Merging capital and O&M budgets to optimize life cycle costing.
- Establishing procurement policies consistent with green practices, and review/revise annually.
- Establishing partnerships with regulators to review and revise regulations to reflect impacts on human health and environmental quality.
- Establishing an internal green building rating system.
- Establishing a permanent position to oversee compliance with green building standards.
- Providing ongoing green building training for staff.
- Integrating and balancing resource flows to enhance life cycle efficiency.
- Designing for flexibility so that future changes can be implemented efficiently.

## *Conclusion*

The procurement of architectural and engineering services is the best place to leverage the resources of an entire project toward increased resource efficiency. Designers respond to what the customer asks for, and careful specification of Statements of Work and deliverables for A&E teams is where owners tell the design community that they want green buildings. Requests for proposals that require and provide budgets for green design services will enhance interest and capability in green building among design firms. Owners sometimes say they want a green building, but then do not include the additional tasks or budget to allow the design team to truly pursue that goal. The Statement of Work, and its accompanying budget estimate, are necessary precursors to a successful green building project.

1. "Cost Analysis of Inadequate Interoperability in the U.S. Capital Facilities Industry." NIST. August 2004.

2. Harris, Cyril M., ed. *Dictionary of Architecture and Construction, 2nd Edition*. McGraw-Hill Inc. 1993.

3. Energy Policy Act of 1992.

4. Doug Balcomb, NREL, Personal communications. Energy-10 available from Sustainable Buildings Industry Council. www.sbicouncil.org

5. Charles Eley, Eley and Associates.

6. Greg Kats, Leon Alevantis, Adam Berman, Evan Mills, Jeff Perlman. "The Costs and Financial Benefits of Green Buildings: A Report to California's Sustainable Building Task Force." October 2003.

7. Doug Balcomb, NREL, Personal communications. Energy-10 available from Sustainable Buildings Industry Council. www.sbicouncil.org EPA and NPS emissions factors.

8. The Cost of LEED, A Report on Cost Expectations to Meet LEED 2009 for New Construction and Major Renovations (NC v2009) Tsoi/Kobus & Associates, Cambridge MA, S. Oppenheimer, S. Mills-Knapp, I. Lenova, AHA Consulting Engineers, Lexington, MA, R. Andrews, Vermeulens Cost Consultants, Toronto, ON, J. Vermeulen, C. Chiarelli, BuildingGreen Brattleboro VT, Published by BuildingGreen LLC, J. Newman, N. Malin.

# Chapter 9

# Rating Systems, Standards & Guidelines

*Joseph Macaluso, CCC*

A building can be considered green without a single standard actually applied to it. In fact, to reduce costs, green buildings are often built using a rating system strictly as a guide without ever formally registering the building. Rating systems, however, do offer a way to measure how green a building is and can supply recognition and validation of that level of commitment.

Rating systems, standards, and guidelines can be classified into two groups: those that relate to specific building components, and those that relate to the building as a whole entity. They range from those that assess specific properties of individual building materials and systems, to those that assess the entire buildings' overall environmental performance. The broader the assessment, the unavoidably more subjective it is. As one architect active in sustainable design put it, "You can have a building that is zero carbon, the greenest, most energy conserving, and not be LEED® rated because you don't have the other stuff."[1]

The Leadership in Energy and Environmental Design (LEED), developed by the U.S. Green Building Council (USGBC), and ENERGY STAR®, a joint program of the U.S. Environmental Protection Agency and the U.S. Department of Energy, are probably the two most recognized whole building rating systems. LEED, which considers many green attributes, is an example of a **multiple attribute** rating system, whereas ENERGY STAR is generally limited to energy efficiency, and would be considered a **single attribute** rating system.

Federal, state, and municipal agencies across the country, such as the General Services Administration, Department of Energy, Department of Health and Human Services, and the Environmental Protection

Agency, have taken an early lead in incorporating energy efficiency and sustainability by developing their own green building guidelines into the design and construction of new facilities. In addition, most states and many major cities have incorporated green into their internal building requirements for new construction. These green guidelines can be used as benchmarks for green building incentive programs and can help to build the green infrastructure necessary to mainstream green building practices.

Overall, such initiatives appear to be working. When the first edition of this book was published in 2002, green building regulations of any kind were limited to a few small communities. Today, many states have some type of green building orders, bills, or laws, such as mandates to exceed current energy codes; strive for LEED certification; or achieve minimum LEED or Green Globe ratings. Eighteen states have adopted laws and regulations mandating LEED Silver Certification for certain publicly owned buildings.[2] They are: Arizona, California, Connecticut, Hawaii, Illinois, Indiana, Kentucky, Massachusetts, Maryland, New Jersey, New Mexico, Nevada, Rhode Island, South Carolina, South Dakota, Utah, Virginia, and Washington. Other regions have a variety of green requirements in place for both public *and* privately owned buildings (including Oklahoma, California, Boston, Baltimore, and Washington D.C.).

California has recently adopted the first statewide mandatory green building code, named CALGreen, effective January 1st 2011. Though many states incorporate energy efficiency requirements into their building codes, the California code also sets standards relating to responsible site development, water conservation, resource conservation, and indoor environmental quality. It covers all new construction, with the exception of hospitals. The code is two-tiered, with a baseline standard and a more ambitious voluntary level. If the building passes, property owners can label their buildings as having complied with the code. Municipalities with more stringent green building regulations, such as San Francisco, will take priority over the state code. It is expected that the code will increase the price of a new home by $1,500.[3] However, building owners can save on the cost by electing not to use a third party rating system in addition to the California code.

The trend in green building has been for ideas to start off as recommendations, followed by guidelines for government-owned buildings, followed by legislation for all buildings. Today's voluntary guidelines will evolve into tomorrow's regulations, raising the bar for what is considered green in the future.

There can indeed be challenges incorporating green components into building design, beginning perhaps with local building codes. Building codes are usually prescriptive, which means that some green components may not be allowable in certain locations, even if they function as well as traditional components in a more earth-friendly way. If code officials are willing to consider green alternatives, a lengthy review process is often required. Some believe that, to encourage innovation and the use of green building products, building codes should be more performance-oriented. In other words, a building component or system approval should be based on how well it performs a function, not on conformance to narrowly defined lists of materials and installation procedures.[4] Furthermore, building codes take time to revise and often do not reflect the current environmental sensitivity. The overriding factor is that building codes traditionally cover health, safety and welfare as they relate to construction and occupancy, while green building codes take into account the health, safety, and welfare of the entire planet. It's not a given that building professionals will accept this broader perspective, but the same was true of the Americans with Disabilities Act (ADA) in the 1990s, which also expanded the scope of existing building codes. Complying with the provisions was, at first, a big challenge to the industry. Now the ADA is looked at no differently than any of the other building codes and regulations. It is quite likely that green building codes will follow the same path.[5]

Regardless of what rating, standard, or guideline system is used, one should always ask: is the assessment being done by a first-party, second-party, or third-party organization ? A first-party assessment comes directly from an organization that is associated with the entity making the claim, or may benefit from the claim. A second-party assessment is not performed by an interested party. It might be done by a trade association, for example, and thus provides a level of independence from those who would directly benefit from a positive assessment. A third-party assessment is done by an independent party that has no financial interest in the outcome of the assessment. There can be no direct payments, shares, loans, or grants from, nor ties to, the company whose product or service is being assessed.[6]

These four principles should be applied when evaluating an assessment system:

1. Science-based – Results/decisions must be reproducible by others using the same standard.

2. Transparent – The standards and process for awarding the certification should be transparent and open for examination.

3. Objective – The certification body should be free of conflict.

4. Progressive – The standard should advance industry practices, not simply reward business as usual.[7]

## Whole Building Multiple Attribute Ratings

**Build green. Everyone profits.**

# LEED® Green Building Rating System

*www.usgbc.org*

The LEED Green Building Rating System is the best known, nationally recognized benchmarking system in North America. As of this printing, there are over 1,900 LEED-certified projects with over 15,000 registered for certification.[8] This number is sure to increase with the recent release of LEED rating systems for mid-rise homes, schools, retail buildings, health care facilities, and neighborhood development programs.

The following is a breakdown of LEED designations: *(See Figures 9.1 and 9.2.)*

- LEED-NC: New Construction, for commercial, institutional, and high-rise residential buildings.
- LEED-EB: Existing Buildings, which includes criteria for maintenance, operations, and refurbishments.
- LEED-CS: Core and Shell, which covers a building's structure, envelope, and basic mechanical/electrical/plumbing systems. Appropriate for speculative buildings.
- LEED-CI: Commercial Interiors, for tenant fit-outs.
- LEED-H: Homes, a collaborative effort with local green homes programs, includes single and multiunit versions.
- LEED for Schools: for K–12 school facilities.
- LEED for Retail, which includes new construction, and commercial interiors versions.

A LEED rating is achieved through earning points in each of these seven categories:

1. SS      Sustainable Sites
2. WE      Water Efficiency
3. EA      Energy & Atmosphere
4. MR      Material & Resources
5. EQ      Indoor Environmental Quality
6. ID      Innovation & Design *
7. RP      Regional Priority **

*Though not a separate facet of green building, an Innovation & Design category is included to encourage creative approaches.*

** *Though not a separate facet of green building, a Regional Priority Credits category was added in 2009 to offer an opportunity to earn bonus points for achieving credits in any of the existing categories that address geographically-specific environmental priorities for the area in which the building is located.*

| LEED NC – Categories | Possible Points |
|---|---|
| Sustainable Sites | 26 |
| Water Efficiency | 10 |
| Energy & Atmosphere | 35 |
| Materials & Resources | 14 |
| Indoor Environmental Quality | 15 |
| Innovation & Design Process | 6 |
| Regional Priority Credits | 4 |
| Total | 110 |

| LEED EB – Categories | Possible Points |
|---|---|
| Sustainable Sites | 26 |
| Water Efficiency | 14 |
| Energy & Atmosphere | 35 |
| Materials & Resources | 10 |
| Indoor Environmental Quality | 15 |
| Innovation in Upgrades, Operations & Management | 6 |
| Regional Priority Credits | 4 |
| Total | 110 |

| LEED CI – Categories | Possible Points |
|---|---|
| Sustainable Sites | 21 |
| Water Efficiency | 11 |
| Energy & Atmosphere | 37 |
| Materials & Resources | 14 |
| Indoor Environmental Quality | 17 |
| Innovation Design Process | 6 |
| Regional Priority Credits | 4 |
| Total | 110 |

| LEED CS – Categories | Possible Points |
|---|---|
| Sustainable Sites | 28 |
| Water Efficiency | 10 |
| Energy & Atmosphere | 37 |
| Materials & Resources | 13 |
| Indoor Environmental Quality | 12 |
| Innovation Design Process | 6 |
| Regional Priority Credits | 4 |
| Total | 110 |

**Figure 9.1**
LEED Rating Types

| LEED – Points Required for Ratings | | | | |
|---|---|---|---|---|
| | Certified | Silver | Gold | Platinum |
| ALL | 40-49 | 50-59 | 60-79 | 80-110 |

**Figure 9.2**
LEED Points Required for Ratings

Within each category, there are subcategories including prerequisites. For example, the Sustainable Sites category contains a prerequisite for Erosion and Sediment Control and also several other subcategories, including Site Selection and Storm Water Management, for earning points if applicable. The rating system is flexible in that it is performance-based, and does not force the applicant into following a narrowly defined set of specifications. The structure and categories in the LEED rating system are often used as a basis for the newer rating systems that are being developed by other entities. For ease of comparison, categories of all rating systems in this chapter are arranged in the same order as in the LEED rating system.

The rating process starts with registering the project. It is recommended that registration be completed as early as the pre-schematic design stage, so that the project can be tracked along the way. Registration can be completed directly through the USGBC's website. Registration provides access to an interactive PDF file that allows the registrant to assign individual team members or groups access rights to specific areas of the LEED application and scorecard for their appropriate credits. The authorized team members can add documentation, perform calculations, and submit the information through LEED Online. After registration, and after all the credits have been documented, the applicant submits the information for the formal review and ruling. If the applicant needs an interpretation for a specific credit, the fee is $220 for the interpretation, and $500 for an appeal. However, a dedicated website that is available once a project is registered for LEED lists rulings on other interpretations and can be checked without charge before requesting a paid interpretation. *(See Figure 9.3 for registration and certification fees.)*

The USGBC produces, maintains, and administers the LEED rating system in the United States. The Canada Green Building Council (CaGBC) **www.cagbc.org** is responsible for the Canadian version of the rating system. Though similar in format and intent, there are differences between the Canadian and U.S. versions of LEED. For example, the Canadian version of LEED for New Construction offers credits for $CO_2$ monitoring in the Indoor Environmental Quality section, and for Durable Building in the Materials & Resources section, whereas the U.S. version does not. The green building councils are comprised of well-respected, nationally recognized proponents of sustainable building, from a broad spectrum of manufacturers, building professionals, building owners, and financial institutions. *(See Appendix for more on LEED.)*

Other World Green Building Council Members with rating standards include:

- Australia – Green Star
- Germany – German Sustainable Building Certification
- Japan – Comprehensive Assessment System for Building Environment Efficiency (CASBEE)
- New Zealand – Green Star NZ
- South Africa – Green Star SA
- United Kingdom – BREEAM

In addition, Green Building Councils are well-established in Argentina, Cuba, India, Mexico, Taiwan, and United Arab Emirates, with emerging councils in Columbia, Italy, the Netherlands, Poland, Romania, Spain, and Vietnam.

| LEED Registration Fees | | | |
|---|---|---|---|
| Square Footage | < 50,000 | 50,000 – 500,000 | > 500,000 |
| Members* | $900 | $900 | $900 |
| Non-Members | $1,200 | $1,200 | $1,200 |

| LEED Certification Fees | | | |
|---|---|---|---|
| New Construction, Commercial Interiors, Core & Shell, and Schools | | | |
| Square Footage | < 50,000 | 50,000 – 500,000 | > 500,000 |
| Design Review | | | |
| Members* | $2,000 | $.040/Square Foot | $20,000 |
| Non-Members | $2,250 | $.045/Square Foot | $22,500 |
| Expediting Fee Add | $5,000 | $5,000 | $5,000 |
| Construction Review | | | |
| Members* | $500 | $.010/Square Foot | $5,000 |
| Non-Members | $750 | $.015/Square Foot | $7,500 |
| Expediting Fee Add | $5,000 | $5,000 | $5,000 |
| Combined  Design & Construction Review | | | |
| Members* | $2,250 | $.045/Square Foot | $22,500 |
| Non-Members | $2,750 | $.055/Square Foot | $27,500 |
| Expediting Fee Add | $10,000 | $10,000 | $10,000 |

*Membership dues ranges from $300 to $12,500 depending on whether the applicant is a public, non-profit or private entity and the gross annual sales volume if applicant represents is a private firm.

**Figure 9.3**
LEED Fees

| LEED Certification Fees | | | |
|---|---|---|---|
| Existing Buildings | | | |
| Square Footage | < 50,000 | 50,000 – 500,000 | > 500,000 |
| Initial Certification Review | | | |
| Members* | $1,500 | $.030/Square Foot | $15,000 |
| Non-Members | $2,000 | $.040/Square Foot | $20,000 |
| Expedited Fee Add | $10,000 | $10,000 | $10,000 |
| Recertification Review | | | |
| Members* | $750 | $.015/Square Foot | $7,500 |
| Non-Members | $1,000 | $.020/Square Foot | $10,000 |
| Expedited Fee Add | $10,000 | $10,000 | $10,000 |

| LEED Precertification Fees | | | |
|---|---|---|---|
| Core & Shell | | | |
| Square Footage | < 50,000 | 50,000 – 500,000 | > 500,000 |
| Members* | $3,250 | $3,250 | $3,250 |
| Non-Members | $4,250 | $4,250 | $4,250 |
| Expedited Fee add | $5,000 | $5,000 | $5,000 |

| LEED Registration Fees | | |
|---|---|---|
| Homes | | |
| Type of Housing | Single Family | Multifamily |
| Members* | $150 | $450 |
| Non-Members | $225 | $600 |

| LEED Certification Fees | | |
|---|---|---|
| Homes | | |
| Type of Housing | Single Family | Multifamily |
| Members* | $225 | $.035/Square Foot |
| Non-Members | $300 | $.045/Square Foot |

| LEED On-site inspection | | |
|---|---|---|
| Type of Housing | Single Family | Multifamily |
| Members & Non-Members | Market pricing from provider | |

*Membership dues ranges from $300 to $12,500 depending on whether the applicant is a public, non-profit or private entity and the gross annual sales volume if applicant represents is a private firm.

**Figure 9.3 (cont.)**
LEED Fees

## The Living Building Challenge
### *www.ilbi.org*

The Living Building Challenge is administered by the International Living Building Institute, founded in 2009 by the Cascadia Region Green Building Council. The standard is not designed to compete with LEED, but rather is intended as a way of raising the bar even further. It's more stringent than LEED Platinum, and there are no credits, only prerequisites. *(See Figure 9.4.)* Instead of basing certification on modeled or anticipated performance as most other standards (LEED now requires a commitment to provide energy and water consumption performance records for at least three years for new buildings), the Living Building Challenge is based on actual performance. Therefore, buildings must be operational for at least twelve months *before* being evaluated. Access to the portions of the website that contain the Published Standard, User's Guide, and other resources is available to Cascadia Members for $125, and non-members for $150.

## Green Globes™
### *www.thegbi.org/greenglobes*

The roots of this rating system can be traced to a British rating system called BREEAM (Building Research Establishment Environmental Assessment Method). It was created in 1990 as a way for building owners and managers to self-assess the environmental performance of existing buildings. It was adapted for use in Canada as the BREEAM Green Leaf rating system, which, in turn, was used as a basis for the web-based Green Globes rating system in 2002 for new buildings. In 2003, the Canadian government recommended, though did not formally approve, the use of Green Globes for projects between $1,000,000 and $10,000,000 and LEED for projects over $10,000,000. The Green Globes rating system has been adapted for use in the United States with the Green Building Initiative as the licensor.[9] Currently there are over 100 Green Globes buildings in the United States.

These are the seven areas of assessment (with each further broken down into sub areas) :

1. Site
2. Water
3. Energy
4. Emissions, Effluents & Other Impacts

| Living Building Challenge 16 Prerequisites (based on version 1.3) |
|---|
| **SITE** |
| 1. Responsible Site Selection prohibits development on or near ecological sensitive areas, and on areas defined as prime farmland or within the 100-year flood plain. |
| 2. Limits to Growth requires development only on greyfield or brownfield sites. |
| 3. Habitat Exchange states that for each acre of development, an equal amount of land must be set aside for habitat protection. |
| |
| **ENERGY** |
| 4. Net Zero Energy requires 100% of the building's energy needs supplied by on-site, renewable energy on a net annual basis. |
| |
| **MATERIALS** |
| 5. Materials Red List identifies and requires exclusion of a "Red List" of chemicals, commonly found in building materials, which pose serious risks to human and ecological health. |
| 6. Construction Carbon Footprint requires offsetting the embodied carbon footprint of all construction-related activities. |
| 7. Responsible Industry requires all wood products to be FSC-certified or come from salvaged sources. |
| 8. Appropriate Materials/Services Radius identifies a series of geographic radii in which all materials and services for the project must be sourced. |
| 9. Leadership in Construction Waste requires diversion of construction waste from landfill/incinerator disposal. |
| |
| **WATER** |
| 10. Net Zero Water requires 100% of occupants' water use from captured precipitation or reclaimed sources. |
| 11. Sustainable Water Discharge requires 100% of storm water and building water discharge to be managed on-site. |
| |
| **INDOOR QUALITY** |
| 12. Civilized Environment requires operable windows that provide access to fresh air and daylight for every occupiable space. |
| 13. Healthy Air/Source Control requires strategies to eliminate pollutant introduction into the indoor environment. |
| 14. Healthy Air – Ventilation requires design of the building to deliver air change rates in compliance with California Title 24 requirements. |
| |
| **BEAUTY & INSPIRATION** |
| 15. Beauty and Spirit requires projects to include design features intended solely for human delight and the celebration of culture, spirit and place appropriate to the function of the building. |
| 16. Inspiration and Education requires publicly-available educational materials highlighting the performance and operation of the Living Building project. |

**Figure 9.4**
Living Building Challenge

5. Resources

6. Indoor Environment

7. Project Management

Green Globes is a self-assessment type of system using a web-based tool. If the score is verified by a third party, the Green Globes logo and brand can be attached to the project. A score is generated at two separate phases of the project, design and construction, without having to wait for a formal review and ruling.

Based on the score, a rating of between one and four Green Globes are earned (five in the Canadian version). Instead of a prescribed sum, as in LEED, the score is based on a percentage of applicable points. For example, if only 100 of the 115 points are applicable in the Site area of assessment, the score would be a percentage of the 985 total applicable points, not the 1,000 total possible points. Unlike LEED, Green Globes includes points in its base categories for integrated pest management, composting organic waste, monitoring $CO_2$, and acoustic comfort. Green Globes places greater emphasis on energy use. *(See Figures 9.5 and 9.6.)*

The cost of a subscription to the Green Globes software is from $3,500–$4,000 per building. The cost of a combined design and construction third-party assessment ranges from $7,000 to more than $15,000, plus assessors' travel costs, depending on the size and complexity of the project. *(See Figure 9.7.)*

**Figure 9.5**
Green Globes® Areas of Assessment

| Green Globes – Areas of Assessment | Points |
| --- | --- |
| Site | 115 |
| Water | 85 |
| Energy | 380 |
| Emissions, Effluents, & Other Impacts | 70 |
| Resources | 100 |
| Indoor Environment | 200 |
| Project Management Process | 50 |
| Total | 1,000 |

| Green Globes – Ratings | | | |
|---|---|---|---|
| 1 Globe | 2 Globes | 3 Globes | 4 Globes |
| 36%–55% | 56%–70% | 71%–85% | 86 + % |

**Figure 9.6**
Green Globes Ratings

| Green Globes Subscription Per Building | |
|---|---|
| NewConstruction | $4,000 |
| Existing Building | $3,500 |

| Green Globes Third Party Assessment Fees | | | | | | |
|---|---|---|---|---|---|---|
| **New Construction** | | | | | | |
| Square Footage | <100,000 | 100,000 to <200,000 | 200,000 to <300,000 | 300,000 to <400,000 | 400,000 to <500,000 | >500,000 |
| **Design Assessment** | | | | | | |
| | $3,500 | $4,000 | $4,500 | $5,500 | $6,500 | $7,500 |
| **Construction Assessment** | | | | | | |
| | $3,500 | $4,000 | $4,500 | $5,500 | $6,500 | $7,500 |
| **Design & Construction Assessment** | | | | | | |
| | $7,000 | $8,000 | $9,000 | $11,000 | $13,000 | $15,000 |
| Expediting Fee | $2,500 | $2,500 | $2,500 | $2,500 | $2,500 | $2,500 |

| Green Globes Third Party Assessment Fees | | | | | | |
|---|---|---|---|---|---|---|
| **Existing Building** | | | | | | |
| Square Footage | <100,000 | 100,000 to <200,000 | 200,000 to <300,000 | 300,000 to <400,000 | 400,000 to <500,000 | >500,000 |
| Certification | $4,000 | $5,000 | $6,000 | $8,000 | $10,000 | $11,000 |
| Re-Certification | $3,500 | $4,000 | $4,500 | $5,500 | $6,500 | $7,500 |
| Expediting Fee | $2,500 | $2,500 | $2,500 | $2,500 | $2,500 | $2,500 |

**Figure 9.7**
Green Globes Fees

R-2000 is an official trademark of Natural Resources Canada. Used with permission.

# R-2000
## *www.r-2000.org*
R-2000 is a voluntary Canadian residential standard established by Natural Resources Canada, with a goal of "efficient use of energy, improved indoor air quality, and better environmental responsibility in the construction and operation of a house."[10] To date, about 10,000

R-2000 homes have been built. The houses must be built by trained and licensed R-2000 builders. After completing the R-2000 builders' course, builders must register, build, and certify a demonstration home before becoming licensed R-2000 builders.

R-2000 sets stringent standards for levels of insulation, air-tightness, window performance, HVAC sizing, venting, and standby loss. These requirements often exceed current Canadian building codes and regulations. For example, energy performance targets for the combined space and water heating is based on the size, location, and fuel type of the house. Compliance is calculated using HOT2000™ software by a licensed R-2000 plan evaluator. Water conservation requirements include water-saver or ultra-low flush toilets and low-flow showerheads and faucets.

In addition to the basic requirements, the builder must incorporate at least three of these nine R-2000 indoor air quality features:

1. Low-emission carpeting

2. Air filtration systems

3. Low-emission paints and varnishes

4. Low-emission floor adhesives

5. Low-emission cabinets and vanities

6. Low-emission flooring

7. Low-emission particleboard underlayment

8. Sub-slab depressurization system (to control radon and soil gases)

9. Indoor moisture control measures

Each of these features contains specific R-2000 requirements. For example, paints and varnishes must be water-based, or meet or exceed Environmental Choice standards.

The R-2000 builder must also incorporate at least two environmental features from a list that includes the following:

- Recycled content insulation (choice of fiberglass, cellulose, mineral fiber, or plastic)
- Recycled content sheathing and drywall (choice of fiberboard, siding, or drywall)
- Recycled content steel studs, saw mill cut-off, and urea-formaldehyde-free wood studs and trim
- Foundation/under-slab drainage made with post-consumer glass

- Energy-efficient appliances
- Reduced energy consumption (at least 15% less than the target amount)
- High-efficiency cooling systems and motors

As with the indoor air quality features, each environmental feature has specific R-2000 requirements. For example, the high-efficiency cooling system must have a minimum SEER (Seasonal Energy Efficiency Ratio) of 12.0 for split system air-cooled air conditioners, a minimum of 12.0 EER (Energy Efficiency Ratio) for single-package central air and heat pumps and ground- or water-source air conditioners, a minimum EER of 10.5 for closed-loop systems, and a minimum EER of 11.0 for all other types.

# NAHB Model Green Home Building Guidelines
## *www.nahb.org*

The National Association of Home Builders Model Green Home Guidelines is a comprehensive national guideline recently developed with the participation of more than 60 industry and green building association stakeholders after a review of 28 local green home building programs. One of the goals of the Model Green Home Building Guidelines is to help incorporate green building principles without driving up the cost of construction significantly. Eighty percent of the homes built by the NAHB are located in the United States.

The table in *Figure 9.8* indicates the minimum number of points that must be earned for each of the categories in order to receive a bronze, silver, or gold rating.

| Model Green Home Building Guidelines - Categories | Bronze | Silver | Gold |
|---|---|---|---|
| Lot Design, Preparation, and Development | 8 | 10 | 12 |
| Water Efficiency | 6 | 13 | 19 |
| Energy Efficiency | 37 | 62 | 100 |
| Resource Efficiency | 44 | 60 | 100 |
| Indoor Environmental Quality | 32 | 54 | 72 |
| Operation, Maintenance and Homeowner Education | 7 | 7 | 9 |
| Global Impact | 3 | 5 | 6 |
| Mandatory Additional Points Earned in Category of Choice | 100 | 100 | 100 |

**Figure 9.8**
NAHB Model Green Home Building Guidelines – Categories

the

collaborative

for high

performance

schools

# CHPS
## *www.chps.net*

The Collaborative for High Performance Schools (CHPS), a not-for-profit group based in California, includes utilities, state agencies, school districts, design professionals, and manufacturers working in collaboration with the California Integrated Waste Management Board. The CHPS criteria are important, because schools make up one of the largest segments of construction. CHPS criteria are geared specifically to school buildings (for example, acoustics in classrooms). CHPS created a five-volume *CHPS Best Practices Manual*: Volume I addresses the needs of school districts; Volume II covers climate zones; Volume III contains the actual prerequisites for becoming a CHPS school; Volume IV deals with maintenance and operations issues to provide the best healthy indoor environment, efficiency, and sustainability; and Volume V specifically addresses commissioning procedures.

Executive Order S-20-04 required the California State Architect in the Department of General Services to adopt the guidelines to enable and encourage schools built with state funds to be resource and energy efficient.[11] Although there are obvious similarities, LEED for Schools and CHPS are not interchangeable. A building that may qualify under the CHPS criteria may not qualify for LEED, or vice versa; however, some may actually qualify for a rating by both systems. The differences pertain to energy and water consumption: CHPS baselines are based on California standards, as opposed to the national standards used in LEED. Other states (Massachusetts, New York, Washington, Maine, Vermont, New Hampshire, Rhode Island, and Connecticut) have modified, or are in the process of modifying, the California CHPS standard, based on their specific codes, regulations, climates, constraints, and priorities, and are incorporating the criteria into their own school construction guidelines.[12] (*See Figure 9.9 and the Appendix for more on CHPS.*)

| CHPS – Categories | Points |
|---|---|
| Site | 15 |
| Water | 5 |
| Energy | 20 |
| Materials | 12 |
| Indoor Environmental Quality | 20 |
| District Resolutions | 13 |
| Total (32 point minimum required for CHPS school) | 85 |

**Figure 9.9**
From *CHPS Best Practice Manual*, Volume III, 2006 Edition

# Whole Building Single Attribute Ratings

## Health House®

*www.healthhouse.org*

Health House building criteria was developed by the American Lung Association® for the purpose of fostering homes that have better indoor air quality and also improve the overall outdoor environment. The measures improve the indoor air quality by ensuring proper ventilation, air filtration, moisture control, and healthy humidity levels, and by reducing VOCs (volatile organic compounds). To achieve these goals, the Health House program has produced a scorecard of potential points and ratings.

Following are the ten steps to take for a house to be registered as a Health House:

1. Health House training session

2. Health House builder agreement signed

3. Builder's fee of $2,500 per house for fewer than 50 homes ($1,750 if the house qualifies for another green building program)

4. Construction information submittal

5. Independent framing/foundation site inspection and HVAC rough-in site inspection

6. Performance testing by an independent party, which includes a calibrated blower door test, a duct tightness test, and pressure measurements

7. Progress tracking and documentation

8. Final tracking approval

9. Final sign-off of tracking by builder and Health House staff

10. Builder registration and listing on a Health House website

DESIGNED TO EARN THE ENERGY STAR

The estimated energy performance for this design meets US EPA criteria. The building will be eligible for ENERGY STAR after maintaining superior performance for one year.

## ENERGY STAR® Label for Commercial Buildings

*www.energystar.gov*

The U.S. Environmental Protection Agency (EPA) created the ENERGY STAR® label to promote energy efficiency for individual products, in recognition that increased energy efficiency reduces carbon dioxide emissions. In 1996, the Department of Energy (DOE) joined the effort, and ENERGY STAR evolved into the current voluntary program, maintained by the two agencies in cooperation with private industry.

At the planning stage, ENERGY STAR provides tools and design guidance for architects. For building designers, the EPA offers Target Finder, a tool that provides an energy consumption target for design projects. If a building design meets EPA criteria and the design is at least 95% complete with construction documents, the "Designed to Earn the ENERGY STAR" graphic can be displayed on project drawings and documents.

Once the building has been completed and occupied for at least one year, the owner can enter the building's energy use data into EPA's Portfolio Manager, a free, online tool that generates a standardized energy efficiency rating from 1 to 100. Buildings that rate 75 or better may print and submit the Statement of Energy Performance to the EPA. If a professional engineer verifies that the building meets or exceeds the qualifications for energy efficiency and indoor air quality standards, then the building can receive the ENERGY STAR rating. Since the program began in 1999, about 8,000 commercial buildings and plants have earned the ENERGY STAR rating. They must qualify each year in order to maintain their partnership with the program.

Types of buildings eligible for ENERGY STAR rating include:
- Government
- Financial centers
- Health care
- K–12 schools
- Higher education facilities
- Hospitality and entertainment
- Offices
- Religious
- Retail
- Industrial

## ENERGY STAR® Label for Homes
### *www.energystar.gov*

Houses can also receive an ENERGY STAR label. Since the ENERGY STAR for homes program started in 1997, over 1,000,000[13] houses have earned the ENERGY STAR label. An added advantage of obtaining an ENERGY STAR for homes label is that meeting these performance requirements is a prerequisite for LEED for Homes certification. Eligibility is earned by a scoring system called HERS (Home Energy Rating System). A HERS report is prepared by a trained energy rater and considers factors such as insulation, appliance efficiencies, and window types. The HERS report compares the potential ENERGY STAR house to a computer-simulation of a house with the same dimensions and configuration and that meets the 2004 *International Energy Conservation Code*. This simulation is referred to as the reference house. If the potential ENERGY STAR house compares equally to the reference house, it is assigned a score of 80. From this point, each 5% reduction in energy usage compared to the reference house usage adds a point to the HERS score. As with the ENERGY STAR applications for commercial buildings, a qualified third party must verify the results. To qualify for an ENERGY STAR label a house, generally, must meet these criteria:

- Earn a HERS index of 85 for *International Residential Code* climate zones 1–5, and a HERS index of 80 for *International Residential Code* zones 6–8. (On-site power generation cannot be used to decrease the HERS index to qualify for ENERGY STAR.)
- Pass a thermal bypass inspection checklist.
- Limit ductwork leakage to less than or equal to 6 cfm to outdoors/100 square feet.
- Include at least one ENERGY STAR-qualified product category in heating or cooling equipment or windows, or five or more ENERGY STAR-qualified light fixtures, appliances, lighting fixture equipped ceiling fans, and/or ventilation fans.
- Have no more than 20% of all screw-in lightbulb sockets using compact fluorescent lamps to decrease the HERS index.
- Use a qualified third party to verify the results.

*(Note: Requirements may differ in California, Oregon, Washington, Montana, and Idaho.)*

Builders may also add an indoor air package to their ENERGY STAR-labeled houses. The package features a high level of excellence in the following features:

- Moisture Control:
  - Water managed roofs, walls, and foundations
- Pest Management:
  - Additional screens, caulking, termite shields, and concrete reinforcement
- HVAC System:
  - Best practices used in the installation for ducts and equipment to minimize condensation
  - Whole-house and spot ventilation
  - Air filtrations systems
- Combustion-Venting Systems:
  - Direct vented or power vented gas- and oil-fired equipment
  - Properly vented fireplaces
  - Garages that are fully sealed from living spaces and equipped with continuously operated exhaust fans
  - Carbon monoxide detectors in all sleeping areas
- Building Materials:
  - Protection of building materials stored on site from weather

- Material selection and installation procedures that minimize the risk of moisture damage
- Meeting specifications that reduce chemical content
- Ventilating homes prior to occupancy where installed materials are likely to emit airborne pollutants
- Radon control in high-risk regions
  - Gravel and plastic sheeting below slabs
  - Fully sealed and caulked foundation penetrations
  - Plastic piping running from below grade through the roof
  - A junction box for easy installation of an electric fan to the radon vent pipe, if needed

ENERGY STAR homes are also being built in Ontario, Canada. Canadian ENERGY STAR homes are promoted by Natural Resources Canada. These homes are 30%–40% more efficient than those built to the minimum Ontario Building Code standards.

## WaterSense®
### *www.epa.gov/watersense*

WaterSense, like the basic ENERGY STAR for Homes, is a single attribute partnership program sponsored by the EPA. It is intended to protect the future of the nation's water supply by promoting water efficiency, which is another facet of green building. Also, as with ENERGY STAR, the label is available for homes and individual building products. The WaterSense for Home label is intended for new single-family homes and townhouses, three stories or fewer. The EPA approves program administrators; the administrators train certification providers; and the certifier hires, trains, and oversees the inspectors.

To earn the WaterSense label, new houses must meet its criteria for:
- indoor water conservation, including plumbing systems, fixtures, fittings, appliances, and other water-using equipment;
- outdoor water conservation, including landscape design and irrigation systems, if installed; and
- homeowner education.

## Building Product Labels

In an effort to be considered green, product manufacturers make all kinds of claims in marketing materials. Some claims are legitimate, but many miss the mark—a practice commonly referred to as "greenwashing." In evaluating how environmentally friendly or sustainable a product really is, there are several things to be aware of. The following are some examples:
- Hidden trade-offs – A product may have a particular green attribute, but other aspects of the product may pose serious negative environmental consequences.

- Lack of verifiable evidence – Any products that do not supply readily accessible proof of the claims, either directly or through a third party, should be viewed as suspect.
- Vagueness – Often claims are so poorly defined, or so broad, that they can easily be misunderstood. Examples include "non-toxic" or "all natural," and of course, "green."
- Irrelevance – An example of this would be claims that a product is free of toxic substances that are already banned from use.
- "Lesser of two evils" – This occurs when a product has some sort of green attribute but is inherently dangerous, unhealthy, or bad for the environment.
- Untruths – Environmental claims may be simply false.[14]

## GreenSpec® Listed
### *www.buildinggreen.com*

www.GreenSpec.com

GreenSpec is a compilation of more than 2,000 "environmentally preferable" products selected by editors at Building Green Inc., the publisher of *Environmental Building News*™, a leading newsletter on environmentally responsible design and construction. GreenSpec-listed products are published in the *GreenSpec Directory,* arranged in CSI MasterFormat ™ order. GreenSpec is available in print form or on the Internet as part of the BuildingGreen Suite™ web-based subscription service. In the internet version, products are searchable by CSI format, and LEED credit. To be included in *GreenSpec*, products are evaluated on their entire life cycle, and must meet at least one of the 26 specific criteria that are organized into the following categories (although conforming to any one of the criteria doesn't automatically qualify a product):

- Products made with salvaged, recycled, or agricultural waste content
- Products that conserve natural resources
- Products that avoid toxic or other emissions
- Products that save energy or water
- Products that contribute to a safe, healthy built environment

In the selection process, the editors apply both quantifiable and verifiable standards, when possible. For example, in the 6th edition of GreenSpec, the standard for gas-fired domestic water heaters is an energy factor of .80 or higher. For appliances, the standard is typically higher than what is required by ENERGY STAR. For central air conditioners and heat pumps, the product line must have at least one model with a Seasonal Energy Efficiency Ratio rating of 16 or greater. Check for current standards, since they are periodically evaluated and updated. When an applicable standard is not available, judgment calls are made based on the editors' knowledge. The staff considers not only specific benefits, but also the overall environmental performance.[15] *(More information on GreenSpec and specifying green products and materials can be found in Chapter 11.)*

## ENERGY STAR® Label

The ENERGY STAR program started labeling individual products even before it started labeling houses and commercial buildings. The list of labeled products ranges from traffic lights, to Christmas lights. A substantial portion of ENERGY STAR products cover building *components* such as windows, roofing, and boilers. *Appendix D* lists some of the ENERGY STAR-rated building components and the key criteria that determine eligibility. In addition to the United States and Canada, the ENERGY STAR product label is also being promoted in Australia, New Zealand, Japan, Taiwan, and the European Union.

## WaterSense®
### *www.epa.gov/watersense*

Under the WaterSense program, the EPA labels individual building products and fixtures that are particularly water efficient—both for commercial and residential use. These high-performance products are generally found to be 20% more water efficient than other products on the market. Product categories include faucets, dishwashers, commercial steam cookers, showerheads, urinals, toilets, and landscape irrigation controls.

## Forest Stewardship Council
### *www.fscus.org*

The FSC logo identifies products that contain wood from well-managed forests certified in accordance with the rules of the Forest Stewardship Council. The council was established in 1993 to promote the responsible management of the world's forests. It is an independent, non-governmental not-for profit organization. Specifically, it is concerned with ecological, social, and economic aspects of the forest management practices used to produce wood products. These products are tracked from the logging sites through to the end-user. The council has adopted criteria that a company must follow in order for its products to be certified. The company harvesting the product must do the following:

- Meet all applicable laws
- Have legally established rights to the harvest
- Respect indigenous rights
- Maintain community well-being

- Conserve economic resources
- Protect biological diversity
- Have a written management plan
- Engage in regular monitoring
- Maintain high conservation value forests
- Manage plantations to alleviate pressures on natural forests

Generally, the forest must be managed to maintain ecological productivity. Management must minimize waste and avoid damage to other forest resources. A complete environmental assessment must be performed before the start of any site-disturbing activities. Safeguards must be in place to protect endangered species. Environmentally friendly pest control should be used, and chemical pesticides avoided. The FSC website includes a searchable database of FSC-certified products and certificate holders with up-to-date information on the validity of FSC certificates. There is even a separate section on FSC building products and where to find them.

# Greenguard®
## *www.greenguard.org*

Greenguard evolved from a third-party product certification program called AQSpec™, which simply identified products that met general product emission standards of the State of Washington and the U.S. Environmental Protection Agency for the EPA's headquarters project. In 2000, AQSpec was replaced by the Greenguard registry and shortly afterwards became the independent, third-party, Greenguard Certification Program℠, for testing low-emitting products and materials. Greenguard Environmental Institute, also an independent, non-profit organization, is responsible for establishing the standards that define low chemical and particle emissions for indoor goods used in the Greenguard Certification Program℠. In 2005, the Greenguard Children & Schools℠ was established, taking into account the unique characteristics of school buildings, and the sensitive nature of school building occupants. In 2006, Greenguard Building Construction℠ was established to address concerns about mold in new construction throughout the design, construction, and operation of a building. Greenguard Institute is a national standards developer authorized by the American National Standards Institute.

Currently there are more than 260 manufacturers that offer Greenguard Certified® products. Rated building products include:

- Adhesives
- Air filters
- Bedding
- Ceiling systems

- Doors
- Flooring
- Furniture
- Insulation
- Office furnishings and equipment
- Movable walls
- Acoustic panels
- Finishes
- Wall covering
- Window treatments

# Global Ecolabelling Network
## *www.globalecolabelling.net*

Ecolabelling is performed by individual member organizations on all types of products, both consumer and commercial. These products include road materials, flooring, wallboard, insulation, windows, burners, boilers, water heaters, appliances, and other building components. The Global Ecolabelling Network members use specific criteria to determine whether a product results in a lower environmental burden and impact in relation to comparable products. If the product meets these goals, it may display a label signifying that it meets the criteria set by the individual ecolabelling organization. The Global Ecolabelling Network is a nonprofit association composed of 26 ecolabelling organizations. Formed in 1994, its goal is to "improve, promote, and develop the ecolabelling of products and services." Members of the Global Ecolabelling Network must:

- Be based solely on voluntary participation for potential licensees.
- Be run by not-for-profit organizations without commercial interests.
- Exhibit independence from undue commercial interests.
- Have a source of funding that will not create a conflict of interest.
- Seek advice from and consult with stakeholder interests.
- Have a legally protected logo.
- Determine criteria based on an assessment of the overall life of a product category.
- Allow open access to potential licensees from all countries.
- Establish criteria levels that encourage the production and use of products and services that are significantly less damaging to the environment than other products.
- Conduct periodic reviews and, if necessary, update both environmental criteria and categories, taking into account technological and marketplace developments.

## Environmental Choice
## Global Ecolabel Network Member
### *http://www.terrachoice-certified.com/en/*

The EcoLogo™ is issued on products that are certified by The Environmental Choice Program, a Canadian organization established in 1988. With over 3,000 products carrying the EcoLogo label alerting consumers to environmentally preferable products, it is North America's most widely recognized multi-attribute environmental product label. "A product or service may be certified [issued the EcoLogo] because it is made or offered in a way that improves energy efficiency, reduces hazardous by-products, uses recycled materials, or because the product itself can be reused."[16]

The Appendix lists EcoLogo building components and key criteria that determine eligibility. EcoLogo also maintains requirements for product longevity, as well as the inclusion of instructions for proper use to maximize the environmental benefits of the product, where applicable.

## Green Seal
## Global Ecolabel Network Member
### *www.greenseal.org*

Green Seal is a non-profit organization that certifies a wide variety of products, including building components such as occupancy sensors, photovoltaic modules, residential central air conditioning systems, chillers, heat pumps, windows, window films, and paints. Green Seal-certified air conditioners, heat pumps, and chillers must meet minimum efficiency requirements. The chemical composition of paints is evaluated for substances that are harmful to the environment. Requirements are also set for the content of recycled material used in the packaging.

The Green Seal organization employs life cycle analysis when developing these standards. Green Seal also has created a set of standards specifically aimed at the environmental practices of lodging properties. Its mission is "to achieve a more sustainable world by promoting environmentally responsible production, purchasing, and products." Products that conform to these standards are allowed to display the Green Seal label. The Green Seal label meets the criteria for ISO 14020 and 14024 standards for Ecolabelling and the U.S. Environmental Protection Agency's criteria for third-party certifiers of environmentally preferable products.

## *Other Global Ecolabel Network Members*

Many ecological labeling programs throughout the world are members of the Global Ecolabel Network. The particular standards used for determining the award of a label vary, and are usually based on government or industry standards. These individual labels cover a variety of product categories, including building products. There are Ecolabel programs in 24 different countries.

Multi-nation members of the network members include the European Union "flower" and Nordic Swan Ecolabels. The European Union label represents countries throughout the European Union, Norway, Lichtenstein, and Iceland. The Nordic Swan label represents Denmark, Finland, Iceland, Norway, and Sweden.

## Rate It Green

*Buy green confidently.*

Rate It Green is a fairly new rating system with a different approach to rating green building products. Instead of a central rating authority that hands down a rating, Rate It Greens asks the users of the product to review and rate it (much as you would on amazon.com®). The ratings are posted on their website and scored based on these reviews. The categories are:

- How green is this service/environmental impact
- Quality of service and end product
- Customer service
- Lifetime cost/overall value
- Corporate policies
- Overall

*Measurement & Management Standards*

## Natural Step
*www.naturalstep.org*

Dr. Karl-Henrik Robèrt, a Swedish cancer researcher, developed the Natural Step program in the 1980s, which is based on four basic system conditions that form a framework for a sustainable society.

1. Substances from Earth's crust must not systematically increase in the biosphere.
2. Substances produced by society must not systematically increase in the biosphere.
3. Nature's function and diversity must not be systematically impoverished by physical displacement, over-harvesting, or other forms of ecosystem manipulation.
4. Resources must be used fairly and efficiently in order to serve basic human needs globally.

This framework allows a business to test its practices against an overall goal of sustainability.

Using this framework, the Natural Step organization provides communities and businesses with education and training to develop strategic planning to help them make smart decisions that will move them towards sustainability. This includes performing gap analysis through a sustainability perspective, and providing strategies and planning to close the gaps. The Natural Step Academy provides learning programs using the science based systems approach to sustainable development.

## Backcasting

In an attempt to apply the Natural Step principles to building construction practices, the Oregon Natural Step Network looked at current green building standards, which are all based on incrementally improving the level of sustainability using current methods and technology. In looking for an alternative to current rating systems, this group aims to enhance current green building approaches and may help develop the green building standard of the future. **Backcasting** achieves results by visualizing the desired outcome.[17] The A-B-C-D method to applying the Natural Step Framework consists of four steps: Awareness and Visioning, Baseline Mapping, Creative Solutions, Decide on Priorities.[18] In the case of a commercial building, the group produced the following results:

- Two separate system flow charts—one for the construction of the building, and the other for the operation of the building. The flow charts show materials, transportation, and energy flowing in, with products/services and solid waste flowing out. Flowing both in and out are water, air, and habitat.

- Two separate matrixes—one for construction, and one for operation, indicating in detail how each in-flow and out-flow violates the four basic Natural Step principles. As an example, water coming into the building from wells and rivers, and flowing out in the form of waste/storm water violates Natural Step System Conditions 3 and 4. *(See Figure 9.10.)*

| Natural Step Matrix | | | System Condition | | | |
|---|---|---|---|---|---|---|
| Area | Item | Violation examples | 1 | 2 | 3 | 4 |
| Habitat | | | | | | |
| Water | | | | | | |
| Energy | | | | | | |
| Air | | | | | | |
| Materials | | | | | | |
| Transportation | | | | | | |

**Figure 9.10**
Matrix Used for Both Construction and Operation

- Guidelines that enable full alignment of the four Natural Step principles. For example, the guidelines for water in-flow and out-flow goals can be: A water budget that does not exceed what naturally falls on the site. If the needs exceed the site limits, the difference may be purchased from other sites that have excess water, as long as the process has no damaging impact on the natural systems. The quality, temperature, and rate of flow on the grounds of the site and leaving the site must have no damaging impact on the natural systems of the watershed. The guidelines are intended to describe the end results required to attain a state of "full alignment" and specific methods of how these measures can be attained. The goal is to create a target to shoot for.[19]

## ISO 14000 Series Standards

ISO is not an acronym. The word is actually a Greek term that means "equal." The full name for the organization is the International Organization for Standardization. Established in 1947, it is truly an international organization that consists of representatives from throughout the world. Its purpose is to develop voluntary technical standards, which help promote fair trade. The 14000 series standard encompasses a wide range of environmental issues, as shown below:

- 14010    Environmental auditing general principles
- 14020    Environmental label and declaration principles
- 14030    Environmental performance evaluation
- 14040    Environmental management, life cycle assessment principles, and framework
- 14050    Environmental management vocabulary

ISO also publishes standard 7330, which is used for the determination of acceptable ranges for temperature, humidity, and air velocity for indoor environments.

## ASTM Standards E 2114 & E 2129

ASTM (American Society for Testing and Materials), now ASTM International, is another venerable standards organization. It was formed in 1898 and is one of the largest standards development organizations in the world. ASTM Standard E 2114 encompasses standards for terminology and product selection for green buildings. ASTM E 2129 sets standards for data collection for sustainability of green building products.

## ASHRAE Standards

ASHRAE (American Society of Heating, Refrigerating, and Air-Conditioning Engineers) publishes basic standards for heating, ventilation, and other mechanical building components. (*See Chapter 5 for solar power and heating standards.*) ASHRAE publications include standards that relate to green building construction, such as those for airborne contaminants, CFC emission reduction, commissioning, energy management systems, energy conservation, indoor air environment, and solar energy.

Of special interest to those involved in green building construction is ASHRAE 90.1 (current version is 90.1-2007) *Energy Standard for Buildings Except Low-Rise Residential Buildings.* This code sets requirements for energy efficiency and methods for determining compliance. It covers the building envelope systems (walls, roofs, etc.), HVAC systems (heating, ventilation, and air-conditioning), lighting systems, and hot water systems for new building construction and major additions.

The code consists of basic requirements for these systems. After these requirements are met, additional ones must be complied with by choosing amongst three alternate methods: prescriptive, system performance, or energy cost budget methods. The **prescriptive method,** which is component-oriented, is the simplest method for demonstrating compliance. The **system performance method** allows some trade-offs between components, although it's more difficult to use than the prescriptive method. The **energy budget method** allows trade-offs between systems to arrive at an overall building performance, but is the most difficult to use, and requires computer modeling.

(Note: The description provided is a summary. When using this code, the actual text and other supporting materials from the most current version should be studied and understood. Courses are given periodically that explain it in detail.)

In fact, the *Model Energy Code* and *International Energy Conservation Code* both reference ASHRAE 90.1 for commercial and high-rise residential buildings. The regulations regarding construction of new federal buildings, 10CFR 434 and 435, codify the ASHRAE 90.1 voluntary standards for private buildings and make them mandatory for federal projects. A number of states have adopted or incorporated the *Model Energy Code* or ASHRAE 90.1 into their building codes. To see which states have adopted these codes, check the website, **www.energycodes.gov** and click on the status of state energy codes hyperlink.

Also important is ANSI (American National Standards Institute)/ASHRAE Standard 105-2007, *Standard Methods of Measuring, Expressing, and Comparing Building Energy Performance.* It provides a method to compare energy performance that can be used for any building, proposed or existing, and allows different methods of energy analysis to be compared.[20]

ASHRAE, IESNA (Illuminating Engineering Society of North America), and the U.S. Green Building Council have recently published Standard 189.1, *Standard for the Design of High-Performance Green Buildings Except Low-Rise Residential Buildings.* This new standard has a broader scope than ASHRAE 90.1 and covers site sustainability, water use efficiency, energy efficiency, indoor environmental quality, and impacts on the atmosphere, materials, and natural resources.[21] It's intended to set forth minimum requirements for the design of sustainable buildings, can be incorporated into enforceable building codes, and may eventually become a LEED prerequisite.

## International Performance Measurement & Verification Protocol

The IPMVP protocol was developed with the help of 20 national organizations from 25 different countries for use as a framework for measuring and verifying energy and water conservation, as well as indoor air quality measures, throughout the world.

## International Code Council

The ICC was established in 1994 with the purpose of developing a single, national, comprehensive building code. The advantage of developing a single code is that code officials, architects, engineers, and contractors could work with a consistent set of requirements throughout the country instead of several different codes. As such, the ICC is the organization responsible for the *International Building Code*, which many states and cities are adopting, some of which are making minor modifications to adapt the code to their specific special conditions. In addition to the building code, the ICC also produces guidelines and other technical manuals. Of interest to green building practitioners is the *ICC International Energy Conservation Code.* This section covers many of the same topics as ASHRAE 90.1, but there are differences in the requirements specified in the two codes. The ICC has also partnered with the National Association of Home Builders to create the voluntary Green Building Standard, which is similar to the Model Green Building Home Guidelines but includes more mandatory items and adds a level for higher scoring projects. ICC has recently developed the *International Green Construction Code* for commercial development; it uses the *California Green Building Standards Code* as a key reference document. It is written to be used as an enforceable code throughout the United States and beyond. The *International Green Construction Code* allows the ASHRAE standard 189.1 to be used as an alternative compliance path.

## Underwriters Laboratories

Underwriters Laboratories (UL) has provided independent safety certification for over 100 years. Its UL label is a familiar sight, appearing on 66,000 manufacturers' products and services each year. Recognizing the need for independent environmental claims validation, UL recently created the UL Environment™ subsidiary. In addition to validating environmental claims through existing standards, UL plans to create its own standards for doors, wallboard, suspended ceilings, and other building products.

*Conclusion*  The project team has a large array of sustainability guidelines, standards, and rating systems available. The choice of a standard guideline or rating system will have a direct impact on the overall design, down to the selection of individual components. A big part of that decision will be based on the balance of the cost of sustainable features against the project budget. Often financial incentives are available for incorporating specific sustainable features into the project, but are only available for a limited amount of time. After the selection of a rating system is made, it is important that the project specifications are written to ensure that building materials, installation, and components combine to meet the sustainable goals of the project.

1. Pogrebin, Robin. "The New York Question: How Green Is My Tower?" *New York Times*, April 16, 2006.

2. Angela Stephens, Sites & Harbison, PLLC. "States Require Architects and Contractors to Design and Construct Public Buildings to Achieve LEED Silver Certification, Design Construction Data," November/December 2009.

3. Kristina Shevory. "California Adopts Green Building Codes" *New York Times, Green Inc.*, January 15, 2010. Quoted cost attributed to David Walls, executive director of the California Building Standards Commission.

4. *Environmental Building News*, Volume 10, Number 9, September 2001.

5. Diane Mastrull, "National Green Building Code is in the Works" *The Philadelphia Enquirer*, November 26, 2009.

6. Stephens, Jeff. *Ecostructure Magazine*, November/December 2004.

7. Ibid.

8. Naverarro, Mireya. "Some Buildings Not Living Up to Green Label." *New York Times*, August 31, 2009 and www.usgbc.org/ LEED

9. *Environmental Design and Construction Magazine*, March 2005.

10. Canadian Home Builders Association www.chba.ca/NewHome/ WhyBuyNew/Energy_Efficiency/index.php

11. *CIWMB's Role with High Performance Schools*, White Paper, May 31, 2006 http://www.ciwmb.ca.gov/agendas/ mtgdocs/2006/05/00020533.doc

12. Koch, Christina. *Eco-Structure, Small Steps Toward a Brighter Future*, September/October 2005.

13. *Energy Star website,* www.energystar.gov

14. Green Paper by TerraChoice Environmental Marketing Inc., November 2007.

15. *Environmental Building News*, Volume 9, Number 1, January 2000, revised February 2001.

16. *Great Lakes Untied website,* www.glu.org/en/node/152

17. "Using the Natural Step as a Framework Toward the Construction and Operation of Fully Sustainable Buildings – Version 10," Oregon Natural Step Construction Industry Group, October 2004.

18. *Natural Step website,* www.naturalstep.org/backcasting

19. "Using the Natural Step as a Framework Toward the Construction and Operation of Fully Sustainable Buildings – Version 10," Oregon Natural Step Construction Industry Group, October 2004.

20. Consulting-Specifying Engineer, August 27, 2007.

21. Jeffery Yoders, "ASHRAE Publishes First Green Building Standard" *Building Design & Construction*, January 25, 2010.

# Chapter 10

# Budgeting & Financing Construction

*Joseph Macaluso, CCC*
*Andy Walker, PhD, PE*

Green buildings present the same budgeting challenges that conventional buildings do, but with some added twists. For example, since sustainability is a main objective, how do you decide which sustainable features should get special consideration? A popular approach is to get the most "bang for the buck" by incorporating as many low- or no-cost green measures as possible or, for LEED® projects, to earn the most credits at the lowest cost. Sometimes, however, in order to highlight a particular green feature, a bit of "conspicuous conservation" may be employed—even if it's not the most cost effective strategy. Also, there's the question of which rating system, if any, will be used, and what rating level should be the goal? Funding and financing are often tied to specific rating systems and levels, so this will factor into the choice. The challenge is to find a balance between lower initial costs vs long-term savings, all the while striving for the greenest building and staying within the budget. After all, what good is a green building if it can't be built?

Estimators are well suited for being part of a green project team. Building involves architects, engineers, and other skilled professionals—all vital to the process—but when it comes to determining cost, the task falls not to architects, engineers, economists, or accountants, but to estimators. This often requires the estimators to work with other building professionals in order to distill all the facets of building down to the bottom line. With green building, the group of professionals is expanded, and the scope goes beyond human capital, to include earth capital as well.

Estimators should be brought into the design process as early as possible to help the designers decide which green strategies (or LEED points) are most cost effective. The cost of mechanical, plumbing, and site work systems tends to be influenced more by green attributes than other building components. Some material and product selections start much sooner than they would with conventional buildings, to assure that the sustainable preference for using locally sourced materials is met. Therefore, the estimator will be called in to obtain actual quotes sooner. As a consequence, cost estimates on green buildings are often more detailed and accurate earlier on in the process than with conventional buildings.[1]

When working on LEED projects, cost estimates are required in order to determine eligibility for specific credits. To earn credit in the Material Reuse category, a percentage is required to document the amount of salvaged, refurbished, or reused materials. To find the percentage, the cost of the reused materials is divided by the cost of all the materials on the project. The quotient will determine if that requirement is met for the credit. The quotient method is used to determine if the requirements for other LEED credits have been met, as well.

For Recycled Content credits, a percentage of recycled content (post-consumer recycled content plus one-half of the pre-consumer content) is required, based on the cost of the total of the materials in the project. The recycled content value of a material assembly, however, is determined by weight. The recycled fraction of the assembly is multiplied by the cost of the assembly to determine the recycled content value. Post-consumer material is defined as waste material generated by households or by commercial, industrial, and institutional facilities in their role as end-users of the product, which can no longer be used for its intended purpose. Pre-consumer material is defined as material diverted from the waste stream during the manufacturing process. Excluded is reutilization of materials such as rework, regrind, or scrap generated in a process and capable of being reclaimed within the same process that generated it.

In the Regional Materials section, a percentage of building materials or products extracted, harvested, or recovered, as well as manufactured, within 500 miles of the project site (based on cost) is required for these credits. If only a fraction of a product or material is extracted, harvested, recovered, or manufactured locally, then only that percentage (by weight) will contribute to the regional value.

In the Rapidly Renewable Materials section, credits require a percentage of the total value of all building materials and products used in the project, based on cost, be derived from rapidly renewable materials (made from plants that are typically harvested within a ten-year cycle or shorter). Under the Certified Wood section, a percentage of wood-based materials and products in wood building components must be certified in accordance with the Forest Stewardship Council's (FSC) principles and criteria. These components include, but are not limited to, structural and general dimensional framing, flooring, sub-flooring, wood doors, and finishes. The specific percentages required for these credits depend on the LEED system and rating level that is being sought. Mechanical, electrical, plumbing components, specialty items, and equipment are not included in the calculations, and only materials permanently installed in the project are included. Furniture may be included, depending on the LEED rating system used and the level sought.

## Initial Costs

It's difficult to make blanket statements about green building costs because of the thousands of components that make up a building, and the countless design options. How those components are selected and interconnected, along with the green strategies used, greatly affect both initial and future building costs. One recent study analyzed 600 buildings, comparing the overall costs of those considered "green" (those seeking LEED ratings) to those that were not. Not surprisingly, there was a wide range in square foot costs—in both green buildings and non-green buildings—even within the same usage categories. But globally, there was no statistical difference in the square foot cost of the buildings between those that were green and those that were not.

Here are several recent reports documenting the cost of green building versus conventional construction:

- In a comprehensive analysis of the financial costs and benefits of green building, Greg Kats reported to the California State Agencies' Sustainable Building Task Force that a minimal up-front investment of about 2% of construction costs typically yields life cycle savings of over ten times the initial investment. Kats reported that LEED certification might add less than 1% to building cost; Silver, 2.1%; Gold, 1.8%; and Platinum, 6.5%.[2]
- Another California study, "Managing the Cost of Green Buildings," reported cost premiums of up to 2.5% for Certified, up to 3.5% for Silver, up to 5% for Gold, and up to 8.5% for Platinum LEED ratings, with emphasis on the observation that these costs have been declining in recent years.[3]
- A study for redevelopment of the previous Stapleton Airport in Denver concluded that a complete system of energy-efficient, sustainable, and healthy upgrades would add about 6.5% to the price of a $150,000 home, but that it would save $70–$100 per year in energy costs. A "stretch" of 2% increase in the buyer's debt-to-income ratio is allowed by an Energy Efficient Mortgage, so the same homeowners could qualify for the $163,000 cost.[4]

- A detailed cost estimate for David Eakin of GSA by Steven Winter Associates indicated a premium on the building cost of up to 1% for LEED Certified, 0% to 4.4% for Silver, and 1.4% to 8.1% for Gold for new courthouse buildings. For major office building renovations, the study found an additional cost of 1.4% to 2.1% for Certified, 3.1% to 4.2% for Silver, and 7.8% to 8.2% for Gold. Prior to this study, GSA had been allowing 2.5% increase in cost for green buildings.[5]

- Lisa Fay Matthieson and Peter Morris evaluated the cost of achieving a Silver LEED rating at a 1% increase in construction cost; Gold, a 2.7% increase; and Platinum, a 7.8% increase in a detailed study of a laboratory building in California. However, this same study concluded in an analysis of 138 buildings that any increase in cost due to building green is small compared to the random variation in building costs.[6]

- As if to prove that point, *Environmental Building News* devoted an issue to design strategies, building practices, and material substitutions that cost no more than conventional practice.[7] One example was that a beneficial window on the south side cost the same as a detrimental window on the west side.

While a 2% increase in building cost appears in many of the studies, there is clearly no percentage "rule of thumb" that is appropriate for all cases, and there is no substitute for a cost estimate to ensure that the budget is sufficient to meet the project goals.

> The average premium for green buildings is slightly less than 2%... The majority of this cost is due to the increased architectural and engineering (A&E) design time necessary to integrate sustainable building practices into projects.
> — Greg Kats, A Report to California's Sustainable Building's Task Force, The Costs and Financial Benefits of Green Building

Overall, the cost of building is trending down. Green building practices once added as much as 20% to the construction cost of the building, but with the increased availability of green materials and green building systems, this has dropped to the much more manageable ranges cited.[8]

## Future Costs

Analyzing building costs should include not only first costs, but also future costs that occur over the life of the facility and its systems (or "assemblies"). These costs include operation, maintenance, disposal, and all the incidental expenses associated with the building. This life cycle costing process is discussed further in the Cost Estimating Overview section of this chapter and in Chapter 13.

In the private sector, often the initial purchaser of a building is not the ultimate user. Therefore, most of the emphasis is on first costs, not future costs—with the exception of the owner-occupied building. In the public sector, where buildings are almost always owner-occupied, the entire life cycle cost of the facility will more likely be considered; in fact for federal agencies, life cycle cost analysis is often required. This is one of the reasons why green buildings were adopted early on, and are still more frequently embraced, in the public sector. Other factors are the numerous voluntary and mandatory green design guidelines established by government agencies for use on their own their projects.

## Low-Cost Green Strategies

A green approach to designing, building, and maintaining a facility or home need not be any more costly than conventional building and can actually have lower initial costs in many cases. Even if these individual steps are not enough to win a LEED designation on their own, they will reward building owners with various types of cost savings—from lower first cost, to reduced energy and water use, to good public relations and customer satisfaction.

The measures described in this section are economical in terms of both first costs and life cycle costs. It is important, however, to also consider green strategies with higher first costs since they can often provide substantial long-term savings, not only in reduced utility costs, but in the comfort, health, and productivity of building users. Also worth noting, once again, is that a key factor in a successful, cost-saving, green facility is the integration, early in the building design process, of all systems for optimal results.

## Orient New Buildings Optimally
Site new buildings and position windows to take best advantage of natural daylight, solar heat gain, and prevailing breezes. Natural light, typically strongest on the south wall, provides psychological benefits, while reducing the energy cost of artificial light.

## Construction Materials
### Reduce the Amount of Needed Materials
Renovating an existing building instead of building a new one saves materials and energy, reduces waste, and can shorten the time required for regulatory review and approvals. There can be some challenges in remodeling an older building with green goals in mind. For example, the building's orientation on the site or historic preservation standards may restrict the opportunities for new techniques for daylighting and optimizing energy efficiencies. On the other hand, many older buildings were designed with large windows to maximize light and ventilation

before the days of air conditioning and fluorescent fixtures. Serious structural problems or hazardous materials are another issue that can substantially increase costs.

Using standard-dimension materials in the building design minimizes waste. This not only saves money on materials purchased, but reduces the cost for debris disposal.

Leave structural materials uncovered—for example, concrete floor slabs, wood beams, and concrete wall panels. There are substantial savings in this approach, even after factoring in special texture or color treatments. Forgoing carpet, drywall, and ceiling tiles also reduces the opportunity for mold growth.

Avoid drop ceilings to gain opportunities for daylighting and possibly lower the total building height (taking full advantage of available floor-to-floor height). Surface treatments, including fireproofing and paint, as well as pendant light fixtures, will offset some of the savings.

Plan for open layouts and reduce the number of interior walls to optimize natural light penetration and make spaces more flexible for future changes in use. Special treatments may be needed to contain sound in separate-use areas.

## Reuse/Recycle

"Deconstruct" when demolishing a building to prepare for a new structure. Salvage materials from a remodeling project to reduce disposal/landfill fees for building renovation debris. Many salvaged materials can be sold, or at least given away, and while the time and cost of careful removal is greater than for standard demolition practices, the tax benefits and reduced disposal costs can result in substantial net savings. Deconstruction costs can be 30%–50% less than demolition.

Another option is obtaining salvaged materials, such as lumber, hardware, and code-appropriate plumbing and light fixtures, from another site. Some extra time is needed to separate and store these materials, and labor costs tend to be higher when installing some salvaged items. (*See Chapter 3 for more on deconstruction.*)

Use engineered lumber, which is made of recycled or scrap pieces of wood, as well as cheaper, faster-growing trees. If bonded with toxic glue, these materials should be sealed to prevent off-gassing. Engineered wood is stronger than ordinary lumber, and more resistant to warping and splitting.

Use concrete with recycled fly ash instead of Portland cement. If existing slabs, foundations, or other concrete structures must be demolished on the site to prepare for new construction, consider crushing the concrete on site for reuse as fill in specific areas or sub-base for roads. Always consider recycled products, from roofing to decking, to insulation, paint, and many others.

The project team should set waste management goals for every project and require a plan from the contractor. The methods might include having materials delivered without cardboard packaging or designating specific materials that will be recycled on-site or returned to manufacturers and suppliers. Specific targets and associated costs and savings should be established.

The cost of installing recycling bins for building users is relatively low and reduces the volume and cost of standard refuse removal, while keeping these materials out of the waste stream. Check with local recycling centers and waste authorities to identify what materials can be recycled and how they must be separated.

## Use Environmentally Friendly Materials

Low- or no-VOC (volatile organic compounds) paints, caulks, and joint compound are widely available, as are recycled carpet pad, tile, and insulation, mostly without significant difference in cost from conventional choices. Carpet squares allow for future savings through selective replacement of worn areas. Formaldehyde-free or sealed materials are the best choice for counters and cabinets. Some natural products, such as resins, beeswax, shellac, and linseed and tung oils, may be a bit more expensive, but have lower toxicity and are better for air quality.

Select or add high R-value insulation to minimize heat flow through the ceiling, walls, and floor and reduce air conditioning and heating demand. Check current prices on alternative insulation materials such as recycled cotton and newspaper. (*See Chapter 2 for a comparison of insulation types.*)

Framing lumber is often from old-growth species like white pine and Douglas fir. Spruce is typically less expensive and may also be grown locally, for additional green value. Look for affordable, certified lumber, or at least make sure treated lumber is sealed to prevent off-gassing of VOCs. (If wood needs to be treated to prevent termites, Timbor, made from boric acid, is considered a low-toxicity product.) Using native materials, including wood (and stone), should reduce costs because there is no need for shipping. It also generates less pollution.

# Division 08 - Windows

In selecting the features that pay back on initial investment, look for high insulation value (R-value: aim for R-5 or R-6) and a low-E (or low-emissivity) coating, which allows light to pass through, but reflects heat. (Select windows based on the orientation of each of the building's walls and the amount of solar radiation, as well as the local climate.) It is best to stay away from polyvinyl chloride (PVC) window frames, since this material releases dioxins in manufacture and when incinerated.

Invest in operable windows for natural ventilation that can reduce the need for air conditioning and maximize the benefits of fresh air. Position windows to enable cross-ventilation. Include sunscreens or overhangs to shade windows that face south, thereby reducing heat gain in summer.

Caulk windows, doors, and any other openings in the building envelope with a low-toxicity material to prevent air leaks.

## Daylighting

This technique, capturing natural light to minimize artificial light, is most effective with tall windows and windows positioned close to corners so they can bounce light off of the nearest wall. Skylights are good options in corridors and stairwells.

# Division 11 - Appliances

Choose ENERGY STAR®-rated appliances, they generally consume 10%–15% less energy and water than other models and often do not cost much more than less efficient models.

# Division 22 - Plumbing

Smaller-diameter supply piping is not only less expensive than larger diameter, but brings water where it is needed more quickly and reduces waste. Instant hot water heaters can save money, depending on the application.

Relatively inexpensive carbon filters can be added to sinks to remove chemicals, heavy metals, chlorine, and many forms of bacteria and parasites. Garbage disposals are inefficient because they require running water and deposit organic materials into septic tanks and sewage treatment plants. Composting is a better solution.

Among the cheapest and easiest water-savers are low-flow showerheads and faucet aerators. Each of these devices can cut water use by about 50%, while maintaining good water pressure. (To get an idea of the volume of water saved, a family of four can save roughly 20,000 gallons of water per year by switching to low-flow showerheads and 22,000 gallons with low-flow toilets.) When fixtures need replacing, choose water-conserving models. Toilets older than ten years might be worth replacing even if they are still functioning, as they are major water users. Some water utilities offer rebates for water-conserving fixtures.

For renovation projects, check for and repair leaks. Inspect all systems, including bathroom fixtures, appliances, sprinklers, and all indoor and outdoor faucets. Even one ongoing leak can increase water consumption by ten percent in a typical residence.

## Division 23 - HVAC

Model the building and integrate all systems, including building orientation (for passive solar heat gain), siding and roofing, high-performance glazing, and insulation, to maximize energy efficiency. Right-size HVAC systems accordingly. Over-sized systems are not only more expensive, but inefficient.

The layout and proper sealing of ductwork plays a big role in HVAC efficiency. Ductwork should pass through conditioned air as much as possible. Install roof ventilation intakes in a location that is the least exposed to pollutants, such as high-traffic areas. Select control systems that can be modified in the future, as needed.

Ceiling fans can improve ventilation and comfort at about 10% of the energy cost of air conditioning. With seasonal adjustments, they can draw warm air up during summer and push it down in winter.

## Division 26 – Lighting

In addition to daylighting, task lighting is another way to realize savings. The number of ambient light fixtures can be reduced if effective task lighting is provided, to be used as needed. Savings occur in both the power required for the lighting and the reduced heat load. Use compact fluorescent bulbs (CFLs) instead of incandescent lamps. They can last 10 times longer and use 66% less energy. This can add up to a savings of $20 over three years (for a 23-watt CFL bulb versus a 100-watt incandescent) for just one bulb. They are also an easy and inexpensive retrofit.

For outdoor lighting, select motion sensor fixtures that are only on when needed. A safety-conscious landscape plan may allow you to reduce the number of light fixtures. (Security features include elements such as fencing, prickly bushes in front of ground-floor windows, and trees whose canopies start at least ten feet off the ground, combined with low ground cover.) Fewer light fixtures mean lower initial cost, utility cost, and light pollution.

## Divisions 31 & 32 - Earthwork & Exterior Improvements

Try to minimize removing/bringing in fill from and to the site. Allow for storm water absorption and reduce paving costs by providing permeable landscaping, minimizing the width and extent of paved roadways and parking, and/or using porous paving materials. (Rarely used overflow parking areas could have a gravel surface or be planted with a durable, low-growing groundcover.) These approaches are less costly than building storm sewers and detention ponds and more environmentally responsible than channeling runoff into sewers. Swales can be used, with plantings to help absorb rainwater and prevent erosion. (Check local regulations on runoff early in the process.) Rainwater can also be collected and stored in cisterns for landscape watering or use in servicing HVAC equipment.

If possible, build on a site that already has utility, water, and sewer lines. If more than one structure is to be built on the site, it is most efficient, in terms of utilities and paving, to cluster them together. This approach also allows for open, undisturbed natural spaces that enhance the property. If a space-efficient smaller building can fill the need, substantial savings can be achieved in first construction cost and life cycle (energy/water/maintenance) costs.

Investigate the surrounding area for unhealthy conditions such as underground chemical leaks from tanks or landfills; neighboring sites that are heavily treated with pesticides and high-voltage power lines that produce electromagnetic radiation. Addressing these issues to provide a healthy new facility may be costly—or not possible.

Consult the landscape architect and contractor early in the planning to determine which trees and other plantings on the site should and can be protected. The savings may be worth the effort, especially for large trees that would be difficult and costly to replace. Trees also contribute to the property's value and can reduce the cooling load by providing shade in summer. Try to make "green" areas with plantings as large as possible, rather than having small, isolated plant beds and trees. The larger areas provide for better absorption of runoff and more wildlife diversity.

Plant native flowers, groundcover, or grasses when annuals or other plantings are removed or when new planting areas are being installed. Generally, the cost of native plants is less than or equal to the cost of "foreign" varieties. Native plants will typically require less than 50% of the water needed for non-native varieties and will also save money because they need less maintenance, fertilizer, and pesticides. For new landscapes, consider drip irrigation or rainwater (and/or gray water) collection systems instead of sprinkler systems. (See "Lighting" for outdoor lighting and landscape features that enhance security.)[9]

## Cost Estimating Overview

Cost estimating is required to set, adjust, and then manage the budget for a building project. It is an integral part of the project effort, starting with early program development. For green buildings, early design stage estimating can be a more complex process, since an integrated design is so crucial to the facility's successfully meeting its sustainability, budget, and building use goals.

Different techniques are used to create estimates at various stages of the project. As the program evolves, the method of estimating should progress, from conceptual and approximate, to specific and detailed. The process begins with the Order of Magnitude estimate, followed by the Occupant Unit, the Square Foot and Assembly estimates, and finally the Unit Price, or detailed, estimate. Estimate accuracy should increase as details about the project are defined. A general rule is to be as precise as the details will allow, and to spend the time required as the details warrant. (*See Figure 10.1.*)

## Organizing the Estimate: Work Breakdown Structures

The budget's line items should be appropriately categorized as the level of detail increases. (The term line item in budgeting and estimating refers to the description and costs associated with a particular item. The word line is used because these costs are usually represented on a single row or horizontal line in a budget or estimate.) The line item can be as broad as the foundation, walls, or roof in preliminary estimates, or it can be as specific as rebar ties, drywall taping, or snow guards in detailed estimates. One useful tool to manage these line items, or details, is called a work breakdown structure, or WBS. This is a hierarchical breakdown of a project that contains successive levels of detail. Each level is a more narrowly defined breakdown of the preceding level. The estimator can use either an existing WBS or a

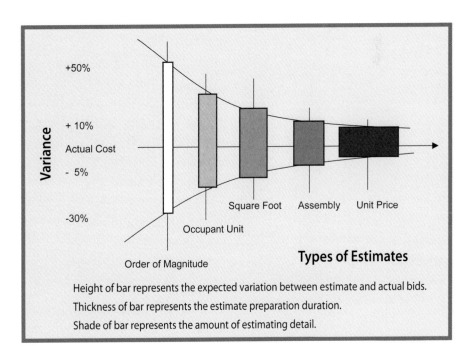

**Figure 10.1**
Types of Estimates and Their Accuracy

project specific system. The WBS provides a way to incorporate project details as they become available without having to prepare an entirely new estimate or budget at each new level. The first level, 1, can further be defined in a second level of detail that will begin with 1.1, 1.2, and 1.3, etc. The next would be 1.1.1, 1.1.2, and 1.1.3, and so forth.

The two most popular WBS formats used for construction are the Construction Specifications Institute's (CSI) MasterFormat and the UNIFORMAT II system, adopted by the American Society of Testing and Materials (ASTM). MasterFormat is based on materials for the related installation tasks, such as wood, concrete, and masonry, whereas UNIFORMAT II is based on installation of complete building systems, such as substructure (a basement foundation or slab), building shell (a roof, exterior wall, or window), and so forth. In addition to these popular formats, some architectural, engineering, and construction firms use their own form of WBS. Most top-level divisions in any WBS will follow a logical sequence. For example, in UNIFORMAT II, Substructure – Division A, precedes Shell – Division B. The advantage of using an established WBS is that they are usually used for project specifications and cost databases, so the estimate will be more efficiently prepared and better coordinated with the project documentation. When working on a LEED project, you will find that project literature is often arranged on a WBS that is based on the LEED credit numbering system.

## Order of Magnitude Cost Estimates

Before any construction budget is developed, a figure must be established as a starting point to begin discussion of costs for the proposed project. This type of "ballpark" figure is typically referred to as an Order of Magnitude estimate and may be somewhat anecdotal in nature. Costs may be estimated per classroom and derived from recent projects, or from published sources, such as RSMeans cost data. Order of Magnitude estimates should be expected to fall in the range between 30% below to 50% above what the actual cost of the project will turn out to be. This estimate may or may not include owner costs, such as legal, architectural, and engineering fees; changes to the original plans and specifications; or other post-bid-award costs.

The costs included in any estimate should be spelled out as clearly as possible, even at this early stage. A cost escalation factor should be added to adjust for increased costs, because the proposed project will be built at some point in the future, and the projects used as a basis for the estimate were built at some point in the past. Because there are virtually no details to consider, examine, or analyze, an Order of Magnitude estimate can be arrived at in a matter of minutes.

Early estimates can have a lot of influence because they are used in feasibility studies and initial project budgeting. The estimate shouldn't be based on overly optimistic assumptions, as it is human nature to remember the first (or lowest) cost mentioned. If the estimate is too low, it can cause problems throughout the project.

## Occupant Unit Cost Estimates

As a building design evolves, the number of occupants the facility will serve is a key piece of information. Estimates that use a common unit relating to the facility's occupants are called Occupant Unit, End Product Unit, End Unit, or Capacity estimates. Costs are expressed in terms of costs per the common unit, which can be seats for auditoriums, beds for hospitals, rental rooms for hotels, or students/desks for schools.

The first step is to gather data on as many recently completed similar projects as possible. The preliminary Occupant Unit estimate will have to be adjusted, or factored, to account for cost escalation between the time the other facilities were completed and the proposed construction time frame for the new building being estimated. This adjustment requires calculating an escalation rate for each of the completed projects, from the midpoint of their construction to the expected midpoint of the proposed new project's construction. In addition, regional labor and material cost differences must be taken into account—between each of the completed projects and those project locations and the location of the proposed new project.

## Square Foot Estimates

Square foot construction costs are based on the gross square footage of building area. Generally, basements, sub-basements, mechanical spaces, stair bulkheads, and other enclosed spaces should be included in the total square footage. Balconies, canopied areas, and open terraces should be counted as one half of their total square footage. The space above auditoriums and gymnasiums or the like that extends beyond the first floor should not be included in the square footage. If there is an interstitial (between floors) space without any equipment in it, it should also not be included. If, however, the interstitial space houses equipment that would otherwise need dedicated space, the area should be included in the square footage. When working with square foot costs, square foot costs will tend to be lower for larger buildings because of the decreasing relative contribution of exterior walls and the economies of scale that come with a larger building.

When working with square foot estimates, site construction and site improvements (CSI MasterFormat Division 02, UNIFORMAT II Division G), costs should not be included, but rather added as a separate figure, since there is no direct relationship between the amount of site construction and site improvements required for a specific size building. As a matter of expedience, however, site work is sometimes included in the square foot cost. Notes accompanying square foot estimates should always indicate whether the estimate is based on gross square footage of the building or on program area, and whether or not site work is included in the cost per square foot.

The square foot estimating method has an expected accuracy range of 20% below to 30% above the actual cost of the project. Estimate preparation time for a new project would typically be about one day.

## Assemblies Cost Estimates

At the design development stage, after the program and schematic design have been completed by the architect, and preliminary plans are starting to be prepared it is time to consider the major systems to be used in the facility. Will the building be air-conditioned? What type of heating system will be used? Will the exterior of the building be brick, concrete block, or another material? During this stage of development, cost estimates are necessary to determine not only the overall building cost, but the cost for major building systems. The Assemblies (or Systems) estimating method is often used at this stage to evaluate the relative costs of major systems and their impact on the project budget.

The assemblies estimate method breaks down a building into individual building systems. Each of these systems, or assemblies, is further broken down into sub-assemblies. For example, a partition assembly is comprised of studs, drywall, and other components. To expedite the estimating process for this partition assembly, these components are all combined and priced out in a common unit, such as a square foot of wall. The estimate may show a single cost for the whole assembly or include a breakdown of all the components that make up the assembly, depending on how much information is available or the level of detail required. Normally, Assemblies cost estimates are organized by the UNIFORMAT II WBS, or a variation of it. The Assemblies estimating method has an expected accuracy range from 10% below to 20% above the actual cost of the project. Preparing an Assemblies estimate for a typical new green project could take about one week.

## Unit Price Cost Estimates

The Unit Price estimate is the most detailed and accurate of the estimating methods, and should be used when the plans and specifications are more than 65% complete. It is not uncommon to have two or three versions of an estimate prepared as the level of plans and specifications progresses to completion. For example, estimates may be prepared at the 75%, 90%, and 100% levels of completion.

The unit price estimate will include costs for each individual item of work. A breakdown of material, labor, and equipment should be provided for each line item. Major headings and subheadings are used to subtotal individual costs. With this type of estimate, the contractor's overhead, profit, owner costs, potential construction change orders (construction contingencies), and potential design changes (design contingencies) are all provided as separate line items. The project plans can be separated into general construction, mechanical, and electrical categories, and estimated by estimators specializing in those trades. Computer software allows several users to work on the same project simultaneously.

The accuracy of Unit Price estimates should fall in a range from 5% below to 10% above actual costs. Estimate preparation time for a unit price estimate of a typical new project is approximately a month, but that time can be reduced significantly if a large estimating staff is assigned to the project.

Unit price estimating is also useful for estimating renovation work, because there is such a variation of existing conditions and scope of work from project to project. For preliminary estimates, sizeable allowances and contingencies are advised, because of the many unknowns, such as unforeseen existing conditions that will affect the renovation cost. Occupant unit, square foot, or assemblies estimating methods can be used to derive preliminary renovation costs for spaces like kitchen and administrative areas, but this approach requires access to a large database of similar projects.

## *Accounting for All Unit Costs*

It is important to define which cost items are included in any type of cost estimate. Many terms have different meanings to different people, so it should never be assumed that a particular cost is included in any estimate. The following is a general outline of costs included in construction budgets: (*See Figure 10.2.*)

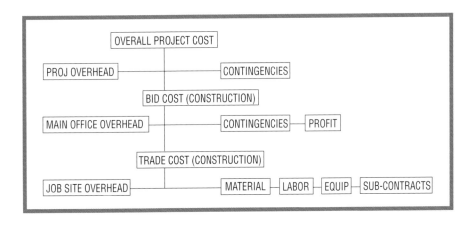

**Figure 10.2**
Project Cost Organizational Chart

The builder's bid costs include:
- Builder's direct costs
- Builder's indirect costs
- Builder's overhead and profit
- Builder's contingencies

Construction costs include builder's bid costs, plus:
- Architectural and engineering fees
- Project management/oversight fees
- Change order costs

Project costs include construction costs, plus:
- Furnishings and equipment costs
- Land acquisition costs and fees
- Project administration costs
- Legal fees
- Financing costs
- Environmental studies costs
- Permits

While the builder's bid amount is usually straightforward, construction and project budgets vary considerably in terms of what is included. Therefore, every estimate should include a basis of the estimate statement with the following information:
- *Purpose*: a clarification of how the estimate is to be used, the standards of accuracy, and the intended purpose of the estimate, e.g., a study, a bid, a budget, and so forth.
- *Scope of Work*: a brief overview of what is included in the estimate and what portion of a larger project the estimate may represent
- *Assumptions and Exclusions*: a list of assumptions made because of incomplete design information, and a listing of anything excluded from the estimate
- *Time/Cost Association*: the project schedule and escalation rates that were assumed in the estimate
- *Contingency Development*: the method and/or rates used to develop contingencies
- *Significant Findings*: a notice of any items of significant risk, concern, or interest that the estimator is aware of in regard to the estimate.[10]

As the project progresses, and the estimating method changes from Order of Magnitude, to Occupant Unit Cost, to Square Foot, to Assemblies, to Unit Price, the basis of the estimate should become more and more detailed.

# Contingency Allowance

A contingency is the amount added to an estimate and budget to cover costs that are likely to be incurred, but are difficult or impossible to precisely predict. The two major categories are costs due to design changes, and costs due to unforeseen construction conditions. These contingencies should be included in the totals for all estimates. Order of Magnitude, Capacity (e.g., cost per student or work station), and Square Foot estimates will have these costs built into their totals. Assemblies estimates may have contingencies included in the totals for each system or added to the overall total as separate line items at the end of the estimate. Unit Cost estimates list contingencies as separate line items, and may include two contingencies:

1.  Design Contingency to cover additional costs for possible design changes. The amount varies with the stages of design. At first, a larger design contingency will be used. As the design is better defined, the contingency should be reduced to near zero as the design is finalized.

2.  Construction Contingency to cover the additional costs of unforeseen conditions, such as utility pipes, underground storage tanks, or large rock ledges on the site, which have to be removed in order for the work to continue. This contingency will be reduced somewhat as field conditions are better understood, and typically will end up at 5%–10% of total construction costs for most new projects.

Sometimes an Owner's Contingency is also included in the estimate and budget to specifically cover costs directly attributed to the owner. In a Guaranteed Maximum Price (GMP) contract agreement, budget contingencies may be categorized as Owner's Contingency and Builder's Contingency. The former is for costs over and above the base budget for which the owner is responsible, and the latter would be for costs over and above the base budget for which the builder is responsible.

For Assemblies and Unit Price estimating, it is helpful to create a customized cost database for a particular facility, so that it can be used for future estimating projects. The assemblies in RSMeans books and software can be modified easily to reflect variations in design standards. All third-party cost data, whether Occupant Unit, Square Foot, Assemblies, or Unit Price, must be adjusted to account for escalation and regional differences, including productivity differences. These factors are available in RSMeans Cost Data books. Typically occupant unit and square foot cost data is arranged according to the type of facility, assembly data by UNIFORMAT II, and unit price data by MasterFormat.

## Value Engineering & Life Cycle Cost Analysis

Along with the design team, the construction project estimating staff should have a working knowledge of value engineering (VE) and life cycle cost analysis (LCCA), and should be expected to be called on to participate in these studies. Though often used to complement one another, VE and LCCA are really two distinct tools. Both are thorough, logical, structured, and systematic decision-analysis processes that can be used to understand and possibly reduce the true overall cost of a facility.

The use of VE and LCCA studies is growing in all types of construction projects and the trend is likely to continue. Value engineering is used to examine a project's required functions, proposed design elements, and construction costs. The focus of a VE study is to provide for the facility's essential functions, while exploring cost savings through modification or elimination of nonessential design elements. VE is specifically spelled out in Public Law 104-106, which states "Each executive agency shall establish and maintain cost-effective value engineering procedures and processes." Specific sustainable design attributes can be included as part of the required functions of the project in a VE study. LCCA is a way of looking at the total cost of a design choice or choices. It includes first cost, operation, maintenance and repair costs, and financing costs over the serviceable life of the design. LCCA is helpful in sustainable building, as a tool to more accurately compare the true costs of competing alternates. LCCA is used to evaluate alternatives that meet the facility's functional and technical requirements with reduced cost or increased value, including consideration of maintenance and operating costs over the life of the facility.[11] LCCA guidelines are recommended or required by many states (including Massachusetts, New York, California, and Arizona) and municipalities for energy-related components such as HVAC, electrical, window, and insulation systems in publicly funded projects. In the state of Alaska, all public facilities are required to employ LCCA for the major systems of a building. The federal government bases cost-effectiveness on the requirements of regulation 10CFR436. Measures are considered cost-effective if the ratio of life cycle savings to investment cost (savings-to-investment ratio) is greater than one, and requires implementing the alternative with the lowest life cycle cost, favoring energy-efficient options. (More on LCCA in Chapter 12.)

## Financial Analysis Introduction

### Break-Even Analysis

Break-Even Analysis or Payback Period analysis is probably the simplest way of looking at one or more design choices for a project. It tells you how long it will take to earn back or break-even on an additional cost through savings or additional revenue. The formula is the First Cost or Additional Cost/Annual Cash Flow or Savings = the Payback Period or Break-Even. The advantage to this method is that it is quick and simple. The disadvantages are that it does not consider benefits that occur after the payback period and that it does not consider the time value of money. A way to get around this problem is to factor in the Net Present Value, complicating the analysis somewhat. Payback Period or Break-Even analysis is helpful in sustainable, green building in determining which option has a shorter payback duration.

## Net Present Value (NPV)

NPV is a way to determine a choice's net value in today's dollars. All costs and benefits, which may be spread-out in time, are adjusted to its "present value" by using discount factors to account for the time value of money.

## Rate on Investment (ROI)

ROI is another simple way to evaluate the efficiency of an investment, or to compare different types of investments. To calculate ROI, the benefit, or return is divided by the cost of the investment. The result is expressed as a percentage. The formula is ROI = (Gain from investment - Cost of investment)/Cost of investment.

## Financing Options

Financing can convert a future stream of savings into the required initial investment for green building systems. Whether the higher cost is justified by fuel cost savings or other benefits depend largely on the terms of the financing arrangement. The most common financing options for green building projects include:

- Grants
- Loans
- Equipment leases
- Energy savings performance contracts
- Chauffage (end-use purchase)
- Utility energy service contracts

Grants are offered by federal, state, and local governments as well as not-for-profit groups. They are most often used as a means to foster innovative approaches to green building. The obvious advantage of grants is that they do not have to be repaid; however, it can be a challenge finding a grant that a particular project will qualify for. Some consultants specialize in finding grants and loans for green buildings.

For homeowners, mortgage loans can offer several advantages in the financing of green construction. Interest rates are kept low through the participation of Federal Loan Associations, plus interest rates on home mortgages are tax-deductible, lowering the effective project cost. Also, mortgage terms of up to 30 years are much longer than personal loans, which have terms of 10 years or less.

Building homes to an established green standard often increases the construction costs, but the energy-saving features and the stringent specifications can also make the house more affordable by reducing monthly expenses, plus add value to the house. Energy-Efficient Mortgages (EEM) take this into account and allow applicants to apply for larger loans. These mortgages are available through the Federal National Mortgage Association (Fannie Mae), the Federal Home Mortgage Loan Corp. (Freddie Mac), the U.S. Department of Housing and Urban Development (HUD), and the U.S. Department of Veterans Affairs (VA). EEMs work well for lower and moderate income level families, where energy costs typically represent a large percentage of a family's expenses. They allow for a 2% increase in the debt-to-income ratio used in the calculations for eligibility. EEM loan limits vary by lender, but FHA mortgage limits range from approximately $200,000 to $360,000 for single family homes (depending on the county where the property is located). A variation of the EEM is called an Energy Improvement Mortgage which can be used to cover the costs of adding energy improvements to an existing home by financing the energy saving upgrades by incorporating them into the mortgage when purchasing the house or when refinancing it.

In order to qualify for an EEM loan, homes must be evaluated with a Home Energy Rating System (HERS) report. The HERS report is used to determine how energy efficient the house is, or, if part of the mortgage is to be used to finance energy improvements, to weigh the increased energy efficiency from the improvements against the cost of those improvements. If the house is not yet built, a projected rating is performed on the energy improvements not yet installed. The projected rating is calculated on the expected energy savings. After the house is completed or after the energy improvements are made, a confirmed rating is calculated. This rating is based on an on-site inspection.[12]

Homes located in urban areas are typically closer to businesses, schools, shopping, and recreation. Therefore, it's more convenient to walk or use inexpensive public transportation. Urbanites tend to have fewer cars and drive fewer miles per household than families living in areas that are spread out. Less automobile use means less pollution, a goal of sustainable development. The money that would have been consumed by automobile expenses can be applied toward the purchase of a home. With this in mind, Fannie Mae has also teamed up with the Natural Resources Defense Council, the Center for Neighborhood Technology, and the Surface Transportation Policy Project to create the Location Efficient Mortgage® (LEM). LEMs are also well-suited to lower and moderate income families who spend a significant portion of their living expenses on transportation costs. LEMs are currently available in neighborhoods within Chicago, Seattle, Los Angeles, and the San Francisco Bay Area. LEMs can be written for up to $300,000 and can be used to purchase not only detached homes, but also town homes and owner-occupied condominiums. LEMs feature a low 3% down payment, and greater flexibility in qualification criteria, but require the home to be located in a densely populated area near public transportation. A worksheet is used to determine the additional buying power of particular neighborhoods. Borrowers must also participate in pre-purchase counseling about homeownership and location efficiency and participate in an annual survey.[13]

Homeowners can also utilize a federal loan program called Clean Renewable Energy Bonds (CREBs) to finance green building strategies such as solar power and efficient irrigation projects. CREBs are issued with a 0% interest rate and the borrower pays back only the principal. The bondholder receives tax credits instead of interest.[14]

Property Assessed Clean Energy (PACE) legislation has created a new type of financing for both commercial and residential property owners through municipal governments. It works by allowing municipalities to float bonds that fund available cash for energy improvement loans. This is used to fund 15-20 year loans for energy improvements. These loans are paid back through a surcharge on the property owner's real estate taxes. This approach provides financing to the property owners without a financial burden on the municipality. It is attractive to investors because, since they're secured by long term tax liens that are senior in right to the mortgage, they are very safe. States where PACE is available include California, Colorado, Illinois, Louisiana, Maryland, Nevada, New York, Ohio, Oregon, Texas, Vermont, Virginia, and Wisconsin.

Leases are an effective way to obtain energy-efficient equipment or green products without a large capital investment. For example, it might be possible to lease carpet, which would be recycled, rather than to purchase it outright. Or, in the case of solar voltaic equipment, under a lease arrangement the cost of maintenance can be included, so that the owner has the financial security of fixed monthly equipment costs and does not have to deal with maintenance headaches.

In an energy performance contract (EPC), an energy services company (ESCO) develops, implements, and finances (or arranges financing) for an energy efficiency project or a renewable energy project and uses the stream of income from the cost savings or renewable energy produced to repay the cost of the project. Actually, the ESCO concept started over 100 years ago in Europe, but, with the focus on energy efficiency and renewable energy that's developed over the past ten years, interest has increased recently in the ESCO concept. ESCOs are unusual for new construction because the utility bills, and thus the energy savings, aren't established yet. However, using building modeling software, it is possible to estimate the savings and base the payments to the ESCO on the modeled amount.[15]

A Chauffage arrangement involves purchasing an end-result rather than purchasing the equipment to produce that end result. Examples include purchasing hot water (in $/BTU) from a solar water heating system or purchasing the electricity produced by a photovoltaic system. Such arrangements (to purchase hot water from solar heating) have been set up at several prisons, including Tehachapi California State Prison, Phoenix Federal Correctional Institution, and Jefferson County Jail in Colorado. (*See Chapter 5 for more on solar energy.*)

Local utility companies should always be consulted when initiating a green building project. They often offer rebates for efficient equipment and may also offer design assistance services and consultation on the effects of rate structures on the cost-effectiveness of green options.

## Incentive Programs

There has been much research on the health and societal costs associated with pollution and resource use. Several years ago, the National Park Service attempted to assign financial costs of air pollution. In today's dollars, those costs work out to be $17.40 per ton of carbon dioxide, $1.10 per pound of sulfur dioxide, and $4.70 per pound of nitrogen oxides.[16] In a recent study on green schools, values of approximately $12.00 per ton of carbon dioxide, $0.60 per pound of sulfur dioxide, and $1.30 per pound of nitrogen oxides were used.[17] Studies of green buildings calculated the 20-year net present value of reduced emissions at $0.50 per square foot.[18]

The wide range of estimated costs is due to the many assumptions that must be employed. However, the cost of these emissions can be as much as half of the total operating costs of a building. Therefore, the building industry has not been able to develop a comprehensive, uniform mechanism for accurately assigning all of the environmental costs associated with a particular building, making it difficult for government entities to determine any sort of "environmental tax." Hence, there is normally no direct financial penalty for not building green. The exception is the county of Arlington, Virginia, which has created a fund to assist green building by assessing those developers that do not commit to achieving a LEED rating a fee of $0.045 per square foot of building area.[19]

Using the carrot instead of the stick to encourage green practices, federal, state, and local governments, as well as utility companies, offer incentive programs in an effort to defray the additional cost of green systems. Some argue that incentives are not necessary and may actually hinder the development of new green technologies in the sense that the credits can create an artificial market; if the incentive is taken away, it could be damaging to these fledgling industries. There is also concern that these incentives send a subtle message to the public that these technologies are not yet cost-effective, when they may in fact be not only cost-effective, but cost-advantageous.[20] In spite of these concerns, many feel that incentives are needed to offset the initial high cost of new technological advances until they become more cost-efficient.

Green building incentives are offered to government entities, manufacturers, builders, owners or end users, and can take several forms. They can be in the form of grants, low interest loans, property tax relief, income tax credits and deductions, or more favorable depreciation rates on equipment. Many of these programs offer indirect financial incentives by providing both information and technical and marketing assistance. Most of the direct financial incentives are offered for energy and water resource conservation, because, by reducing the demand for these resources, state and local governments can reduce infrastructure costs, and thereby reduce the tax and utility rate burden on a community. Incentives based on holistic green building approaches or green building rating systems are less common.

For home builders, regional green building programs sponsored by building trade organizations are available in some areas. These programs offer indirect financial incentives by partnering local home builders with trade associations, investors, and local government, to provide technical assistance, and marketing opportunities—including project identification through the use of recognized rating systems and their logos. Guidelines used for these programs often follow the format though not the exact content used in the LEED rating system.

Financial incentive programs tend to be limited in both scope and duration. However, new incentive programs tend to open up as old ones expire. The green building team must be constantly vigilant to new offerings and mindful of the limited duration of the incentives. The team should include someone with expertise in tracking down and applying for environmental and energy-related loans, grants, and funding from both government and private sources. Several consultant services specialize in finding and obtaining loans and grants.

## Federal Incentive Programs

The National Energy Policy Act of 2005 amended by the Emergency Economic Stabilization act of 2008 and the American Recovery and Reinvestment Act of 2009 have had a significant effect on green building. Significant funding has been channeled already toward green building via state funding or tax incentives to companies and consumers, though it should be noted that many of the programs have or are about to expire. Those that do remain offer benefits to the owners of business, farms, and homes that install renewable and energy efficient systems.

For overall energy efficiency, a tax credit of up to $1.80 per square foot is available to businesses on new and existing commercial buildings that are built to save 50% of heating, cooling, ventilation, water heating, and interior lighting energy costs compared to buildings that meet ASHRAE Standard 90.1-2001.

For fuel cells, tax credits are available to businesses for up to 30% of the costs. For micro-turbines, credits are available for up to 10% of the cost. For solar water heating, photovoltaic, and some solar lighting systems, a tax credit is available to businesses and homeowners for up to 30% of the costs as well as wind turbines, and geothermal heat pumps. Companies for which taxes are not a major economic factor might be able to partner with one that has a tax liability to take advantage of the credits.[21]

## State & Utility Company Incentive Programs

Most states offer rebates, loans, grants, and tax credits to encourage water conservation, energy conservation, the use of renewable forms of energy, or environmental conservation measures. To find out more about these offers, visit the individual states' websites. One example of a state-sponsored organization is the New York State Energy Resource Development Authority (NYSERDA). It offers technical assistance for the Green Building Tax Credit and other loans, grants, and incentives for improving energy efficiency and encouraging green building design and building systems.

Business electricity customers in a utilities service territory can often take advantage of rebates available for purchasing and installing energy-efficient equipment in new buildings or replacing equipment in existing buildings. Rebates are available through utility companies for energy-efficient cooling equipment, lighting equipment, premium efficiency electric motors, and variable frequency drives, and through the customized efficiency programs for projects not covered by the standard conservation programs.

Policies that promote residential and commercial photovoltaic projects include net metering (getting the full retail value for PV power) and rebates that directly reduce the price per DC watt (for example, $1.50/Watt for Xcel customers in Colorado).

Financial incentives are also often available from utilities or state agencies for recommissioning and energy design assistance.

The following websites offer more information on incentives:

- Database of State Incentives for Renewable Energy: www.dsireusa.org

- Solar Energy Industry Association: www.seia.org/Legislation.html
- Tax Incentive Assistance Project: www.energytaxincentives.org

## *Some Examples*

**New York:** New York State's Green Building Tax Credit program allows tax credits for green building construction. In addition to the whole building, tax credits are also available for individual building system components. The program is aimed at large commercial and multifamily projects. The state has formulated a set of specific standards for what constitutes a green building for the purposes of the tax credit that include energy efficiency, indoor air quality, recycling, and compliance with existing regulations. The whole building tax credits are available for up to 7% of the allowable costs, capped at $150/SF for the base building (mechanical rooms, main lobbies, elevators, stairways, etc.), and $75/SF for tenant areas.

For fuel cells that service green facilities, the applicant can receive a 30% tax credit of allowable costs. Allowable costs are capped at $1,000/kw of capacity.

For integrated photovoltaic modules, a 100% tax credit of the allowable incremental costs is offered. Allowable costs are capped at $3/watt capacity.

A 25% tax credit of the allowable incremental costs is available for nonintegrated photovoltaic modules. Allowable costs are capped at $3/watt capacity.

For new air conditioning equipment using non-ozone-depleting refrigerant servicing green spaces, a tax credit is currently offered at 10% of the allowable cost.

There is a cap of $2,000,000 combined component credit per building, and a cap on the total yearly program funding available.

**Maryland:** Maryland's Green Building Tax Credit is for buildings that:

1. Use no more than 65% of the energy attributed to buildings that comply with the ASHRAE 90.1-1999 standard

2. Are certified as LEED Version 2.0 Silver or higher

3. Meet LEED:
    a) Sustainable Sites, Credit 8 Light Pollution
    b) Water Efficiency, Credit 3.1 Water Reduction
    c) Materials and Resources, Credit 2.1 Construction Waste Management

4. Comply with all state, county and local building and construction regulations and processes

## Local Incentive Programs

Municipalities and counties are another source of financial incentives. Some cities offer Integrated Design Assistance and Energy Efficiency Programs. For example, in lieu of tax incentives, Arlington County, Virginia, rewards developers with allowances to build higher-density projects if buildings are LEED-rated.[22] The higher the LEED rating, the higher the density Floor Area Ratio (FAR) allowed. FAR is the relationship between the amount of useable floor area permitted in a building and the area of the lot on which the building stands. It's obtained by dividing the gross floor area of a building by the total area of the lot. For office space the FAR ranges from .05 for LEED certified to .45 for LEED Platinum, and for residential the FAR ranges from .10 for LEED certified to 0.5 for LEED Platinum. This higher density allows more rental units to be built per floor area, which translates to a higher rent roll. The increased rental income can offset the higher first costs of building green.[23]

Austin, Texas, not only provides technical assistance and free publicity to developers that incorporate green design features, but also offers rebates on a wide variety of products and services. Residential projects are reviewed by the Green Building Program and receive ratings from one to four stars, depending on the design's degree of sustainability. Rebates are dependent on the completion of the project, and the amount of energy and water savings realized.[24]

In Chicago, Illinois, the Chicago Department of Construction and Permits has implemented an innovative program that can reduce the time it takes to process permits for green buildings to less than 30 business days and even as little as 15 days. This reduction in time can indirectly reduce the cost of the project by reducing its overall duration. Applicants that demonstrate an extraordinary level of green features may be able to have consultant code review fees waived, which can range from $5,000 to $50,000 depending on the size, type, and complexity of the project. (*See Figure 10.3.*)

Seattle, Washington's Priority Green program provides technical, permitting assistance, and priority land use and building permit review for innovative green building projects. The Downtown Density Bonus allows some density and building height increases for buildings that achieve a LEED silver rating.[25]

The government is not the only source of incentive programs. The private sector can also help. The Enterprise Green Communities is a good example of a not-for profit based incentive program. Enterprise Community Partners (then called the Enterprise Foundation) was started in 1982 to provide funding, technical expertise, and political action to help promote affordable housing. Enterprise Community

| PROJECT TYPE | BENEFIT TIER I | BENEFIT TIER II | BENEFIT TIER III |
|---|---|---|---|
| | Expedited permit[1] (goal < 30 days) | Consultant review fee paid up to $25,000 Expedited permit[1] (goal < 30 days) | Consultant review fee 100% waived[1] Expedited permit (goal < 30 days) [1] |
| **Residential** Market Rate Single Building (<10 units) | Not applicable | Chicago Green Homes ★ ★ + 2 Menu Items | Chicago Green Homes ★ ★ ★ + 3 Menu Items |
| Market Rate Multiple Buildings (<10 units/building) | Not applicable | Chicago Green Homes ★ ★ + 3 Menu Items | Chicago Green Homes ★ ★ ★ + 3 Menu Items |
| 20% Affordable Development (<10units/building) | Not applicable | Chicago Green Homes ★ ★ + 2 Menu Items | Chicago Green Homes ★ ★ ★ + 3 Menu Items |
| Market Rate Multifamily (including hotels) | LEED Certified[2] + 2 Menu Items | LEED Silver[2] + 2 Menu Items | LEED Platinum[2] + 2 Menu Items |
| 20% Affordable Multifamily | Chicago Green Homes ★ ★ + 2 Menu Items | Chicago Green Homes ★ ★ ★ + 2 Menu Items | LEED Silver[2] + 2 Menu Items |
| **Institutional** Hospitals | LEED Certified[2] + 2 Menu Items | LEED Silver[2] + 2 Menu Item | LEED Platinum[2] or LEED Gold + 2 Menu Items |
| Community Centers and Schools | LEED Certified[2] + 1 Menu Item | LEED Silver[2] + 1 Menu Item | LEED Platinum[2] or LEED Gold[2] + 2 Menu Items |
| **Industrial** | Not applicable | LEED Certified[2] + Energy Star Roof + 1 Menu Item | LEED Gold[2] or LEED Silver + 2 Menu Items |
| **Commercial** Retail over 10,000 square feet (footprint) | LEED Certified[2] + Energy Star Roof + 2 Menu Items | LEED Silver[2] + 25% Green Roof + 2 Menu Items | LEED Gold[2] + 50% Green Roof + 2 Menu Items |
| Retail under 10,000 square feet (footprint) | LEED Certified[2] + 1 Menu Item | LEED Silver[2] + 1 Menu Item | LEED[2] Platinum or LEED Gold + 2 Menu Items |
| Office over 80 feet tall | LEED Certified[2] + 50% Green Roof + 2 Menu Items | LEED Silver[2] + 75% Green Roof + 2 Menu Items | LEED Platinum[2] or LEED Gold + 75% Green Roof + 2 Menu Items |
| Office under 80 feet tall | LEED Certified[2] + 2 Menu Items | LEED Silver[2] + 2 Menu Items | LEED Platinum[2] or LEED Gold + 3 Menu Items |

1 Applicant must contact DOB at beginning of construction documents to fully benefit.

2 All LEED projects must earn a minimum of 2 points under Energy and Atmosphere Credit 1: Optimize Energy Performance.

* Projects consisting solely of installation of a green roof or renewable energy equipment on an existing building are also eligible for the Green Permit Program.

**Figure 10.3**
The Chicago Dept. of Construction and Permits Green Permit Program provides an incentive to build green by streamlining the permit process timeline. Note the higher the LEED rating, the quicker the permit can be processed.

Partners receives donations from large corporations like Home Depot, Kresge, and major banks. It uses these donations to provide funding for affordable housing projects. The funding comes in the form of grants, loans, and Low Income Housing Tax Credits (LIHTC) equity. In 2004, the Enterprise Green Communities was launched as a five year program using the Green Criteria (*see Appendix*) as a requirement for participating in the program and receiving LIHTC equity. The criteria are similar to the LEED for homes rating system and are referenced in the criteria. Under this program they have built over 14,500 homes and have trained 4,500 housing professionals. They have now started on the second generation of Green Communities, another five-year program. The criteria for the next generation of Enterprise homes will be published on their web site at www.enterpisenextgen.org. The goal is to produce or preserve 75,000 green houses, commercial, and community buildings.

## Conclusion

Building green requires a high degree of advance thought, knowledge, research, collaboration, analysis, paperwork, and legwork to assess and maximize both the ecological and economic advantages. Specific requirements of funding partners must be met in order to secure their loans, grants, and assistance. Preparing a good set of project specifications is critical to making sure that the goals of both the green building ratings system and the funding partners are met—not to mention the design and function of the project as a whole for the owner, building users, and community. This chapter dealt primarily with the direct costs of building green; however, there are many other indirect costs and benefits associated with building green which Chapter 15 will delve into in more detail.

1. *Estimating Projects Seeking LEED Certification – An Update*, DCD magazine, Joseph J. Perryman MRICS MAPM LEED-AP.

2. Greg Kats, Leon Alevantis, Adam Berman, Evan Mills, Jeff Perlman. "The Costs and Financial Benefits of Green Buildings: A Report to California's Sustainable Building Task Force." October 2003.

3. Geof Syphers, Mara Baum, Darren Bouton, Wesley Sullens. "Managing the Cost of Green Buildings." KEMA. October 2003.

4. David Johnson. *Building Green in a Black and White World.* Home Builder Press, National Association of Homebuilders, Washington D.C.

5. Steven Winter Associates, GSA. "LEED Cost Study submitted to General Services Administration." October 2004.

6. Lisa Fay Matthieson and Peter Morris, "Costing Green: A Comprehensive Cost Database and Budgeting Methodology." Davis Langdon. 2004.

7. *Environmental Building News*. Building Green. May 1999.

8. *The New York Question: How Green Is My Tower?*, New York Times, Robin Pogrebin, April 16, 2006.

9. Global Green Sustainable Design Competition for New Orleans "Top 20 No- or Low-Cost Green Building Strategies." http://competition.globalgreen.org/green_building/ 05_twenty_strats_1.php
Environmental Building News "Building Green on a Budget" May 1999. http://www.buildinggreen.com/features/lc/low_cost.html
Global Green "A Blueprint for Greening Affordable Housing: Developer Guidelines for Resource Efficiency and Sustainable Communities." http://`www.globalgreen.org/media/publications/housing.pdf

10. Dysert, Larry and Bruce Elliott "The Estimate Review and Validation Process" Cost Engineering Morgantown, WV, January 2002.

11. Alphonse J. Dell'Isola and Stephen J. Kirk, *Life Cycle Costing for Facilities*, Reed Construction Data, 2003.

12. http://www.natresnet.org/ratings/default.htm

13. http://www.locationefficiency.com

14. *Going Green Without Going Broke – Combating the Green Premium*, Leigh A. Poltrock, Esq., Cohen & Grisby, PC – March 19, 2009.

15. Bertoldi, P and Rezessy, S. 2005. *Energy Service Companies in Europe*. Status report 2005. European Commission, DG JRC, Institute for Environment and Sustainability, Renewable Energies Unit. EUR 21646 EN.

16. *National Park Service Denver Service Center Guideline 94-04*, revised September 1997. (Costs Escalated to 2006 using the Bureau of Labor Statistics CPI calculator and rounded to the nearest tenth of a dollar.)

17. *National Review of Green Schools: Costs, Benefits, and Implications for Massachusetts*, Greg Kats, December 2005, Capital E.

18. Ibid

19. http://www.arlingtonva.us/DEPARTMENTS Environmental Services/epo/EnvironmentalServicesEpoGreenBuildings.aspx

20. Environmental Building News, June 2000.

21. http://www.energytaxincentives.org

22. http://www.arlingtonva.us

23. Governing, January 2002.

24. http://www.ci.austin.tx.us

25. http://www.seattle.gov

# 11 Specifying Green Products & Materials

## Mark Kalin, FAIA, FCSI, LEED AP

Green, greener, greenest? Is it more important for a product to have high recycled content, a minimum carbon footprint, or be sustainably manufactured? What are life cycle assessments, environmental product declarations, and carbon-neutral products? There are more questions than answers. Fifteen years ago, Kalin Associates authored *GreenSpec – Specifications for Environmental Sustainability*. Today we have completed over 150 projects seeking USGBC LEED certification, and a few answers have emerged:

1. Performance should remain the number one criterion for product selection.

2. Performance, cost, and availability determine which products are actually installed.

3. Achieving LEED certification is a matter of careful planning and clear specifications.

4. Project owners look to the entire team to make sustainable choices.

Every U.S. president has had an environmental policy. Our favorite was President Clinton's:

> Our vision is of a life-sustaining earth. We are committed to the achievement of a dignified, peaceful, and equitable existence. We believe a sustainable United States will have an economy that equitably provides for satisfying livelihoods and a safe, healthy, high quality life for current and future generations. Our nation will protect its environment, its natural resource base, and the functions and viability of natural systems on which all life depends.

Green, greener, greenest? You will need to make the necessary choices. This chapter provides information to help building design and construction professionals select and specify green building products. Topics include:

- Building product manufacturers and green products
- What are green products?
- Who selects green products?
- When are green products selected?
- Green product checklists
- Greening your firm
- Green product short-form specifications

## Building Product Manufacturers & Green Products

Claims by the product manufacturer that their products are environmentally friendly must be carefully evaluated. Several cases in point follow.

**Claim 1: Sheet lead is a green product.** When we requested information from product manufacturers, one of the first responses was from a trade organization from the lead industry. They maintained that lead was a green product because it was a natural material and had a successful history of long-term performance. They recommended we include lead in our list, but we didn't. Is lead a green product? Do we accept the claims of the supplier, which include that there are very few, if any, EPA regulations against using lead in buildings? Or do we consider that lead content is regulated in commercial and residential paint products, as even small chips of lead paint are believed to cause brain damage in young children? Or that installers are required to regularly have their lead levels checked? Or that lead doesn't migrate in the soil, and its use for hundreds of years verifies the manufacturer's claims?

**Our Opinion:** Lead is not acceptable in an elementary school or any location where a young child can touch it. Lead is not acceptable as a roofing material where water runoff will enter a watershed or other environmentally sensitive areas. As major producers continue to eliminate lead from their product lines, the choice will be made for us, and alternative alloys with tin and zinc will replace lead.

**Claim 2: Carpet pad manufactured from virgin urethane is greener than rebonded carpet cushion.** Manufacturers of carpet cushion claim that less energy is required to manufacture carpet pad from virgin urethane than the energy and adhesives required to fabricate rebonded carpet pads. Should we only recommend the use of virgin urethane pads?

**Our Opinion:** Virgin urethane pads have more uniform density. Don't feel obligated to use rebonded carpet pads. Depending on your perspective, both may be seen as green.

Claim 3: Latex paints are a greener choice than oil-based paints with higher volatile organic content (VOC) emissions. Water-based latex paints are considered greener than oil-based paints. However, manufacturers of oil-based paint claim longer service life and less repainting over the life cycle of the building. The cleanup of oil-based paints is controlled, while latex paint waste is frequently flushed down drains where the algaecides and fungicides in the paint kill the bacteria at the sewage treatment plant. Should we use oil-based paints?

Our Opinion: Zero-VOC and latex formulations have advanced paint technology significantly. Since most commercial repainting is done for new tenants or a new color scheme, longer service life isn't necessarily the determining factor. The choice may be made for us, as state and regional limits on VOCs are established.

Claim 4: Linoleum is green because it is made of natural components. The last linoleum plant in the U.S. closed in the 1930s (as vinyl asbestos tile pushed it from the marketplace), and now linoleum is manufactured primarily in Europe. Should we count the embodied energy in manufacturing as well as the fuel costs of transportation in our product selection? The manufacturing process for linoleum is energy-intensive; is the extra cost worth higher wear performance?

Our Opinion: Although an increase for the demand in linoleum has instigated manufacturing in the U.S. again, selection based on green criteria should include more than just the use of natural ingredients. It's ultimately the designer's choice.

Claim 5: PVC is a green choice for roofing and waterproofing. Use of PVC for roofing and waterproofing in Europe is considered a hazard, but high-performing PVC systems are readily available in the U.S. PVC didn't exist 80 years ago, but now each of us has a measurable amount of PVC in our bodies. Do we know the answer?

Our Opinion: PVC roofing and waterproofing systems perform well and should be considered, as the intended purpose is to keep the building dry (to avoid all the material and health hazards of uncontrolled water in a building). But PVC contains dioxin which is a potent carcinogen, and associated with the manufacturing of PVC, as well as with disposal and accidental combustion in building fires or landfills. If your goal is to reduce the amount of PVC in your building, start on the inside rather than the outside with PVC-free flooring, wall base, casework, computers, pens, chairs, and furniture; yet without plastics, the planet could not sustain its current population.

Claim 6: Forest Stewardship Council (FSC) certified wood is the green choice for your projects. There's even a USGBC LEED point you can earn for using certified wood. However, certified wood in architectural species has thus far been available only at a premium price. Most of the certified forests are mid-sized, and not all species are readily available. The program is excellent, but critics, such as the Canadian government and others, believe they have been managing their forests for decades, and the wood they produce meets other sustainable wood programs without being FSC certified. On a recent LEED project, once it was determined that 50% of the wood would not be certified, the requirement was abandoned for the entire project. Note that the current LEED (version 2009 as of this printing) still requires a minimum of 50% FSC certified wood content for credit, but now includes prorated FSC Mixed Credit products within the calculation.

**Our Opinion:** Why should only one certification agency be included in LEED? The Sustainable Forestry Initiative (SFI), developed by members of the American Forest and Paper Association, is one of several with legitimate credentials. The difference between "green" and "LEED" becomes more apparent.

Identifying green products, just like defining sustainability, is an exercise in subjectivity. There are many different definitions of green, such as being 100% recycled and recyclable; using less energy in manufacture; improving the building users' health through reduction in toxic materials; or employing more energy-efficient methodologies for heating, cooling, and lighting. *(See Chapters 1 and 2 for green building definitions, and more on green materials and products.)*

Green is all of the above and more. By our definition, green products are those with excellent performance that maintain or improve the human environment while diminishing the impact of their use on the natural environment—in other words, *sustainable*.

## What Are Green Products?

Materials in use for sustainable design run the gamut from cotton insulation, to recycled asphalt paving, to photovoltaic arrays. Many products offer a green component that is at best incremental, offering performance or some other characteristic that is only slightly better than the conventional product. Use of these products by designers and contractors results in a positive effect that is now measurable.

In our experience, green product characteristics fall into six categories, and many products have benefits in multiple categories. Note that these categories are somewhat subjective, and a product that falls into three categories is not necessarily any more green than a product that falls into only one category.

1. Green process

2. Improved sustainability

3. Recycled content

4. Recyclable

5. Low toxicity

6. Biodegradable

**Green Process:** The product is manufactured with consideration for exposure of workers to chemicals, source of materials, energy-efficient production methods, use of recycled materials in packaging, reclaiming manufacturing waste, and prudent use of energy. Since many of these approaches actually save the manufacturer money, these principles are incorporated as manufacturing facilities are upgraded. Even manufacturers of plastics can effectively claim their manufacturing as a green process. *(See Chapter 9 for more on green product rating standards.)*

**Improved Sustainability:** The product is renewable and makes good use of available resources. Use of wood from well-managed forests for building framing is an example of renewable and sustainable product selection. Sustainability considers the whole instead of specifics, emphasizing relationships rather than pieces in isolation. Sustainable design considers environmental and human health and well-being, in addition to the traditional criteria of function, cost, and aesthetics. While environmentalists have focused attention on the degradation of natural systems, advocates of sustainability generally believe in trading destructive behaviors for healthy ones and developing in ways that are beneficial ecologically and economically.

Sustainability can be illustrated by systems as well as individual products, such as those used to improve the energy performance of the building. For example, the current energy code of the *Massachusetts State Building Code* requires an air barrier in the exterior wall assembly and continuous insulation located outboard of the metal studs in a brick veneer-steel stud wall assembly. An air barrier can be established simply by taping the joints and perimeter of the exterior gypsum sheathing, but only by using a tape with a very low permeability and a high-performing permanent adhesive. Many architects have chosen to put a continuous air and vapor barrier membrane over the entire wall, again improving the long-term energy performance of the building and reducing the risk of premature failure of the exterior wall. Since the insulation is outside of the membrane, this allows the elimination of fibrous insulation in the metal stud cavity and the vapor barrier behind the interior drywall. Some prefer to limit fibrous insulation, and most acknowledge that an interior vapor barrier is frequently breached during installation or by wall outlets or other utility penetrations. (For construction details illustrating the concept [in Autocad format], refer to **www.pacerepresentatives.com,** a manufacturers' collaborative website.) The assembly improves the longevity of the exterior wall, decreases the risk of mold in the exterior wall, and improves the energy performance of the building.

**Recycled Content:** The product is fabricated with post-consumer materials or post-industrial by-products. Many products, ranging from steel, to finish materials, to carpet cushion, are manufactured with recycled content. For example, synthetic gypsum board is manufactured from gypsum deposited on the interior of smokestacks at coal-fired power plants during scrubbing. This gypsum is chemically the same as naturally occurring gypsum and does not have to be mined. Considering the overall energy consumption and shipping costs of using synthetic gypsum board, it makes most sense to use it within 500 miles of its manufacturing location. One large gypsum manufacturer claims that over 30 percent of its overall production is synthetic gypsum board. The company recommends that designers consider using their standard products if the project location is more than 500 miles from a synthetic gypsum plant, because the cost of shipping will outweigh the advantage of using recycled materials.

Other post-consumer materials include items such as plastic wood products fabricated using recycled plastic bottles. Products such as structural steel are always fabricated with both post-industrial (waste scrap) and post-consumer (salvaged steel) content.

**Recyclable:** The product can be reused or reprocessed after use and refabricated. We are most familiar with recyclable soda cans and bottles, but the same can apply to asphalt paving, masonry, metal framing, insulation, gypsum wallboard, acoustical ceiling panels, toilet compartments, and even carpet. Extruded polystyrene insulation manufacturers claim their product can be reused in roofing assemblies, since the material is not affected by moisture. Most major manufacturers of gypsum wallboard and acoustical ceiling panels provide facilities to recycle construction waste from their products.

**Low Toxicity:** The product is less toxic than comparable products used for the same purpose. Toxic fumes from site-mixed products, coatings, adhesives, and sealants containing such chemicals as formaldehyde and styrenes are a real threat to health, especially in remodeling projects where the building may be occupied while the work is being performed. Exposure to such products as carpet adhesives and high-performance paints has caused problems ranging from discomfort to long-term disability.

All products are now required to have Material Safety Data Sheets (MSDS) listing their components and potential hazards, but many architects have no training in interpreting them. Many hospitals and some manufacturing companies require MSDS submittals before they will allow a product at their construction site or manufacturing facility. Wood particleboard manufactured with resins that do not contain formaldehyde offers a less toxic environment for chemically-sensitive individuals and even for artwork stored in museums. *(See Chapter 7 for more on airborne toxins.)*

**Biodegradable:** The product returns to the earth naturally under exposure to the elements. The abandoned barn in the field eventually collapses and disappears. The subway car is dumped into the ocean as a marine habitat, and over time the steel corrodes. We expect our buildings to last a lifetime, but it is not necessary for products to last thousands of years.

## Who Selects Green Products?

Product selection is different from specification writing. The specifier may know the method to communicate product selection to the contractor, but cannot complete the specification until a product is selected. A frequent criticism of specifications by contractors is that there is too much boilerplate, and too little product specifics.

Selection of building products is difficult. Considerations of cost, performance, and aesthetics are critical. For a detailed methodology of product selection by performance or prescriptive methods, refer to *The Project Resource Manual (PRM) - CSI Manual of Practice,* produced by the Construction Specifications Institute and available at **www.csinet.org** The same methodology applies to green products. Who makes the selection?

**The Owner:** Corporate owners and owners of retail chains choose products frequently. Their experience with hundreds of locations gives them the knowledge of what works. One retail chain delivers the carpet adhesive to each of their stores under construction, for example, as lawsuits from tripping hazards are a major concern. Corporate and retail clients are also interested in consistent brand identity and the buying power that comes with multiple locations. Most individual building owners rarely select products and usually allow the architect to make product selections. Institutional projects have facility management staffs and sometimes student committees who champion green product research and selection.

**The Architect:** The architect's professional license addresses the need to protect public health, safety, and welfare. Product selection is largely the architect's responsibility. If a waterproofing material must withstand 50 feet of hydrostatic head, for instance, the architect must find a product that performs. If the building code requires fire-retardant treatment for roof sheathing, it is the architect's responsibility to specify a fire-retardant product. The contractor is not responsible for code compliance for product selection. Since many green products are relatively new, the architect must perform significant research or find verification that the product is suitable and code-compliant.

**The Specification Writer:** There are over 1,700 products in a typical project specification for a building. The design architect generally selects products that meet the most critical performance requirements or products of visual importance. In reality, the specification writer selects many of the other products, based on the materials already researched in their master specifications, recent projects, or field experience. For most manufacturers, it is important to have their name included in the specifications. A specifier who finds a green product that is suitable for use may incorporate that product into the master specification and use it on every project. In reality, the specification writer shares the responsibility for product selection with the architect, as part of the design team.

**The Contractor/Subcontractor:** Contractors and subcontractors have significant product knowledge. They can assist the architect or specification writer during product selection and specification and frequently suggest substitutions during construction. The value of their contribution to the product selection process should not be underestimated, as one specific product can succeed or fail depending on the situation. A major building product manufacturer indicated that six out of seven product failures they investigate are attributed to inappropriate use of the product. For example, moisture-resistant gypsum board should not be used for ceilings in toilet rooms. The product was researched, specified, bid, purchased, and installed—and then failed because it was the wrong product for that purpose. There are no spec police; experienced professionals should make product selections.

**The Product Manufacturer:** The product manufacturer is the expert. The architect, specifier, or contractor can never know the product as intimately as its manufacturer. The manufacturer should assist in recommending green products based on their knowledge of where and how the product is to be used. For example, a carpet installation on a slab-on-grade will require a vapor barrier, while a carpet installation on an elevated slab may or may not. A low-emitting adhesive may have a more limited installation temperature range than that of a solvent-based adhesive. Water-based epoxies may be suitable for toilet rooms, but not for the food service area.

## When Are Green Products Selected?

There are five phases in a typical construction project, and selection requirements for green products depend on the phase. *(See Chapter 8 for more on the green project team and sequence.)* The following selection process should be considered for all products, green or not:

1. **Schematic Design:** Prepare outline specifications or a project description. Determine the owner's requirements for green design, budget impact, and possible need for green products to meet industry green evaluation programs, such as the U.S. Green Building Council LEED Certification, GreenGlobes, or the

Green Guide for Health Care. Green products and alternative mechanical and electrical systems often involve an initial premium price, with justification usually based on life-cycle costs. *(See Chapter 13 for life cycle cost evaluation methods.)*

2. **Design Development:** Update outline specifications or prepare a draft of full specifications. Verify project requirements, including the essential evaluation of the green products' performance requirements. Explore information on product options and features.

3. **Construction Documents:** Prepare full specifications, illustrating the requirements for green products. Re-evaluate detailed information, compatibility with adjacent materials, and material performance. If the contractor is not familiar with the product, additional details and installation instructions will be needed.

4. **Bid and Award:** Assist with sourcing green products and answering bidders' questions. The contractor may require phone numbers, websites, or sources for green products unfamiliar to them. Bidders must be advised which products are required, and which are intended to contribute to LEED credits.

5. **Construction Administration:** Enforce your specifications. Be wary of substitutions that, while meeting other performance criteria, cannot meet green requirements. Verify that green products are ordered on time, and that the installers are factory-trained or acceptable to the manufacturer. For a USGBC project, maintain project documentation for final submittal for LEED certification. This will require collection of specific manufacturer information on VOC content limits, usually described in the manufacturer's MSDS (Material Safety Data Sheet) or MLC (Manufacturer's Letter of Certification). For items where the manufacturing location and source of materials is important, an affidavit from the manufacturer should be required. The subcontractor will be required to separate labor and material costs for LEED calculations.

## *A Green Product Checklist*

One of the easiest ways to get started selecting green products is to develop a checklist of choices. While a checklist could be dozens of pages long, Figure 11.1 (at the end of the chapter) is limited to a smaller number of reasonable choices that can be used in many projects. The checklist is intended to help the design team select green products efficiently for construction projects. The 120 green choices are listed in CSI MasterFormat order. After completion of this checklist, the author (usually the designer or project architect) should circulate it to the project team and specification writer for comments. Since these choices might also be included in your firm's master specifications, refer to the specifications for specific products, manufacturers, websites, and telephone numbers for each item.

## Greening Your Firm

How do you get to green? The following examples relate the relative success of four firms as they approach sustainable design and green product selection.

**Firm 1:** The principals of the architectural firm make a commitment to sustainable design and green products. They decide to internally evaluate all of their projects based on the LEED Rating System of the U.S. Green Building Council or other rating system such as Green Globes. Green review is added to their quality assurance program.

*Six months later:* The firm finds that the LEED criteria for sustainable design closely match their existing designs. Sensitivity to context and energy efficiency have been considered in their projects for many years. The LEED rating system points out some new opportunities, but there are no major changes in the design or document production processes. Green products selected for projects are frequently value-engineered out, and their corporate owners don't seem particularly committed to green, nor to the claims of increased productivity with sustainable design. Green grows slowly in the firm because only a few are committed to sustainability.

**Firm 2:** A firm specializing in government work notes that their clients are requiring evidence of experience with green design as a selection criterion for architects. The marketing principal convenes a meeting of project managers, and an organized effort is made to achieve LEED certification for a project and green their specifications. Designers and project managers in the firm are encouraged to learn green principles, so they can "talk the talk."

*Six months later:* Several LEED projects are under way, and the engineering disciplines in the firm are pleased to have the opportunity to do more energy modeling and to work with the designers to improve overall performance of the buildings. However, green efforts are generally limited to key people, and the rest of the firm waits for the trickle-down influence of those in senior positions. The firm has established its green credentials, and use of the firm's green specifications gradually increases.

**Firm 3:** A committee of interior designers in a multidisciplinary firm meets monthly to discuss green topics. Speakers are invited, staff attends green seminars, and a consultant is hired to create a database of green products to be made available on the firm's intranet. Green articles in magazines are constantly circulated to appropriate staff.

*Six months later:* The enthusiasm of the green committee spreads to most of the younger staff in the firm. Individuals contribute to a common database, and even small contributions build the firm's green deliverables. The firm subscribes to numerous magazines, and the librarian routes articles according to the interest areas expressed by individual staff. The green dynamic continues to grow in the firm, and a certain green pride develops. Projects meet their green targets.

**Firm 4:** The principal responsible for maintaining the firm's details on energy performance and exterior wall assemblies expands his long-standing commitment to building technology by adding sustainable design to his criteria. Green products are added to the firm's master specifications. LEED projects accelerate the process. The firm creates a position for a green researcher.

*Six months later:* All projects are reviewed during design for energy performance and green opportunities. The technology principal has much success requiring individual project architects to evaluate their projects for green. During bidding and construction, some contractors object to the special materials and increased inspections during construction, but the firm enforces its policies. Research backs up product selection and detailing. Buildings with improved energy performance and careful product selection are designed, constructed, and put into service.

## Conclusion

The responsibility for selecting and specifying sustainable building products and systems lies with the entire design team. Owners, architects, engineers, contractors, and building product manufacturers all contribute, based on their unique views of the project. Owners who make green credentials part of their designer and contractor selection process have the most success. Emerging professionals with the energy to investigate and try new products move the green industry forward. Contractors who understand building technology embrace buildings that perform better and processes such as commissioning which improve building performance. As our population increases and as the available resources are consumed, the imperative for sustainable design is ever more apparent. The responsibility is yours and mine, moving green to greener one project at a time.

# A Green Product Checklist

DATE:_____ PROJECT NAME: _____

COMPLETED BY: _____

## DIVISION 01 - GENERAL

- ☐ Certification: require USGBC LEED V3 [New Construction] [Existing Buildings] [Commercial Interiors] [Core and Shell] [Schools] [Retail] [Healthcare] [Homes] [Neighborhood Development] certification at [certified] [silver] [gold] [platinum] level.
- ☐ Green Globes: require [final structure in compliance] [work consistent] with Green Globes – US level [Two Globes] [Three Globes] [Four Globes] requirements.
- ☐ EPA Rating: comply with Energy Star [new home] [building label] qualifications.
- ☐ EPA Rating: comply with WaterSense recommendations.
- ☐ EPA National Performance Track: comply with EPA performance track criteria and environmental management system.
- ☐ Health Care: comply with Green Guide for Health Care (GGHC) recommendations.
- ☐ Health Care: comply with Hospitals for a Healthy Environment H2E Award criteria.
- ☐ During Construction: implement construction pollution and IAQ controls.
- ☐ During Construction: implement a construction waste management system.
- ☐ Commissioning Before Occupancy: implement construction pollution and IAQ controls.
- ☐ Final Cleaning: implement green housekeeping practices for final cleaning procedures.
- ☐ System Performance After Construction: implement commissioning.
- ☐ Substitutions: require impact on green design goals for proposed substitutions.

## DIVISION 02 - EXISTING CONDITIONS

- ☐ Disassemble components and existing structures for reuse
- ☐ Verify hazardous materials are disposed of legally in licensed landfills

## DIVISION 03 - CONCRETE

- ☐ Permanent insulating concrete formwork
- ☐ Reusable concrete formwork
- ☐ FSC-certified formwork
- ☐ Rebar supports fabricated from recycled steel
- ☐ Rebar supports fabricated from recycled plastic
- ☐ Cellular concrete
- ☐ Recycled aggregate in concrete mix
- ☐ Coal fly ash or ground granulated furnace slag in concrete mix
- ☐ Low-VOC concrete hardening and curing compounds

## DIVISION 04 - MASONRY

- ☐ Glass block shapes fabricated from recycled plastics
- ☐ Glass bricks fabricated from recycled glass
- ☐ Simulated stone fabricated from recycled materials
- ☐ Concrete masonry units with integral insulation
- ☐ Concrete masonry units fabricated from recycled materials
- ☐ Autoclaved aerated concrete masonry units
- ☐ Brick fabricated from cleaned, petroleum-contaminated soils
- ☐ Salvaged brick reuse
- ☐ Paving blocks fabricated from recycled rubber
- ☐ Masonry cavity drainage material fabricated from recycled materials
- ☐ Locally sourced stone

## DIVISION 05 - METALS

- ☐ Structural steel with recycled content
- ☐ Steel decking with recycled content
- ☐ Cold-formed metal framing with recycled content
- ☐ Metal fabrications and ornamental metal fabricated with recycled content

## DIVISION 06 - WOOD, PLASTICS, AND COMPOSITES

- ☐ Certified wood for framing, Forest Stewardship Council (FSC)
- ☐ Certified wood for interior architectural woodwork, Forest Stewardship Council (FSC)
- ☐ Certified wood for exterior architectural woodwork, Forest Stewardship Council (FSC)
- ☐ Arsenic- and chromium-free pressure-treated wood
- ☐ Engineered framing fabricated from small wood pieces
- ☐ Sheathing fabricated from recycled waste paper
- ☐ Sheathing fabricated from recycled waste paper, fire-retardant
- ☐ Structural insulated panels
- ☐ Floor decking fabricated from recycled wastepaper
- ☐ Underlayment fabricated from recycled wastepaper
- ☐ Underlayment fabricated from recycled materials
- ☐ Salvaged and reclaimed wood (for timbers and interior woodwork)
- ☐ Medium density fiberboard fabricated with recycled and recovered wood fibers
- ☐ Particleboard fabricated with recycled and recovered wood fibers
- ☐ Medium density fiberboard fabricated with no added urea-formaldehyde
- ☐ Particleboard fabricated with no added urea-formaldehyde

**Figure 11.1 (cont.)**

- Rapidly renewable agrifiber board fabricated with no added urea-formaldehyde
- Rapidly renewable bamboo wall paneling
- Wood trim fabricated from veneered finger-jointed wood
- Low emitting wood adhesives, interior use
- Countertop materials fabricated from recycled materials

## DIVISION 07 - THERMAL AND MOISTURE PROTECTION

- Fiberglass insulation fabricated with recycled glass
- Fiberglass insulation fabricated with no added urea-formaldehyde
- Mineral wool insulation manufactured with recycled material
- Cellulose insulation with recycled material and borate-based primer
- Cotton batt insulation manufactured with recycled material
- Biobased spray insulation manufactured with plant based soy content
- Spray foam air barrier insulation and sealant
- Foamed-in-place insulation
- Extruded polystyrene insulation, non-ozone depleting
- Polyisocyanurate insulation, non-ozone depleting
- Exterior water-repellent sealers with low VOCs
- Air and vapor barrier membrane at exterior building envelope
- Recycled rubber roofing slates
- Fiber-cement roofing shingles
- Metal wall and roof panels manufactured with recycled content
- Green roof systems
- Solar reflective materials for roof surfaces, Energy Star qualified
- Roof walkway pads fabricated from recycled materials
- Joint fillers fabricated from recycled materials
- Low emitting joint sealers, interior use

## DIVISION 08 - OPENINGS

- Steel doors and frames with recycled content
- Wood doors with certified wood, Forest Stewardship Council
- Wood doors fabricated from hardboard
- Wood doors fabricated with recycled content cores
- Wood doors fabricated with agrifiber board cores
- Wood doors fabricated with no added urea-formaldehyde
- Fiberglass doors
- Aluminum framing systems fabricated with recycled content aluminum
- Skylights for daylighting
- High-performance wood windows, Energy Star qualified
- High-performance vinyl replacement windows, Energy Star qualified
- High-performance fiberglass windows, Energy Star qualified
- High-performance insulating glass, with low-e coating

## DIVISION 09 - FINISHES

- Low emitting adhesives, interior use
- Gypsum board fabricated with synthetic gypsum
- Gypsum board fabricated at local plant
- Ceramic tile with recycled content
- Terrazzo flooring with recycled content
- Acoustical ceiling panels and suspension systems with recycled content
- Wood flooring with certified wood, Forest Stewardship Council (FSC)
- Wood flooring finishes, low emitting
- Engineered wood flooring with recycled content and no added urea-formaldehyde
- Salvaged and reclaimed wood flooring
- Rapidly renewable cork flooring
- Rapidly renewable bamboo flooring
- Linoleum flooring
- Recycled rubber flooring
- PVC-free flooring, wall base, and accessories
- Resilient flooring systems with FloorScore certification
- Carpet system with CRI Green Label Plus certification
- Carpet system with SGS Cool Carpet climate neutral or ANSI-NSF 140 certification
- Carpet fabricated with recycled materials
- Carpet fabricated with natural materials (wool)
- Carpet tile fabricated with recycled materials
- Carpet backing fabricated without styrene butadiene (SBR) latex
- Carpet cushion fabricated from recycled materials
- Cork wall covering
- Recycled fiberboard wall panels
- Sisal wall coverings
- Acoustical wall panels with recycled content
- Sound control board fabricated from recycled newsprint
- Interior paints with zero-VOC content
- Exterior paints with zero-VOC content

## DIVISION 10 - SPECIALTIES

- Bulletin boards fabricated from cork
- Toilet compartments fabricated from recycled HDPE plastic
- Wall protection systems with PVC-free materials
- Lockers fabricated from recycled HDPE plastic

**Figure 11.1 (cont.)**

☐ Electric hand dryers in toilet rooms
☐ Shower curtains fabricated of cotton

## DIVISION 11 - EQUIPMENT
☐ Dock bumpers fabricated from recycled vehicle tires
☐ Appliances with Energy Star labels

## DIVISION 12 - FURNISHINGS
☐ Manufactured casework fabricated with FSC certified wood
☐ Manufactured casework with no added urea-formaldehyde
☐ Anti-fatigue mats fabricated from recycled materials
☐ Entry mats fabricated from recycled vehicle tires
☐ Permanent entryway systems with drain pans
☐ Window treatment systems with photosensors, automated operation
☐ Window treatment systems with PVC-free materials

## DIVISION 13 - SPECIAL CONSTRUCTION
☐ Solar water heaters
☐ Photovoltaic systems, rooftop mounted modular units
☐ Photovoltaic systems, integrated into building envelope

## DIVISION 14 - CONVEYING SYSTEMS
☐ Machine-room-less traction elevators
☐ Holeless hydraulic elevators

## DIVISION 22 - PLUMBING
☐ Waterless urinals
☐ Ultra low flow toilets
☐ Composting toilets
☐ Gray water recycling system
☐ Heat-sensing flow consumption fittings
☐ Underfloor air distribution system-displacement ventilation system
☐ Low emitting joint sealers, interior use
☐ Low emitting paints, interior use
☐ Commissioning

## DIVISION 23 - HVAC
☐ Energy modeling
☐ Locate ductwork inside building enclosure
☐ Insulate and seal ductwork
☐ Low emitting joint sealers, interior use
☐ Low emitting paints, interior use
☐ Commissioning

## DIVISION 26 - ELECTRICAL
☐ Energy efficient lighting fixtures and bulbs
☐ Occupancy sensors
☐ Perimeter daylighting controls
☐ Low emitting joint sealers, interior use

☐ Low emitting paints, interior use
☐ Commissioning

## DIVISION 31 - EARTHWORK
☐ Recycled subbase materials
☐ Containment structures fabricated from recycled materials
☐ Retaining walls fabricated from recycled plastic
☐ Geomembrane liner fabricated with recycled geotextiles
☐ Geotextiles fabricated from recycled materials
☐ Soil stabilization mat fabricated from recycled plastic

## DIVISION 32 - EXTERIOR IMPROVEMENTS
☐ Rubber paving manufactured from recycled tires
☐ Porous paving manufactured from recycled plastic
☐ Rubber paving fabricated from post-consumer recycled rubber
☐ Brick paving fabricated from cleaned oil-contaminated soils
☐ Glass pavers fabricated from recycled glass
☐ Plastic pavers fabricated from recycled plastic
☐ Rubber unit pavers fabricated from post-consumer vehicle tires
☐ Stepping stones fabricated from recycled rubber
☐ Locally sourced stone for paving and site walls
☐ High albedo (solar reflectance) materials for exterior surfacing
☐ Irrigation hosing fabricated from recycled vehicle tires
☐ High efficiency irrigation system design using [gray water] [harvested rainwater]
☐ PVC-free pipe material options: HDPE and PEX
☐ Play equipment fabricated from recycled components
☐ Granulated rubber play surfacing fabricated from recycled tires
☐ Fencing fabricated from PVC-free HDPE recycled plastic or composite lumber
☐ Bicycle racks
☐ Site furnishings fabricated with recycled content
☐ Erosion control mats fabricated from recycled fibers
☐ Organic fertilizers
☐ Landscape edging fabricated from recycled plastic
☐ Landscape timbers fabricated from recycled plastic
☐ Mulch fabricated from recycled hardwood blend
☐ Mulch fabricated from recycled newspapers
☐ Root barriers fabricated from recycled polypropylene
☐ Soil amendments composed of recycled or composted materials
☐ Native or adapted climate appropriate planting materials
☐ Xeriscaping, landscaping to minimize the use of water and chemicals

**Figure 11.1 (cont.)**

# SECTION 011000
# GREEN PRODUCT SHORT-FORM SPECIFICATIONS

**PART 1 GENERAL**

## 1.1 SUMMARY

A. The green products included in this Section are provided for example only. No endorsement of individual products is intended. Verify product selections and current availability with the product manufacturer before including this text in a project specification. In a typical specification, these products would be included in the appropriate specification section, and not grouped together in a single section. This is a source list; additional product performance requirements, features and attributes would be listed in a full specification.

B. For databases of self-reported green information, consider GreenFormat by The Construction Specifications Institute, www.greenformat.org, ARCATgreen, www.arcat.com, and Building Green, www.buildinggreen.com

## 1.2 SUBMITTALS

A. Product Data: Submit manufacturer's product data and installation instructions for each material and product used. Include sustainable design characteristics.

B. Shop Drawings: Submit shop drawings indicating material characteristics, details of construction, connections, and relationship with adjacent construction.

C. Samples: Submit two representative samples of each material specified indicating visual characteristics and finish. Include range samples if variation of finish is anticipated.

## 1.3 QUALITY ASSURANCE

A. Comply with governing codes and regulations. Provide products of acceptable manufacturers which have been in satisfactory use in similar service for three years. Use experienced installers. Deliver, handle, and store materials in accordance with manufacturer's instructions.

**PART 2 PRODUCTS**

## 2.1 CONCRETE CONTAINING POZZOLAN ADMIXTURES

A. Concrete Containing Coal Fly Ash: Provide coal fly ash in concrete mix, in a percentage acceptable to project structural engineer. Provide coal fly ash from one of the following or approved equal:
1. Member, American Coal Ash Association, Syracuse, NY, telephone 315-428-2400
2. Boral Material Technologies, San Antonio, TX, telephone 210-349-4069
3. Hanson Aggregates South Central Region, Dallas, TX, telephone 800-441-0005
4. Mineral Solutions, Eagan, MN, telephone 800-437-5980
5. The SEFA Group, West Columbia, SC, telephone 800-884-7332
6. VFL Technology, Dagsboro, DE, telephone 302-934-8025

B. Concrete Containing Ground Granulated Blast Furnace Slag: Provide blast furnace slag in concrete mix, in percentage acceptable to project structural engineer

## 2.2 CONCRETE MASONRY UNITS

A. Autoclaved Aerated Concrete Masonry Units: provide lightweight insulating autoclaved concrete masonry by one of the following or approved equal:
1. ACCO Aerated Concrete Systems, Inc., Apopka, FL, telephone 888-901-2226, www.accoaac.com
2. SafeCrete AAC, Ringgold, GA, telephone 706-965-4587, www.safecrete.com
3. E-Crete, Tempe, AZ, telephone 480-596-3819, www.e-crete.com
4. Texas Contec, Inc., San Antonio, TX, telephone 877-926-6832, www.texascontec.com

B. Concrete Masonry Units with Recycled Content: provide units with structural grade expanded shale, clay or slate content, equal to SmartWall Systems, manufactured by one of the following producers, certified by the Expanded Shale Clay and Slate Institute:
1. Camosse Masonry Supply, Worcester, MA 01604-1597, telephone 508-755-6193
2. A. Jandris & Sons, Inc., Gardner, MA 01201, telephone 978-632-0089
3. Medway Block Co., Inc., Medway, MA 02053, telephone 508-533-6701

**Figure 11.1 (cont.)**

C. Concrete Masonry Units with Integral Insulation: provide units by one of the following or approved equal:

    1. IMSI System, as manufactured by Insulated Masonry Systems, Inc., Scottsdale, AZ, telephone 602-970-0711

    2. Sparfil Wall System II, as manufactured by Sparfil Blok Florida, Inc., Tampa, FL, telephone 813-963-3794

    3. ThermaLock Concrete Block, as manufactured by ThermaLock Products, North Tonawanda, NY, telephone 716-695-6000

## 2.3 RECYCLED CONTENT IN METALS

A. Recycled Content of Steel (2007) according to the Steel Recycling Institute:

    1. Basic Oxygen Furnace (BOF), for manufacturing steel studs: 32.7% total recycled content = 25.5% post consumer and 6.8% post industrial

    2. Electric Arc Furnace (EAF), for manufacturing structural steel and rebars: 93.3% total recycled content = 56.9% post consumer and 31.4% post industrial

B. Stainless Steel: stainless steel for building products includes approximately 60% recycled content, both post-industrial and post-consumer, according to the Specialty Steel Industry of North America

C. Aluminum: Post-industrial aluminum is commonly available with approximately 50–75% recycled content at little or no additional cost. Post-consumer aluminum may not be readily available to the building industry.

D. Copper: Copper for building products (except copper wire) includes approximately 50–75% recycled content, both post-industrial and post-consumer. The three major producers of copper sheet products in the U.S. are Hussey Copper Ltd., Leetsdale, PA; Luvata (formerly Outokumpu American Brass Co.), Buffalo, NY; and Revere Copper Products Inc., Rome, NY.

E. Zinc: Zinc for building products includes approximately 30% recycled content, both post-industrial and post-consumer. The two major producers of zinc sheet products in the U.S. are Rheinzink and Umicore Building Products (VM Zinc), which fabricates in Mesa, AZ, and Allentown, PA.

## 2.4 WOOD AND LUMBER MATERIALS

A. Certified Wood: provide wood products from managed forests complying with requirements of the Forest Stewardship Council Principles and Guidelines for certified wood building components; Forest Stewardship Council, Washington, DC, telephone 877-372-5646; www.fscus.org

B. Salvaged and Reclaimed Wood Suppliers: subject to compliance with requirements and, unless noted otherwise, give preference to products manufactured within a 500 mile radius of the project site.

    1. Benson Woodworking Engineered Timber Structures, Walpole, NH 03608, telephone 603-756-3600, www.bensonwood.com

    2. Carlisle Wood Plank Floors, Stoddard, NH 03464, telephone 800-595-9663, www.wideplankflooring.com

    3. Longleaf Lumber LLC, Somerville, MA 02143, telephone 617-625-3659, www.longleaflumber.com

    4. Old Wood Workshop LLC, Pomfret Center, CT 06259, telephone 860-974-3622, www.oldwoodworkshop.com

    5. Sylvan Brandt LLC, Lititz, PA 17543, 717-626-4520, www.sylvanbrandt.com

C. Hardwood Veneer Plywood Fabricated without Urea-Formaldehyde: provide Purebond, by Columbia Forest Products, Portland, OR 97201, telephone 800-547-4261, www.cfpwood.com

D. Medium Density Fiberboard (MDF) Fabricated from Wood Residuals and without Formaldehyde: provide Medite II for interior applications, Medex for use in high moisture applications, as manufactured by SierraPine Ltd, Roseville, CA, telephone 800-676-3339, www.sierrapine.com

E. Agrifiber Board: Industrial grade particleboard fabricated from agricultural residue, including harvested wheat straw and sunflower hulls, and non-formaldehyde-based resin, complying with ANSI A208.1, Grade M3 Acceptable products are as follows:

    1. Environ Biocomposites Manufacturing LLC, Mankato, MN 56001, tel. 800-324-8187, www.environbiocomposites.com

## 2.5 WOOD PRESERVATIVE TREATMENTS

A. Pressure-Treated Wood, Arsenic- and Chromium-Free: provide pressure-treated wood produced in accordance with AWPA U1, use category as applicable, and the following or approved equal:

    1. Standard Product: Preserve Brand treated wood products with ACQ treatment

    2. Water-Repellent Product: Preserve Plus, water-repellent, retention of 0.31 pounds per cubic foot

    3. Manufacturer: CSI Chemical Products, telephone 704-522-0825, www.treatedwood.com

    4. Retention Rate:

        a. Above Ground Deck Support: 0.40 pounds per cubic foot for decking, fence boards, handrails, and similar items

**Figure 11.1 (cont.)**

b. Ground Contact Fresh Water: 0.40 pounds per cubic foot for fence posts, landscaping, piers, docks, and similar items

c. Permanent Wood Foundations: 0.60 pounds per cubic foot for wood foundations and crawl spaces

d. Poles: 0.60 pounds per cubic foot for building and distribution poles

2.6 COUNTERTOP MATERIALS

A. Countertops Materials: provide one of the following or approved equal:

1. Alkemi, by Renewed Materials LLC, Cabin John, MD 20818, www.renewedmaterials.com, 60% recycled aluminum and resin content

2. IceStone, Inc., Brooklyn, NY, www.icestone.biz; 75% recycled glass content

3. CaesarStone USA, Sun Valley, CA 91352; limited colors up to 35% recycled content

4. Silestone by CosentinoUSA, Stafford, TX 77477; limited colors up to 35% recycled content

5. Vetrazzo, Richmond, CA 94804, www.vetrazzo.com; 85% recycled glass content

6. Zodiaq, by duPont, Wilmington, DE 19805; limited colors up to 25% recycled content

2.7 FIBERGLASS INSULATION

A. Fiberglass Insulation Manufactured with Recycled Glass: provide one of the following or approved equal:

1. CertainTeed Corporation, Valley Forge, PA, telephone 800-233-8990, www.certainteed.com; 20–25% recycled glass content

2. Johns Manville Corporation, Denver, CO, telephone 800-654-3103, www.jm.com; 25% recycled glass content

3. Fiberglass Building Insulation by Guardian Fiberglass, Inc., Albion, MI; 20–25% recycled glass content

4. Fiberglass Insulation by Ottawa Fibre, Inc., Ottawa, Ontario, Canada, telephone 613-736-1215, www.ofigroup.com; 60–80% recycled glass content

5. Pink Fiberglass Building Insulation by Owens Corning, Toledo, OH, 800-438-7465, www.owenscorning.com; 30% recycled glass content

2.8 MINERAL WOOL INSULATION

A. Mineral Wool Batt Insulation Manufactured with Recycled Material: provide one of the following or approved equal:

1. ThermaFiber LLC, Wabash, IN, telephone 888-834-2371; 75% recycled content

2. Rock Wool Manufacturing Company, Leeds, AL; 75% recycled content

3. Roxul Inc., Milton, Ontario, Canada, telephone 800-265-6878; 75% recycled content

B. Mineral Wool Spray-Applied Insulation Manufactured with Recycled Material: provide one of the following or approved equal:

1. ThermaTech by ThermaFiber LLC, Wabash, IN, telephone 888-834-2371; 75% recycled content

2. Thermal-Pruf, Dendamix, and Sound-Pruf by American Sprayed Fibers, Inc., Merrillville, IN, telephone 800-824-2997; 100% recycled content

3. Sloss Blowing Wool by Sloss Industries Corp., Alexandria, IN, telephone 800-428-6404

2.9 CELLULOSE INSULATION

A. Cellulose Insulation Manufactured with Recycled Material: Provide one of the following or approved equal:

1. International Cellulose Corporation, Houston, TX, telephone 800-444-1252

2. Members of the Cellulose Insulation Manufacturers Association, Dayton, OH, telephone 888-881-2462

2.10 FOAMED-IN-PLACE INSULATION

A. Foamed-in-Place Insulation: provide one of the following or approved equal:

1. PurFill 1G by Todol Products, Natick, MA; tel. 508-651-3818, www.todol.com; containing no urea-formaldehyde and no CFCs

2. SuperGreen Foam by Foam-Tech, Div. of H.C. Fennell, N. Thetford, VT, tel. 802-333-4333, www.foam-tech.com; containing no formaldehyde, CFCs or HCFCs

3. Zerodraft Z1-24 Foam Sealant by Zerodraft, div. of Canam Building Envelope Specialists, Inc., Mississauga, Ontario, Canada, tel. 877-272-2626, www.canambuildingenvelope.com; containing no added urea-formaldehyde and no CFCs

B. Spray-Applied Bio-Based Insulation: provide low-density, open-cell polyurethane foam insulation, containing 20-25% soy content, equal to one of the following or approved equal:

1. BioBase 501, by BioBased Systems, Spring Valley, IL 61362, telephone 800-803-5189, www.biobased.net

2. HealthySeal 500, by BioPolymers, LLC, www.healthyseal.com

**Figure 11.1 (cont.)**

3. Sealection 500, by Demilec USA, LLC, Arlington, TX  76011, telephone 817-640-4900, www.sealection500.com

C. Spray-Applied Air Barrier Foam Insulation: provide one of the following or approved equal:

    1. WALLTITE by BASF Polyurethane Foam Enterprises LLC, www.basf.com

    2. Heatlok, by Demilec USA, LLC, Arlington, TX  76011, telephone 817-640-4900, www.sealection500.com

## 2.11 RIGID INSULATION

A. Extruded Polystyrene Insulation, Non-Ozone Depleting Substances:

    1. Styrofoam High Performance by Dow Chemical Co., Midland, MI, telephone 800-441-4369; 15% recycled glass content, no HCFC or CFC content

    2. Foamular by Owens Corning, Toledo, OH, 800-438-7465, www.owenscorning.com; 20% recycled glass content, no HCFC or CFC content

B. Polyisocyanurate Foam Insulation, Non-Ozone Depleting Substances: ACFoam, as manufactured by Atlas Roofing Corp., Atlanta, GA, telephone 770-952-1442

## 2.12 THERMOPLASTIC POLYOLEFIN (TPO) ROOFING SYSTEMS

A. Thermoplastic Polyolefin (TPO) Roofing Systems: provide one of the following or approved equal:

    1. Sure-Weld TPO, by Carlisle SynTec Inc., Carlisle, PA  17013, telephone 800-4-syntec, www.carlisle-syntec.com

    2. UltraPly TPO, by Firestone Building Products Company, Indianapolis, IN 46240, telephone 800-428-4442, www.firestonebpco.com

    3. Stevens EP, by Dow Roofing Systems, Holyoke, MA  01040, telephone 800-621-7663, www.dowroofingsystems.com

    4. VersiWeld, by Versico Inc., Carlisle, PA  17013, telephone 800-992-7663, www.versico.com

## 2.13 GREEN ROOF SYSTEMS

A. Green Roof Systems: provide green roof system by one of the following or approved equal:

    1. Garden Roof Assembly by American Hydrotech, Inc., Chicago, IL, telephone 800-877-6125

    2. Green Roof-Roofscape by Barrett Company, Millington, NJ, telephone 800-647-0100

    3. SopraNature by Soprema USA, Inc., Wadsworth, OH, telephone 800-356-3521

    4. Green Shield Green Roof System, by The Garland Company, Cleveland, OH, telephone 800-321-9336

## 2.14 HIGH-PERFORMANCE WINDOWS

A. High-Performance Wood Windows: provide high-performance windows as manufactured by one of the following or approved equal:

    1. Heat Smart, as manufactured by Loewen Windows, Steinbach, Canada, telephone 800-563-9367, www.loewen.com

    2. High-Performance Wood Windows, as manufactured by Marvin Windows and Doors, Fargo, ND, telephone 800-346-5128, www.marvin.com

    3. Designer Series SmartSash, as manufactured by Pella Corporation, Pella, IA, telephone 800-847-3552, www.pella.com

    4. High-Performance Wood Windows, as manufactured by Weathershield Manufacturing Inc., Medford, WI, telephone 800-477-6808, www.weathershield.com

B. High-Performance Vinyl Replacement Windows: provide high-performance windows as manufactured by one of the following or approved equal:

    1. Gilkey Window Company, Cincinnati, OH, telephone 513-769-4527, www.gilkey.com

    2. Kensington Windows, Vandergrift, PA, telephone 800-444-4972

    3. Stanek Vinyl Windows Corp., Cuyahoga Heights, OH, telephone 216-341-7700, www.stanekwindows.com

    4. Thermal Industries, Inc., Pittsburgh, PA, telephone 800-245-1540, www.thermalindustries.com

C. High-Performance Fiberglass Windows: provide high-performance windows as manufactured by one of the following or approved equal:

    1. Accurate Dorwin, Winnipeg, Canada, telephone 204-982-8370, www.accuratedorwin.com

    2. Fibertec Window Mfg. Ltd., Concord, Canada, telephone 905-660-7102, www.fibertec.com

    3. Integrity, from Marvin Windows and Doors, Fargo, ND, telephone 800-346-5128, www.integritywindows.com

    4. Thermotech Fiberglass Fenestration, Carp, ON, Canada, telephone 888-930-9445, www.thermotechfiberglass.com

**Figure 11.1 (cont.)**

2.15 HIGH-PERFORMANCE INSULATING GLASS

A. High-Performance Insulating Glass: provide products by the following or approved equal:

1. Comfort E2, Comfort T1 and Solar Glass by AFG Industries, Kingsport, TN, telephone 800-251-0441

2. INE Neutral Low-E Glass by Interpane, Clinton, NC, telephone 800-334-1797

3. Pilkington Energy Advantage by Pilkington NA, Toledo, OH, telephone 800-526-6557

4. Sungate 500, Solarban 60, Solarban 70, Solarban 70XL, and Azurlite by PPG Industries, Pittsburgh, PA, telephone 800-377-5267

5. VE1-2M and Superwindow by Viracon, Owatonna, MN, telephone 800-533-2080

6. Superglass with Heat Mirror by Southwall Technologies, Palo Alto, CA, telephone 800-365-8794

2.16 SYNTHETIC GYPSUM BOARD

A. Synthetic Gypsum Board: Provide synthetic gypsum board fabricated from gypsum reclaimed from manufacturing processes and recycled paper facings, manufactured by one of the following or approved equal:

1. Gypsum Wallboard, as manufactured by G-P Gypsum Corp. (Wheatfield, IN and Savannah, GA, plants), Atlanta, GA, telephone 404-652-4000

2. Gold Bond Gypsum Wallboard, as manufactured by National Gypsum Co. (Shippingport, PA, or Baltimore, MD plants), Charlotte, NC, telephone 800-628-4662

3. Sheetrock Brand Gypsum Panels, as manufactured by United States Gypsum Co. (Aliquippa, PA, Washingtonville, PA, and Montreal, QC, and others), Chicago, IL, telephone 800-606-4476

2.17 TILE WITH RECYCLED CONTENT

A. Ceramic and Porcelain Tile with Recycled Content: provide one of the following or approved equal:

1. Eco-Cycle Ceramic Tiles, as manufactured by Crossville Ceramics, Crossville, TN, telephone 615-484-2110

2. Armstone Confetti, as manufactured by PermaGrain Products, Inc., Newtown Square, PA, telephone 610-353-8801; 90% recycled content

3. Terra Classic and Terra Traffic Tiles, as manufactured by Terra Green Ceramics, Richmond, IN, telephone 317-935-4760

B. Glass-Silicate Tile with Recycled Content: provide one of the following or approved equal:

1. Aurora Glass, Eugene, OR 97402. 100% recycled glass, 86% post-consumer. A charitable endeavor of St. Vincent de Paul society. All profits are returned to the community through housing, education, and other social programs.

2. Bedrock Industries, Seattle, WA 98119. 100% recycled glass, 50% post-consumer and 50% post-industrial.

3. Environmental Stone Products, Allentown, WI 888-629-1969. Glass tile made from recycled glass and silica.

4. Futuristic Tile, Allenton, WI 800-558-7800. Glass-silicate tile from 100% post-consumer recycled glass.

5. Oceanside Glass Tile, Carlsbad, CA 92008. 85% post-consumer recycled glass.

6. Sandhill Industries, Boise, ID 83716. 100% post industrial plate glass.

2.18 ACOUSTICAL CEILINGS

A. Acoustical Ceiling Systems with Recycled Content: provide acoustical ceilings with percentage recycled content listed for mineral wool, cellulose fiber, glass fiber, metal panels, and suspension systems:

1. Manufacturer: USG Corporation, Chicago, IL, telephone 312-606-4000, www.usg.com

   a. Product: ClimaPlus Ceilings (X-Technology), 62–78% recycled content

   b. Product: Frost, 70% recycled content

   c. Product: Glacier, 71% recycled content

   d. Product: F Fissured, 71% recycled content

   e. Product: Specialty Aluminum Panels, 70% recycled steel content

   f. Product: Donn Aluminum Suspension Systems, 95% recycled steel content

   g. Product: Steel Suspension Systems, 25% recycled steel content

2. Manufacturer: Armstrong World Industries, telephone 877-276-7871, www.armstrong.com

   a. Product: Cirrus HRC, 82% recycled content, reclaimable

   b. Product: Ultima, 70–80% recycled content, reclaimable

   c. Product: Endura, 73% recycled content, reclaimable

   d. Product: Fine Fissured Open Plan, 72% recycled content, reclaimable

   e. Product: Stratus, 72% recycled content, reclaimable

   f. Product: Sanserra, 66% recycled content, reclaimable

   g. Product: Ceramaguard, 38% recycled content, reclaimable

**Figure 11.1 (cont.)**

h. Product: Clean Room Mylar, 31–70% recycled content

i. Product: MetalWorks, 25% recycled content, reclaimable

j. Product: Steel Suspension Systems, 30% recycled steel content

k. Product: Aluminum Suspension Systems, 50% recycled aluminum content

3. Manufacturer: Certainteed Ceilings (Celotex and Ecophon), Valley Forge, PA, telephone 800-233-8990, www.certainteed.com-products-ceilings

a. Products: Cashmere, 82–88% recycled content, reclaimable

b. Products: Symphony m, 82–88% recycled content

c. Products: Gyptone, 85% recycled content

d. Products: Ecophon, 75% recycled content

e. Products: Adagio, 58–65% recycled content

f. Products: Baroque, 52–62% recycled content, reclaimable

g. Products: Fissured, 52–62% recycled content, reclaimable

h. Products: Sand, 52–62% recycled content, reclaimable

i. Product: Suspension Systems, 25% recycled steel content

## 2.19 RESILIENT FLOORING

A. Linoleum Tile Flooring: ASTM F 2195. Provide linoleum tile in color and pattern selected and as follows:

1. Manufacturer: Armstrong World Industries, Lancaster, PA, telephone 877-276-7871, www.armstrong.com

2. Product: Marmoleum, by Forbo Industries, Hazleton, PA, telephone 800-842-7839, www.forbo-industries.com

3. Product: Linoleum xf, by Johnsonite Inc. (a division of Tarkett), Chagrin Falls, OH, telephone 800-899-8916, www.johnsonite.com

B. Linoleum Sheet Flooring: ASTM F 2034. Provide linoleum sheet in color and pattern selected and as follows:

1. Manufacturer: Armstrong World Industries, Inc., Lancaster, PA, telephone 877-276-7876, www.armstrong.com

2. Product: Marmoleum, by Forbo Industries, Hazleton, PA, telephone 800-842-7839; www.forbo-industries.com

3. Product: Linoleum xf, by Johnsonite Inc. (a division of Tarkett), Chagrin Falls, OH, telephone 800-899-8916, www.johnsonite.com

C. Biobased Resilient Tile Flooring: Provide biobased (PVC-free) composition tile in color and pattern selected and as follows:

1. Product: Migrations, by Armstrong World Industries, Lancaster, PA, telephone 877-276-7871, www.armstrong.com

2. Product: MCT, by Forbo Industries, Hazleton, PA, telephone 800-842-7839, www.forbo-industries.com

## 2.20 RAPIDLY RENEWABLE FLOORING

A. Bamboo Flooring: provide one of the following or approved equal:

1. MOSO Bamboo Flooring, MOSO International NA, Ltd., Seattle, WA  98112, www.moso-bamboo.com

2. Plyboo Bamboo, Smith & Fong Company, S. San Francisco, CA  94080, www.plyboo.com

3. Teragren Bamboo, Teragren LLC, Bainbridge Island, WA  98110, www.teragren.com

B. Cork Flooring: provide one of the following or approved equal:

1. Dodge Cork Tile, Dodge-Regupol, Inc., Lancaster, PA  17601, telephone 866-883-7780, www.regupol.com

2. Expanko Cork Co., Parkesburg, PA  19365, telephone 610-436-8300, www.expanko.com

3. Wicanders Natural Cork, by Amorim Flooring North America, Inc., Hanover, MD  21076, telephone 800-828-2675, www.wicanders.com

## 2.21 WOOD FLOORING FINISHES

A. Wood Flooring Finishes, Low-Emitting Types: provide one of the following or approved equal:

1. Polyureseal BP, by American Formulating & Manufacturing Co., San Diego, CA, telephone 800-239-0321, www.afmsafecoat.com

2. Bona Series waterborne polyurethane wood floor finishes, by BonaKemi USA, Aurora, CO  80011, telephone 800-872-5515, www.bonakemi.com

3. StreetShoe, by Basic Coatings, Inc., Toledo, OH  43607, www.basiccoatings.com

## 2.22 FLOORING ADHESIVES

A. Adhesive for Ceramic Tile, Resilient Tile, Linoleum, Carpet, and Other Flooring Materials, Low-Emitting and Low-Odor without Solvents: provide tile adhesive recommended by flooring manufacturer, or one of the following or approved equal:

**Figure 11.1 (cont.)**

1. Ad-vanced Air Tech Adhesives, by Advanced Adhesive Technology Inc., Dalton, GA, telephone 706-226-0610

2. SAF-T Series, by Capitol USA, Dalton, GA, telephone 800-831-8381, www.capitolusa.com

3. Safe-Set Series, by Chicago Adhesive Products Co., Romeoville, IL, telephone 800-621-0220, www.chapco-adhesive.com

4. Safe-Coat Series, by American Formulating & Manufacturing Co., San Diego, CA, telephone 800-239-0321, www.afmsafecoat.com

5. Envirotec Healthguard Adhesives, by W.F. Taylor Co., Inc., Fontana, CA, telephone 800-868-4583, www.wftaylor.com

6. GreenLine Series, by The W.W. Henry Co., Aliquippa, PA 15001, telephone 800-232-4832, www.wwhenry.com

7. Ultra-Bond ECO Series, by Mapei Corporation, Deerfield Beach, FL 33442, telephone 800-426-2734, www.mapei.com

## 2.23 CARPET

A. Carpet Fabricated with Recycled Materials: provide one of the following or approved equal:

1. BPS High Recycled Content Broadloom, by Bentley Prince Street, City of Industry, CA 91746, telephone 800-423-4709, www.bentleyprincestreet.com

2. Carpet with Encore SD Ultima and Karakul, by J&J/Invision, Dalton, GA 30722, telephone 800-241-4586, www.jj-invision.com

3. Commercial Carpet with ColorStrand by Mohawk Industries, Calhoun, GA, telephone 800-622-6227

4. Carpet with EcoTec 6 Backing, by Shaw Contract Group, Dalton, GA 30722, telephone 800-257-7429, www.shawcontractgroup.com

B. Wool Carpet: provide wool carpet by one of the following or approved equal:

1. Classic Weavers, Dalton, GA, telephone 706-277-7767

2. Dresso USA, Inc., Wayne, PA, telephone 215-526-9517

3. Floorgraphix Inc., Cartersville, GA, telephone 404-386-0310

4. Louis De Poortere, Atlanta, GA, telephone 404-688-6331

5. U.S. Axminster, Greenville, MS, telephone 601-332-1581

C. Carpet Tile Fabricated with Recycled Materials: provide one of the following or approved equal:

1. BPX Carpet Tile with GlasBac RE, by Bentley Prince Street, City of Industry, CA 91746, telephone 800-423-4709, www.bentleyprincestreet.com

2. ER3 RS Modular Tile, by Collins & Aikman Floorcoverings, a Tandus Company, Dalton, GA, telephone 800-248-2878, www.tandus.com

3. Earth Square, by Milliken Carpet, LaGrange, GA, telephone 877-327-3639

4. i2 Cool Carpet Tile, Carpet Tile with GlasBac RE, and FLOR Terra with Ingeo PLA Fiber, by Interface Flooring Systems, Atlanta, GA, telephone 866-281-3567, www.interfaceinc.com

5. EcoSolution Q and EcoWorx, by Shaw Contract Group, Dalton, GA 30722, telephone 800-257-7429, www.shawcontractgroup.com

D. Natural Fiber Carpets: provide sisal, coir, hemp, jute, and reed carpets from one of the following or approved equal:

1. Design Materials, Inc., Kansas City, KS 66106, telephone 800-654-6451, www.dmikc.com

2. Earth Weave Carpet Mills, Inc., Dalton, GA 30722, telephone 706-278-8200, www.earthweave.com

3. Sisal Rugs Direct, Excelsior, MN 55331, telephone 888-613-1335, www.sisalrugs.com

## 2.24 CARPET CUSHION

A. Carpet Cushion Fabricated from Recycled Materials: provide one of the following or approved equal:

1. EcoSoft Carpet Cushion, by Invista Commercial Flooring, Kennesaw, GA, 30144, telephone 800-438-7668, www.antron.invista.com

2. Ethos, by Collins & Aikman Floorcoverings, a Tandus Company, Dalton, GA, telephone 800-248-2878, www.tandus.com

3. Syntex, Hartex, PL and DublBac Series, by Leggett & Platt, Inc., Nashville, TN 37202, telephone 615-634-1600, www.leggett.com

4. Endurance II, by Shaw Contract Group, Dalton, GA 30722, telephone 800-257-7429, www.shawcontractgroup.com

**Figure 11.1 (cont.)**

## 2.25 INTERIOR PAINTS

A. Interior Latex Paints with Zero-VOC Content: provide one of the following or approved equal:

1. Pristine Eco-Spec, by Benjamin Moore & Co., Montvale, NJ, telephone 800-344-0400, www.benjaminmoore.com

2. Pure Performance, by PPG Architectural Finishes, Pittsburgh, PA, telephone 888-774-7732, www.ppg.com

3. Harmony, by Sherwin-Williams, Cleveland OH, telephone 800-321-8194, www.sherwin-williams.com

4. Safecoat, by American Formulating & Manufacturing Co., San Diego, CA, telephone 800-239-0321, www.afmsafecoat.com

5. Enviro-Cote, by Kelly-Moore Paint Co., Sacramento, CA 95838, telephone 800-874-4436, www.kellymoore.com

B. Interior Transparent Finishes with Low-VOC Content: provide one of the following or approved equal:

1. Safecoat Clear Finishes, by American Formulating & Manufacturing Co., San Diego, CA, telephone 800-239-0321, www.afmsafecoat.com

C. Interior Water-Based Multi-Color Paints: provide one of the following or approved equal:

1. Polomyx All Acrylic (previously Zolatone Waterbase), by Surface Protection Industries International, North Billerica, MA, telephone 888-765-6699

2. Aquafleck, by California Paints, Cambridge, MA

## 2.26 TOILET PARTITIONS

A. Toilet Partitions with Recycled Content Solid Plastic: provide one of the following or approved equal:

1. Poly-Pro Plus Solid Resin, Capitol Partitions, Inc., Columbia, MD, telephone 410-740-8870, www.capitolpartitions.com

2. Sanypoly Solid Resin, Santana, Scranton, PA, telephone 800-368-5002, www.hinyhider.com

3. Yemm & Hart, Marquand, MO, telephone 573-783-5434, www.yemmhart.com

## 2.27 LOCKERS

A. Lockers with Recycled Content Solid Plastic: provide one of the following or approved equal:

1. The Mills Company, a subsidiary of Bradley Corporation, Menomonee Falls, WI 53052. 800-272-3539, www.bradleycorp.com

2. Sanypoly Solid Resin, Santana, Scranton, PA, telephone 800-368-5002, www.hinyhider.com

3. Yemm & Hart, Marquand, MO, telephone 573-783-5434, www.yemmhart.com

## 2.28 HAND DRYERS

A. Electric Hand Dryers: provide electric hand dryers by one of the following or approved equal:

1. XLerator Electric Hand Dryer by Excel Dryer, Inc., East Longmeadow, MA, telephone 413-525-4531

2. Electric Hand Dryer by World Dryer, Berkeley, IL, telephone 800-323-0701

3. Dyson Airblade, Chicago, IL 60654, www.dysonairblade.com

## 2.29 GRAY WATER SYSTEM

A. Graywater Recycling System: System shall recycle gray water from non-toilet bathroom and laundry waste water for exterior below-grade irrigation system. Provide system by one of the following or approved equal:

1. M-1000, M-100, as manufactured by Agwa Systems Inc., Burbank, CA, telephone 818-562-1449

2. ReWater System, as manufactured by ReWater Systems, Inc., Palo Alto, CA, telephone 415-324-1307

## PART 3 EXECUTION

## 3.1 INSTALLATION

A. Install materials and systems in accordance with manufacturer's instructions and approved submittals. Install materials and systems in proper relation with adjacent construction and with uniform appearance. Coordinate with work of other sections.

B. Restore damaged components. Clean and protect work from damage.

## 3.2 CONSTRUCTION WASTE MANAGEMENT

A. Comply with the requirements of Division 1 Section, Construction Waste Management, for removal and disposal of construction debris and waste.

**Figure 11.1**

# Chapter 12
# Commissioning the Green Building

*Arthur Adler, PE, CEM*

There is the potential for installation and operations problems in all newly constructed buildings. Green buildings may include special systems and equipment that are not familiar to the owner, maintenance staff, or some members of the design and construction team. Consulting an independent, qualified commissioning agent during the programming phase can save time and money and, perhaps most important, ensure that the building functions properly and is easy to maintain and operate as designed.

Commissioning is often thought of as a series of tests conducted on equipment prior to the turnover of systems to the building owner at the end of a construction project, but final testing of systems is only one aspect of commissioning a building. ASHRAE defines commissioning as the process of ensuring that systems are designed, installed, functionally tested, and capable of being operated and maintained to conform to the design intent. The process begins with planning and includes design, construction, start-up, acceptance, and training, and can be applied throughout the life of the building.[1]

There are a number of commissioning resources available that employ different methods of accomplishing the same goal—providing a building that operates as intended—with full documentation and training on all systems. The sources that are referred to most often by owners and commissioning providers are:

- Portland Energy Conservation Incorporated (PECI)
- California Commissioning Guides (2006 available online for free)
  - New Buildings
  - Existing Buildings

- California Commissioning Collaborative – Retrocommissioning Tool Kit (2007/2008 available online for free)
- ASHRAE
- Guideline 0-2005–The Commissioning Process
- Guideline 1.1-2007–HVAC&R Technical Requirements for the Commissioning Process
- Building Commissioning Association
- Building Commissioning Handbook, 2nd Edition
- SMACNA
- HVAC Systems Commissioning Manual, 1st Ed., 1994

Not all aspects of each of these guidelines are required. Owners may choose to have the commissioning agent perform some of these activities and eliminate others. Not surprisingly, cost is the primary reason for reducing the commissioning scope, although it can be argued that the less thorough the commissioning, the higher the costs will be in change orders, energy consumption, and maintenance over the life of the building.

LEED® 2009 for new construction and major renovations (described in Chapter 9) includes two levels of commissioning: fundamental and enhanced.

These basic commissioning activities are prerequisites to achieving any rating:

- Engage an independent Commissioning Authority (CxA) with documented experience on at least two projects. (For projects under 50,000 sq. ft., the CxA may be part of the design team.)
- The CxA must report results directly to the owner.
- The CxA is to collect and review the owner's project requirements and basis of design documentation.
- Develop and include commissioning requirements in the construction documents.
- Develop and implement a commissioning plan.
- Verify the installation and performance for each commissioned system.
- Complete a summary commissioning report.

The commissioning process must be completed for the following energy-related systems:

- Heating, ventilating, air conditioning and refrigeration systems, and associated controls
- Lighting and daylighting controls
- Domestic hot water systems
- Renewable energy systems (e.g., wind, solar)

To receive *two* extra points for commissioning (enhanced commissioning), the following additional activities must be performed:

- Prior to the construction documents phase, designate an independent CxA.
- Conduct at least one focused review of the design prior to the mid-construction documents phase, and back-check the review comments in the subsequent design submission.
- Conduct a selective review of contractor equipment submittal documents for equipment to be commissioned. Perform the review concurrently with the design engineer.
- Develop a systems manual which provides future operating staff with the information required to understand and optimally operate the commissioned systems.
- Verify that the training requirements for the project have been completed.
- Review the operation of the building with operations staff within 10 months of substantial completion. Include a plan for resolving outstanding commissioning-related issues.

Consult the LEED *Reference Guide for Green Building Design and Construction*, 2009 edition for detailed guidance on the rigor expected for design and submittal reviews and creation of the systems manual.

Commissioning tasks should be structured to meet the requirements of the project, and not just the points for a rating system. The more complex the components and systems, the more detailed the commissioning effort should be. For all projects that utilize the sustainable design approach, the commissioning agent should be hired during the programming phase so that he or she can provide input and help define what the building should and should not be able to do. In this way, attributes that may be deemed desirable by some may be negated by the commissioning agent prior to the design team spending any time incorporating these features into the design. Hiring the commissioning agent at this early stage of the process will provide the greatest benefit to the owner.

## Approach

This chapter describes the commissioning-related activities that can be performed during each step of a *complete* commissioning process. (As previously mentioned, some owners may choose to perform only selected steps due mainly to cost considerations.) The primary steps in the life of a project are listed and described below, as they relate to building commissioning:

1. Programming
2. Design

3. Construction

4. Acceptance

5. Post-acceptance

## The Programming Phase

### Hiring the Commissioning Agent (CxA)

The owner or company procuring commissioning services should request the following information from each potential commissioning agent:

- A list of the "green" projects the company has worked on. (A CxA who has worked on green projects may have a better understanding of the process and be able to add more value.)
- A list of the specific phases of the project that each team member was involved in.
- A resumé for each individual who will be working on the project. (A CxA with experience programming and installing building control systems is recommended.)
- A copy of a final commissioning report completed by members of the commissioning team.

### Commissioning Checklist

The purpose of the commissioning checklist, Figure 12.1, is to help plan and keep track of the activities that will be carried out by the commissioning agent. Depending on timing and budget, certain commissioning activities may be eliminated or reduced in scope. This list can be helpful in planning which activities will be used, and then checking them off as they are completed.

## The Design Phase

The commissioning agent should ask questions of all parties involved in the systems to be commissioned during development of each phase of the construction documents. The CxA is also responsible for making sure that all aspects of commissioning have been properly incorporated into the specifications.

### The Design Intent Document

More recently this document has been referred to as the Owner's Project Requirements (OPR). It explains the ideas, concepts, and criteria considered important to the owner. It provides detailed design parameters that the systems must be able to attain when the project is complete. It clarifies the final goals of the system operation to the CxA, as well as to all parties involved in the project's design. The design engineer is solicited for input and feedback to clarify the design intent. The document becomes the basis for functional testing and defining system performance.

| | Check Items That Apply | Notes on Percent Testing, Hours of Training, etc. |
|---|---|---|
| **Programming Phase** | | |
| CxA Participation in the Sustainable Process | | |
| **Design Phase** | | |
| Design Intent Document | | *(Created by A/E?)* |
| Commissioning Plan | | |
| Commissioning Specifications | | |
| Construction Documents Review | | *(Specify at which stages?)* |
| **Construction Phase** | | |
| Coordinate and Direct Commissioning Activities | | |
| Review Construction Meeting Minutes | | |
| Review Equipment Submittals and Manufacturer checklist | | |
| Conduct Commissioning Scoping Meetings | | *(Number of meetings)* |
| Test Procedures | | *(List tests)* |
| Review of Control System Programming | | *(Review for each system type)* |
| Create Test Procedures | | |
| Test Procedure Review | | |
| O&M Manual Review | | |
| Training | | *(List systems and hours (video?)* |
| Equipment Start-up and Pre-Functional Testing | | *(List systems to be witnessed and percent of each type)* |
| **Acceptance Phase** | | |
| Conduct Commissioning Meetings | | *(Number of meetings)* |
| Functional Performance Testing | | |
| Retesting | | *(List equipment and percent of each type to be tested)* |
| Systems Manuals | | |
| Final Commissioning Report | | *(List percent allowance)* |
| | | *(List level of detail to be added)* |
| | | *(List topics to be included)* |
| **Post-Acceptance Phase** | | |
| Seasonal Testing | | |
| Interview Facility Staff and Recommend Improvements | | |
| Trend Analysis | | |

**Figure 12.1**
Commissioning Checklist

The design intent is always evolving. For green buildings, it is critical to work with the owner to discuss and develop a document that provides the following:

- Project schedule and budget including the commissioning process scope and budget
- Project documentation including user requirements and Systems Manual
- Occupancy requirements and schedules
- Training requirements for Owner's personnel
- Warranty requirements
- Benchmarking requirements and statistical tools that are to be used
- Operation and maintenance criteria for the facility and capabilities of the staff
- Quality requirements of materials and construction
- Allowable tolerance in facility system operations for lighting, temperature and humidity
- Energy efficiency and environmental sustainability goals
- Adaptability for future facility changes and expansion
- Systems integration requirements, especially across disciplines
- Acoustical, vibration and seismic requirements
- Accessibility, communication and security requirements
- Applicable codes and standards

The design intent evolves into the basis of design and selection of system types and sizes. The architect, engineer, and owner begin to evaluate the performance requirements that will be required of each system. This is not a trivial exercise. Space heating and cooling loads are greatly affected by the design of the building envelope (insulation values of the roof, walls, and windows), and the internal loads (such as lighting, computers, and people). The CxA should make sure that the design team has discussed all of the energy-saving options available. Electric and gas utilities may provide incentives for specifying energy efficient equipment, systems, and buildings.

Most high-performance equipment has an additional cost, which may be offset over the life of the equipment due to lower energy consumption. Selecting equipment with lower loads can also translate into space savings through smaller heating and cooling systems.

Here are some of the energy-related items that should be evaluated:

- Orientation of the building including location and size of windows
- Daylight harvesting
- Double- or triple-pane glass with low-E coating

- Additional insulation in the walls and ceilings
- Condensing boilers serving systems designed for low temperature hot water
- High-performance chillers and cooling towers
- High-efficiency motors with variable frequency drives
- Occupancy based controls for lighting and HVAC
- Energy-saving sequences, such as static pressure reset, condenser, and chilled and hot water reset enthalpy-based economizer
- ENERGY STAR®-compliant office equipment

After energy-related issues have been discussed, materials must be chosen for the building interior and exterior. The engineer and architect should work with the owner to define which elements are priorities relative to the budget. The CxA should ask questions about each item selected to determine if it will be maintainable, and if the product has been installed in other buildings. Some materials that should be reveiwed closely include the following:

- Caulking and sealants (Consider the maximum allowable level of VOCs and their lifespan.)
- Carpets (Consider the minimum requirement for recycled fiber and maximum VOC level.)
- Paints (environmentally-friendly with low-VOC level)

The level of effort at this stage of the process by the CxA should be equivalent in rigor to that during the functional testing phase. Making changes to materials or systems at this stage of the process is always less expensive than after construction begins.

## Commissioning Plan

The commissioning plan is a document (or group of documents) prepared by the CxA that defines the commissioning process in the various phases of the project. The plan is continually adjusted as the construction of the subsystems and other parts of the building progress. Every portion of the commissioning process is included in the commissioning plan. The plan includes schedules, responsibilities, documentation requirements, communication and reporting protocols, and the level of testing to be completed. Portions of the commissioning plan are incorporated into the commissioning specifications, including systems to be tested and the responsibility of each party relative to the commissioning process.

A draft commissioning plan is prepared prior to the start of the construction phase to ensure that commissioning activities are incorporated into the construction schedule. The CxA must spend time with the construction manager (CM) to make sure that all commissioning activities are inserted into the construction schedule.

This is critical to ensure that commissioning does not slow down the project.

The major categories addressed by the commissioning plan are:

- Introduction
- Systems to be commissioned
- Commissioning team
- Scope and team member responsibilities
- Documentation requirements
- Verification test procedures
- Operations and maintenance manuals
- Training
- Schedule

## Commissioning Specifications

Detailed testing requirements must be incorporated into the specifications so that contractors can budget the proper amount of time for functional performance tests in their pricing. One source for this documentation is the Model Commissioning Plan adopted by the U.S. Department of Energy.[2] This document recommends specification sections where commissioning activities should be described:

| | |
|---|---|
| 0800 | Supplementary Conditions |
| 01700 | Project Closeout |
| 15010 | Mechanical General |
| 15990 | Testing, Adjusting, and Balancing |
| 15997 | Mechanical Testing Requirements |
| 16010 | Electrical General |
| 16997 | Electrical Testing Requirements |
| 17100 | Commissioning Process |

In the new 2004 Construction Specifications Institute (CSI) MasterFormat™ edition[3], additional locations in each section are allocated for commissioning, including:

| | |
|---|---|
| 01 91 00 | Commissioning (part of Life Cycle Activities) |
| 23 08 00 | Commissioning of HVAC |
| 25 08 00 | Commissioning of Integrated Automation |
| 26 08 00 | Commissioning of Electrical Systems |

## Construction Documents Review

The construction documents should be reviewed by the CxA at the 50% and 95% completion stages to ensure that commissioning tasks have been properly coordinated, and to comment on accessibility of equipment for maintenance and adequacy of metering, as well as proper placement of devices. For green buildings, it is important to review not only individual systems and components, but their interrelationships. Conducting a thorough review and research of new products at this stage of a project can save a lot of time, money, and aggravation later.

For example, large atriums with lighting fixtures, smoke detectors, or fans installed high above the floor may require a lift for servicing. Tile specified for the finished flooring must be strong enough to support the concentrated wheel load of a lift without cracking. The ability to reach all fixtures from a lift must also be evaluated.

Specified materials such as paints, sealants, ceiling tiles, carpeting, and furnishings may have certain characteristics that cause them to off-gas VOCs or other potentially harmful chemicals. Architects may inadvertently specify green products that are new and may be untested. The CxA should ask the engineer and architect to determine if they have considered the possible side effects of the new products being specified. Have the MSDS (Material Safety Data Sheets) been requested as part of the submittal package? Have qualified material substitutions been identified?

If a specified system has not been used extensively in the past, such as a well water heat pump system, then a series of questions must be asked: Has all information been requested relative to the well flow rate capacity, conductivity, environmental permitting, filtration pipe size, and serviceability? Is the heat pump reliable? Does it have adequate heating capacity and temperature output? The engineer should have performed a "worst case" analysis to determine the heat available when both the well temperature and outside air temperature are cold. An additional heat source may be required. As with any other system that is not commonly installed in buildings, an expert may need to be consulted to discuss all the pros and cons.

Areas that the commissioning agent should focus on include these:
- Clear and rigorous design documentation, including detailed and complete sequences of operation
- An HVAC, fire, and emergency power response matrix that lists all equipment and components (e.g., air handlers, dampers, and valves) with their status and action during a fire alarm and under emergency power
- Access for reading gauges, entering doors and panels, and observing and replacing filters and coils
- Required isolation valves, dampers, interlocks, and piping to allow for manual overrides, simulation of failures, and seasonal testing conditions

- Sufficient monitoring points in the building automation systems (BAS), even beyond those necessary to control the systems, to facilitate performance verification and operation and maintenance (O&M)
- Adequate trending and reporting features in the BAS
- Pressure and temperature plugs close to controlling sensors for verifying their calibration
- Pressure gauges, thermometers, and flow meters in strategic areas to facilitate verification of system performance and ongoing O&M
- Pressure and temperature plugs in less critical areas or on smaller equipment where gauges and thermometers would not be necessary
- Specification of the locations and criteria for duct static pressure sensors and hydronic differential pressure sensors
- Adequate balancing valves and dampers, flow metering, and control stations and control system functions to facilitate and verify reliable test and balance
- Specification of required startup and testing functions to be performed by the manufacturer's field service personnel, such as chillers and generators
- Complete O&M documentation requirements in the specifications
- Complete training requirements in the specifications

## The Construction Phase

During the construction phase of the project, the building systems are installed, started up, and undergo pre-functional performance testing. Weekly construction meeting minutes are reviewed by the CxA to make note of punch list items relative to maintenance and usability of the systems being commissioned. Topics related to commissioning checklists, training plans, and operation and maintenance data are also reviewed.

### Coordinate & Direct Commissioning Activities

The CxA coordinates and directs commissioning activities according to the approved commissioning plan. Regular communication between the Construction Manager (CM) and CxA is critical to transfer scheduling information and provide up-to-date information on change orders, submittal status, and scheduled meetings. This allows commissioning activities to be carried out without delaying the project completion, while limiting formal written correspondence.

### Review Construction Meeting Minutes

The CxA reviews and comments, as appropriate, on all construction meeting minutes. It is important for the CxA to be kept up-to-date on any changes being discussed so that he or she can provide input prior to the recommendation becoming a change in the scope. To make sure that commissioning concerns are addressed by the engineers and contractors, a separate section should be added to the construction meeting minutes to track CxA questions and comments.

## Review Equipment Submittals & Manufacturer Checklists

The CxA should review equipment submittals for compliance with the design intent and the specifications. It is especially important that any substitutions for green components be reviewed for compliance with the specification.

The CM should provide copies of equipment submittal data to the engineer and CxA at the same time. The CxA should provide a response to the owner and engineer before the engineer issues review comments. This will allow the engineer to incorporate all relevant CxA comments into a single document that is, then, sent to the contractor.

## Conduct Commissioning Scoping Meetings

The CxA is responsible for calling commissioning scoping meetings with the contractors to review any outstanding documentation issues, as well as upcoming testing and training. These meetings are held, as required, during the construction phase to discuss issues that the CxA has identified or items relating to equipment startup scheduling, O&M manuals, or training. Late in the construction phase, when contractors are more familiar with their role in the commissioning process, it may be possible to incorporate these meetings into the weekly construction meeting. This approach shows respect for the contractors' time, which makes them more likely to support the commissioning process and provides the CxA with the necessary information.

## Test Procedures

Details of specific operational attributes of the equipment to be installed are incorporated into the pre-functional and functional test procedures.

Manufacturers of major mechanical equipment, such as chillers, boilers, photovoltaic arrays, and emergency generators, have start-up and test procedures that have been developed specifically for the equipment. Therefore the CxA does not need to develop pre-functional test procedures for this equipment, but should review and understand how the equipment's operation will interface with other systems. This information will be used to write functional performance tests for integrated systems.

## Review of Control System Programming

This is a critical component of the standard commissioning procedure that can be used to minimize misunderstandings between the engineer's specified sequence of operation and that programmed by the controls contractor. After the controls contractor has completed programming, a field meeting is held between the CxA and the controls programmer/technician. The CxA asks the controls programmer how each sequence was programmed, and records the response. All interlocks, delays, and control routines are reviewed for each type of unit or system. Many issues are identified during this review, and the programmer is given the opportunity to revise the code, or the design engineer is asked if programming meets the original intent. As a result, there are fewer unexpected problems during functional testing, fewer deficiencies, and fewer retests (not to mention less paperwork and finger-pointing). The results of this meeting will allow the CxA to align test procedures to reflect the control system programs.

## Create Test Procedures

The CxA prepares test procedures based on manufacturer recommendations and the specified sequence of operations. At a minimum, test procedure forms should include space to record the following:

- System and equipment or component name(s)
- Equipment location and ID number
- Project name and date
- Participating parties
- A copy of the specification section describing the test requirements
- A copy of the sequence of operations or other specified parameters being verified
- Required pre-test field measurements
- Instructions for setting up the test
- Set points, alarm limits, schedules
- Specific, step-by-step test procedures in a clear, sequential, and repeatable format
- Acceptance criteria of proper performance with a "Yes/No" check box to allow for clearly marking whether proper performance of each part of the test was achieved
- A section for comments
- Signatures and date block for the CxA

Additional information for developing test procedures can be found at the PECI website, which has recently added guides for functional testing[4] and control systems design.[5]

## Test Procedure Review

The CxA distributes a draft copy of the test procedures to the engineers and contractors for review and comment prior to creating and issuing a final version.

## O&M Manual & Contractor Test

Contractors will be requested to submit O&M manuals to the CM and CxA as soon as the equipment submittals have been reviewed and approved. The CxA should review and comment on the O&M manuals. Contractors are asked to submit for review any pre-functional test forms that meet the specifications and are typically used for the start-up of major equipment and systems. O&M manuals will become an integral part of the Systems Manual that is developed by the CxA.

## Training

Prior to scheduling training, the O&M manuals and a training plan must be submitted by contractors to the CM, CxA, and A/E. The training plan should indicate:

- Equipment to be included
- Intended audience
- Location
- Objectives
- Subjects covered (e.g., description, duration of discussion, and special methods)
- Duration of training on each subject
- Instructor for each subject and their qualifications
- Methods (e.g., classroom lecture, video, site walk-through, actual operational demonstrations, or written handouts)

The CxA reviews the manuals and plan, and then audits the training sessions to ensure that the O&M personnel understands the operation of each system. Videotaping training sessions is recommended so that future operation and maintenance personnel can be easily introduced to the systems and the ways in which they were designed to operate. Each training session should have an agenda, a sign-up sheet with participant contact information, and an evaluation to provide feedback to the training organizers and instructors.

## Equipment Start-up & Pre-Functional Testing

Start-up and pre-functional tests of major equipment, such as boilers, chillers, and large fan and pumping systems, are performed by the contractor or manufacturer's representative and typically witnessed by the CxA. Test results are recorded by the contractor and included with the O&M manual. Contractors maintain a master deficiency list of tests that are either incomplete or have failed. The CxA can comment on how the tests were executed and any open issues that prevented the tests from being completed successfully.

## The Acceptance Phase

After the building systems have been started up, and pre-functional performance testing has been successfully completed, the contractors sign off on each system, stating that it is ready for functional performance testing.

## Functional Performance Testing

The purpose of functional performance testing is to determine if the performance defined in the design intent documentation has been met. Each system is tested through all modes of system operation (for example, seasonal, occupied/unoccupied, warm-up/cool-down, and so forth, as applicable). This includes every individual interlock and conditional control logic, all control sequences, both full- and part-load conditions, emergency conditions, and simulation of all abnormal conditions for which there is a required system or controls response.

Testing may be accomplished by traditional manual testing (for example, changing a set point and immediately observing a response) and short-term monitoring using the energy management system (EMS) trending capabilities. Portable data loggers may also be used to gather data. The best method, however, is to specify any points that provide energy consumption or temperature information and include them as part of the EMS trends. The monitoring requirements are detailed in the functional performance tests. As each individual check or test is accomplished, the CxA observes and records the physical responses by the system and compares them to the specified sequences to verify the test results.

The verification of the testing, adjusting, and balancing (TAB) report is an integral part of functional performance testing. The CxA requests that the TAB contractor demonstrate the results of random balancing readings, which are recorded by the CxA and compared to the TAB report values.

As an extension of actual tests, the controls contractor's trend logs, developed in the EMS, are evaluated by the CxA for control, stability, and conformance with the design intent. This is a key element in evaluating the long-term operation and performance of the systems.

When individual system functional performance has been verified, the integrated or coordinated response between each system is checked. For example, fire and smoke alarm interactions with HVAC equipment should be tested under all modes of operation.

Typically, the operation of all major and critical equipment is functionally tested. Usually, a percentage (typically 25%) of terminal equipment, such as variable air volume boxes, fan coil units, and radiation, is put through full functional testing. All systems that are either new or green should be fully tested to ensure optimum performance.

## Retesting

Portions of systems that fail functional performance tests are retested after the contractor indicates in writing that the deficiency has been resolved. Typically, a budget is set aside for re-running functional tests. Actual failure rates cannot be predicted. However, for multiple equipment items such as rooftop units or VAV boxes, portions of the test that fail on more than one piece of equipment will not be executed on subsequent equipment until the contractor submits in writing that all equipment of this type has been reviewed for the deficiency. Clauses can and should be added to the specifications that limit the number of retests (usually one) for each type of equipment. Additional retests should be paid for by the responsible contractor. The CxA is obligated to identify the parties responsible for the failed tests.

## Systems Manuals

Operation and maintenance manuals that are assembled by contractors are not always well-organized or easy to use. Systems Manuals or Recommissioning & Energy Management Manuals should be created by the CxA using the O&M manuals and organizing the information by system. A brief description of how each system operates is typically added to the front of each section, along with a schematic diagram with all equipment identified, the operational sequence, and maintenance requirements and the frequency with which they should be performed. The front of the manual should include contact information on contractors that were responsible for installing and testing each system. Manuals should also provide cut sheets and identify suppliers of major equipment and replacement parts. A troubleshooting guide is another important component, listing problems that may arise, possible causes and solutions, and criteria for deciding when equipment should be repaired, and when it must be replaced. Portland Energy Conservation Incorporated (PECI) publishes a series of O&M best practice manuals that can be helpful in defining how systems are maintained.[6]

## Final Commissioning Report

The commissioning report is intended to be the primary record document for commissioning for each specific system and the building as a whole. Information in the report should include the following:

- Name, address, firm, and phone number of CxA
- Description of installed systems

- List and description of commissioning tasks
- Commissioning plan
- Completed design intent document
- Completed pre-functional test checklists
- Completed functional performance tests
- All non-compliance forms
- Summary of commissioning findings
- Recommendations for system recommissioning
- Analysis of the performance of each system
- Recommendations for system improvements
- Summary of operator training
- Sequence documentation
- Site visit reports
- Blank functional checklist forms for recommissioning

## The Post-Acceptance Phase

### Perform Seasonal Testing

Portions of systems that are weather-dependent should be retested during the opposite season from the one in which they were originally tested. For example, if an air handling unit was commissioned during the summer, a follow-up test should be performed during the winter for items such as the heating valve and damper controls. These components would have been verified for proper operation during the summer, but their stability of control would not have been confirmed. One of the primary means of documenting the proper operation of each system over time is by plotting and reviewing trend data in a program such as Microsoft® Excel. Control of temperature and pressure loops can be demonstrated under all load conditions through summer and winter, occupied and unoccupied periods.

### Interview Facility Staff

The facility operations and maintenance staff should be interviewed during quarterly operational reviews conducted through the first year of operation. These personnel are required to maintain a log of issues including:

- Changes in the building usage, installed equipment, and occupancy
- Documentation of any changes in set points, control sequences, or overrides
- Trouble finding or using equipment maintenance procedures
- System servicing and maintenance documentation and problems
- Documentation of comfort complaints

This information will help the CxA provide the building operations personnel with an understanding of the changes or issues and a more focused approach to addressing them. It is important to document and address problems as soon as possible while equipment is still under warranty.

## Recommend Improvements

During the warranty period, needed improvements and enhancements to the operation of commissioned systems are identified. The CxA should make the recommendations based on a review of system operations and interviews with the operating personnel and building occupants. Any implemented changes should be documented in the systems manual (O&M manual) by the CxA.

## Conclusion

Commissioning of green buildings is more important than for any other type of structure due to the myriad of new products, systems, and technologies that are incorporated. Making sure that the operations personnel understands how to properly maintain and operate the building can mean the difference between having an environment in which people thrive; are happy, productive, and healthy; and one where the building is more costly to operate or makes occupants sick. The commissioning agent must put him/herself in the place of the building owners and occupants and ask more questions earlier in the design and construction process to help avoid problems.

1. ASHRAE Guideline 0-2005, "The Commissioning Process."
2. Complete Guide Specifications, *www.peci.org*
3. Construction Specifications Institute, *www.csinet.org*
4. Functional Testing Guide, *www.peci.org*
5. Control System Design Guide, *www.peci.org*
6. O&M Best Practice Series, *www.peci.org*

# Analyzing Economic & Environmental Impacts

# Chapter

# *13* Economic Analysis & Green Buildings

## Sieglinde K. Fuller, PhD

Building economics, value engineering, and cost engineering are the three main fields that explicitly include an economic evaluation in building-related project analyses. The common theme that ties the three disciplines together is that each is concerned with improving the allocation of resources by implementing only projects that are cost-effective. A number of methods can be used to measure economic efficiency.

**Life Cycle Cost** (LCC) analysis is one of the most straightforward and easily understandable methods of evaluation; it is used in all three of these fields. Certified value specialists and cost engineers also often present their economic analysis results in terms of **Payback Period** (PB) or **Internal Rate of Return** (IRR). Building economists usually also include measures of **Net Savings** (NS) and **Savings-to-Investment Ratio** (SIR) to cover all aspects of an economic analysis. Except for payback, all of these supplementary measures are consistent with the life cycle costing principle of assessing the long-term costs of ownership. The payback measure usually ignores costs and benefits that are incurred after payback of initial costs is achieved.

LCC analysis has been widely recognized as a valuable tool for evaluating the economic performance of energy and water conservation and renewable energy projects undertaken by federal, state, and local governments and the private sector. The method applies to any project, public or private, where future operational cost savings are traded off against higher initial capital investment costs. This is usually the case also for green building components, which may cost more initially, but save money and have a positive impact on the environment in the long run by reducing energy use, resource depletion, and waste.

The LCC method described in this chapter is fully consistent with the *Standards on Building Economics*, published by the American Society for Testing and Materials (ASTM).[1] These same standards are followed in the BLCC5[2] (Building Life Cycle Cost Program) for evaluating energy and water conservation and renewable energy projects, and in BEES[3] (Building for Environmental and Economic Sustainability), a life cycle assessment tool for evaluating the environmental and economic impact of building materials. *(See Chapter 14 for more on BEES.)* This chapter presents an overview of the principles and method of life cycle costing. *(See the Resources for more information.)*

## Economic Efficiency

Figures 13.1a through 13.1c show three complementary concepts of economic efficiency. Figure 13.1a displays total owning and operating costs associated with a range of energy efficiency levels. As the level increases, investment costs rise at an increasing rate. The cost of energy consumption is reduced, but at a decreasing rate. The total cost curve is the vertical summation of the investment cost and operating costs associated with any level of energy efficiency. The lowest point on the total LCC cost curve, Q*, is the level of energy efficiency that minimizes life cycle costs.

**Figure 13.1a**

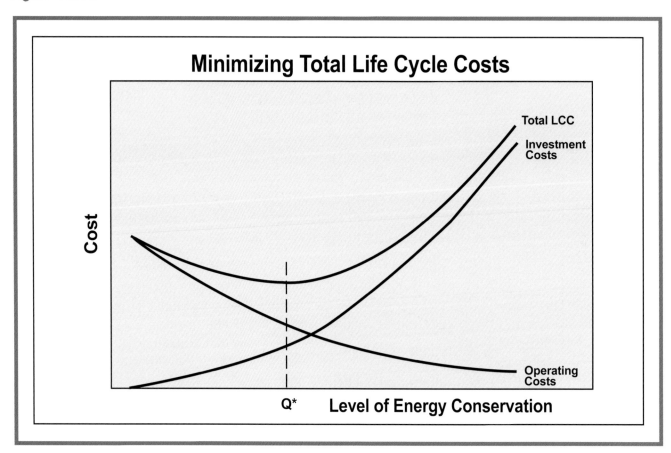

Figure 13.1b shows that the most cost-effective level of energy consumption can also be determined by maximizing net savings. The investment cost curve is the same as in Figure 13.1a. The savings curve is the difference between the operating cost at the zero level of investment and the operating cost at any other level of investment. The economically optimal level of energy efficiency is the level for which net savings are greatest, the level at which the curves are most distant, again at Q*.

The two curves in Figure 13.1c show that each additional unit of energy efficiency results in smaller and smaller increments in savings, and greater and greater additions to cost. The point at which the last increment in cost increases savings by the same amount is the economically optimal level, Q*.

In all three cases, it pays to increase investment if the level of energy efficiency is to the left of Q*. To the right of Q*, reducing investment lowers life cycle costs and increases net savings. Economists refer to the level of investment, Q*, where LCC is minimized, NS is maximized, and incremental investment is equal to incremental savings, as the "economically efficient level" of investment for a given project.

**Figure 13.1b**

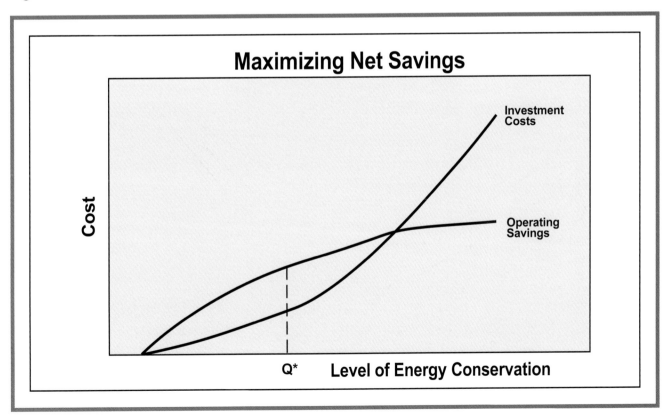

*Discounting* Because of inflation and the real earning power of money, a dollar paid or received today is not valued the same as a dollar paid or received at some future date. For this reason, costs and savings occurring over time must be "discounted." **Discounting** adjusts cash flows to a common time, often the present, when an analysis is performed, or a decision has to be made. The conversion of all costs and savings to time-equivalent "present values" allows them to be added and compared in a meaningful way.

To make future costs and savings time-equivalent, they must be adjusted for both inflation and the real earning power of money. One approach is to first eliminate the effects of inflation from the estimated dollar amounts and state them in "constant dollars." The discount rate used to calculate present values needs to be a "real" discount rate, excluding inflation; it adjusts only for the real earning power of money. A different approach, recommended when taxes are included in the analysis or when budget allocation is an issue, is the "current-dollar approach," where the rate of inflation is included in the dollar amounts, and the discount rate is a "nominal" rate that also includes inflation. Both approaches, if applied correctly and consistently to all cash flows in the analysis, yield the same present-value results.

**Figure 13.1c**

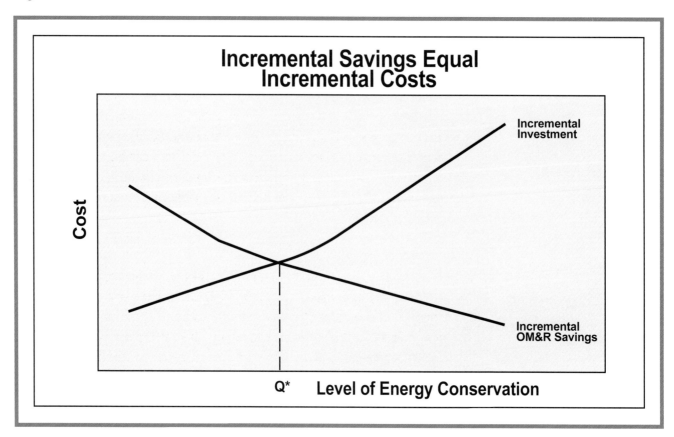

Incremental Savings Equal Incremental Costs

## Discount Rate

The discount rate used to adjust future costs and savings to present value is the rate of interest that makes the investor indifferent between cash amounts received or paid now or in the future. Most people would prefer receiving $100 today rather than later. There is an "opportunity cost" associated with deferring receipt of funds in that you give up the interim use of, or earnings on, the funds. By determining the future amount that causes you to be willing to forego a present amount, it is possible to calculate your **Minimum Acceptable Rate of Return** (MARR) or the opportunity cost of money. The greater your earning opportunities from alternative investments, the higher your MARR will be. Individuals, firms, and institutions set the discount rate to reflect their MARR.

## Study Period

The study period is the time during which the effects of a decision are of interest to a decision-maker. There is no one correct study period, but it must be long enough to enable a correct assessment of long-run economic performance. Often, the life of a building or system under analysis determines the length of the study period. Replacement costs and residual values are used to equalize the study period for buildings or systems with different lives. All alternatives have to be evaluated over the same study period.

## Uncertainty & Risk

LCC analyses are performed early in the decision-making process, and the input data used is therefore inherently subject to uncertainty and risk. The results are presented deterministically, implying a level of accuracy that may not be warranted. Some simple techniques exist for taking uncertainty and risk into account. Sensitivity analysis, for example, tests how outcomes differ as the uncertain input values are changed. This technique provides a range of outcomes and break-even values for savings and costs. If probabilities can be attached to input values, a more sophisticated risk analysis can be performed that includes a measure of the likelihood of a deviation from the "best-guess" outcome.[4]

## Measures of Economic Evaluation

### Life Cycle Cost

LCC analysis takes into account all costs of acquiring, operating, maintaining, and disposing of a building or building system. The LCC concept requires that all costs and savings be evaluated over a common study period and discounted to present value before they can be meaningfully compared. Figure 13.2 is a diagram of this process.

From a decision standpoint, the LCC of a design alternative has meaning only when it is compared to the LCC of a base case fulfilling the same basic performance requirements. *(See Figure 13.3.)* The basic criterion for determining whether a design alternative that increases capital investment and lowers future operating costs is cost-effective is that the savings generated by the investment must be greater than the additional investment cost. This will ensure that the total life cycle cost of the energy-saving or green alternative is lower than that of the base case. If several alternatives are being considered, the most cost-effective alternative is the one with the lowest life-cycle cost.

**Figure 13.2**
Life Cycle Costing
at a Glance

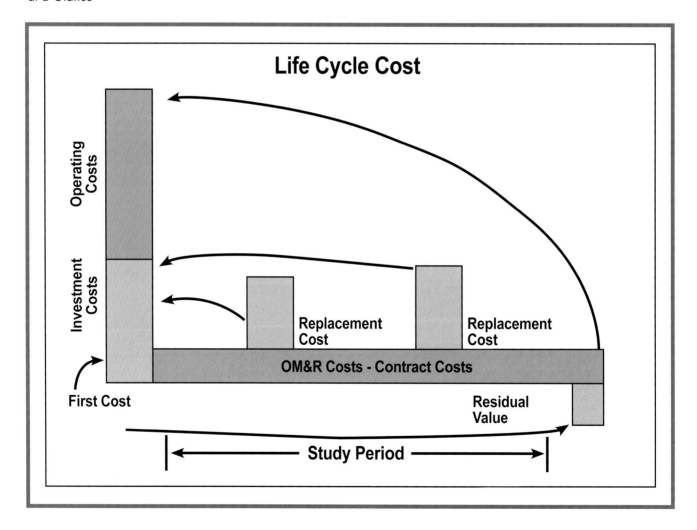

     **Green Building: Project Planning & Cost Estimating**

## Supplementary Measures of Economic Evaluation

Lowest LCC is a measure of economic efficiency that is relatively easy to calculate and interpret. It is the method prescribed by the Federal Energy Management Program (FEMP) of the U.S. Department of Energy (DOE) and other government agencies to evaluate energy and water conservation projects. To supplement LCC, additional measures of economic performance can be used to determine the comparative cost-effectiveness of capital investments. Several widely used measures are Net Savings (NS), Savings-to-Investment Ratio (SIR), Internal Rate of Return (IRR), and Payback Period (PB). These measures are meaningful only in relation to a base case and are consistent with the LCC methodology if they use the same study period, discount rate, and escalation rates.

### Net Savings

Net Savings (NS) is a measure of long-run profitability of an alternative relative to a base case. The NS can be calculated as an extension of the LCC method as the difference between the LCC of a base case and the LCC of an alternative. It can also be calculated directly from differences in the individual cash flows between a base case and an alternative. For a project alternative to be cost-effective with respect to the base case, it

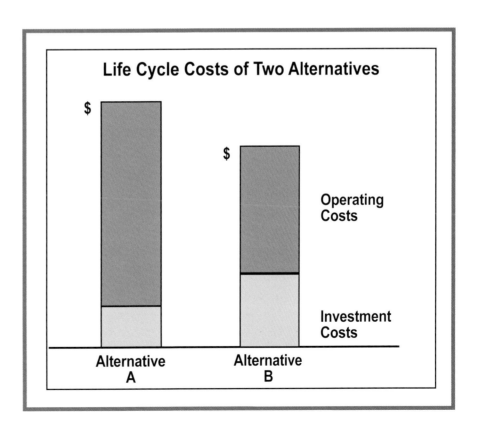

**Figure 13.3**

**Chapter 13** . Economic Analysis & Green Buildings          **343**

must have an NS greater than zero. Even with a zero NS, the minimum required rate of return has been achieved because it is accounted for in the NS computation through the discount rate.

## Savings-to-Investment Ratio

The Savings-to-Investment Ratio (SIR) is a dimensionless measure of performance that expresses the ratio of savings to costs. The numerator of the ratio contains the operation-related savings; the denominator contains the increase in investment-related costs. An SIR greater than 1.0 means that an alternative is cost-effective relative to a base case. The SIR is recommended for setting priorities among projects when the budget is insufficient to fund all cost-effective projects. The projects are ranked in descending order of their SIRs.

## Internal Rate of Return

Internal Rate of Return (IRR) measures solve for the interest rate that will equate the stream of costs and savings. The calculated interest rate is compared against a specified minimum acceptable rate of return, usually equal to the discount rate. The calculation of the traditional IRR assumes that any proceeds from the project can be reinvested at the calculated rate of return over the study period. A widely used version of the IRR is the Adjusted IRR (AIRR) or Overall IRR (OIRR); it uses the discount rate rather than the calculated rate of return as the reinvestment rate. The AIRR is used in the same way as the SIR.

## Payback Period

The Payback Period (PB) measures the length of time until accumulated savings are sufficient to pay back the cost. **Discounted Payback** (DPB) takes into account the time value of money by using time-adjusted cash flows. If the discount rate is assumed to be zero, that is, if the opportunity cost of money is not taken into account, the method is called **Simple Payback** (SPB). Since both the DPB and the SPB ignore all costs and savings that occur after payback has been achieved, they are not entirely consistent with the LCC measure. They should be used only as a screening measure, followed up with a full LCC analysis.

## Basic Steps in LCC Analysis

The basic steps in an LCC analysis are:
- Identify feasible alternatives.
- Establish assumptions and parameters.
- Specify costs and estimate in dollars.
- Discount costs to present values.
- Compute LCC for each alternative.
- Select the alternative with the lowest life-cycle cost.

Depending on the circumstances, one may also want to calculate supplementary measures of economic performance, perform an uncertainty assessment, and add a narrative describing non-monetary costs and savings.

## Identify Feasible Alternatives

Only energy-saving or green alternatives that are technically sound and practical may be included in the set of candidates to be evaluated. This presumes that they satisfy the technical performance requirements set out in the project description, and that there are no physical or other constraints that would eliminate an alternative for reasons other than economics.

## Establish Assumptions & Parameters

The assumptions and parameters that apply to all inputs should be clarified and documented at the outset. They include:

- Length of study period
- Base date
- Length of planning/construction period
- Service date
- Treatment of inflation
- Operational assumptions for building or building system
- Energy and water price schedules

## Specify Costs & Estimate in Dollars

### Relevant Effects

The most challenging part of an LCC analysis is determining the economic effects of a design change to a building or building system and estimating the associated costs. Only costs that are relevant to the decision and significant in amount need to be included. Because LCC analysis is performed early in the design process, engineers and analysts rely on estimating guides and databases for initial and operating cost estimates. Careful engineering judgment must be applied when determining the relevant effects of energy conservation and other green building features, and when estimating their costs.

### Types of Costs

The cost components typical for building-related LCC analyses are:

- Initial investment costs
- Capital replacement costs
- Residual values, such as resale or salvage values or disposal costs
- Operating, maintenance, and repair costs
- Energy costs

- Water costs
- Taxes
- Non-monetary costs

All costs included in the analysis are expressed in base-year dollars. These base-year amounts will be multiplied by discount factors that incorporate the discount rate and any applicable escalation rate.

## Cost Categories

The method used to classify the cost components of an LCC analysis will depend on what role they play in the mechanics of the methodology. The most important categories distinguish between investment-related and operational costs, annually recurring and non-annually recurring costs, and initial and future costs.

### Investment-Related Costs & Operational Costs: For the purpose of entering data for an LCC analysis, costs are usually divided into investment-related costs and operational costs. Acquisition costs, including costs for planning, design, and construction, are investment-related, as are residual values, such as resale value, salvage value, or disposal costs. Under the FEMP rule, capital replacement costs are also defined as investment-related. Energy and water costs, maintenance costs, and repair costs are considered operational. This distinction is useful when computing economic measures that evaluate long-run savings in operational costs in relation to the capital investment costs needed to implement the project.

### Annually Recurring & Non-Annually Recurring Costs: Some of the costs included in an LCC analysis are recurring, such as energy, routine maintenance, and repair. They are lumped together into annual amounts for the purpose of discounting. Non-annually recurring costs are those that may occur only one time during the life cycle, such as acquisition costs and residual values, or several times, such as replacement or major repair costs. This categorization is needed for choosing the appropriate pre-calculated discount factors used to convert future costs to present values.

### Initial & Future Costs: In a third classification, acquisition costs are designated as initial costs, and all other costs as future costs, a useful classification both for selecting discount factors and for relating a project's initial investment costs to its future operational costs.

### Taxes: In the case of private-sector projects, taxes may have an impact on the economic viability of projects in two ways:
- As a mechanism for providing direct financial subsidies.
- Through regular tax laws, such as property tax laws, sales taxes, and income tax laws.

In the case of conservation or green projects for federal, state, or local governments, taxes can be disregarded in an LCC analysis.

**Non-Monetary Costs & Benefits:** Non-monetary costs and benefits are project-related effects for which there may not be an objective way to assign a dollar value. Examples of non-monetary costs might include the loss of productivity due to noisy HVAC equipment or insufficient lighting. Examples of non-monetary benefits might include good employee morale because of a beautiful view, an indoor garden, or good public relations due to owning a green building. Even though these non-monetary costs and benefits cannot directly be included in the LCC calculations, they should be documented in narrative form and taken into consideration in the decision-making.

## Discount Costs to Present Values

The basic equation for discounting dollar amounts to present values is

$$PV = F_t / (1+d)^t$$

where $F_t$ = cost or savings in future year t, and d = discount rate.

If a cost of $5,000 is to be incurred in five years, an amount of $3,918 will have to be included in the analysis as a present value if the (real) discount rate is 5%. The interest rate at which an investor feels adequately compensated for trading money now for money in the future is the appropriate rate to use as a discount rate.

Multiplicative discount factors for various types of discounting operations are available from look-up tables in cost engineering, economics, and finance textbooks and are usually included in LCC computer programs.

When performing an LCC analysis, three types of future cash flows are most commonly encountered, each requiring a different type of present-value factor:

1. A one-time amount is multiplied by the **Single Present Value** (SPV) factor to compute its present value. An example of a one-time amount is a replacement cost or a salvage value.

   *Example:* Find the present value of a replacement cost ($C_0$) of $5,000 (constant base-year dollars) occurring eight years from the base date, using a real discount rate of 3.0%.

   $$PV = C_0 \times SPV8$$
   $$PV = \$5,000 \times 0.789 = \$3,945$$

2. An annual amount as of the base-year is multiplied by the **Uniform Present Value** (UPV) factor to find the present value of a stream of costs over the study period. An example is an operating and maintenance cost that remains the same (apart

from inflation) from year to year. Recurring costs are treated as annual amounts discounted to the base date from the year of their occurrence.

*Example:* Find the present value of a series of maintenance costs ($A_0$) of \$3,500 recurring annually over a time period of 15 years using a real discount rate of 3%.

$$PV = A_0 \times UPV15$$
$$PV = \$3,500 \times 11.94 = \$41,790$$

3. An annual amount ($A_0$) that varies from year to year at some known rate is multiplied by the **Modified Uniform Present Value** (UPV\*) factor. The rate of change can be either constant or variable from year to year. An amount changing at a constant rate may be an operating cost that increases annually due to expected higher maintenance costs. An example of an amount that changes at a variable rate each year is the energy cost of a building. The FEMP UPV\*, for example, includes varying energy price projections published annually by DOE's Energy Information Administration (EIA) by U.S. region, energy type, and rate type.

*Example:* Find the present value of an annual electricity cost of \$12,000 for a project located in Maryland and priced at a commercial rate. The study period is 25 years.

$$PV = A_0 \times UPV*25 \ (FEMP\ 2006)$$
$$PV = \$12,000 \times 15.81 = \$189,720$$

Figure 13.4 is a summary of present-value factors.

## Compute LCC for Each Alternative
### *LCC Formulas*
The general formula for the LCC present-value model is:

$$LCC = \sum_{t=0}^{N} \frac{C_t}{(1+d)^t}$$

where:

LCC = Total LCC in present value dollars of a given alternative

$C_t$ = Sum of all relevant costs, including initial and future costs, less any positive cash flows occurring in time t

N = Number of periods in the study period

d = Discount rate used to adjust cash flows to present value

A simplified formula for building-related projects can be stated as follows:

$$LCC = I + Repl - Res + E + W + OM\&R$$

where:

| | | |
|---|---|---|
| LCC | = | Total LCC of a given alternative |
| I | = | Investment costs |
| Repl | = | Capital replacement costs |
| Res | = | Residual value (resale, salvage value) less disposal costs |
| E | = | Energy costs |
| W | = | Water costs |
| OM&R | = | Non-fuel operating, maintenance, and repair costs in present values. |

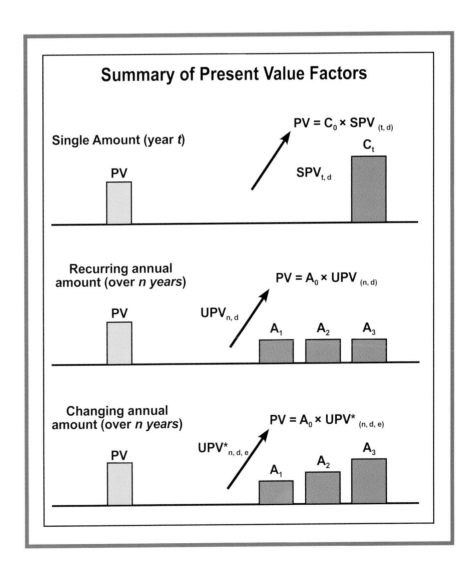

**Figure 13.4**
Summary of Present
Value Factors

## LCC Example

The following example applies the LCC method to the comparison of a conventional HVAC system base case with an energy-saving alternative. The system with the lower LCC will be accepted as the cost-effective system. The HVAC system is to be installed in a federal office building in Washington, D.C. The parameters and assumptions common to both the base case and the alternative are as follows:

**Location:** Washington, D.C.

**Discount rate:** Current FEMP discount rate: 3.0% real for constant-dollar analysis

**Energy prices:** Fuel type: Electricity at $0.08/kWh, local rate as of base date

**Rate type:** Commercial, FEMP UPV* factor, Region 3

**Cash-flow convention:** End-of-year occurrence for annually recurring amounts

**Useful lives of systems:** 20 years

**Study period:** 20 years

**Base date:** April 2006

The data summary and LCC calculation for conventional HVAC design, the base case, is as follows:

| Cost Items | Base Date Cost | Year of Occurance | Discount Factor[5] | Present Value |
|---|---|---|---|---|
| (1) | (2) | (3) | (4) | (5) = (2) x (4) |
| Initial investment cost | $103,000 | Base Date | already in PV | $103,000 |
| Capital replacement (fan) | $12,000 | 12 | $SPV_{12}$  0.701 | $8,412 |
| Residual value (salvage) | ($3,500) | 20 | $SPV_{20}$  0.554 | ($1,939) |
| Electricity: | | | | |
| 250,000 kWh at $0.08 | $20,000 | annual | FEMP UPV*$_{20}$ 13.45 | $269,000 |
| OM&R | $7,000 | annual | $UPV_{20}$ 14.88 | $104,160 |
| | | | | |
| Total LCC | | | | $482,633 |

In this example, the LCC of $482,633 for the conventional design serves as a baseline against which the LCC of the energy-saving alternative system will be compared.

The data summary and LCC calculation for energy-saving HVAC design, the alternative, is as follows:

| Cost Items | Base Date Cost | Year of Occurance | Discount Factor[6] | Present Value |
|---|---|---|---|---|
| (1) | (2) | (3) | (4) | (5) = (2) x (4) |
| Initial investment cost | $110,000 | Base Date | already in PV | $110,000 |
| Capital replacement (fan) | $12,500 | 12 | $SPV_{12}$ 0.701 | $8,762 |
| Residual value (salvage) | ($3,700) | 20 | $SPV_{20}$ 0.554 | ($2,050) |
| Electricity: | | | | |
| 162,500 kWh at $0.08 | $13,000 | annual | FEMP $UPV*_{20}$ 13.45 | $174,850 |
| OM&R | $8,000 | annual | $UPV_{20}$ 14.88 | $119,040 |
| Total LCC | | | | $410,602 |

## Select Alternative with the Lowest Life Cycle Cost
### LCC Criterion
The LCC criterion for choosing one design over another is the lowest life cycle cost. If one assumes that the input values are reasonably certain, and there are no non-monetary costs or benefits that need to be taken into account, one would select the energy-saving HVAC system for installation. If some of the input values are uncertain, sensitivity analysis can be used to calculate a range of possible LCCs.

## Selection Criteria for Supplementary Measures

Since the Net Savings measure is simply the difference in present-value LCCs between a base case and an alternative, it can easily be calculated by subtracting the LCC of the alternative from the LCC of the base case. Thus the Net Savings for the alternative are:

$$NS_{Alt} = \$482,633 - \$410,602$$

$$NS_{Alt} = \$72,031$$

This means that the energy-saving design saves $72,031 in present-value dollars over the 20-year study period, over and above the 3.0% minimum acceptable real rate of return. If the LCC of an alternative is lower than the LCC of the relevant base case, it will have positive Net Savings, a Savings-to-Investment Ratio greater than one, an Internal Rate of Return greater than the discount rate, and a Payback Period shorter than the study period. An SIR of 10.99, an AIRR of 16.12%, and a PB period of two years have been computer-calculated for this example, as shown in the BLCC5 FEMP analysis in Figure 13.5.

## Computer-Supported LCC Analysis

Various computer programs are available that greatly facilitate LCC analysis. NIST, under sponsorship of DOE/FEMP, developed the Building Life Cycle Cost Program BLCC5. The program follows the LCC principles reviewed in this chapter and contains federal criteria established by legislation and recommended in Executive Order 13123 for "Greening the Government through Efficient Energy Management." Agency-specific discount rates, inflation rates, discounting conventions, and energy price escalation rates are built in as defaults for analyzing FEMP and MILCON (military construction) projects, funded either through appropriations or financed through private-sector energy savings performance contracts (ESPC) or utility energy services contracts (UESC). Since most of the default values in BLCC5 can be edited, the program can also be used by private-sector LCC practitioners. Specific private-sector modules that include tax and financial analyses will be added to BLCC5 in the future.

Figures 13.5 and 13.6 indicate how the LCC analysis may be approached in BLCC5.

The current version of BLCC5 is BLCC 5.3-09. It contains the following six modules with agency-specific defaults, which may be edited if not applicable to a particular project.

1. **FEMP Analysis; Energy Project:** For energy and water conservation and renewable energy projects under the FEMP rules based on 10 CFR 436.

2. **Federal Analysis; Financed Project:** For Federal projects financed through energy savings performance contracts (ESPCs) or utility energy services contracts (UESCs).

3. **OMB Analysis:** Projects subject to the Office of Management and Budget (OMB) Circular A-94 for non-energy, Federal Government construction projects, but not water resource projects.

4. **MILCON Analysis; Energy Project:** For energy and water conservation and renewable energy projects in military construction.

5. **MILCON Analysis; ECIP Project:** For energy and water conservation projects under the Energy Conservation Investment Program (ECIP).

6. **MILCON Analysis; Non-Energy Project:** For military construction designs that are not primarily intended for energy or water conservation.

The BLCC5 program calculates life cycle costs, net savings, savings-to-investment ratio, internal rate of return, and payback period. The program's hierarchical data input structure serves as a guideline for data entry. Built-in defaults are provided for agency-specific discount

## Comparison of Present-Value Costs
### PV Life-Cycle Cost

| | Base Case | Alternative | Savings from Alternative |
|---|---|---|---|
| **Initial Investment Costs:** | | | |
| Capital Requirements as of Base Date | $103,000 | $110,000 | -$7,000 |
| **Future Costs:** | | | |
| Energy Consumption Costs | $269,015 | $174,860 | $94,155 |
| Energy Demand Charges | $0 | $0 | $0 |
| Energy Utility Rebates | $0 | $0 | $0 |
| Water Costs | $0 | $0 | $0 |
| Recurring and Non-Recurring OM&R Costs | $104,150 | $119,029 | -$14,879 |
| Capital Replacements | $8,417 | $8,767 | -$351 |
| Residual Value at End of Study Period | -$1,996 | -$2,132 | $136 |
| | ------------ | ------------ | ------------ |
| Subtotal (for Future Cost Items) | $379,585 | $300,524 | $79,062 |
| | ------------ | ------------ | ------------ |
| **Total PV Life-Cycle Cost** | $482,585 | $410,524 | $72,062 |

## Net Savings from Alternative Compared with Base Case

| | |
|---|---|
| PV of Non-Investment Savings | $79,277 |
| - Increased Total Investment | $7,215 |
| | ------------ |
| **Net Savings** | $72,062 |

## Savings-to-Investment Ratio (SIR)

**SIR** =  10.99

## Adjusted Internal Rate of Return

**AIRR** =  16.12%

## Payback Period
### Estimated Years to Payback (from beginning of Service Period)

Simple Payback occurs in year     2

Discounted Payback occurs in year  2

## Energy Savings Summary
### Energy Savings Summary (in stated units)

| Energy Type | -----Average Base Case | Annual Alternative | Consumption----- Savings | Life-Cycle Savings |
|---|---|---|---|---|
| Electricity | 250,000.0 kWh | 162,500.0 kWh | 87,500.0 kWh | 1,749,760.4 kWh |

**Figure 13.5**
FEMP Analysis on an Energy Project

rate, inflation rate, discounting convention, and inflation adjustment. DOE energy price forecasts are incorporated by region, along with fuel type and rate type. The program calculates region- and end-use-specific emissions reductions, and provides detailed reporting capability that can be used for project documentation.

## Conclusion

Anybody concerned with the economic efficiency of buildings will recognize that making decisions on the basis of first cost only, or even on the basis of simple payback as it is generally used, does not optimize the allocation of the resources available for improving our built environment. Initial construction costs *and* future operational and repair costs determine the value of a building. The overview presented in this chapter introduces the concepts and techniques of life-cycle costing, a method of economic evaluation especially well suited to weighing future cost reductions and benefits of green building features against higher initial investment costs. Supporting computer programs

**Figure 13.6**
Summary of Present
Value Factors

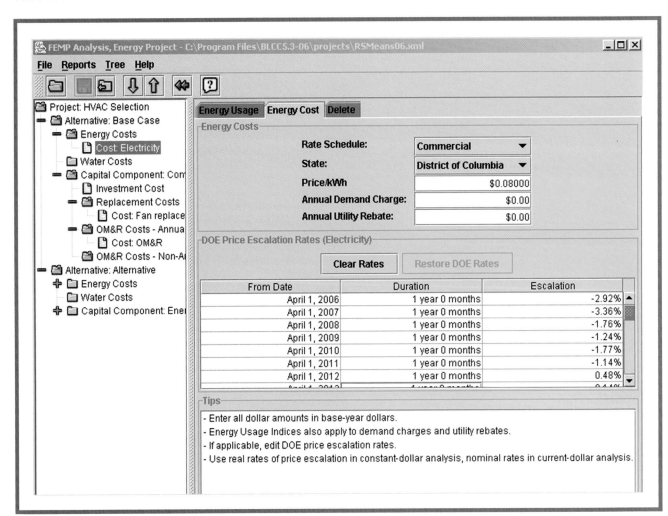

facilitate the application of an approach that is systematic, as well as practical, problem-solving. In combination with well-researched estimates of cost data, life cycle costing leads to financially responsible decision making.

1. *Standards on Building Economics*, Fourth Edition. 1999. American Society for Testing and Materials, 100 Barr Harbor Drive, West Conshohocken, PA.

2. Building Life-Cycle Cost Program, BLCC5.3-06. 2006. National Institute of Standards and Technology, Gaithersburg, MD, updated annually on April 1.

3. *Building for Environmental and Economic Sustainability.* BEES3.0d. 2002. National Institute of Standards and Technology. Gaithersburg, MD.

4. *Techniques for Treating Uncertainty and Risk in the Economic Evaluation of Building Investments.* 1995. National Institute of Standards and Technology Special Publication 757. Gaithersburg, MD, (in-depth description of how to account for uncertainty and risk in life cycle cost analyses).

5. The discount factors used in the examples are from *Price Indices and Discount Factors for the Federal Energy Management Program.* April 2006. The factors are calculated with the 2006 FEMP discount rate of 3.0 percent (real) and the latest DOE energy price escalation rates.

6. Ibid.

# Chapter *14* Evaluating Products Over Their Life Cycle

*Barbara C. Lippiatt*

Selecting building products based on minimum life cycle economic impacts is relatively straightforward. Products have been bought and sold in the marketplace, which has established their first cost, and sound analytical procedures to quantify life cycle cost have been developed and employed for over 20 years. In addition to initial cost, future costs that contribute to life cycle cost include the cost of energy, operation and maintenance, labor and supplies, replacement parts, and eventually the cost of decommissioning or recycling the system. Chapter 13, "Economic Analysis & Green Buildings," addresses in detail the economic aspects of life cycle costing.

But how do we include life cycle environmental impacts in our purchase decisions? Environmental impacts, such as global warming, indoor air quality, water pollution, and resource depletion, are, for the most part, economic externalities. That is, their costs are not reflected in the market prices of the products that generated the impacts. Moreover, even if there were a mandate today to include environmental "costs" in market prices, it would be nearly impossible to do so due to difficulties in assessing these impacts in classical economic terms. How do you put a price on clean air and clean water? What, ultimately, is the price of human life, and how do we value the avoidance of its loss? Economists have debated these questions for decades, and a consensus does not appear imminent.

While environmental performance cannot be measured on a monetary scale, it can be quantified using the evolving, multi-disciplinary approach known as **environmental life cycle assessment** (LCA). All stages in the life of a product are analyzed: raw material acquisition, manufacture, transportation, installation, use, and recycling and waste management. The National Institute of Standards and Technology BEES (Building for Environmental and Economic Sustainability) tool[1] applies an LCA approach to measure the environmental performance of building products, following guidance in the International Organization for Standardization (ISO) 14040 series of standards for LCA.[2] BEES separately measures economic performance using the American Society for Testing and Materials (ASTM) standard life cycle cost (LCC) approach.[3] These two performance measures are then synthesized into an overall performance measure using the ASTM standard for Multi-Attribute Decision Analysis.[4] For the entire BEES analysis, building products are defined and classified based on UNIFORMAT II, the ASTM standard classification for building elements.[5]

## Measuring Environmental Performance

Environmental life cycle assessment is a "cradle-to-grave" systems approach for measuring environmental performance. It is based on the belief that all stages in the life of a product generate environmental impacts and must therefore be analyzed. The stages include:

- Raw materials acquisition
- Product manufacture
- Transportation
- Installation
- Operation and maintenance
- Recycling and waste management

An analysis that excludes any of these stages is limited because it ignores the full range of upstream and downstream impacts of stage-specific processes.

The strength of environmental life cycle assessment is its comprehensive, multi-dimensional scope. Many sustainable building claims and strategies are now based on a single life cycle stage or a single environmental impact. A product is claimed to be green simply because it has recycled content, or accused of not being green because it emits volatile organic compounds (VOCs) during its installation and use. These single-attribute claims may be misleading because they ignore the possibility that other life cycle stages, or other environmental impacts, may yield offsetting effects.

For example, the recycled content product may have a high embodied energy content, leading to resource depletion, global warming, and acid rain impacts during the raw materials acquisition, manufacturing, and transportation life cycle stages. LCA thus broadens the environmental discussion by accounting for shifts of environmental problems from one life cycle stage to another, or one environmental medium (land, air, or water) to another. The benefit of the LCA approach is in implementing a trade-off analysis to achieve a genuine reduction in overall environmental impact, rather than a simple shift of impact.

The general LCA methodology involves four steps. The **goal and scope definition** step spells out the purpose of the study and its breadth and depth. The **inventory analysis** step identifies and quantifies the environmental inputs and outputs associated with a product over its entire life cycle. Environmental inputs include water, energy, land, and other resources; outputs include releases to air, land, and water. However, it is not these inputs and outputs, or *inventory flows*, that are of primary interest. We are more interested in their consequences, or impacts on the environment. Thus, the next LCA step, **impact assessment**, characterizes these inventory flows in relation to a set of environmental impacts. For example, impact assessment might relate carbon dioxide emissions, a *flow*, to global warming, an *impact*. Finally, the **interpretation** step combines the environmental impacts in accordance with the goals of the LCA study.

> **LCA Methodology Steps**
> 1. Goal & scope definition
> 2. Inventory analysis
> 3. Impact assessment
> 4. Interpretation

## Goal & Scope Definition

The goal of the BEES LCA is to generate relative environmental performance scores for building product alternatives sold in the United States. These scores are combined with economic performance scores to help the building community select environmentally and economically balanced building products.

The scoping phase of any LCA involves defining the boundaries of the product system under study. The manufacture of any product involves a number of unit processes (e.g., ethylene production for input to the manufacture of the styrene-butadiene bonding agent for stucco walls). Each unit process involves many inventory flows, some of which themselves involve other, subsidiary unit processes.

The first product system boundary determines which unit processes are included in the LCA. In the BEES approach, the boundary-setting rule consists of a set of three decision criteria. For each candidate unit process, mass and energy contributions to the product system are the primary decision criteria. In some cases, cost contribution is used as a third criterion.[6] Together, these criteria provide a robust screening process.

The second product system boundary determines which inventory flows are tracked for in-bounds unit processes. Quantification of *all* inventory flows is not practical for the following reasons:

- An ever-expanding number of inventory flows can be tracked. For instance, including the U.S. Environmental Protection Agency's Toxic Release Inventory (TRI) data would result in tracking approximately 200 inventory flows arising from polypropylene production alone. Similarly, including radionucleide emissions generated from electricity production would result in tracking more than 150 flows. Managing such large inventory flow lists adds to the complexity, and thus the cost, of carrying out and interpreting the LCA.

- Attention should be given in the inventory analysis step to collecting data that will be useful in the next LCA step, impact assessment. By restricting the inventory data collection to the flows actually needed in the subsequent impact assessment, a more focused, higher quality LCA can be carried out.

Therefore, in the BEES model, a focused, cost-effective set of inventory flows is tracked, reflecting flows that will actually be needed in the subsequent impact assessment step.

Defining the unit of comparison is another important task in the goal and scoping phase of LCA. The basis for all units of comparison is the **functional unit**, defined so that the products compared are true substitutes for one another. In the BEES model, the functional unit for most building products is 1 SF (0.09 m²) of product service for 50 years.[7] Therefore, for example, the functional unit for the BEES roof covering alternatives is covering 1 SF (0.09 m²) of roof surface for 50 years. The functional unit provides the critical reference point to which all inventory flows are scaled.

Scoping also involves setting data requirements. Data requirements for the BEES study include:

- **Geographic coverage:** The data is U.S. average data.
- **Time period:** The data is a combination of information collected specifically for BEES within the last 10 years, and from the well-known Ecobalance LCA database created in 1990.[8] Most of the Ecobalance data is updated annually. No data older than 1990 is used.
- **Technology:** When possible, the most representative technology is studied. Where data for the most representative technology is not available, an aggregated result is used based on the U.S. average technology for that industry.

## Inventory Analysis

Inventory analysis entails quantifying the inventory flows for a product system. Inventory flows include inputs of water, energy, and raw materials, and releases to air, land, and water. Data categories are used to group inventory flows in LCAs. For example, in the BEES model, flows such as aldehydes, ammonia, and sulfur oxides are grouped under the air emissions data category. Figure 14.1 shows the categories under which data is grouped in the BEES system. For each product included in BEES, up to 400 inventory flow items are tracked.

A number of approaches may be used to collect inventory data for LCAs.[9] These range from:

- Unit process- and facility-specific: data collected from a particular process within a given facility that is not combined in any way.
- Composite: data collected from the same process combined across locations.
- Aggregated: data collected combining more than one process.
- Industry-average: data derived from a representative sample of locations believed to statistically describe the typical process across technologies.
- Generic: data without known representation, but that is qualitatively descriptive of a process.

Since the goal of the BEES LCA is to generate U.S. industry-average results, generic product data is collected primarily using the industry-

**Figure 14.1**
BEES Inventory Data Categories

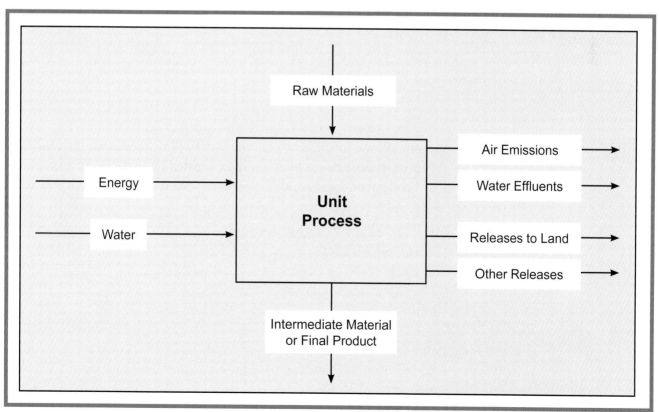

average approach. Manufacturer-specific product data are collected primarily using the unit process- and facility-specific approaches, then aggregated to preserve manufacturer confidentiality. Data collection is done under contract with Environmental Strategies and Solutions (ESS) and PricewaterhouseCoopers/Ecobalance, using the Ecobalance LCA database, which covers more than 6,000 industrial processes gathered from actual site and literature searches from more than 15 countries. Where necessary, the data is adjusted to be representative of U.S. operations and conditions.

Approximately 90% of the data comes directly from industry sources, with about 10% from generic literature and published reports. The generic data includes inventory flows for electricity production from the average U.S. grid, and for selected raw material mining operations (e.g., limestone, sand, and clay mining operations). In addition, ESS and Ecobalance gathered additional LCA data to fill data gaps for the BEES products. Assumptions regarding the unit processes for each building product are verified through experts in the appropriate industry to assure the data is correctly incorporated in BEES.

## Impact Assessment

The impact assessment step of LCA quantifies the potential contribution of a product's inventory flows to a range of environmental impacts. BEES takes primarily an Environmental Problems approach to impact assessment, as developed within the Society for Environmental Toxicology and Chemistry (SETAC). It involves a two-step process:[10]

1.  **Classification** of inventory flows that contribute to specific environmental impacts. For example, greenhouse gases, such as carbon dioxide, methane, and nitrous oxide, are classified as contributing to global warming.

2.  **Characterization** of the potential contribution of each classified inventory flow to the corresponding environmental impact. This results in a set of indices, one for each impact, that is obtained by weighting each classified inventory flow by its relative contribution to the impact. For instance, the Global Warming Potential index is derived by expressing each contributing inventory flow in terms of its equivalent amount of carbon dioxide.

The BEES model uses this Environmental Problems approach where possible because it enjoys some general consensus among LCA practitioners and scientists.[11] The U.S. EPA Office of Research and Development has developed TRACI (Tool for the Reduction and Assessment of Chemical and other environmental Impacts), a set of state-of-the-art, peer-reviewed U.S. life cycle impact assessment methods that has been adopted in BEES 4.0.[12] Ten of the 11 TRACI impacts follow the Environmental Problems approach:

- Global warming potential
- Acidification potential
- Eutrophication potential (unwanted addition of mineral nutrients to the soil or water, which can lead to undesirable ecosystem shifts)
- Fossil fuel depletion
- Habitat alteration
- Criteria air pollutants
- Smog
- Ecological toxicity
- Human health toxicity
- Ozone depletion

Water intake is assessed in TRACI, and adopted in BEES 4.0, using the Direct Use of Inventories Approach, meaning that the life cycle inventory results are used as is in the final interpretation step. BEES also assesses Indoor Air Quality, an impact not included in TRACI because it is unique to the building industry. Indoor Air Quality is also assessed using the Direct Use of Inventories approach, for a total of 12 impacts for most BEES products.

## Interpretation

At the LCA interpretation step, the impact assessment results are combined. Few products are likely to dominate their competition in all impact categories. One product may out-perform the competition in terms of fossil fuel depletion and solid waste, but may fall short relative to global warming and acidification, and fall somewhere in the middle on the basis of indoor air quality and eutrophication. To compare the overall environmental performance of competing products, the performance measures for all impact categories may be synthesized. *(Note that in BEES, synthesis of impact measures is optional.)*

Synthesizing the impact category performance measures involves combining "apples and oranges." Global warming potential is expressed in carbon dioxide equivalents, acidification in hydrogen ion equivalents, eutrophication in nitrogen equivalents, and so on. How can these diverse measures of impact category performance be combined into a meaningful measure of overall environmental performance? The most appropriate technique is **Multiattribute Decision Analysis** (MADA). MADA problems are characterized by trade-offs, as is the case with the BEES impact assessment results. The BEES system follows the ASTM standard for conducting MADA evaluations of building-related investments.[13]

MADA first places all impact categories on the same scale by normalizing them. Within BEES, each impact category is normalized using U.S. EPA data corresponding to its TRACI set of impact assessment methods. These data estimate the per capita annual contribution to each impact in the United States, and are used to place each product-specific impact category performance measure in the context of all U.S. activity, contributing to that impact. All performance measures are thus translated to the same scale, allowing comparison across impacts.

Normalized impact scores may also be compared across building elements if they are first scaled to reflect the product quantities to be used in the building under analysis over the same time period. For example, consider the global warming scores for roof coverings and chairs. If these scores are each first multiplied by the quantity of their functional units to be used in a particular building (roof area to be covered and seating requirements, respectively), they may then be compared. Comparing across elements can provide insights into which building elements lead to the larger environmental impacts and thus warrant the most attention.

MADA computes a weighted average environmental performance score after weighting each impact category by its relative importance to overall environmental performance. In the BEES software, the set of importance weights is selected by the user. Several derived, alternative weight sets are provided as guidance, and may be used either directly or as a starting point for developing user-defined weights. The alternative weight sets are based on an EPA Science Advisory Board study, a Harvard University study, and a set of equal weights, representing a spectrum of ways in which people value various aspects of the environment.

## Measuring Economic vs Environmental Performance

Measuring the economic performance of building products is more straightforward than measuring environmental performance. Published economic performance data is readily available, and there are well-established ASTM standard methods for conducting economic performance evaluations. First, cost data is collected from the latest edition of the RSMeans' annual publication, *Building Construction Cost Data*, and future cost data is based on the latest data published by Whitestone Research in *The Whitestone Building Maintenance and Repair Cost Reference*, supplemented by industry interviews. The most appropriate method for measuring the economic performance of building products is the life cycle cost (LCC) method. *(See Chapter 15 for full coverage of LCC.)* BEES follows the ASTM standard method for life cycle costing of building-related investments.[14]

It is important to distinguish between the time periods used to measure environmental performance and economic performance, which are different. Recall that in environmental LCA, the time period begins with raw material acquisition and ends with product end-of-life. Economic performance, on the other hand, is evaluated over a fixed period (known as the *study period*) that begins with the purchase and installation of the product, and ends at some point in the future that does not necessarily correspond with product end-of-life.

Economic performance is evaluated beginning at product purchase and installation because this is when out-of-pocket costs begin to be incurred, and investment decisions are made based on out-of-pocket costs. The study period ends at a fixed date in the future. For a private investor, its length is set at the period of product or facility ownership. For society as a whole, the study period length is often set at the useful life of the longest-lived product alternative. However, when all alternatives have very long lives (e.g., more than 50 years), a shorter study period may be selected for three reasons:

1.  Technological obsolescence becomes an issue.

2.  Data becomes too uncertain.

3.  The further in the future, the less important the costs.

In the BEES model, economic performance is measured over a 50-year study period, as shown in Figure 14.2. This period is selected to reflect a reasonable amount of time over which to evaluate economic performance for society as a whole. The same 50-year period is used to evaluate all products, even if they have different useful lives. This is one of the strengths of the LCC method. It adjusts for the fact that different products have different useful lives when evaluating them over the same study period.

For consistency, the BEES model evaluates the use stage of environmental performance over the same 50-year study period. Product replacements over this 50-year period are accounted for in the environmental performance score, and end-of-life solid waste is prorated to year 50 for products with partial lives remaining after the 50-year period.

The LCC method totals all relevant costs associated with a product over the study period. Alternative products for the same function, such as floor covering, can then be compared on the basis of their LCCs to determine which is the least costly means of providing that function over the study period. Categories of cost typically include costs for purchase, installation, maintenance, repair, and replacement. A negative cost item is the *residual value*. The residual value is the product value remaining at the end of the study period. In the BEES model, the residual value is computed by prorating the purchase and installation cost over the product life remaining beyond the 50-year period.[15]

The LCC method accounts for the time value of money by using a discount rate to convert all future costs to their equivalent present value. Future costs must be expressed in terms consistent with the discount rate used. There are two approaches. First, a *real* discount rate may be used with constant-dollar costs (e.g., Year 2002). Real discount rates reflect the portion of the time value of money attributable to the real earning power of money over time, and not to general price inflation. Even if all future costs are expressed in constant Year 2002 dollars, they must be discounted to reflect this portion of the time value of money. Second, a *market* discount rate may be used with current-dollar amounts (e.g., actual future prices).

Market discount rates reflect the time value of money stemming from both inflation and the real earning power of money over time. When applied properly, both approaches yield the same LCC results. The current version of BEES computes LCCs using constant Year 2002

**Figure 14.2**
BEES Study Periods for Measuring Building Product Environmental and Economic Performance

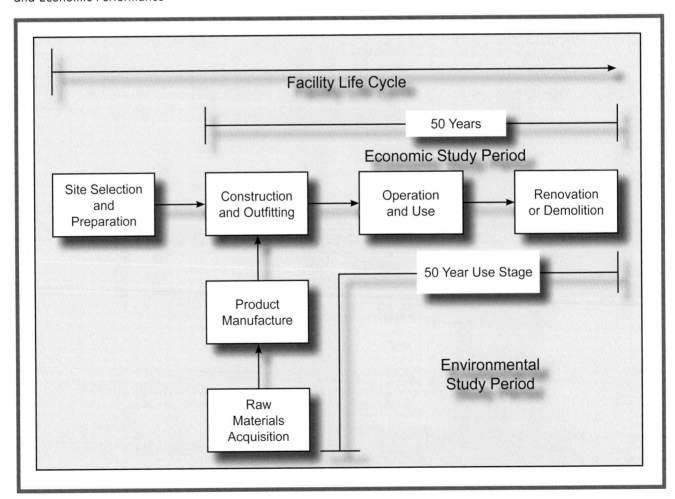

**Green Building: Project Planning & Cost Estimating**

dollars and a real discount rate. As a default, it uses a real rate of 3.9%, the 2002 rate mandated by the U.S. Office of Management and Budget (OMB) for most federal projects.[16]

## Overall Performance: Economic & Environmental

The BEES overall performance score combines the environmental and economic results into a single score, as illustrated in Figure 14.3. Before combining the two, each is placed on a common scale by dividing by the sum of corresponding scores across all alternatives under analysis. In effect, then, each performance score is rescaled in terms of its share of all scores, and is placed on the same relative scale from 0 to 100. Then the environmental and economic performance scores are combined into an overall score by weighting environmental and economic performance by their relative importance and taking a weighted average. The BEES user specifies the relative importance weights used to combine environmental and economic performance scores and may test the sensitivity of the overall scores to different sets

**Figure 14.3**
BEES Overall Performance Score Breakdown

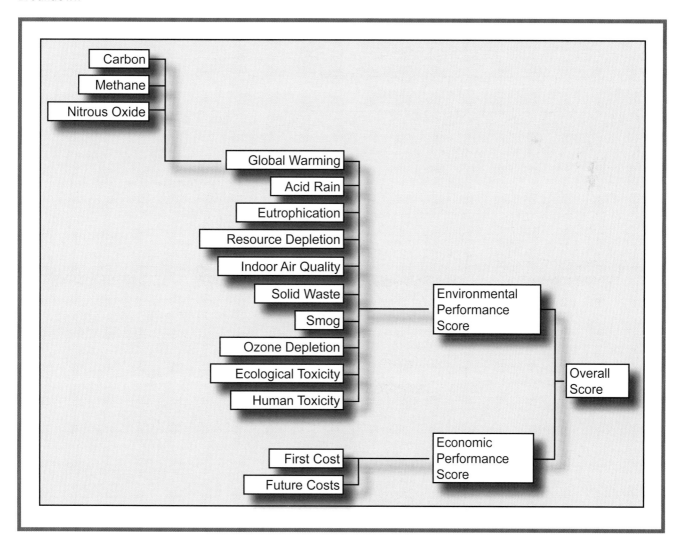

of relative importance weights. Figures 14.4 through 14.6 show three BEES summary graphs illustrating how BEES reports environmental, economic, and overall performance, respectively, based on user-defined importance weights.

## Limitations

Properly interpreting the BEES scores requires placing them in perspective. There are inherent limits to applying U.S. average LCA and LCC results and in comparing building products outside the design context.

The BEES LCA and LCC approaches produce U.S. average performance results for generic and manufacturer-specific product alternatives. The BEES results do not apply to products manufactured in other countries where manufacturing and agricultural practices, fuel mixes, environmental regulations, transportation distances, and labor and

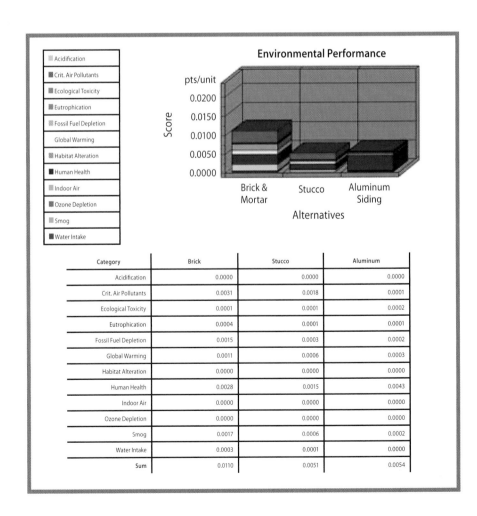

| Category | Brick | Stucco | Aluminum |
|---|---|---|---|
| Acidification | 0.0000 | 0.0000 | 0.0000 |
| Crit. Air Pollutants | 0.0031 | 0.0018 | 0.0001 |
| Ecological Toxicity | 0.0001 | 0.0001 | 0.0002 |
| Eutrophication | 0.0004 | 0.0001 | 0.0001 |
| Fossil Fuel Depletion | 0.0015 | 0.0003 | 0.0002 |
| Global Warming | 0.0011 | 0.0006 | 0.0003 |
| Habitat Alteration | 0.0000 | 0.0000 | 0.0000 |
| Human Health | 0.0028 | 0.0015 | 0.0043 |
| Indoor Air | 0.0000 | 0.0000 | 0.0000 |
| Ozone Depletion | 0.0000 | 0.0000 | 0.0000 |
| Smog | 0.0017 | 0.0006 | 0.0002 |
| Water Intake | 0.0003 | 0.0001 | 0.0000 |
| Sum | 0.0110 | 0.0051 | 0.0054 |

**Figure 14.4**
BEES Summary Graph:
Environmental Performance

material markers may differ.[17] Furthermore, all products in a generic product group, such as vinyl composition tile floor covering, are not created equal. Product composition, manufacturing methods, fuel mixes, transportation practices, useful lives, and cost can all vary for individual products in a generic product group. The BEES results for the generic product group do not necessarily represent the performance of an individual product.

The BEES LCAs use selected inventory flows converted to selected local, regional, and global environmental impacts to assess environmental performance. Those inventory flows that currently do not have scientifically proven or quantifiable impacts on the environment are excluded. Examples are mineral extraction and wood harvesting, which are qualitatively thought to lead to loss of habitat and an accompanying loss of biodiversity, but whose impacts may not have been quantified. If the BEES user has important knowledge about these or other potential environmental impacts, this information should be brought into the interpretation of the BEES results.

During the interpretation step of the BEES LCA, environmental impacts are optionally combined into a single environmental performance score using relative importance weights. These weights necessarily incorporate values and subjectivity. BEES users should routinely test the effects on the environmental performance scores of changes in the set of importance weights.

The BEES environmental scores do not represent *absolute* environmental performance. Rather, they represent proportional differences in performance, or *relative* performance, among competing

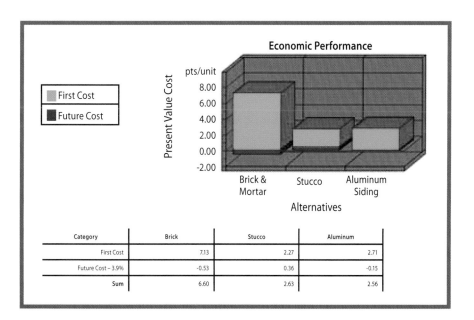

**Figure 14.5**
BEES Summary Graph:
Economic Performance

| Category | Brick | Stucco | Aluminum |
|---|---|---|---|
| First Cost | 7.13 | 2.27 | 2.71 |
| Future Cost – 3.9% | -0.53 | 0.36 | -0.15 |
| Sum | 6.60 | 2.63 | 2.56 |

alternatives. Consequently, the overall performance score for a given product alternative can change if one or more competing alternatives are added to, or removed from, the set of alternatives under consideration. In rare instances, rank reversal, or a reordering of scores, is possible.

Finally, since they are relative performance scores, no conclusions may be drawn by comparing overall scores across building elements. That is, if exterior wall finish Product A has an overall performance score of 30, and roof covering Product D has an overall performance score of 20, Product D does not necessarily perform better than Product A (keeping in mind that lower performance scores are better). This limitation does *not* apply to comparing environmental performance scores across building elements, as noted above.

There are inherent limits to comparing product alternatives without reference to the whole building design context. First, this approach may overlook important environmental and cost interactions among building elements. For example, the useful life of one building element (e.g., floor coverings), which influences both its environmental and economic performance scores, may depend on the selection of related building elements (e.g., subflooring). There is no substitute for good building design.

Environmental and economic performance are but two attributes of building product performance. The BEES model assumes that competing product alternatives all meet minimum technical performance requirements.[18] However, there may be significant

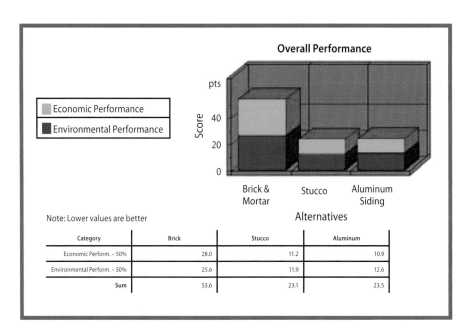

**Figure 14.6**
BEES Summary Graph:
Overall Performance

| Category | Brick | Stucco | Aluminum |
|---|---|---|---|
| Economic Perform. – 50% | 28.0 | 11.2 | 10.9 |
| Environmental Perform. – 50% | 25.6 | 11.9 | 12.6 |
| Sum | 53.6 | 23.1 | 23.5 |

Note: Lower values are better

differences in technical performance, such as acoustical performance, fire performance, or aesthetics, which may outweigh environmental and economic considerations.

## Conclusion

Applying the BEES approach leads to several general conclusions. First, environmental claims based on single impacts, such as recycled content alone, should be viewed with skepticism. These claims do not account for the fact that one impact may have been improved at the expense of others. Second, measures must always be quantified on a functional unit basis as they are in BEES, so that the products being compared are true substitutes for one another. One roof covering product may be environmentally superior to another on a pound-for-pound basis, but if that product requires twice the mass as the other to cover one square foot of roof, the results may reverse. Third, a product may contain a negative-impact constituent, but if that constituent is a small portion of an otherwise relatively benign product, its significance decreases dramatically. Finally, a short-lived, low-first-cost product is often not the cost-effective alternative. A higher first cost may be justified many times over for a durable, maintenance-free product. In sum, the answers lie in the trade-offs.

1. BEES is developed by the National Institute of Standards and Technology (NIST) Building and Fire Research Laboratory with support from the U.S. EPA Environmentally Preferable Purchasing Program. The current version, BEES 4.0, aimed at designers, builders, and product manufacturers, includes actual environmental and economic performance data for nearly 200 building products spread across a range of building applications. The BEES software and manual may be downloaded free of charge from **www.bfrl.nist. gov/oae/software/bees.html**

2. International Organization for Standardization, Environmental Management—Life-Cycle Assessment—Principles and Framework, International Standard 14040, 1997; ISO Environmental Management—Life-Cycle Assessment—Goal and Scope Definition and Inventory Analysis, International Standard 14041, 1998; and ISO Environmental Management—Life-Cycle Assessment—Life Cycle Impact Assessment, International Standard 14042, 2000.

3. American Society for Testing and Materials. *Standard Practice for Measuring Life-Cycle Costs of Buildings and Building Systems.* ASTM Designation E 917-99, West Conshohocken, PA, 1999.

4. American Society for Testing and Materials, *Standard Practice for Applying the Analytic Hierarchy Process to Multiattribute Decision Analysis of Investments Related to Buildings and Building Systems,* ASTM Designation E 1765-98, West Conshohocken, PA, 1998.

5. American Society for Testing and Materials. *Standard Classification for Building Elements and Related Sitework UNIFORMAT II.* ASTM Designation E 1557-97, West Conshohocken, PA, September 1997.

6. While a large cost contribution does not directly indicate a significant environmental impact, it may indicate scarce natural resources or numerous subsidiary unit processes potentially involving high energy consumption.

7. All product alternatives are assumed to meet minimum technical performance requirements (e.g., acoustic and fire performance).

8. Ecobalance, Inc. DEAMTM 3.0: Data for Environmental Analysis and Management. Bethesda, MD, 1999.

9. U.S. Environmental Protection Agency, Office of Research and Development. *Life Cycle Assessment: Inventory Guidelines and Principles.* EPA/600/R-92/245, February 1993.

10. SETAC-Europe, Life Cycle Assessment, B. DeSmet, et al. (eds.), 1992; SETAC. *A Conceptual Framework for Life Cycle Impact Assessment.* J. Fava, et al. (eds.), 1993; and SETAC. *Guidelines for Life Cycle Assessment: A Code of Practice.* F. Consoli, et al. (eds.), 1993.

11. SETAC. *Life-Cycle Impact Assessment: The State-of-the-Art.* J. Owens, et al. (eds.), 1997.

12. U.S. Environmental Protection Agency. *Tool for the Reduction and Assessment of Chemical and Other Environmental Impacts (TRACI): User's Guide and System Documentation, EPA/600/R- 02/052.* U.S. EPA Office of Research and Development, Cincinnati, OH, August 2002.

13. American Society for Testing and Materials. *Standard Practice for Applying the Analytic Hierarchy Process to Multiattribute Decision Analysis of Investments Related to Buildings and Building Systems* ASTM Designation E 1765-98, West Conshohocken, PA, 1998.

14. American Society for Testing and Materials. *Standard Practice for Measuring Life-Cycle Costs of Buildings and Building Systems* ASTM Designation E 917-99, West Conshohocken, PA, 1999. Note that the Building Life-Cycle Cost (BLCC) software discussed in the next chapter also follows this ASTM standard method in conducting its life-cycle costing evaluations.

15. For example, a product with a 40-year life that costs $10 per 0.09 square meters ($10 per square foot) to install would have a residual value of $7.50 in year 50, considering replacement in year 40.

16. Office of Management and Budget (OMB). "Circular A-94," *Guidelines and Discount Rates for Benefit-Cost Analysis of Federal Programs.* Washington, DC, October 27, 1992 and OMB Circular A-94, Appendix C, 2002.

17. BEES *does* apply to products manufactured in other countries and sold in the United States. These results, however, do not apply to those same products as sold in other countries because transport to the United States is built into their BEES life cycle inventory data.

18. Environmental and economic performance results for wall insulation, roof coverings, and concrete beams and columns do consider technical performance differences. For wall insulation and roof coverings, BEES accounts for differential heating and cooling energy use. For concrete beams and columns, BEES accounts for different compressive strengths.

# Chapter

# 15 Evaluation, Analysis & Data Tools

## Joseph Macaluso, CCC
## M. Magda Lelek, PE, CEM

One of the hallmarks of green building is the extra thought given early on and throughout the design process. It means thinking beyond current codes, standards, and conventional wisdom. Sustainable building systems and components are analyzed and evaluated in greater detail and on more levels than those of traditional buildings. Computer software can improve the efficiency of virtually all aspects of this analysis. In fact, in some areas, such as energy modeling, the analysis can be so complex that software is essential to the process.

Government sources, environmental groups, and third-party software developers have created software in both stand-alone programs and ones that can be integrated into Computer Assisted Drafting/Design (CADD or CAD) software. Many of these programs are available at no charge or at a reasonable cost. Product manufacturers also offer low- or no-cost software to assist architects, engineers, estimators, facility owners, managers, and other team members in evaluating energy efficiency and other environmental aspects of their products.

This chapter is an overview of the more popular tools currently available to help with analysis, planning, design, selection, and estimating appropriate to green building systems and materials. Additional software packages can be found at the Energy Efficiency & Renewable Network website of the Department of Energy (DOE): **www.eere.energy.gov/buildings/tools_directory**

There are too many helpful websites to list in this chapter but some of them are listed in the Appendix. One that stands out is the Green Building Advisor, which combines Green Basics, Blogs, Green Homes, Product Guide, Strategy & Details, and Q&A, all on one website. And, if you just can't get enough green building in your life, Greenergy2030 offers green social networking to meet up with like-minded people and share information at **www.greenergy2030.com**

## Building Information Modeling

Building Information Modeling (BIM) software is a big deal for green building on several levels. Through BIM, the collaborative design approach, often encouraged by green building supporters, is not only possible, but practical. Early CAD software started the process, revolutionizing design and drafting by replacing the traditional pencil on paper with more efficient electronic designing and drafting. Three dimensional renderings were possible, but involved extra steps; therefore, CAD was primarily used for two dimensional drawings (2D). BIM made it easier to design in three dimensions (3D). The addition of time properties (4D) brought construction sequencing and scheduling capabilities. Adding cost properties (5D) brought estimating capabilities. Linking data to objects in the drawings added even more intelligence, which allowed not only visual simulation of the construction process, but also simulation of energy use and lighting properties. Although legal issues still need to be worked out, the central database on BIM-based projects allows all team players to share the same information, eliminating inconsistencies and duplication of effort. Team access to the central database also helps in the coordination of any issues that arise during construction. Without BIM, sharing information is possible but difficult, as there is no central database.

There is virtually no limit to the information that can be associated with objects included in a BIM model. Information such as distance from a manufacturing source, environmental life cycle properties, and reused material content allows architects, engineers, and consultants to determine percentages. Cost and content percentages can be calculated based on individual components, systems, and the entire building. For estimators, quantity take-off reports can be generated from the BIM model, eliminating time consuming manual counting and measuring. The report can be used directly, or imported into construction cost estimating software or spreadsheets.

Software packages that apply the BIM concept include Autodesk Revit Architecture (**www.usa.autodesk.com**), Autodesk Green Building Studio, Autodesk Ecotect Analysis (**www.autodesk.com/ecotect/analysis**), and others. Some of the packages are developed mainly as design tools while others are more of analysis tools focusing on daylight analysis, acoustical analysis, thermal comfort analysis, energy analysis, and other aspects of building functions. Pricing of these packages varies and so does the learning curve.

BIM does require a substantial investment in time and money. However, as in CAD, "reader" programs are available for those that only need to view, measure, or review BIM files. For preliminary building modeling, Google offers a free easy-to-use program called SketchUp. A version with more features and capabilities is available for $500. Programs from other sources, called "plugins," are available that expand the capabilities of the software, including those that allow modeling of energy usage, lighting characteristics, and total carbon footprint. Open Studio is a free plugin for SketchUp provided by the U.S. Department of Energy, that simplifies the creation and editing of building geometry for its EnergyPlus software (see below). Integrated Environmental Solutions (**www.iesve.com**) and Greenspace Research (**www.greenspaceresearch. com**) also offer free plugins for SketchUp, as well as integrated building performance analysis tools for a fee.

For Estimators, quantity take-off (QTO) software tools permit efficient extraction material quantities from the BIM model into a report, or exportation into estimating software or even electronic spreadsheets. The Reed SmartBIM QTO (**www.reedconstructiondata.com/bim**) also links materials being taken off to the RSMeans *CostWorks* database, while multiplying the quantities by the unit costs. Of course, both quantities can be refined by the cost estimator. The software costs about $500 per user.

## *Whole Building Energy Evaluation*

## DOE-2 & eQUEST

DOE-2 software is designed to predict hourly energy use and energy cost of a building, using hourly weather data, a description of the building and its HVAC equipment, and the utility rates structure. It is widely recognized as the industry standard. DOE-2 is available with a range of user interfaces.

The DOE-2 based programs can be used for the analysis of all types of buildings for both a new design and for existing facilities. It can be used to calculate hourly, daily, monthly, seasonal, and annual load profiles or building energy consumption estimates for individual building components or for the entire building.

The DOE-2 based programs are useful for comparing alternative building designs, systems, or components, including individual design features such as building geometry, location/orientation, construction materials, HVAC systems and controls, utility selection, and other design options. The DOE-2 software can also be helpful in later stages during project implementation, building commissioning, measurement, and verification, and to quantify savings for potential monetary incentives from local utilities. For existing buildings, the software may be helpful in building energy consumption and end uses diagnostics for the purpose of building operation optimization and energy conservation. The latest versions of DOE-2 programs (DOE-2.2 and eQUEST) can also be used for modeling photovoltaic (PV) systems.

Various DOE-2 based programs can be used for LEED® building analysis for energy efficiency-related credits. They can also be used for *Energy Code* compliance analysis, life cycle cost analysis (overall or individual building components), and indirectly for pollution production/reduction analysis.

At this time, there are two versions of the DOE-2 software available. DOE-2.1E is the older version, and DOE-2.2 is the newest building energy use simulation and cost calculation engine. In the "plain" version, the programs are machine-independent "batch" executables and require considerable experience and learning curve to use effectively, but offer expert users great flexibility. There are some commercial versions and Windows®-based interfaces developed that use DOE-2 "simulation engines." DOE-2.2 is the "simulation engine" contained within eQUEST®, and PowerDOE. eQUEST® is a complete interactive Windows implementation of the DOE-2 program that can be used in two modes. The "wizard" mode can be used for a variety of building analyses even by less experienced building modelers, and the "detailed" mode allows full access to the complete features of the DOE-2.2 program and is better suited to more advanced users. PowerDOE is a previous generation, Windows-based application for DOE-2.2. It is still available but, as of this book's printing, has not been updated since 2001. An example of the commercial versions of DOE-2.1E is **VisualDOE 4.0** program.

eQUEST, DOE-2.2, and DOE-2.1E are available for download at no charge at **www.doe2.com**. Other DOE-2 based software programs are typically available for a fee that varies based on the hardware platform and software vendor. Visit their website for more information on the available DOE-2 software, pricing, and capabilities.

Input for a DOE-2 based building model can be grouped into three sections: loads, systems, and economics.

The load inputs include:
- Building envelope: building location/orientation, building geometry, construction materials, and windows details, including shading
- Internal loads: occupants, plug loads, lights, other
- Schedules: internal loads, shading devices, other

The systems inputs include:

- HVAC system: type, size, performance (DX or chilled water, constant volume or VAV, packaged or central stations, terminal units type, etc.), and control strategies (temperature control, fan control, schedules, set points, OA control, etc.)
- Physical plant: equipment selection (type, size, performance) for chillers, boilers, cooling towers, district steam/CHW, domestic hot water heaters and equipment control (schedules, set points, sequence of operation, etc.)
- Process loads: type (steam, hot water, chilled water, etc.), size, schedules

The economics inputs include:

- Utility rates/rate structures: electricity, natural gas, fuel oil, purchased steam, purchased chilled water, other
- Equipment cost: first cost, maintenance costs, major overhaul costs

DOE-2 programs allow numerous design alternatives/iterations to be performed at any level of design development. The programs provide great flexibility in analysis, offering better system trade-off analysis as they take into account interaction among all building components (e.g., fenestration area, lighting, daylighting, cooling load, cooling equipment size).

If required, a very detailed and precise energy model can be created, although the time and effort involved in providing such a high level of detail needs to be weighed against the potential impact and benefit it will have on the analysis for which the model is used. The time required for the model development depends on the level of detail desired and on the purpose for which the model is created.

Once a model is created, some changes can be made with the "stroke of a key," a big advantage over manual/spreadsheet analysis. Building geometry/envelope input typically is considered the most time-consuming component, but again, the extent of the effort will depend on the level of detail required. Also with features offered by some of the programs (for example, the eQUEST wizard features), many building envelope components can be developed with fairly small effort.

There are many users of the DOE-2/eQUEST programs worldwide, and various forums are available for exchange of information related to building energy consumption simulation. One popular forum is the **BLDG-SIM@gard.com** mailing list where building energy modelers exchange opinions and post questions. More information about this and similar mailing lists can be found at **http://onebuilding.org**

## Energy-10™

Energy-10 is a user-friendly whole-building energy evaluation software that helps to perform hourly energy simulations in order to quantify, analyze, assess, and illustrate the effects of changes in building insulation, windows, lighting systems, and mechanical systems, as well as daylighting, passive solar, and natural ventilation—by individual component and on the building in total. It is best suited for residential and small buildings under 10,000 square feet and is best used at the conceptual design stage. The program provides the results in the form of summary tables, as well as up to 20 graphics that compare the current design to a base design.

Energy-10 is the result of collaboration between the National Renewable Energy Laboratory, Lawrence Berkley National Laboratory, and Berkeley Solar Group. It is easier to use and less expensive than DOE-2, but is not as robust. The cost of the software is approximately $375. The Energy-10 website is **www.energy-10.com**

## EnergyPlus™

EnergyPlus performs energy use simulation, load, heat balance, and mass balance calculations. It includes simulation time steps of less than an hour. The modular structure of the program will facilitate third-party development. The software produces text output files that offer the advantage of being easy to adapt to spreadsheet and text reports for further development. Solar thermal, multi-zone airflow, photovoltaic, and fuel cell simulations are expected to be added. The basic program requires a degree of computer literacy. The software is available at no cost at the DOE website, **www.eere.energy.gov/buildings/energyplus**

There are some graphical user interfaces currently in development or already available that use the EnergyPlus simulation engine to perform building energy consumption analysis. Information about them is available at the EnergyPlus website mentioned above. Some of them focus on specific aspects of energy modeling (for example evaluating the fenestration system for a building) and some offer more comprehensive building analyses. An example of the latter type of a software package is DesignBuilder. It is available for purchase at prices that vary depending on the licensing option selected. Information about DesignBuilder is available at **www.eere.energy.gov/buildings/energyplus**

## SPARK

SPARK (Simulation Problem Analysis Research Kernel) is a highly sophisticated program that can model more complex building envelopes and mechanical systems than DOE-2 or EnergyPlus. The software is an equation-based, object-oriented simulation environment and runs up to 10–20 times faster than other simulation programs. The basic program is available at no cost. The potential drawback is that it requires a high degree of computer literacy to use. To download the software, visit the Lawrence Berkeley National Laboratory website at **http:// simulationresearch.lbl.gov**

## HOT3000™

HOT2000 and it successor, HOT3000, simulation software is designed primarily for low-rise residential buildings to evaluate the effectiveness of heating and cooling, including passive solar systems. They do not require a high level of computer literacy. HOT2000 and HOT3000 are used to determine if a house is energy efficient enough to qualify for the R-2000 label. The software generates detailed monthly and annual tables on heat loss HVAC loads and the cost of energy use.

HOT2000 and HOT3000 can compare up to five different fuel types and several different HVAC systems. Four different types of houses can be compared. HOT3000 is available in both English and French, as a free download making it popular in Canada as well as the United States. Other software in the family includes Hot2® EC, for performance compliance, and HOT2XP, which has an easy-to-use graphical interface and generates results that can be further fine-tuned with HOT2000. To download the software at no charge, visit the Natural Resources Canada website at **http://canmetenergy-canmetenergie.nrcan-rncan.gc.ca/eng/software_tools.html**

## Green Footstep

Sponsored by the Rocky Mountain Institute, Green Footstep is a free and easy-to-use web-based tool that calculates the amount of greenhouse gases a building contributes to the atmosphere. It allows designers to set goals and evaluate how a design or changes in a design affect the greenhouse gasses. It can be used all the way from pre-design to occupancy. It considers the site, design, construction, and operation of the building. It compares the native conditions, to the existing conditions, to the building design. **www.greenfootstep.org**

## Building Systems Evaluation

Programs such as RESFEN, WINDOW, and THERM are available for analysis of fenestration at no charge from the Lawrence Berkeley National Laboratory. Links to order these programs and for additional information can be found at **http://windows.lbl.gov/software/resfen/ resfen.html** For solar water heating, FRESA and RETScreen® are two computer programs used for preliminary analysis for renewable energy applications. Both of these programs are available at no cost, FRESA at the DOE website, **www1.eere.energy.gov/femp/renewable_energy/ renewable_software.html** and RETScreen® at **www.retscreen.net/ang/ menu.php**

The hourly energy simulation program, TRNSYS, is widely used for precise engineering data and economic analysis and to optimize parameters of solar water heating system design. The cost is approximately $4,000 for commercial use and $2,000 for educational use. The website is **http://sel.me.wisc.edu/trnsys**

These programs, along with Energy-10, are also used for photovoltaic modeling. PV*SOL®, PVcad, and PV-DesignPro are some other popular programs used in photovoltaic systems. T*SOL® is a program used to simulate solar thermal systems. Free demonstration versions of PV*SOL and T*SOL (available in English, French, and other languages) can be downloaded at **www.valentin.de** and PVcad is available at no cost at **www.iset.uni-kassel.de** PV-DesignPro is part of the Solar Design Studio software package and costs approximately $250. It's available at **www.mauisolarsoftware.com**

There are several computer programs available to help develop strategies for reducing a building's water usage. One of them is called Watergy, a simple spreadsheet the designer uses to identify areas for potential water and energy savings. The program calculates the cost of these strategies and the payback period. Watergy is a free download available at **www1.eere.energy.gov/femp/information/download_watergy.html**

## Codes & Standards Compliance Evaluation

REScheck is a quick and easy way to check to see if a typical single- or multi-family residential building is in compliance with the *Model Energy Code* and the *International Energy Conservation Code*. The program generates a report that lists project data and compliance results.

COMcheck is designed to check compliance with commercial building energy codes, such as ASHRAE 90.1 and the *International Energy Conservation Code*.

The REScheck and COMcheck series are Windows®-based, and can be downloaded at no charge. In addition to these desktop software packages, web-based versions of REScheck and COMcheck are also available. The desktop and web-based versions are all available at no charge at **www.energycodes.gov**

As discussed in Chapter 9, the HERS rating system and subsequent report is used to determine energy efficiency of homes for compliance with requirements of the ENERGY STAR® and Energy Efficient Mortgage programs. Two popular software packages used to generate the HERS report are REM/Rate™ and TREAT. The Residential Energy Services Network (RESNET) accredits HERS rating software and HERS rating providers. The RESNET website is **www.natresnet.org**

Some larger Architectural and Engineering firms have developed their own software to comply with LEED's document-intensive process. But tracking can also be accomplished through spreadsheets or project management software, which is well suited for keeping track of submittals, drawings, receipts, product specification sheets, and the like. This should only get better, as project management software companies have already begun to update their software to include LEED credit tracking capabilities. [1]

Some LEED credits and Living Building Challenge prerequisites credits are earned by using locally sourced products and materials. To determine the distance of the materials source you can measure on Google Earth, a free download. And then, the radius from the job site can be plotted on a map with free software called, interestingly enough, Free Map Tools. Another helpful feature of this software is the ability to plot and calculate distances both by land transportation, or "as the crow flies." **www.freemaptools.com**

## Life Cycle Analysis

Life cycle cost analysis is a significant factor in green building design and construction. The typically higher initial costs of many green approaches are weighed against future savings. BLCC5 is a program developed by the National Institute of Standards and Technology (NIST) to perform life cycle analysis of buildings and building components. This program is useful for comparing alternate designs that have higher initial costs, but lower operating costs over the life of the building. BLCC5 is very useful in evaluating water and energy conservation projects, as well as renewable energy strategies. The software compares two or more competing alternate designs and determines which has the lowest life cycle cost and, therefore, which is the most economical in the long run. The software is Windows®-based and is available at no cost through the DOE website (previously noted).

A thorough analysis of the environmental aspects of building systems requires a study of all their environmental impacts throughout their entire life span, from manufacturing to disposal. Athena Environmental Impact Estimator software is used to assess the environmental impact of buildings at the early stages of design, using the Athena Institute's life cycle analysis database. If an energy simulation has been completed, the data can be entered into the software for use in building operation calculations. Currently the software covers four geographic regions in the United States, a U.S. average, and most of Canada, by region. Results of calculations can be displayed in summary tables and graphs. The software, including reports and interpretive support, is available for about $700 (plus $300 for the interpretive support) at **www. athenaSMI.ca**

Because environmental issues are often tied to costs, several software packages try to employ an integrated approach. As described in Chapters 13 and 14, the BEES model is a technique used to analyze both economic and environmental impacts and blend them into a rational decision-making scoring system. The BEES software contains pertinent data and the computational engine that generates the BEES score. The current version contains a database of over 200 building products.

The BEES software produces graphics that combine the environmental and economic life cycle performance scores for user-selected alternate building products. Graphics also show individual environmental impact flows, as well as economic first and future costs. The Windows®-based software is available at no cost from the DOE website. The software includes generic and brand-specific items and EPA methods for evaluating environmental impacts and uses an absolute scoring system which allows comparisons across building elements.

## Ad Hoc Analysis

Versatility is the reason why electronic spreadsheets are the workhorses of engineering, architectural, and construction management offices, for ad hoc analysis is frequently required in green building construction. Third party vendors, such as @Risk supply Excel add-ins for advanced and complex statistical analysis. Spreadsheet templates are often used to save set-up time in life cycle costing, value engineering, and LEED analysis. Breakeven analysis, capital budget return on investment, lease vs. buy analysis, decision matrix, and risk analysis templates can be downloaded from the Microsoft Office Online website. Often overlooked are the built-in statistical and financial functions, which can save a considerable amount of time. On Excel 2007® they can be accessed by clicking on the Formulas tab, then on the Function Library Group; clicking on the Financial Commands will display all the financial functions available. On older versions they can be accessed by clicking on the Insert tab, then on the Function menu, and scrolling through and selecting the Financial category.

## Case Studies & Databases

Case studies provide information on specific buildings and unique conditions, while cost databases provide statistically normalized cost data in the form of a mean or median from many data samples of buildings, systems, or individual components to provide an expected average cost. Case studies are particularly useful because of the uniqueness of green buildings, providing insight into the technologies and techniques used on a particular project. Cost data from both case studies and databases may need to be adjusted to a specific location and point of time in order to be to be useful as a reference.

Building Green Incorporated is the publisher of *Environmental Building News* (EBN), an independent monthly newsletter devoted to sustainable building. EBN offers *GreenSpec*® and searchable archives on a CD of all back issues of *Environmental Building News*. *GreenSpec* is a directory of 2,000 green building products screened by the editors of EBN, and a guideline specification for environmentally preferable products. Building Green Incorporated also offers the *BuildingGreen Suite*, a web-based subscription service with access to high performance building case studies (over 200 green building projects), *GreenSpec*, and the EBN archives. (**www.buildinggreen.com**)

*Design Cost Data* magazine is another good source for green case studies, with the advantage of cost breakdowns by CSI division. In conjunction with the magazine is an electronic cost database available to subscribers. DC&D Technologies also produces a software package called D4Cost that allows users to modify actual case studies to reflect different construction dates, locations, and sizes. Several case studies from DC&D can be found in the "Case Studies" section of this book.

Whitestone Research offers maintenance and repair cost databases and cost models for entire buildings and building systems in their data books and software. This information can be very helpful for use in life cycle costing. Their website is **www.whitestoneresearch.com**

RSMeans *CostWorks* CDs and cost data books are excellent sources for conventional building costs that can be used for comparisons with green components. They are also useful because green building approaches often incorporate conventional building materials and components. To see the full range of RSMeans products and services, visit their website at **www.rsmeans.com** *(See appendix A for instructions on using Means cost data.)*

## Creating Project Cost Databases

In addition to specific software packages, the project team should use spreadsheets and database software to create a cost database, or add to the existing project cost database, for reference and estimating the cost of future projects. The advantage of capturing actual project costs is that the "provenance" of the information (time, location, and conditions) is known first-hand. The data is more likely to be reliable and relevant, therefore, requiring fewer corrections and adjustments.

In particular, green building component and system information should be captured and saved with as much detail as possible, as this information is not as easy to come by, as it is for more generic items. Individual unit costs should be organized using the material-based CSI MasterFormat™ work breakdown structure; while building assemblies should follow the systems based on UNIFORMAT™ structure for ease of retrieval and use. It may also be helpful to use a LEED-based work breakdown structure. Line items should be broken down into material costs, unit labor hours, composite wage rate, and equipment costs. It is important to include date, location, and conditions as part of each individual line item record. Breaking down the costs in this manner allows for easy adjustments to be made to wage rates, productivity, cost escalation, location and field conditions, so that they can be easily adapted for future estimates and cost analysis.

## Conclusion

The software presented in this chapter represents just some of the many useful tools in the evaluation, compliance, and analysis of green building data. Often, because of the expense and time required to purchase and learn new programs, conventional wisdom dictates that the investment should be made only when it is needed for a particular project. However, it is recommended that software be purchased *before* it is absolutely needed for a particular project. This allows users to become familiar with it ahead of time, gaining valuable experience in a more relaxed atmosphere, instead of trying to figure out how features work with a deadline looming, thus avoiding the potential of missed deadlines or costly mistakes.

When using software for the first time, start off with a small job and have a contingency plan in place for performing the work manually, or even concurrently using software you are familiar with. As more experience is gained, users should experiment with some of the more advanced features of the software, even though these may not be required for a particular problem. These features may be required on future projects. With a little time and experience, users will find that keeping current with the latest computer software can greatly enhance and streamline green building projects.

1. Houston, Neal. *Software Advice Track LEED,* Volume 3, Credits in Project Management Software

# Chapter

# *16* The Greening of Commercial Real Estate

*Phil Waier, PE, LEED AP*

The commercial real estate industry is the latest segment to embrace the green movement. The various "green" rating systems have raised awareness of resource usage and provided a road map and recognition for reduced consumption, with the USGBC LEED program gaining the greatest acceptance. Adopters of, and attitudes toward, sustainable construction have been evolving. Rating systems provide benchmarks for comparing buildings and heighten our focus on the resources required to construct and operate them. The earliest adopters of LEED or sustainable development were the government and institutions, such as universities and hospitals. These owners have a long-term investment in their buildings, often occupying them until they are so obsolete that it is no longer technically feasible to remodel them. The next tier of adopters was corporate owners. They built corporate headquarters designed to be showcase buildings with the latest sustainable technologies. High profile commercial organizations such as Walmart, Goldman Sachs, Macy's, and Wachovia, have shown that it is good business to build green.

While the green movement is beginning to age, there are still some growing pains. The design community is working with increasingly educated buyers, some with reasonable expectations, and others wanting to push the envelope for sustainability. The green movement has spurred numerous new technologies, resulting in design changes and new methodologies. The commercial real estate industry is continually monitoring these changes and their impact on the bottom line. As a result of new technologies employed and familiar technologies applied in new ways, additional risk is being placed on the developer by owners requesting avant-garde design, and the design community is under greater risk, designing to enhanced requirements. This can result in increased design fees. A recent survey of design fees indicated that there is a 3% design fee increase. This increase is attributable to the additional time required to design to enhanced operating performance, and the associated risk. As green design becomes more commonplace, that differential will decrease. Some organizations, experienced in green design, would argue that a differential no longer exists.

The design changes may be the result of an altruistic desire for sustainable construction or a response to meeting the requirements rating system such as LEED, Green Globes, or Energy Star. (*See Chapter 9 for more on rating systems.*) The numerous reasons for building green are included in the analysis that real estate professionals prepare before initiating a project. Just as ordinary citizens are concerned about the environment, real estate investors are searching for socially conscious investment vehicles. Green building REITs (Real Estate Investment Trusts) and investment funds have been established to address these needs. Due to heightened demand and funding sources, the commercial real estate industry has begun to embrace green construction. In fact, the momentum is such that Class A office space will soon be defined with a green requirement.

Interest in sustainable development by the commercial real estate organization is based upon many factors, ranging from altruistic to financial, with the emphasis on financial. The following highlights the factors that have promoted the adoption of green commercial construction and factors limiting adoption.

## The Role of Government

### Government Leadership

The federal government has taken a leadership position in adopting green construction practices. Prior to LEED, the U.S. Department of Energy (DOE) established the Energy Star Rating System. Energy Star compares energy consumption among building types in the same region. Those within the lowest 25% of usage are awarded an Energy Star Certification. It is important to note that the focus of Energy Star is energy usage and is, therefore, not a complete rating system, such as LEED and Green Globes. The federal government also significantly impacts the rate of green construction by virtue of the legislation it enacts and the policies it makes. As a property owner and tenant, the government was an early adopter of green construction. Government agencies were among the first to incorporate the LEED rating system into new facility construction.

Government leasing policies have promoted the leasing of space in energy efficient buildings. This practice has evolved to encourage that new leases be signed in buildings that are LEED certified, if available. As a result, commercial real estate developers in areas with a high concentration of government offices are developing their buildings using LEED standards.

In addition to influencing real estate investment through its role as owner and tenant, the government also has regulatory powers. State and local governments can influence where buildings are constructed, by zoning, and how they are constructed through codes and regulations. The following is a sample of development regulations:

- Boston, requires LEED-NC certification for all new public and private building construction of 50,000 square feet or greater.
- Los Angeles mandates that new construction greater than 50,000 square feet meets LEED standards and provides for expedited permit processing when LEED silver certification is met.
- Washington, D.C., requires that, for privately owned, nonresidential projects having 50,000 or more square feet of gross floor area and involving new construction or substantial improvements, a green building checklist be submitted as part of the building permit application. The checklist will document the elements of green building that are to be integrated into the project. These projects must meet the LEED-NC 2.2 or the LEED-CS 2.0 standards at the silver level.

## Government Incentives

Governments (state and local) provide incentives for building green. These incentives usually relate to expedited zoning approvals and building permit review. Zoning densities can also be increased or taxes decreased, if green requirements are met.

When making a decision on whether or not to build green, it is important to consider federal, state, local, and commercial incentives. One of the best sources of incentive data is the Database of State Incentives for Renewables and Efficiency (DSIRE). This database is funded by the DOE and maintained by the North Carolina Solar Center at North Carolina State University.

The database at **www.dsireusa.org** provides location-specific incentives in each state. A typical listing of available financial incentives follows:

- Green building incentives
- Local grant programs
- Property tax incentives
- Sales tax incentives
- State grant programs
- State rebate programs
- Utility rebate programs
- Other incentives unique to the location

For example, New York State lists incentives provided by a variety of organizations, such as the New York State Energy Research and Development Authority and numerous power companies. These incentives range from grants for 50% of the project value to utility rebates.

Another incentive of building green is permitting. These benefits range from permit filing assistance to expedited permit processing and a reduction in inspection fees. Examples of cities providing expedited permitting include Washington, D.C., Chicago, Jacksonville, and Seattle.

## Owner/Investor Interests

The green building movement provides benefits to building owners, real estate management firms and tenants. Studies have shown that energy is the single greatest operating expense, typically accounting for 32% of the operating budget. As the U.S. economic recession continues, green and energy efficient buildings will continue to maintain high occupancies, as tenants focus on lower utility costs and a reduction in their carbon footprint. Building greenness is measured by either of two different scales: LEED or Green Globes. Each of these rewards energy efficiency based upon a reduction from a norm. Approximate percentage reductions based upon the LEED system range from Certified/Silver at 24% to 33% to Gold/Platinum at 47% to 60%.[1]

## Reduced Operating Costs

Operating costs represent approximately 15% of the total annual cost of a building; employees working in the building account for the other 85%. While 15% is a small percentage, any savings go directly to the bottom line. Energy savings from green buildings generally range from 20% to 40%. In 2007, Real Estate Research (RREEF) reported that the average utility cost for a private office building is $2.26 per square foot. Based upon a 200,000 square foot office building, the savings, assuming a 30% reduction, would be $135,000 per year. Johnson Controls reports that a modern central heating and energy control system alone can reduce energy costs by 5% to 15%, depending on the building. [2]

In addition to energy conservation measures, green building techniques include the following:

- Flexible open space floor plans
- Use of locally sourced materials
- Use of rapidly renewable products

These designs look to minimize the use of new materials for office renovations, thus reducing cost and creating less construction waste.

# Higher Rents and Reduced Vacancy Rates

Another attraction to building green is higher financial rewards. These rewards vary by geographic location, based upon the local perception and adoption of sustainability. They can generally be summarized as follows:

- Comparatively fast absorption period
- Attraction and retention of high quality tenants
- Competitive rents
- Above average occupancy rates

A 2007 study conducted by RREEF Research, using data mined from the CoStar database, supports the findings listed above. RREEF notes that the comparison of traditional buildings to Energy Star and green buildings has flaws, based upon high owner occupancy of green buildings and their age. "Despite these limitations, clear patterns emerge: for every sector tested, vacancy rates for both Energy Star and LEED buildings are below those of conventional buildings. Overall, the vacancy rate in all sectors together is 6.1% for LEED space and 8.0% for Energy Star buildings, compared to 8.6% for all buildings."[3]

Similarly, RREEF, using CoStar data, analyzed vacancy and rental rates for LEED and LEED Class A buildings vs all Class A (LEED and non-LEED).

|  | Vacancy Rate | RentalRate/S.F. |
|---|---|---|
| LEED Class A | 7.4% | $39 |
| All Class A (LEED and non-LEED) | 11.6% | $29 |

In this case, again, the flaws identified above are present. "Still the data reveals consistent patterns supporting anecdotal evidence that green buildings lease up quicker, at higher rents, and maintain higher occupancies."[4]

## Attracting and Keeping Tenants

Green buildings are attractive investments, based upon vacancy and rental rates. In addition, absorption time to fully lease a new green building is less than for a traditional building. When all the costs of a vacancy are added together, this reduction can have a significant impact on financial performance. The following are the costs associated with a vacancy:

- Lost rent
- Real estate commissions
- Tenant improvement costs
- Marketing
- Vacant spaces contributing to building operating budget

Considering the cost of replacing a tenant, it is financially advantageous for building owners and operators to work with tenants to ensure their continued occupancy. One way owners foster higher retention rates is to keep variable cost down by focusing on energy conservation. In USGBC LEED certified buildings, owners must monitor energy usage to ensure optimal performance via a commissioning process at the end of one year's occupancy or retro commissioning. Due to changes in occupancies and usage, it is necessary to adjust building automation systems for peak performance.

Another factor contributing to tenant retention is employee satisfaction. Owners are initiating recycling and environmentally conscious cleaning programs in their buildings to meet the demands of an increasingly environmentally conscious workforce.

## Resale Value

Since the higher upfront costs commonly associated with green construction are a deterrent, a life cycle cost analysis is often performed to demonstrate the merits of building green. The problem is that a typical life cycle cost analysis is based on 20 years, while the typical investor's investment time frame may be less than 10 years. Therefore, life cycle costs can be a hard sell.

A study conducted by Capital E Analysis calculated the 20-year net present value (NPV) life cycle savings per square foot of LEED Bronze/Silver building and Gold/Platinum LEED Certified building compared to a traditional design. The 20-year NPV life cycle saving based upon design considerations was approximately $16.00 per square foot. The estimated incremental cost of construction was $4.00 per square foot, resulting in a net savings of $12.00 per square foot. Capital E also estimated the 20-year NPV productivity saving of $36.89/S.F. and $55.37/S.F. for Certified/Silver and Gold/Platinum respectively. The construction savings are much easier to document than the productivity savings, though most occupants of green building would agree that they exist.

It must be pointed out that many green upgrades have a return on investment (ROI) of five years or less. Adobe Headquarters in San Jose invested $1.4 million in energy retrofits that resulted in $1.2 million annual savings. In addition, they received $380,000 rebate in the first year.

## Insurance

In addition to the incentives provided by governments and utilities, insurance companies are providing green building incentives. The Fireman's Fund announced that they are offering a 5% reduction in green building insurance premiums.

Owners of green buildings need to pay special attention to their property insurance policy. Many owners believe that green buildings are just like any other building and, therefore, their standard commercial building insurance policy will cover losses. Many insurance companies are creating policies for green buildings that address their specific needs. The following are examples of green building risks that may not be included in a standard policy.

## Recertification Costs

Certified buildings require commissioning as a LEED prerequisite. Some certified buildings also earned LEED IAQ, Credit 3.2 (indoor air quality) by flushing the building with outside air prior to occupancy. Maintaining the certification when a loss occurs requires that the building be recommissioned and flushed, if that is one of the earned certification credits. Building flushing is not only a cost issue but also a time issue. Credit 3.2 requires flushing with 14,000 cubic feet of outdoor air per square foot of floor area. At the least, it probably requires the addition of temporary air handling equipment and, possibly, a delay in occupying the building. Recertification coverage should also be considered as a policy rider.

## Business Interruption

Business interruption insurance is an essential element of most business insurance policies. Insurance companies have parameters for the duration of reconstruction. If green materials or systems require replacement, the time for reconstruction may exceed insurance company standards, therefore requiring the owner to absorb the cost of additional time in temporary facilities.

## On-Site Power Generation

Some green building projects also include on-site power generation. In many cases, power generated on site may also be added to the grid, resulting in income to the project. If a power-generating source is disabled or destroyed, coverage can be provided not only for the repair or replacement of the generating equipment, but also for the loss of income.

## Vegetative Roofs

Buildings with green "vegetative" roofs also require additional coverage. Traditional policies may address the loss of landscape elements such as grass, shrubs, and trees. This coverage, if included, will most likely not extend to the replacement vegetative roofs. An endorsement for green roof replacement should also include the roof membrane.

In general, when insuring a green building, owners should check with their insurance agents to ensure the proper coverage is provided. Many insurance companies, including Firemen's Fund, Zurich N.A. and Lexington Insurance, are offering green endorsements.

## Health and Productivity

When corporations analyze their operating costs, they find that facilities costs account for 15% of costs, while employee expenses, which include attracting, training, and compensation, account for nearly 85%. Therefore, the health and productivity advantages of a green building can be significant. The major benefits of green are defined by LEED Indoor Environmental Quality (IEQ), which comprises the following major elements:

- Indoor air quality
- Thermal comfort
- Acoustics
- Lighting, including natural light and views

These attributes contribute to making workers more productive and healthier. It should be noted that not all green buildings address each of these elements.

An additional factor of IEQ includes careful attention to the materials used in operations and maintenance. Buildings can be built with green attributes, but if they are not maintained with environmentally friendly chemicals, or if pollutant sources are not addressed, the benefits may not be realized. In short, IEQ requires a systems approach that starts with design and construction and extends to operation, maintenance, and occupant activity.

A 2009 study from the University of California, San Diego, surveyed 2,000 workers from green buildings throughout the country. These workers have worked in both traditional buildings and their current green building environment. The researchers queried issues of productivity and health. Approximately 50% reported that they were more productive working in a green environment. Of those, 12% strongly agreed they were more productive. The remaining 50% noted little change. Similarly, Lockheed Aircraft relocated a known group of workers from a traditional building to a newly constructed green building, and absenteeism dropped 15%. As stated previously, a Capital E study estimated that the 20-year NPV productivity savings associated with a LEED building can range from $37 to $55/S.F.

Another green building study conducted at the 585,000 S.F. Lockheed Martin office facility reported that absenteeism for a known group of employees dropped 15% when relocated into a building that was both energy efficient and naturally lighted. Based upon the 2,700-employee occupancy, reduced absenteeism paid for the additional building cost in the first year.

The IEQ benefits of a green building exist beyond the office environment. Studies by retailers confirm that sales of products in naturally lighted areas exceed those in other areas. Similarly, worker productivity in factories and student learning in schools improve with natural lighting.

## Attracting and Keeping Employees

Due to the high cost of recruiting and training new employees, it is in the employer's best interest to retain existing employees. Providing a comfortable, healthy work space is one retention element. A recent survey by **Monster.com** found that more than 75% of Canadians surveyed said they would leave their current job for an employer who is more environmentally friendly.[5]

## Reduced Operating Costs

Tenants are becoming more sophisticated in lease negotiations. The existing economy has allowed tenants to seek the best space at the best price. This usually translates to a property that includes some green elements. One of the most significant elements is energy efficiency. Tenants expect lower energy bills and expect that potential spaces include existing or planned strategies for energy reduction.

## Environmental Image

Tenants react to the environmental pressures placed upon them by their employees, customers, and business associates. Employees are reacting to environmental concerns at home by using compact fluorescent lightbulbs and driving more fuel-efficient automobiles. These concerns are brought into the workplace with the expectation that their employer shares their concerns. Similarly, customers measure the environmental consciousness of the companies with whom they do business. Business associates, such as Dell Computers and WalMart, expect their suppliers to be environmentally conscious. Both of these major purchasers of vendor products are requesting sustainable initiatives from their suppliers, such as reducing the amount of packaging or reducing greenhouse gas emissions.

## *Factors Limiting the Adoption of Green*

The primary factors limiting the growth of LEED Certified buildings are as follows:

- Building cost
- The certification process
- Understanding the benefits
- Risk
- Valuation process

Despite numerous studies to the contrary, there is an ongoing perception that LEED Certified *building cost* is substantially more than traditional building cost. The studies by Capital C, Davis Langdon and GSA all report the additional cost to be between 2% to 6%. A 2007 opinion survey conducted by the world business council, based upon reports from 146 green buildings, places the median additional cost of green buildings at less than 2%, compared to the 17% public perception.[6]

Another deterrent is the LEED *certification process* and its cost. Owners are overwhelmed by the rating system and its requirements. It should be noted that the process has been streamlined by a web-basing. In its earliest days, there were few architects and engineers familiar with the LEED process and requirements. The number of LEED accredited professionals has grown to over 31,000. This results in more professionals with experience in the design and construction of certified buildings and thus a reduction in cost. The average increase in construction costs for LEED certified design is 2%.[7]

Due to the still relatively small number of LEED certified projects (less that 2% of new construction), there is not a lot of data that attests to the energy and resource savings *benefits* of these buildings. The 146-building study referenced above concluded that 80% of the buildings in the study had energy savings in excess of 20%.[8] As engineers, architects, and contractors become experienced in the resource use reduction, the savings related to LEED certification become more predictable. A thorough commissioning program at the completion of construction and at the one year of occupancy date will further guarantee the projected savings. (*See Chapter 12, "Commissioning the Green Building."*)

The *risk* associated with LEED certified buildings relates to the proposed building meeting the certification level required by the owner and the subsequent energy use reductions being at the levels projected, using the energy modeling programs. Achieving the required certification level requires a strategic plan based upon input from the entire design team, using Integrated Project Design (IPD), and the contractor. It is advisable to provide some cushion in calculating certification points in order to address contingencies.

The final factor may be the *valuation process*. The three basic approaches to value are cost, sales, and income.

The use of cost is very difficult at this time, simply because there is limited information available for the cost of green construction and, furthermore, how much the market will pay for the sustainable components. The incremental cost of a green building is different for each building, because, while the greenness is measured against the USGBC point scale, there are numerous ways to achieve the points.

The sales approach presents similar challenges. There is currently a limited number of green buildings constructed throughout the country. Most of these buildings are owned either by governments or institutions. A second set of green buildings are owned as corporate headquarters. Each of these categories do not turn over with any frequency; therefore sales data, if available, is not reliable.

The lack of data for either of the two above methods leaves only the income approach. This is best analyzed using discounted cash flow (DCF). The DCF utilizes the cash flow forecast to analyze income and value changes.

The absence of significant market data makes all of the above valuation methods tenuous. There will have to be many more green commercial buildings constructed, bought, and sold before valuators can place a premium valuation on sustainable construction. In the meantime, valuators will have to depend upon their knowledge of the marketplace and value-adds in a specific project (such as significant energy use reduction) to credibly value a property.

## Green Investment Instruments

Some investors believe in green construction but do not want to own property outright. This want is being addressed by the creation of REITs that build or purchase only LEED or Energy Star certified properties. Recent RREEF research reports that the demand for socially conscious investment vehicles has grown tenfold in the past decade, to almost $1.6 trillion.

The most commonly sited REITs are as follows:

ProLogis (industrial)
- Simon Property Group (retail centers)
- SL Green (office)
- Liberty Property Trust (office)
- Archstone-Smith (residential)

A recent study revealed that nearly 60%+ of U.S.-based REITs are currently purchasing, or intending to purchase, properties that include sustainable strategies.[9]

## Conclusion

The growth of the green movement in commercial real estate has been greatly boosted by both federal and state governments, which are encouraging and requiring sustainable construction. In support of this, building codes are being rewritten to require better energy efficiency.

Professional organizations, such as the American Society of Heating, Refrigeration, and Air-Conditioning Engineers (ASHRAE), are also promulgating new standards, for example, ASHRAE 189.1, "Standard for the Design of High-Performance Green Buildings." Another big assist to the greening of commercial real estate comes from well-known businesses that choose green buildings as their corporate headquarters. Such buildings are often showplaces of the latest in green technology and serve to bring these innovations before the public eye, leading to more demand.

The commercial real estate industry is responding as tenants demand energy efficient green buildings, which have the additional benefits of providing a healthier, more productive workplace. Owners, as well, recognize the financial benefits of owning green buildings: competitive rents, faster absorption, less turnover, and higher quality tenants. Finally, investors are acknowledging the benefits of green construction and placing their funds with organizations that focus on these properties.

The green building movement is not a passing trend—it is common sense. It has permanently changed the building construction industry and the standards by which owners, tenants, and investors evaluate property.

1. Compass Resource Management, February 2007, "Towards a Green Investment Fund."

2. National Real Estate Investor, July 2005, "It Pays to Be Green."

3. RREEF Research, November 2007, "The Greening of U.S. Investment Real Estate."

4. Ibid.

5. Ibid.

6. Good Energies, "Greening Buildings and Communities: Costs and Benefits."

7. Ibid.

8. Ibid.

9. RREEF Research, November 2007, "The Greening of U.S. Investment Real Estate."

*Part*

# 4 Case Studies

**Case Study 1:** Reprinted with Permission from *Design Cost Data*, www.dcd.com/Nov-Dec 2008, ©2008 DC&D Technologies, Inc.

# Clemson University – ICAR Collaboration 3
## Greenville, South Carolina

### Architect

Pazdan-Smith Group Architects

The CU-ICAR Campus will be Clemson University's center for automotive engineering research. Clemson has partnered with The Furman Co., a private-sector developer, to create several multi-tenant buildings on the site to house automotive industry professionals that are interested in collaboration with the Center. Pazdan-Smith Group provided design services for CU – ICAR Collaboration 3.

Clemson University charged the client to develop a multi-tenant office building that would be a secondary, non-dominate companion to support and house the multiplicity of automotive industry research that would take place in conjunction with the Carol Campbell Graduate Engineering Center. However, while being secondary to the main campus building, the building would also need to be an exceptional architectural design that would exhibit the characteristics of innovation and research at a highly visible location along Interstate 85. The building would need to provide students and automotive industry researchers with great opportunities for collaboration. By designing the building to include highly visible circulation routes and multiple opportunities for spontaneous contact between students and fellow researchers, the building encourages the phenomenon of "chance encounters," which have proven to be a key component to the success of a creative research environment.

The building's interior includes 72,961 square feet of laboratory space on the ground level, including a twenty foot clearance high-bay area with a 5 ton crane, combined with 44,682 square feet of class-A office space on the second level. Planning for the future, the building's structural and circulation systems were designed with flexibility to add two additional levels of multi-tenant office space for a total of four stories and 208,000 square feet.

In the spirit of engineering, the building was designed and built to be a model for efficiency and performance. The building was designed to greatly exceed present efficiency standards. To achieve this objective, a thorough and all-encompassing approach would be needed. In addition to using state-of-the-

art mechanical equipment, components such as underfloor air distribution and engineered, exterior sunshading systems would need to be incorporated. Final energy modeling showed that Collaboration 3's energy efficiency is almost twenty percent better than ASHRAE 90.1 (2004) standards.

The exterior materials consist of various materials that include a high level of recycled material including aluminum storefront and curtainwall, glass, black closure size brick masonry units and steel paneling. The structural design is a steel frame with castellated beams and composite slabs. Final calculations show that the building was constructed with over a third of its material, by cost, made from post-consumer and pre-consumer recycled content.

The project team chose to make water efficiency an integral part of the building design. Outdoors, landscaping was designed to include low-water-demand native and indigenous plantings that would not require the installation of permanent irrigation systems. Indoors, by using high-efficiency fixtures, waterless urinals and occupant sensors, an expected water-use reduction of nearly 50% beyond standards set forth in the 1992 Energy Policy Act was attained.

The building has been certified LEED® Core and Shell Gold by the U.S. Green Building Council, the first in the state.

### LEED®
### Core and Shell Gold

### Manufacturers

**DIV. 7:** *Metal Composite Wall Panels:* Centria.
**DIV. 8:** *Entrances & Storefronts:* Vistawall; *Glass:* Guardian; *Sun Screens:* Armetco; *Panels, Trim, Clips:* Greenscreen.
**DIV. 9:** *Access Floors:* Tate.
**DIV. 10:** *Elevators:* Schlindler.

# EDUCATIONAL EU081152

## Clemson University – ICAR Collaboration 3

## Architect

Pazdan-Smith Group Architects
200 East Broad Street, #300, Greenville, SC 29601
www.pazdan-smith.com

## Construction Team

**Structural & Civil Engineer:**
Britt, Peters & Associates, Inc.
550 South Main Street, #301, Greenville, SC 29601

**General Contractor:**
Harper Corporation
35 West Court Street, #400, Greenville, SC 29601

**Mechanical & Electrical Engineer:**
Talbot & Associates Consulting Engineers, Inc.
916 West Fifth Street, Charlotte, NC 28202

**Landscape Architect:**
Innocenti & Webel
188 Dug Hill Trail, Tryon, NC 28782

## Project General Description

**Location:** Greenville, South Carolina

**Date Bid:** Jan 2006

**Construction Period:** Oct 2006 to Sep 2007

**Total Square Feet:** 117,643 **Site:** 3.5 acres.

**Number of Buildings:** One.

**Building Size:** First floor, 72,961; second floor, 44,682, total, 117,643 square feet.

**Building Height:** Varies.

**Basic Construction Type:** New/Steel frame with concrete slabs.

**Foundation:** Slab-on-grade.

**Exterior Walls:** Brick, curtainwall. **Roof:** Membrane.

**Floors:** Concrete. **Interior Walls:** Metal stud drywall.

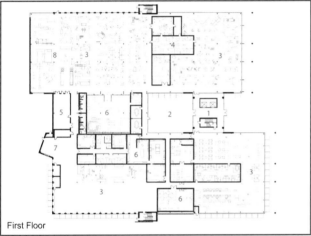

First Floor

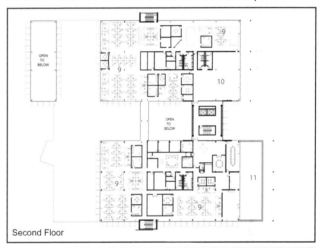

Second Floor

| C.S.I. Divisions | | | COST | % OF COST | SQ.FT. COST | SPECIFICATIONS |
|---|---|---|---|---|---|---|
| | | PROCUREMENT & CONT. REQ. | 1,111,966 | 11.62 | 9.45 | — |
| 1. | 1. | GENERAL REQUIREMENTS | 312,688 | 3.27 | 2.66 | Administrative requirements, quality requirements, temporary facilities & controls, product requirements, execution & closeout requirements. |
| 3. | 3. | CONCRETE | 866,093 | 9.05 | 7.36 | Forming & accessories, reinforcing, cast-in-place. |
| 4. | 4. | MASONRY | 230,307 | 2.41 | 1.96 | Unit, corrosion-resistant, manufactured. |
| 5. | 5. | METALS | 1,866,018 | 19.50 | 15.86 | Structural metal framing, joists, decking, cold-formed metal framing, fabrications, decorative, structural steel supports for 5-ton crane (crane purchased & installed by owner). |
| 6. | 6. | WOOD, PLASTICS & COMPOSITES | 186,451 | 1.95 | 1.58 | Rough carpentry, architectural woodwork. |
| 7. | 7. | THERMAL & MOISTURE PROTECTION | 659,507 | 6.89 | 5.61 | Dampproofing, thermal protection, roofing & siding panels, membrane roofing, flashing & sheet metal, roof & wall specialties & accessories, joint protection. |
| 8. | 8. | OPENINGS | 1,264,503 | 13.21 | 10.75 | Doors & frames, entrances, storefronts & curtain walls, hardware, glazing. |
| 9. | 9. | FINISHES | 352,437 | 3.68 | 3.00 | Plaster & gypsum board, tiling, ceilings, flooring, painting & coating. |
| 10. | 10. | SPECIALTIES | 819,362 | 8.56 | 6.96 | Interior, safety, exterior, other. |
| 12. | 12. | FURNISHINGS | 5,797 | 0.06 | 0.05 | Furnishings & accessories, other. |
| 14. | 14. | CONVEYING SYSTEMS | 192,257 | 2.01 | 1.63 | Elevators (2 passenger). |
| 15. | 21. | FIRE SUPPRESSON | 172,692 | 1.80 | 1.47 | Water-based fire-suppression, fire-extinguishing. |
| 15. | 22. | PLUMBING | 322,040 | 3.37 | 2.74 | Piping & pumps, equipment, fixtures. |
| 15. | 23. | HVAC | 830,306 | 8.68 | 7.06 | Piping & pumps, air distribution, air cleaning devices, central heating, central cooling, central HVAC. |
| 16. | 26. | ELECTRICAL | 376,537 | 3.93 | 3.20 | Medium-voltage distribution, low-voltage transmission, electrical & cathodic protection, lighting. |
| | | **TOTAL BUILDING COST** | **9,568,961** | **100.00** | **$81.34** | |
| 2. | 31. | EARTHWORK | 133,388 | | | Earth moving, earthwork methods. |
| 2. | 32. | EXTERIOR IMPROVEMENTS | 188,195 | | | Bases, bollards & paving, improvements. |
| 2. | 33. | UTILITIES | 84,019 | | | Water, sanitary sewerage, storm drainage. |
| | | **PROJECT COST** | **9,974,563** | | | **(Excluding architectural and engineering fees)** |

# Home & Hospice Care of Rhode Island
## Providence, Rhode Island

## Architect

Vision 3 Architects

Photos Courtesy of Aaron Usher

Home & Hospice Care of Rhode Island is the state's largest and most comprehensive provider of hospice and palliative care, and is the third oldest hospice in the country. In 2006, Home & Hospice purchased 1085 North Main Street in Providence, with plans to consolidate their hospice facility, administrative offices, and education and bereavement center into one building. On May 31, 2009, a crowd of nearly 500 people celebrated the grand opening of Home & Hospice's new headquarters.

The renovation of the four-story building is currently pursuing LEED® Gold certification and is expected to be the first fully operational LEED certified health care facility in Rhode Island. Sustainable design aligns with Home & Hospice's philosophy on the cycles of life and the cycles of nature. During design, Home & Hospice consulted with a cultural anthropologist on critical design issues.

The first, major sustainable design commitment Home & Hospice made was to convert an abandoned building, instead of building new. "Not only does reusing an existing facility significantly divert demolition and construction waste from landfills," states David Sluter, CEO of New England Construction, contractor for the renovation, "it enhances the neighborhood by converting a vacant building into a thriving healthcare facility that is open to community use." Throughout construction, 92.6% of all construction waste was recycled. In addition, 95% of the existing wall, floor, and roof construction was reused. "When walking through the new Home & Hospice," says Diana Franchitto, President and CEO of Home & Hospice Care of Rhode Island, "you would never believe that 95% of what you see existed here before. Everything looks brand new."

Other sustainable design features include a reflective roof to prevent heat absorption; low-flow water fixtures with motion sensors; high-performing and energy-efficient building mechanical and electrical systems; and low or no VOC-emitting carpets, paints, adhesives, and wood products. Home & Hospice has also committed to obtaining at least 35% of their electricity from renewable sources, and using only green cleaning methods and products to reduce chemicals in the environment.

Besides the project's sustainable design features, the goal of the project was to provide a facility in which Home & Hospice Care could fulfill their mission to provide compassionate, professional, state of the art physical, emotional and spiritual care for all people facing life-threatening illness. "Vision 3 Architects wrapped the entire design of the facility around this mission," affirms Keith Davignon, Principal of Vision 3 Architects. "We listened closely to Home & Hospice's staff, and provided them with a comfortable and dignified environment for patients and their families."

"Our new home reflects thoughtful planning geared toward the needs of our patients, families and staff. Our goals included creating a sustainable hospice environment that offers patients and family members comfort, peace and plenty of space for reflection and quiet time," states Franchitto. "With the creativity and guidance of Vision 3 and New England Construction, we've achieved these goals and look forward to continuing our important role in the state's health care scheme."

**LEED® GOLD Pending**

# MEDICAL MD091148

## Home & Hospice Care of Rhode Island

### Architect

Vision 3 Architects
225 Chapman Street, Providence, RI 02905
www.vision3architects.com

### Construction Team

**Structural Engineer:**
Odeh Engineers, Inc.
1223 Mineral Spring Avenue, North Providence, RI 02904

**General Contractor & Cost Estimator:**
New England Construction
293 Bourne Avenue, Rumford, RI 02916

**Electrical & Mechanical Engineer:**
Creative Environment Corp.
50 Office Parkway, East Providence, RI 02914

### Project General Description

**Location:** Providence, Rhode Island
**Date Bid:** Apr 2008
**Construction Period:** Aug 2008 to May 2009
**Total Square Feet:** 47,734 **Site:** 1.41 acres.
**Number of Buildings:** One.
**Building Size:** First floor, 12,400; second floor, 12,924; third floor, 11,205; fourth floor, 11,205; total, 47,734 square feet.
**Building Height:** First floor, 11'4"; second floor, 10'8"; each additional floor, 10'8"; floor to floor, 10'8"; total, 43'11".
**Basic Construction Type:** Renovation/Steel Frame.
**Foundation:** Cast-in-place. **Exterior Walls:** Brick.
**Roof:** TPO/Ballasted. **Floors:** Concrete.
**Interior Walls:** Metal stud drywall.
**Projected and/or Modeled Energy Usage KBTU/SF/yr:**
.036556

| DIVISION | COST | % OF COST | SQ.FT. COST | SPECIFICATIONS |
|---|---|---|---|---|
| GENERAL REQUIREMENTS | 1,230,143 | 16.25 | 25.77 | Mobilization, change orders, temporary facilities, permits, insurance, fees, superintendent. |
| CONCRETE | 88,230 | 1.17 | 1.85 | Forming & accessories, reinforcing, cast-in-place. |
| MASONRY | 49,490 | 0.65 | 1.04 | — |
| METALS | 459,528 | 6.07 | 9.63 | Structural steel. |
| WOOD, PLASTICS & COMPOSITES | 607,719 | 8.03 | 12.73 | Rough carpentry, finish carpentry, architectural woodwork. |
| THERMAL & MOISTURE PROTECTION | 188,098 | 2.49 | 3.94 | Waterproofing & dampproofing, roofing. |
| OPENINGS | 484,745 | 6.40 | 10.16 | Glass work, storefront & windows, doors, frames & hardware. |
| FINISHES | 878,018 | 11.60 | 18.39 | Plaster & gypsum board, ceilings, flooring, wall finishes, painting & coating. |
| SPECIALTIES | 61,311 | 0.81 | 1.28 | Fire place, toilet accessories, toilet partitions, signage, fire extinguishers. |
| EQUIPMENT | 5,133 | 0.07 | 0.11 | Kitchen. |
| CONVEYING SYSTEMS | 189,715 | 2.51 | 3.97 | Elevators (2 existing refurbished). |
| FIRE SUPPRESSON | 196,608 | 2.60 | 4.12 | — |
| PLUMBING | 518,630 | 6.85 | 10.87 | — |
| HVAC | 1,839,798 | 24.30 | 38.54 | — |
| ELECTRICAL | 771,995 | 10.20 | 16.17 | — |
| **TOTAL BUILDING COSTS** | **7,569,161** | **100%** | **$158.57** | |
| EXISTING CONDITIONS | 154,000 | | | Demolition, abatement demolition. |
| EARTHWORK | 336,992 | | | Excavation and backfill. |
| EXTERIOR IMPROVEMENTS | 48,650 | | | Landscaping. |
| **TOTAL** | **8,108,803** | | | (Excluding architectural and engineering fees) |

### Regional Cost Trends
*This project, updated to December 2009 in the selected cities of the United States.*

| EASTERN U.S. | Sq.Ft. Cost | Total Cost | CENTRAL U.S. | Sq.Ft. Cost | Total Cost | WESTERN U.S. | Sq.Ft. Cost | Total Cost |
|---|---|---|---|---|---|---|---|---|
| **Atlanta GA** | $144.94 | $6,918,712 | **Dallas TX** | $144.94 | $6,918,712 | **Los Angeles CA** | $185.87 | $8,872,230 |
| **Pittsburgh PA** | $158.58 | $7,569,885 | **Kansas City KS** | $150.06 | $7,162,901 | **Las Vegas NV** | $168.82 | $8,058,264 |
| **New York NY** | $204.63 | $9,767,593 | **Chicago IL** | $182.46 | $8,709,437 | **Seattle WA** | $180.75 | $8,628,040 |

**Subscribe to DCD and get immediate access to this project and over 1,300 more in the DCD Archives, a powerful cost modeling tool for conceptual estimating, cost validating, project feasibility, or budgeting.**

# Radnor Middle School
## Wayne, Pennsylvania

### Construction Manager
Reynolds Construction Management, Inc.
### Architect
Blackney Hayes Architects

Photos Courtesy of Reynolds Construction Management, Inc.

Radnor Township School District, located in southeastern Pennsylvania, serves the children of St. Davids and parts of Wayne, Rosemont, Bryn Mawr, Villanova, Ithan, Newtown Square, and Radnor. They have accepted the goal of inspiring and empowering students within the district to become lifelong learners. Until 2005 the District had been utilizing a middle school that was originally constructed in 1923 and the Administration and School Board recognized the need for a new facility. The District hired Reynolds Construction Management, Inc. to provide pre-construction and construction management services on a new state-of-the-art middle school.

Radnor Township School District asked Reynolds to provide assistance in developing their preliminary budget. Reynolds' team of electrical, mechanical, plumbing, architectural and structural estimators worked with the District to create a budget that could be used by the District as they started the selection of a design team and made decisions regarding the project's financing.

The design team, led by Blackney Hayes Architects of Philadelphia, began the design for the new middle school and Reynolds provided assistance to the District by ensuring that the design matched the original intent, program and budget. Reynolds also worked closely with the District and the design team to develop the correct bidding strategy for the project. The key consideration was to determine the appropriate number of bid packages for the project that would maximize participation and competition among bidders. Once the correct number of bid packages had been agreed to, Reynolds held a number of pre-bid meetings where they provided more in-depth information to interested contractors and ensured that the prospective bidders understood the bid documents and the construction schedule. This process led to more precise and lower bids from the contractors and provided Radnor Township School District the best possible price on their project.

Upon completion of the pre-construction and bidding phases, Reynolds provided the District with on-site management and supervision of the contractors. Through the direction

and expertise of Reynolds, the Radnor Township School District received the new middle school on schedule and within budget.

The middle school is designed and utilizes materials that are in-tune with the center of downtown Wayne and the nearby residential neighborhoods. The new facility uses many of the latest technologies for lowering energy and operating costs, while improving indoor air quality and creating an optimal learning environment for the District's students. Even though the new building is 4-stories high, its scale was broken down through geometric shifts and use of the site's topography to decrease the apparent height at street level.

Environmentally sustainable design and construction have been a hallmark of recent projects at Radnor Township School District and the new Radnor Middle School is no exception. The building includes many "green" features

such as geo-thermal heating and cooling, a partially vegetated roof, recycled materials, heat, motion and light sensors and other features that will help the District achieve their goal of a gold level certification from the US Green Building Council's LEED® program.

### LEED® GOLD

### Manufacturers

**DIV. 4:** *Brick:* McAvoy Brick Company; *Architectural Block:* Beavertown Block Company; *Gray Block:* Fizzano Brothers.
**DIV. 7:** *Membrane & Vegetated Roof:* Magco Inc., a Tecta America Company.
**DIV. 8:** *Windows:* Eagle; *Curtainwall, Entrances:* Kawneer.
**DIV. 9:** *Carpet:* Collins & Aikman; *VCT:* Armstrong; Expanko Cork.
**DIV. 14:** *Elevators:* Thyssen Krupp.

# EDUCATIONAL EU081150

## Radnor Middle School

### Construction Manager
Reynolds Construction Management, Inc.
3300 North Third Street, Harrisburg, PA 17110
www.reynoldsconstruction.com

### Architect
Blackney Hayes Architects
150 S. Independence Mall West, #1200, Philadelphia, PA 19106
www.blackneyhayes.com

### Construction Team
**Structural Engineer:**
Pennoni Associates
2041 Avenue C, #100, Bethlehem, PA 18107

**MEP Engineer:**
Concord Engineering Group, Inc.
520 South Burnt Mill Road, Voorhees, NJ 08043

**Civil Engineer:**
Gilmore & Associates, Inc.
350 East Butler Avenue, New Britain, PA 18901

**Education Planner:**
Ingraham Dancu Associates
1265 Lakevue Drive, Butler, PA 16002

**Cost Estimator:**
International Consultant Inc.
221 Chestnut Street, #200, Philadelphia, PA 19106

### Project General Description
**Location:** Wayne, Pennsylvania
**Date Bid:** Oct 2005
**Construction Period:** Jan 2006 to Sep 2007
**Total Square Feet:** 188,822

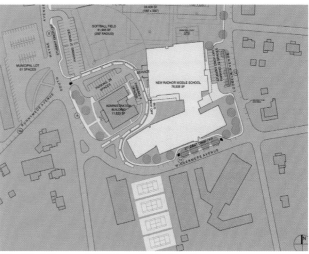

**Site:** 10.421 acres (9.173 less right of way).
**Number of Buildings:** One.
**Building Size:** First floor, 65,141; second floor, 52,485, third floor, 41,580; fourth floor, 29,616; total, 188,822 square feet.
**Building Height:** First floor, 14'; second, third, fourth, 13'4"; total, 54'.
**Basic Construction Type:** New/Composite structural steel.
**Foundation:** Cast-in-place.
**Exterior Walls:** CMU, brick, limestone.
**Roof:** Vegetated roof assembly, asphalt shingles, membrane. **Floors:** Concrete.
**Interior Walls:** CMU (Classrooms), metal stud drywall (Offices), movable partitions.

| C.S.I. Divisions | | | COST | % OF COST | SQ.FT. COST | SPECIFICATIONS |
|---|---|---|---|---|---|---|
| | | PROCUREMENT & CONT. REQ. | — | — | — | — |
| 1. | 1. | GENERAL REQUIREMENTS | — | — | — | Price & payment procedures, administrative requirements, quality requirements, temporary facilities & controls, product requirements, execution & closeout requirements, performance requirements (cost spread through General Trades). |
| 3. | 3. | CONCRETE | 4,226,928 | 14.00 | 26.11 | Cast-in-place (600 cubic yards foundation & walls, 3,700 cubic yards floors). |
| 4. | 4. | MASONRY | 7,339,900 | 20.85 | 38.87 | Unit, manufactured. |
| 5. | 5. | METALS | 5,055,000 | 14.36 | 26.77 | Structural metal framing, joists, decking, cold-formed metal framing, fabrications. |
| 6. | 6. | WOOD, PLASTICS & COMPOSITES | 1,291,378 | 3.00 | 1.87 | Rough carpentry, architectural woodwork. |
| 7. | 7. | THERMAL & MOISTURE PROTECTION | 1,056,582 | 2.67 | 4.97 | Dampproofing & waterproofing, thermal protection, steep sloop roofing, roofing & siding panels, membrane roofing, flashing & sheet metal, roof & wall specialties & accessories, fire & smoke protection, joint protection. |
| 8. | 8. | OPENINGS | 1,526,174 | 5.67 | 10.57 | Doors & frames, specialty doors & frames, entrances, storefronts, & curtain walls, windows, hardware, glazing, louvers & vents. |
| 9. | 9. | FINISHES | 3,287,144 | 9.34 | 17.41 | Plaster & gypsum board, tiling, ceilings, flooring, wall finishes, acoustic treatment, painting & coating. |
| 10. | 10. | SPECIALTIES | 234,796 | 0.34 | 0.62 | Information, interior, safety, storage, other. |
| 11. | 11. | EQUIPMENT | 363,350 | 1.03 | 1.92 | Foodservice, education & scientific, entertainment, athletic & recreational, other. |
| 13. | 13. | FURNISHINGS | 511,823 | 1.45 | 2.71 | Casework, furnishings & accessories, multiple seating. |
| 14. | 14. | CONVEYING SYSTEMS | 117,398 | 0.33 | 0.62 | Elevators 2 (1 passenger, 1 freight/passenger). |
| 15. | 21. | FIRE SUPPRESSON | 560,000 | 1.59 | 2.97 | Water-based fire-suppression system, fire-extinguishing systems, fire pumps. |
| 15. | 22. | PLUMBING | 1,188,400 | 3.38 | 6.29 | Piping & pumps, equipment, fixtures, pool & fountain systems. |
| 15. | 23. | HVAC | 4,924,200 | 13.99 | 26.08 | Facility fuel systems, piping & pumps, air distribution, air cleaning devices, central heating, central cooling, central HVAC, decentralized HVAC equipment. |
| 16. | 26. | ELECTRICAL | 2,857,780 | 8.12 | 15.13 | Power generating & storing equipment, lighting. |
| 16. | 27. | COMMUNICATIONS | 660,487 | 1.88 | 3.50 | Structured cabling, data, voice. |
| | | **TOTAL BUILDING COST** | **35,201,340\*** | **100.00** | **$186.43** | |
| 2. | 31. | EARTHWORK | 5,832,365 | | | Site clearing, earth moving, earthwork methods, excavation support & protection, special foundations & load-bearing elements. |
| | | **PROJECT COST** | **41,033,705** | | | **(Excluding architectural and engineering fees)** |

\* General Trades submitted in one lump sum of $11,739,800. The lump sum of $11,739,800 (submitted as General Trades) was divided by percentages (Concrete 42%; Wood, Plastics, & Composites 3%; Thermal & Moisture Protection 8%; Openings 17%; Finishes 28%; Specialties 1%, and Conveying Systems 1%) using a comparable LEED® middle school from DCD.

**Subscribe to DCD and get immediate access to this project and over 1,300 more in the DCD Archives, a powerful cost modeling tool for conceptual estimating, cost validating, project feasibility, or budgeting.**

**Case Study 4:** Reprinted with Permission from *Design Cost Data*, www.dcd.com/Sept-Oct 2009, ©2009 DC&D Technologies, Inc.

# Riverbend Elementary School
Yuba City, California

## Architect
Nacht & Lewis Architects

Photos Courtesy of Donald Satterlee Photography

The Riverbend Elementary School is modeled around a K-8 curriculum model. This program presents unique challenges in dealing with such diverse age groups. Special attention was required to address the unique needs of younger kindergarten children and the advanced curriculum needs of 7th & 8th graders.

The school is organized in small grade-level clusters around a central courtyard. Facilities include an administrative and counseling office, library, multi-purpose room with performing arts capabilities and a full-size independent gymnasium. Site amenities include generous turf playfields, a running track and equipment areas for the individual grade levels.

Sustainable design elements were also fundamental in the projects development. Natural daylight is abundant in virtually all spaces on the campus. High efficiency mechanical systems, low-water use plumbing fixtures, and automatic lighting controls contribute to a facility that exceeds the energy requirement of California Title 24 by better than 30%. The school is also recognized by the Collaborative of High Performance Schools for its energy conscious design and sustainable features.

The design goals were to create a new model for an elementary school campus that would focus on sustainability, provide a sense of community and that promote student achievement; and to create a facility that would reflect the School District's commitment to the community and to planning for the future.

The school site is located several hundred yards west of the Feather River and on the edge of new suburban development. The Feather River, its landforms and vegetation, became the design inspiration for the hardscape and landscape design of the campus. There is a symbolic levee in the center of the campus and

the selection of trees, ground covers, and paving patterns were selected specifically to relate to the river environment giving the school and the students a unique sense of place.

The sustainability components of the project were developed using the Collaborative for High Performing Schools' Best Practices Manual and from the U.S. Green Building Council LEED® program. The building forms and materials are derived from the local agricultural vernacular and are reinterpreted looking towards the future. The roof forms and materials become the integrated support structure for more than 300 kvA of thin film photovoltaic panels producing enough power to lower the utility costs to run the school by over 30%.

The Gymnasium, Administration Building and the Library Building were site built and maintained the campus's focus on green design with an emphasis on energy efficiency and day-lighting. All three buildings incorporate large amounts of translucent insulated window panels, which let diffused light in and lowered the energy loss typical of traditional windows. The building forms were designed based on the layout of thin film photovoltaic panels that are integrated directly into the metal roofing system without the need for additional structural supports. The PV system is designed to provide up to 100% of the peak electrical demand of the campus on a bright day and more than 30% of the campus's annual energy needs. Based on the success of the PV system the district is looking into opportunities to expand the system at other schools.

This project was designed as a model of Green Design and sustainability for public schools in California and scored 38 points in the Collaborative for High Performing Schools rating system. The buildings on campus combine community wide centralized planning,

high efficiency equipment and environmental controls, translucent glazing, and rooftop photovoltaic panels and the elimination of potable water for landscape irrigation. The campus is an active laboratory of sustainable design ideas and is used in the educational curriculum of the students.

This elementary school campus is based on a 'super sized' Kindergarten thru 8th grade model. Recent studies have identified decreased student performance in traditional elementary/middle/high school models. As our society becomes more fragmented and transient, students have been looking to their schools as a form of stability and continuity. By keeping kids on a single campus through out their elementary school years, they benefit from the availability and familiarity of the schools support systems and it has been shown that the K-8th grade model promotes increased parent participation in the child's education.

Riverbend Elementary School is the 2008 recipient of the Leroy F. Greene "Award of Merit" for the Coalition for Adequate School Housing Design and Planning Awards.

## Manufacturers

**DIV. 7:** *Metal Roofing:* **Garland**.
**DIV. 8:** *Glass Low E:* **PPG**; *Entrances & Storefronts, Windows, Curtainwall:* Kawneer; *Daylighting:* **Kalwall**.
**DIV. 9:** *Carpet:* Collins & Aikman; *VCT:* Armstrong.

### Extended Product Information
*Metal Roofing:* **Garland**
See advertisement on page 24.
*Glass Low E:* **PPG**
See advertisement on page 3.
*Daylighting:* **Kalwall**
See advertisement on page 23.

# EDUCATIONAL EU090920

## Riverbend Elementary School

### Architect

Nacht & Lewis Architects
600 Q Street, #100, Sacramento, CA 95811
www.nlarch.com

### Construction Team

**Owner:**
Yuba City School Unified District
750 Palora Avenue, Yuba City, CA 95991

**General Contractor:**
Sundt Construction
2860 Gateway Oaks Drive, #300, Sacramento, CA 95833

**Structural Engineer:**
Buehler & Buehler Structural Engineers
600 Q Street, #200, Sacramento, CA 95811

**Mechanical Engineer:**
Capital Engineering Consultants, Inc.
11020 Sun Center Drive, Rancho Cordova, CA 95670

**Electrical Engineer:**
The Engineering Enterprise
853 Lincoln Way, #105, Auburn, CA 95603

### Project General Description

**Location:** Yuba City, California
**Date Bid:** Apr 2006 **Construction Period:** Apr 2006 to July 2007
**Total Square Feet:** 86,000 **Site:** 21 acres.
**Number of Buildings:** 13 – 3 site built, 10 modular. 46 classrooms seating 1,300 students; Auditorium, 4,946 sq. ft. seating 733 occupants; Gym, 5,968 sq. ft. seating 771 occupants.
**Building Size:** First floor, 86,000; total, 86,000 square feet.
**Building Height:** First floor, 38'6"; total, 38'6".
**Basic Construction Type:** New/Structural steel braced frame (CHPS Certified).
**Foundation:** Cast-in-place, slab-on-grade.
**Exterior Walls:** CMU, storefront, cement plaster.
**Roof:** Metal, modified bitumen. **Floors:** Concrete.
**Interior Walls:** Metal stud drywall.
**Projected and/or modeled energy usage KBTU/SF/yr:** 102.17 kBTU/sq.ft.yr.

| C.S.I. Divisions | | | COST | % OF COST | SQ.FT. COST | SPECIFICATIONS |
|---|---|---|---|---|---|---|
| | | PROCUREMENT & CONT. REQ. | — | | | — |
| 1. | 1. | GENERAL REQUIREMENTS | 4,469,155 | 27.27 | 51.97 | Summary, price & payment procedures, temporary facilities & controls, product requirements, execution & closeout requirements. |
| 3. | 3. | CONCRETE | 1,977,230 | 12.06 | 22.99 | Forming & accessories, reinforcing, cast-in-place, cast decks & underlayment, grouting. |
| 4. | 4. | MASONRY | 239,688 | 1.46 | 2.79 | Unit. |
| 5. | 5. | METALS | 1,984,420 | 12.11 | 23.07 | Structural metal framing, joists, decking, cold-formed metal framing, fabrications, decorative metal. |
| 6. | 6. | WOOD, PLASTICS & COMPOSITES | 107,995 | 0.66 | 1.26 | Rough carpentry, finish carpentry, architectural woodwork, plastic fabrications. |
| 7. | 7. | THERMAL & MOISTURE PROTECTION | 531,653 | 3.24 | 6.18 | Dampproofing & waterproofing, thermal protection, weather barriers, roofing & siding panels, modified bitumen built-up roofing, flashing & sheet metal, roof & wall specialties & accessories, fire & smoke protection, joint protection. |
| 8. | 8. | OPENINGS | 545,827 | 3.33 | 6.35 | Doors & frames, specialty doors & frames, entrances, storefronts, & curtain walls, windows, hardware, glazing. |
| 9. | 9. | FINISHES | 1,734,885 | 10.58 | 20.17 | Plaster & gypsum board, tiling, ceilings, flooring, wall finishes, acoustical treatment, painting & coating. |
| 10. | 10. | SPECIALTIES | 181,396 | 1.11 | 2.11 | Information, interior, safety, storage. |
| 11. | 11. | EQUIPMENT | 489,450 | 2.99 | 5.69 | Vehicle & pedestrian, commercial, foodservice, educational & scientific, athletic & recreational, collection & disposal. |
| 12. | 12. | FURNISHINGS | 66,806 | 0.41 | 0.78 | Casework, furniture, multiple seating. |
| 13. | 13. | SPECIAL CONSTRUCTIONS | 48,918 | 0.30 | 0.57 | Special purpose rooms. |
| 14. | 14. | CONVEYING SYSTEMS | 8,675 | 0.05 | 0.10 | Lifts. |
| 15. | 21. | FIRE SUPPRESSON | 216,000 | 1.32 | 2.51 | Water-based fire-suppression systems, fire-extinguishing systems. |
| 15. | 22. | PLUMBING | — | — | — | Included in HVAC: Piping & pumps, equipment, fixtures, gas & vacuum systems for laboratory & healthcare. |
| 15. | 23. | HVAC | 1,711,774 | 10.44 | 19.90 | Air distribution, air cleaning devices, decentralized HVAC equipment. |
| 16. | 26. | ELECTRICAL | 2,076,682 | 12.67 | 24.15 | Medium-voltage distribution, facility power generating & storing equipment, electrical & cathodic protection, lighting. |
| | | **TOTAL BUILDING COSTS** | **16,390,554** | **100.00** | **$190.59** | |
| 2. | 2. | EARTHWORK | 3,554,167 | | | |
| 2. | 32. | EXTERIOR IMPROVEMENTS | 856,396 | | | |
| | | **TOTAL** | **20,801,117** | | | |

(Excluding architectural and engineering fees)

# Seven Generations Office Park, Building A
## Fort Collins, Colorado

### Architect
RB+B Architects, Inc.

Seven Generations LLC of Fort Collins, Colorado asked RB+B Architects, Inc. to design a campus of three high performance core and shell office buildings (two 10,000-square-foot one-story buildings and one 36,000-square-foot two-story building) that could be built on a traditional construction budget. This developer believed that offering high performance office space at the same cost as traditional office space would give them an edge in the market place and would help them spread the word in the community that building in a more sustainable way is not only the right thing to do to combat climate change, but economically viable. In a collaborative effort, the project team produced a designed that was "Design to Earn the ENERGY STAR" and has achieved LEED-CS® Platinum Level Certification. The nationally recognized ENERGY STAR and LEED® programs were utilized to validate the project's high performance claims.

The site is within walking distance of basic services and open space was preserved where possible. A local bike path coupled with bike racks and showers support alternate methods of transportation. Preferred parking for Fuel Efficient Vehicles was provided to encourage reduced fossil fuel use by building occupants. A concrete parking lot was utilized to reduce heat island effect around the campus.

The building utilized raised access floors for under floor air distribution (UFAD), which is more efficient and controllable than traditional overhead air distribution. Extensive daylighting reduced the need for electric light during daylight hours. A high performance building envelope reduced the heating and cooling loads and the size of the mechanical equipment. Low flow plumbing fixtures such as dual flush toilets and 1/8 gallon per flush urinals maximized water

Photos Courtesy of RB+B Architects, Inc.

efficiency within tenant spaces to reduce the burden on municipal water supply and wastewater systems, and drought tolerant landscaping reduced the use of water on the site. A small demonstration solar array helped offset some of the building's electrical usage.

### LEED-CS Platinum
### Manufacturers

**DIV. 4:** *Brick:* Interstate Brick, Besalite Block.
**DIV. 7:** *Membrane:* Firestone; *EIFS:* BASF.
**DIV. 8:** *Entrances & Storefronts:* Tubelite; *Glazing:* **PPG**.
**DIV. 9:** *Access Floor:* Tate.

**Extended Product Information**
*Glazing:* **PPG**
See advertisement on page 3.

# OFFICE OF081144

## Seven Generations Office Park, Building A (Shell)

## Architect

RB+B Architects, Inc.
315 East Mountain Avenue, #100, Fort Collins, CO 80524
www.rbbarchitects.com

## Construction Team

**Structural Engineer:**
Larsen Structural Design
10820 Prima Drive, Fort Collins, CO 80524

**Construction Manager General Contractor:**
Dohn Construction, Inc.
2642 Midpoint Drive, Unit A, Fort Collins, CO 80525

**Mechanical, Electrical & Plumbing Engineer:**
Beaudin Ganze Consulting Engineers
251 Linden Street, Fort Collins, CO 80524

**LEED Consultant:**
Institute for the Built Environment
Guggenheim Hall, Colorado State University,
Fort Collins, CO 80523

**Energy Consultant:**
Enermodal Engineering, Inc.
1325 E. 16th Avenue, Denver, CO 80218

## Project General Description

**Location:** Fort Collins, Colorado

**Date Bid:** Dec 2006

**Construction Period:** Mar 2007 to Nov 2007

**Total Square Feet:** 10,000 **Site:** 3.6 acres.

**Number of Buildings:** One (one completed of three planned).

**Building Size:** First floor, 10,000; total, 10,000 square feet.

**Building Height:** First floor, 20' 10"; total, 20' 10".

**Basic Construction Type:** Structural Steel/IIN.

**Foundation:** Cast-in-place, reinforced concrete, slab-on-grade. **Exterior Walls:** CMU, brick, EIFS.

**Roof:** Membrane.

**Floors:** Concrete, raised floor over slab-on-grade.

**Interior Walls:** Metal stud drywall.

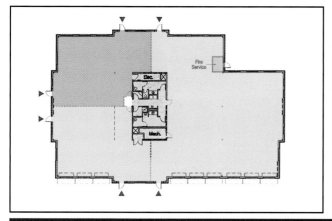

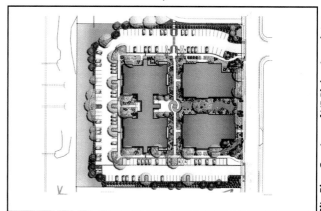

Site Plan Courtesy of VF Ripley Associates

| | | C.S.I. Divisions | COST | % OF COST | SQ.FT. COST | SPECIFICATIONS |
|---|---|---|---|---|---|---|
| | | PROCUREMENT & CONT. REQ. | 117.109 | 8.56 | 11.71 | — |
| 1. | 1. | GENERAL REQUIREMENTS | 115,623 | 8.45 | 11.56 | Summary, price & payment procedures, administrative requirements, quality requirements, temporary facilities & controls, product requirements, execution & closeout requirements, performance requirements. |
| 3. | 3. | CONCRETE | 163,084 | 11.92 | 16.31 | Forming & accessories, reinforcing, cast-in-place, precast. |
| 4. | 4. | MASONRY | 63,360 | 4.63 | 6.34 | Unit. |
| 5. | 5. | METALS | 194,156 | 14.19 | 19.42 | Structural metal framing, joists, decking, cold-formed metal framing, fabrications, decorative. |
| 6. | 6. | WOOD, PLASTICS & COMPOSITES | 9,049 | 0.66 | 0.90 | Rough carpentry, finish carpentry, architectural woodwork. |
| 7. | 7. | THERMAL & MOISTURE PROTECTION | 114,404 | 8.36 | 11.44 | Dampproofing & waterproofing, thermal protection, weather barriers, membrane roofing, flashing & sheet metal, roof & wall specialties & accessories, joint protection. |
| 8. | 8. | OPENINGS | 72,644 | 5.31 | 7.26 | Doors & frames, entrances, storefronts & curtain walls, hardware, glazing. |
| 9. | 9. | FINISHES | 149,178 | 10.90 | 14.92 | Plaster & gypsum board, tiling, ceilings, flooring, painting & coating. |
| 10. | 10. | SPECIALTIES | 7,311 | 0.53 | 0.73 | Information, interior. |
| 11. | 11. | FURNISHINGS | 2,884 | 0.21 | 0.29 | — |
| 15. | 21. | FIRE SUPPRESSON | 16,995 | 1.24 | 1.70 | Water-based fire-suppression systems, fire-extinguishing systems. |
| 15. | 22. | PLUMBING | 114,902 | 8.40 | 11.49 | Piping & pumps, equipment, fixtures. |
| 15. | 23. | HVAC | 167,730 | 12.26 | 16.77 | Piping & pumps, air distribution, central HVAC equipment. |
| 16. | 26. | ELECTRICAL | 60,063 | 4.38 | 6.01 | Medium voltage distribution, electrical & cathodic protection, lighting. |
| | | **TOTAL BUILDING COST** | **1,368,492** | **100.00** | **$136.85** | |
| 2. | 31. | EARTHWORK | 77,248 | | | Site clearing, earth moving, earthwork methods. |
| 2. | 32. | EXTERIOR IMPROVEMENTS | 377,635 | | | Bases, bollards, & paving, improvements, irrigation, planting. |
| 2. | 33. | UTILITIES | 155,959 | | | Water, sanitary sewerage, storm drainage, electrical. |
| | | **PROJECT COST** | **1,979,334** | | | **(Excluding architectural and engineering fees)** |

# Washington Public Utilities Districts Association

Olympia, Washington

### Design/Build General Contractor

Mountain Construction

### Design Manager & Architect

Helix Design Group, Inc.

Photos Courtesy of Matt Todd Photography

Among the goals for the new headquarters for the Washington Public Utility Districts Association (WPUDA) was to enhance their public image as a good steward of both their financial resources and the environment, and broaden its leadership role in these areas by demonstrating that prudent, sustainable design is "practical thinking" and not "fringe thinking".

The home of Washington's 27 Public Utility Districts, the WPUDA achieved this goal and more with their new headquarters earning the LEED® Platinum rating, the first in the State of Washington.

The program requirements were accommodated within the quarter-acre brownfield development site by incorporating below-grade parking and construction close to property lines and adjacent buildings.

The design reflects the residential quality of the surrounding neighborhood while incorporating modern design elements as the area makes the transition to a more commercial district. The key design element for the project is the treatment of scale. The structure has been broken down into smaller, more residential elements, utilizing changes in materials/textures, setbacks and multiple wall planes, hipped roof planes and bracketed window awnings. The office windows are of a residential size and spacing while the glass entry facade reflects a more commercial quality.

Numerous innovative features were required to earn LEED® Platinum, the highest available green building design rating, such as:

**Solar power:** 159 roof-mounted photovoltaic (solar power) panels projected to generate 40% to 50% of the building's power requirements.

**Glass:** Engineered glass assembly that reflects solar heat and 95% of harmful UV rays without darkening like tinted glass.

**Water:** The plaza water feature is fed by rainwater. Like a natural stream, it will be al-

lowed to go dry in the summer. Landscaping is not irrigated.

**Heat Island reduction:** Roofing material reflects solar radiation and heat build-up in the urban area.

**Natural light:** Design, glass and skylights provide natural light to 90% of workspaces.

**No off-gassing:** Carpet, paint and other materials were selected to eliminate harmful chemical gases in areas where people work.

**Heating/Cooling:** Ultra high efficiency HVAC system with no ozone-depleting refrigerants, high pollutant air filtration and operable windows for healthy air.

### Green Building Achievements

- 50% Renewable energy.
- 52% Reduction in generated waste-water.
- 61% Reduction in potable water use.
- 69% Energy optimization.
- 89% Construction waste diverted from landfills.
- 17% Recycled content of construction materials.
- 71% FSC certified wood.
- 59% Materials manufactured locally, and of those, 62% harvested locally.
- 90% Work areas with natural daylight.
- 100% Work areas with outside view.

### LEED® Platinum

### Manufacturers

**DIV. 7:** *Metal:* AEP; *Manufactured Siding:* James Hardie.
**DIV. 8:** *Windows:* Milgard; *Storefront:* United States Aluminum.
**DIV. 9:** *Carpet Tile:* Shaw Work Life Collection.
**DIV. 26:** *Photovoltaic Panels:* REC Silicon.

# CIVIC CV081126

## Washington Public Utilities Districts Association

### Design/Build General Contractor

Mountain Construction
7457 South Madison Street, Tacoma, WA 98409
www.mountainconst.com

### Design Manager & Architect

Helix Design Group, Inc.
6021 12th Street East, #201, Tacoma, WA 98424
www.helixdesigngroup.net

### Construction Team

**Structural and Civil Engineer:**
Sitts & Hill Engineering, Inc.
2901 South 40th Street, Tacoma, WA 98409

**LEED Manager, Mechanical & Design/Build HVAC:**
Sunset Air, Inc.
5210 Lacey Boulevard, Lacey, WA 98503

**Electrical Engineer:**
Electric Systems LLC
5011 S. Burlington Way, Tacoma, WA 98409

**Plumbing Engineer:**
Tacoma Plumbing & Heating, Inc.
1817 112th Street E, #G, Tacoma, WA 98445

### Project General Description

**Location:** Olympia, Washington
**Date Bid:** June 2006
**Construction Period:** Sep 2006 to Sep 2007
**Total Square Feet:** 20,168 **Site:** 0.25 acres.
**Number of Buildings:** One.
**Building Size:** Subterranean, 8,912; first floor, 5,310; second floor, 5,946; total, 20,168 square feet.
**Building Height:** Subterranean, 9'4"; first floor, 14'; second floor, 11'; total, 42' from grade to roof.

FIRST FLOOR

**Basic Construction Type:** New/Wood Frame.
**Foundation:** Slab-on-grade. **Exterior Walls:** CMU.
**Roof:** Metal. **Floors:** Wood.
**Interior Walls:** Wood stud drywall.

| C.S.I. Divisions | | | COST | % OF COST | SQ.FT. COST | SPECIFICATIONS |
|---|---|---|---|---|---|---|
| | | PROCUREMENT & CONT. REQ. | 858,751 | 22.51 | 42.58 | — |
| 1. | 1. | GENERAL REQUIREMENTS | 346,000 | 9.07 | 17.16 | Administrative requirements, quality requirements, temporary facilites & controls, product requirements. |
| 3. | 3. | CONCRETE | 386,000 | 10.12 | 19.14 | Forming & accessories, reinforcing, cast-in-place, precast, grouting, cutting & boring. |
| 4. | 4. | MASONRY | 112,000 | 2.94 | 5.55 | Unit. |
| 5. | 5. | METALS | 176,000 | 4.61 | 8.73 | Structural metal framing. |
| 6. | 6. | WOOD, PLASTICS & COMPOSITES | 465,000 | 12.19 | 23.06 | Rough carpentry, finish carpentry, siding & trim. |
| 7. | 7. | THERMAL & MOISTURE PROTECTION | 163,000 | 4.27 | 8.08 | Dampproofing & waterproofing, thermal protection, steep slope roofing, roofing & siding panels, membrane roofing, flashing & sheet metal. |
| 8. | 8. | OPENINGS | 135,000 | 3.54 | 6.69 | Doors & frames, entrances, storefronts & curtain walls, windows, roof windows & skylights, hardware. |
| 9. | 9. | FINISHES | 195,000 | 5.11 | 9.67 | Plaster & gypsum board, tiling, ceilings, flooring, wall finishes, painting & coating. |
| 10. | 10. | SPECIALTIES | 36,000 | 0.94 | 1.79 | Interior, safety. |
| 11. | 11. | EQUIPMENT | 20,000 | 0.52 | 0.99 | Commercial. |
| 12. | 12. | FURNISHINGS | 23,000 | 0.60 | 1.14 | Casework. |
| 14. | 14. | CONVEYING SYSTEMS | 50,000 | 1.31 | 2.48 | Elevators (1). |
| 15. | 21. | FIRE SUPPRESSON | 83,000 | 2.18 | 4.12 | Water-based fire suppression. |
| 15. | 22. | PLUMBING | 60,000 | 1.57 | 2.97 | Piping & pumps, equipment, fixtures, pool & fountain plumbing systems. |
| 15. | 23. | HVAC | 182,000 | 4.77 | 9.02 | Piping & pumps, air distribution, air cleaning devices, central heating, central cooling, central HVAC. |
| 16. | 26. | ELECTRICAL | 525,000 | 13.75 | 26.03 | Medium-voltage distribution, facility power generating & storing equipment. |
| | | **TOTAL BUILDING COST** | **3,815,751** | **100.00** | **$189.20** | |
| 2. | 2. | EXISTING CONDITIONS | 48,000 | | | Demolition & structure moving. |
| 2. | 31. | EARTHWORK | 301,000 | | | — |
| 2. | 32. | EXTERIOR IMPROVEMENTS | 119,000 | | | — |
| | | **PROJECT COST** | **4,283,751** | | | (Excluding architectural and engineering fees) |

# Appendix A: HVAC Equipment Efficiency Tables

| Residential Central Air Conditioner FEMP Efficiency Recommendation | | |
|---|---|---|
| Product Type[a] | Recommended Level[b] | Best Available |
| Split Systems | 11.0 or more EER<br>13.0 or more SEER[c] | 14.6 EER<br>16.5 SEER[c] |
| Single Package | 10.5 or more EER<br>12.0 or more SEER[c] | 12.2 EER<br>16.0 SEER[c] |

[a] Split system and single package units with capacity under 65,000 BTU/h are covered here. This analysis excludes window units and packaged terminal units.
[b] This efficiency recommendation meets ENERGY STAR® specification effective October 1, 2002.
[c] SEER (seasonal energy efficiency ratio) is the total cooling output (in BTU) provided by the unit during its normal annual usage period for cooling divided by the total energy input (in Wh) during the same period. Based on DOE test procedure, see 10 CFR 430, Sub-Part B, Appendix M. Federal Energy Management Program (FEMP) http://www.eren.doe.gov/femp/procurement/index.cfm

**Figure A.1**
Courtesy of the Federal Energy Management Program (FEMP). Reprinted with permission

| Residential Air-Source Heat Pump FEMP Efficiency Recommendation[a] | | |
|---|---|---|
| Product Type | Recommended[a] | Best Available[b] |
| Split Systems | 8.0 or more HSPF<br>11.0 or more EER<br>13.0 or more SEER | 9.6 or more HSPF<br>14.9 EER<br>17.4 SEER |
| Single Package[c] | 7.6 or more HSPF<br>10.5 or more EER<br>12.0 or more SEER | 8.3 HSPF<br>12.0 EER<br>15.6 SEER |

[a] This efficiency recommendation meets ENERGY STAR® specification effective October 1, 2002. SEER (seasonal energy efficiency ratio) is the total cooling output (in BTU) provided by the unit during its normal annual usage period for cooling divided by the total energy input (in Wh) during the same period.
[b] The best available models are split systems. The best available HSPF and best available SEER apply to different models. HSPF (heating seasonal performance factor) is the total heating output (in BTU) provided by the unit during its normal annual usage period for heating divided by the total energy input (in Wh) during the same period.
[c] Single package gas and electric units are covered here. This analysis excludes window units and other ductless systems. Federal Energy Management Program (FEMP) http://www.eren.doe.gov/femp/procurement/index.cfm

**Figure A.2**
Courtesy of the Federal Energy Management Program (FEMP). Reprinted with permission

| Water Cooled Chiller FEMP Efficiency Recommendation[a] | | |
|---|---|---|
| Compressor Type and Capacity | Part Load Optimized Chillers | |
| | Recommended IPLV[b,c] (kW/ton) | Best Available IPLV[b,c] (kW/ton) |
| Centrifugal (150–299 tons) | 0.52 or less | 0.47 |
| Centrifugal (300–2,000 tons) | 0.45 or less | 0.38 |
| Rotary Screw >= 150 tons | 0.49 or less | 0.46 |
| Compressor Type and Capacity | Full Load Optimized Chillers | |
| | Recommended Full Load[d] (kW/ton) | Best Available Full-Load[d] (kW/ton) |
| Centrifugal (150–299 tons) | 0.59 or less | 0.50 |
| Centrifugal (300–2,000 tons) | 0.56 or less | 0.47 |
| Rotary Screw >= 150 tons | 0.64 or less | 0.58 |

[a] Depending on the application, buyers should specify chiller efficiency using either full-load or integrated part-load values as shown (see text).
[b] Values are based on standard reference conditions specified in ARI standard 550/590-98.
[c] Integrated part load value (IPLV) is a weighted average of efficiency measurements at various part-load conditions, as described in ARI Standard 550/590-98. These weightings have changed substantially from the previous standard, ARI 550-92, lowering IPLV ratings by 10%–15% for the same equipment.
[d] Full load efficiency is measured at peak load conditions described in ARI Standard 550/590-98. Federal Energy Management Program (FEMP) http://www.eren.doe.gov/femp/procurement/index.cfm

**Figure A.3**
Courtesy of the Federal Energy Management Program (FEMP). Reprinted with permission

| Commercial Heat Pump FEMP Efficiency Recommendation | | |
|---|---|---|
| Product Type and Size | Recommended Level[a] | Best Available[b] |
| Air-source[c] < 65 MBTU/h | 12.0 SEER or more 7.7 HSPF or more | 13.2 SEER 8.5 HSPF |
| Air-source 65–135 MBTU/h | 10.1 EER or more 10.4 IPLV or more 3.2 COP or more | 11.5 EER 13.4 IPLV 4.0 COP |
| Air-source 136–240 MBTU/h | 9.3 EER or more 9.5 IPLV or more 3.1 COP or more | 10.5 EER 12.4 IPLV 3.3 COP |
| Water-source[d] 65–135 MBTU/h | 12.8 EER or more 4.5 COP or more | 14.5 EER 5.0 COP |

[a] Efficiency levels for air-source units sized between 65 and 240 MBTU/h meet ASHRAE 90.1 minimum efficiency requirements.
[b] The best available EER and best available COP apply to different models.
[c] Only units with 3-phase power supply are covered in this category.
[d] Water source heat pumps covered here use cooling towers and boilers as the heat transfer sink or source in a closed loop piping system. This may increase boiler energy use by lowering the return water temperature. Auxiliary pumping energy is not included in the WSHP efficiency rating. EER (energy efficiency ratio) is the cooling capacity (in BTU/hour) of the unit divided by its electrical input (in watts) at standard peak rating conditions. SEER (seasonal energy efficiency ratio) and IPLV (integrated part-load value) are similar to EER, but weigh performance during the cooling season. COP (Coefficient of Performance) is the heating capacity (in BTU/h) at standard heating conditions divided by its electrical input (also in BTU/h). HSPF (Heating Seasonal Performance Factor), like SEER, weighs heating performance at various conditions. Federal Energy Management Program (FEMP) http://www.eren.doe.gov/femp/procurement/index.cfm

**Figure A.4**
Courtesy of the Federal Energy Management Program (FEMP). Reprinted with permission

**Figure A.5**
Courtesy of the Federal Energy
Management Program (FEMP).
Reprinted with permission

| Ground Source Heat Pump FEMP Efficiency Recommendation | | | | |
|---|---|---|---|---|
| Product Type | Recommended | | Best Available[a] | |
| | EER[b] | COP[c] | EER[b] | COP[c] |
| Closed Loop | 14.1 or more | 3.3 or more | 25.8 | 4.9 |
| Open Loop[d] | 16.2 or more | 3.6 or more | 31.1 | 5.5 |

[a] The best available coefficient of performance (COP) and best available energy efficiency ratio (EER) for the open-loop system apply to different models.
[b] EER is the cooling capacity (in BTU/hour) of the unit divided by its electrical input (in watts) at standard (ARI/ISO) conditions of 77°F entering water for closed-loop models and 59°F entering water for open-loop systems.
[c] COP is the heating capacity (in BTU) of the unit divided by its electrical input (also in BTU) at standard (ARI/ISO) conditions of 32°F entering water for closed-loop models and 50°F entering water for open-loop equipment.
[d] Open-loop heat pumps, as opposed to closed-loop models, utilize "once-through" water from a well, lake or stream. Federal Energy Management Program (FEMP) http://www.eren.doe.gov/femp/procurement/index.cfm

**Figure A.6**
Courtesy of the Federal Energy
Management Program (FEMP).
Reprinted with permission

| Commercial Boiler FEMP Efficiency Recommendation[a] | | | |
|---|---|---|---|
| Product Type (Fuel/ Heat Medium) | Rated Capacity (BTU/h) | Recommended Thermal Efficiency ($e_t$)[b] | Best Available[c] Thermal Efficiency ($e_t$) |
| Natural Gas Water | 300,000–2,500,000 | 80% $e_t$ | 86.7% $e_t$ |
| | 2,500,001–10,000,000 | 80% $e_t$ | 83.2% $e_t$ |
| Natural Gas Steam | 300,000–2,500,000 | 79% $e_t$ | 81.9% $e_t$ |
| | 2,500,001–10,000,000 | 80% $e_t$ | 81.2% $e_t$ |
| #2 Oil Water | 300,000–2,500,000 | 83% $e_t$ | 87.7% $e_t$ |
| | 2,500,001–10,000,000 | 83% $e_t$ | 85.5% $e_t$ |
| #2 Oil Steam | 300,000–2,500,000 | 83% $e_t$ | 83.9% $e_t$ |
| | 2,500,001–10,000,000 | 83% $e_t$ | 84.2% $e_t$ |

[a] This recommendation covers low- and medium-pressure boilers used primarily in commercial space heating applications. It does not apply to high-pressure boilers used in industrial processing and cogeneration applications.
[b] Thermal efficiency (et), also known as "boiler efficiency" or "overall efficiency," is the boiler's energy output divided by energy input, as defined by ANSI Z21.13. In contrast to combustion efficiency (ec), et accounts for radiation and convection losses through the boiler's shell.
[c] These "best available" efficiencies do not consider condensing boilers, which are generally more efficient but are not readily ratable with ANSI Z21.13. Federal Energy Management Program (FEMP) http://www.eren.doe.gov/femp/procurement/index.cfm

| Commercial Unitary Air Conditioner FEMP Efficiency Recommendation | | |
|---|---|---|
| Product Type and Size[a] | Recommended Level | Best Available |
| <65 MBTU/h (3 phase) | 12.0 SEER or more[b] | 14.5 SEER |
| 65–135 MBTU/h | 11.0 EER or more<br>11.4 IPLV or more | 11.8 EER<br>13.0 IPLV |
| >135–240 MBTU/h | 10.8 EER or more<br>11.2 IPLV or more | 11.5 EER<br>13.3 IPLV |

[a] Only air-cooled single-packaged and split system units used in commercial buildings are covered. Water source units are not covered by ENERGY STAR® but look for efficiency ratings that meet or exceed these levels for air source units.

[b] When operating conditions are often close to rated conditions or in regions where there are high demand costs, look for units with the highest EER ratings that also meet or exceed this SEER. EER (energy efficiency ratio) is the cooling capacity (in BTU/hour) of the unit divided by its electrical input (in watts) at the Air Conditioning and Refrigeration Institute's (ARI) standard peak rating condition of 95°F. SEER (seasonal energy efficiency ratio) and IPLV (integrated part-load value) are similar to EER but weigh performance at different (peak and off-peak) conditions during the cooling season. Federal Energy Management Program (FEMP) http://www.eren.doe.gov/femp/procurement/index.cfm

**Figure A.7**
Courtesy of the Federal Energy Management Program (FEMP). Reprinted with permission

| Air Cooled Chiller FEMP Efficiency Recommendation[a] | | |
|---|---|---|
| | Part Load Optimized Chillers | |
| Compressor Type and Capacity | Recommended[b]<br>IPLV[c] (kW/ton) | Best Available[b]<br>IPLV[c] (kW/ton) |
| Scroll (30–60 tons) | 0.86 or less | 0.83 |
| Reciprocating (30–150 tons) | 0.90 or less | 0.80 |
| Screw (70–200 tons) | 0.98 or less | 0.83 |
| | Full Load Optimized Chillers | |
| Compressor Type and Capacity | Recommended<br>Full Load (kW/ton) | Best Available<br>Full Load (kW/ton) |
| Scroll (30–60 tons) | 1.23 or less | 1.10 |
| Reciprocating (30–150 tons) | 1.23 or less | 1.00 |
| Screw (70–200 tons) | 1.23 or less | 0.94 |

[a] Depending on the application, buyers should specify chiller efficiency using either full-load or integrated part-load values as shown (see text).

[b] Values are based on standard rating conditions specified in ARI Standard 550/590-98. Only packaged chillers (i.e., none with remote condensers) are covered.

[c] Integrated part-load value (IPLV) is a weighted average of efficiency measurements at various part-load conditions, as described in ARI Standard 550/590-98. These weightings have changed substantially from the previous standard, ARI 590-92, lowering IPLV ratings by 10%–15% for the same equipment. Federal Energy Management Program (FEMP) http://www.eren.doe.gov/femp/procurement/index.cfm

**Figure A.8**
Courtesy of the Federal Energy Management Program (FEMP). Reprinted with permission

**Residential Ground-Source Heat Pump FEMP Efficiency Recommendation**

| Product Type | Recommended | | Best Available[a] | |
|---|---|---|---|---|
| | EER[b] | COP[c] | EER[b] | COP[c] |
| Closed Loop | 14.1 or more | 3.3 or more | 25.8 | 4.9 |
| Open Loop[d] | 16.2 or more | 3.6 or more | 31.1 | 5.5 |

[a] The best available coefficient of performance (COP) and best available energy efficiency ratio (EER) for the open-loop system apply to different models.
[b] EER is the cooling capacity (in BTU/hour) of the unit divided by its electrical input (in watts) at standard (ARI/ISO) conditions of 77°F entering water for closed-loop models and 59°F entering water for open-loop systems.
[c] COP is the heating capacity (in BTU) of the unit divided by its electrical input (also in BTU) at standard (ARI/ISO) conditions of 32°F entering water for closed-loop models and 50°F entering water for open-loop equipment.
[d] Open-loop heat pumps, as opposed to closed-loop models, utilize "once-through" water from a well, lake or stream. Federal Energy Management Program (FEMP) http://www.eren.doe.gov/femp/procurement/index.cfm

**Residential Gas Furnace FEMP Efficiency Recommendation**

| Product Type | Recommended AFUE[a,b] | Best Available AFUE |
|---|---|---|
| Residential Gas Furnace[c] | 90% or more | 97% |

[a] AFUE (annual fuel utilization efficiency) is a measure of heating efficiency on an annual basis. The DOE test procedure defines AFUE as the heat transferred to the conditioned space divided by the fuel energy supplied.
[b] Based on DOE test procedure, see 10 CFR, Sub-Part B, Appendix N.
[c] Residential gas furnaces include those fired by natural or propane gas, with input ratings less than 225,000 BTU/hour. Federal Energy Management Program (FEMP) http://www.eren.doe.gov/femp/procurement/index.cfm

**Electric Water Heater FEMP Efficiency Recommendation**

| Storage Tank Volume) | Energy Factor[a] | Annual Energy Use[b] |
|---|---|---|
| Less than 60 gallons | 0.93 or higher | 4,721 kWh/year or less |
| 60 gallons or more | 0.91 or higher | 4,825 kWh/year or less |

[a] Energy Factor is an efficiency ratio of the energy supplied in heated water divided by the energy input to the water heater.
[b] Based on DOE test procedure (10 CFR 430, Sub-Part B, Appendix E). Federal Energy Management Program (FEMP) http://www.eren.doe.gov/femp/procurement/index.cfm

**Gas Water Heater FEMP Efficiency Recommendation**

| Storage Type (rated volume) | Energy Factor[a] | Annual Energy Use[b] |
|---|---|---|
| 50 gallons or less | 0.62 or higher | 242 therms[c]/year or less |

[a] Energy factor is an efficiency ratio of the energy supplied in heated water divided by the energy input to the water heater.
[b] Based on DOE test procedure (10 CFR 430, Sub-Part B, Appendix E).
[c] 1 therm = 100,000 BTU Federal Energy Management Program (FEMP) http://www.eren.doe.gov/femp/procurement/index.cfm

# Appendix B: Additional Information on Standards & Guidelines

## List of ENERGY STAR® – Qualified Building Products & Equipment and Summary Specifications (March 2004)

| Building Envelope | |
| --- | --- |
| Roofing | Low Slope roofs must have an initial solar reflectance of > 0.65. After 3 years, the solar reflectance must be > 0.50. |
| | Steep Slope roofs must have an initial solar reflectance of > 0.25. After 3 years, the solar reflectance must be > 0.15. |
| Windows, Doors, and Skylights for the Northern Climate Zone | Windows and doors must have a U-factor* of 0.35 or below; there is no SHGC* requirement for this climate zone. |
| | Skylights must have a U-factor* of 0.60 or below; there is no SHGC* requirement for this climate zone. |
| Windows, Doors, and Skylights for the North/Central Climate Zone | Windows and doors must have a U-factor* of 0.40 or below and a SHGC* of 0.55 or below. |
| | Skylights must have a U-factor* of 0.60 or below and a SHGC* of 0.40 or below. |
| Windows, Doors, and Skylights for the South/Central Climate Zone | Windows and doors must have a U-factor* of 0.40 or below and a SHGC* of 0.40 or below. |
| | Skylights must have a U-factor* of 0.60 or below and a SHGC* of 0.40 or below. |
| Windows, Doors, and Skylights for the Southern Climate Zone | Windows and doors must have a U-factor* of 0.65 or below and a SHGC* of 0.40 or below. |
| | Skylights must have a U-factor* of 0.75 or below and a SHGC* of 0.40 or below. |
| **Residential Appliances** | |
| Clothes Washers | Minimum Modified Energy Factor (MEF) of 1.42. |
| Dishwashers | At least 25% more efficient than minimum federal government standards. |
| Full Size Refrigerators, 7.75 cubic feet or greater | At least 15% more energy efficient than the minimum federal government standard (NAECA). |
| Full Size Freezers, 7.75 cubic feet or greater | At least 10% more energy efficient than the minimum federal government standard (NAECA). |
| Compact Refrigerators and Freezers Less than 7.75 cubic feet and 36 inches or less in height | At least 20% more energy efficient than the minimum federal government standard (NAECA). |
| **Commercial Foodservice** | |

**B.1**

| | |
|---|---|
| Commercial Solid Door Refrigerators and Freezers | Energy efficiency is measured in kWh/day. Specifications based on unit internal volume<br><br>Refrigerators < 0.10V + 2.04 kWh/day.<br><br>Freezers < 0.40V + 1.38 kWh/day.<br><br>Refrigerator-Freezers < 0.27AV - 0.71 kWh/day.<br><br>Ice Cream Freezers < 0.39V + 0.82 kWh/day. |
| Commercial Hot Food Holding Cabinets | Energy efficiency is measured in watts/ft3.<br><br>Maximum Idle Energy Rate is 40 watts/ft3. |
| Commercial Fryers | Open deep-fat gas fryers must have a heavy load (French fry) cooking energy efficiency of > 50% and an Idle Energy Rate of < 9,000 Btu/hr.<br><br>Open deep-fat electric fryers must have a heavy load (French fry) cooking energy efficiency of > 80% and an Idle Energy Rate of < 1,000 watts. |
| Commercial Steam Cookers | Only 3-, 4-, 5-, and 6-pan units currently qualify to earn the ENERGY STAR.<br><br>Electric steam cookers must have a cooking energy efficiency of at least 50%, and the maximum idle rate (measured in kW) varies depending on the number of pans.<br><br>Gas steam cookers must have a cooking energy efficiency of at least 38%, and the maximum idle rate (measured in Btu/hr) varies depending on the number of pans. |
| **HVAC** | |
| Boilers | Rating of 85% AFUE* or greater (about 6% more efficient than the minimum federal standards) |
| Furnaces | Rating of 90% AFUE* or greater (about 15% more efficient than the minimum federal efficiency standards) |
| Light Commercial HVAC | Covers central air conditioners and heat pumps used in small office buildings, clinics and medical care facilities, hotels, dorms, military barracks, retail strip malls, and other locations (i.e., units rated at 65,000 Btu/h or up to 250,000 Btu/h as well as three-phase equipment rated below 65,000 Btu/h).<br><br>Energy-efficiency specifications based on equipment type and size category. |
| Air-Source Heat Pumps | > 8.0 HSPF/ > 13 SEER/ > 11 EER* for split systems<br><br>> 7.6 HSPF/ > 12 SEER/ > 10.5 EER* for single package equipment including gas/electric package units |
| Geothermal Heat Pumps | Open Loop: >3.6 COP (H); >16.2 EER (C)*<br><br>Closed Loop: >3.3 COP (H); >14.1 EER (C)*<br><br>Direct Expansion (DX): >3.5 COP (H); >15 EER (C)* |
| Room Air Conditioners | At least 10% more energy efficient than the minimum federal government standards. |
| Central Air Conditioners | > 13 SEER/ > 11 EER* for split systems<br><br>> 12 SEER/ > 10.5 EER* for single package equipment including gas/electric package units |
| Programmable Thermostats | Capability of maintaining two separate programs (to address the different comfort needs of weekdays and weekends) and up to four temperature settings for each program. |
| Residential Ceiling Fans | Specification defines residential ceiling fan airflow efficiency on a performance basis: CFM of airflow per watt of power consumed by the motor and controls. Efficiency is measured on each of 3 speeds.<br><br>At low speed, fans must have a minimum airflow of 1,250 CFM and an efficiency of 155 CFM/watt.<br><br>At medium speed, fans must have a minimum airflow of 2,500 CFM and an efficiency of 110 CFM/watt.<br><br>At high speed, fans must have a minimum airflow of 5,000 CFM and an efficiency of 75 CFM/watt.<br><br>Integral or attachable lighting, including separately sold ceiling fan light kits, must meet certain requirements of the RLF specification. |

**B.1 (cont.)**

| | |
|---|---|
| Ventilating Fans | Range hoods (up to 500 cfm): maximum allowable sound level of 2.0 sones; minimum efficacy level of 2.8 cfm/Watt |
| | Bathroom and utility room fans (10 to 80 cfm): maximum allowable sound level of 2.0 sones; minimum efficacy level of 1.4 cfm/Watt; minimum rated airflow at 0.25 static w.g. 60% of 0.1 static w.g. airflow |
| | Bathroom and utility room fans (90 to 130 cfm): maximum allowable sound level of 2.0 sones; minimum efficacy level of 2.8 cfm/Watt; minimum rated airflow at 0.25 w.g. 70% of 0.1 static w.g. airflow |
| | Bathroom and utility room fans (140 to 500 cfm [max]): maximum allowable sound level of 3.0 sones; minimum efficacy level of 2.8 cfm/Watt; minimum rated airflow at 0.25 w.g. 70% of 0.1 static w.g. airflow |
| | In-line fans (single-port & multi-port): no sound or airflow requirement; minimum efficacy level of 2.8 cfm/watt |
| | Light sources must use pin-based fluorescent technology and meet specific performance criteria based on system efficacy per lamp ballast combination, lamp start time, lamp life, color rendering index, correlated color temperature, noise, maximum total lamp wattage (excluding night lights), and maximum night light wattage.* |
| | Warranty provided must be a minimum of 1 year |
| Dehumidifiers | Energy efficiency is measured in liters of water removed per kWh of energy consumed. |
| | Ranges from > 1.20 to >1.50 L/kWh for standard capacity units. |
| | > 2.25 L/kWh for high capacity units. |
| **Electrical** | |
| Transformers | Low-Voltage Dry-Type Transformer Manufacturing Partners: Energy efficiency specifications based upon kVA, differing for single versus three-phased equipment. |
| Residential Light Fixtures | Energy-efficiency specifications based on specific performance characteristics relating to the lamp, ballast, and fixtures as a whole. |
| | The fixture, lamps, and ballast must be tested in accordance with the appropriate IESNA, ANSI, and UL reference standards, and must meet OSHA/NRTL safety and reliability guidelines. |
| | Includes a written 2-year manufacturer warranty covering repair and replacement of defective parts of the fixture housing or electronics (excluding the lamp). |
| Compact Fluorescent Lamps (CFLs) | Product testing criteria for medium screw-based CFLs include: efficacy, lumen output, lifetime (minimum 6,000 hours), color rendering index, color temperature, power factor and start time. |
| | Must also comply with product packaging requirements set by the FTC and ENERGY STAR. |
| | Product includes a two-year warranty for residential applications. |
| | ENERGY STAR CFL criteria references standards set by: ANSI, CIE, IESNA and UL. |
| Exit Signs | Operates on 5 watts or less per face. |

**B.1 (cont.)**

# LEED for New Construction, v2.2
# Registered Project Checklist

Project Name:
Project Address:

| Yes | ? | No | | | | Points |
|---|---|---|---|---|---|---|
| | | | **Sustainable Sites** | | | **14 Points** |
| Y | | | Prereq 1 | **Construction Activity Pollution Prevention** | | Required |
| | | | Credit 1 | **Site Selection** | | 1 |
| | | | Credit 2 | **Development Density & Community Connectivity** | | 1 |
| | | | Credit 3 | **Brownfield Redevelopment** | | 1 |
| | | | Credit 4.1 | **Alternative Transportation**, Public Transportation Access | | 1 |
| | | | Credit 4.2 | **Alternative Transportation**, Bicycle Storage & Changing Rooms | | 1 |
| | | | Credit 4.3 | **Alternative Transportation**, Low-Emitting and Fuel-Efficient Vehicles | | 1 |
| | | | Credit 4.4 | **Alternative Transportation**, Parking Capacity | | 1 |
| | | | Credit 5.1 | **Site Development**, Protect of Restore Habitat | | 1 |
| | | | Credit 5.2 | **Site Development**, Maximize Open Space | | 1 |
| | | | Credit 6.1 | **Stormwater Design**, Quantity Control | | 1 |
| | | | Credit 6.2 | **Stormwater Design**, Quality Control | | 1 |
| | | | Credit 7.1 | **Heat Island Effect**, Non-Roof | | 1 |
| | | | Credit 7.2 | **Heat Island Effect**, Roof | | 1 |
| | | | Credit 8 | **Light Pollution Reduction** | | 1 |

| Yes | ? | No | | | | Points |
|---|---|---|---|---|---|---|
| | | | **Water Efficiency** | | | **5 Points** |
| | | | Credit 1.1 | **Water Efficient Landscaping**, Reduce by 50% | | 1 |
| | | | Credit 1.2 | **Water Efficient Landscaping**, No Potable Use or No Irrigation | | 1 |
| | | | Credit 2 | **Innovative Wastewater Technologies** | | 1 |
| | | | Credit 3.1 | **Water Use Reduction**, 20% Reduction | | 1 |
| | | | Credit 3.2 | **Water Use Reduction**, 30% Reduction | | 1 |

| Yes | ? | No | | | | Points |
|---|---|---|---|---|---|---|
| | | | **Energy & Atmosphere** | | | **17 Points** |
| Y | | | Prereq 1 | **Fundamental Commissioning of the Building Energy Systems** | | Required |
| Y | | | Prereq 2 | **Minimum Energy Performance** | | Required |
| Y | | | Prereq 3 | **Fundamental Refrigerant Management** | | Required |
| | | | Credit 1 | **Optimize Energy Performance** | | 1 to 10 |
| | | | Credit 2 | **On-Site Renewable Energy** | | 1 to 3 |
| | | | Credit 3 | **Enhanced Commissioning** | | 1 |
| | | | Credit 4 | **Enhanced Refrigerant Management** | | 1 |
| | | | Credit 5 | **Measurement & Verification** | | 1 |
| | | | Credit 6 | **Green Power** | | 1 |

continued…

**B.2** *(Courtesy of U.S. Green Building Council. Reprinted with permission.)*

| Yes | ? | No | | | |
|---|---|---|---|---|---|
| | | | **Materials & Resources** | | **13** Points |

| | | | | | |
|---|---|---|---|---|---|
| **Y** | | | Prereq 1 | **Storage & Collection of Recyclables** | Required |
| | | | Credit 1.1 | **Building Reuse**, Maintain 75% of Existing Walls, Floors & Roof | 1 |
| | | | Credit 1.2 | **Building Reuse**, Maintain 100% of Existing Walls, Floors & Roof | 1 |
| | | | Credit 1.3 | **Building Reuse**, Maintain 50% of Interior Non-Structural Elements | 1 |
| | | | Credit 2.1 | **Construction Waste Management**, Divert 50% from Disposal | 1 |
| | | | Credit 2.2 | **Construction Waste Management**, Divert 75% from Disposal | 1 |
| | | | Credit 3.1 | **Materials Reuse**, 5% | 1 |
| | | | Credit 3.2 | **Materials Reuse**, 10% | 1 |
| | | | Credit 4.1 | **Recycled Content**, 10% (post-consumer + ½ pre-consumer) | 1 |
| | | | Credit 4.2 | **Recycled Content**, 20% (post-consumer + ½ pre-consumer) | 1 |
| | | | Credit 5.1 | **Regional Materials**, 10% Extracted, Processed & Manufactured Regic | 1 |
| | | | Credit 5.2 | **Regional Materials**, 20% Extracted, Processed & Manufactured Regic | 1 |
| | | | Credit 6 | **Rapidly Renewable Materials** | 1 |
| | | | Credit 7 | **Certified Wood** | 1 |

| Yes | ? | No | | | |
|---|---|---|---|---|---|
| | | | **Indoor Environmental Quality** | | **15** Points |

| | | | | | |
|---|---|---|---|---|---|
| **Y** | | | Prereq 1 | **Minimum IAQ Performance** | Required |
| **Y** | | | Prereq 2 | **Environmental Tobacco Smoke (ETS) Control** | Required |
| | | | Credit 1 | **Outdoor Air Delivery Monitoring** | 1 |
| | | | Credit 2 | **Increased Ventilation** | 1 |
| | | | Credit 3.1 | **Construction IAQ Management Plan**, During Construction | 1 |
| | | | Credit 3.2 | **Construction IAQ Management Plan**, Before Occupancy | 1 |
| | | | Credit 4.1 | **Low-Emitting Materials**, Adhesives & Sealants | 1 |
| | | | Credit 4.2 | **Low-Emitting Materials**, Paints & Coatings | 1 |
| | | | Credit 4.3 | **Low-Emitting Materials**, Carpet Systems | 1 |
| | | | Credit 4.4 | **Low-Emitting Materials**, Composite Wood & Agrifiber Products | 1 |
| | | | Credit 5 | **Indoor Chemical & Pollutant Source Control** | 1 |
| | | | Credit 6.1 | **Controllability of Systems**, Lighting | 1 |
| | | | Credit 6.2 | **Controllability of Systems**, Thermal Comfort | 1 |
| | | | Credit 7.1 | **Thermal Comfort**, Design | 1 |
| | | | Credit 7.2 | **Thermal Comfort**, Verification | 1 |
| | | | Credit 8.1 | **Daylight & Views**, Daylight 75% of Spaces | 1 |
| | | | Credit 8.2 | **Daylight & Views**, Views for 90% of Spaces | 1 |

| Yes | ? | No | | | |
|---|---|---|---|---|---|
| | | | **Innovation & Design Process** | | **5** Points |

| | | | | | |
|---|---|---|---|---|---|
| | | | Credit 1.1 | **Innovation in Design**: Provide Specific Title | 1 |
| | | | Credit 1.2 | **Innovation in Design**: Provide Specific Title | 1 |
| | | | Credit 1.3 | **Innovation in Design**: Provide Specific Title | 1 |
| | | | Credit 1.4 | **Innovation in Design**: Provide Specific Title | 1 |
| | | | Credit 2 | **LEED® Accredited Professional** | 1 |

| Yes | ? | No | | | |
|---|---|---|---|---|---|
| | | | **Project Totals** (pre-certification estimates) | | **69** Points |

**Certified:** 26-32 points, **Silver:** 33-38 points, **Gold:** 39-51 points, **Platinum:** 52-69 points

**B.2 (cont.)** *(Courtesy of U.S. Green Building Council. Reprinted with permission.)*

| Product | Key Green Attributes |
|---------|---------------------|
| **Sitework** | |
| Composting systems for residential waste | Design for maximizing anaerobic activity |
| Drainage pipe | Recycled content requirements |
| Drought resistant planting systems | Contains recycled components<br>No significant leaching of hazardous compounds if waste tires are used<br>Demonstrate reduced watering needs |
| Recreational equipment and outdoor furniture | Recycled and post consumer plastic content requirements |
| **Metals** | |
| Steel | Contains 50% or > recycled content,<br>Contains 15% or > post-consumer content<br>Embodied energy < or = 7.5 MJ/kg hot band state "gate to gate"<br>Embodied energy < or = 11.5MJ/kg final finished steel roll state "gate to gate" |
| **Wood Substitutes** | |
| Particle board from agricultural fiber | Must use 100% agricultural fiber as the cellulose fiber source, and must employ the criteria statement "particle board from agricultural residue" wherever the Ecologo is used<br>Formaldehyde emission restrictions |
| **Insulation** | |
| Cellulose | Contains 80% or > recycled content |
| Fiberglass | Contains 45% or > recycled content |
| Mineral wool | Contains 35% or > recycled content, 50% or > for loose-fill or spray on type |
| Extruded polystyrene | Contains 20% or > recycled content |
| Expanded polystyrene | Must implement a program for recovery of post-consumer and/or pre-consumer waste that can be re-introduced into the manufacturing process |
| Polyisocyanurate | Contains 15% or > recycled content (plastic component only) |
| Closed cell spray polyurethane foam | Contains 5% or > recycled content |
| Aluminum reflective | Contains 15% or > recycled content (plastic layer content) |
| Acoustical insulation | Non toxic<br>Recycled and post consumer material content requirements |
| **Finishes** | |
| Commercial non-modular carpets | No VOC emissions<br>Specific coating requirements<br>Use of recycled materials<br>Recovery of manufacturing effluent |
| Commercial modular carpets | |
| Other virgin wood substitute flooring | |
| Cork flooring | |
| Rubber based textile flooring | |

**B.3**

| | |
|---|---|
| Bamboo flooring | No VOC emissions including formaldehyde > .5mg/m2/hr<br>Not coated with products that are manufactured or formulated with arsenic, cadmium, lead, mercury, or nickel, and contain suspected carcinogens or mutagens |
| Gypsum wallboard | Recycled material content |
| Paints varnishes and stains | Restrictions on aromatic solvents, formaldehyde, halogenated solvents<br>Restrictions VOC content and output<br>Restrictions on manufacturing release of BOD & TSS<br>Instructions on use and disposal |
| Alternative wood treatments | Nontoxic<br>Biodegradable<br>No VOC output<br>Restrictions on components to low impact compounds |
| Gypsum wallboard | Recycled material content |
| **Equipment** | |
| Washing machines | Not exceed maximum power consumption of 2.0 kWh/cycle<br>Not exceed maximum EnerGuide rating or 315 kWh<br>Not exceed 15.0 liters/kg of water consumption (based on max drum volume and normal loads)<br>Not exceed operating time of 60 minutes/cycle<br>Not exceed rating of 0.5 g/cycle per (AHAM test)<br>Not exceed residual moisture of 65% for machines with drum volume of 31 liters or 60% for machines with drum volume > 31 liters |
| Dishwashers | Perform at a minimum of at least 0.5 cycles per kWh as per AHAM<br>Not exceed maximum EnerGuide rating or 558 kWh<br>Not exceed 25.0 liters/kg of water consumption per normal cycle<br>Filter 100% of used water<br>Not exceed noise levels of 60.8 dBa<br>Not exceed detergent consumptions 30 g per cycle or be equipped with automatic dispensing capabilities that do not exceed this amount of detergent use |
| **Furnishings** | |
| Mattresses | Use only steel innersprings which have been repaired and heat treated<br>Manufacturer must comply with reuse of the following:<br>steel innersprings 55% by weight<br>urethane foam 4% by weight<br>cotton liners 10% by weight<br>Direct all cotton liners which have been removed from mattresses to paper manufacturing facilities |
| Demountable partitions | Low VOC and formaldehyde emissions<br>Plastic components CFC free<br>Manufactured in facilities with waste reduction strategies |
| Office furniture and panel systems | Low VOC and formaldehyde emissions<br>Plastic components CFC free<br>Manufactured in facilities with waste reduction strategies<br>New wood products traded according to the Convention on International Trade in Endangered Species<br>Content stamping of plastics |

**B.3 (cont.)**

| Mattresses | Use only steel innersprings which have been repaired and heat treated<br>Manufacturer must comply with reuse of the following:<br>steel innersprings 55% by weight<br>urethane foam 4% by weight<br>cotton liners 10% by weight<br>Direct all cotton liners which have been removed from mattresses to paper manufacturing facilities |
|---|---|
| **Heating, Cooling, & Ventilating Equipment** | |
| Water conserving products | Maximum flow rates |
| Hot water storage tanks | Minimum energy factors<br>Insulation material restrictions |
| Hot water storage tanks, indirect gas fired | Low stand-by loss<br>Foam insulation material must be produced with non-ozone depleting blowing agents |
| Hot water heating boilers, gas fired | Combustion efficiency of at least 88%<br>Low emissions of NOx and CO |
| Heaters and furnaces, gas fired | Energy efficiency:<br>at least 78.5% for vented room heaters<br>at least 78.9% for gravity and fan type wall furnaces<br>at least 80% for gravity and fan type direct vented wall furnaces |
| Heating/cooling systems for buildings | Specific reduced energy consumption requirements<br>Energy source requirements<br>Pollutant output and use restrictions i.e. CFC, NOx, SOx<br>Water use and contamination restrictions |
| Thermostat control | Provide evidence of energy efficiency |
| Exhaust fans | Minimum energy efficiency of 3.6 cubic feet per minute/watt |
| | |

**B.3 (cont.)**

# CHPS Criteria Summary

| Category | Class | Credit/Prerequisite | Points |
|---|---|---|---|
| Sustainable Sites (15) | 1. Site Selection (6) | SS1.0: Code Compliance | P |
| | | SS1.1: Environmentally Sensitive Land | 1 |
| | | SS1.2: Greenfields | 1 |
| | | SS1.3: Central Location | 1 |
| | | SS1.4: Joint-Use of Facilities | 1 |
| | | SS1.5: Joint-Use of Parks | 1 |
| | | SS1.6: Reduced Footprint | 1 |
| | 2. Transportation (3) | SS2.1: Public Transportation | 1 |
| | | SS2.2: Bicycles | 1 |
| | | SS2.3: Minimize Parking | 1 |
| | 3. Stormwater Management (2) | SS3.0 Construction Site Runoff Control | P |
| | | SS3.1: Limit Stormwater Runoff | 1 |
| | | SS3.2: Treat Stormwater Runoff | 1 |
| | 4. Outdoor Surfaces (2) | SS4.1 Reduce Heat Islands – Landscaping Issues | 1 |
| | | SS4.2: Reduce Heat Islands – Cool Roofs | 1 |
| | 5. Outdoor Lighting (1) | SS5.1: Light Pollution Reduction | 1 |
| | 6. Schools as Learning Tools (1) | SS6.0: Educational Display | P |
| | | SS6.1: Demonstration Areas | 1 |
| Water (5) | 1. Outdoor Systems (2) | WE1.0: Create Water Use Budget | P |
| | | WE1.1: Reduce Potable Water for Landscaping | 1-2 |
| | 2. Indoor Systems (3) | WE2.1: Reduce Sewage Conveyance from Toilets and Urinals | 1 |
| | | WE2.2: Reduce Indoor Potable Water Use | 1-2 |
| Energy (20) | 1. Energy Efficiency (15) | EE1.0: Minimum Energy Performance | P |
| | | EE1.1: Superior Energy Performance | 1-13 |
| | | EE1.2: Natural Ventilation | 1 |
| | | EE1.3: Energy Management Systems | 1 |
| | 2. Alternative Energy Sources (3) | EE2.1: Renewable Energy | 1-3 |
| | 3. Commissioning and Training (2) | EE3.0: Fundamental Building Systems Testing and Training | P |
| | | EE3.1: Enhanced Commissioning | 1-2 |

## B.4

Courtesy of the Collaborative of High Performance Schools (CHPS) from the CHPS
Best Practice Manual, Volume III, 2006 Edition.

| Category | Class | Credit/Prerequisite | Points |
|---|---|---|---|
| Materials (12) | 1. Recycling (0) | ME1.0: Storage and Collection of Recyclables | P |
| | 2. Construction Waste Management (2) | ME2.0: Construction Waste Management | P |
| | | ME2.1: Construction Site Waste Management | 1-2 |
| | 3. Building Reuse (3) | ME3.1: Reuse of Structure and Shell | 1-2 |
| | | ME3.2: Reuse of Interior Partitions | 1 |
| | 4. Sustainable Materials (7) | ME4.1: Recycled Content | 1-2 |
| | | ME4.2: Rapidly Renewable Materials | 1 |
| | | ME4.3: Organically Grown Materials | 1 |
| | | ME4.4: Certified Wood | 1 |
| | | ME4.5: Salvaged Materials | 1-2 |
| | | ME4.6 Alternative: Environmentally Preferable Products | ½ -7 |
| Indoor Environmental Quality (20) | 1. Lighting and Daylighting (6) | EQ1.1: Daylighting | 1-4 |
| | | EQ1.2: View Windows | 1 |
| | | EQ1.3 Electric Lighting | 1 |
| | 2. Indoor Air Quality (9) | EQ2.0: Minimum Requirements | P |
| | | EQ2.1: Increased Ventilation Effectiveness | 2 |
| | | EQ2.2: Low-Emitting Materials | ½ -4 |
| | | EQ2.3: Chemical and Pollutant Source Control | 1 |
| | | EQ2.4: Ducted Returns | 1 |
| | | EQ2.5: Filtration | 1 |
| | 3. Acoustics (3) | EQ3.0: Minimum Acoustical Performance | P |
| | | EQ3.1: Improved Acoustical Performance | 1 or 3 |
| | 4. Thermal Comfort (2) | EQ4.0: ASHRAE 55 Code Compliance | P |
| | | EQ4.1: Controllability of Systems | 1-2 |
| Policy and Operations (13) | 1. District Level Credits (6) | PO1.1: CHPS Resolution | 1 |
| | | PO1.2: Environmental Education Resolution | 1-2 |
| | | PO1.3: Periodic Assessment of Environmental Conditions | 1 |
| | | PO1.4: Equipment Performance | 1-2 |
| | 2. Transportation (2) | PO2.1: Buses | 1 |
| | | PO2.2: Low Emission School Buses | 1 |
| | 3. Project Level Credits (5) | PO3.1: Maintenance Plan | 1-3 |
| | | PO3.2: Green Power | 2 |

## Total Available CHPS Points     85

B.4 (cont.)

# Resources

## Green Building/ Sustainability

**Advanced Building Technologies**
http://www.advancedbuildings.org

**American Institute of Architects Committee on the Environment (AIA COTE)**
202-626-7300 or 800-AIA-3837
http://www.aia.org/cote

**Applied Building Science–WSU Energy Program**
360-956-2000
http://www.energy.wsu.edu/buildings

**Architects/Designers/Planners for Social Responsibility (ADPSR)**
510-845-1000
http://www.adpsr.org

**BUILT GREEN®**
425-460-8238
http://www.builtgreen.net

**Center for Maximum Potential Building Systems (CMPBS)**
512-928-4786
http://www.cmpbs.org

**Center for Neighborhood Technology**
773-278-4800
http://www.cnt.org

**Center for Sustainable Systems**
734-764-1412
http://css.snre.umich.edu

**Cleveland Green Building Coalition**
216-961-8850
http://www.clevelandgbc.org

**Congress for the New Urbanism**
312-551-7300
http://www.cnu.org

**Development Center for Appropriate Technology**
520-624-6628
http://www.dcat.net

**Ecohaus**
800-281-9785
http://www.ecohaus.com

**Environmental Health Watch**
216-961-4646
http://www.ehw.org

**Environment Web Directory**
http://www.webdirectory.com

**Georgia Tech's Sustainable Facilities & Infrastructure Program**
404-894-8089
http://maven.gtri.gatech.edu/sfi

**Global Green USA Headquarters**
310-581-2700
http://www.globalgreen.org

Green America, National Association of Home Builders Research Center
800-638-8556
http://www.nahbrc.com

Green America –
National Green Pages™
800-584-7336
www.greenamericatoday.org

Green Clips
415-928-7941
http://www.greenclips.com

Greener Buildings
www.greenerbuildings.com

The Green Guide
800-647-5463
http://www.thegreenguide.com

Green Home
202-544-5336
www.greenhome.org

Green Roundtable/Nexus
617-374-3740, ext. 4
http://www.greenroundtable.org

GreenSeal
202-872-6400
http://www.greenseal.org

GreenSource
866-664-8243
www.greensource.construction.com

International Initiative for Sustainable Built Environment
www.iisbe.org

Los Angeles Sustainable Building Initiative
http://www.sustainla.org

National Environmental Directory
http://www.environmentaldirectory.net

Oikos Green Building Source
800-346-0104
http://www.oikos.com

Pennsylvania Governor's Green Government Council (GGGC)
717-783-9981
http://www.gggc.state.pa.us

Portland Bureau of Planning & Sustainability
503-823-7222
http://www.portlandonline.com

Process Guidelines for High-Performance Buildings
http://sustainable.state.fl.us/fdi/edesign/resource/index.html

Regenerative Ventures
510-644-9300
www.regen-net.com

Santa Monica Green Building Design & Construction Guidelines
310-458-8549
http://greenbuildings.santa-monica.org

Scottsdale, Arizona's Green Building Program
480-312-7080
http://www.ci.scottsdale.az.gov/greenbuilding

Seattle Sustainable Building Policy
http://www.cityofseattle.net/sustainablebuilding/SBpolicy.htm

Smart Communities Network
National Center for Appropriate Technology
406-494-4572
www.ncat.org

Smart Growth
202-962-3623
http://www.smartgrowth.org
http://www.smartcommunities.ncat.org

Sustainable Buildings Industry Council
202-628-7400
http://www.sbicouncil.org

Sustainable Building Sources
http://www.greenbuilder.com/general/BuildingSources.html

Sustainable Development International
+44 (0) 20 7871 0123
http://www.sustdev.org

Sustainable Product Purchasers Coalition
http://www.sppcoalition.org

Urban Ecology, Inc.
415-617-0158
http://www.urbanecology.org

U. S. Department of Energy: Energy Efficiency and Renewable Energy Network
800-342-5363
http://www.eere.energy.gov

U.S. Green Building Council
202-828-7422
http://www.usgbc.org

# Indoor Air Quality (IAQ)

Air Infiltration & Ventilation Centre
+32 (2) 655 77 11
http://www.aivc.org

American Council for Accredited Certification (ACAC)
888-808-8381
http://www.acac.org

American Lung Association
202-785-3355
http://www.lungusa.org

American Society of Heating, Refrigerating & Air-Conditioning Engineers (ASHRAE)
800-527-4723
http://www.ashrae.org

Building Science Corporation
978-589-5100
http://www.buildingscience.com

California Indoor Air Quality Program
http://www.cal-iaq.org

EPA Indoor Air Quality
202-343-9370
http://www.epa.gov/iaq

Healthy Indoor Air for America's Homes
406-994-3451
http://www.montana.edu/wwwcxair

Indoor Air Quality Association
(IAQA)
301-231-8388
http://www.iaqa.org

Indoor Environment Notebook
765-285-5780
*IAQ questions answered by Thad
Godish, Ph.D., Ball State University*
http://web.bsu.edu/ien

Institute of Inspection, Cleaning &
Restoration Certification
360-693-5675
http://www.iicrc.org

International Society of Indoor Air
Quality & Climate–ISIAQ
831-426-0148
http://www.isiaq.org

MidAtlantic Environmental Hygiene
Resource Center
215-387-4096
http://www.mehrc.org

National Institute of Building
Sciences (NIBS)
202-289-7800
http://www.nibs.org/projects.html

National Safety Council Air Quality
Program
800-621-7615
http://www.nsc.org

OSHA Indoor Air Quality
800-321-6742
http://www.osha.gov

Restoration Industry Association
443-878-1000
http://www.ascr.org

World Health Organization
41-22-791-21-11
http://www.who.int/indoorair/en

# Energy Efficiency &
# Renewable Energy

Air Conditioning and Refrigeration
Institute (ARI)
703-524-8800
http://www.ari.org

Alliance for Energy and Economic
Growth
202-463-5642
http://www.yourenergyfuture.org

Alliance to Save Energy
202-857-0666
http://www.ase.org

American Council for an Energy-
Efficient Economy (ACEEE)
202-507-4000
http://www.aceee.org

American Solar Energy Society, Inc.
(ASES)
303-443-3130
http://www.ases.org

American Wind Energy Association
202-383-2500
http://www.awea.org

Building Enclosure Technology &
Environment Council (BETEC)
National Institute of Building
Sciences
202-289-7800
http://www.nibs.org/betec.html

Center for Renewable Energy &
Sustainable Technology
Renewable Energy Policy Report
202-293-2898
http://www.crest.org

Database of State Incentives for
Renewable Energy
Lists, by state, renewable energy
incentives for homeowners and
businesses.
http://www.dsireusa.org

Efficient Windows Collaborative
Alliance to Save Energy
202-530-2254
http://www.efficientwindows.org

Energy Central Network
303-782-5510
http://www.energycentral.com

Energy Conservation in Buildings &
Community Systems
202-586-9449
http://www.ecbcs.org

Energy Efficiency & Renewable
Energy (EERE)
877-337-3463
http://www.eere.energy.gov

Energy Efficient Building Association
952-881-1098
http://www.eeba.org

Energy Ideas Clearinghouse
800-872-3568
http://www.energyideas.org

Energy Star
888-782-7937
http://www.energystar.gov

National Wind Technology Center
303-384-6979
http://www.nrel.gov/wind

Northeast Sustainable Energy
Association
413-774-6051
http://www.nesea.org

Northwest Energy Efficiency Alliance
800-411-0834
http://www.nwalliance.org

Online Fuel Cell Information Center
202-785-4222
http://www.fuelcells.org

Portland Energy Conservation
Incorporated
503-248-4636
http://www.peci.org

Renewable Energy Policy Project
& Center for Renewable Energy &
Sustainable Technology
202-293-2898
http://www.crest.org

Southface Energy Institute
404-872-3549
http://www.southface.org

U.S. Department of Energy
202-586-5000
http://www.energy.gov

## Building Rating Systems, Codes, Standards & Guidelines

**American Lung Association**
Health House® Program
800-788-5864
http://www.healthhouse.org

**American National Standards Institute (ANSI)**
202-293-8020
http://www.ansi.org

**American Society for Testing & Materials (ASTM)**
610-832-9585
http://www.astm.org

**American Society of Heating, Refrigerating & Air-Conditioning Engineers, Inc. (ASHRAE)**
404-636-8400
http://www.ashrae.org

**Building Research Establishment Environmental Assessment Method (BREEAM)**
http://www.breeam.org

**Collaborative for High Performance Schools (CHPS)**
415-957-9888
http://www.chps.net

**Climate Cool**
Climate Neutral Network
http://www.climateneutralnetwork.org

**EarthCraft House**
404-604-3636
http://www.earthcrafthouse.com

**Efficiency Valuation Organization**
http://www.evo-world.org

**Energy Efficient Building Association**
Criteria for Energy & Resource

Efficient Buildings
952-881-1098
http://www.eeba.org

**Energy Star**
888-782-7937
http://www.energystar.gov

**Environmental Choice Program**
800-478-0399
http://www.environmentalchoice.com

**Forest Stewardship Council**
612-353-4511
http://www.fscus.org

**Global Ecolabelling Network**
613-247-1900
www.globalecolabelling.net

**Global Reporting Initiative**
http://www.globalreporting.org

**Green Globes**
The Green Building Initiative
877-424-4241
www.thegbi.org

**GREENGUARD**
800-427-9681
http://www.greenguard.org

**Green Seal**
202-872-6400
http://www.greenseal.org

**GreenSpec**
Building Green
802-257-7300
http://www.buildinggreen.com/menus

**International Code Council (ICC)**
202-370-1800
http://www.iccsafe.org

**International Organization for Standardization (ISO)**
+41 (22) 749 01 11
http://www.iso.org

**National Association of Home Builders – Model Green Home Guidelines**
800-368-5242
www.nahb.org

**National Conference of States on Building Codes & Standards, Inc.**
703-437-0100 x238
http://www.ncsbcs.org

**The Natural Step**
503-241-1140
http://www.naturalstep.org

**New York City Department of Design and Construction**
http://www.nyc.gov/html/ddc/html/ddcgreen

**Sustainable Buildings Industry Council**
Green Building Guidelines
202-628-7400
http://www.sbicouncil.org

**U.S. Green Building Council's Leadership in Energy & Environmental Design (LEED)**
800-795-1747
http://www.usgbc.org

## Government Organizations

**Air Force Center for Environmental Excellence**
http://www.afcee.brooks.af.mil

**Energy Efficiency & Renewal Energy Network**
877-337-3463
http://www.eere.goe.gov

**Energy Information Administration**
202-586-8800
http://www.eia.doe.gov

**ENERGY STAR (EPA)**
888-782-7937
http://www.energystar.gov

**Fannie Mae**
202-752-7000
http://www.fanniemae.com

**Federal Energy Management Program**
http://www1.eere.energy.gov/femp

Intergovernmental Panel on Climate Change
+41 (22) 730 8208/84/54
http://www.ipcc.ch

Natural Resources Canada
613-995-0947
http://www.nrcan.gc.ca

New York State Energy Research & Development Authority (NYSERDA)
518-862-1090
http://www.nyserda.org

Office of Building Technology, State & Community Programs
http://www.eere.energy.gov/buildings

Partnership for Advancing Technology in Housing (PATH)
800-245-2691
http://www.pathnet.org

U.S. Department of Energy (DOE)
202-586-5000
http://www.energy.gov

U.S. Housing & Urban Development Department (HUD)
202-708-1112
http://www.hud.gov

## Professional Associations

Affordable Comfort Incorporated
724-627-5200
http://www.affordablecomfort.org

Air Conditioning Contractors of America
703-575-4477
http://www.acca.org

Air Conditioning, Heating & Refrigeration Institute (AHRI)
703-524-8800
http://www.ahrinet.org

Alternative Fluorocarbons Environmental Acceptability Study
http://www.afeas.org

American Architectural Manufacturers Association
847-303-5664
http://www.aamanet.org

American Council for an Energy-Efficient Economy
202-507-4000
http://www.aceee.org

American Gas Association
202-824-7000
http://www.aga.org

American Institute of Architects
800-242-3837
http://www.aia.org

American Society of Heating, Refrigerating & Air-Conditioning Engineers, Inc. (ASHRAE)
404-636-8400
http://www.ashrae.org

American Society of Mechanical Engineers
800-843-2763
http://www.asme.org

American Solar Energy Society
303-443-3130
http://www.ases.org

American Wind Energy Association
202-383-2500
http://www.awea.org

Association of Energy Engineers
770-447-5083
http://www.aeecenter.org

Association of Higher Education Facilities Officers (APPA)
703-684-1446
http://www.appa.org

Building Owners & Managers Association (BOMA)
202-408-2662
http://www.boma.org

Edison Electric Institute
202-508-5000
http://www.eei.org

Energy & Environmental Building Association
952-881-1098
http://www.eeba.org

Gas Appliance Manufacturers Association (GAMA)
703-524-8800
http://www.ahrinet.org

International Facility Management Association (IFMA)
713-623-4362
http://www.ifma.org

Manufactured Housing Institute
703-558-0400
http://www.mfghome.org

National Association of Demolition Contractors
800-541-2412
http://www.demolitionassociation.com

National Association of Energy Service Companies
202-822-0950
http://www.naesco.org

National Association of Home Builders (NAHB)
800-368-5242
http://www.nahb.com

National Association of Housing & Redevelopment Officials
877-866-2476
http://www.nahro.org

National Association of State Energy Officials (NASEO)
703-299-8800
http://www.naseo.org

National Center for Appropriate Technology (NCAT)
800-275-6228
http://www.ncat.org

Natural Resources Defense Council (NRDC)
212-727-2700
http://www.nrdc.org

Residential Energy Service Network
760-806-3448
http://www.natresnet.org

Solar Energy Industries Association
202-682-0556
http://www.seia.org

Weatherization Assistance Program
Technical Assistance Center
202-624-5867
http://www.waptac.org

## Other Organizations

**Economic Input-Output Life Cycle
Assessment**
Green Design Institute, Carnegie
Mellon University
412-248-2299
http://www.eiolca.net

**Environmental Building Association
of N.Y. State, Inc.**
518-357-8926
http://www.eba-nys.org

**Habitat for Humanity International**
800-422-4828
http://www.habitat.org

**United Nations Environment
Programme (UNEP)**
http://www.unep.org

**World Business Council for
Sustainable Development**
+41 (22) 839 3100
http://www.wbcsd.ch

## Research Organizations

**Brookhaven National Laboratory**
631-344-8000
http://www.bnl.gov

**Building & Fire Research Laboratory**
(National Institute of Standards and
Technology)
301-975-5900
http://www.nist.gov.bfrl

**Buildings Technology Center**
Oak Ridge National Laboratory
http://www.ornl.gov/btc

**Carnegie-Mellon Green Design
Institute**
412-268-2299
http://gdi.ce.cmu.edu

**Electric Power Research Institute**
800-313-3774
http://www.epri.com

**Florida Solar Energy Center**
321-638-1000
http://www.fsec.ucf.edu

**Lighting Research Center**
518-687-7100
http://www.lrc.rpi.edu

**National Association of Home
Builders Research Center**
800-638-8556
http://www.nahbrc.org

**National Renewable Energy
Laboratory (NREL)**
303-275-3000
http://www.nrel.gov

**Rocky Mountain Institute**
970-927-3851
http://www.rmi.org

**U.S. EPA Environmentally Preferable
Purchasing Program (EPP)**
http://www.epa.gov/opptintr/epp

## Publications: Magazines & Newsletters

*The Air Conditioning, Heating &
Refrigeration News*
800-837-8337
http://www.achrnews.com

*Appliance Design Magazine*
248-633-4818
http://www.appliancedesign.com

*Appliance Magazine*
http://www.appliance.com

*Architectural Record*
212-904-2594
http://archrecord.construction.com

*The Architectural Review*
http://www.arplus.com

*Builder Magazine*
202-452-0800
http://www.builderonline.com

*Building Design & Construction*
630-288-8000
http://www.bdcnetwork.com

*Building Operating Management
Magazine*
800-727-7995
http://www.facilitiesnet.com/bom

*Buildings Magazine*
319-364-6167
http://www.buildings.com

*Design Cost Data*
800-533-5680
http://www.dcd.com

*EcoIQ*
408-865-0888
http://www.ecoiq.com/magazine/
index.html

*Engineered Systems*
847-763-9534
http://www.esmagazine.com

*Environmental Building News*
802-257-7300
http://www.BuildingGreen.com

*Environmental Design &
Construction*
847-763-9534
http://www.edcmag.com

*Green Builder Magazine*
513-407-5611
http://www.greenbuildermag.com

*Green @ Work*
561-693-4469
http://www.greenatworkmag.com

*Heating/Piping/Air Conditioning
(HPAC Engineering)*
216-696-7000
http://www.hpac.com

*Home Energy Magazine*
510-524-5405
http://www.homeenergy.org

*Home Furnishings News*
212-979-4800
http://www.hfnmag.com

*Home Power Magazine*
800-707-6585
http://www.homepower.com

*Interiors & Sources Magazine*
319-364-6167
http://www.interiorsandresources.com

*The Journal of Light Construction*
802-879-3335
http://www.jlconline.com

*Natural Home*
800-340-5846
http://www.naturalhomemagazine.com

*New Village*
510-420-1361
http://www.newvillagepress.net

*Remodeling Magazine*
202-452-0800
http://www.remodeling.hw.net

*Residential Architect*
202-452-0800
http://ra.hw.net

*Solar Today Magazine*
303-443-3130
www.ases.org

*Sustainable Facility*
847-763-9534
http://www.energyandpowermanagement.com

*The Urban Ecologist*
415-617-0161
http://www.urbanecology.org

## Publications: Books

*A Better Place to Live: New Designs for Tomorrow's Communities.* Michael Corbett. Published by Rodale Press, 1981. A guide to building and planning considerations for more sustainable development and living.

*Architecture and the Environment: Bioclimatic Building Design.* David Lloyd Jones. Published by The Overlook Press, 1998. Fifty examples of architecture throughout the world built according to bioclimatic—or green—guidelines. Past, present, and future examples are accompanied by charts of building energy features, energy performance, and environmental health features.

*Biomimicry: Innovation Inspired by Nature.* Janine M. Benyus. Published by Harper Perennial, 2002. Biomimicry shows how nature offers countless examples of how to design our products, our processes, and our lives. Benyus, a noted science writer, explains how this new science is transforming everything from harnessing energy to feeding the world. www.biomimicry.net

*Building Air Quality, A Guide for Building Owners and Facility Managers.* Published by EPA and NIOSH. http://www.cdc.gov/niosh/baqtoc.html

*Building Green: A Complete How-To Guide to Alternative Building Methods.* Clarke Snell and Tim Callahan. Published by Lark Books, 2005. Hands-on manual of working with alternative green materials and sustainable approaches, such as straw bale, cob, cord wood, and living roofs, with over 1,000 photographs.

*Climatic Considerations in Building and Urban Design.* Baruch Givoni. Published by John Wiley & Sons Publishers, 1998. Comprehensive reference on building and urban climatology.

*Creating the Not So Big House: Insights and Ideas for the New American Home.* Sarah Susanka. Published by Taunton, 2002. Explores the modern home and how to create intimate, livable spaces without owning massive homes. Profiles 25 house designs from around the country.

*The Death and Life of Great American Cities.* Jane Jacobs. Published by Random House, 2002. Offers valuable lessons not yet learned about building healthy, safe, and habitable cities.

*Design with Nature.* Ian L. McHarg. Published by John Wiley & Sons, 1995. Presents a thorough analysis of the relationship between the built environment and nature. This was one of the first books to bring forward planning concepts in environmental sensitivity, and has since served as the guide for a number of developments including Civano in Tucson, Arizona.

*EBN Archives CD-ROM.* Edited by Alex Wilson and Nadav Malin. This CD-ROM includes all back issues of *Environmental Building News*, with a cumulative index, a comprehensive green building products directory, and detailed bibliography of green building resources. http://www.buildinggreen.com

*Ecological Design.* Sim Van der Ryn and Stuart Cowan. Published by Island Press, 1995. This book discusses how the living world and humanity can be reunited by making ecology the basis for design. Design principles are presented that can help build a more efficient, less toxic, healthier, and more sustainable world.

*The Ecology of Building Materials.* Bjorn Berge, translated by Filip Henley. Published by Architectural Press, 2001. An in-depth review of building materials' composition and properties from an ecological perspective. Includes recommendations of environmentally friendly construction methods, as well as materials and a wide offering of alternative, and often historic methods.

*Environmental Design Charrette Workbook.* Donald Watson. Published by the American Institute of Architects, 1996. Highlights design workshops dealing with energy efficiency, building technology, environmental approaches to landscaping, waste prevention and resource reclamation, and planning and cultural issues.

*Environmental Remediation Estimating Methods, 2nd Edition.* Richard R. Rast. Published by RSMeans, 1997. Estimating guidance for over 50 types of remediation technologies—from air sparging and air stripping to drum removal, excavation and extraction, landfill disposal, piping, UST closure, transportation, and more.

*Environmental Resource Guide.* The American Institute of Architects. Published by John Wiley & Sons, Inc., 1998. Provides a comprehensive guide to resources for environmental building, updated three times a year. Project reports present case studies that incorporate environmental

concepts and technologies. Material reports detail the environmental aspects and life cycle of building materials.

*Green Architecture.* James Wines. Published by Taschen, 2000. A discussion about what makes a building green, complete with a wide range of images and case studies.

*Green Architecture: Design for an Energy-Conscious Future.* Brenda and Robert Vale. Published by Bulfinch Press, 1991. Provides an overview of resource-conscious building and an exploration of the relationship between the built environment and such critical problems as power supply, waste and recycling, food production, and transportation.

*Green Building: A Primer for Builders, Consumers, and Realtors.* Bion D. Howard. Published by Building Environmental Science and Technology. http://www. energybuilder.com/greenbld.htm

*Green Building Materials: A Guide to Product Selection and Specification, 2nd Edition.* Ross Spiegel and Dru Meadows. Published by John Wiley & Sons, 2006. A hands-on guide to today's wide range of green building materials including what they are, where to find them, and how to use them effectively.

*Green Building Products: The GreenSpec Guide to Residential Building Materials, 2nd Edition.* Alex Wilson, BuildingGreen, Inc., and Environmental Building News. Published by New Society Publishers, 2006. Product directory and review of green materials for residential homebuilding.

*Green Building Resource Guide.* John Hermannsson, AIA. Published by Taunton Press, 1997.

*Green Development: Integrating Ecology and Real Estate.* Rocky Mountain Institute: Alex Wilson, Jenifer L. Uncapher, Lisa McManigal, L. Hunter Lovins, Maureen Cureton, William D. Browning. Published by John Wiley & Sons Inc. 1998. Every stage of the development process is examined in detail: market research, site planning, design, approvals, financing, construction, marketing, and occupancy.

*Green Developments CD-ROM.* Rocky Mountain Institute, 2001. Enables viewers to explore 200 individual green real-estate development case studies. It features photographs, plans, and drawings along with video and audio clips of projects, resources, web links, financing, marketing, and approvals highlights, and an introduction to the green development approach and sustainable building.

*The Green House: New Directions in Sustainable Architecture.* Alanna Stang and Christopher Hawthorne. Published by Princeton Architectural Press, 2005. An exploration of green residential design, featuring more than 20 home plans.

*Greening the Government Through Efficient Energy Management.* Executive Office of the President, Executive Order 13123, June 1999.

*GreenSpec Directory, 6th Edition.* From the editors of *Environmental Building News.* Published by BuildingGreen, Inc. A comprehensive product directory with manufacturers' literature, and guideline specification, for building professionals.

*The Harris Directory*. The Harris Reports. A Web database of more than 5,000 recycled and pollution-preventing materials for home, office, and garden; including products that contain less toxic ingredients and offer safer cleaning options. http://www.harrisdirectory.com

*Healthy House* books. John Bower. Published by the Healthy House Institute. A number of books on how to design, build, and create a healthy house can be found at http://www.hhinst.com/booksvideos.html

*Historic Preservation: Project Planning & Estimating*. Swanke Hayden Connell Architects. Published by RSMeans, 2001. Expert guidance on managing historic restoration, rehabilitation, and preservation—and determining and controlling the cost. Includes restoration techniques for over 75 materials.

*The HOK Guidebook to Sustainable Design, 2nd Edition*. Sandra F. Mendler, AIA and William Odell, AIA. Published by John Wiley & Sons, 2006. A comprehensive, practical guide for architects, engineers, planners, interior designers, and landscape architects to integrate sustainable architecture in their work.

*Homemade Money: How to Save Energy and Dollars in Your Home*. Richard Heede and the staff of the Rocky Mountain Institute. Published by Brick House Publishing Company, 1995. Describes practical ways to save energy and dollars in an existing or new residence.

*How Buildings Learn: What Happens After They're Built*. Stewart Brand. Published by Penguin, 1995. Discusses how buildings adapt over time. Photos of case studies are used throughout to show before/after states of buildings. Design principles are described for creating an adaptable/flexible building.

*Life-Cycle Costing Manual for the Federal Energy Management Program, NIST Handbook 135*. S.K. Fuller and S.R. Peterson. Published by the National Institute of Standards and Technology, 1995. http://www.fire.nist.gov/bfrlpubs/build96/art121.html

*Natural Capitalism: Creating the Next Industrial Revolution*. Paul Hawken, Amory Lovins, & L. Hunter Lovins. Published by Little, Brown and Company, 1999. This groundbreaking book describes a future in which business and environmental interests increasingly overlap, and in which companies can improve their bottom lines and help solve environmental problems. http://www.rmi.org

*Natural Ventilation in Buildings: A Design Handbook*. Edited by Francis Allard. Published by James & James, 1998. This book describes the real potential of natural ventilation, its appropriate use, design and dimensioning, and how to overcome barriers.

*The New Natural House Book: Creating a Healthy, Harmonious, and Ecologically Sound Home*. David Pearson. Published by Fireside, 1998. A handbook for a healthy, environmentally benign, natural home; including principles, elements, and spaces.

*The Next American Metropolis: Ecology, Community, and the American Dream, 3rd Edition*. Peter Calthorpe. Published by Princeton Architectural Press, 1995. Places the "American Dream" of a suburban home for the nuclear family in its historical and ecological context. It suggests mechanisms of transit-oriented development including mixed-use, pedestrian-friendly pockets. Features case studies from across the United States.

*The Once and Future Forest: A Guide to Forest Restoration Strategies*. Leslie Jones Sauer. Published by Island Press, 1998. Developed by landscape design firm Andropogon Associates, this is a guidebook for restoring and managing natural landscapes. Focusing on remnant forest systems, it describes methods of restoring and linking forest fragments to re-create a whole landscape fabric.

*The Passive Solar Energy Book*. Edward Mazria. Published by Rodale, 1979. A complete guide to the passive solar home, greenhouse and building design.

*A Practical Guide for Commissioning Existing Buildings*. Available at http://www.PECI.org

*A Primer on Sustainable Building*. Dianna Lopez Barnett and William D. Browning. Published by Rocky Mountain Institute, 1995. Provides an overview for architects, builders, developers, students, and others interested in environmentally responsive home building and small commercial development. Topics include: site and habitat restoration, transportation integration, food–producing landscapes, energy efficient design, materials selection, indoor air quality, cost implications, and more.

*Rural by Design.* Randall Arendt, et al. Published by APA Planners Press, 1994. Advocates creative, practical land-use planning techniques to preserve open space and community character. Case studies demonstrate how rural and suburban communities have preserved open space, established land trusts, and designed affordable housing appropriate for their size and character.

*Ten Shades of Green: Architecture and the Natural World.* Peter Buchanan and Kenneth Frampton. Published by Architectural League of NY, 2006. Case study of ten buildings that illustrate how environmental responsibility and green design influence modern architectural pursuits.

*Value Engineering: Practical Applications.* Alphonse J. Dell'Isola. Published by RSMeans, 1997. Provides techniques to control costs and maximize quality in facilities design, construction, and operations.

*Visions for a New American Dream.* Anton Nelessen. Published by APA Planners Press, 1994. Provides practical information to help planners and designers create small communities that combine the best design principles of the past with the technological advances of the present to combat suburban sprawl.

# Glossary

**abatement**
The encapsulation or removal of building materials containing pollutants (such as lead or asbestos) to prevent the release of or exposure to fibers.

**activated charcoal (activated carbon)**
A material obtained principally as a by-product of the paper industry and used in filters for absorbing smoke, odors, and vapors. (**activated charcoal filtration** A filtration system that pulls certain chemicals and components from the air.)

**active walls**
Building walls that act as a generator or collector of energy. An example is a double glass wall that collects solar energy and reflects excess heat when the desired interior envelope temperature has been reached. This combination reduces a facility's net heating and cooling load.

**adaptable building**
A building that can be easily updated or modified to meet changing needs or requirements.

**adobe**
Earthen, sun-cured brick. A relatively labor-intensive, but low-embodied energy material, adobe absorbs excess heat during hot days and releases it during cool nights, thereby moderating a building's internal temperature.

**air door**
An invisible barrier of high-velocity air that separates different environments. Sometimes called *air walls*, air doors are typically used for garage-type or larger doors to reduce infiltration and ex-filtration.

**airflow retarders**
Continuous materials, such as gypsum board, sheathing materials, rigid insulation, and sprayed foam insulation, that resist differences in air pressure caused by mechanical systems, the stack effect, and wind.

**albedo**
The ratio of reflected light on a surface compared to the total amount of light.

**annual fuel utilization efficiency (AFUE)**
A seasonal efficiency rating that is an accurate estimation of fuel used for furnaces and direct-fired forced hot air systems. It measures the system efficiency and accounts for startup, cool-down, and other operating losses.

**audio masking system**
Reducing distracting sounds and increasing speech privacy through the use of sound-masking equipment or software. Some systems provide protection from laser beams and other high-tech sound detection devices.

**backcasting**
A creative thinking process in which the desired result of a project is first envisioned, and then different means of achieving it are proposed. Solutions tend to be less constrained by preconceived ideas.

**balance point**
The temperature outside at which the heat lost from a building equals the heat gained from the occupants and equipment inside.

**battery charge controller**
A device that modulates the charge current into a battery to protect against overcharging and the associated loss of electrolytes. A low-voltage disconnect protects the battery from becoming excessively discharged by disconnecting the load.

**BEES (Building for Environmental and Economic Sustainability)**
A methodology that considers multiple environmental and economic impacts over the building product's entire life cycle to develop a rational decision-making scoring system.

**biodegradable**
Capable of breaking down and decaying naturally and returning to the earth.

**biological wastewater management**
Using natural or simulated wetlands to purify wastewater through biological processes.

**biophilia**
A field of research that studies the correlation between building ecology (specifically more "natural"

environments that feature views to nature, daylight, and fresh air) and good health.

**black water**
Wastewater from toilets and other plumbing fixtures that may be contaminated with bacteria or other harmful organisms.

**blast furnace slag**
A waste product of steel production that can be used to replace aggregate in concrete mix to reduce energy consumption and solid waste.

**BLCC**
A National Institute of Standards and Technology (NIST) software program that performs life-cycle analysis of buildings and components, useful for comparing alternate designs that have higher initial costs, but lower operating costs over the life of the building.

**BREEAM (Building Research Establishment Environmental Assessment Method)**
A whole building standard for the UK used to assess the environmental performance of buildings.

**brownfield sites**
Abandoned or underused industrial sites that often require remediation of hazardous waste or other pollutant contamination prior to reuse.

**building ecology**
The environment inside a building, such as air quality, lighting, and acoustics, and its effect on a building's occupants and the overall environment.

**building integrated photovoltaics (BIPV)**
Substituting a conventional part of building construction with photovoltaic material. Shingles,

standing seam metal roofing, spandrel glass, and overhead skylight glass are some examples.

**carbon absorption**
A water treatment system most often used for residential applications that removes the odor and unpleasant taste sometimes found in municipal water supplies. Carbon filters are not certified for removing VOCs, lead, coliform, or asbestos.

**carbon dioxide ($CO_2$)**
An odorless, incombustible gas emitted by respiration, organic decomposition, and fossil fuel combustion. Among its uses are fire extinguishers, aerosols, and refrigeration. Carbon dioxide is considered a greenhouse gas, because it traps radiation and effects global warming.

**CASBEE (Comprehensive Assessment System for Building Environmental Efficiency)**
A whole building standard and labeling tool used in Japan and developed by the Japan Sustainable Building Consortium (JSBC).

**certified forest product**
A product created from materials obtained from forests that have met specific environmental guidelines, and that are certified for use in green construction. *See also* **Forest Stewardship Council.**

**certified wood**
Wood from well-managed forests that replenish, rather than deplete, old growth timber.

**CFL** *See* **compact fluorescent lamp.**

**chilled water system**
A cooling system in which the refrigerant expands through a thermal expansion valve. In order for the system to operate, the refrigerant must be compressed from a low temperature gas to a high temperature.

**chlorofluorocarbons (CFCs)**
Chemicals traditionally used in air conditioners, paints, aerosol sprays, and other products. CFCs destroy ozone molecules in the upper atmosphere, thereby contributing to global warming.

**chromated copper arsenate (CCA)**
A highly-toxic chemical made up of chromium, copper, and arsenic. The EPA has classified CCA as a restricted use product for certified pesticide applicators only. Pressure-treated wood, formerly treated with CCA, now uses a different, less toxic process for residential applications.

**cistern**
A tank used to collect and store rainwater for reuse, typically for landscape watering.

**clean energy**
Energy obtained from a renewable source that produces zero or low emissions and has minimal environmental impact.

**Climate Neutral™ Network (CNN)** A nonprofit organization whose mission is to help achieve a net-zero impact on the earth's climate. Its Climate Cool™ brand identifies select products that eliminate or offset greenhouse emissions throughout their life cycle.

**cob**
Earth and straw molded by hand into sculptural walls that work well in hot, dry climates, along the same principle as adobe. Cob can be used in other climates, but the building may require supplemental insulation or additional heating or cooling.

**combustion efficiency**
A measurement of output versus energy consumed for boilers and hot water heaters.

**commissioning**
The process of ensuring that building systems are designed, installed, functionally tested, and capable of being operated and maintained to conform to the design intent.

**commissioning plan**
A document or group of documents prepared by a commissioning agent that defines the commissioning process in the various phases of the project.

**commissioning report**
The primary record document for commissioning for each specific building system, as well as the facility as a whole. The report should include a description of installed systems and commissioning tasks, the commissioning plan, completed pre-functional test checklists and functional performance tests, and findings and recommendations.

**compact fluorescent lamp (CFL)**
Efficient light bulbs that use far less energy than standard, incandescent bulbs. CFLs typically provide 8,000 hours of usage, compared to less than 2,000 for incandescent bulbs.

**compost**
Organic fertilizer created from plants and other biodegradable materials that decompose naturally.

**composting toilet**
A toilet that requires little or no water and composts waste into fertilizer.

**conduction**
The transfer of heat across a solid substance. Every material has a specific conductivity (U-value) and resistance (the inverse of the U-value, called R-value). Metal is a particularly good conductor.

**convection**
The transfer of heat in a fluid or gas, such as in air, experienced as a cold draft next to a leaky window or an open door. Methods of preventing convective heat transfer include sealing gaps around windows, doors, electrical outlets, and other openings in the building envelope.

**cool roof**
A roof made of materials (typically light in color) that have a high thermal emittance and solar reflectance. Cool roofs can substantially reduce a building's cooling load.

**daylighting**
Admitting natural light into a space, including distributing light at uniform levels, avoiding glare and reflections, and controlling artificial light to achieve energy and cost savings.

**daylight transmittance**
The percentage of visible light that a glazing transmits.

**dead band widening system**
A control system for boilers and furnaces that allows for a wide system dead band, or time delay, from set point. Burners can be shut off and stay on for longer periods of time, with fewer cycles. Avoiding short boiler cycling increases the net system efficiency.

**deconstruction**
A green building strategy that involves reuse of construction materials salvaged from buildings that are being demolished or remodeled. New building designs may include plans for deconstruction and later reuse of materials.

**desiccant system**
A type of air filtration system that removes waterborne contaminants.

**design charrette**
A focused, team effort to complete an architectural design in a short period of time by addressing the project's goals, needs, and limitations to find creative, but realistic solutions.

**Design for the Environment (DfE)**
A model for environmentally sensitive building design developed by the U.S.

Environmental Protection Agency. The purpose of DfE is to analyze and improve performance, while reducing the environmental risks of products and practices.

## direct expansion system (DX)

A cooling system with refrigerant that expands through a thermal expansion valve. The heat is then removed from the airstream by way of the airstream DX coil.

## direct solar gain

Solar heating achieved when sunlight enters a room directly and heats the room or is stored in walls or floors.

## discounting

Adjusting cash flows to a common point in time (often the present) when an analysis is performed, or a decision has to be made in the green building design process. The conversion of all costs and savings to time-equivalent "present values" allows them to be added and compared in a meaningful way. To make future costs and savings time-equivalent, they must be adjusted for both inflation and the real earning power of money.

## diurnal flux

Temperature fluctuation between the day and night hours.

## DOE-2

A sophisticated U.S. Department of Energy software program designed to predict a building's hourly energy usage and cost, given weather data, a description of the building and its HVAC equipment, and the utility rates structure.

## down-cycling

Using one product's materials to make other products, such as turning plastic soda containers into park benches (rather than recycling into soda containers). This approach is preferable to disposing of materials directly into landfills, but less favored than recycling.

## drip irrigation

A landscape watering system that uses low water pressure and flexible tubing placed on the ground. These systems conserve water by targeting the roots of plants, rather than letting water evaporate as sprinklers would do.

## dual-flush toilets

Toilets that conserve water by allowing different settings for liquid versus solid waste.

## earth coupling

The practice of building into the ground to take advantage of the vast thermal mass of the earth, which remains a constant temperature at a certain depth below grade (depending on the climate).

## earthen flooring

Earth compacted with fibers such as straw and conditioned with natural oils to form a stable, hard flooring surface.

## earth sheltering

The practice of building into the ground or earth-berming to protect a building from inclement weather and strong wind. It takes advantage of the vast thermal mass of the ground, which remains at a constant temperature at a certain depth below grade (depending on the climate).

## EcoEffect

A Swedish national environmental assessment system that focuses on energy consumption and life cycle cost analysis.

## EcoProfile

A whole building standard for Norway.

## electric screw compressor

An electric-powered rotary compressor that uses less electricity than traditional reciprocating refrigeration compressors (typically .7–.95 kWh/ton hr).

## electric scroll compressor

An electric-powered rotary compressor that uses less electricity than traditional reciprocating refrigeration compressors (typically .9–1.4 kWh/ton hr).

## electrostatic precipitator

A type of filtering device that captures smoke and dust particles in an interior space. It electrically charges, or "ionizes," the particles as they pass through a screen, so that they are attracted to electrically charged plates.

## embodied energy

The energy needed to produce a building product, not accounting for transportation, durability, reuse, and recycling.

## emissivity

A product's ability to emit thermal radiation, expressed as a fraction between zero and one. Most non-metallic solids have a high emissivity, while shiny metals have the lowest. Fenestrations that reflect radiant rays have a low emissivity. *See also* **low-emissivity [low-E] coatings.**

## end-use/least cost

A major green consideration when designing a building and selecting products. This factor involves an evaluation of the end users' needs and explores different ways of achieving them at the lowest cost with the greatest efficiency over time.

## energy efficiency ratio (EER)

A measure of energy efficiency in the cooling mode that represents the ratio of total cooling capacity to electrical energy input.

## energy modeling

Using computer modeling software to analyze alternative energy systems to help determine the most efficient design. It typically involves not only mechanical and electrical systems, but building orientation, materials, lighting, and landscaping.

**energy recovery**
A process whereby energy from one source is used to provide energy for another process.

**energy recovery ventilator (ERV)**
Mechanical equipment that is added to the ventilation system, featuring a heat exchanger to provide controlled ventilation into a building, while increasing energy efficiency.

**energy savings performance contract (ESPC)**
A contracting partnership between an agency/consumer and an energy services company (ESCO) in which the ESCO evaluates the facility's energy needs and consumption and identifies strategies for improvement. The ESCO often helps pay for the initial cost of implementation in exchange for a share of the energy savings.

**ENERGY STAR®**
A U.S. Environmental Protection Agency and Department of Energy whole building standard for rating the energy efficiency of appliances, electronics, lighting, homes, commercial buildings, and industrial facilities. As of the printing of this book, the ENERGY STAR® label applies to more than 40 product categories.

**ENERGY-10™**
A whole-building energy analysis software program that performs hourly energy simulations in order to quantify, analyze, assess, and illustrate the effects of changes in building insulation, windows, lighting systems, and mechanical systems, as well as daylighting, passive solar, and natural ventilation for building and homes less than 10,000 SF. Developed by the National Renewable Energy Laboratory's (NREL) Center for Building and Thermal Systems.

**EnergyPlus**
Stand-alone energy analysis software that includes simulation time steps of less than an hour, including solar thermal, multi-zone airflow, photovoltaic, and fuel cell simulations.

**engineered wood**
Composite wood product made from pieces of recycled/reconstituted/scrap wood and fibers bonded together with adhesive to create a durable and resource friendly substitute for raw-sawn lumber.

**enthalpy wheels**
Also referred to as *heat wheels*, a heat recovery system that removes moisture from the ambient air while also cooling the ventilated air by passing all incoming air over a desiccant-coated wheel. This process removes up to 85% of heat/moisture.

**environmental audit**
An assessment of a facility's compliance with local and national environmental requirements.

**environmental building consultant**
A specialist in sustainable building design who makes recommendations regarding the impact of building materials as they are produced, including waste generated in the construction process and over the product life cycle.

**Environmental Choice**
A Canadian ecolabeling organization, first established in 1988, that provides market incentives to suppliers and manufacturers of environmentally-sound products and services. The EcoLogo is issued to Environmental Choice-certified products after third-party verification.

**Environmental Protection Agency (EPA)**
The U.S. government agency that develops and enforces environmental standards and regulations enacted by Congress.

**evaporative cooling**
Drawing heat from the air to vaporize water, making the resultant air cooler, but more humid.

**external insulation finish system (EIFS)**
Commonly known as synthetic stucco, an exterior non-load-bearing wall finish system composed of a continuous insulation layer, base coat, and finish. Though touted for its insulating and energy-savings qualities, EIFS must be carefully installed according to manufacturer's guidelines to avoid water penetration.

**fiber optics**
The transmission of light pulses through bundles of fine, transparent glass or plastic fibers. One green application of fiber optics is its use in allowing sunlight from roofs to penetrate different areas of the core of buildings. Fiber optic lighting does not add to the building's heat load like conventional incandescent lights.

**filtering faucet**
A faucet that filters out particles to improve the taste, appearance, and safety of water.

**fixed solar collection systems** Systems mounted to the ground or roof at an angle optimal to receive direct sunlight. Although immovable, these systems are often favored for their simplicity and lower cost versus tracking-type systems.

**flow form features**
Artistic, decorative water features that can be incorporated into a building's ecology to maintain a pleasant humidity level, atmosphere, and acoustics.

**fly ash**
A waste product from coal-fired power plants. Up to 70% of the aggregate used in traditional concrete mixes can be replaced with fly ash to reduce

energy consumption and solid waste and increase chemical resistance and strength.

### Forest Stewardship Council (FSC)

An international organization formed in 1993 that is concerned with ecological, social, and economic aspects of the forest management practices used to produce wood products. In order to earn Forest Stewardship Council certification, a wood product must meet certain criteria as it moves from the logging site through to the end-user.

### formaldehyde

A toxic, colorless, pungent-smelling chemical used to manufacture building materials and products, such as glue in fiberboard. Sources of formaldehyde include building materials (such as cabinetry); smoking; household products; and the use of un-vented, fuel-burning appliances, such as fork lifts, gas stoves, and kerosene space heaters.

### geothermal heat

A system for heating buildings in which an underground water tank uses subsurface ground temperatures to keep the system water at a moderate temperature, thus requiring less energy to heat the water to hot enough temperatures to warm the building.

### glare

The difference in luminance ratio between a window and its adjoining space. Also refers to light hitting a person's eyes directly from a fixture, causing discomfort and reducing visual acuity.

### glazing

Window covering materials, such as glass and clear films, that allow light to enter, while providing weather protection.

### Global Ecolabelling Network

A nonprofit association composed of 26 ecolabeling organizations that use specific criteria to determine whether a product results in a lower environmental burden and impact in relation to comparable products.

### gray water

Wastewater recycled from appropriate sinks, showers, baths, and laundry, which can be used for watering plants, cooling HVAC equipment, and other purposes.

### Green Globes®

A web-based rating system used to assess the sustainability and environmental friendliness of a building design. After third-party verification of the score, the Green Globes logo and brand can be awarded to the project.

### green process

Manufacturing products with consideration for the source of materials, energy-efficient manufacturing methods, use of recycled materials in packaging, and reclaiming manufacturing waste.

### green products

Sustainable products that minimize the impact on the natural environment.

### green roof

Also called a *living roof*, a roof with a layer of soil and plantings that dissipates solar heat, provides good insulation, absorbs rainwater runoff, generates oxygen, and protects and therefore extends the life of the roofing material below. It can also give the roof space a garden-like appearance. The roofing becomes its own ecosystem with soil and plantings.

### Green Seal

A nonprofit organization and member of the Global Ecolabelling Network that certifies a wide variety of products, including building components, such as occupancy sensors, photovoltaic modules, residential central air conditioning systems, chillers, heat pumps, windows, window films, and paints.

### Green Star

A whole building standard and rating system for Australia's commercial and residential buildings, created by the Green Building Council of Australia.

### GREENGUARD

An independent, third-party certification program for testing products and materials for emissions of particles and chemicals, created by the GREENGUARD Environmental Institute™, an ANSI-accredited standards developer.

### GreenSpec Directory™

A compilation of over 2,000 energy-efficient, environmentally-friendly building products selected by the editors of *Environmental Building News*. Greenspec also contains guideline specification language.

### harvested rainwater

Rainwater collected in a storage unit that can be treated and used for a variety of applications, such as flushing toilets, serving HVAC units, washing clothes, and irrigation.

### Health House®

Building criteria developed by the American Lung Association® to encourage the construction of houses that have better indoor air quality and improve or reduce the impact on the overall environment. Health House analyzes ventilation, air filtration, moisture control, and healthy humidity levels, as well as reducing VOCs (volatile organic compounds).

### heat mirror technology

A type of window design that uses a low-emissivity coated film product suspended inside or between panes of an insulating glass unit. This is a lower-cost alternative to low-E glass double-pane units.

## heat recovery ventilators
Ventilators that capture heat from the exhausted air (or pre-cool the incoming air, depending on the climate).

## heat sink system
An energy recovery system that uses the exhaust over a thermal heat sink, then switches the incoming air to travel over the heat sink that was heated by the exhaust air.

## high-mass construction
A building construction approach using masonry, adobe, or other building materials that can lessen the extremes of diurnal flux, especially in arid climates.

## high-performance building
A building that is energy-efficient, healthy, and comfortable for its occupants.

## HK-BEAM
Acronym for Hong Kong Building Environmental Assessment Method, a voluntary whole building standard that analyzes and labels the environmental performance of buildings.

## Home Energy Rating System (HERS)
A scoring system established by the Residential Energy Services Network (RESNET) in which a home built to the specifications of the HERS Reference Home (based on the 2006 *International Energy Conservation Code*) scores a HERS Index of 100, while a net zero energy home scores a HERS Index of 0. The lower a home's HERS Index, the more energy-efficient it is.

## HOT2000™
Simulation software designed primarily for low-rise residential buildings that evaluates the effectiveness of cooling and heating systems, including thermal effectiveness and passive solar systems. HOT2000 is also used as the compliance software for the Canadian R-2000 program.

## hybrid photovoltaic generator system
A power system that combines solar photovoltaics with a conventional generator system to minimize life cycle costs. It takes advantage of the low operating cost of a photovoltaic array and the on-demand capability of a generator. To optimize cost, a PV system can incorporate a generator to run infrequently during cloudy periods. The PV array typically provides 70%–90% of the annual energy, and the generator provides the remainder.

## indigenous materials
Locally produced materials that support green building goals by reducing energy use and pollution from transportation, while boosting the local economy.

## indirect gain
Solar heating achieved without allowing the sun's rays to directly enter the space, achieved by installing glazing a few inches in front of a south-facing high-mass wall.

## indoor air quality (IAQ)
The measure of a building's air in terms of elements that affect occupant health, including factors such as proper humidification, odor, mold, and off-gassing of chemical agents.

## infill
Building on a vacant site or underutilized parcel of land within an established urban area rather than on the outskirts in order to promote more efficient use of existing infrastructure.

## infiltration
The entering and/or escaping of air from one space to another or from the outdoors, usually due to pressure or temperature differential. Infiltration can occur in routes established during construction, or over time as buildings settle or move slightly, and cracks are established.

## insolation
Amount of solar energy that reaches Earth's surface per unit of time, typically measured in BTUs per square foot per day or per hour.

## International Performance Measurement & Verification Protocol (IPMVP)
A leading international standard used in more than 40 countries. The IPMVP was developed by the Efficiency Valuation Organization (EVO) for use as a framework for measuring and verifying energy and water conservation, as well as indoor air quality.

## inverter
Power conditioning equipment for photovoltaic systems used to convert DC power from the photovoltaic arrays, wind turbines, water turbines, fuel cells, or batteries to AC power for the appliances. A rotary inverter is a DC motor driving an AC generator. More common are static inverters, which use power transistors to achieve the conversion electronically.

## isolated heat gain
Solar heating achieved using an attached sunspace, such as a greenhouse.

## land stewardship
Managing land and its resources with sustainability as the goal.

## LEED®
Leadership in Energy and Environmental Design (LEED), a U.S. Green Building Council rating system for commercial, institutional, and high-rise residential buildings. Used to evaluate environmental performance from a "whole building" perspective over a building's life cycle.

## leichtlehm
Literally translated from German as "light loam," this mixture of clay and straw is pressed and hardened to create a strong, natural building material.

### life-cycle assessment (LCA)

A multi-disciplinary approach to measuring environmental performance that analyzes all stages in the life of a product: raw material acquisition, manufacture, transportation, installation, use, recycling, and waste management.

### light pipes

Pipes lined with highly reflective film used to reflect light from a roof aperture to a space that may not be directly beneath the roof and which cannot therefore accommodate a standard skylight. Light pipes are generally used in small spaces like bathrooms or hallways.

### light pollution

The glare from inefficient outdoor lights, especially around highly populated areas, making it difficult to discern the features of the night sky.

### light shelves

A daylighting system based on sun path geometry, used to bounce light off a ceiling, project light deeper into a space, distribute light from above, and diffuse it to produce a uniform light level below.

### light to solar gain ratio (LSG)

The ratio of visible light transmittance to the solar hear gain coefficient (SHGC). LSG measures the ability of glazing to provide light without excess solar heat gain.

### linoleum

A natural, durable type of flooring that is made of pieces of cork mixed with linseed oil and resin.

### low-emissivity (low-E) coatings

Coatings applied to glass that allow the transmission of short-wave energy (visible light), but have a low emissivity-to-long-wave infrared radiation (heat). The result is a reduction in the facility's net heating and cooling requirements. The lower the emissivity, the lower the resultant U-value of the window.

### low-flow toilet

An economically and environmentally efficient toilet that uses less water per flush than a conventional model.

### Material Safety Data Sheet (MSDS)

An informational form published by manufacturers of hazardous materials to describe their dangers and safe handling procedures.

### maximum power point (MPP)

In photovoltaic systems, the point at which the most possible current is drawn from a cell, and the voltage subsequently drops off. The MPP changes slightly with temperature and intensity of sunlight. Most photovoltaic (PV) systems have power conditioning electronics, called **maximum power point trackers (MPPT)**, that constantly adjust the voltage in order to maximize power output. Simpler systems operate at a fixed voltage close to the optimal voltage.

### micro-hydro power

Power generated by moving water, usually on a fairly small scale, such as energy harnessed from a local river to power a small town.

### mold

Small organisms occurring naturally indoors and out, including on plants, foods, and leaves. In excessive quantities in an indoor environment, mold can be a health hazard. *See also* stachybotrys.

### NAHB Model Green Home Building Guidelines

National Home Building guidelines developed to help builders incorporate green building principles without significantly increasing construction costs.

### native landscape

Plantings that are selected because they have adapted to thrive in the local environment without irrigation, fertilizer, or pesticides, and that provide storm water management. *See also* xeriscaping.

### Natural Step

An international organization first developed in Sweden by oncologist Dr. Karl-Henrik Robèrt in 1989 that promotes a framework of sustainability, focusing on responsible, future-conscious use of Earth's natural resources. The U.S. membership is held by the Oregon Natural Step Network.

### net metering

Allowing electric meters of power generating facilities, such as solar or wind power, to turn backwards when more energy is produced than customers consume. Net metering allows customers to use the excess energy their own system generates to offset their consumption over an entire billing period, not just at the time the electricity is produced.

### net savings (NS)

A measure of long-run profitability of an alternative relative to a base case. It can be calculated as an extension of the life-cycle costing (LCC) method as the difference between the LCC of a base case and the LCC of an alternative.

### night-time ventilation

Cooling buildings with outside air at night to minimize the cooling load during the day. Ventilation can be achieved naturally via temperature drops, wind, cross-ventilation, and stack effect, or through use of wind towers and mechanical ventilation.

### non-potable substitution system

A system that uses by-product water to replace potable water for systems that do not require fresh water.

**off-gassing**
The release of airborne particulates, often from installed construction materials such as carpeting, cabinetry, or paint, that can cause allergic reactions and other health problems in building occupants.

**orientation**
The siting of a building relative to compass direction and, therefore, to the sun, which can impact heating, lighting and cooling costs.

**passive solar heating**
Design strategies that contribute to the requirements of the heating load without requiring an energy input to operate (no pumps or fans). For example, architectural elements, such as windows, insulation, and building mass, operate without the need for power input. Passive solar designs are categorized as direct gain, sunspaces, or Trombe walls.

**payback period (PB)**
Measures the length of time until accumulated savings are sufficient to pay back the initial cost. Discounted payback (DPB) takes into account the time value of money by using time-adjusted cash flows. If the discount rate is assumed to be zero, the method is called simple payback (SPB).

**performance-based fee**
A fee structure that rewards a consultant's effort to minimize a project's life-cycle cost. The designer's fee is based on a measurement, such as energy use or operating cost of the completed facility.

**perfluorooctane sulfonate (PFOS)**
A potentially toxic organic compound shown to persist and bioaccumulate in human and animal tissue, most often used as a stain-repellant and to treat carpeting, leather, paper, and other materials. PFOS was phased out by some U.S. manufacturers beginning in 2001 after research revealed its hazardous effects.

**photovoltaics (PV)**
Devices that convert sunlight directly into electricity. PVs generate power without noise, pollution, or fuel consumption, and are useful where utility power is not available, reliable, or convenient.

**plastic curtains**
Curtains or strip doors that reduce infiltration and exfiltration within a building. These barriers typically consist of several strips of heavy plastic (often transparent or translucent) that form a fairly tight seal, yet allow easy passage.

**precycling**
Proactive approach of selecting products and materials according to their potential for lessening the amount of material that goes into the waste stream and for future recycling. Precycling includes buying in bulk, avoiding one-time use products, and choosing products that are biodegradable and have the least amount of throw-away packaging, for example.

**pressure reset system**
A control system for boilers and furnaces that allows wide fluctuations in pressure. As a result, the burners can be shut off for longer periods and stay on for longer amounts of time, with fewer cycles. Avoiding short cycles increases the net system efficiency.

**R-2000**
A voluntary Canadian standard established by Natural Resources Canada with the goal of improving energy efficiency and water quality in home construction and use.

**Radiance®**
A ray-tracing software program developed by the U.S. Department of Energy and Lawrence Berkeley National Laboratory that analyzes and displays light level contours of lighting design. It is used by architects, engineers, and researchers to analyze illumination, visual quality and appearance of designed spaces, and new technologies.

**radiant cooling**
An efficient cooling system that typically involves running cool water through a building's floors, walls, or ceilings.

**radiant floor heating**
An efficient heating system that uses heated water piped underneath flooring, also referred to as hydronic radiant floors.

**radiation**
The transfer of heat from a warmer body to a cooler one. One way to minimize radiation heat transfer is by using reflective surfaces, such as light-colored roofing materials.

**rammed earth**
Earth formed into thick, durable monolithic building walls that are energy-efficient and fire-resistant. Typically used in hot, dry climates, rammed earth walls are composed of screened engineered soil and cement, formed to be 18" or 24" thick. If used in cooler climates, rammed earth may require supplemental insulation or additional heating or cooling.

**reclaimed lumber**
Wood building materials removed from a deconstructed building in such a way that they can be reused for non-structural purposes.

**recycled content**
Products such as steel, plastic lumber, and carpet cushion, fabricated with post-consumer materials or post-industrial by-products.

## recycling

Reusing, reprocessing, or refabricating products after their initial use. Examples of recycled products include some types of tile, glass, asphalt paving, masonry, metal framing, insulation, toilet compartments, and carpet.

## reflective roof

Roofing treated with a special coating that reflects the sun's heat away from the building, reducing the building's heat gain and prolonging the life of the roof.

## reset controls

Controls for hot water systems that inversely monitor the hot water loop set point as compared to the outdoor temperature. For example, the system may be set for 180°F when the outdoor temperature is 0°F, and, inversely, the loop temperature could be 120°F when the outdoor air temperature is 45°F.

## rice hull ash

A by-product from burning agricultural rice waste that can be used in applications similar to cement.

## roof washer

A system for diverting rainwater at the start of each rainfall away from collection tanks and cisterns, so that only the cleaner water that follows is collected for reuse.

## R-value

The measurement of insulation effectiveness. The higher the R-value, the better the insulating performance.

## savings-to-investment ratio (SIR)

A dimensionless measure of performance that expresses the ratio of savings to costs, recommended for establishing priorities among projects. The numerator of the ratio contains the operation-related savings; the denominator contains the increase in investment-related costs.

## seasonal energy efficiency ratio (SEER)

A measure of energy efficiency that represents the total cooling of a central air-conditioner or heat pump in BTUs during the normal cooling season, as compared to the total electric energy input (in watt-hours) consumed during the same period.

## selective glazing

Window material, such as glass, that screens out the infrared and ultraviolet portions of the solar spectrum, but allows visible light to pass. Selective glazing is recommended if a clear appearance is desired, or if a high visible transmittance is required to meet daylighting goals.

## selective surface

A blackened metal foil that has a high absorbtivity in the short wavelength solar spectrum, but a low emissivity in the long wavelength infrared spectrum, thus reducing radiant heat loss off the surface. Used in Trombe walls for passive solar heating or in solar collectors to heat water.

## sick building syndrome (SBS)

A building condition whereby occupants are exposed to health problems that can be attributed to poor air quality. SBS can be caused by off-gassing of volatile organic compounds (VOCs) from construction materials, poorly vented combustion appliances, equipment and chemicals, or molds and microbial organisms.

## site preservation

Minimizing the effect of a new building on the building site (environment).

## smart house

An automated home that conserves energy by using electronic sensors that regulate the operation of systems including HVAC, lighting, appliances, security, etc.

## solar collectors, high-temperature

Large solar collector systems that surround an absorber tube with an evacuated borosilicate glass tube to minimize heat loss, and often utilize mirrors to concentrate sunlight on the tube. High-temperature systems are required for absorption cooling or electricity generation, but are also used for mid-temperature applications such as commercial or institutional water heating.

## solar collectors, low-temperature

Unglazed and uninsulated solar thermal collectors that operate at up to 18°F (10°C) above ambient temperature. Most often used to heat swimming pools.

## solar collectors, mid-temperature

Flat plate solar thermal collectors with cover glass and insulation that produce water 18°–129°F (10°–50°C) above the outside temperature, and are most often used for heating domestic hot water.

## solar heat gain coefficient (SHGC)

The percentage of solar energy either directly transmitted or absorbed and re-radiated into the building, ranging from 0.0–1.0. (The lower the number, the lower the solar heat gain). SHGC has replaced the older term *shading coefficient* (SC); SHGC = 0.87*SC.

## solar heating

Methods of heating using the sun, including passive solar (direct, indirect, and isolated gain), solar water heating, and solar ventilation air preheating.

## SPARK (Simulation Problem Analysis Research Kernel)

A sophisticated software program developed by the Lawrence Berkeley National Laboratory that can model complex building envelopes and mechanical systems, used by building technology researchers and energy consultants.

## stachybotrys
A greenish-black, potentially hazardous mold found on cellulose products (such as wood or paper) that have remained wet for several days or longer.

## stack effect
The movement of air caused by the difference between outside and inside building temperatures. As warmer air rises, it causes high pressure at the top of a building and low pressure at the bottom. At points of greater pressure differential, such as the attic and basement, it is especially crucial to seal air leaks and use airflow retarders.

## statement of work
A written statement describing the procurement of architectural and engineering services, including preliminary or schematic design, design development, and construction document preparation.

## straw bale
A low-embodied-energy farming by-product that can be used to build highly insulated (R-50), fire- and termite-resistant walls. Paired with stucco exterior and drywall interior, straw bale is a plentiful green construction alternative to lumber.

## sun-hours
The number of kilowatt-hours per square meter per day.

## sunspace
Interior building space where temperatures are permitted to vary beyond a limited range of "comfort" conditions. When the mass overheats with warmth from the sun, the additional stored energy is retrained to help warm the building when outdoor temperatures cool off. Sunspaces tend to be used less often than regular work or living space, so direct heat gain is not as much of an issue.

## sun-tempered buildings
Buildings designed using standard construction methods, but oriented optimally on the site and featuring carefully designed windows to reduce heating load.

## sustainability
A central characteristic of green building design that focuses on use of renewable, resource-efficient, environmentally friendly, and healthy products.

## sustainable design
Design that considers environmental and human health and well-being, as well as resource efficiency, in addition to the traditional criteria of function, cost, and aesthetics.

## temperature differential
The difference in temperature between two spaces within a building, or between the indoor and outdoor temperature. Temperature differential causes natural convection currents and air to migrate through cracks and open doors, windows, or other means of egress.

## thermal chimney
A chimney that uses solar energy to heat air, which then rises and is exhausted through the roof. A natural convection loop occurs as cooler air is drawn into the building (sometimes through a cool underground duct) to replace the exhausted hot air.

## thermal mass cooling
A method suited to climates with wide diurnal temperature swings. It involves running cool nighttime air across a large indoor building mass, such as a slab. The cool thermal mass then absorbs heat during the day.

## thermal storage capacity
A material's capacity to store the sun's heat for later use.

## thermosyphon system
A solar-powered water heating system that requires no pump or electricity to run.

## third-party commissioning
Independent assessment of systems to ensure that their installation and operation meets design specifications and that they are as efficient as possible. *See also* **commissioning.**

## tracking solar collection systems
Solar collection systems that are typically pole-mounted to the ground and that track the east-west movement of the sun for maximum energy collection.

## transpired solar collector
A low-cost, high-performing solar collector made of a painted metal plate perforated with small holes. Outdoor air for ventilation is heated as is it drawn in through the perforated collector.

## Trombe wall
A sun-facing wall made of stone, concrete, or other thermal mass material that collects heat during daylight hours and releases it to the space behind the wall over a 24-hour period.

## ultraviolet lighting system
An air filtration system that kills mold and bacteria in the airstream.

## urban heat islands
Asphalt-laden, typically urban areas, which are several degrees hotter than surrounding locations.

## urban sprawl
Uncontrolled spread of development outward from urban centers into more natural areas in an inefficient, unplanned, and wasteful way.

## urea-formaldehyde foam insulation (UFFI)
Insulation used in wall cavities as an energy conservation measure during the 1970s that has relatively

high indoor concentrations of formaldehyde.

## U.S. Green Building Council (USGBC)
A national organization and consensus-based rating system that promotes adoption of green building practices, sustainable technologies, and standards.

## U-value
Measurement of heat loss or gain due to the differences between indoor and outdoor air temperatures (BTUs/hr/SF). U = 1/R (The lower the U-value, the better the insulating performance.)

## vapor barriers
Materials used to prevent the passage of vapor or moisture into a structure or another material, thus preventing condensation and reducing latent loads on air conditioning systems. Polyethylene, the foil facing on insulation, and asphalt-impregnated building paper can serve as vapor barriers.

## ventilation
The movement of air into and out of a building, accomplished by mechanical ventilation or infiltration. Under current standards (usually ASHRAE guidelines), ventilation requirements for the building depend on the space's usage, type, and or the projected occupancy.

## vestibule
A passageway or anteroom serving as an air lock at a building's entrance. Vestibules minimize the infiltration and ex-filtration of exterior conditions into the space within the building envelope.

## visible transmittance (VT)
A window rating that includes the amount of visible light that is transmitted. VT ranges between 0 and 1, and the higher rating indicates more light transmitted.

## volatile organic compounds (VOCs)
Chemicals that are harmful when released (off-gassed) from building products after installation. Most paints, coatings, and adhesives for finishes such as flooring and wall coverings off-gas VOCs that can cause headaches, nausea, and throat and eye irritation. Low- or zero-VOC products are increasingly available.

## waste-to-energy
Conversion of waste products to energy (steam, heat, or electricity) by incineration.

## water efficiency
Products or fixtures, such as low-flow toilets and faucets, that use less water than traditional products while still sustaining the same performance.

## whole-building
Integration of a building's systems to maximize sustainable and/or economic functioning by considering many factors including use of energy and other resources, building materials, site preservation, and indoor air quality so that a structure can run at its maximum efficiency; enhance user health, comfort, and productivity; and have the least impact on the environment.

## whole-house fan
A fan (typically centrally located in the attic ceiling of a house) that draws fresh outside air into the living space, flushes hot air up to the attic, and exhausts it to the outside.

## wind electric system
A single turbine, smaller than the utility-scale models, but much more efficient than the old-fashioned windmill, producing clean, affordable electricity for a rural home, farm, or business.

## window tinting
Film applied to windows to reduce the amount of solar heat transmission through the glass by increasing the solar reflection (not necessarily visible reflection) and solar absorption of the glass.

## wingwall
An outside wall attached perpendicular to exterior walls near windows to direct air into the windows for ventilation purposes.

## xeriscaping
Landscaping featuring native, drought-tolerant, well-adapted plant species, especially in dry climates, to avoid the need for irrigation. Xeriscaping typically calls for less fertilizer and fewer pest control measures than traditional landscapes.

## zero-water urinal
An energy-efficient, wall-mounted urinal that uses no running water, other than for occasional servicing to clean the unit.

# Index

## O

occupants, needs of, 83-84

off-gassing, 35, 36, 39, 50, 176-178

Ontario Building Code, 251

opaque insulated fenestration, 95

open space, 16, 390

operating efficiency, 390

operation and maintenance, 229

operations and maintenance budget, 231

orientation, of buildings, 4, 8, 130, 209, 217, 220, 269, 273, 322

oriented strand board (OSB), 35

outdoor lighting, 22, 60-61

## P

paints, 50, 203, 297
    low-emission, 245

parking lots, 18

particleboard, low-emission, 245

passive heating and cooling, 12

passive solar heating, 9, 11, 29, 122, 129-135, 221

passive walls, 78

paving, 18, 63

payback period, 163, 164, 282-283, 337, 344

performance goals, 214

permit, for deconstruction, 80

pest control, 62, 250

photometrics, 110

photosynthesis, 27

photovoltaics (PV), 5, 12, 18, 44, 53-55, 122, 137-145
    cells and modules, 139-141
    system components, 141

plants
    improving air quality with, 181-182
    watering with gray water, 196-197

plastic curtains, 96

plastic, recycled, 37

plug loads, 61-62

plumbing, 57-58, 272-273

ponds, 63

Portland Energy Conservation Incorporated, 317

post-acceptance phase, of commissioning, 332-333

potable water, 45, 116-117

PowerDOE, 378

process, green, 298-299

product manufacturers, green, 296-298

productivity, 304, 347, 386

products, green
    checklist for, 296, 306-316
    economic vs. environmental performance, 364-367
    environmental performance of, 358-364
    evaluating over life cycle, 357-371
    overall performance of, 367-371
    selection, 301-302
    specifying, 295-316

programming, 319-320

public transit, 18

purification systems, water, 195-196

PVC, 46, 48, 297

## R

R-2000®, 244-246

Radiance®, 194

radiant cooling, 12

radiant heat, 101

radon control, 251

rainwater
    collection, 34, 44-46, 117-118
    healthy use of, 196-197

rammed earth, 64, 65

rating systems, 233-235

real estate, commercial, 387-398

recycled, furniture, 201-202

recycling, 14, 27, 29, 30, 230, 298

reflective coatings, 44

reflective roof, 8, 90-92, 183

refrigeration, 102-103

regulators, partnering with, 231

renewable energy, 12-13, 16
    distribution and generation of, 113

REScheck, 382

reservoirs, 63

RESFEN, 381

resilient flooring, 50

RESNET, 382

RETscreen, 149, 154, 381

rice hull ash, 32

Rocky Mountain Institute, 381

roofs, 44, 74, 90-93
    noise and, 198-199

runoff, 15, 33, 62, 117, 197

R-value, 9, 33, 34, 37, 38, 39, 47, 94, 95, 271

## S

safety, of deconstruction, 75

salvaged materials, 71-80

savings-to-investment ratio, 282, 337, 343, 344, 351

schematic design, 213, 219, 220-224

Seasonal Energy Efficiency Ratio (SEER), 246

security, 13

selective surfaces, 135

sewage treatment, 15, 19

sheathing, 35

solar heat gain coefficient (SHGC), 9, 46, 47, 131, 137, 187

showerheads, low-flow, 57, 116

sick building syndrome, 19-20

single present value, 347

site
    assessment, 72-74
    selection and development, 15-18
    work, 62, 266, 278

skylights, 47, 187

SMACNA, 318

Society for Environmental Toxicology and Chemistry, 362

software, design process, 177

solar energy, 12, 16, 47
    systems, 53, 121-155, 218

solar heat gain, 7, 86-87, 135

Solar Rating and Certification Corporation (SRCC), 149

solar thermal systems, 102

solar ventilation air preheating, 152-154

solar water heating, 11, 53, 122, 145-151

SPARK, 380

specialties, Division 10, 50-51

specifying, of green products and materials, 295-316

sprawl, 16, 18

stack effect, 40

standards, building, 233-262, 382-383

statement of work, 213

steel studs, recycled-content, 245

storm water, 15, 18, 62
  collection, 117

straw bale, 30, 39, 63-64

sub-slab depressurization system, 245

sun control devices, 51

sunspaces, 130, 133-134

sun-tempered building design, 130

sustainability, 299

# T

T*SOL, 382

takeoffs, 217

team building, 210-211

team, design
  decision-making, 223-224
  establishment of, 199-200
  selection of, 216
  statement of work, 216-219

technology and information sharing, 210

temperature differential, 85

terrorism, 13

testing, adjusting, and balancing (TAB) report, 324, 330

The Collaborative for Higher Performance Schools (CHPS), 247, 429-430

THERM, 381

thermal & moisture protection, Division 07, 37-46

thermal chimneys, 11-12

thermal comfort, 171, 182-183

thermal solar collection systems, 128-129

thermal storage mass, 132

third-party commissioning, 13

toilets, 50, 57, 116

tracking solar collection systems, 128-129

training, green, 231

transpired collector principle, 151-152

TREAT, 382

trees, used in green design, 87, 137

TRNSYS, 149, 381

Trombe walls, 11, 130, 134-135

tube lights, 22

# U

U.S. Department of Energy, 165, 194, 233, 248, 324, 343, 375, 377, 388

U.S. Department of Health and Human Services, 233

U.S. Environmental Protection Agency (EPA), 69, 201, 233, 248, 296, 360, 362

U.S. Green Building Council, 234, 236

UFFI, urea-formaldehyde foam insulation, 176

ultraviolet light, 10, 46, 179, 195

uniform present value, 347-348

urethane, virgin, 296

U-value, 9, 47, 95, 131, 134, 187

# V

value engineering, 225, 282

vapor diffusion retarders, 41

vapor migration, 85

varnishes, low-emission, 245

ventilation, 20, 58, 84-86

vestibules, 96

volatile organic compounds (VOCs), 20, 28, 30, 36, 43, 50, 176, 195, 201, 202, 203, 271, 323, 358

# W

wall covering, 50

wall finishes, 203

walls, noise and, 198-199

waste management, 271

water cooling, 103

water quality, 195-196

water, conservation of, 115-118

Watergy, 382

waterproofing, 41-43, 93

wetlands, 16, 19, 63

whole-house air filters, 180

whole system design, 4

wind power, 12, 16, 114, 157-170

wind turbines, 55, 56, 160, 162-164

WINDOW, 381

windows, 5, 9-10, 14, 42, 46-48, 85, 271-272
  daylighting and, 187-188
  efficiencies of, 130-132
  noise and, 198-199

wood, certified, 8, 34, 46, 35, 200, 201

wood flooring, 50

wood studs, urea-formaldehyde-free, 245

# X

xeriscaping, 197